Istanbul 1432 / 2011

© Erkam Publications 2011 / 1432 H
A translation of "İmandan İhsana Tasavvuf"

Published by:
Erkam Publications
Ikitelli Organize Sanayi Bölgesi
Turgut Özal Cd. No: 117 Kat: 2/C
Başakşehir, Istanbul, Turkey
Tel: (+90 212) 671 07 00 pbx
Fax: (+90 212) 671 07 48
E-mail: info@islamicpublishing.net
Web site: http://islamicpublishing.net

All rights reserved. No part of this publication may be reproduced, stored in a retrieval system, or transmitted in any from or by any means, electronic, mechanical, photocopying, recording or otherwise, without the prior permisson of the copyright owner.

ISBN   : 978-9944-83-363-9

The author : Osman Nuri Topbaş
Translator : Erdinç Atasever, Hikmet Yaman
Copy Editor : Suleyman Derin
Graphics   : Ali KAYA (Worldgraphics)
Printed by : Erkam Printhouse

SUFISM
A PATH TOWARDS
THE INTERNALIZATION OF FAITH
(IHSÂN)

Osman Nuri Topbaş

ERKAM PUBLICATIONS

"*In the name of The Almighty, the Merciful, the Compassionate*

By the sun and its morning brightness and by the moon when it follows the sun, and by the day when it displays the sun and by the night when it enshrouds the sun!

By the heaven and He Who built it and by the earth and He Who extended it! By the soul and He Who shaped it and inspired it to wickedness and righteousness!

Prosperous is he who purifies it, and failed has he who seduces it."
(Ash-Shams, 1-10)

The things by which the Almighty takes an oath in the Quran have special significance in Islamic religious terminology, but the subjects that follow these things possess even profounder meanings. This is the same case in the Quranic verses above, but with a subtle difference: The Almighty takes seven consecutive oaths in these verses and even employs the particle (*qad*) to intensify the meaning before talking about the real subject, which is the soul (*nafs*) and says, "Prosperous is he who purifies it, and failed has he who seduces it." (Ash-Shams, 9-10)

It is quite interesting that no topic in the Quran other than the purification of the soul precedes such consecutive Divine oaths, seven in number again. This Quranic occurrence is enough to indicate the significance and necessity of the purification of the soul for man's eternal salvation. Thus this book, entitled "From Faith (*iman*) to Internalization of Faith (*ihsan*)", is a collection of explanations of this delicate topic, as proffered by the saints of the Lord, through their verbal articulations, as well as actual practices.

Preface

Praise be to the Almighty, Who has breathed into man of His spirit and granted him a metaphysical reflection and profound contemplation; and peace be upon Prophet Muhammad -upon him blessings and peace- who, as the quintessential example of human beings, enjoyed the receipt of these Divine gifts the most.

There is no doubt that Sufism represents the heart, essence and spiritual dimension of Islam. Islam elevates the human characteristics of spirituality and love inherent in the hearts of believers up to their zeniths, especially when this essence and spirit of Islam take the form of practice in the actions of capable people. This means that Sufism embodies one of the most fruitful trees of knowledge and gnosis in the garden of Islam. Depending upon its addressee, Sufism has accordingly been articulated in three main formats:

a) Primarily for the elite.

b) For both the elite and the common people.

c) Primarily for the common people.

Some Sufi works are written mainly for the elite steeped in an advanced intellectual background in the Sufi way. In this context, we can mention *Fusus al-Hikam* and *al-Insan al-Kamil* by Ibn Arabi (d. 1240) and Abdulkarim al-Jili (d. 1403), respectively. Some others, such as the *Mathnawi* of Jalaladdin Rumi (d. 1273), are written for both the elite and common people; the latter can benefit from like works in proportion to the level of their understanding. This second type of works helps those who have studied exoteric sciences comprehend the ultimate objective of their knowledge, which is the knowledge of the Almighty. Still some other works, such as *Anvar ul-Ashiqin, Muhammediye*, and *Nafakhat al-Uns* by Ahmed Bican (15th century), Yazicioglu Mehmet (d. 1451), and Abdurrahman Jami (d. 1492), respectively, are written primarily for the common people. These works aim at contributing towards establishing a solid theoretical and practical ground for the common people, who already have a basic understanding of religious precepts, and to improve their spiritual perfection.

Such variety in the nature of traditional works on Sufism stems from the efforts to enable different levels of human society to understand Islam truly in accordance with their intellectual capacities. Thus, both the elite and common people comprehend and practice Islam, as its profound contents require this, and to quote an expression used by the ancients to describe their two-dimensional knowledge, become "two-winged".

With such multidimensionality, Sufism addresses every class of human society. On the one hand it keeps the society awake against lethargy and inactivity at times of socio-economical ease and comfort, while, on the other hand, it provides relief for people through mapping out a way to reconsider events, often seemingly disastrous, in times of difficulty. On one hand, Sufism keeps practicing believers away from a deceiving feeling of security and self-assurance regarding their ultimate destinies while on the other hand, it shines hope onto sinners through the unlimited Divine mercy and forgiveness. Such was the case in Anatolia during the Mongolian invasions, which wrought injustice and suffering on the land. But it was during the same time period when many influential Sufi figures and institutions came to the scene to soothe the Anatolians and console their unbearable pains.

In this day and age when humanity is surrounded by troubles and afflictions of a similarly huge nature, the Sufi way can no doubt help human beings deal with these problems, by introducing theoretical and practical solutions to their difficulties. Indeed, many of our brethren, who have only recently escaped the yokes of atheism, need and seek spiritual treatment, like wounded birds. Likewise, many people in both East and West, who for a long time suffered from the materialist ideology, have now grown an avid interested in getting to know Islam as represented by the earliest Sufi figures. Growing affectionate to what they subsequently see in the vivid examples of such figures, more often than not, they end up sincerely embracing Islam.

Preface

All these points indicate that Sufism represents an indispensable manifestation of Islam and no less priceless gift of blessing and perfection at the hands of believers. Therefore, Sufism holds an essential significance to help Muslims improve the state of their religiosity, in addition to the fact that it presents an accurate and complete form of Islam to non-Muslims in drawing their attention to Islam and carving out a passage for them to embrace the religion. To be sure, in its truest form, the Sufi way acts like a mirror of heart that reflects the life of the Blessed Prophet -upon him blessings and peace- onto the following generations until the Day of Judgment. For this reason, the inspiration and love of Allah, glory unto Him, and His Messenger -upon him blessings and peace- have always been vibrant in the hearts of believers since the beginning of Islam, a vivacity set to remain therein for eternity. Only as a result of this fact does Islam continue to maintain its existence and influence, in spite of the material weakness of contemporary Muslims with respect to this-worldly conditions.

Both apparent and hidden enemies of Islam have been attempting to separate Sufism from Islam, which in actual fact coexist like the body and spirit. They claim that Sufism introduces a different world-view from Islam. Their flawed portrait of the Sufi way engenders certain misconceptions in those who are interested in the matter yet are unaware of the factual reality underlying it. An honest and unspoiled presentation of Sufism is therefore an essential undertaking in the modern world. In addition to correcting misconceptions about Sufism, this book aims at presenting the inherent beauties of this tradition, already briefly mentioned above, to interested minds and hearts. In this sense the Sufi tradition is like a boundless ocean; it overflows with scholarly works which truthfully present the authentic conceptions and practices that are integral to the way.

Adhering to this scholarly tradition, we have here attempted to offer a little contribution to it, even if our effort be like a single drop in an ocean. Attaining to the value of a single drop would more than suffice for the author of book, so long as the book functions like a bridge in connecting hearts to Divine presence; after all, the Sufi way is essentially a state-of-mind (*hal*) rather than words expressed (*qal*).

In this context the work will first give a general content of Sufism, and then proceed to explain the main concepts of this Islamic tradition, such as knowledge of the Divine (*marifatullah*), love of the Divine (*muhabbatullah*), purification of the soul (*tazkiyatu'n-nafs*), purification of the heart (*tasfiyatu'l-qalb*), exemplary Sufi courses of action (*uslub*), and the like. Naturally, precedence in the examples we present belongs to the Blessed Prophet -upon him blessings and peace-, followed by the greats figures of Islam, who are none other than heirs of the Prophet –upon him blessings and peace- and this tradition. We have occasionally dealt with some doubtful and opposing views regarding certain subtle Sufi concepts, but only as far as the related arguments – not the holders of these views as individuals – are concerned. Furthermore, we have called careful attention to some inappropriate and inadequate practices by certain figures, who under the rubric of Sufism, in fact hold positions distant from traditional the spiritual training Sufism has to offer. As it will be seen, we have argued that this occurrence stems either from the ignorance or the heedlessness of those figures involved.

To cut a long story short, although this work is written formally by the author, it is in fact nothing but a compilation by saints of the Lord. All the inspirations and beauties in the work mirror exquisite reflections the spiritual heart-worlds of saints onto us. Our function merely consists of an effort of putting these reflections together and presenting them in accordance with the contemporary needs and conditions. Consequently, we have benefitted profusely from previous works on Sufism, as well as from many friends of ours, who, for us, are virtually like "living books". It is with pleasure and gratitude that we acknowledge this fact.

And finally, we should note that our sincere prayers for the 'people' the Lord mentioned throughout in this work and for our friends from the academia who lent their support in bringing this project to fruition.

O Lord! In spite of our insufficient and lackluster attempt to explain the notions of the Sufi way, give us Your blessings and render our words influential upon the minds of our readers! O Lord! Grant us and our readers Your sublime and unlimited favor, by means of this humble, heartfelt attempt!

Amin!

Osman Nuri TOPBAS

Uskudar, Istanbul, 2002

CHAPTER ONE

WHAT IS SUFISM?

A- THE ORIGIN OF SUFISM
B- THE DEFINITION OF SUFISM
  1- The Sufi way personifies exemplary character traits (akhlaq) and propriety (adab).
  2- The Sufi way is about purifying the heart and the soul.
  3- The Sufi way is a ceaseless spiritual combat.
  4- Sufism means sincerity (ikhlas)
  5- Sufism means standing upright on the straight path (istiqamah)
  6- The Sufi way is (rida) and submission (taslimiyyah)
C- THE SUBJECT MATTER OF SUFISM
D- THE GOAL OF SUFISM
E- THE NECESSITY OF SUFISM
F- THE RELATION OF SUFISM TO OTHER SCHOLARLY DISCIPLINES
  1- Islamic Disciplines
    a- *Theology (Kalam)*
    b- *Quranic exegesis (Tafsir)*
    c- *The Sayings and Practice of Prophet Muhammad -upon him blessings and peace- (Hadith-Siyar)*
    d- *Jurisprudence (Fiqh)*
  2- Natural Sciences
  3- Literature
  4- Fine Arts
    a- *Music*
    b- *Architecture*
    c- *Calligraphy*
  5- Philosophy
G- Beneficial Knowledge

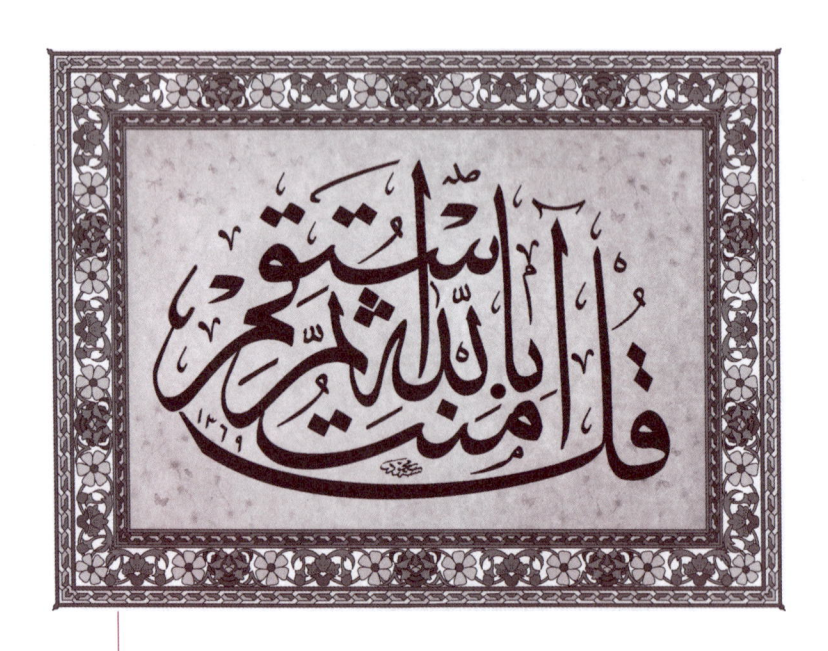

"Say, I affirm my faith in The Almighty and then remain steadfast to it."
(قل آمنت بالله ثم استقم) (*Muslim, İman 62*)

What is Sufism?

You have had a good example in The Almighty's Messenger for whosoever hopes for The Almighty and the Last Day, and remembers The Almighty often. (Al-Ahzab, 21)

A. THE ORIGIN OF SUFISM

In addition to His innumerable blessings, Allah, glory unto Him has granted human beings a unique quality, an extremely precious and subtle quality at that. The Almighty mentions this fact in the Quran when He declares, "I have breathed into him of My spirit." (al-Hijr, 29) In return, the Almighty wants His servants to sincerely love and worship Him, so that they receive a portion of the knowledge of from Him and thereby reach Him.

The Almighty has also given human beings certain special qualities in order to guide them to this direction. In addition to this general guidance, He also entrusted some of His servants, who were given even further special qualities, with the mission of prophethood. This is an additional Divine favor to human beings. During the times when there shall no longer hail any Prophets from among them, the Lord has continued gracing ordinary human beings by designating some of His righteous servants, who are in fact heirs to the prophets, to guide them to the right path.

The institution of prophethood marks an incomparable blessing of the Divine to mankind. In order to render prophethood all-embracing for humankind entire, the Almighty inaugurated this celebrated institution with Adam -upon him peace-, the first human being and, at once, the first prophet. After being articulated by more than a hundred-and-twenty-four-thousand prophets, this sacred path of guidance underwent a process of gradual perfection, compliant with the social and intellectual progress of mankind. And it was with the prophethood of the last prophet, Muhammad -upon him blessings and peace-, that this chain of Divine guidance reached its ultimate perfection.

Prophet Muhammad -upon him blessings and peace- possesses two distinctive characteristics that separate him from other prophets. Firstly, his light was created even before the creation of Adam -upon him peace-. Secondly, in terms of his bodily manifestation, he was the final prophet to appear on Earth. Prophet Muhammad -upon him blessings and peace- therefore represents the first as well as the last pages of the book of prophethood. To put it in another way, the institution of prophethood was launched with the Muhammadan Light (*Nur-i Muhammadi*), the very first entity to exist, and was ended with the Muhammadan Corporeality (*Cisman-i Muhammadi*); his appearance on the spatio-temporal conditions of the world. These two unique characteristics make him the last prophet in the temporal sense, but also the first one in terms of his original creation.

Since the underlying motivation for the entire creation to come into existence is the Muhammadan Light itself, the Almighty created the Blessed Prophet -upon him blessings and peace- with a unique quality, on the basis of which he has been designated as "the beloved" (*habibi*) of the Lord. By subjecting his exceptional earthly existence to a close training, both inwardly and outwardly, the Almighty sent the Blessed Prophet Muhammad -upon him blessings and peace- to humanity as a gift.

The exemplary character and personality of the Blessed Prophet -upon him blessings and peace- represent the unreachable apex of human characteristics, including those that are fathomable by ordinary human comprehension. The reason underlying this is the fact that the Almighty made him a quintessential example (*uswa hasana*), the most perfect model, for the entire human race. Being an example for the human race entire, the Almighty therefore made the Blessed Prophet -upon him blessings and peace- experience every aspect thinkable of human life, a life experience that included his birth as a vulnerable orphan, all the way to him later reaching the authoritative political and religious leadership of

What is Sufism?

his community. Therefore, every person, from different levels of society, can find a good example for himself in the life of the Prophet -upon him blessings and peace-, and learn lessons from it.

In the Quran, the Almighty declares that the Blessed Prophet -upon him blessings and peace- represents the best example for the entire humankind, for every person, from the beginning of his prophethood to the Last Day:

$$لَقَدْ كَانَ لَكُمْ فِى رَسُولِ اللّٰهِ اُسْوَةٌ حَسَنَةٌ$$

$$لِمَنْ كَانَ يَرْجُوا اللّٰهَ وَ الْيَوْمَ الْاٰخِرَ وَ ذَكَرَ اللّٰهَ كَثِيرًا$$

"You have a good example in The Almighty's Messenger for whosoever hopes for The Almighty and the Last Day, and remembers The Almighty often." (al-Azhab, 21)

This means that all human beings stand in need of properly learning the characteristics of the Blessed Prophet -upon him blessings and peace-, so that, through the blueprint set by his life and deeds, they can attain religious and moral perfection. In a broader sense, such perfection refers to the nature of the Sufi course of conduct. Every person should practice what he or she has learned in proportion to his or her capacity. This process starts with a simple imitation (*taqlid*) and ends in realization (*tahqiq*), which ultimately occurs in accordance with and to the degree of the love and spiritual intimacy that a person feels for the Blessed Prophet -upon him blessings and peace-. Innumerable spiritual blessings and disclosures beckon in sharing the same feelings with the Prophet -upon him blessings and peace-. Being able to partake in some share of the physical, spiritual, and moral characteristics of the Prophet -upon him blessings and peace- to the extent our capacities allow, is the highest kind of honor attainable in this world and the world to come.

Allah, glory unto Him, created the Blessed Prophet -upon him blessings and peace- upon the best natural disposition (*fitrah*), both inwardly and outwardly, and trained him accordingly. The Prophet -upon him blessings and peace- underlines this aspect of his personality, when he says, "My Lord has educated me, and how superbly has He educated me!"[1]

The Blessed Messenger -upon him blessings and peace- lived in a terribly violent and ignorant society for forty years before actually receiving prophethood. Still, he was under constant Divine protection and reared by Divine education. Never was he involved in any kind of blameworthy action for which the pre-Islamic society of Ignorance was known. Furthermore, in order to prepare him better for the heavy responsibility of prophethood, he had his chest cleft and his heart was cleansed and filled with spiritual blessings and lights.

Even before his prophethood, the Messenger of Allah -upon him blessings and peace- led a highly respectable lifestyle and believed in the oneness of The Almighty. Especially right before his reception of prophethood, he had increased his complete devotion to the Almighty, by retreating into seclusion in a cave on the Mount of Hira for long periods of time, on a regular basis, in order to contemplate on the essential questions for humanity. The outward reason behind his willful seclusion were his heartfelt sufferings from the wickedness, injustice and misery of the society in which he lived, taking their toll on his profoundly compassionate heart that exuded mercy towards all beings. As for the inward and real reason behind his seclusion, it was a preparatory stage in order to receive the Divine Message, namely the Quran, from the Almighty into the pure heart of the Blessed Prophet -upon him blessings and peace-. The disclosures and inspirations that his heart received during this momentous period of his lifetime guided his heart towards spiritual purification and made it a receptacle for Divine revelation. Becoming ready for revelation, his graceful heart then received spiritual signs and inspirations in the form of truthful visions for six months. The curtains of veiling the secrets of the spiritual realm were thereby parted for the Prophet -upon him blessings and peace-. This process helped him improve his unique inborn capacity for receiving revelation enabling to bear a huge burden otherwise hopelessly beyond the capacity of ordinary people; similar in ways to how iron turns to steel by virtue of the inherent characteristics it possesses.

---

1   Suyuti, *Jamiu's-Saghir*, I, 12

What is Sufism?

The Blessed Prophet -upon him blessings and peace- combined the authorities and duties of all previous prophets in his personality and conduct. The nobility of lineage and conduct, the perfection of morals and disposition, reached their apex in his person. He established legal regulations. He taught how to cleanse the heart and purify the soul, which incidentally is the essence of Sufism. He also taught the correct way to worship the Almighty and pray to Him with a pure heart. Through his exemplary lifestyle, he embodied and represented a perfect form of morality. His age of forty marked a significant turning point not only for himself but also for humankind entire.

The essence of Sufism consists of uplifting our spiritual dimension to a certain degree of maturity and making it receptive to the knowledge and love of the Lord, and thereby imparting onto it that certain blend required for reuniting with the Real. Such a perfect blend is the spirit that will save us; a blend which, at once, is a sacred inheritance bequeathed to us from the caves of Hira and Thawr. It was during specific times and at specific places, not only reserved to Hira and Thawr, that the Blessed Prophet -upon him blessings and peace- went through an intense spiritual training, essential in preparing him for the weight of Quranic revelation; and it was this training constituted that the fruitful basis for purifying his heart and cleansing his soul.

Before receiving the Quranic revelation, the Blessed Prophet -upon him blessings and peace- had already reached a certain degree of spiritual maturity and moral perfection. However, after his return from the cave of Hira where he openly received the Divine Instruction for the first time, the Prophet -upon him blessings and peace- attained a much higher perfection, incomparable even to the exceptional characteristics he already possessed prior to his prophethood. There, the Prophet -upon him blessings and peace- had entered an intense and profound spiritual connection with the Almighty; he was given an enchanting taste of the light of Divine oneness and knowledge, elevating him to the peak of the spiritual state of being conscious of the Lord, imbibing a deep sense of piety in his every particle. Set in motion thereby, he would offer deeds of worship at night

Sufism: A Path Towards the Internalization of Faith (Ihsân)

until daybreak until his legs would get swollen. Even when he is eyes were shut to asleep, his heart was always alert and awake in a deep, rousing contemplation of the Lord Almighty.

In fact, through the content of the revelation of the Holy Quran, replete with knowledge and wisdom, the Blessed Muhammad -upon him blessings and peace- left even the most elite of his contemporaries helpless and in awe; and through his personal lifestyle and actions, he virtually became a miraculous ocean of virtue, unrivalled in both past and future. No invention until the Last Day will be able to falsify the Prophet -upon him blessings and peace-, nor will any educator be able to reach his standard of conduct.

This spiritual maturity of the Blessed Prophet -upon him blessings and peace- underwent a gradual increase until ultimately reaching its peak; and by means of the Ascension (*Miraj*), a unique gift from the Beloved (*Mahbub*) to another (*Habib*), he became a "traveler of eternity". On that night, as the special guest of his Lord, the Prophet -upon him blessings and peace- went beyond all the spatio-temporal limitations of the world by which human beings are bound, and attained the reality of the secret mentioned in the Holy Quran as "two bows'-length away, or nearer". (an-Najm, 9)[2]

This immense Divine gift, called *Isra* and *Miraj*, was a present to the Prophet -upon him blessings and peace- and took place in accordance with a Divine regulation that decreed the temporary removal, for him, of all kinds of limitations set for human beings. On this occasion, the worldly conceptions of space and time disappeared, and a journey and visions that would normally take the lifespans of billions of human beings, took place within a very short period of time. The Prophet -upon him blessings and peace- travelled beyond the frontiers of the "Worlds", "Throne", and "Lote-Tree" and received the

---

[2] *Qaba qawsayni aw adna*: At the night of *Miraj*, the Blessed Prophet -upon him blessings and peace- was uniquely allowed to cross beyond the point of the Lote-Tree (*Sidrat al-Muntaha*). No other created being, including Jibril –upon him peace-, was ever allowed to come this close to the Almighty. The Quranic statement, "two bows'-length away, or nearer", denotes a confidential meeting between the Almighty and the Prophet -upon him blessings and peace-. Grasping the reality of this meeting lies beyond the capacity of ordinary understanding.

unprecedented privilege of being disclosed with the vision of the Lord and with talking to Him directly without any intermediary.

It was such spiritual maturity and perfection that the Almighty bestowed on the Blessed Prophet -upon him blessings and peace-. These Almighty-given characteristics continually accompanied him throughout his communicating of the Divine message to human beings and in his avid yearning to guide humankind entire onto the straight path. The Prophet's -upon him blessings and peace- genuine desire and consciousness for fulfilling the heavenly duty he was entrusted with, delivered him to the zenith of human perfection. On the way, he categorically rejected all kinds worldly offers proposed to steer him away from delivering this message. In his eyes, worshipping The Almighty in the most proper sense of the term was preferable to everything else.

An event which took place in the early days of his prophethood perfectly explains the Blessed Prophet's -upon him blessings and peace- priorities. The idolaters of Mecca sent a proposal to him through his paternal uncle Abu Talib, in order to dissuade him from, and put a stop to, his prophetic activities. In response to this proposal, the Blessed Prophet -upon him blessings and peace- said to his uncle, in a resolute tone, "I swear in the name of the Lord, my dear uncle, that even if they were would place the sun in my right hand and the moon in my left, I would never give up delivering this message. Either the Almighty makes this message spread all over the world and thus I complete my duty, or I breathe my last on this path."[3]

Following their unsuccessful attempt, the idolaters, still ill-at-ease with the birth of Islam and its impending growth, took their proposal a step further. This time they came to the Blessed Prophet -upon him blessings and peace- and declared, "If you want to be rich, we can give you all the wealth in the world and you will be the richest man among the entire tribes in Arabia. If you have a desire for political leadership, we can make you our leader and you can be the ruler of Mecca. Should you wish to marry to a noble woman, we can wed you to the noblest and most beautiful woman in Quraysh…allowing you to pick and choose. We are ready to do everything you want…so long as you simply put an end to this all."

---

3   Ibnu'l-Athir, *al-Kamil fi't-Tarikh*, II, 64.

The unconditional and final response of the Blessed Prophet -upon him blessings and peace- to the ludicrous offers of the flesh made by the idolaters, was his declaration, "I do not expect anything from you; wealth, property, authority, leadership, nor women. The only thing I want is for you to stop worshipping those powerless idols and to start worshipping the Almighty alone."[4]

There is no doubt that these statements and actions present the most consummate examples for all human beings, especially in being firmly stable on faith and consciousness of duty, as well as an ideal and pure state of servitude. The improper proposals in question were about attaining some worldly pleasures in return for those of the eternal world. The history of humankind is full of examples of those who sold their ideals out in return for meager expectations and prosperities of the world.

The Holy Quran and its exemplary practice by the Blessed Prophet -upon him blessings and peace- constitute the essential principles of Islam. The former, being a theoretical source of guidance until the Last Day, begins by praising the Lord of all Worlds and ends by purifying the heart from all sorts of negative attributes and enjoining man to take refuge in the Lord, submissively and unconditionally. The latter represents the practical source of guidance for mankind; for following the Blessed Prophet -upon him blessings and peace- is the only means to acquire true happiness both Here and in the Hereafter. Nothing belonging to this world, however precious it may seem, can ever compare to this salvation; eternal and thus irreplaceable in nature.

The Holy Quran was delivered first to the Blessed Prophet -upon him blessings and peace-, and then through him, to entire humankind. The Quran is a Divine Word that calls mankind to acquire knowledge of the Lord and reach Him by following a natural reasoning on the basis of arriving at the Producer through the product, the Cause through the effect, the Artist through the art, and the Creator through creation. Consequently, the Holy Quran teaches the precise and proper way to frequently remember the Lord and to lead an observant and pious life, in which one minds the Divine commands as if he sees the Lord in front of him, and thereby acquire the love and approval of the Divine.

---

4   Ibn Hisham, *as-Sirah*, I, 236.

What is Sufism?

One should keep in mind that the single source of Divine love is the Blessed Prophet -upon him blessings and peace-; since to love the Prophet -upon him blessings and peace- is tantamount to loving the Lord, and likewise, obeying or disobeying the Prophet -upon him blessings and peace- is equal to obeying or disobeying the Almighty.

As mentioned above, the reason of the creation of existence was the Creators' love for the Muhammadan Light, the first entity ever to be created. All of creation, therefore, was created for the sake of and as a cover for the Muhammadan Light. Mankind represents the most elite part of all creation in terms of receiving Divine gifts. The zenith of all mankind, in the same respect, it is the Muhammadan existence, in other words, the tangible existence of the Blessed Prophet –upon him blessings and peace- on Earth. Man includes the characteristics of all beings, for which reason he has also been referred to as "the little world" or "the micro cosmos". The human being is therefore comprehensive creation in terms of containing the qualities, both good and evil, of all beings. At the same time, the human being represents the choicest portion and cream of all creation, because it is like a seed that includes a huge plane-tree inside, or in equal measure, like an individual that potentially includes a society within himself. On the basis of such unique characteristics, mankind holds the title of "the pearl of creation" (*ashraf-i makhluqat*); yet the Muhammadan existence goes far beyond this advanced point. Those who met the Blessed Prophet -upon him blessings and peace- in person were able to either distinguish his inner reality or act blind towards it, depending on the acuteness or the bankruptcy of their physical and moral abilities. Looking at him, some were able to discern and appreciate the goodness of him; while there were others, who would dismally fail and only see something bad. Abu Bakr and Ali ibn Abi Talib –Allah be well-pleased with them- had really met the same person as Abu Jahl did, but the former two saw completely different things in comparison to Abu Jahl. So deep was the love through which Abu Bakr and Ali –Allah be well-pleased with them- beheld the Blessed Prophet -upon him blessings and peace- that the two became the first link of the golden chain of the Sufi way.

Sufism: A Path Towards the Internalization of Faith (Ihsân)

Sufism aims at attaining an outward as well as inward togetherness with the Blessed Prophet -upon him blessings and peace-; a state of togetherness grounded on a boundless love for him. The primal concern of Sufism therefore centers on the spirituality of the Prophet -upon him blessings and peace-, both inwardly and outwardly, and guides believers to receive a portion from his spirituality conducive to reaching that state of togetherness with him. In other words, the Sufi way aims at underpinning faith with a sincere and intense love and fulfilling the deeds of worship amid a deep reverence towards the Almighty and pursuing an observant life. It is the inspiring reflections of this sublime gift that begun with the "Divine breath" breathed for the first time into Adam -upon him blessings and peace-, and which reached its perfection in the Blessed Prophet -upon him blessings and peace-. To be able to comprehend the reality of the spiritual and existential command that comprises the core of *tasawwuf*, it is imperative that one acquires a deep and detailed knowledge of the life of the Blessed Prophet -upon him blessings and peace.

The Blessed Prophet -upon him blessings and peace- represents the quintessential example for mankind in every aspect of life, including his prowess in educating people and purifying their hearts. As a prophet, he was entrusted with many duties for which he exercised numerous commands. Among these duties, especially four kinds come to the fore:

1. Receiving Divine revelation (*wahy*): The Blessed Prophet -upon him blessings and peace- received the revelation from the Almighty through the archangel Jibril –upon him peace-. This receipt of divine revelation, which took place on the basis of Divine will, came to an end with the departure of the Prophet -upon him blessings and peace- from this world.

2. Explaining the Quranic teachings: The Holy Quran contains concise judgments and realities, which the Blessed Prophet -upon him blessings and peace- explained and elaborated during his years of prophetic duty. Muslim scholars (*mujtahid*) have assumed this scholarly authority after the passing away of the Prophet -upon him blessings and peace-. The purpose of explaining Quranic teachings is to render them actual and practicable in life. Carried out by authoritative Muslim scholars, this undertaking is called "independent reasoning" (*ijtihad*). In principle, *ijtihad* is a continual process in Muslim society, but its incumbency depends upon the availability of qualified scholars at a given time. In any case, this duty belongs to knowledgeable Muslim scholars who have attained to the level required of *ijtihad*.

3. Carrying out administrative responsibilities: In order to implement Divine commands and prohibitions on individual and collective issues, the establishment of an administrative structure was necessary for the Blessed Prophet -upon him blessings and peace-. The Islamic government he thus established was assumed, after him, by his righteous successors or caliphs.

4. Purifying the souls of mankind: The Blessed Prophet -upon him blessings and peace- was able to touch the hearts of people and influence them, through the spiritual command he was given. After his departure from this world, subsequent Muslim generations took all of his responsibilities upon themselves, only with the exception of receiving and delivering Divine revelation. This last duty, that of reaching people's hearts and purifying them, was among his essential responsibilities, and it is natural to expect it to continue on until the Final Hour; for a balanced religious life can only be based on a harmony of the outward and the inward. It is especially this duty that has been carried out and perpetuated by Sufis, the source and principles which come directly from the Prophet's –upon him blessings and peace- practice of the instructions of the Quran. Sufis have placed special emphasis on spiritually-oriented religious teachings to help people become better human beings and more mature Muslims. Islam will doubtless continue to the Last Day, and endless journey which naturally and necessarily includes its spiritual dimension. It is exactly in this context that the continual existence of Sufism and its authoritative representatives form an essential part of this journey.

The Blessed Prophet -upon him blessings and peace- represents the ultimate perfection of humankind with regards to exoteric and esoteric virtues in servanthood, worship, social interactions, and morality. For thirteen years in Mecca, the Prophet -upon him blessings and peace- underwent a kind of preparatory spiritual training; and when he was immigrating to Medina, he became subjected to a further spiritual training

Sufism: A Path Towards the Internalization of Faith (Ihsân)

in the cave of Thawr, where he was to witness certain Divine disclosures. This cave functioned for him as a special place to experience Divine wisdoms and advanced spiritual realities. The Prophet -upon him blessings and peace- stayed in the cave for three days. His companion was Abu Bakr -Allah be well-pleased with him-, the noblest of mankind after the prophets. From start to end, this companionship was a great honor and privilege for Abu Bakr, underlined by the Quran's reference to him as "the second of the two" in the cave (at-Tawbah, 40). The Quran also mentions the Prophet's -upon him blessings and peace- comforting of Abu Bakr –Allah be well-pleased with him-,

$$\text{لاَ تَحْزَنْ اِنَّ اللهَ مَعَنَا}$$

"Sorrow not; surely The Almighty is with us." (at-Tawbah, 40) This Quranic statement further indicates the fact that the Prophet -upon him blessings and peace- taught the secret meaning and inner gist of togetherness with the Almighty. According to the Sufi understanding, this incident was the earliest example for remembrance of the Almighty in silence (*dhikr-i khafi*) and an indication of how such a deep state of togetherness with the Almighty imparts tranquility onto hearts. Sufis draw further emphasis on the fact that, historically speaking, the cave of Thawr was the birthplace of the transferal of spiritual secrets from one heart to the other in the Islamic tradition. Thus, accordingly, Abu Bakr –Allah be well-pleased with him- was the earliest Muslim figure to receive spiritual training directly from the Blessed Prophet -upon him blessings and peace-, one of the integral reasons as to why he is celebrated as the most authoritative Muslim, after the Prophet -upon him blessings and peace- himself, in the traditional chain of transmission of the Sufi way. The cave of Thawr, therefore, virtually became a particular place in the world from which a servant could reach his Lord, Who is beyond all kinds of spatio-temporal conceptions.

The Sufis further relate that similar to his teaching of the principles of remembrance of the Lord in silence (*dhikr-i khafi*) to Abu Bakr –Allah be well-pleased with him-, the Blessed Prophet -upon him blessings and peace- also instructed the remembrance of the Lord aloud (*dhikr-i jahri*) to Ali ibn Abi Talib -Allah be well-pleased with him-. On the basis of such a historical background, the instructions regarding the remembrance of the

What is Sufism?

Lord, which are of primary importance in Sufi training, have their origin in the teachings of the Blessed Prophet -upon him blessings and peace-, which, in turn, have been passed on by two of the earliest and most reputable Muslim religious authorities.

In characterizing the essence of religion, Sufism has in fact been present since Prophet Adam -upon him peace- to Prophet Muhammad -upon him blessings and peace-. Many principles of Sufism readily present themselves in the life of each prophet. As for its appearance as theoretical and practical discipline as it is known today, however, Sufism was systematized for the first time in the second century after the Hegira; that is the Blessed Prophet's -upon him blessings and peace- emigration from Mecca to Medina in 622 A.D.

None of the Islamic theological and legal schools (*madhhab*) of thought came into existence during the lifetime of the Blessed Prophet -upon him blessings and peace-. At the same time, however, the Prophet -upon him blessings and peace-did issue certain theological and legal principles for his Companions to make them more knowledgeable in matters concerning Islam. These instructions were not written down during his lifetime and compiled as systematic scholarly disciplines. After a certain period of time, however, students of the great scholars of Islamic jurisprudence, for instance, started collecting the opinions of their teachers and putting them together. This process marked the beginning of the emergence of Islamic schools of thought, where the opinions of a great scholar were collected under his name, by which each scholarly legacy came to be known as; such as the Hanafi, Shafii, Maliki, and Hanbali schools of Islamic jurisprudence. In accommodating for the needs of practical life, these legal schools were subsequently embraced by the masses.

Similar to other Islamic disciplines, *tasawwuf* encourages people to follow the abstinence and piety of the earliest Muslim generations, who in effect had practiced the essence of Sufism. In time, Muslim people generally found themselves all the more engaged in matters and pursuits of the world, where those who had managed to remain steadfast on religious objectives were reduced to a small minority in their society. This last group, the saints, burdened the responsibility of warning people against the deceiving pleasures of the world and offered precious advice to guide them onto their essential direction. They did not aim specifically at establishing a new way of

Sufism: A Path Towards the Internalization of Faith (Ihsân)

thinking or an organized spiritual order. Their sole objective was pursuing a decent life in accordance with Quranic and prophetic instructions. Appreciating their exemplary religiosity, both their contemporaries and subsequent generations embraced these saintly advices, by attending their spiritual sessions and taking lessons from both their words and deeds. This process culminated in acknowledging saints as spiritual guides and teachers. People who welcomed such eminent religious figures in their practice of religion then started collecting the words and instructions of their masters and systematized them as a spiritual discipline. In the end, Sufi orders came into existence bearing the names of their masters, such as the Qadiriyya, Mawlawiyya, Naqshbandiyya, and the like.

The word *tariqah* means a method (literally "way" or "path") which each branch of Sufism uses to reach the Lord by helping flourish the moral and religious characteristics innate to human beings. Depending on their methodologies, there are three kinds of *tariqah*s:

1. **The path for the good** (*tariq-i akhyar*): These are the *tariqah*s that focus on the deeds of worship and piety.

2. **The path for the virtuous** (*tariq-i ebrar*): These are the *tariqah*s that concentrate on purifying the human soul through spiritual exercises and services.

3. **The path for lovers** (*tariq-i shuttar*): They are the *tariqah*s that aim at attaining the same goal through love.

Each of these three kinds of *tariqat*s welcomes people in accordance with their personal characteristics. Each person joins a *tariqat* that is the most suitable for his spiritual purification and perfection. Since people are of different temperaments, it is only natural that there should be different *tariqat*s. The Almighty says in the Quran,

لِكُلٍّ جَعَلْنَا مِنْكُمْ شِرْعَةً وَ مِنْهَاجاً

"To each of you We prescribed a law (*shir'a*) and a method (*minhaj*)." (al-Maida, 48)

The word *minhaj* in the Quranic verse has been defined as an "illuminated way", specifically denoting the path of servanthood that should

What is Sufism?

be followed in order to gain spiritual closeness with the Lord. A celebrated Sufi adage in fact states that "The number of the ways to the Lord is as great as the number of breaths of every created being."

On the other hand, Quranic judgments are of three types:

1. Creedal (the principles of faith)
2. Legal or jurisprudential
    a) of worship
    b) Social interactions
    c) Punishments
3. Ethical or comprehension of the heart (*fiqh-i kalbi*)

Fiqh-i kalbi means the betterment of one's inner world or morality, constituting thereby the inner dimension of creedal and practical principles. *Fiqh-i kalbi* aids to mature human action to the point of producing righteous deeds (*amal-i salih*). According to the Quran, piety (*taqwa*), abstinence (*zuhd*), and the beautifying or internalization of faith (*ihsan*) represent the most significant characteristics of praiseworthy states of the heart.

Piety (*taqwa*), in the sense of constantly being conscious of Allah, glory unto Him, means protecting the heart by means of diligently observing Divine commands and prohibitions in a state-of-mind acutely aware of the ceaseless responsibility before the Almighty.

Abstinence (*zuhd*) is to empty the heart of everything other than of the Lord.

Beautifying or internalizing faith (*ihsan*) is to embark upon a ceaseless spiritual contemplation with an awareness of being under constant Divine surveillance.

(اَلْاِحْسَانُ أَنْ تَعْبُدَ اللّٰهَ كَأَنَّكَ تَرَاهُ فَإِنْ لَمْ تَكُنْ تَرَاهُ فَإِنَّهُ يَرَاكَ)

The Blessed Prophet -upon him blessings and peace- says, "Ihsan is to worship the Lord as if you see Him; for even if you do not see Him, He sees you." (*Bukhari*, Iman, 37, *Muslim*, Iman 1) In other words, *ihsan* refers to training the psyche to the point where one feels and knows that he is being watched by the Almighty every step he takes. Such a psychological condition improves the state of the heart and enables a believer to organize his entire life in accordance with Divine regulations. It is through this process that the heart becomes purified; and from this perspective, Sufism is about leading the heart to purification.

Religion aims at bettering people and refining them spiritually. One can fulfill this objective only after one comes to a profound realization of being the servant of the Almighty. According to the Islamic understanding, the ideal human being is he who embodies the attributes of the Lord as his own; and the way to this ideal passes exclusively through the spiritual education of the heart. In order to render the essence of the heart a polished mirror in reflecting these Divine traits, the servant needs to reserve a central place for the remembrance of the Lord (*dhikr*) in his heart. Turning the heart towards the Almighty in this manner, ultimately allows it to enjoy the reflections of these brilliant manifestations.

Islam keeps the door of spiritual advancement open for believers through *zuhd*, *taqwa*, and *ihsan*. Otherwise, had Islam required and implemented only exoteric regulations for believers and closed the door to the Lord in an absolute manner, reaching the Lord would have been impossible for those graced with a spiritual capacity in this direction, which would have been a great injustice indeed. And this would have proven an insurmountable barrier between the Almighty and His devout servants. But on the contrary, the line of communication between the Almighty and His servants is unreservedly open, in many ways, to those who have the capacity to reach Him; a capacity whose fulfillment marks the ultimate level of perfection for human beings. Since the acts and judgments of the Almighty are full of wisdom, it is unthinkable that He should close the way to Himself, for His dedicated servants, entirely shut.

In one respect, for pious servants, *ihsan* represents a spiritual *miraj* or ascension of spiritual intimacy to their Lord, insofar as the term refers to a steady psychological condition man is called on to embody, in which he becomes conscious of the closeness of the Lord at all times. This notion of *ihsan* is grounded on its aforementioned definition given by the Blessed

What is Sufism?

Prophet -upon him blessings and peace-, where *ihsan* is explained as the mindset of worshipping the Almighty as if one sees Him right before his eyes; and though he might not see the Lord, the Lord does indeed thoroughly see everything, including him. Those who comprehend this inner signification of *ihsan* regulate their entire lives accordingly, whereby they provide a continuous dwelling place for *ihsan* deep in their hearts.

From this point of view, *ihsan* is a spiritual reality, which Sufis seek to attain. Striving for this purpose ultimately enables one to obtain a deep spiritual connection with the Lord and whosoever establishes such a sound connection with Him becomes 'a friend of His', a saintly character who assumes the attributes of the character traits of the Lord as his own. A servant unable to taste a spiritual maturity of this caliber becomes stuck in the exoteric surface understanding of the religion and remains only on the level of imitation. Nonetheless, the Blessed Prophet's -upon him blessings and peace- moral and spiritual characteristics were not only put into practice by the Companions they were also diligently passed onto following generations. Every single Muslim therefore enjoys irrevocable access to and the opportunity to experience the spiritual dimension of Islam; and in this sense, there is no elitism in the Islamic religious tradition.

In light of the elucidations offered thus far, we may give an outline the basic understanding of Sufism in traditional Muslim circles as follows: Being based on the Quran and thus indigenous to Islam, Sufism is an essential dimension of the Islamic religious tradition. In stark contrast to this authentic understanding and legitimacy of Sufism, however, some look to the origin or origins of Sufism outside of Islam. They speculate on various potential origins, based on etymology or historical contacts. They, for instance, assert that Sufism comes from the ancient Greek word "*sophia*", a term alleged to be the Arabic "*tasawwuf*". In similar vein, there are others who try to conjure an origin for Sufism in the pre-Islamic Judeo-Christian religious tradition; and still others who claim that the Sufi way has roots in Hindu mysticism. The common denominator of all these approaches is that they remain superficial in understanding and appreciating the essence of Sufism.

Muslim scholars have in fact presented a copious amount of solid and convincing arguments in duly exposing the origin of the word "*tasawwuf*" as embedded in Islamic sources. It has been commented, for instance,

Sufism: A Path Towards the Internalization of Faith (Ihsân)

that etymologically speaking, the term "*tasawwuf*" is derived from the Arabic words "*safa*", "*safwah*", and "*istafa*", all of which denote 'purity' in differing significations. Some Muslim scholars draw a sound historical relation between the word "*tasawwuf*" and a fraction of the earliest Islamic community, whose members specifically devoted themselves to constant acts of worship and abstinence, who were referred to as the "*ahlu'-suffa*", literally "the people of purity". It is reported that they would wear woolen mantles; in other words, mantles made from "*suf*", the Arabic word for wool. A "*sufi*" or a "*mutasawwif*", in this sense, is a person who wears woolen clothing, on the basis of the historical fact that the "*ahlu'-suffa*" would prefer the same clothing, out of abstinence and humbleness.

As a fundamental principle, Muslim scholars base their personal interpretations of religious notions on the ground of the Quran and the Sunnah. Thus, just like a Muslim jurisprudent who does not stray from the Quran and Sunnah when affording rulings in Islamic legal matters through independent reasoning (*ijtihad*), Sufis base their spiritual interpretations of religious topics unswervingly upon the Quran and the Sunnah. In this regard the Sufis are no different to jurisprudents, insofar as both are expected to act with feelings of piety and the consciousness of the Lord (*taqwa*) and underpin their arguments with evident proofs from the Quran and the Sunnah.

On some occasions, however, some Sufi writers with insufficient knowledge of conventional or exoteric Islamic disciplines and momentarily intoxicated under the grip of spiritual ecstasy, may make errors of judgments or utter intricate, baffling statements. Sufi orders whose sheikhs were knowledgeable scholars also of exoteric sciences, were able to remain immune to such mistakes. The Naqshbandiyya and similar Sufi orders that keep themselves very close to the outward principles of the Quran and the Sunnah have coined a widespread rule in this regard, that says, "The stable foot of the compass is the Shariah (the Law)." Rumi similarly elaborates:

"We are like compasses. Our stable foot stands firm on the Shariah, and with the other, we travel amid the seventy-two nations on earth. The Shariah is like a candle; it illuminates and shows the way. One cannot move forward only by taking the candle in one's hand, but one cannot proceed without taking it in the hand either. Once you begin to progress under the light of the Shariah…it is this that which we call tariqah."

*S*ufism is the effort to pursue a lifestyle that is harmonious with the essence of religion, by virtue of purifying oneself from material and moral defects, and embodying, in their place, a beauty of moral conduct.

B. THE DEFINITION OF SUFISM

Sufism is a zest or a state-of-mind, rather than a mere statement; a matter of existential embodiment rather than simply knowing. The more one savors and experiences the Sufi way, the deeper one becomes in the knowledge pertaining to spiritual realities. It is otherwise impossible to provide a comprehensive explanation of the reality of Sufism by means only of words. Therefore, saints of various intellectual and cultural backgrounds have offered a variety of definitions of the Sufi way, reflecting their personal spiritual states at that given moment; which makes Sufism a highly multidimensional discipline.

Saints and their disciples progress on the spiritual path compliant with their inborn and acquired capacities, and in proportion to the spiritual inspirations their hearts experience. From this perspective, one may easily come across different explanations of the same religious matters given by a number of different saints, to the extent that these explanations are conditioned by and depend upon their peculiar spiritual states and also upon the specific character of the Divine manifestations they receive in their hearts. Nonetheless, each of these various definitions of the Sufi path given by saints is correct and justified by the personal experience of each. As for an objective perception of the essence of Sufism today, one may only arrive at a broad understanding of it, based again on the various definitions saints have articulated in the past.

Sufism: A Path Towards the Internalization of Faith (Ihsân)

Considering the shared aspects of the various definitions of the Sufi way, we may say that Sufism is a discipline that leads believers to moral perfection by virtue of improving their inner, spiritual dimensions and directs towards attaining a proximity to the Real by helping them embody exemplary moral traits and conduct, guiding them thereby to the knowledge of Lord.

Below are just a few definitions of Sufism offered by saints in accordance with the spiritual manifestations they were privileged with:

1. **The Sufi way personifies exemplary character traits (*akhlaq*) and propriety (*adab*).**

Saving a believer from blind imitation (*taqlid*) in matters of faith, exemplary character traits give birth to the consciousness of *ihsan*, which itself imparts uprightness and integrity to the thoughts and acts of human beings. *Ihsan* is to permanently implant a mindset in the heart of a believer, crystallized by a constant awareness of the Lord, as if the believer sees Him. Gradually, *ihsan* becomes an essential and governing force behind all the actions and behavior of a believer throughout his life. Abu'l-Husayn an-Nuri explains Sufism accordingly when he says, "Sufism consists not of forms and sciences but of good moral qualities (*akhlaq*). If it were about forms, one would have taken it by means of personal striving; if it were about sciences, one would have learned it by means of conventional education. For this reason, neither can forms nor science merely make one reach the purpose. Sufism is to succeed in embodying the qualities of the Lord." The special emphasis an-Nuri places on his definition is thus the strong connection between the Sufi way and the embodiment of exemplary character traits it leads to.

Even though one might not find the term *tasawwuf* mentioned during the lifetime of the Blessed Prophet -upon him blessings and peace-, its essence and reality nonetheless did exist. What we mean by the expression "exemplary moral qualities" is none other than the moral qualities of the Noble Messenger -upon him blessings and peace-; qualities which the believer is expected to embody at the expense of his deficient traits. The integrity of the Blessed Prophet's -upon him blessings and peace- morality is confirmed by the Quran:

$$وَ اِنَّكَ لَعَلٰى خُلُقٍ عَظِيمٍ$$

"And indeed, you are of a great moral character." (al-Qalam, 4)

What is Sufism?

Similarly, when inquired about the morals of the Blessed Prophet -upon him blessings and peace-, Aisha –Allah be well-pleased with her- replied said, "His morals were that of the Quran." (*Muslim*, Musafirin, 139) When a servant embodies the exemplary moral traits laid down by in the Quran and abides by the Quranic principles, he virtually becomes the Quran come-to-life. Contemplating on the meaning of the Quran, reciting it in reverence, and practicing its instructions represent the apex of good morality.

The Blessed Prophet -upon him blessings and peace- was sent by the Almighty with the mission of enlightening the universe entire, the whole spatio-temporal scope, from the very onset his prophethood until the Final Hour. Thanks to reliable historical and scholarly records, we are gifted today with a strenuously detailed account of the Prophet's -upon him blessings and peace- life and times. Upon glancing at these records, one is unmistakably struck by many an extraordinary aspect of his life; fitting, as he represents the quintessential perfection of humankind and morality. The Blessed Prophet -upon him blessings and peace- himself highlights his universal mission when he states, "I have been sent for nothing but to perfect good morals." (Imam Malik, *Muwatta*, Husnu'l-Khulq 8). Confirming this is the verse of the Holy Quran, which refers to the Blessed Prophet -upon him blessings and peace- as "the quintessential example" (*uswah hasanah*): "You have a quintessential example in The Almighty's Messenger for whosoever hopes for The Almighty and the Last Day, and remembers The Almighty often." (al-Ahzab, 21)

Even after the physical departure of the Blessed Prophet -upon him blessings and peace-, the Lord will always hail saintly scholars from among people, as a gift to humankind and more importantly, to perpetuate the practice of good morals. These scholars are described in a *hadith* as "the heirs of prophets" (*warathatu'l-anbiya*)[5]. The Blessed Prophet -upon him blessings and peace- offers a further description of such scholars, saying, "The most perfect believer with respect to faith is he who exudes the best

---

5   The term "*warathatu'l-anbiya*'" denotes the real scholars who, both inwardly and outwardly, personify prophetic conduct and above all, the morals of the Blessed Prophet -upon him blessings and peace-, and exhibit an exemplary way of life in all respects, in both theory and practice; as the *hadith* in question reads, "…*real* scholars are heirs to prophets." *Abu Dawud*, Ilm, 1.

moral traits." *(Ahmad ibn Hanbal, Musnad, II, 250)* These words allude to the fact that good morals are the fruits of faith and the signs of its perfection. Consequently, saints are spiritual guides who have been privileged with the good fortune of having personified the moral qualities of the Blessed Prophet -upon him blessings and peace-. Correlated is the definition of the Sufi way offered by Abu Muhammad al-Jariri, according to which it is "… to embody good morals and to refrain from the immoral."

As demanding an undertaking it is to beautify heart with good morals and cleanse it from the immoral, it is nevertheless essential in order to attain to eternal happiness and salvation. In highlighting the grueling nature of this awaiting task, Abu Hashim as-Sufi says, "Eradicating an existing conceit from the heart is more difficult than digging a mountain with a needle." Similar are the words of Abu Bakr al-Kattani: "Sufism is about morality. A person morally better than you is at the same time a person spiritually purer than you."

The history of mankind is replete with the manifestations of the exemplary conducts of prophets. Prophet Yusuf -upon him peace-, for instance, exemplifies one of the most remarkable instances of moral excellence in history. As reported by the Quran, Yusuf –upon him peace- not only did not retaliate against his brothers who had, years ago, committed the terrible crime of throwing him into a well in the middle of nowhere, he displayed an unrivalled show of mercy and forgiveness when meeting them years down the track, assuring them that "No blame will there be upon you today. The Almighty will forgive you; and He is the most merciful of the merciful." *(Yusuf, 92)*

The ultimate goal a Sufi strives for is to emulate Ibrahim -upon him blessings and peace- in purging his heart of everything worldly and filling it with obedience to Divine commands; Ismail -upon him peace- in unconditional submission to the Almighty and contentedness with Divine fate; and Ayyub -upon him peace- in enshrouding the heart in unyielding patience. Spiritually, it is to personify the sorrow of Dawud -upon him peace- and the abstinence of Isa -upon him peace-.

A Sufi's heart ought to imitate the heart of Musa –upon him peace-, in being immersed in spiritual joy and yearning for the Lord in His remembrance, and above all, the heart of the Blessed Prophet -upon him blessings

What is Sufism?

and peace- in sincerity, love and devotion for Allah, glory unto Him. Abu Hafs al-Haddad gives an inclusive summary of all these descriptions when he says, "Sufism is about good propriety (*adab*)." In explanation of *adab*, Rumi says,

> O gentleman! Beware that adab is the soul in your body;
>
> Adab is the eye of the Men of the Lord and the light of their hearts.
>
> If you want to crush Satan's head, open your eyes and see;
>
> It is adab that depresses Satan.
>
> If you cannot find adab in a man, he is not in fact a human being.
>
> It is adab that separates mankind from animals.

In the same context Rumi also says,

> My reason asked my heart, "What is faith (iman)?"
>
> My heart whispered into the ear of my reason, "Faith is all about propriety (adab)."

Another poet versifies,

> Adab is a crown sent down from the Lord's light;
>
> Place it on your head and be spared from all plights.

For a long time, therefore, it has been customary to have a cautionary signboard at Sufi lodges that read, "*Adab Ya-Hu!*"; a motto with a multidimensional meaning. While it reminds the reader how essential it is to live a life of propriety, from another vantage, it is at the same time a plea, in the sense of "O Lord, give us *adab*!

2. The Sufi way is about purifying the heart and the soul.

Since man has come to this world for trial, he is afflicted, until death, with the presence of the ego or the lower self (*nafs*), which contains innumerable negative aspects. Even if one reaches the highest point of sainthood, he always remains face to face and under the threat of three main obstacles: the temporal world, ego and Satan. He is always vulnerable to the deceiving tricks, whispers and traps set by these three elements. The merit of servanthood starts the moment a believer turns his heart to the Lord, and by eliminating the dangers caused by the three aforementioned elements, thereby saves himself from the deceptive glitters of worldly pleasures.

The purification of the heart and soul is an essential undertaking in rectifying the evil inclinations existent in human nature and subsequently planting the seeds of piety (*taqwa*) therein. For this reason, every human being is responsible for acquiring knowledge of the Almighty, in proportion to his personal capacity. This responsibility also includes moving a step beyond the conventional knowledge of the Almighty to attain the real knowledge of Him, and to complement this with righteous deeds. Such is the meaning of "servanthood", in the truest sense. Actualizing this kind of servanthood requires one to embark upon purifying the heart and soul; and this entails a by-passing or a purging of the obstacles set by the ego and tuning all desires to the eternal. Such is the only way to reach the Lord both Here and in the Hereafter.

The innate nature of the heart is that it is the precinct of the Divine Gaze; in other words, it is the point on which the Sight of the Lord is fixed, so to speak. As such, the heart is open and receptive to Divine inspiration on the condition that it is cleansed of every kind of worldly desires and selfish concerns. A heart dominated by these meager desires is spiritually impure and therefore unreceptive to the inspirations and disclosures coming from the way of the Lord. Living up to this principle does not necessarily require that one loves no person other than the Lord; though having said that, those triumphant in attaining a heart of purity at the end of this road have developed an immunity against the love of anything else other than the Lord (*masiwa*). Given that common human beings, however, cannot entirely erase their love for 'things' of the world from their hearts, it is hoped that they will in fact benefit from these metaphorical loves, as long as they do not allow them to weigh heavier than their love for the Real.

Recalling the function and status of the heart, both spiritual and material, will help us better appreciate the vitality of purifying it. The Blessed Prophet -upon him blessings and peace- states, "There is a piece of flesh in human body…if good then so is the whole body; and if bad, so the entire body becomes bad. Beware…that this (piece of flesh) is the heart." (*Bukhari, Iman, 39*)

Rumi gives a symbolic explanation of the same reality and states that when a person tries to fill an empty sack, he needs to make sure that the sack does not have any holes; otherwise his efforts are useless. Likewise, Rumi continues, human deeds become meaningful and lead to eternal salvation only if performed with a purified heart; for the rewards of deeds depends on the intention, and the intention itself is a deed exclusive to the heart. In light of this strong connection, one needs to correct his intention and adorn it by means of sincerity; but this is not a simple undertaking. Only qualified masters can guide one in the process of purifying the heart, at the end of which one can attain the desired spiritual state. Saints train their disciples in educating the heart, helping them reach the spiritual perfection of *ihsan*, where they acquire a spiritually innervated heart that feels the presence of the Lord at all times.

Reaching this said level of spiritual perfection requires the purification of the heart from all desires and objects other than the Almighty. A heart endowed with such quality starts perceiving subtle and deep realities and becomes the locale for the manifestation of Divine Names and spiritual secrets, the depth of which depend on the depth of spiritual maturity the heart has acquired. Knowledge of the Divine (*marifatullah*), which is to know the Lord in and through the heart, appears inside a heart of such caliber; and this appearance signals the beginning of the transformation of ordinary knowledge (*ilm*) into real knowledge or wisdom (*irfan*).

The Quran declares that only those who humbly present themselves to the presence of the Almighty with a sound and purified heart, will be able to reach eternal salvation:

يَوْمَ لاَ يَنْفَعُ مَالٌ وَ لاَ بَنُونَ اِلاَّ مَنْ اَتَى اللهَ بِقَلْبٍ سَلِيمٍ

"The Day when there will not benefit [anyone] wealth or children, but only one who comes to The Almighty with a sound heart." (as-Shuara, 88-89) In contrast, hearts that are contaminated by evils and hardened from becoming distant from the Lord are bound to perish, as the Quran pronounces, "By the soul and He who shaped it and inspired it to wicked-

Sufism: A Path Towards the Internalization of Faith (Ihsân)

ness and righteousness! Prosperous is he who purifies it, and failed has he who seduces it." (as-Shams, 7-10) In line, the Quran also reveals, "Then woe to those whose hearts are hardened against the remembrance of the Lord. Those are in manifest error." (az-Zumar, 22). Inspired by these Quranic proclamations are the words of Abu Said al-Kharraz, which shed great light onto our current discussion: "A perfect man is the one whose heart Lord has purified and filled with spiritual light."

3. The Sufi way is a ceaseless spiritual combat.

Belonging to Junayd al-Baghdadi, the above definition underlines the fact that Sufism is a lifelong struggle (*jihad*) against the evil temptations of the ego. This struggle aims at bringing all the evil aspects of the ego under control. Taken in the conventional sense, a battle lasts for only a certain period of time; yet the battle against the ego has no ceasefire until death. The Quran instructs, "And worship your Lord until there comes to you the certainty [i.e., death]." (al-Hijr, 99) The Almighty warns His servants against heedlessness, insofar as it opens gates of the heart to the tricks of the ego and leaves it vulnerable.

$$\text{وَ اذْكُرْ رَبَّكَ فِى نَفْسِكَ تَضَرُّعًا وَ خِيفَةً وَ دُونَ الْجَهْرِ مِنَ الْقَوْلِ بِالْغُدُوِّ وَ الْاٰصَالِ وَ لاَ تَكُنْ مِنَ الْغَافِلِينَ}$$

The Lord states in the Quran, "And remember your Lord within yourself in humility and in fear without being apparent in speech in the mornings and the evenings. And do not be among the heedless." (al-Araf, 205)

In the same context the Blessed Prophet -upon him blessings and peace- uses the term "the greater *jihad*" when describing the imperative struggle to be undertaken against the ego. As they were returning from the battle of Tabuk, referred to as the 'Battle of Hardship' owing to its painstaking nature, the Prophet -upon him blessings and peace- turned to Companions and said, "Now we are returning from the smaller *jihad* to the greater *jihad*." The companions felt amazed and asked the Blessed Prophet -upon him blessings and peace-, "What could be a greater *jihad* than this one?" to which the Prophet Blessed Prophet –upon him blessings

What is Sufism?

and peace- responded, "Indeed, we are now returning from the smaller *jihad* to the greater *jihad*…the *jihad* against the ego."[6]

In expressing his thoughts on the significance of the delicate balance Islam establishes between the smaller and greater *jihad*s, the contemporary thinker Roger Garaudy says, "Sufism is a completely Islamic spiritual education and, in fact, refers to an inner struggle against all kinds of natural temptations that put a person away from the original purpose of his creation and enslave to him to the ego. In Islamic terminology, this exertion is called 'the greater *jihad*'. As for 'the smaller *jihad*', it is undertaken against all kinds of authority, wealth, and false pieces of knowledge that place Muslims away from the path of their Almighty; Muslims carry out the smaller *jihad* in order to make an effort to actualize the unity and harmony of the path of their Lord. It is the balance between these two types of *jihad* (greater and smaller) that assures the happiness and soundness of individual and social life."[7]

4. Sufism means sincerity (*ikhlas*)

Sufism means sincerity in the presence of the Lord. In its terminological sense, sincerity refers to offering all acts of worship solely for the sake of the Almighty, without any other consideration intruding on the heart. The operation of cleansing all kinds of worldly expectations from the heart and focusing only on the pleasure of the Lord is a required and central virtue in Islam. The mere objective of all acts of worship is to attain the pleasure of the Lord; and if a person loses his concentration and allows the intrusion of secondary, trivial concerns, the proper term to describe this situation would be insincerity or lip-service. Acts of worship offered with a mindset are worthless in the sight of the Divine. Sincerity is, therefore, the most important feature in rendering a deed of worship accepted by the Lord.

Sincerity is to protect the heart against all kinds of worldly desires and aspirations and render closeness to the Lord the only motivation that stirs the heart into practice. Sincerity further leads the servant to the pleasure of the Lord, the ultimate good ever attainable. In the Quran, the Almighty repeatedly underlines the vital significance of sincerity in acts of worship

---

6   Suyuti, *Jamiu'-Saghir*, II, 73
7   R. Garaudy, *Islam'in Vaad Ettikleri*, 47.

Sufism: A Path Towards the Internalization of Faith (Ihsân)

performed by His servants and reveals, "Indeed, We have sent down to you the Book, [O Muhammad], in truth. So worship The Almighty, [being] sincere to Him in religion;" (az-Zumar, 2) and "Say, 'Indeed I have been commanded to worship The Almighty, [being] sincere to Him in religion.'" (az-Zumar, 11) The Quranic verses further reveal that on the brink of being expelled from the presence of the Almighty, Satan retorted, "My Lord, because You have put me in error, I will surely make [disobedience] attractive to them [i.e., mankind] on earth, and I will mislead them all. Except, among them, Your sincere and purified servants." (al-Hijr, 39-40)

Sufism is to salvage oneself from the hands of the ego by doing every single thing for the sake of the Almighty and by acknowledging the fact that all blessings and honor come only from Him. Regardless of the spiritual level or station one might be at, one must always be weary of giving in to self-importance and conceit, a mindset that is reminiscent of the Divine revelation the Blessed Prophet -upon him blessings and peace- received when returning, to Medina, from the victory of Badr:

فَلَمْ تَقْتُلُوهُمْ وَ لٰكِنَّ اللّٰهَ قَتَلَهُمْ وَ مَا رَمَيْتَ اِذْ رَمَيْتَ وَ لٰكِنَّ اللّٰهَ رَمٰى

"And you did not kill them, but it was The Almighty Who killed them. And you threw not, [O Muhammad], but it was The Almighty Who threw." (al-Anfal, 17)[8] Therefore, a servant must always be aware of his vulnerability and his state of being a created human, and realize that every blessing, victory and success comes only from the Almighty as a gift. Beguiled into thinking otherwise will only diminish the rewards of deeds, if not make them disappear entirely.

Failure to conduct oneself sincerely in deeds of worship and allowing the ego to gain the upper hand incurs disastrous consequences, as made mention in a _hadith_ narrated by Abu Hurayra –Allah be well-pleased with him-, where the Blessed Prophet -upon him blessings and peace- says,

---

[8] According to the reports, when the battle began, the Prophet Muhammad -upon him blessings and peace- prayed and threw a handful of dust at the enemy, which struck the eyes of the enemy and stupefied them. The verse was revealed right after this incident.

What is Sufism?

"The first of men (whose case) will be decided on the Day of Judgment will be a man who died as a martyr. He will be brought (before the Judgment Seat). The Almighty will make him recount all the blessings He had bestowed upon him in life and he will recount each of them appreciatively. The Almighty will then ask, 'What did you do in return?' He will reply, 'I fought for You until I died as a martyr.' To that the Almighty will reply, 'You are lying. You fought for the sake of being called a 'brave warrior'; and so were you called.' Then the Almighty will decree and the man will be dragged with his face downward and cast into Hell. Then will be brought forward a man who had acquired knowledge, passed it onto others and recited the Quran. He will be brought; and the Almighty will make him recount His blessings and the man will recount them appreciatively. Then the Almighty will ask, 'What did you do in return?' He will say, 'I acquired knowledge and disseminated it and recited the Quran seeking Your pleasure.' The Almighty will say, 'You are lying. You acquired knowledge so that you might be called a scholar, and you recited the Quran only so that you might be called a reciter; and so were you called.' Then the Divine order will be passed against him and he will be dragged with his face downward and cast into the Fire. Then will be brought a man whom The Almighty had made abundantly rich and had granted every kind of wealth. He will be brought and the Almighty will make him recount His blessings and he will recount them appreciatively. The Almighty will then ask, 'What did you do in return?' He will say, 'I spent money in every cause in which You wished that it should be spent.' The Almighty will say, 'You are lying. You did so that you might be looked up to as a generous fellow; and so it was said.' Then will The Almighty pass orders and he will be dragged with his face downward and thrown into Hell." (*Muslim*, 'Imara, 152)

In the same context, Rumi says, "O heedless! I wish you had turned your face sincerely towards the Almighty when you fell prostrate in worship and known thoroughly the real meaning of saying, 'Exalted is my Lord, freed of all kinds of deficiencies i.e., if you had prostrated yourself in worship with your heart, not just with your body!"

Acts of worship that are not performed in sincerity are morally defective and are contaminated with idolatry. The key to purifying acts of worship is sincerity. Any given deed offered insincerely is of no benefit to the offerer. After the affirmation of true faith, the most emphasized Quranic command is the act of ritual prayer; yet those who offer ritual prayer devoid of sincerity are sternly warned, as made explicit in the following: "So woe to those who pray [but] who are heedless of their prayer." (al-Maun, 4-5) True to this spirit, Junayd al-Baghdadi says, "Sincerity means purifying a deed from moral corruption." Another saint throws light on the subtle balance to be upheld in any given act of worship when he says, "Being pretentious and self-congratulating with respect to being sincere is itself a kind of insincerity." Insofar as the mindset of sincerity is concerned, the biggest danger looms when a servant begins to hold an unshakeable conviction in his own piety. In this connection, the Messenger of Allah –upon him blessings and peace- says, "Be sincere in religion. If you do so, then even a small amount of deeds would be enough for you." (Hakim, *Mustadrak*, IV, 341) In another, *hadith* the Prophet -upon him blessings and peace- underlines the same principle in the words, "Verily the Almighty does not look to your faces and your wealth, but looks to your heart and to your deeds." (*Muslim*, Birr, 34)

5. Sufism means standing upright on the straight path (*istiqamah*)

In Sufi terminology, *istiqamah* is to hold tightly onto the Quran and Sunnah. In the Quran, the Almighty commands the Blessed Prophet –upon him blessings and peace- and the believers with *istiqamah*, declaring,

$$\text{فَاسْتَقِمْ كَمَآ اُمِرْتَ وَ مَنْ تَابَ مَعَكَ وَ لاَ تَطْغَوْا}$$

"So stand firm [in the straight path] as you have been commanded, [you] and those who have turned with you [to The Almighty]; and do not transgress." (Hud, 112).

It has been reported that regarding this chapter of the Quran the Prophet –upon him blessings and peace-, "Chapter Hud made me age" (*Tirmidhi*, Tafsir Surah, 56/6). Commentators have explained the Divine command that placed the Blessed Prophet –upon him blessings and peace- under so heavy a spiritual burden[9], as "O Prophet, you must act in accordance with the morals and regulations of the Quran morality and regulations and represent a living example of uprightness, so that there

---

9   Qurtubi, *al-Jami*, IX, 107.

should not be any doubt and uncertainty regarding your personality. Do not pay attention to the hurtful remarks that come your way from the idolaters and hypocrites and instead let the Almighty deal with them. Stand firm and upright on the straight path with regards to your social and individual responsibilities, as you are commanded and do not deviate from the straight path. Do not fear any kind of difficulty that you might think would prevent you from fulfilling your prophetic mission. No matter how great an obstacle you may encounter, your Lord, and your Lord alone, is your helper."[10]

Regarding this Quranic verse, Abdullah ibn Abbas –Allah be well-pleased with him- comments, "In the intensity in which it addresses the Messenger of Allah –upon him blessings and peace-, there no other Quranic statement more forceful and challenging than this" (Nawawi, *Sharh-i Sahih Muslim*, II, 9). Although this address, on the surface, is directed straight at the Prophet -upon him blessings and peace- himself, the challenge it conveys actually covers all believers; and from this vantage, the apprehension the Blessed Prophet –upon him blessings and peace- was not of his own well-being but, more so, the well-being and ability of his followers to remain unwavering on the upright path. In any case, the Prophet's –upon him blessings and peace- personal uprightness is already confirmed by the Quran, which declares him as being "…on a straight path." (Yasin, 4) Therefore, what had actually made the Blessed Prophet –upon him blessings and peace- age was the unfathomable care he felt for the eternal salvation of his followers.

Since the Blessed Prophet -upon him blessings and peace- was designated as the final prophet of mankind, his message will remain forever alive, as the exclusive guide in showing mankind the way to straight path that shall lead them to the Almighty. The Quran avows that the Lord's love and compassion for human beings depends on their obedience to the Blessed Prophet -upon him blessings and peace-, as mentioned in the following verses,

---

10   Elmalılı M. Hamdi Yazır, *Hak Dini Kur'an Dili*, IV, 2829-2830.

Sufism: A Path Towards the Internalization of Faith (Ihsân)

قُلْ اِنْ كُنْتُمْ تُحِبُّونَ اللّٰهَ فَاتَّبِعُونِى يُحْبِبْكُمُ اللّٰهُ وَ يَغْفِرْ لَكُمْ ذُنُوبَكُمْ وَ اللّٰهُ غَفُورٌ رَحِيمٌ

"Say [O Muhammad], 'If you do love the Lord, then follow me, [so] The Almighty will love you and forgive you your sins. For The Almighty is All-forgiving, All-merciful;'" (Al-i Imran, 31)

"Say, 'Obey The Almighty and obey the Messenger … If you obey him, you will be [rightly] guided.'" (an-Nur, 54)

It is within this framework that Dhunnun-i Misri says, "Whoever follows the Sunnah of the Messenger of Allah, glory unto Him, in practice proves the truth of his love for the Lord." The words of Bayazid Bistami are of a similar tone: "Even if you see a person sitting cross-legged high in the air, look at whether or not he observes Divine commands, follows the Sunnah and observes the limits set by the Almighty's rights. Should you fail to detect these, do not announce his sainthood, merely on the basis of his extraordinary performance." The essence and blissful consequence of remaining steadfast on "the Straight Path" is indicated by the Quran, which assures that "…whoever obeys the Almighty and the Messenger, those will be with the ones upon whom the Almighty has bestowed favor of the prophets, the steadfast affirmers of truth, the martyrs, and the righteous. Ah! What a beautiful fellowship!" (an-Nisa, 69). As the Quranic verse indicates, the straight path, the observing of which rests on obeying the Lord and His Messenger, is the path that the 'chosen' people follow. The gist of standing firm on the straight path is faith and piety of a kind that imparts a continual consciousness of the Lord, and only in the heart do these two elements reside. Standing firm on the straight path, therefore, denotes the process of uniting such a heart with the body. Faith, sincerity and moderation in the heart compel one to stand steady on the straight path and render that stand permanent.

The Blessed Prophet –upon him blessings and peace- has said, "As long as the tongue does not stand firm on the straight path, the heart cannot do so; and as long as the heart does not stand firm on the straight path, faith cannot be strong." (Ahmad ibn Hanbal, *Musnad*, III, 198) A Companion once sought the advice of the Blessed Prophet -upon him blessings and peace-, who then counseled him to say, "…I affirm my faith in the Almighty and then remain steadfast to it." (*Muslim*, Iman, 62)

Neither is there any spiritual state higher than consistently standing firm on the straight path under all circumstances, nor is there any Divine command more difficult in realizing. Standing firm on the straight path is to uphold moderacy in all deeds of worship, without venturing into extremity or insufficiency, and remaining relentless on the path of Allah, glory unto Him. It also and essentially includes performing Divine commands as perfectly as one's personal capacity allows. Owing to its painstaking difficulty, standing firm on the straight path has therefore been considered the greatest extraordinary feat (*karamah*) a saint can ever exhibit. Saints have always attached great importance to this notion of remaining upright; in other words, of being persistent and patient in following the enlightening path of the Blessed Prophet -upon him blessings and peace-. Rumi explains this fact very nicely when he says,

As long as my soul stays in my body,
I am a servant of the Quran and a dust under the Blessed Prophet's feet;
If anyone relates from my words anything other than this,
I am free of his words and himself.
If anyone goes to sit a table other than the Prophet's table,
Beware that Satan will eat from the same pot together with him;
Because the food eaten in any table other than the table of wisdom
Gets stuck in the eater's throat…and even pierces through it.

6. The Sufi way is (*rida*) and submission (*taslimiyyah*)

The term *taslimiyyah* denotes submission, obedience and accepting something without any disagreement. The word Islam comes from the same root. Sufism strives to establish the sentiments of contentment and submission to the Lord deep in the heart, so as to open up an avenue for the servant to come closer to his Lord and constantly feel the Divine Gaze watching over him at all times. Life on Earth is filled with pains, concerns and afflictions, not to mention the fact of having to deal with the innumerable kinds of traps installed by the ego. All these may start decreasing, only when the servant embraces contentment and submission; as they reduce the pain of afflictions to a bare nothing, the moment the servant begins to appreciate that all sufferings are rather blessings in disguise handed out by the Lord. That is when pain becomes a motive for celebration, rather than complaint.

Taslimiyyah further indicates the wholehearted acceptance, by a servant, of everything the hand of fate deals out to him; a resignation towards everything predestined, only of course after taking the necessary precautions from beforehand. The most vivid example of the practice of *taslimiyyah* is perhaps to be found in the attitudes both Ibrahim -upon him peace- and his son Ismail -upon him peace-. Upon being called by the Divine to sacrifice his son, Ibrahim –upon him peace- accepted the chilling command without hesitation, while Ismail –upon him peace- was ever resigned to the Divine command that decreed his sacrifice. The Holy Quran pays homage to their exemplary attitudes, where they are both praised for having "…submitted their wills to the Almighty." (as-Saffat, 103)

A servant should submit himself to the commands and prohibitions of the Almighty and rest content with everything the Almighty inevitably decides for him. Receiving difficulties and trials with patience and placing all trust in the Lord, are indispensable. After all, the path to spiritual perfection is mapped out with trials. In connection, Shaqiq al-Balkhi says, "If only one knew of the rewards for suffering, he would never wish to get rid of it." Well aware of the subtle balance and intimacy of all opposing notions, saints have viewed both grief and pleasure from the same perspective. Since overstressing sadness and, in like measure, exaggerating joy are actually nothing but traps of the ego, it is vital to receive all things in contentment and submission, knowing that what destined to always and irrevocably takes place.

Passion and Divine love are another two aspects integral to *taslimiyyah*, to the degree that a lover always welcomes and enjoys everything, good or bad, that comes from the beloved and looks upon it as an opportunity to prove the genuineness of his love. It was perhaps the same idea that motivated Abu Ali Rudbari to say, "Sufism means kneeling down at the door of the beloved and waiting sincerely and submissively, even if it is certain that the beloved will eventually tell the lover to go away." A servant with a heart brimming over with love embraces everything that comes from his Lord; an embracing whose intensity depends on the depth of his love for Him. Ibrahim's -upon him peace- genuine and loving submission

What is Sufism?

the Almighty transformed a raging fire into a rose garden, within a second. Yaqub's -upon him peace- contentment and submission to Divine predestination made the excruciating pain of separation from his precious son Yusuf -upon him peace- sufferable, as he responded simply by saying, "So patience is most fitting." (Yusuf, 18).

Sufis have made submission to the Almighty a central notion in their lives, as in the words of Rabia al-Adawiyya, "A lover unconditionally obeys his beloved." This means that *taslimiyyah* is a matter of obeying with love. The Companions perfected their levels of their righteousness in and through their love, obedience and faith in the Blessed Prophet -upon him blessings and peace-, by virtue of which they duly became ideal figures to guide the following Muslim generations.

In light of the aforementioned definitions of Sufism, we may conclude by stating that the Sufi way demands that a believer make effort to put the essence of the religion to practice through purifying himself of material as well as immaterial contaminations and assuming good character traits in their place. This way, a believer reaches a comprehensive understanding of all physical and spiritual events that take place and gains an insight to secrets which can otherwise not be grasped by use of the rational faculty alone. Sufism is the struggle to overcome the ego and to let the heart shine its inherent potential to enjoy unlimited spiritual pleasures. From another vantage, the Sufi way is also a kind of scholarly discipline, elaborating on how the flesh chains the spirit into a prison and locks the gates, preventing it from comprehending the realities and wisdoms that underlie surrounding events. In providing the human spirit the key to unlock the gates of the flesh, the Sufi way leads the spirit out of that prison and allows it to explore the lessons and wisdoms embedded in all types of observable events, teaching it the correct way of appraising and re-evaluating them, from an insightful and spiritual panorama.

Ibrahim Effendi, the renowned Sheikh of the Sufi Lodge of Aksaray, eloquently voices the assorted definitions of the Sufi path in the following lines:

Being a Sufi, at the onset, is freedom from material existence,
At the end, it is to rise to throne of the heart

Being a Sufi, at the onset, is to strip away the flesh,
At the end, it is to enter the Lord's palace of secrets.

*Being a Sufi, is to remove the fading garment of the body,
In return for a pure existence, and the light of the Lord...*

*Being a Sufi, is to kindle the candle of the heart with a flame Divine,
And hence throwing it in the fire of love, to burn forever more...*

*Being a Sufi is save oneself from the grip of the ego,
And hence to follow the Law and attain to true faith.*

*Being a Sufi is acquaintance with the ways of the Lord;
And hence to reach out a helping hand and cure to the needy.*

*Being a Sufi is to unlock the flesh with the key of the Lord's Name,
And to usher it in through the gates of nothingness.*

*Being a Sufi is to turn the Sufi words to action,
Where each word uttered becomes a portion of life.*

*Being a Sufi is to learn to interpret the dreams and the word,
To become a secret, in one's own right, in the seat of life.*

*Being a Sufi is to become joyous and bewildered in Divine presence,
To be in amazement before the secrets of the Divine.*

*Being a Sufi is to cleanse the heart of everything other than the Lord,
To turn the heart into His Throne through faith*

*Being a Sufi is to reach East and West in the blink of an eye;
To hence care for all people and offer them shelter.*

*Being a Sufi is to witness the Lord's presence in every particle,
To hence be a sun shining upon all creation.*

*Being a Sufi is to understand the languages of all creation;
To assume to role of Solomon in the realm of intellect.*

*Being a Sufi is to seize the firmest handle, to burden the greatest duty;
To hence reflect on the Quran and convey the news of Divine Mercy.*

*Being a Sufi is to treat all beings through the secret name of the Lord;
The ability to absorb the commands of the Quran.*

*Being a Sufi is to seek the Lord in every gaze thrown,
To hence turn difficulty into ease for the fellow human being.*

What is Sufism?

*Being a Sufi is to turn the heart into a depository of Divine knowledge
To lead a drop, the human being is, into the vast ocean.*

*Being a Sufi is to burn entire existence in the fire of negation;
And then to revive through the light of affirmation".*

Being a Sufi is to call to the path, to say "sufficient is the Lord" (ar-Rad, 43),
To nurture delight for the inevitable "return". (al-Ghashiyah, 28)

*Being a Sufi is to return to life after dying a thousand times each day,
To act as a reviver for corpses from all creation.*

*Being a Sufi is to annihilate existence into the existence Divine,
To conceal oneself in the intimacy of being "even nearer".* (an-Najm, 9)

*Being a Sufi is to surrender the soul to the beloved and become free;
To remain with the beloved forever more.*

*Being a Sufi, Ibrahim, is to become a real servant of the Lord;
To embrace and remain loyal to the Law of Muhammad.*

> The subject matter of Sufism is as vast and deep as an ocean; for it covers everything related to the human soul and spirit.

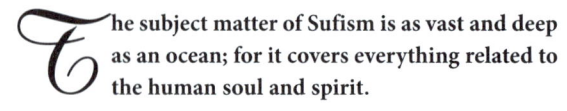

C. THE SUBJECT MATTER OF SUFISM

The variety of definitions and explanations that have been provided of Sufism indicate the breadth of its subject matter. It might therefore be said that the subject matter of Sufism is as vast and deep as an ocean; for it covers everything related to the human soul and spirit. Essentially, it sees to the spiritual states passed by the wayfaring disciple during his spiritual journey, in the beings with whom he meantime gets in touch with, in the experiences he encounters and in the ways he finds, knows, and serves his Lord; though this would only be brief number of the otherwise great breadth of topics the subject matter of Sufism includes. Still, at the risk of being succinct, we may nonetheless proceed to expand on the primary subject matter of the Sufi path.

Above all, the Sufi path engages in the spiritual states and stations a disciple passes by in the process of perfecting his unripe spirit to ripeness, by means of purifying his heart and soul. In other words, Sufism deals with the exact ways of purifying the heart and soul and obtaining inner and outer enlightenment, to enable the actions of the Sufi to accord with Divine pleasure and thereby grant him eternal happiness. The gist of this consists in embodying an exceptional moral conduct and tapping in to the knowledge of spiritual realities. At its core, Sufism thus seeks to ensure one tastes the zest of *ihsan*, of internalizing faith, and enjoying its indescribable pleasure.

To put it in another way, the Sufi path is about the principles and ways to understand the Divine wisdoms, secrets and intentions concealed in names and attributes of Allah, glory unto Him, as well as their abounding manifestations throughout the universe. In this context, Sufism talks about notions related to the unseen, the spirit, the heart and the soul; as well as spiritual experiences like insight (*kashf*), inspiration (*ilham*), spiritual witnessing (*mushahada*), ecstasy (*wajd*), and love (*'ishq*), and no less, the spiritual states attained as a result of undergoing these experiences.

In short, Sufism is concerned with imparting the spiritual ability to behold and witness of the names and attributes of the Lord and to acquire Divine knowledge (*marifatullah*), offering man a real insight into the universe, the Quran, as well as himself, by taking him through a journey at the end of which awaits spiritual maturity.

The aim of the Sufi way is impart the zest of morality onto the heart of a believer; a zest for mercy, affection, generosity, forgiveness and gratitude.

D. THE AIM OF SUFISM

On glancing at the comprehensive definition and subject matter of Sufism, it is easy to see that it carries a significant and sublime objective for humankind. The implementation of this objective began with as early as the first prophet and was perpetuated by all the prophets through to the final prophet, and after him, by saints. One may encapsulate this objective as, 'embodying the duty of servanthood to the Almighty in the best manner possible'. Judging from this approach, Sufism typifies the highest aim of humankind; the objective to free each and every human being from moral defects and endow them with the attributes or moral traits of the Lord and His Messenger -upon him blessings and peace- and thereby enable them to attain to the pleasure of the Almighty. This entails that the ego be subjected to the authority of religion and attuned to offering deeds of worship with sincerity, as befits the notion of *ihsan*. This purifies the heart and steers it in the direction of spiritual realities, and ultimately, to the pleasure of Allah, glory unto Him.

Insofar as his original essence is concerned, man has been created as the best of all creation and 'in the best nature' (at-Tin, 4); yet, on the other hand, with an ever-looming potential to alienate itself from his original reason of existence, man has a tendency to defy and corrupt its otherwise incorrupt nature and become even more bewildered than animals. Therefore, the only criterion to determine the honor and value of man is faith (*iman*) and, afterwards, good morality (*akhlaq*). The duty of prophets has consisted of purifying the hearts and souls of their followers and equipping them with faith and good morals. Being the heirs to the prophets, saints continue and uphold the practice of this blessed duty

What is Sufism?

and represent living examples of prophetic teachings by teaching and practicing the knowledge of the heart in their communities.

Sufis try to follow the Blessed Prophet -upon him blessings and peace- in every manner, both outwardly and inwardly. In their communities, they perform the theoretical and practical duties fulfilled at one time by prophets. The Blessed Prophet –upon him blessings and peace- alludes to the integrity of their mission when he says, "The real scholars are heirs to the prophets." (*Abu Dawud*, 'Ilm, 1) Sufism therefore partakes in the aim of prophets; that of leading people to the direction of spiritual maturity by safeguarding them from sensual, egotistical desires and immorality.

In a *hadith al-qudsi*, the Almighty declares, "This religion is the religion that I approve. Most fitting of this religion are generosity and good morals… so promote these two qualities as long as you follow this religion." (Haythami, *Majma'u al-Zawa'id*, VIII, 20) Compliant with this Divine command, the Sufi way aims to impart the zest of morality onto the heart of a believer; a zest for mercy, affection, generosity, forgiveness and gratitude.

A further aim of Sufism is to help those, who have an inborn spiritual capacity, in improving themselves on the path of abstinence and piety. Sufi teachings guide such people in the direction of spiritual betterment and maturity, by enabling them to suppress the desires of their ego and draw nearer to their Lord; and thereby guiding them in the way of acquiring the knowledge of the Divine. Inspiring Sufis in this regard is the Quranic verse,

إِنَّا عَرَضْنَا الْأَمَانَةَ عَلَى السَّمٰوَاتِ وَ الْأَرْضِ وَ الْجِبَالِ فَاَبَيْنَ اَنْ يَحْمِلْنَهَا وَ اَشْفَقْنَ مِنْهَا وَ حَمَلَهَا الْاِنْسَانُ اِنَّهُ كَانَ ظَلُومًا جَهُولاً

"Indeed, We offered the Trust to the heavens and the earth and the mountains, and they declined to bear it and feared it; but man [undertook to] bear it. Indeed, he was unjust and ignorant." (al-Ahzab, 72) Likewise, the aim of the Sufi way is to save people from tyranny, against both themselves and other, and ignorance and equip them with the characteristics perfection. The antonym of tyranny (*zulm*) is justice (*adl*), which refers to the validity and balance of the deeds offered by a servant. While the antonym of ignorance (*jahl*), on the other hand, is knowledge (*ilm*), in order to

Sufism: A Path Towards the Internalization of Faith (Ihsân)

become a truly knowledgeable person, one needs to absorb both exoteric and esoteric sciences. In this context Ghazzali says, "The heirs to prophets are those who possess a combined knowledge of both exoteric and esoteric sciences."

The salvation of man depends on purging the bad characteristics existent in the ego and on performing deeds in accordance with the criteria laid down for valid righteous deeds (*amal salih*), and no less, on putting knowledge into practice, exclusively through which one becomes a better human being. In Sufi terminology, this implies transforming ordinary knowledge into *irfan*, i.e. gnosis or wisdom. In the final analysis, Sufism deals with theoretical and practical instructions to bring this project to life. Saints are those who realize this objective through perfecting the quality and intensity of their faith and piety; though they are quite few in number. In the Quran, the Almighty alludes to them when He declares,

$$\text{اَلَا اِنَّ اَوْلِيَاءَ اللهِ لَا خَوْفٌ عَلَيْهِمْ}$$
$$\text{وَ لَا هُمْ يَحْزَنُونَ الَّذِينَ اٰمَنُوا وَ كَانُوا يَتَّقُونَ}$$

"Unquestionably, on the friends of the Lord there is no fear, nor will they grieve; those who believe and feel [constantly] the consciousness of the Lord." (Yunus, 62-63)

Properly manifested in the heart, faith saves a believer from all kinds of superstition and brings him closer to his Lord. Piety, in the sense of having a constant consciousness of the Lord, on the other hand, purifies the heart from all else besides the Lord. In this way, the heart of a believer assumes a quality where it becomes 'the precinct of the Divine Gaze' and a recipient, thereby, of the Divine inspirations and wisdoms.

The Day when there will not benefit [anyone] wealth or children, but only one who comes to The Almighty with a sound heart. (as-Shuara, 88-89)

E. THE NECESSITY OF SUFISM

Sufism represents the essence and spiritual dimension of Islam; like the core of a fruit that gives its taste. It is a well-known fact that man fundamentally has two existential dimensions: the body and soul. Each of these dimensions has natural requests and inclinations. Islam does not deny these, as they come from birth and creation; instead it recognizes them as natural facts. Islam, however, does aim at improving positive inclinations, while reducing negative inclinations and temptations to the smallest degree possible and directing them towards a positive end. And conducive to this objective, Islam sets certain principles.

If man ignores his spiritual dimension and designs his whole life merely in accordance with his bodily needs and expectations, he cannot reach happiness and tranquility, since he needs to do something to meet the irrepressible needs of his spiritual existence. Religion provides a balanced schedule between the material and immaterial worlds. On the one hand, it leads human being towards the immaterial world, but on the other hand, it does not deny nor ignore the necessities in relation to this material world. Rather, religion redefines bodily, material inclinations and adds celestial meanings to them. When a man gets used to looking at everything from a materialist perspective, he starts analyzing everything, even the most abstract and subtle ones, from a materialist perception. He fails to see the very immaterial reality behind the material existence. This is, in fact, one of the main reasons behind the opposition of many to the Sufi way.

In its original, uncorrupted form, human perception is attracted to spiritual secrets and abstract realities, as well as to material and concrete beings. The central point is then whether or not a man satisfies the needs

Sufism: A Path Towards the Internalization of Faith (Ihsân)

of his soul, as eagerly as he would satisfy his bodily needs. Today many Westerners, struggling with moral crises and corruption despite having reached the peaks of material welfare, have found themselves dragged to the pits of atheism. Even in Rome, the center of Catholic Christianity, atheists constitute a sizable group in society, only because they have been deprived of satisfaction between their spiritual and immaterial needs. The main reason underlying this predicament is the fact that they have lost the connection between the Divine origin and their heart. Since the current version of their religion has been misrepresented and distorted through human interference, it has lost its untouched Divine form and can therefore no longer satisfy natural human needs. And for this reason, many Westerners do not feel a deep-seated enjoyment of their religion; nor do they reach real happiness and tranquility.

A person who remains deprived of the inner or spiritual enjoyment religion provides views everything, even the most abstract things, from a materialist viewpoint and analyzes them in a crude and formal manner. Consequently, such an understanding of religion remains empty and bone-dry.

As for Sufism, it leads man towards the spirit and soul. It opens a suitable way to personal capacity for spiritual satisfaction. If we ignore the spiritual dimension of religion, which gives satisfaction to man, we would reduce it to the level of human systems based on personal interests. In this case, we would be promoting only the external and worldly benefits of acts of worship and servanthood, at the expense of disregarding the main goal that satisfies the heart. Then, for instance, daily prayer, fasting and almsgiving would be depicted as a certain physical practice, diet, and social assistance, respectively. Such an understanding and practice of religion is always doomed to be highly opportunistic nature. This is not to entirely disregard these consequential benefits altogether; yet they are never the main objectives, but only offshoots of these deeds.

If we pay attention only to the outward benefits of religion, we would entirely miss the main point of offering deeds of worship; and since this jaded perspective would move us away from the essence of Islam, an understanding of the kind would no longer be Islamic. The essence of the religion is about meeting the needs of the human spirit and satisfying the innate human disposition regarding its religious orientation. And the way to furnish the practice of the instructions of religion with a spiritual profundity is Sufi training. Early Muslim believers, who sought to reach a profundity in religion, found some means to attain to it and eventually systematized Sufi education.

Putting all beings on a hierarchical scale of perfection from the simplest to the most advanced, one finds that the human being represents the peak point of this order. But even within human beings, there are many different types and levels with respect to their inborn capacities and inclinations. This is a necessary social arrangement for the facilitation of life on Earth. Based on His unquestionable knowledge and design, the Almighty has created human beings with various potentials, not only with respect to their outward capabilities, but also with respect to their inward or spiritual capabilities. He does not require anything beyond their capacities from His servants, but nonetheless does put certain responsibilities over their shoulders in proportion to their abilities.

The Almighty, Whose mercy is exceeds His wrath, has an unlimited mercy for His entire creation. For this reason, in holding His servants liable with certain responsibilities, the Almighty takes their minimum level of capacities into consideration. In other words, He sets the basic limits in proportion with the capacities of the weakest human being. On the other hand, however, for those who are naturally able to carry responsibilities more than ordinary people, it is only natural that there should be a way to let them improve themselves so that they could flourish and enjoy their spiritual potentials. Otherwise, being restricted from meeting the needs of their spirit would be injustice towards them. Therefore, in addition to the common responsibilities they share with ordinary believers before the Law (*Shariah*), they are nevertheless offered a way of improving their souls in abstinence, piety and internalizing faith. And the Sufi way is just that, which at once, provides both the rational and religious grounds for its necessity.

The peace and serenity of the heart depends on the level of spirituality it has reached. Its realization demands that a servant undergo a spiritual training, insofar as full of knowledge and wisdom, insight into the highest religious realities thus spiritual perfection only begins to trickle inside the heart through an implementing of certain practices. Even in the case of prophets, who were designated among mankind as living models, went through a unique, preparatory process before they ever received Divine revelation. In order for the heart to become receptive to spiritual manifestations, it needs to be refined from its density and hardness to a certain blend of delicacy and sensitivity. True to this process, before he received the mission of prophethood, the Blessed Prophet -upon him blessings and peace- would consistently enter a spiritual retreat. Likewise, Musa -upon him peace- underwent a phase of religious contemplation before he talked to the Almighty. Similarly, before he became the ruler of Egypt, Yusuf -upon him peace- remained in prison for twelve years, in which he endured sufferings of many kinds. And in the end of this period, his heart severed all concerns and relations from all else besides the Almighty.

Before his ascension to the heavens, the Blessed Prophet -upon him blessings and peace- was given insight, by the Divine, into the mystery underlying the Quranic chapter *Inshirah* (Expansion). His chest was cleft open, after which his blessed heart was cleansed and filled with knowledge and wisdom, in preparation for the extraordinary occurrences he was about to witness of Divine secrets and spiritual realities, too subtle and therefore beyond ordinary human perception.

The Blessed Prophet -upon him blessings and peace- had the kindest and purest heart any human being had ever possessed, a fact admitted to by even the most ingrained unbelievers of his time. In spite of this, he still had to undergo a spiritual operation in order to be fully equipped to behold the exposition of the magnificent secrets that were to be exhibited for him by the Almighty, for which he underwent the operation known as *Shaqq-i Sadr* (Expansion of the Breast)[11]. This operation, at once, emphasizes the importance of the spiritual world. Even prophets, exclusive

---

11   *Shaqq-i Sadr* also called *Sharh-i Sadr*, is a term referring to an operation performed by angels on Prophet Muhammad -upon him blessings and peace-. During this operation, the angles cleaved open the Prophet's chest -upon him blessings and peace- and filled it with Divine light and tranquility, so as to impart onto it a spiritual expansion. The Prophet -upon him blessings and peace- underwent this operation twice in his lifetime; first during his childhood and second right before his ascension to heavens. The Qur'an refers to this incident saying, "Have We not expanded for you [O Muhammad] your chest." (Inshirah,1)

in being privileged with the attribute of innocence (*isma*), were made to undergo a process of purifying their hearts before entering the presence of the Almighty.

If the prophets, who were chosen servants of the Almighty, had to undergo a process of inner purification, then we can imagine the necessity and importance of this undertaking for ordinary human beings; for one cannot come close to the Subtle (*Latif*)• with an unsubtle and harsh heart. This is comparable to the case of a person who has lost the sense of sight and smell and who therefore cannot enjoy the delicate fragrance of a rose; or the inability to see a beautiful scene through a vapory window. Thus, in order to become receptive to Divine secrets and wisdoms, the heart needs to be entirely refined of in-subtleness and harshness, evocative of the declaration of the Almighty, in the Quran, which reads, "The Day when there will not benefit [anyone] wealth or children, but only one who comes to The Almighty with a purified heart." (as-Shuara, 88-89) And only by means of spiritual education does the heart assume a purity of the kind.

Strolling along a shore, one can stumble upon a great number of stones, almost embedded in the sand, that have interminably been polished by the splashing waves, which not only has smoothened the stones of all their defects, they have also imparted onto them a durable, granite-like strength. Similar is the case of a raw piece of diamond. Only after being cut through with the skillful strokes of a craftsman does it reach its inner potential of brilliance and transparency. Likewise, in order to obtain a little amount of gold, one must sift a huge amount of soil. What we mean is that every single thing in this world goes through some kind of a process of refinement and purification. The heart is no different; for in order to attain to its Quranic quality of purity, it must be subjected to a spiritual education.

A spiritually uneducated heart is a raw and cold iron. Giving it a certain shape demands that it be placed in a fire to burn away its rust, and a few, competent strikes to transform its hard, stubborn quality to softness. Only after such a sequence can one furnish it with the intended shape. Likewise is the case of the heart; in order to perfect its inherent quality, it needs to be placed under certain spiritual trainings, after which it begins to witness the realm of realities, invisible to ordinary vision and impermeable to the rational faculties. This unique kind of vision or witnessing is purely a matter of spiritual experience and perception.

To be able to reach this level of perfection, one needs to strengthen and mature the capacity of one's heart. In a similar fashion, if an ordinary and untrained person attempts to perform a physical motion that normally requires long practice, he may end up breaking his bones; yet the same motion can easily be performed by a trained athlete without any risk. Any given physical ability can be achieved by concentrating the entire strength of the body onto a single point. Correspondingly, for the heart to acquire the necessary spiritual ability, all its strength must concentrate on the remembrance of Allah, glory unto Him, and love for His Messenger -upon him blessings and peace-. The Quran hints at this prerequisite when it declares,

$$\text{اِنَّمَا الْمُؤْمِنُونَ الَّذِينَ اِذَا ذُكِرَ اللّٰهُ وَجِلَتْ قُلُوبُهُمْ}$$
$$\text{وَ اِذَا تُلِيَتْ عَلَيْهِمْ اٰيَاتُهُ زَادَتْهُمْ اِيمَانًا وَ عَلٰى رَبِّهِمْ يَتَوَكَّلُونَ}$$

"The believers are only those who, when The Almighty is mentioned, their hearts become fearful, and when His verses are recited to them, it increases them in faith; and upon their Lord they rely." (al-Anfal, 2)

Guiding the heart atop this high level of perfection involves a process of cleansing it and keeping it distant from sin and instilling in it a spiritual maturity; since a hard, untrained heart cannot get in proper touch with the Lord. An elementary school student cannot understand the content of the books studied by law school students, simply because his mind has not reached the level of maturity required for their comprehension. He still has long years of education in front of him. Similarly, an immature and raw heart needs a certain kind of education and training before it can ever begin to comprehend the intricate subtleties on the path of the Lord. It is this education or training that is the hallmark of the Sufi path.

The sole focal point is hence the heart; the quality of which the Lord pays attention to in all conduct and deeds of worship, as testified to by the words of the Blessed Prophet -upon him blessings and peace-: "Verily the Almighty does not look at your bodies and your appearances, but He look at your hearts" (*Muslim*, Birr, 33). This goes for all kinds of conduct. If a servant, for instance, eats with the intention of gaining strength to duly fulfill his deeds of worship, even his eating itself is considered a type of worship. Working to earn a livelihood for one's family in a lawful manner is also a type of worship; and every move made for that purpose is met with by a reward from the Almighty, as his intention, which is an act exclusive to the heart, is good.

Similar to this is clothing. Wearing an *imamah*, for instance, is a part of Sunnah or the authentic practice of the Prophet –upon him blessings and peace-. A person who wears an *imamah*, however, should look to mature his spiritual dimension and personify this formal Sunnah in his moral conduct, through exhibiting, for instance, affection and mercy, among numerous others. Mere formality is, otherwise, insufficient on its own; it might even lead a person to ostentation. Yunus Emre expresses this fact wonderfully, when he says, "If becoming a dervish was wearing a turban and cloak, we would buy them at little expense."

In a similar fashion, the veiling of women is a requirement in Islam. A Muslim woman, however, should be veiled not just formally and outwardly, but also spiritually and inwardly. While her body is veiled, a woman's morality might in fact be meager and naked. If a woman is ignorant and brazen, she may easily put aside her veil when the times become difficult or when her ego finds a way to dominate her. Whilst veiling herself, she must maintain her mission of womanhood, since she is entrusted with the responsibility over the nurturing of her children and housekeeping. For this reason, a solid moral fiber is essential for her in every aspect of life. Without a doubt, her morals ought to go hand-in-hand with her formal veiling, which she must observe, lest she transgress the limits set by the Almighty. With that said, insofar as the commands of the Almighty are concerned, covering up is not the end of the road but only part and perhaps the beginning of it.

To cite another example, building a mosque is considered a huge charity in Islam, but if the benefactor acts not out of moral maturity but only to promote the selfishness of his ego in a self-congratulatory manner, Allah forbid, the value of his charity becomes very little and almost nothing. Indeed, the Almighty belittles and humiliates those who, in their deeds, promote only themselves and always say 'I'; though, in contrast, He praises those who say, "O Lord! This is but your favor and kindness." The sole criterion, therefore, of rendering all human actions acceptable in the Sight of the Divine is their underlying intention and moral quality.

With all the aforementioned accounts now in the backdrop, we may arrive at the conclusion that Sufism plays a significant religious role in human life; for it is a spiritual system of education whose motivation is to teach the precise and appropriate manner of how every single action ought to be executed, that is to say, under the constant mindset of being in a state of worship, and how every act of worship is to be offered in a spiritually refined way. There are, in fact, two complementary dimensions in every single deed of worship: form and essence or spirit. In the Quran, Allah, glory unto him, does not provide detailed information regarding the formal requirements of worship, such as the number of times one is supposed to kneel and prostrate in a single daily prayer. But He does inform us about the required moral and spiritual qualities we must embody when offering them, leaving the teaching of their formal requirements to the practice of the Blessed Prophet –upon him blessings and peace-.

Even a hypocrite can fulfill the mere formal or outward requirements of a given deed of worship. The chief hypocrite Abdullah ibn Ubayy ibn Salul, for example, would frequent the Mosque in Medina to offer his daily prayers behind the lead of the Blessed Prophet -upon him blessings and peace-; yet this offering was a sheer matter of formality, lacking the embodiment of real essence behind the deed. Acts of worship offered only to meet formalities do not have any merit in the presence of the Almighty. Their acceptability depends on the unity of form and essence.

A careful analysis of both the Quranic verses and the Prophetic sayings on the pillars of Islam, such as daily prayer, fasting, almsgiving and pilgrimage, reveals that it is imperative for a servant to unite their outward and inward requirements in his deed. In relation to daily prayer, for instance, the Quran declares, "Indeed, prayer restrains from immorality and wrongdoing." (al-Ankabut, 45) A person is unable to restrain himself from wrongdoings despite punctually offering his daily prayers, lacks sincerity in his deed. The Almighty is stern concerning those who outwardly offer the daily prayers, yet insincerely: "So woe to those who pray, [but] who are heedless of their prayer." (al-Maun, 4-5) Similar is another Quranic verse: "Certainly will the believers have succeeded: They who are during their prayer humbly submissive." (al-Muminun, 1-2)

According to the requirements laid down by above verses of the Quran, the primary characteristic of those who are bound for salvation is that they offer ritual prayers submissively. Performing a prayer in a complete manner demands that one implements its outward and inward requirements in unity. We can picture two persons offering prayer at the same time and place; yet that is not to say that there is no great difference between the two performances. In explaining the inner requirements of a ritual, the Prophet -upon him blessings and peace- states, "A person performs prayer; but only one half, one third, one fourth, one fifth, one sixth, one seventh, one eighth, one ninth, even one tenth of his prayer is written for him [as reward]." (Ahmad ibn Hanbal, *Musnad*, IV, 321) In the Quran, the Almighty identifies believers as those "…who carefully maintain their prayers." (al-Muminun, 9)

Together with, though venturing beyond its external meaning, Rumi provides an esoteric interpretation of the above Quranic verse and says, "They maintain their states during prayer, even after completing the prayer. The daily prayers, that show us the straight path and restrain us from wrongdoing, are performed five times a day. But the lovers are always in prayer; for the passion in of Divine love burning inside their hearts cannot be snuffed out in five splashes; nor would it disappear with five-hundred-thousand." Similarly, Yunus Emre describes the prayers of those awakened from heedlessness in the following lines:

Our imam is love, our congregation in the heart;
The qiblah is the Beloved, the prayer incessant.

In fact, a standard ritual prayer lasts approximately up to ten or fifteen minutes. Still, a servant is expected to maintain his religious concentration even after completing his daily prayers, lest his heart be exposed to the intrusion of ill-thoughts that gradually throw it back into heedlessness, immorality and even -Allah forbid – disbelief. For this reason, the servant should relentlessly busy his heart busy with Divine remembrance and always remain mindful of Him.

Sufism: A Path Towards the Internalization of Faith (Ihsân)

The heedless, on the other hand, do not have a heart endowed with the quality of being submissive to and mindful of the Almighty even during ritual prayer, let alone outside it. On this subject, the following story is quite meaningful.

A dervish, proceeding on the path of spiritual maturity, was offering ritual prayer in a mosque in the middle of the night. Then it suddenly started raining and with the raindrops pelting down onto the roof, his heart began longing for home. At that moment, a cautionary voice inside of him said, "This prayer of yours is no good for us because you have sent your beautiful part (heart) home and left here merely your body." This recalls the words of the Blessed Prophet -upon him blessings and peace-: "There are many who pray deep into the night but staying up late sleepless is all they gain." (Ahmad ibn Hanbal, *Musnad*, II, 373) Ultimately, it all comes down to moral and spiritual maturity.

Comparable is the case of fasting, comprised of both outward and inward dimensions, which must be taken into account when offering one. The Blessed Prophet –upon him blessings and peace- assures that such a consummate offering of fasting erases all kinds of sins previously committed: "Whoever fasts during the month of Ramadan, believing in its merit and expecting its return only from the Almighty, will have his past sins forgiven." (*Bukhari*, Sawm, 6) Otherwise, fasting is merely an experiment of starvation. Rather, the purpose of fasting is to acquire a forceful sense of piety; a sense of being conscious of the Lord at all times (*taqwa*). Attesting to this is the Quran itself: "O you who believe! Fasting is prescribed to you as it was prescribed to those before you that you may attain piety." (al-Baqarah, 183)

From this perspective, fasting should not be performed only with the stomach, but with the entire organs of the body, and most importantly, the heart. Through contemplating on the significance of the blessings given by the Almighty, the heart is expected to comprehend the spiritual depth of the notion of fasting. Fasting is a type of training to flourish good moral characteristics in man, like mercy and affection. If a person fasts without displaying such characteristics, his fasting becomes a matter of formality. Gossiping and backbiting, especially, whilst fasting, prevents the deed from receiving any rewards and reduces it to nothing. The Blessed

Prophet -upon him blessings and peace- underlines the importance of this fact saying, "There are many of those who fast, but the only result of their fasting is hunger and thirst." (Ahmad ibn Hanbal, *Musnad*, II, 373) This *hadith* is another indication of the necessity of upholding the moral and spiritual dimensions of fasting.

The significance of the moral and spiritual dimensions of deeds of worship can also be observed in almsgiving (*zakat*), a manifestation and proof of a believer's altruism. When He talks about the characteristics of the believers in the Quran, the Almighty says, "And from their properties was [given] the right of the [needy] petitioner and the deprived." (ad-Dhariyat, 9)

If a believer is person of spiritual strength, on handing out the required alms from his wealth, he does so with the mindset of restoring the rights the needy and deprived and not as if he is doing them a favor; he further feels appreciation and gratitude towards them for giving him the opportunity to purify his wealth. Only by embodying this mindset can a believer take hold of the real meaning and virtue of almsgiving. To be sure, the receiver does help the benefactor in providing an avenue for him to fulfill an obligatory deed of worship and to protect him from misfortunes and troubles, as well as enabling him to acquire eternal rewards. When offering any form of charity, a truly mature believer acts in accordance with the *hadith*, "Charity reaches The Almighty's Hand [of power] before it reaches the hand of the needy." (Tabarani, *Mujam al-Kabir*, IX, 109)[12] To be able to grasp the secret of this *hadith*, the believer acts insightfully and knows that everything he gives goes, in reality, to the Almighty. And such is the confirmatory basis of the spiritual dimension of almsgiving, a sensitivity that only comes through with moral and spiritual maturity.

When giving something away as charity, the great saints would even wrap it in a nice cover and give it in secret, mindful of the fact that the Almighty would receive it first before the needy. Such are some of the manifestations the moral sensitivity and kindness Islam imparts. Alluding to the etiquette in offering charity, the Almighty emphasizes the same point in the Quran by declaring, "He (The Almighty) receives charities." (at-Tawbah, 104)

---

12   For a similar narration see also *Bukhari*, Tawhid, 23.

In stark contrast, if a person offers charity without any awareness of delicate etiquette he needs to embody and in a conceited way that rubs salt onto the wound of the needy, it would mean obliterate all his potential rewards, as Islam sternly condemns such arrogance and insensitivity. A Muslim should always be an epitome of kindness and sensitivity; yet then again, these characteristics depend on the moral and spiritual level of the person.

Supreme moral and spiritual character traits are more perceptible during pilgrimage. On the surface, pilgrimage comes across as a deed of worship dominated by formal and physical aspects, like wearing the pilgrim's garb (*ihram*), circumambulating (*tawaf*), standing on the hill of Arafat, offering sacrifice, going to Muzdalifa, and so on. These, however, comprise only the external aspects of pilgrimage. When we look into the spiritual dimension of this act of worship, by taking part in it, we are reminded of the Final Hour and the Day of Judgment, through which we are called upon to contemplate on the Divine reckoning and to reflect on and reevaluate the days of our lives that have passed thus far.

In a mosque, believers stand in the same line of prayer, regardless of their social standing. Still, a quick look at what each person wears by suffices to provide enough evidence for us to make an accurate estimation of what the social standing of each and every person actually is. But conducting guesswork of the kind is impossible during the annual pilgrimage. Millions of people stand shoulder to shoulder, enshrouded in the same type of clothing, without giving away the least clue as to what their social standings in this world might be. The pilgrims are guided towards such deep-seated sensitivity and kindness that as long as they are enshrouded in the pilgrim's garb, they are disallowed from doing certain things they are normally free to do at all times else. For instance, pilgrims are not allowed to pluck any grass and hunt any animals; they are not even allowed to point out the location of game to a hunter. Idle chatting and vain activities are also forbidden so that the heart may concentrate only on higher realities.

On a similar note, sacrificing an animal with the intention of seeking closeness to the Lord also has both outward and inward requirements, as is the case with all other acts of worship. Although the process of sacrificing an animal comprises certain rituals one must follow, the chief aspect of this act is the performer's intention, whose place is, again, in the heart. It is the quality of the intention which determines whether or not the sacrifice is accepted in the presence of the Almighty. The Divine instruction in this regard is clear:

$$\text{لَنْ يَنَالَ اللهَ لُحُومُهَا وَ لاَ دِمَآ ؤُهَا وَ لٰكِنْ يَنَالُهُ التَّقْوٰى مِنْكُمْ}$$

"It is not their meat, nor their blood that reaches the Almighty; it is your piety that reaches Him." (al-Hajj, 37)

In light of the above Quranic verse, we may say that if a person sacrifices an animal under social duress, that is, an anxiety over the possible backlash of the Muslim community should he abstain from fulfilling the requirement, his deed will not grant him the pleasure of the Almighty. A vivid example of this is mentioned in the Quran in the accounts of Prophet Adam's -upon him blessings and peace- two sons. Cain had presented a sacrifice to Allah, glory unto Him, but halfheartedly, merely to comply with the rule. And expectedly his sacrifice was rejected. His brother, Abel, on the other hand, presented his own sacrifice sincerely and righteously, consequent upon which his sacrifice was accepted. The related Quranic verse reads, "And recite to them the truth of the story of the two sons of Adam. Behold! They each presented a sacrifice [to The Almighty]: it was accepted from one, but not from the other. Said the latter, 'Be sure I will kill you.' 'Surely', said the former, 'The Almighty only accepts from the righteous.'" (al-Maida, 27)

All the above mentioned points indicate that the acceptability and integrity of all acts of worship depend primarily on moral and spiritual maturity and consciousness in which they are offered. This serves as a strong testimony to the necessity of spiritual education and the indispensability of purifying the heart.

In this conjunction, however, there is to be found a further delicate point. It is true that all deeds of worship ought to be performed with sincerity and piety, free from the devastating intrusion of any kind of ostentation. But it would even be a worse mistake for the servant to stop short at

Sufism: A Path Towards the Internalization of Faith (Ihsân)

offering the obligatory deeds of worship due to the fear that he may not live up to the required standards and hence render all his efforts futile. One is not expected to discard the duty of offering deeds of worship; much rather, he is expected to put in his best effort to enhance their quality as much as possible through adjusting his inner world by virtue of increasing his level of sincerity and piety. The path of spiritual progress is, after all, full of difficulties, and it demands a great struggle against sensual tendencies. There is no such thing as reaching the ultimate level swiftly and with leisurely ease. Sincerity is the highest point of spiritual advancement and climbing to this point requires a gradual, step-by-step progress. And as essential as it is to apply personal effort on this path, it is more important to pray to receive Divine help and guidance.

In view of the fact that the quality of one's deeds relies on his moral and spiritual condition, the Sufi way extends an indispensable helping hand in guiding the heart towards its proper direction and reason for existence. It is thus not surprising to observe that attempts which portray Islam as a dry and empty collection of regulations always end up in a downright rejection of the Sufi way. Such a conclusion is only a natural outcome of their sterile course of thinking.

That mistakes, misuses and misrepresentations figure in all scholarly disciplines is an unquestionable fact of matter. Religious disciplines are no different, including Sufism, the essence and spiritual dimension of Islamic learning. Yet, authorities in any given field can distinguish right from wrong regarding the matter under question. In this manner, any deliberate or absentminded attempt to show that certain arbitrary mistakes and misuses are in fact peculiar to the field of Sufism, would be dubious. Competence and incompetence in the persons involved can be found across all scholarly fields; and there is no justifiable reason to single out Sufism in this regard and employ some incompetent cases in point to devalue its position within the spectrum of Islamic religious disciplines.

There might be some incompetent people who refer to themselves as Sufis and act supposedly on its behalf, though in reality they might in fact only be exploiting it. There is no reason to generalize their particular situations and extend it to the eligible Sufis of competence who practice this discipline strictly in line with the Islamic religious tradition. Rejecting

What is Sufism?

Sufism as an Islamic field on this ground alone is therefore implausible. To downright reject the Sufi way due to certain misrepresentations is comparable to rejecting the entire field of medicine due to some medical mistreatments; and there indeed might be some practitioners in the field of medicine, who misuse and exploit this discipline. Therefore both theoretically and practically, it is unfeasible to disclaim Sufism as not being essential to Islamic learning.

The Sufi way cannot be understood based on the practices of self-acclaimed Sufis, incompetent and of ill-intent, who stake a claim to being eligible representatives of this tradition. Since Sufism can be understood and observed only by those of spiritual depth, even the simplest minds can distinguish the authentic Sufi way from the inauthentic, based on the enormous difference of quality between their practices.

Sufism cannot be understood on the basis of casual generalizations either, as it is a matter of heart, a state-of-mind founded upon passion and love. To describe Sufism in a way that does justice to it, to those who do not have the least share of love is ultimately a vain endeavor; comparable to describing colors to person who was born blind.

The more man moves away from contemplating on his inner world, the more he becomes a powerless imitator. Neither can he understand his own reality, nor can he plunge into the depths of his soul. The best he can do is to try to imitate those around. Unable to even enjoy the great potential lying dormant in his heart, he is all the more distant from setting an example within his community. Gaining closeness to the Lord and reaching Him becomes possible, only after nurturing a sublime moral quality that renounces all kinds of temporal desires and concerns.

At its core, Sufism is a science about mankind. When a man sets himself free from earthly concerns and concentrates on his soul and spirit, he finds himself before the gates of the palace of wisdoms and realities. The real Sufis are those who understand the Quran and make it their distinctive guide in upholding their true faith. A Sufi is a person who feels responsible in the presence of the Lord for the eternal wellbeing of the community in which he lives.

On one occasion, the saint Najmaddin Kubra joined his disciples to offer the funeral prayer of a righteous man who had just passed away.

Towards the end of the prayer, when, ritually, they started reminding the dead of the required information in the grave, Kubra smiled. His disciples were surprised to see Kubra smile on such an occasion and could not help but ask him of the reason. First, he did not want to explain the reason, but when his students insisted, Kubra said, "The heart of the man reminding the dead of the required information was dead and heedless, while the heart of the dead was awake and mindful. I was astonished at the fact that a heedless person was trying to help someone mindful, whose heart in reality was awake."

In a sense, the case of those who reject Sufism supposedly for the sake of upholding the integrity of knowledge, is as astounding as the case of a dead heart trying to revive a heart that is already alive. Already proven is the success of Sufis throughout centuries in keeping religious life alive, passing it onto following generations, guiding the general public and delivering the message of Islam. A contemporary Muslim scholar testifies to this fact and confesses, "I was brought up in a rational manner. My jurisprudential studies and investigations made me reject everything that was not explained and proved to me in a convincing way. Undoubtedly to this day, I fulfill my religious responsibilities, such as daily prayers and fasting, not on account of sufistic motivations but from a jurisprudential obligation. I say to myself, 'The Almighty is my Lord, my Protector. He has commanded me to do these and I have to do them. Other than that, rights and responsibilities are mutually dependent. The Almighty has decreed these for me so that I could benefit from them, which means I am responsible for thanking Him.'

But since I started living in the West, in Paris to be precise, I was astounded to observe that it is the words of Sufis like Ibn Arabi and Rumi that primarily lead Christians to embrace Islam; not the views of Muslim jurisprudents or theologians. I have stood witness to this on many an occasion. On being asked a question regarding a certain Islamic topic, my answer would always prove unconvincing if based on rational proofs and reasoning. But offering a sufistic explanation would always prove successful; though in time, I lost my efficiency in this regard. I nonetheless realized that greater service to Islam, at least in today's Europe and Africa, lied not in the sword or reason but in the heart, namely in Sufism; as was the case during the time of Ghazan Khan following the blistering devastation of Muslim lands in the hands of Hulagu.

Upon this observation, I started examining some works of Sufism; and this opened the eye of my heart. I realized that the path of Sufism during the lifetime of the Blessed Prophet -upon him blessings and peace- and in the practice of eminent Sufi figures, was not too busy oneself with certain scholarly words and formulations, but to proceed on the swiftest path leading man to the Lord and to seek the ways to improve human character. Man looks for reasons behind the responsibilities placed on his shoulders. Rational and material explanations regarding the metaphysical world move us away from the goal. It is only metaphysical or spiritual explanations that satisfy human beings."[13]

In light of these words, we can draw the conclusion that any attempt to reject Sufism, whose agreement with the Quran and Sunnah is unquestionable, is tantamount to cutting down a fruitful tree, a grave sin to commit indeed. In the words of Rumi, "Do not blame the rose, if your nose cannot smell."

Another important aspect of Sufism in our contemporary world lies in the method it applies in correcting human character and behavior, conducive to transforming one into a better human being. Our noble *Shariah* aims at guiding human beings by drawing to their attention to the awaiting rewards and punishments both in this life and in the Hereafter. As for Sufism, it uses affection and love. The contemporary human being suffers in the spiritual depression of being distanced from religion and under the excruciating burden of sin. Undeniable is the fact that extending forgiveness, lenience and affection will exercise a greater effect in correcting and saving such people. From this perspective, today's world stands in dire need of the Sufi method, both theoretically and practically, as much as it needs spiritual realities. Educating and guiding people under the shade of mercy, tolerance and affection would undoubtedly culminate in a universal success. Approaching these vulnerable souls suffering under the tyranny

---

[13] M. Aziz Lahhabi, *Islam Sahsiyetciligi*, trans. I. Hakki Akin, pp. 114-115, footnote 8, Istanbul, 1972. This footnote exists in a letter written by Muhammad Hamidullah to the translator, dated September 27, 1967. (Taken from Mustafa Kara, *Metinlerle Gunumuz Tasavvuf Hareketleri*, pp. 542-543)

of reason and sensuality in an Islamic manner and using such positive and encouraging notions to lead them to a better direction, will surely yield more fruitful results than threatening them with certain punishments.

Since Sufism regards the immorality and transgression of humankind as a side effect of a lack of love, its method prioritizes positive notions and endorses them as bases for delivering the Islamic message. By nature, human beings always yearn for affection; they therefore embrace the approaches adopted over the centuries by saints like Abdulqadir Jilani, Yunus Emre, Bahauddin Naqshbandi and Rumi.

The below anecdote is moving in terms of reflecting modern man's yearning and love for saints of the yester-years. Muhammad Iqbal, the great contemporary Muslim intellectual and a Rumi enthusiast, was on board on a flight to Turkey. The moment the plane entered the Turkish airspace, the great thinker stood up from his seat and remained standing for a while. When the people accompanying asked him as to why he had done so, Iqbal evocatively replied, "These are the lands of Rumi's grave and of the meritorious people who burdened the great responsibility of protecting Islam against its enemies. Were it not for the Turks, Islam would have receded back into the Arabian Peninsula. Out of the great respect I have in my heart for this great scholar and people, I felt compelled to stand up in reverence."

The moving example above shows that a true Sufi may exercise an influence that stands the test of time over many centuries. Many centuries after his passing away, Rumi, one of the greatest representatives of the Sufi way, drew the admiration of another great mind of the caliber of Iqbal. The fact that Rumi's teachings could wield a momentous influence in helping Iqbal shape his character and adorn it with love, passion, sensitivity, and knowledge, in a sense, attests to the necessity of the Sufi path in our own time. Sufism unites hearts from the East to the West, maturing and exalting them in the process; and this is an undeniable reality that encompasses all ages and generations.

To be a Sufi is to be equipped with exoteric sciences and realities and to thereby reach beyond the climes of the heart-world.

F. THE RELATION OF SUFISM TO OTHER SCHOLARLY DISCIPLINES

Scholarly disciplines come into existence consequent upon the inborn interest human beings have for inquiry. Each of these disciplines investigates laws and principles regarding the realities in the area of its specialty. Through its investigation each discipline reaches, intentionally or unintentionally, certain points in common with Sufism, which itself incorporates and covers the same given field from broader perspective; that is from the vantage of wisdom. This mutuality is not relevant only to religious sciences, but also to all other sciences, theoretical and practical, ranging from fine arts to philosophy. In this relation, we will now look briefly into the relation of Sufism to other scholarly disciplines under five categories.

1. SUFISM AND OTHER ISLAMIC DISCIPLINES

The purpose of religion is to make man acquainted with his Creator to mankind, to inform him of the obligations and responsibilities he has in Divine presence and to guide him to organize his social interactions in accordance with Divine will. Corresponding with this is the goal of Sufism; to lead a believer to this direction and endow him with a moral and spiritual strength to help him actualize these religious goals. Sufism also provides a spiritual background and explanation for the external aspects of religious commands and spiritually motivates a believer to offer his duties with a passionate sincerity and piety. As is therefore expected, the Sufi way is inextricably connected with all other branches of Islamic learning. An

Sufism and Theology

The subject matters of Islamic theology are primarily the Almighty's essence, attributes and oneness. Since it is principally related to creedal topics, theology is regarded as the most important Islamic discipline (*ashrafu'l-ulum*). One of the basic goals of theology is establishing intellectual bases for endorsing true beliefs and rejecting false ones. Therefore, one of Islamic theology's main functions is to respond to the critiques and opposition directed against Islam and to convince people of that Islam is a true and authentic religion revealed by the Almighty. The goal of Sufism is similar; it aims at knowing Allah, glory unto Him, Who has perfect attributes and is free from any kinds of defect, but through the heart.

Theology tries to find solutions to creedal issues on the basis of the Quran and Sunnah and by use of the human rational faculty. In this regard, theologians' position may be comparable to that of philosophers. Yet, unlike the latter, the former do not use human reason independently from religion; instead, they put reason under the service of religion. Nevertheless, through its logical move from cause to effect, the rational faculty of man is not sufficient, on its own, to enable one to reach the truth. This is a journey of knowledge that requires the utilization of other means, first and foremost the heart.

Exactly at the point where reason arrives at a dead-end and cannot proceed to figure out the solution, the heart takes the lead and ensures man proceeds on this journey to see the solution for himself. In the Sufi path, these solutions manifest in the heart, in the form of spiritual unveilings and inspirations; and it goes without saying that the way in which these clarifying solutions are comprehended must be in agreement with the Quran and Sunnah. Eventually, at the end of this epistemological process, Sufism leads a servant to a satisfactory finale.

To be sure, Muslim theologians also acknowledge the necessity of the heart as an authentic instrument of knowledge. In this regard, as has already been mentioned, they differ from philosophers, the majority of whom acknowledge only the faculty of reason as an instrument of knowledge. Historically speaking, there are many theologians who theoretically acknowledge the validity of spiritual explanations, not to mention many others to have personally practiced the Sufi way.

In effect, the mental activity of man, his reason and judgment, are always derived from the sensory impressions received from the material world. He thus tries to reach the truth by means of drawing similarities and discerning opposites. Reaching and grasping, however, the existence and realities of metaphysical beings, of which ordinary human mental activity does not have previous impressions, is impossible in this manner. The human faculty of reason, therefore, cannot satisfy man's inborn inclinations towards reaching the Real, save to a limited extent. In relation to metaphysical realities, to which ordinary human reason does not have access, man can improve his level of intellectual satisfaction and perfect it through spiritual inspirations and manifestations that are impressed upon the heart. The main function of Sufism comes into existence at this point, for it provides an indispensable service to man in making him reach out to realities of a more advanced nature, which otherwise stand beyond the capacity of ordinary human reason. Sufism actualizes this possibility by invigorating man through Divine remembrance and thus renders the heart suitable to receive spiritual unveilings and inspirations. In this context, mainly with respect to the essential and performative attributes of the Almighty, Sufism is not only closely connected to Islamic theology; it further improves the theological explanations and hence human satisfaction, especially with regards to the metaphysical issues for which the human faculty of reason cannot provide sufficient answers.

Sufism addresses people in proportion to their intellectual capacities and enriches general theological arguments for the use and satisfaction of competent minds. It strengthens a person's belief and conviction in the existence and oneness of the Almighty. Fakhruddin Razi, a prominent Muslim theologian and exegete, elucidates the relation between Sufism and Islamic theology and says, "Even though the methodologies of theologians are not sufficient enough to attain to reality, they are still the necessary first steps to be taken as a prelude to Sufism. Religious perfection can be attained through a healthy transition from exoteric religious sciences to the esoteric ones; the latter being based on knowledge of the underlying realities of things."[14]

Sufism and Quranic Exegesis (*Tafsir*)

The science of Quranic exegesis explores the meanings of Quranic revelations and elaborates on them. The Holy Quran is a Divine guidance for mankind and its expressions comprise a depth of meaning. From this perspective, *tafsir* functions like a pharmacy for Sufism. Sufism aims at purifying and perfecting the inner dimension of man, an aim which the field of *tafsir* complements by providing the required prescriptions and medicine. In its application and analysis of topics, as well as in establishing its foundational methodology, Sufism relies principally on the Quran.

By offering instructions in every aspect of life, the Holy Quran leads mankind to attain to the pleasure of the Lord. It informs man the exact manner of leading a life dominated by the ever-present feeling of responsibility before the Almighty, of offering deeds of worship in the most sincere manner thinkable and pursuing life of piety adorned by an unremitting remembrance of the Divine. These considerations are equally central to the Sufi way.

As has already been underlined, the primary aim of a Sufi is to reach the Lord through the heart. And the authentic Sufi conception acknowledges the Holy Quran, the touchstone of human life, whose brilliant verse call for the deepest of all reflections, as the exclusive means to lead man to this direction. Reciting the Quran is an indispensable part of a Sufi's life; it is the first thing he is required to do in the earliest hours of the morning. Capturing the subtle meanings conveyed by the Quranic verses, however, requires, in turn, a purified heart.

Since through his moral conduct the Blessed Prophet -upon him blessings and peace- was the Quran come-to-life, saints, being dedicated to moral perfection, strive to regulate every aspect of their lives in accordance with the ideal the Prophet –upon him blessings and peace- provided. By

---

14 Muhammad Salih al-Zarqan, *Fakhr al-Din al-Razi wa-ara'uhu al-kalamiyya wa-al-falsafiyya*, p. 76 (taken from Muhammad Abid al-Jabiri, *Arab-Islam Kültürü'nün Akıl Yapısı*, p. 626.)

practicing and actualizing the Quran in every dimension of their lives, they become living Qurans in their own right.

As the Holy Quran is their main source of blessing and inspiration, Sufis have contributed immensely to *tafsir* literature, providing an invaluable service for enriching this literature through bringing the allegorical meanings of the verses of the Quran to light. Sufi commentators of the Quran have worked meticulously on unearthing the subtle meanings and inner wisdoms of Quranic expressions. Of course, their undertaking should not be confused with an attempt to imprison the illimitable Divine Words within limited human expressions; this was never their intention, insofar as a Sufi would never even think of devaluing the priceless expressions of the Quran. Furthermore, the Sufi methodology does not justify arbitrary and baseless interpretations. The general principles for a proper spiritual commentary as has been set by Sufi masters, is as follows:

1) The inner meaning posited for any given Quranic statement must not contradict the external message of the given verse.

2) The suggested meaning must have a place the general content of the Quran and Sunnah.

3) The wording and context of the given Quranic verse must be suitable for the proposed allegorical meaning.

As some authoritative examples of Sufi commentaries of the Quran, we may mention the *Haqaiqu't-Tafsir* of Abu Abdullah Rahman as-Sulami, the *Lataifu'l-Isharat* of Qushayri and the *Ruhu'l-Bayan* of Ismail Hakki of Bursa. In addition to these complete commentaries of the Holy Quran, there are many others that include allegorical interpretations of specific Quranic verse, such as the works of Ibn Arabi and Rumi. Doubtless is the fact that the Quran is the inimitable word of the Almighty that has come directly from His attribute of Speech (*kalam*). Therefore, however competent a commentary may be, in the final reckoning, it is still a commentary; the reflections and words of a human being which cannot encompass the entirety of the semantic world of the Quran.

As human beings, we cannot completely understand the reality of the Almighty's essence and attributes. Likewise is the case of understanding the Quran. Being a product of the Lord's unique attribute of Speech, the Quran cannot be comprehended by any mind and rephrased by any tongue, however well-gifted they might be. Our grasp of the real meaning of the Quran might is comparable to taking a drop from a vast ocean; and this is highlighted by the Quran itself: "And if all the trees on earth were pens and the ocean [were ink], with seven oceans behind it to add to its [supply], yet would not the Words of the Almighty be exhausted [in the writing]; for The Almighty is Exalted in might and wisdom." (Luqman, 27)

We might argue that the Almighty uses a higher level of speech to address human beings than their own conventional level, so that they could concentrate on the timeless and infinite aspects of Divine Speech and appreciate it in proportion to their level of understanding. The Blessed Prophet -upon him blessings and peace- explains this peculiarity of the Quranic style and states, "There is no end to the appearance of the Quran's meanings." (*Tirmidhi*, Fadailu'l-Quran, 14) Rumi says, in similar fashion that "…it is possible to transcribe the text of the Quran with a little amount of ink; but when it comes to expressing all the secrets comprised therein, an unlimited amount of ink of the size of immeasurable oceans would not suffice; nor would all the trees on earth as pens."

The abovementioned Quranic and prophetic statements indicate that the Quran in fact comprises the entirety of all realities and truths in the form of a nucleus. Had this inner signification of the Quran been given an explicit mention, its size would exceed all boundaries. For this reason, the Quran mentions some truths in an explicit manner, while alluding to others only implicitly. Only those who are firmly grounded upon knowledge can discover these secrets; those who possess a profound insight to understand the realities embedded in the Quranic phrases and who execute its commands with a sound mind and heart.

Enumerating the scholarly qualifications required to embark upon an interpretation of the Quran, scholars of the methodology of *tafsir* include a branch they refer to as 'God-given (*wahbi*) knowledge', an expertise bestowed exclusively upon the exceptional servants of Allah, glory unto Him. This kind of knowledge is attained only by virtue of embodying piety, modesty and abstinence, and remaining in a ceaseless battle against the ego. Indicating this is a *hadith* which states, "Whoever practices that which he knows, the Almighty teaches him that which he does not know."

What is Sufism?

(Abu Nuaym, *Hilya*, X, 15) This effectively means that one cannot attain a portion of the secrets of the Quran, so long as he does not embark upon purifying from immoral traits and shortcomings like conceit, jealousy, love of the world, and so forth. For the Quran says, "I will turn My signs away from those who are arrogant on the earth without right." (al-Araf, 146)

Sufism and the Sayings and Actions of the Blessed Prophet -upon him blessings and peace- (*Hadith-Siyar*)

The science of *hadith* focuses on the sayings, actions, confirmations and physical and moral characteristics of the Blessed Prophet -upon him blessings and peace-. As is valid for all the other Islamic scholarly disciplines, *hadith* constitutes the second most important authoritative source for Sufism after the Holy Quran. *Hadith* collections contain authentic accounts of all aspects of the Prophet's –upon him blessings and peace-life, be they physical, moral, and spiritual. From this perspective, it is not very hard to arrive at a conclusion that *hadith*s play a decisive role in the formation and development of Sufism. *Hadith*s that convey good moral qualities such as abstinence (*zuhd*), moral scrupulousness (*wara*), internalization of faith (*ihsan*), modesty (*tawaddu*), altruism (*ithar*), patience (*sabr*), gratitude (*shukr*), and trust in the Almighty (*tawakkul*) constitute the grounds of mystical theories and practices. These have a close relevance to Sufism, as they present the words and deeds of the Blessed Prophet -upon him blessings and peace-. It is there that the inseparable connection between Sufism and the science of *hadith* becomes most evident.

As was mentioned during the discussion of the relation of Sufism to Quranic exegesis, the foremost aim of Sufis is to seek closeness to and ultimately reach the Lord. They are aware that the journey of Divine love cannot be undertaken, except by following in the footsteps of the Blessed Prophet -upon him blessings and peace-. Sufis, therefore, follow the Prophet -upon him blessings and peace- under all circumstances and enjoy making use of the records of *hadith* that present glimpses of his exemplary words and deeds.

To follow the Blessed Prophet -upon him blessings and peace- is to feel an extreme love for him and to prefer him over everything else. There are many Quranic verses that underline the necessity of loving and obeying the Prophet -upon him blessings and peace. Concrete examples how one ought to love and obey the Blessed Prophet -upon him blessings and peace- can be found only in the scholarly sources of *hadith* and prophetic biography. Not only with respect to offering acts of worship and social interactions but also with respect to possessing good moral character traits, the Blessed Prophet -upon him blessings and peace- is the most perfect human being who ever graced this life. In detailing and confirming these fine aspects of the Prophet's –upon him blessings and peace-works of *hadith* and prophetic biography are indispensable.

The meticulously recorded words of the Prophet -upon him blessings and peace- have come to our day, thanks to the narrative reliability of Muslim generations. In addition to his profound words, the actions and behavior of the Prophet -upon him blessings and peace- were also reported, in detail, by his Companions, and passed onto one generation after another to this day. The exemplary qualities observed in the conduct of great Sufis were inspired by none other than the Prophet's -upon him blessings and peace- ideal characteristics; the pattern each believer must emulate as much as his capacity allows, since the Blessed Prophet -upon him blessings and peace- was sent as a perfect example for humankind entire. Those who can properly actualize this ideal are indeed exceptional individuals, for understanding the spirit of the Prophet's –upon him blessings and peace- instructions and embodying them diligently in their lives. The fact that Sufis strive to lead people to this prophetic direction through their theoretical and practical teachings suffices to prove that they always act in accordance with the essence of the Sunnah.

The praiseworthy conduct of Sufis is but a reflection from the Prophet's –upon him blessings and peace- typical qualities and living practices as transmitted in the textual records of *hadith*. From this vantage, the actions and behavior of exemplary Sufis are to be considered as the living commentaries of the words and conduct of the Blessed Prophet –upon him blessings and peace-. To put it in another way, by embodying the contents of the transmitted *hadith*s, Sufis uphold and perpetuate prophetic practices in different times and places.

What is Sufism?

Even before the appearance of Sufism as a scholarly discipline, both Sufis and scholars of *hadith* compiled works entitled *Kitabu'z-Zuhd* (The Book of Abstinence), which acts as a bridge connecting Sufism to the science of *hadith*.

On the other hand, Muslim mystics enriched the field of *hadith* by affording allegorical interpretations of various *hadith*s and expanding on their spiritual meanings. And although scholars of *hadith* have generally rejected this kind of possibility, some Sufis further argued that it was possible to personally receive *hadith*s from the Blessed Prophet -upon him blessings and peace- under his spiritual influence and command. According to this approach, this would occur through spiritual unveilings.

In Islamic intellectual history, we find many Sufi scholarly figures, like Hakim Tirmidhi and Kalabadhi, who presented works in the fields of both *hadith* and Sufism. Furthermore, there are many authorities in the field of *hadith*, who produced works in line with the Sufi methodology. The great Imam Bukhari -may Allah have mercy on him-, for instance, who compiled the most authoritative work in the field of *hadith* unanimously regarded as the second most important Islamic religious scripture after the Holy Quran – had an exemplary custom in writing down each *hadith* he had memorized. Before proceeding to transcribe each *hadith*, the Imam would perform two units of prayer to ask the Almighty to bestow upon him a conviction regarding the authenticity of the record in question. Only after a sincere supplication and spiritual conviction with respect to the report would the great Imam include the given narration in his work.[15] Similarly, another great hadith scholar Ahmad ibn Hanbal is said to have taken three *hadith*s directly from the Blessed Prophet –upon him blessings and peace- in a dream.[16]

Sufism and Islamic Jurisprudence (*Fiqh*)

Fiqh literally denotes knowing, understanding and comprehending. During the early days of Islam, the word *fiqh* would encompass all kinds

---

15 See Ibn Hajar, *Hady al-Sari Muqaddima Fathu'l-Bari*, p. 489; Ibn Hajar, *Taghliq al-Taliq*, V, 421.
16 See *Majmū' al-Hadith*, manuscript 110a-112b.

Sufism: A Path Towards the Internalization of Faith (Ihsân)

of knowledge, both temporal and spiritual, a person needed; and one who had amassed an expertise in knowledge in its broadest significance was referred to as a *faqih*, in the sense of an *alim* or a scholar. In this context, a *faqih* was person with insight into the wisdom underlying being and physical occurrences, as well as an intellectual capacity to discern and acknowledge his religious rights and responsibilities. Accordingly, Imam Abu Hanifa defines *fiqh* as "…a person's knowledge of the things in favor of and against him with regards to religion."

The central aspect of this knowledge was to 'know the Lord', the knowledge most essential to human happiness. Thus, Abu Hanifa's writings on creedal topics were later compiled by his students under the title of "*al-Fiqhu'l-Akbar*", or 'the greatest *fiqh*'. In the early days of Islam, that was what the term *fiqh* meant. In time, however, when the body of Islamic knowledge became immensely extensive, the word *fiqh* acquired its terminological sense and scholars of *fiqh* began to exclude creedal and ethical discussions from *fiqh* and restricted its usage to practical and legal matters. And today, this is what is meant by *fiqh*.

Sufism is no different in the sense of relating to the knowledge of things in favor of and against human beings. In addition to the mutual epistemological ground it shares with *fiqh*, Sufi knowledge includes both internal and external aspects of religious matters. *Fiqh* gives us information about the external requirements for practical religious topics, such as ritual ablution, ritual prayer, fasting and so forth. As for Sufism, it imparts knowledge with regard to their internal requirements; to clean and purify the heart in order to prepare one for the spiritual contentment, knowledge and inspiration that beckon in the practice of these deeds. The Sufi path thereby functions as the ground for the sincere and perfect devotion to be embodied when offering these deeds. On account of this, Sufism is also called "internal *fiqh*" (*al-fiqh al-batin*) or "the *fiqh* of conscience" (*al-fiqh al-wijdani*), insofar as it constitutes the spiritual basis and essence of *fiqh*.

There is no doubt that the ultimate goal of the science of *fiqh* is to ensure that deeds of worship are offered with a certain blend and quality, so that they are accepted in Divine presence. This perfection of quality comes only from a spiritual maturity that Sufism gets one to strive for. In this subtle context, *fiqh* and Sufism function complementarily to each other; for the fundamental goals of Sufism is making a believer reach metaphysical and spiritual realities through the practice of the external deeds and behaviors *fiqh* lays down as obligatory. Putting the requirements of *fiqh* to practice cannot yield the desired results without acquiring the moral and spiritual maturity outlined by Sufism.

In the case of daily prayer, for instance, the science of *fiqh* describes its external requirements, such as cleanliness and executing the ritual in an acceptable order. Furthermore, *fiqh* outlines the necessity of intention, which itself is an internal requirement. But in doing so, *fiqh* does not keep itself busy with the detailed spiritual requirements of prayer, such as purifying the heart from ostentation and jealousy, however necessary they may be for a consummate prayer and complementary to its external requirements. Sufism organizes the inner requirements of prayer and tries to harmoniously combine their external and internal aspects. Since *fiqh* is a branch of Shariah, imperative for all believers to follow, it basically regulates the outward aspects of religion on which human responsibility is based. Be that as it may, it is the inner quality in which one conducts himself that renders the fulfilling of this responsibility accepted by the Lord; an inner quality the Lord wills to see in His servants.

Scholars of *fiqh* unearth the religious rulings that regulate all acts of worship, as well as social interactions, like marriage, divorce, trading, and punishments. They examine and systematize these rulings. Complementarily, Sufis provide the moral and spiritual background of these rulings and emphasize the importance of the required spiritual mindset to adopt when offering them. It is none other than the Holy Quran that inspires Sufis in this regard; for it is the Quran that first and foremost places emphasis on the inner and spiritual aspects of deeds of worship.

Of course, all this does not mean that Sufis do not consider the science of *fiqh* important; nor does it mean that they are not sufficiently interested in Islamic legal studies. On the contrary, great Sufi figures were at the same time competent scholars in the traditional exoteric disciplines, including *fiqh*. We might, for instance, mention the names of Ghazzali, Ibn Arabi, Rumi, Imam Rabbani, and Khalid Baghdadi in this context.

Those unable to comprehend the real content of outward religious rulings and spiritual realities claim that there is a huge difference and even an unbridgeable opposition between the science of *fiqh* and Sufism. Indeed, there are some dramatic examples of this situation in Islamic religious history. As far as the relationship between the real scholars of *fiqh* and competent Sufis is concerned, however, there are a host of cases testifying to their mutual respect and recognition. Disagreement and controversy occurs only between the ignorant who think of themselves as infallibly knowledgeable in *fiqh* and the crude Sufis who would regard themselves spiritually perfected.

We will show them Our signs in the horizons and within themselves until it becomes clear to them that it is the T/truth. But is it not sufficient concerning your Lord that He is, over all things, a Witness? (Fussilat, 53)

2. SUFISM AND NATURAL SCIENCES

Natural sciences, whose basic doctrine maintains that sense perceptions are the only admissible basis of human knowledge and whose scientific data are produced under laboratory conditions, might on the surface seem unrelated to Sufism. But the reality of the matter is not quite so.

Every kind of scientific activity that aims at understanding the underlying wisdoms and realities of beings and natural occurrences, reaches only as far as the point where metaphysics begins; and this is the point where natural sciences and Sufism meet. Sufism peers into and reveals the secrets and wisdoms of all beings, the metaphysical dimensions of the universe in general. It leads human beings to a more reliable, comprehensive, and convincing level of knowledge regarding the Almighty and the worlds. In short, Sufism takes man to the realm of reality.

Natural sciences focus on the material and visible world. Things invented through the study of natural sciences are in fact qualities already embedded in those things by the Almighty. This means that every invention pertaining to material world comes into being as a testimony to the power and might of the Creator. Proceeding from this point, we can argue that natural sciences help us appreciate the miracles of Divine art.

On the other hand, Islam explores matter together with its immaterial and metaphysical dimensions. The modern natural sciences of today have verged upon this approach. Every novel invention in this material world opens a metaphysical door to new unknowns and leads the human mind to the infinite realm. Man begins with the sensory impressions offered to him by material world, though in the end he is led to the metaphysical realities underneath. This is especially the case in contemporary times; science has made an extraordinary advance to the point of coming face to face with metaphysics. For this reason, the materialist theories of old devised to imprison reality into the strict confines of matter have lost their credibility. Lavoisier's theory of conservation of mass/matter, for instance, considered an indisputable taboo in the last century, has now lost its validity in scholarly circles. Likewise, 'the law of the eternity of matter', one of the most controversial points of conflict between philosophy and religion, is not able to find passionate supporters anymore. Even science now prefers the theory that matter is not an essential, but only an accidental form. That matter is a condensed form of energy has now been established by the breaking of the atom into pieces, whereby it has become clear that what we call "matter" is in reality an energy that is imprisoned in a certain form. In addition, many new scientific discoveries, especially in the fields of physics, chemistry, biology and astronomy, serve to confirm countless facts already mentioned in religious scriptures, first and foremost the Holy Quran, regarding the nature of things.

New discoveries on human genes indicate that every human being has a kind of individual and particular code; just one example among many others that testify to the incapacitating nature of Divine art in creation. Paying tribute to this is Ziya Pasha, a 19th century Ottoman intellectual and poet:

I glorify He whose art makes minds meek,
And whose might leaves the wise weak…

From the beginning of Islam, Muslims were taught and knew the innate weakness of human capacity with respect to the wonders of Divine art. The possibility that, towards the end of time, such scientific discoveries might come close to the level of miracles is also no secret to them. Yet, every new scientific discovery reinforces human conviction of his incapacity at the face of the majestic art of the Almighty, whose infinite wisdom he then feels compelled to acknowledge. It is this human weakness Ziya Pasha brings to the fore when he says:

What is Sufism?

These Divine wisdoms the tiny mind cannot understand;
For its scales cannot weigh a weight so grand

Sufism reflects on all beings in order to comprehend the metaphysical mysteries underlying their existence; the very threshold natural sciences reach at the end of their inquiries. This interconnectedness renders a positive relationship between Sufism and natural sciences apparent and undeniable.

In fact, the Holy Quran diverts attention to the innumerable secrets and wisdoms in creation. The following Quranic verse, for instance, underlines this fact, declaring,

سَنُرِيهِمْ اٰيَاتِنَا فِى الْاٰفَاقِ وَ فِى اَنْفُسِهِمْ حَتّٰى يَتَبَيَّنَ لَهُمْ اَنَّهُ الْحَقُّ اَوَلَمْ يَكْفِ بِرَبِّكَ اَنَّهُ عَلٰى كُلِّ شَىْءٍ شَهٖيدٌ

"We will show them Our signs in the horizons and within themselves until it becomes clear to them that it is the Truth. But is it not sufficient concerning your Lord that He is, over all things, a Witness? (Fussilat, 53) The word "horizons" in this verse points to external world that encompasses the human being. As for the phrase "within themselves", it indicates wisdoms, lessons, and secrets existent in the biological and spiritual aspects of human existence.

In His Holy Quran, the Almighty highlights the importance of examining external word and thus of paying attention to His signs embedded in His creation. We might mention the following Quranic verses in this regard. "Do they not travel through the earth, so that their hearts [and minds] may thus learn wisdom, and their ears may thus learn to hear? Truly it is not their eyes that are blind, but their hearts which are in their breasts." (al-Hajj, 46) "And We did not create the heavens and earth and that between them in play. We did not create them except in truth (for just ends), but most of them do not understand." (ad-Dukhan, 38-39)

Sufism: A Path Towards the Internalization of Faith (Ihsân)

As far as the creation of human beings is specifically concerned, the Holy Quran underlines that just like it is in the case of all other beings, the creation of human being is directed to certain purposes and just ends, as indicated by the declaration,

$$\text{اَفَحَسِبْتُمْ اَنَّمَا خَلَقْنَاكُمْ عَبَثًا وَ اَنَّكُمْ اِلَيْنَا لاَ تُرْجَعُونَ}$$

"Did you then think that We created you in jest and that you would not be brought back to Us [for account]?" (al-Muminun, 115)

From the macro to the micro level of creation, extraordinary manifestations of Divine art exist in every particle. Sufism aims at providing a universal comprehension of all these realities, in the center of which lies human being. In addition to this theoretical aspect, Sufism aims at maturing a believer's religious and spiritual qualities through certain trainings like the remembrance of Allah, glory unto Him, and a variety of other spiritual meditations. Sufism, therefore, includes both theoretical and practical instructions.

In the Quranic scripture, there are verses that call attention to the wisdoms embedded in the physical world; and every now and then, the Quran resorts to question forms in order to make its statements more emphatic. Even though these emphases may appear to be related primarily to the physical qualities of the things in question, they are not reserved exclusively to that. For that reason, in our inquiries to comprehend the wisdom inherent in the visible qualities of entities, we need a more advanced and able methodology than what natural sciences offer us in this regard. And this fact equally accentuates the need one has to improve the spiritual conditions of his heart in order to make it receptive to this spiritual way of sensing and comprehending. In providing such a possibility and competence for human beings, this is where the Sufi way enters the framework.

As hinted at before, a renowned principle of Sufism considers the visible universe as the manifestation of the Names of the Almighty. Every single being in this world is hence a miracle of art. We might proceed and attempt to write voluminous books to explain the nature and realities of the seemingly ordinary happenings we experience on a daily basis; yet we would still miserably fail in offering a complete picture. When a gazelle eats a mulberry leaf to produce musk, for instance, a silkworm consumes the very same leaf to produce silk. The universe around us abounds in the miracles and signs of Allah, glory unto Him, all within the reach of our observation; though we do not spare sufficient time to properly reflect on them. When one observes a greening grass, a blossoming flower and a tree generously offering its fruits with the purpose of deriving a personal lesson; and when one contemplates on the ways how all these plants take their colors, smells and tastes from the simple earth, one cannot help but be awestruck by the glory of Divine art and power. Sufism encourages human beings to look at the whole creation with an eye to take a lesson. Consequently, Sufis believe that nothing in this world was created in vain, without a purpose, a conviction which they confirm by setting the hearts sail towards that very same purpose.

Similar to the Holy Quran and man, the universe has also come into existence as a composition of the manifestations Divine Names. One might say that all natural sciences ultimately aim towards tapping into the Divine wisdom and law that govern the universe entire, which fundamentally are certain compositions of the manifestations of the Divine Names impressed upon the conditions of the world; as has been stated. Strangely, all natural sciences and most scientists constitutionally suffer from an ingrained weakness to appreciate and duly reflect on these manifestations; as only those who improve and mature their moral and spiritual dimensions, may acquire in their hearts the skill of comprehending the secrets and wisdoms of creation, an existential and epistemological capacity that exceeds far beyond the horizons of natural sciences. To venture beyond these horizons at which natural sciences stop short, Sufism takes the lead; and this is the very point in which the two band together.

It is Sufism that brought Turkish literature into existence, developed and matured it.

3. SUFISM AND LITERATURE

Sufism conducts its spiritual operation in the heart and the Sufis reflect the subtle ideas and insights impressed upon their hearts onto various forms of literary arts, including poetry and prose. Bringing these reflections and teachings to life through words, Sufis have had a durable impact on the minds across centuries, leaving behind many extraordinary pieces of artwork, enriched in both content and form. The immense Sufi contribution to literature has aided humankind in gradually reaching a refined depth of aesthetic taste, through giving voice to the deepest and most sophisticated feelings ever accessible to human sensation.

In the history of Turkish literature, there is a tradition called '*Tekke* Literature', explicitly of a religious nature, which emerged from the lodges of (*tekkes*) of Sufi orders. The linguistic style of *Tekke* literature varies from being quite simple and fluent to lyrical and even didactic. Religious and spiritual symbols are embedded in the products of this tradition. *Munacat* and *Nat* are two of the most common poetry forms of Tekke literature. The main subject matter of the former is the Oneness of The Almighty (*tawhid*) and seeking refuge in Him, while the latter is a passionate expression of love and yearning for the Blessed Prophet -upon him blessings and peace-. Despite this seeming difference of content, all forms *Tekke* literature encourage people to improve their levels of piety, to console and comfort their yearning hearts; and aim at steering them clear from sins and heedlessness, and thereby establishing love, solidarity and peace in society.

Since the tumultuous times of the Mongol invasions, Yunus Emre's poems have functioned as guidance and consolation for people up to this day. Thorough their poems and other forms of literature, Sufis have offered an immense service in passing religious sentiments onto the following generations and keeping moral and spiritual virtues alive. Khoja Ahmed Yesevi, Haci Bayram Veli, Eshrefoglu Rumi and Aziz Mahmud Hudayi are just some of the leading Sufi authors who not only contributed to the flourishing of Islamic-Turkish literature, but also guided believers through their literary output.

As for the tradition of classical or *Diwan* literature, it consists of poetic works written mostly in the form of the metrical system referred to as *aruz*, and expressed in a highly advanced level of artistic style. Despite the fact that it also includes exquisite pieces of art in the form of prose, the main body of the *Diwan* literature consists of rhymed poetry immersed in Sufi ideas. Sufism's decisive influence on the *Diwan* literature is unquestionable, as one can find therein many examples of Islamic spiritual symbolism, skillfully articulated in a highly sophisticated style.

Each poetic form employed in the *Diwan* literature highlights specific religious notions. *Munacat*, for instance, is about the Oneness of the Almighty; and especially the ones written by Sufi poets are filled of spiritual enthusiasm. Similarly, in the case of *nat*, whose main topic is the Blessed Prophet -upon him blessings and peace-, one is met with heartfelt yearnings of prophetic love. Fuzuli, for example, expresses the depth of his longing for the Prophet -upon him blessings and peace- in the following lines from his famous *Su Kasidesi* (Ode of Water), where he traces the ultimate trajectory of flowing water:

All their lives, dashing their heads against one rock to another,
To reach the grounds He walked, like a drifter, flows water

Consequently, under the great influence and inspiration shone upon by Sufism, many celebrated Sufis of the likes of Rumi, Fuzuli, Naili, Nabi, Nahifi and Sheikh Galib, were able to produced exquisite pieces of artwork.

All this gives an idea of the profound enrichment spirituality has bestowed upon all forms of literary art. The moral and spiritual elements of the Sufi way that figure in literary works have enabled made artistic taste of poetry and prose to reach the hearts of the general public. Testifying to this fact is the eminent contemporary scholar of Turkish literature Nihad Sami Banarli, who says, "It is Sufism that brought Turkish literature into existence, developed and matured it." The immense influence Sufism has exercised on literary forms may also be observed in the works of poets who did not have any personal affiliation with Sufism. Nabi, for instance, was a poet who usually wrote on profane topics; though he could not stop himself from writing a *nat*. The first poem that brought Tevfik Fikret fame was in fact a *munacat*.

The Blessed Prophet -upon him blessings and peace- himself encouraged believers to improve their artistic skills and called attention to this dimension of human existence. He especially acknowledged the great influence of poetry on the heart and mind. According to a *hadith* narrated by Aisha -may Allah be well-pleased with her-, the Prophet -upon him blessings and peace- had his Companions build a special pulpit for the poet Hassan ibn Thabit in the mosque. Hassan would sit on this pulpit and give poetical responses to the poems written against the Blessed Prophet -upon him blessings and peace-. For Hassan, the Prophet -upon him blessings and peace- said, "The Almighty supports Hassan through the Holy Spirit, as long as Hassan defends His Messenger." (*Tirmidhi*, Adab, 70; *Abu Dawud*, Adab, 87) The fact that Jibril –upon him peace- accompanies the poet Hassan indicates that if an artist sets out to produce something for the sake of the Almighty, he can receive Divine inspiration and confirmation in what he does.

The essential ingredients of human arts are kneaded by Sufism; they represent reflections of human refinement, sensitivity and profundity in various formats. As is visible in history, human arts have decisive effect upon building civilizations.

4. SUFISM AND FINE ARTS

Artworks are reflections of human spiritual depth and sensitivity onto concrete entities. In the final analysis, every single human art is a certain reflection of thoughts and feelings existent in the human spirit. Artistic refinement and elegance always goes in parallel with spiritual profundity.

The essential ingredients of human arts are kneaded by Sufism in the sense that they represent reflections of human refinement, sensitivity, and profundity in various formats. As seen in history, human arts have decisive effect upon building civilizations. In effect, nations that reached an advanced level of civilizational progress in the past, accomplished this feat not only with respect to politics, economics, and military, but also with respect to sciences and arts. Muslim history is full of examples of such development. Here, we cannot give a detailed exposition of the spiritual patterns reflected onto many kinds of fine arts. Instead, we will rest content with presenting a brief account of the spiritual motifs observable in certain art forms.

Music

Islam does not disallow the flourishing of characteristics innate to human nature; instead, it regulates them to a harmonic order. Like many other aesthetic forms of art, music is one form through which certain characteristics innate to human predisposition find expression. Thus, as is the case with other forms of art, neither can one unconditionally accept music nor reject it.

Sufis acknowledge the undeniable influence of music on man and make use of this art for praiseworthy ends, as outlined by the basic moral and religious principles of Islam. They lead music towards a heavenly objective and make its content and command address the human spirit, rather than the ego. Accordingly, Sufis approve and practice the types of music that are in agreement with these general principles, and disapprove and disallow the types of music that incite and mislead the ego.

Indeed, when directed towards a good end, whether in the form of harmonious instrumental music or accompanied by the lyric poems of *gazel*, *kaside* and *ilahi* patterns, music plays an essential role in elevating the spiritual level of human beings, as it inspires heavenly thoughts and tastes. In this context, music provides many positive benefits. For example, it increases the listener's desire for devotion, reminds him of the Almighty, makes him mindful of sins, imparts onto his heart pure thoughts and blessings, and so on. Especially when music is played at the proper time, as one is overcome by a state of spirituality it exercises an even further positive influence on the human spirit. Owing to its constructive effects on also on the human psyche, Sufis have made use of music for ages, along with their use of other positive means. Coming to existence as a result of the religious and aesthetic interest Sufis took in music was a distinct branch of Islamic music, referred to, broadly, as 'Sufi music'.

We need to mention, however, that there is not a unanimously positive or negative Sufi attitude towards music. While there are some Sufis who absolutely disallow the use of music as a means for spiritual training, there are others who argue that music can be employed for this purpose, so long as certain requirements are followed. They disallow, for instance, the use of stringed musical instruments, but allow the use of percussion, the legitimacy of which they draw from the historical fact that the Blessed Prophet -upon him blessings and peace- allowed his Companions to play the said instruments on certain occasions like battle, in order to spur the Muslim soldiers.

For the sake of refraining from endless debates on this issue, it will suffice to conclude that the use of the melodious human voice is permissible within the religious border lines of legitimacy. It might even be said that endorsing music of the kind is even recommendable within general

What is Sufism?

Muslim circles. It is a natural fact that a call to prayer by *muadhdhin* with a beautiful voice has a greater impact on the listeners. The Prophet's -upon him blessings and peace- course of action in selecting the person to call the faithful to prayer implies further instructions in this regard. While Muslims were discussing the proper means to call the believers to ritual prayer, the Blessed Prophet -upon him blessings and peace- saw a truthful dream in which he was dictated the words of the *adhan*. Though he first informed Abdullah ibn Zayd and Omar ibn Khattab -may Allah be well-pleased with them- of the *adhan*, he did not, however, entrust the duty of reciting it with the two great Companions. It was rather Bilal –may Allah be well-pleased with him- who was entrusted with the duty, from which one may gather that his strong and beautiful voice would have played a major role in his selection; a duty he upheld so long as he remained alive.

With that said, it certainly cannot be argued that music exercises only a positive influence on human beings. Nonetheless, it would not be correct to reject music altogether, simply based on the fact that it is overwhelmingly used, in our times, as a means to incite and provoke the ego.

The following anecdote gives us a general Islamic strategy with respect to the healthy approach to take with regard to music. Khoja Misafir, a disciple of Bahauddin Naqshbandi says, "I was in the service of the respected Bahauddin and but also fond of music in the meantime. On one occasion, together with a number of his other disciples, we came together and with some musical instruments in our hands, we decided to play music in the presence of our venerated master so that we could learn his position in this regard. So, we put our plan into action in his presence. The master did not prevent us from doing so, but simply said, 'We do not do this…yet we do not disallow it either.'"

The perceptive strategy of Naqshbandi implies that believers should be mindful and precautious with music; for it might be misused by way of inciting human sensual desires. As far as Sufism in a more specific context is concerned, we need to underline that there should be a balanced and reasonable approach to music, particularly in our modern times. As is unfortunately observable in the practices of some so-called Sufi groups, the content of Sufism should not be reduced simply to chanting and singing.

Architecture

One of the most widely observable works of fine art which stand testimony to the influence of Sufism is indeed architecture. Architecture comes into existence through the combination of mathematical, geometrical and spiritual talents human beings have which is then melted in a harmonious pot. In other words, architecture represents intellectual and spiritual abilities of man reflected onto and embodied in material things, like stone and wood.

Sufism has had a decisive influence on Islamic architecture in more ways than one. We can, for instance, observe this influence vividly in Suleymaniye Mosque and the complementary buildings that surround it. Peering into this architectural masterpiece through a Sufi eye reveals that the spirit of Islam is deep impressed thereon. Its eye-catching magnificence is combined with a profound spirituality, symbolized with many spiritual facets peeking through every inch of the mosque. So skillfully designed are the central dome of the mosque and its surroundings that starting from its foundations up to the dome we can see a gradual symbolic progression multiplicity to unity, to the One (*Wahid*); the dome which seals the building. The harmony of the central dome with the other domes is quite extraordinary, signifying the Sufi principle 'unity within multiplicity, multiplicity within unity'. The Suleymaniye Mosque thus attractively embodies a series of elegant marks of spirituality, remarkably epitomizing the transition from the multiple to the majestic 'One', and vice versa. In echoing the recitations of the Holy Quran and prayers performed in the mosque, the same dome also symbolizes the Blessed Prophet -upon him blessings and peace- and his function of delivering the Divine message to his followers.

This unique mosque is virtually the meeting point of astonishing human genius and capacity. Tranquility kneaded into majesty in the most consummate fashion has brought a superbly harmonious monument of architectural beauty into existence. With its graceful minarets moving up to the sky, the mosque is like a devout servant who has submissively raised his hands aloft to pray to the Lord.

The internal atmosphere of the Suleymaniye Mosque also casts a profound influence on the human psyche. Many visitors of different religious backgrounds admiringly express the spiritual attraction they feel inside the ambiance of this colossal temple and the comforting inner peace and tranquility that comes over them. It is narrated that the mosque was built on the basis of an order received, in a dream, from the Blessed Prophet -upon him blessings and peace-.

In contrast to mosques of the caliber of Suleymaniye which were built to last until the Final Hour, various types of Sufi institutions such as dervish convents, lodges, and public kitchens served to spiritually enrich the scene of Muslim towns in a different manner. Great and small, many buildings of this type inspire a sense of perishability, simplicity, nothingness, and modesty. They were built in accordance with their function, which means they were spacious enough to facilitate Sufi training; yet they have always been far from giving a sense of majesty, having been built with the intention of inspiring the sense of perishability, instead. Nevertheless, all these buildings offer a display of the manifestations of Islamic spirituality embedded architecture.

Calligraphy

Islamic calligraphy or *husn-i hat* is the art of handwriting the letters of the Holy Quran in accordance with the set aesthetic criteria and in the most beautiful manner imaginable. To put it in another way, Islamic calligraphy represents an exceptional form of art which was born out of the genuine efforts to handwrite the Holy Quran in the most appropriate manner. Throughout Islamic history, Sufi lodges and convents have played a significant role in developing calligraphy. Sufi circles always supported this form of art and have sponsored many prominent calligraphers, who were able to find an ideal environment in Sufi institutions for both perfecting their skills and receiving further education in the art. Meantime, they would also undergo some kind of spiritual training; for a pure and refined heart has always been considered imperative for calligrapher, to enable him to reflect his talent onto letters with a natural, inborn flow that could find its way into the hearts of admiring eyes. Furthermore, the spiritual maturation of a calligrapher, necessary to obtain expertise in the art, required him to go through a difficult apprenticeship to prove his level of patience and submission. For that, he needed a spiritually matured calligrapher to emulate.

Thus, On the basis of such common peculiarities, the art of calligraphy is intimately related to Sufism.

The shared ground between calligraphy and Sufism transpires in the handwriting of a rude and irritable person; it looks skewed and broken, which is a symptom of the spiritual anguish he suffers from deep down. The goal of Sufism is to train and refine the ego and thereby save the human spirit from its tyranny through instilling therein peace and sensitivity. Calligraphers, too, need such peace and sensitivity, as the art of calligraphy is not simply about fine handwriting. Much rather, it is essentially a discipline aimed toward refining souls and to filling hearts with spiritual sensations.

Spiritual strengthening has, in effect, prepared the way for many a gifted artist in attaining to that desired level of maturity and expertise. It was under the spiritual training of Sufi circles that many great masters of Islamic calligraphy of the likes of Sheikh Hamdullah, Karahisari, Yesarizade and Mustafa Rakim attained to that specific maturity. The example below carries great import in reflecting the penetrating influence of Sufism on Islamic arts.

Karahisari, the eminent calligrapher, had been entrusted with the duty of writing the calligraphies of the Suleymaniye Mosque's dome. He put in his ultimate effort to complete his work as perfectly as possible, so that the calligraphies would live up to the magnificence of the great mosque. He took his job tremendously serious; so much so that towards the end of his work, he lost his sight in both eyes. Once the construction of the mosque was complete and was ready to be opened to public service, the Ottoman Sultan Suleyman the Magnificent said, "The honor of opening this holy mosque to public worship must go to our chief architect Sinan, for accomplishing the feat of building this splendid and marvelous mosque." As much as he was a master of architecture, Sinan, however, was also a master of modesty. The humble Sinan instantly remembered Karahisari's matchless sacrifice and politely responded to the Sultan by saying, "Your Majesty, the calligrapher Karahisari sacrificed his eyes while adorning the mosque with his exquisite calligraphies. In my humble opinion, it would be best if you gave him the honor instead!" Sultan Suleyman agreed and gave the unforgettable honor of opening the mosque to Karahisari, amid the heartfelt tears of the onlookers.

In addition to its own artistic standards, the development and continuity of Islamic calligraphy owes a great deal to the spiritual criteria of beauty. From this perspective, the scribing of the Holy Quran and of the description of the personal virtues and the qualities of the Prophet -upon him blessings and peace- (*Hilya-i Sharifah*) constitute the highest level of perfection in Islamic calligraphy. According to the tradition, only those calligraphers who have proved their unparalleled mastery in calligraphy are given the privilege of attempting to scribe the Holy Quran and the *Hilya*. It was this profound conduct of respect that made works of calligraphy forcefully attractive to hearts and souls, convincing them to passionately respond to the Divine command "Read!"

Being the fruit of such a sincere theoretical and practical tradition, since its beginning, the art of calligraphy has been taught with no financial charge to determined students. Every calligrapher regards his service of teaching calligraphy as the obligatory almsgiving of this art and never expects any financial return on the basis of his teaching.

In short, a believer who appreciates even a glimpse of the following *hadith* cannot help but take interest in beauty. The *hadith* says, "Indeed the Almighty is beautiful and loves beauty." (*Muslim*, Iman, 147)

Man craves to express and manifest the inner beauties he nurtures in his inner world. A Muslim artist hence carries a natural desire to allow his profound abilities to transpire in accordance with the given aesthetic criteria and, of course, in a manner that is harmonious with the essence of Islam and clear of the traps of pride and arrogance. All forms of art in accord with the spirit of Islam thus find their due support and protection in Sufi circles. Many forms of fine arts which meet Sufism in the depths of the human intellectual and spiritual world, reach a higher visual and aesthetic level and visual level through the inspirational notions of the Sufi way they absorb in their motifs.

Without the help of spiritual perceptions and feelings, one cannot penetrate into the realm of infinite realities through human reason alone.

5. SUFISM AND PHILOSOPHY

Natural sciences investigate physical entities and occurrences piecemeal and try to present their characteristics within the general principles dubbed as 'laws of nature'. Philosophy is the intellectual discipline that seeks either to combine these scientific principles or to establish more general theories; a branch of learning that makes a constant effort to relate scholarly fields with one another, to expose their deep-down interconnectedness.

From this perspective, philosophy is endorsed as the science of sciences. The sole means philosophy has in its aim to reach a higher truth, however, is the human rational faculty. Although not all philosophical schools assign as high and authoritative a position for human reason as does the philosophical school of rationalism, they nonetheless rely on reason as the only means to search and find truth. Rationalism, in a sense, goes to the extreme point of ascribing a god-like status to reason.

Islam acknowledges human reason or the possession of sanity as one of the fundamental requisites for being held liable for obligations. Still, it also recognizes its innate insufficiency with respect to attaining the ultimate truths, for which it makes it reliant on religious narration or tradition (*naql*), in contrast to the one-sided philosophical approach to the sources of human knowledge. As a form of Islamic understanding and quest for perfection, Sufism pursues certain metaphysical realities, though its rational endeavor strictly follows the religious tradition and does not venture beyond the limits of spiritual unveiling or insight (*kashf*). The fact that fundamental Sufi ideas rely on religious principles necessitates the recognition of Sufi intellectual activities as firmly grounded upon the Islamic narrative tradition.

Even though human reason is offered a leeway to capture and reflect on the wisdom of the narrative tradition, its independent activity in demonstrating Islamic precepts is not seen permissible. For this reason, in order to make the human rational faculty as perfectly useful as possible, Islam decrees that it be corrected with revelation, establishing thereby its legitimate field of activity. Still, the general public, or persons who are uncultivated in this regard, are not required to accept every single idea expounded through one's spiritual insight. Setting the standard here is a Sufi maxim, which declares that "…a spiritual insight is binding only for the person who experiences it and not for others."

It cannot be claimed, in any way, that the ultimate truth is exhausted by the capacity of human reason; for even after reason lies exhausted in its search, the soul is left unsatisfied and continues to explore regardless. This is a natural and inborn human characteristic. For this reason, nearly all intellectual systems, religious or not, acknowledge this aspect of realities that eludes the immediate rational grasp. Renowned is the fact that metaphysical deliberations constitute a significantly large portion of philosophy. But, again, since they have no other medium than human reason to advance in their search, philosophers leave themselves vulnerable to inconsistency. Furthermore, the enterprise of philosophy is reflexive, as each philosopher begins his work by rejecting or disproving the theories of previous philosophers to establish his own personal position, the egoistic arguments in defense of which often betray the underlying self-centeredness underlying it. Nonetheless, used to accomplish this task is again the same tool; reason, which is never free of inconsistencies.

Human reason is indeed like a two-edged sword; one can use it for both good and evil ends. The same human reason which helps man reach the level of "best model" (at-Tin, 4) may also degrade him to the lowly state of 'bewilderment'. (al-Araf, 179) This means that human reason needs to come under discipline, which Divine revelation provides. Only when reason proceeds under the supervision of revelation will it lead man to salvation; leaving the guidance of revelation aside, it will only steer man to destruction. In attaining the pleasure of the Lord, it is therefore imperative for human reason to be guided.

History has been witness to many tyrants, with sound rational capacities, who have yet not felt the slightest remorse for committing the most brutal massacres; for they perceived their brutalities as sound, rational behavior. Hulagu Khan, for one, drowned four-hundred-thousand innocent people in the waters of Tigris, without feeling the least remorse. Before Islam, many Meccan men used to take their daughters to bury them alive, amid the silent screams of their mothers that shed their hearts to pieces. Chopping a slave was no different for them than chopping wood; they even saw it as their natural right. They, too, had reason and feelings, just like us, which however were like the teeth of a wheel working the opposite direction, defiant of expectation.

Demonstrated by all this is the natural need human beings have for guidance and being directed, owing to the positive and negative inclinations and desires within them. The direction given, however, must in turn be compatible with the natural predisposition; and this is possible only through education in the light of Revelation, that is the guidance and enlightening of prophets. Otherwise, a direction conflicting with the natural predisposition will only generate evil.

Since they attempt to explain everything by way of human reason, philosophers cannot guide themselves to the right path, let alone their societies to this direction. After all, if the human rational faculty had a sufficiently power to guide man to the straight path, the institution of prophethood and the emergence prophets would have been unnecessary. From this perspective, reason stands in need of the guidance of revelation.

Realizing the inherent insufficiency of human reason, some philosophers have sought other means to search for truth. One of them was the French philosopher Henry Bergson (d. 1941), who instead regarded human intuition as an epistemological means to attain to truth. This notion strikes a tune with what our past fellow Sufis would call 'inner occurrences' (*sunuhat- i qalbiyya*), which refers to the implementation of the heart as the means to obtain real knowledge. Bergson argues that it would be wrong to reject the factuality of inner occurrences received after a certain kind and period of spiritual training. He asserts that it would be logically baseless to refute the feasibility of the knowledge obtained by the heart, since this knowledge, as is the case with Sufi knowledge, is of a different nature that eludes all empirical analysis. This fact indicates that only a small portion of philosophy comes close to appreciating religious and spiritual thought. The majority of philosophers, on the other hand, do not accept any epistemological means to attain to truth other than the human rational faculty, sparing their entire time of day instead to launch into falsifying each other. In contrast to the scattered nature of philosophy, prophets and saints, who are their rightful heirs, are fed by the same, harmonious origin; enlightened through Divine revelation and inspiration. Prophets, as well as saints, are therefore always in agreement with each other.

Ghazzali, the great Muslim thinker, says, "Once I finished my investigations and analyses in the field of philosophy, I came to the conclusion that this field could not provide sufficient answers to my need. I realized that human reason alone could not properly understand everything and that it would not always fail in the attempt to unveil the curtain that covers the visible side of things." Commenting on Ghazzali's position, Necip Fazıl Kısakürek adds, "As this great thinker, dubbed 'the proof of Islam', had verged upon leaving all kinds of rational and scientific approaches aside and had begun inclining towards the real type of knowledge, he hinted that, '…the real solution lies in seeking shelter in the spirituality of the Prophet of the prophets; all the rest is some kind of deception and illusion. And alas, reason is nothing but just limitation!' This exquisite mind thereupon halted all his questions and found shelter under the spirituality of the Prophet of the prophets, and discovered the infinite." (*Veliler Ordusundan*, p. 213)

To be sure, one can reach a certain level of reality the limited power of reason; yet how could such a limited faculty cover the entire reality? Is there not any reality that exists beyond it? Even though philosophy ultimately seeks answers to metaphysical questions it does not offer any satisfactory answers to the above questions. But since Sufism differs sharply from philosophy in springing from the source of Divine revelation, one can find indeed answers find answers therein to these gnawing questions.

It is The Almighty Who created man and Who knows best knows his nature, needs and limitations. This makes Divine revelation necessary for human reason in its avid desire to behold the truth. Beyond the furthest point reachable by human reason, there exist other realms, which disclose their realities to the heart in the form of spiritual unveilings or insights. Attaining to the realm of infinite realities is therefore impossible without the aid of the spiritual.

Knowing is not to look on but solve wisdoms and secrets.

G. BENEFICIAL KNOWLEDGE

When ordinary knowledge becomes personalized and penetrates into the depths of a sound perception, it reaches the level of gnosis or wisdom (*irfan*). A gnostic (*arif*) is a person cognizant of the secrets and wisdoms of Divine manifestations embedded as knowledge in his heart. Simpler put, an *arif* refers is he who possesses *irfan*. A person knowledgeable in the conventional scholarly disciplines, though not in the spiritual, is rightfully referred to as a scholar, yet not as gnostic. Knowledge possessed by such people is fixed like the written knowledge in books. This situation resembles a seed in a storehouse; it cannot flourish so long as it is kept detached from soil. Since it is kept at a distance from the heart, it is a kind of knowledge that cannot culminate in true contemplation. Knowledge of the kind has therefore rightly been labeled as 'bookish' or 'pedantic knowledge.'

However, all kinds of knowledge are undoubtedly beneficial if they are used in a proper manner and directed towards their opposite end. Yet, insofar as the real happiness and ultimate salvation of humankind in this world and the next is concerned, acquiring only the external aspects of sciences does not provide a sufficient solution. To fill this gap, Islam underlines the spiritual aspects of sciences and demands that they be used in a good and beneficial way for humankind entire, without being exploited for evil purposes. In this context, Islam has coined a term 'beneficial knowledge' (*al-ilmu'n-nafi*) that revamps the entire externalities of human sciences from a transcendental perspective.

The late Mahir Iz calls attention to the insufficiency of a scientific knowledge devoid of deep, spiritual dimension. The only remedy, accordingly, to remove this weakness is to undertake a spiritual training. Iz says, "It is not possible to put trivial aspects of ordinary knowledge together in a harmonious way. Therefore, I have come to the conclusion that even though I should not hold myself back from scientific inquiries, the real kind of knowledge and truth is attainable only under the guidance of spiritually qualified teachers. It was for this reason that having received a spiritual sign, I decided to become a disciple of our respected master Sami Efendi." (*Yillarin Izi*, p. 396)

The inner maturity attained at the end of the spiritual road elevates human perception to a horizon higher than that of exoteric sciences, and the term *marifah* refers to this very horizon: by the exclusive means of certain spiritual practices can one reach this horizon. No matter how eminent a scholar one might be, upon obtaining such a high level of perception, he acknowledges his own weakness, whereby he is effectively cured from the disease of self-conceit. He becomes filled with feelings of awe and weakness in the presence of a horizon that opens up to an exhibition of infinite and intricate realities. Reflecting further with a sound reason, he furthermore realizes that to know is not to simply look on at the outward aspects of a given thing. Much rather, it is to solve its underlying mystery of the great design and coming to an insightful awareness of Divine wisdoms impressed upon creation.

Through a symbolic parable, Rumi offers a splendid explanation of the significance of acquiring the knowledge of the Divine for the eternal happiness of mankind, and of the tragic outcome waiting for those who do not enter the path of its realization. A grammarian boards a boat. He starts talking with the boatman in a smug and conceited manner, which he keeps up throughout the journey. From time to time, he asks the boatman various questions on the intricacies of grammar. Each time the boatman confesses to not know the answer to the question posed, it inflates the grammarian's pride all the more, who pities him, each time, saying, 'What a pity! You have wasted half of your life in ignorance!' Though heartbroken he may be, being the mature and kind man he is, the boatman does not respond to the insulting remarks made by the grammarian and remains silent. With their conversation flowing along these lines, there suddenly erupts a great storm, dragging the boat into a terrifying whirlpool. As the other travelers begin to panic, this time the boatman turns to the grammarian and asks,

'Do you know how to swim, great man?' The grammarian's face grows pale and says with a dim voice, 'No, I do not.' To that the boatman replies, 'I may have laid waste to half of my life by not learning grammar…but you, my friend, have just wasted your entire life by not learning how to swim. If only you knew, grammarian, that what matters in the sea is not the knowledge of grammar but the knowledge of how to swim!'

The knowledge of grammar in this parable symbolizes the worldly and exoteric sciences. Truly beneficial knowledge, however, is the knowledge that meets human needs; and the greatest of all human needs, physically and spiritually, is to attain to the eternal happiness. And this depends on attaining to the pleasure and contentment of the Lord, which, in turn, depends on a perfected faith and deeds.

This story tells us that come the time when our spirit is about to leave our body as we lay on our deathbeds, the only kind of knowledge of benefit to us will not be the spiritless and dry knowledge that only serves to aggravate our egos, but the knowledge that transforms our ordinary learning into *irfan* and thereby meets our eternal needs and desire for happiness.

Before death reaches us, we therefore need to transform all kinds of information that lie dormant in our mental storehouse into beneficial knowledge that would please the Almighty. For at the time when our flesh is about to return its origin, the earth, from whence it came, scattered pieces of learning that have merely provided a comfortable life to our flesh will not help us anymore. At that moment, we need a sound, purified heart. Before death reaches the heart, the heart needs to get rid of the obstacle of the ego and acquire a sound quality. Inability to reach this level is to drown in the vast sea of the Hereafter. But those who save themselves from negative characteristics to the extent of virtually killing their egos, are graciously welcomed by that new realm of existence, immune from all the harm that otherwise comes from it. The Sufi maxim to 'Die before death' is quite illuminative in this regard. Death, in this sense, is to minimize the desires of the ego. Accomplishing this demands a constant self-examination. 'Call yourselves to account before you are called to account' is another spiritual principle of Sufism urging one to review and contemplate on the nature of the never-ending desires of the ego and practice towards rectifying his soul, before it inevitably happens in the impending world to come.

Sufism: A Path Towards the Internalization of Faith (Ihsân)

A scholar reports that he once "...saw Abu Hamid Ghazzali among a group of evidently enlightened people, wearing clothes full of patches and carrying a ewer in his hand. I asked him, 'Was not the position of head-professorship in the Nizamiya Madrasa of Baghdad better than this?' He looked deeply into my eyes for a while and said, 'I am here because when the full moon of happiness rose on the sky of will, the sun of reason showed the way of meeting.'" (Muhammad ibn Abdullah al-Hani, *Adab*, p. 9)

For this reason, the most influential type of knowledge that will lead mankind to happiness and salvation, in this world and the next, is the knowledge of heart that makes one acquainted with the Lord. It is this kind of knowledge that gives birth to a sense of mental and spiritual responsibility with which man fulfills good deeds in the best way possible. Without this profound feeling of sensitivity, science will only serve to destroy mankind, even though they emerged to serve mankind to begin with. Beneficial knowledge, therefore, is a matter of broader horizons and mentality. Without beneficial knowledge, the many potentially useful aspects of human sciences cannot be actualized. On the contrary, they become instruments serving malicious ends. The only way to avoid this hazard is through attaining to that inner maturity and noble characteristics imparted by what we call 'beneficial knowledge.'

There are many cases of systematic exploitation and misrepresentation by persons who despite being knowledgeable, lack the maturity of beneficial knowledge. A person with a law degree, for instance, might act like a ruthless executioner, when in fact he was trained to deliver human rights and justice. Similarly, a person with a medical degree might turn into a human butcher, when it is a cure that people expect from him to deliver. In spite of his knowledge, a ruler might likewise act in an unmerciful and loveless manner towards people under his command. Though they do possess fragments of scientific knowledge, these so-called people of learning commit crimes even beyond the wildest imagination of the illiterate. Yunus Emre hence says:

A person's real purpose for learning,
It is to know the Truth
If you have learned, but still do not know,
Such is a useless effort.

What is Sufism?

Consequently, every person needs first and foremost the enlightenment and inner depth of beneficial knowledge, while he keeps himself busy in learning various sciences so that he could succeed in matters worldly and other-worldly, material and immaterial. In reality, though it might have some temporary and outward benefits, knowledge that leads a person to pride, self-conceit and ultimately to self-destruction, is a great burden to carry. For this reason, the Messenger of the Almighty -upon him blessings and peace- always sought to acquire beneficial knowledge and prayed the Almighty to bestow such knowledge upon him. In this context, the Blessed Prophet -upon him blessings and peace- would utter the following prayer, "O Lord! I ask for beneficial knowledge from You and seek refuge in You from useless knowledge!" (Muslim, Dhikr, 73) Being also the essence of mystical knowledge in Sufism, beneficial knowledge means an effort to equip a servant with abstinence, piety and the internalization of faith. When a believer's knowledge acquires this level of epistemological perfection, it then attains the level of *marifah* or gnosis.

To explain this distinctiveness of spiritual knowledge, Rumi says, "Scholars knowledgeable only of exoteric sciences are aware of the subtleties of geometry, astronomy, medicine, and philosophy, depending on their fields. But these are all pieces of knowledge that belong to the perishable world, which lasts only for a short period of time. Such knowledge cannot have man ascend (*miraj*) to the realms above the seventh heaven. The ignorant, who are slaves to their egos, cannot obtain any knowledge of the way to the Almighty and the spiritual stations in between. Only can the wise Gnostics attain the knowledge of this; and only through their hearts, not through their reason."

Those who are lacking of the inner maturity of beneficial knowledge cannot reach the 'ultimate reality', however well-versed they might be in their scholarly fields. Knowledge truly enlightens its possessor, but only after when its possessor can transfer it from his reason to his heart to mature it therein and to actualize it in the form of moral character traits and righteous deeds. The Almighty says in the Quran, "[O Muhammad] say, 'O my Lord, increase me in knowledge!'" (Taha, 114) This increase in knowledge refers to servant's improvement of his level of religious perfection, of his level of piety and fear before the Divine. The Quran also says, "Only those of His servants who have knowledge fear The Almighty [rightfully]." (al-Fatir, 28) The Blessed Prophet -upon him blessings and peace- states, in relation,

$$\text{اِنَّمَا يَخْشَى اللهَ مِنْ عِبَادِهِ الْعُلَمٰٓؤُا}$$

"Among you I am the one who feels the highest level of piety and knows Him best." (*Bukhari*, Adab, 72)

Thus, a person whose knowledge is not implanted in his heart and which has not taken him to fear and love Allah, glory unto Him, is not really a scholar in the truest sense of the term, however much those around might regard him to be.

The great Imam Ghazzali addresses those who are preoccupied only with the exoteric sciences of the world and waste their lives on their trivial aspects, when he says, "I will feel pity for you, son, should you fail to transform your knowledge of theology, logic, rhetoric, poetry and grammar into wisdom and gnosis (*irfan*). You will have otherwise not received any benefit, but merely wasted the life given to you by the Almighty to worship Him."

Indeed, what is the use of acquiring knowledge if it will ultimately prove worthless in ushering one through Paradise to meet the Lord? Such knowledge would only incur disappointment in the presence of the Almighty. Could knowledge that leads a person to devilish conceit, arrogance and rebellion as were the cases of Balaam the son of Beor and Qarun, really be called knowledge? Certainly not! For this reason, authoritative Muslim figures describe the Islamic conception of knowledge as follows: "Knowledge means comprehension, without which knowledge cannot be actualized. The final destination of comprehension is the knowledge of the Divine (*marifatullah*), the essence of all learning. The closer a science is to this essence, the more laudable it is."

Likewise the eminent Rumi says, "A skillful and knowledgeable person deserves merit…but there is a lesson to be reaped in the case of Satan, whose knowledge did not suffice for him to appreciate the reality of Adam, as he based his verdict exclusively on his outer aspect instead. Many a knowledge and perception acts as a bandit thwarting the seeker of truth from the main path. It is for this reason that the majority of the dwellers of Paradise are those with a pure and sound heart, who were able to protect themselves from the evil of philosophers. So save yourself from pride and self-conceit and get rid of all things useless, so that you receive Divine mercies from above."

No human being can reach reality by the mere activity of reason, as it cannot disentangle itself out of the many enigmas it sees upon observing the universe. Reason does serve an important function in attending to the sensory things of the world; yet without the help of Divine revelation, it is an insufficient means to reach higher reality. Attaining reality is a matter of faith and love, in addition to reason. A sound human rational faculty trained by revelation can take a servant to a certain point in his search for truth. To comprehend greater secrets and wisdoms beyond this point, the servant may take flight only with the wings of his heart.

Reason is like a small gate that leads one to the realm of realities and secrets. Without it, one cannot reach *marifah*; a fool may never lay hold of wisdom. But reason alone does not suffice to lay hold of that wisdom, for it needs to take a further step that requires the intervention of love. The method of travelling beyond conventional, rational learning is outlined by the words of Rumi that urges one to "Sacrifice reason at the feet of *Mustafa* (the Blessed Prophet)." On the path towards the Real, a further spiritual medium beyond human rational faculty is needed.

All Muslim saints confirm that it was love that enabled them to traverse this ocean of existence. We therefore find melodies of love in their statements, again and again. In their eyes, this perishable world is worthless and all but devoid of any significance; and hence their attentions are unswervingly directed to the real aim. Muslim saints are pious servants of the Almighty who undertake, in their times and societies, the prophetic mission of training and purifying souls and presenting living examples of religious instructions.

A believer, whose inner eyes are open, sees the Divine manifestations of the Lord everywhere he looks. This should not be looked upon as something miraculous; it is rather knowledge transformed into gnosis (*marifah*). It is the product of real love entrenched in the heart. By means of the spiritual insight that comes from Divine love, saints the universe entire as a manifestation of Divine power. They peer into and behold the underlying wisdoms and realities of all beings. Such spiritual insight is an unparalleled Divine gift. How else could there be any meaning in life, if a person were not able to understand the silent language of winds, rivers and mountains? How can there be any enjoyment in life for one who is unable to take any lessons from nature? They are all reverberating testimonies of the uniqueness of Divine art. Failure to feel anything at the face of this matchless artwork only exposes an inner rawness and spiritual deficiency.

Sadi Shirazi points to wisdom and invites people to heed to true knowledge, as he says:

In the eyes of awakened, even green leaves are divan (of poetry);
Does not every particle reveal the art of the Divine?

The universe is a splendid exhibition that springs from the Divine. A splendid manifestation of it is the mystery called man, for carrying a heart resplendent with the spiritual gems that offers him the opportunity to mature his soul in this life. Even as he was being stoned by his people, Hallaj was still looking to mature his soul by repenting on behalf of those hurling the stones.

Each tiny particle in the universe incessantly brings us fresh news and greetings from the Divine. From the smile of a little baby to a fluttering butterfly, from the chirping nightingales to the exquisite colors and fragrances of spring, everything is virtually a countless manifestation of Divine joy. The sign of the embodiment of beneficial appears when one begins to read the book of universe through the inner eye and realize that the entire universe is a book of wisdom to draw lessons of Divine manifestations. In the Quran, the Almighty says, "And We did not create the heavens and earth and that between them in play," (ad-Dukhan, 38). "Did you then think that We created you in jest and that you would not be brought back to Us [for account]?" (Muminun, 115)

Compliant with these principles, each scholarly field ought to lead man to a grasp of his reason of existence; and observing the universe and recognizing the Divine majesty therein ought to lead him to the Supreme Creator. A person who does not have access to this insightful horizon cannot be complete, however great his rank or expertise may be in the specific field he is engaged with. The merit of any given science lies in its role in providing inner maturity and moral perfection; only these will benefit man in this world and the next.

All these points show that a servant can acquire beneficial knowledge only after establishing certain inner and spiritual qualities in his heart. This operation is two dimensional. While purifying the ego from all negative character traits like ostentation, self-conceit, covetousness, pride and love of fame, one must at the same time replace them in the heart with the praiseworthy, Muhammad-like moral traits, such as, piety, sincerity, mercy, patience, thankfulness, modesty, contentment, asceticism, moral scrupulousness and trust in the Almighty, among others.

Imam Rabbani offers a short description of the mindset in which beneficial knowledge can grow. He says, "Our first and foremost duty, my brothers, is to correct our faiths in accordance with the Quran and Sunnah. The innovators and the stray assume that their convictions are in agreement with the Quran and Sunnah, when in reality, it could not be more distant."

When a believer has established this mindset, he is then required to learn the precepts of the religion, permissible and impermissible activities, and duties prescribed by the Quran and Sunnah. He is also required to put his theoretical knowledge into practice. In order to be able to actualize all these in a complete manner, the believer needs to embark upon a ceaseless process of purifying his heart and soul. Knowledge of religious precepts is useless unless the faith is correct. Offering good deeds is useless without the knowledge of religious precepts. Purifying the heart and soul is unviable without offering good deeds. And faith, practice and knowledge all are useless without the purification of the heart and soul. It is in this mindset that beneficial knowledge flourishes en route for *marifa*.

O our Lord! We pray that You feed us with beneficial knowledge and protect us from all knowledge that is useless! Include us among those who put their theoretical knowledge into practice! Put us among those blessed and fortunate servants of Yours who transform their knowledge into gnosis (marifa) and attain to the knowledge of You; and thereby complete their spiritual ascension (miraj)!

Amin!

CHAPTER TWO

The Training of Sufism
(Sayr-Suluk)

A- **THE SELF (*NAFS*) AND İTS PURİFİCATİON (*TAZKİYA*)**
   1- **The Reality of the Self**
   2- **The Purification of the Self**
   3- **The States of the Self**
      a- *The Evil-Commanding Self (an-nafsu'l-ammara)*
      b- *The Self-Blaming Nafs (an-nafsu'l-lawwama)*
      c- *The Inspired Self (an-nafsu'l-mulhama)*
      d- *The Tranquil Self (an-nafsu'l-mutmainna)*
      e- *The Satisfied Self (an-nafsu'r-radiya)*
      f- *The Satisfying Self (an-nafsu'l-mardiyya)*
      g- *The Perfect Self (an-nafsu'l-kamila)*

B- **THE HEART (*QALB*) AND İTS PURİFİCATİON (*TASFİYA*)**
   1- **The Nature of the Heart**
   2- **The Types of Hearts**
   3- **The Purification of the Heart**
      a- Halal food
      b- Repentance and prayer
      c- Reading the Quran and obeying its commands
      d- Worshipping with utmost concentration
      e- Reviving the nights through worship
      f- Divine Remembrance and Contemplation (muraqaba)
      g- Love for the Blessed Prophet -upon him blessings and peace-
      h- Contemplating on Death
      i- Being together with the pious and righteous
      j- Possessing Good Morals
   4- **Gazing at the Universe through a Purified Heart**

C- **THE BASIC PRINCIPLES OF SUFI TRAINING**

D- **MURSHID-I KAMIL (A MATURE MASTER) AND METHODS OF SPIRITUAL ENLIGHTENING**
   1- **Murshid-i Kamil**
   2- **Methods of Spiritual Guidance**
      a- Muhabbah (Love) and Rabitah
      b- Getting together (sohbah)
      c- Service (khidmah)
      d- Favorable Inclination (tawajjuh)
      e- Prayer (dua)

E- **THE SUFI MANNERISM**
   1- **The Manner of Guidance and Mercy**
   2- **The Manner of Gentleness and Affection**

But those will prosper who purify themselves. (as-Shams, 14)

The Training of Sufism (*Sayr Suluk*)

Sufism is a spiritual school where the heart and soul is purified in the hands of real educators, the heirs of Prophet Muhammad -upon him blessings and peace-.

Human beings are created in various capacities with the potential talents and abilities each possesses. Sufi masters, therefore, use a variety of training methods compliant with the aspirant's spiritual talents and disposition. It goes without saying that it is impossible to subject human disposition to a complete change; yet it can be matured to a certain important extent if trained by and guided through Divine instructions. Islamic law (*Shariah*) establishes the same general regulations for all Muslims. In addition to and based on these general rules, the Sufi path promotes particular methods of spiritual training in accordance with the personal characteristics of the wayfarer. Here, we need to clarify a subtle and frequently misunderstood point: Sufism does not promote any principles that contradict the *Shariah*. The relationship between the *Shariah* and Sufism may be comparable to a compass. The stable leg of the compass is the *Shariah*, while the other, moveable leg is Sufism. Though the distance between the two legs may increase depending on personal disposition and abilities of the wayfarer, the moveable leg is nonetheless always bound remain loyal to the fixed leg, and never moves beyond its control.

On the other hand, this delicate criterion is applicable only to those who thrive in observing the commands and prohibitions of the Almighty. For this reason, true Sufis are those who rectify their outward aspects while at the same time directing their attention to maturing their inward qualities. Such Sufis constantly strive to embody advanced characteristics, both externally and internally, in a delicately balanced manner. Not only do they acknowledge the importance of correcting and perfecting the external human qualities, they emphasize the significance of improving internal human characteristics, namely the heart; as human actions come into effect through the will, which, in turn, is controlled by the heart.

One of the subtle principles the Blessed Prophet followed -upon him blessings and peace- in spiritual education was to never reproach the interlocutor, even if he be guilty at all fronts. Much rather, the Prophet –upon him blessings and peace- would caution the person in an indirect manner by ascribing the fault to himself. There are numerous reports that detail the admirable and exemplary attitude the Blessed Prophet -upon him blessings and peace- would show in such situations. On many an occasion, for instance, the Prophet -upon him blessings and peace- would express his disapproval of an unpleasant behavior by simply saying, in a very gentle and polite manner, "What is wrong with me that I see you do such and such?" Emulating this exemplary attitude, Sufis call themselves to account on a regular basis but treat others with utmost leniency. Since they are too occupied with inner purity and spiritual education, they approach others, even sinners, with affection and tolerance. Sufis thus strive to get rid of all kinds of sin, though certainly not the sinners themselves. Before correcting negative human characteristics, Sufis try to soften the hearts of their interlocutors through the spiritual power and blessings that emanate from their gatherings, and prepare hearts for the awaiting process of correction and betterment. Sufis, therefore, help others tone their anger and rage while at the same time lend them a helping hand in restoring their sense of repentance.

An incomparable example of spiritual refinement can be found in Yusuf's -upon him blessings and peace- treatment of his brothers. During his reign in Egypt, his brothers, who had once attempted to kill him by throwing him into a deserted well, came to ask his help. To ensure they did not feel uncomfortable, Yusuf -upon him blessings and peace- hid his real identity from them and gave them everything they requested; treating them with dignity, honor, and hospitality. Remember that by that time, Joseph -upon him blessings and peace- had all the power to exact his revenge from his brothers and settle all accounts. But, instead, being the exemplary spiritual guide he was, he displayed an utmost forgiveness, putting everything aside for the sake of the Lord. The Quran recounts the assuring words Yusuf -upon him blessings and peace- said to his brothers

The Training of Sufism (Sayr Suluk)

once his true identity was revealed: "No reproach this day shall be on you; the Lord will forgive you; He is the most merciful of the merciful." (Yusuf, 92) Seeing this noble act, Yusuf's -upon him blessings and peace- brothers felt a deep regret for what they had done many years ago and repented, there and then, of their grave sin. They acknowledged Yusuf's -upon him blessings and peace- excellent qualities and testified to his spiritual merits; the desired result was achieved through this process.

Another exemplary manifestation of the spiritual methods of education Sufis have followed in history is as follows. A group of heedless young men were sitting by Tigris River, drinking, and enjoying their day, when Maruf Karhi, a prominent saint, happened to pass by them. When they saw him coming, the young men thought that the Sheikh would see their inexcusable situation and curse them. Understandably, they felt uncomfortable. Frustrated, however, one man from the group stood up and called out, sarcastically, "Why don't you start your cursing right away, Sheikh, so that we are drawn into the ferocious waters of Tigris and perish once and for all?" Yet, without showing the least sign of irritation, the Sheikh raised his hands up mercifully and prayed, "O Lord! Let these young men be happy in the world to come as well, just as You let them enjoy their time in this world!" Surprised by the Sheikh's reaction, the baffled young men asked "What are you talking about, Sheikh? Your words do not make any sense!" Maruf Karhi, whose simple prayer had already touched the hearts of the young men for its sincerity, replied "Sons... If the Lord wants you to be joyful in the world to come, He leads you towards repentance." Seeing such an unexpected and affectionate response, the young men were sent into a deep contemplation. Overcome by a deep remorse, they ended up giving up the bottle and their musical instruments, repenting for all their previous misdemeanors to become seekers of happiness and salvation, both in this world and the world to come.

As mentioned above, another basic principle of Sufism in spiritual education is to utilize various pedagogical methods in accordance with the disposition of the seeker. The reason why we have a variety of Sufi orders is to be explained by this aspect of human psychology; as depending on the types of personal dispositions, Sufi orders employ a range of educational and instructive methods. For instance, a seeker with an enthusiastic disposition would find greater appeal in the Qadiri type of tutoring, which would allow him to proceed on the spiritual path with greater efficiency. A seeker with a poetic, artistic, and romantic temperament, on the other hand, would find himself more at home in the Mawlawi order. Likewise, a seeker with a sober and calm nature would find the Naqshbandi order more suitable. Therefore, in his spiritual training and progress, the seeker searches and finds the avenue most suitable for his temperament

Human disposition cannot be reset completely. Acknowledging this fact, Sufi masters see themselves responsible only for helping their disciples to become aware of their positive and negative personal qualities, and lead them to heavenly directions through this awareness. Sufi masters work diligently to introduce specific methods for each disciple in treating his personal, spiritual problems.

The Arabs of pre-Islamic times were extremely uncivilized and hardhearted, to such an extent that they could even bury their infant girls alive. They were members of a merciless society in which human rights belonged only to the powerful, while ordinary people had to undergo all kinds of suffering. Through Prophet Muhammad's -upon him blessings and peace- spiritual education, this society found the guidance that would make them the most civilized and distinguished human beings on earth. Thanks to the unspoiled spiritual energy in their hearts, which was inspired by their unconditional love for the Blessed Prophet -upon him blessings and peace-, they offered their acts of worship in an admirably sincere fashion. Celebrated as the Noble Companions (*Ashab- i Kiram*), they left a lasting legacy of exemplary religious and moral standards to the following generations.

Under the Prophet's -upon him blessings and peace- guidance and education, the Noble Companions reached the highest points of spirituality. Abdullah ibn Masud describes their unparalleled spiritual progress, when he says, "We reached such a level that we were able to hear the morsels, going down our throats, praising the Lord."

Sufism, therefore, represents the educational method by which the Blessed Prophet -upon him blessings and peace- trained his Companions in guiding them to religious and spiritual purification. Sufism refers to a spiritual school in which the heart and soul undergo a process of refinement and purification under the guidance of real educators, who are, in effect, the heirs of the Prophet -upon him blessings and peace-. And the training of Sufism (*sayr suluk*) is the term used to describe this spiritual school and the progressive path of becoming a perfected human being.

He who knows his soul knows his Lord.

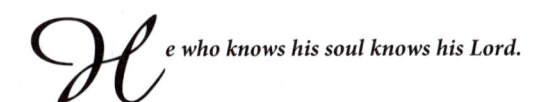

A. THE SELF (*NAFS*) AND ITS PURIFICATION (*TAZKIYA*)

1. THE REALITY OF THE NAFS

The Almighty created Adam -upon him blessings and peace-, the father of all human kind, in Paradise and through him, made man the most honored created being. As a result of this heavenly privilege, however, the Almighty willed that mankind toil to deserve an eternal and blissful life in Paradise. As desired by the Almighty's design in past eternity, Adam -upon him blessings and peace- committed that well-known blunder in paradise, as a result of which he was sent out from Paradise to this world; though paradise remained his original homeland, while this world a land of exile and trial. Man's subsequent return to Paradise has thus become a matter of reward and merit, for which he has to successfully undergo a variety of tests.

For such reasons, among all creation, the Almighty has given human beings unique characteristics. The Almighty willed to design mankind in accordance with the quality of their praiseworthy and blameworthy deeds, ranging from "the lowest of the low (*asfal al-safilin*)" to "the highest of the high (*a'la al-'illiyin*)." In other words, being the pearl of all creation, man possesses an inborn capacity towards good and evil; and thus his high or low position among creation depends on the way he uses his will. The success of man in this undertaking is proportional to his personal success in enhancing his good qualities and, at the same time, curbing his evil aspects. The merit of a human being becomes evident in this battle ground where the good and evil features stake conflicting claims over the control of the person.

According to Sufis, the negative and positive inclinations that exist in man have two locale or focal points in "the animal soul" and "the lordly soul".

The animal soul is a subtle faculty that enables man to stay alive in this world and to keep his biological existence under control. It is also called "life" or "self". Since the animal soul keeps running its basic operations in the human body even while a person is asleep, most of the biological functions in the body are involuntarily carried on during sleep. But the lordly soul leaves the body during sleep, to return to it once again the moment a person wakes up. The animal soul sets the body in motion, makes it speak, and enables it to operate all the other basic bodily functions. The animal soul leaves the body by death. Its location is between the brain and the heart, from where it spreads out to the whole body and undertakes its main operations through the circulating blood. This soul is related to "the temporal and created world (*alamu'l-khalq*)"[17] and constitutes the starting point of human actions. If untrained, this soul may exercise negative influences over a human being.

The lordly soul refers to the human soul which the Almighty had breathed of His spirit. It is this quality that differentiates a human being from the rest of creation. The lordly soul belongs to "the world of unconditioned existence (*alamu'l-amr*)"[18] and accompanies the human body so that man may perform good deeds. By way of, and thanks to, this soul which the human body dresses, man leads a decent and observant lifestyle in servanthood and obedience. The lordly soul does not perish or disappear with the death of the body; though by death the effect of the lordly soul over the body comes to an end.

Man gives directions to his life depending on the exact nature of the battle taking place in his inner dimension between the animal and lordly souls. When the lordly soul wins the battle, man becomes inclined towards

---

17 *Alamu'l-khalq*: This world is bound by time and space and constituted by created beings. *Alamu'l-khalq* is also called "the temporal or visible world". Things that we perceive through our five senses come from this world.

18 *Alamu'l-amr*: This world is free of the concepts of time and matter and has come into existence merely by the Divine command "Be!". It is also designated by the terms "the spiritual or unseen world". Subtle realities such as the intellect, soul, spirit, heart, and secret belong to this world.

good deeds and morality. But when the animal soul takes the control, man becomes inclined towards all kinds of sin and immorality. Man's responsibility for his actions is based on his preferences and decisions between good and evil deeds. Since man is given a capacity to perform his actions in accordance with his free will, and thereby take his animal soul under control to a certain extent, he is liable for what he does and eligible for both reward and punishment.

The human ego constitutes one of the biggest obstacles that stand in front of man in this world of tests and trial. For this reason, in general, we think of the human self, or nafs, as a negative concept. In reality, however, the self has positive qualities embedded in its essence. To make this essence appear in all its glory, man must instead polish the nafs from all kinds of dirt through spiritual purification. Man should continually keep himself busy with striving for good causes in this world so that he could reach a blissful life in the world to come, as every man shapes his own eternal life in this world and reaps whatever he sows. Depending on the quality of his deeds, each person will attain a pleasant or an unpleasant life in the Hereafter. In one respect, we might even say that it is man himself who writes his own destiny in this life.

One of the essential conditions of eternal happiness and salvation for man is to mature the lower self or the ego to a proper degree of ripeness, so as to accustom it to offering good deeds. A self that lacks this ripeness is similar to an aggressive and untamed horse, which takes its rider to destruction, rather than to his intended destination. A saddled horse, on the other hand, properly trained and bridled, takes its rider peacefully to the destination, however dangerous the road might be. Likewise, an untamed and uncontrolled self cannot take its possessor to the sublime and celestial aims of life.

In fact, the self, or nafs, functions as a two dimensional vehicle. While it has a potential to elevate man's value to the peaks of maturity and make him the pearl of all creation, it might also degrade his value to the lowest of the low. The self, therefore, has a potential to head towards both directions, like a two-edged knife. When properly trained it heads towards the good; though if not, it recklessly heads towards evil.

Sufism: A Path Towards the Internalization of Faith (Ihsân)

Every human soul that remains deprived of spiritual guidance and control, functions like a dark curtain of ignorance that covers the surface of realities. But as mentioned above, despite the obstacle of the ego, if a person purifies himself by salvaging his soul from the hands of immoral characteristics, he can reach advanced points even higher than that of angels. For the merit of every end is proportionate to the level of difficulty experienced and of the obstacles overcome for the sake of reaching this end.

Immoral characteristics in the soul interfere with the communication between the Almighty and the servant. Only through the practice of the required spiritual methods can one remain firm against these relentless interferences; and this means an equally relentless struggle against the ego's lowly temptations and desires. Such a course of action requires a persistent and determinate toil. In this context, the Blessed Prophet –upon him blessings and peace- says,

اَلْمُجَاهِدُ مَنْ جَاهَدَ نَفْسَهُ

"[The real] struggler (*mujahid*) is the one who struggles against his own self." (Tirmidhi, *Fadailu'l-Jihad*, 2; Ahmad ibn Hanbal, *Musnad*, VI, 20)

Although the struggle against the lower self, or the ego, does not kill it, it nonetheless takes it under control. In fact, Sufism does not so much aim at utterly destroying the self, as withholding it from transgressing and immunizing it against lowly desires and inclinations. The Sufi way undertakes this operation in accordance with Divine instructions. In this regard, Ghazzali compares man's position with a rider and says, "The nafs is the spirit's saddled beast. If a person lets go of the bridles of the nafs and follows its direction, his destruction becomes unavoidable. If he tries to destroy the self (as it is in the case of certain Hindu religions and mystical philosophies), then he is bound to remain behind on the path of reality, without any saddled beast. Better you hold on tight to the bridles of the beast and make use of it."

Following this course of action in dealing with the self is a requirement, and moreover, an essential part of the prophetic method in human education. The Blessed Prophet -upon him blessings and peace- did not approve of the attitude of refraining totally from eating, drinking and living a family life for the sake of devoting the entire energy to worship. He repeatedly underlined the fact that such a monastic practice of complete self-isolation was not a part of Islam. The Blessed Prophet -upon him blessings and peace- hence showed the possibility and methods of accomplishing spiritual progress whilst leading a life in society.

On the other hand, during the course of this education, which is a difficult struggle indeed, a wayfarer encounters certain states and stations of the nafs. One of the most dangerous afflictions the nafs encounters whilst advancing on the spiritual path is the risk of ascribing an existence to itself and dragging itself thereby into self-conceit. Detrimentally, this is where the hidden arrogance and pride takes control. In the course of struggling against the lower self, even small mistakes are inexcusable, as they allow the lower self to return to its original starting point.

Since the lower self is always on alert and waiting in ambush, one should never feel safe from its deception and harm. For this reason, a believer should constantly be aware of the possible dangers and tricks that come from his own nafs. He should meet them with a sound judgment and rein them in with a determination inspired by Divine revelation.

How can we purify the self, man's saddled beast, when it has innate evil temptations? Furthermore, what kind of spiritual levels are waiting to be reached in the course of this training of purification? Now, it is time for us to focus on these two questions.

The question is whether or not you will be able to acquire a rose-like nature. What this means is that even though you see all kinds of thorns in the garden of this world, you are not to act as a thorn yourself; however severely injured you might be by them. You should instead try to be like a rose, which, despite the chill of winter, blossoms all the same...

2. THE PURIFICATION OF THE LOWER SELF, OR NAFS

The word *tazkiyah* means to cleanse and purify. It also denotes increasing, improving, and a blessing. From this semantic perspective, *tazkiyah* comprises the entire process of spiritual education.

Purifying the nafs means is to cleanse it primarily from unbelief, ignorance, evil thoughts, false convictions and immorality. In other words, the purification of the self is an act of cleansing aimed at eliminating all kinds of theoretical and practical impurities. This process ends in filling the nafs with good religious and moral qualities, such as sound belief, knowledge, gnosis, wisdom and spirituality.

The Sufi purification concentrates on lessening the lowly desires of the nafs, breaking its authority over the body and establishing the spirit's authority instead. This occurs only through practices of abstinence that strengthen the will-power against the lower self; and this involves a strict self-discipline with regards to food, sleep and speech. Sufism thus outlines the methods of disciplining the soul through three interconnected concepts: little of food (*qillatu't-taam*), little of sleep (*qillatu'l-manam*), and little of speech (*qillatu'l-kalam*). In establishing a spiritual authority over the nafs, these rules constitute the earliest steps. It should also be borne in mind that a wayfarer should not exaggerate the practice of these rules. Since our body has been entrusted to us by the Almighty, we have to keep in mind the need to deal with it in moderation.

The Training of Sufism (Sayr Suluk)

In other words, during the process of purifying the lower self, a servant should keep himself away from excess in either direction. He should not overdo spiritual exercises in the name of taking the self under complete control; for Islam commands moderation in all states and actions, and warns people against all kinds of exaggerative behavior. Furthermore, neither is it not possible to eliminate the self all together, nor is this required by religion. Instead, a believer is expected to purify his self in the sense of bridling and training it in accordance with Divine instructions.

The act of training and purifying the self is itself the most decisive factor in determining the nature of man's ultimate end; whether it will be one of destruction or happiness. To fulfill this process of purification, a servant should readily submit himself to Divine will and resist against his lustful passions and indecent expectations. Every believer should be aware of his shortcomings, weaknesses and ignorance. At the same time, he should truly comprehend the absolute glory and power of Allah, glory unto Him, and regulate his actions accordingly. If the believer is successful in this undertaking, then his 'evil commanding self' (Yusuf, 53) becomes purified from immorality and thus turns into a praiseworthy self.

On account of the immense level of difficulty involved, man's struggle for purifying his self is regarded as 'the greater *jihad*', in the sense of being a *jihad* against the lower self. The term was in fact used by the Blessed Prophet -upon him blessings and peace- on their return from the grueling Campaign of Tabuk, where he said to his marching Companions, "Now we are returning from the smaller *jihad* to the greater *jihad*."

Tabuk was indeed an overwhelming campaign. From beginning to end, Muslims found themselves in a highly difficult situation, fighting on two fronts against both the hypocrites and the whispers of Satan. It was a scorching hot summer wreaked by a severe drought. The destination moreover demanded a long march through an area unsuited for travelling on foot. Making matters more difficult was the fact that it was the annual harvest season. When the Companions were informed that an incomparably huge Byzantine army was waiting for them near Tabuk, the battle suddenly looked more challenging than ever. The Muslim army of thirty-thousand men travelled approximately one-thousand kilometers and back. When they were finally returning to Medina, they were virtually reduced to skin and bones, with the campaign taking its toll on their exhausted bodies. It was in this backdrop that the Blessed Prophet -upon him blessings and peace- was making a statement to the Companions by drawing their attention to the greater struggle that awaited them. Naturally, the Companions were left amazed and they asked the Prophet -upon him blessings and peace-, "What could be a greater *jihad* than this one?" To that the Prophet -upon him blessings and peace- responded, "Yes, now we are returning from the smaller *jihad* to the greater *jihad*…the *jihad* against the lower self." [19]

Renowned, on the other hand, is the story of the three Companions who failed to take part in the Tabuk campaign. Even though they had attended all the previous military campaigns, the three Companions failed in their duty to obey the Prophet Muhammad's -upon him blessings and peace- command at this one instance, without any excuse. When the Muslim army came back from the campaign, the three Companions were spiritually excluded from the community; the Blessed Prophet -upon him blessings and peace- and the other Companions severed all communications with them. The three Companions subsequently felt an indescribable remorse over their failure and weakness to join the campaign.[20]

---

[19] Suyuti, *Jamiu's-Saghir*, II, 73

[20] The names of these three Companions were Murarah ibn Rab al-Amri, Hilal ibn Umayyah al-Waqifi and Kaab ibn Malik, the poet. The three Companions had taken part in all the previous battles; except for Kaab -Allah be well-pleased with him-, who was absent only at Badr. The world had suddenly narrowed in their eyes, constricting their hearts, now that they were ignored by the entire Muslim society because of their misjudgment in remaining behind from Tabuk. Worst of all was the fact that the Blessed Prophet -upon him blessings and peace- had shunned them to a point where he did not even respond to their greetings. The entire earth had become estranged; even their wives were like strangers. There was nothing they could do about it, except for weep, day and night. They were like melted candles from their incessant crying. They had done a mistake but that did not distance them from being sincere, upright; neither did it shake their trust in Allah, glory unto Him, nor did it divert them away from remorse and repentance. Fifty days had gone by when they were finally rewarded for their honesty and genuine repentance in the form of the Quranic verse: "And to the three who were left behind, until, when the earth became strait for them, for all its breadth, and their souls became strait for them, and they thought that there was no shelter from God except in Him, then He turned towards them, that they might also turn; surely God turns, and is All-compassionate." (at-Tawbah,118-119) For a more detailed analysis of this subject-matter see Osman Nuri Topbaş, *The Chain of Prophets*, IV, 289-294.

The Training of Sufism (Sayr Suluk)

Now we need to stop and consider that if such an overwhelming physical *jihad* was considered "the smaller *jihad*", and the failure to attend nonetheless came at a great cost for the Companions mentioned, what about the cost of failing to attend "the greater *jihad*"? As mentioned above, the Prophet -upon him blessings and peace-, described man's struggle for purifying his self as "the greater *jihad*". Abandoning this type of jihad would surely incur more tragic consequences for man in the presence of the Almighty. Considering the enormity of this responsibility, every believer of right mind must get his act together, and call himself to account before the Divine Judgment catches him. In this context, the Lord's warning in the Quran is quite powerful: "What, did you think that We created you only for sport, and that you would not be returned to Us?" (al-Muminun, 115) Similarly, another Quranic verse says: "What, does man reckon he shall be left to roam at will?" (al-Qiyamah, 36) The Noble Prophet -upon him blessings and peace- also says, "A mindful person is he who takes his lower self under control, calls it to account, and performs good deeds for the world to come. A foolish person is the one who expects something good from the Almighty in vain, while following the desires of his lower self." (*Tirmidhi*, Qiyamah, 25; *Ibn Majah*, Zuhd, 31)

Consequently, every believer should be mindful of the characteristics of his self and the responsibility he carries for its purification. He should take great care and use the appropriate methods, in order not to fall victim to the nafs in the process. The Almighty warns us against the tricks of the lower self and says:

$$\text{اَرَاَيْتَ مَنِ اتَّخَذَ اِلٰهَهُ هَوٰيهُ اَفَاَنْتَ تَكُونُ عَلَيْهِ وَكِيلاً}$$

"Have you seen the one who has taken his caprice as his god? Will you be a guardian over them?" (al-Furqan, 43) Prophet Muhammad -upon him blessings and peace- also underlines the importance of this fact and says: "Concerning my community, I fear most about the possibility that they will follow the desires of their lower selves." (Suyuti, *Jamiu's-Saghir*, I, 12) Purifying the self is therefore of vital importance and a huge responsibility for every believer. The Almighty mentions this fact in the following verse of the Quran:

Sufism: A Path Towards the Internalization of Faith (Ihsân)

قَدْ اَفْلَحَ مَنْ زَكّٰيهَا وَ قَدْ خَابَ مَنْ دَسّٰيهَا

"Prosperous is he who purifies it (the nafs), and failed has he who seduces it." (as-Shams, 9-10) In other words, he who corrects his self will reach his destination safe and sound, while he who leaves his self to wallow in its excess and arrogance will face utter disappointment. This means that the nafs includes two functions, working in the opposite poles. If one follows it unconditionally, he would end up in an eternal loss. But if one trains the self and takes it under control, he could reach a spiritual level even higher than that of angels. The self is the unique means that can lead one to both directions.

Although all good deeds come with an outward aspect, they always have an essential, inner dimension to be discerned. Charity, for instance, outwardly appears as lending a helping hand to the needy; but actually and inwardly, it inspires the self towards the good and beautiful. In this way, good deeds feel at home in the self and the spirit becomes intimately acquainted with them. Likewise, reciting the Quran, which includes the most beautiful and truthful words, paying careful attention to its advices and putting its instructions into action represent some basic means to correct the self. A servant who organizes his whole life in accordance with the Quran becomes safe from the deceptive whispers of his self and thus pursues the main objective in life, which is none other than to attain to the pleasure of the Lord. His heart then becomes receptive to the Divine disclosures. When the servant attains this high level of spiritual perfection, the unseen realm becomes visible for him and the universe presents itself as it is; an open book of wisdom and wonder. Therefore, every believer should be mindful of the Quranic commands and prohibitions, so that he does not risk his eternal happiness and salvation both in this world and the world to come.

The Holy Quran offers many verses in relation to purification of the soul. The term 'purification' (*tazkiyah*)" in these verses comprises three main aspects:

1. The Almighty's purification.

2. Prophet Muhammad's -upon him blessings and peace- purification.

3. A person's own purification of his nafs.

a. Purification by the Almighty

The Almighty says in the Quran,

$$\text{فَلاَ تُزَكُّوا اَنْفُسَكُمْ هُوَ اَعْلَمُ بِمَنِ اتَّقَىٰ}$$

"Hold not yourselves purified; The Almighty knows very well him who is the Almighty-fearing." (an-Najm, 32) The late exegete Elmalılı Hamdi Effendi gives the following interpretation for this verse: "Do not be proud of yourselves and assume yourselves to be sinless, faultless and purified. For you might have many faults, but not be aware of them." Regarding the same verse of the Quran, Alusi, another exegete, comments, "It is narrated that this verse was revealed concerning a group of people who would say, 'We have our prayer, fasting, and pilgrimage to save us!' It is more appropriate for a servant to keep his acts of worship and good deeds undisclosed, lest they become contaminated with self-conceit and lip-service. But without having such a negative intention, it is fine for the servant to talk about his good deeds to encourage others to do the same."

In another Quranic verse, the Almighty says, "Have you not seen those who claim themselves to be pure? Nay; only The Almighty purifies whom He will." (an-Nisa, 49) Here, it is a self-acclaimed pureness, stemming from pride. In reality, purification is dependent upon a person's piety which itself is consequent upon practice. Piety, in turn, is an inner quality whose reality is known only by the Almighty. For this reason, a pureness declared only by the Almighty is admissible, and not any self-acclaimed assertion of purity. In this context, the Blessed Prophet -upon him blessings and peace- would pray, "O Lord…grant to my soul the sense of Your fear and purify it; for You are its Best Purifier; its Protecting Friend and Guardian." (Muslim, Dhikr, 73) Similarly, another Quranic verse underlines the importance of the Almighty's own purification as follows: "If not for the favor of the Almighty upon you and His mercy, not one of you would have been pure, ever, but The Almighty purifies whom He wills, and The Almighty is All-hearing, All-knowing." (an-Nur: 21)

Sufism: A Path Towards the Internalization of Faith (Ihsân)

All these reports clearly state that purification belongs in reality to the Almighty, Who, by way of His limitless favor and mercy, enables His servant to practice good deeds and guides him to the means of purification. The servant, therefore, should keep himself away from conceit and self-promotion, and instead hold the Almighty as the actual Purifier. The servant should be mindful of the fact that his entire personal efforts towards purification will be useless in the Hereafter, unless the Almighty purifies him. This mindset provides the ultimate means to reach eternal salvation. Even though purification might be attributable to the servant with respect to personal will and effort, and to prophets and spiritual masters with respect to providing guidance and teaching, in the final analysis, purification is attributable only to the Almighty, Who creates the means of purification for His servant and enables him to find these means.

b. Purification by the Messenger of Allah -upon him blessings and peace-

In its description of the Blessed Prophet's -upon him blessings and peace- duties, the Quran mentions the following qualities:

كَمَا اَرْسَلْنَا فِيكُمْ رَسُولاً مِنْكُمْ يَتْلُوا عَلَيْكُمْ اٰيَاتِنَا وَ يُزَكِّيكُمْ وَ يُعَلِّمُكُمُ الْكِتَابَ وَ الْحِكْمَةَ وَ يُعَلِّمُكُمْ مَالَمْ تَكُونُوا تَعْلَمُونَ

"Just as We have sent among you, of yourselves, a Messenger, to recite Our signs to you and to purify you, and to teach you the Book and the Wisdom, and to teach you that you knew not." (al-Baqarah, 151) "Truly the Almighty was gracious to the believers when He raised up among them a Messenger from themselves, to recite to them His signs and to purify them, and to teach them the Book and the Wisdom, though before they were in manifest error." (Al-i Imran, 164)

These Quranic verses clarify the three principal duties the Prophet -upon him blessings and peace- was entrusted with:

a. Conveying the Almighty's Signs to Human Beings

Conveying the Divine revelation prophets receive marks the beginning of their prophethood. Yet, this is also the first step and the basic and broadest ground to enable human beings to reach the desired destination.

b. The Act of Purification

The gist of the belief in the oneness of Allah, glory unto Him, (*tawhid*) can be realized only through cleansing the human lower self from inner filths like unbelief, polytheism, and sin. Furthermore, this Divine message may feel at home only in peaceful and tranquil souls. The best example of this fact can be observed in the lives of the Companions of the Blessed Prophet -upon him blessings and peace-. In spite of having committed the gravest of sins during their pre-Islamic lives, when they found the right guide in the Prophet's -upon him blessings and peace- teaching and spiritual training, they ended up purifying their nafs to become the most distinguished people on earth. Maturing and perfecting themselves, they left a lasting legacy for the Muslim generations to follow; a legacy set to last until the Final Hour.

c. Teaching the Book and Wisdom

At this stage comes the Book, which explains the rules and regulations that mankind ought to follow. This Book is the Holy Quran. A person's spiritual qualities determine his comprehension of the spirit of the Quran. In reality, the Quran is to be read and comprehended by the heart. And as for the eyes, they are simply means for the heart.

Since the Quran, human being, and universe all come into existence through manifestations and disclosures of Divine Names, they represent a limitless treasure of secrets. These secrets and wisdoms open themselves to a person in proportion to his level of spiritual purification and maturity. The teaching of wisdom comes at the end of all these stages; for the Almighty allows only those who have purified their nafs to comprehend the wisdoms and secrets of the Quran. The Quran itself represents the disclosures of Divine Names in the format of "Speech" so that the human mind might have access to them.

The verses of the Quran mention purification together with the teaching of the Book and Wisdom. This fact indicates that those who possess unpurified nafs cannot attain to the true knowledge of things, and most importantly, of the Quran. Their knowledge will not benefit them, even

Sufism: A Path Towards the Internalization of Faith (Ihsân)

if they might possess some bits of it. Since knowledge and wisdom are of invaluable importance, they do not dwell in ordinary places. A heart set to become a dwelling place for knowledge and wisdom, is to be freed of all kinds of useless and dangerous grimes. For this reason, prophets first convey the Divine signs, and then embark upon purifying the hearts of those to whom they have conveyed the signs. It is only at the end of this process that prophets teach the Book and Wisdom to persons who have thus become spiritually purified. The secrets embedded in this universe open themselves gradually only to those who possess a heart purified in the manner mentioned. Those who possess such hearts may even become springs of wisdom in their own right.

The exoteric dimensions of Prophet Muhammad's -upon him blessings and peace- duties and instructions will be maintained until the end of the world, through the attentive efforts of Muslim scholars who recite the Quran and teach others its commands and prohibitions. As for the esoteric dimensions of his activities, they will also be perpetuated until the Last Day, by virtue of the industrious efforts of spiritual masters who undertake the mission of purifying hearts and souls.

c. A Person's Own Purification of His Self

Regarding a person's purification of his own self, the Holy Quran reads, "By the nafs and He Who shaped it and inspired it to wickedness and righteousness! Prosperous is he who purifies it, and failed has he who seduces it [by way of ignorance and sins]." (as-Shams, 7-10) According to the requirements of this Quranic statement, the prosperous and saved ones will only be those whom the Almighty has purified by freeing them of sins and equipping them with His blessings and fear. Another Quranic verse describes the distinguished position of such people in the world to come as follows, "Enter you among My servants! Enter you My Paradise!" (al-Fajr, 29-30) Still another verse says,

$$\text{قَدْ اَفْلَحَ مَنْ تَزَكّٰى وَ ذَكَرَ اسْمَ رَبِّهِ فَصَلّٰى}$$

"Prosperous is he who has purified himself and mentions the name of his Lord, and prays." (al-Ala, 14-15) The command to purify mentioned in

The Training of Sufism (Sayr Suluk)

the last verse is quite significant. The servant is expected to: 1) First cleanse his heart, body and possessions from all negativity and immorality; which 2) results in the unveiling the curtains of ignorance that stand between the servant and the Almighty; 3) after which, with a body nurtured by lawful food and a heart mindful of the Almighty, the servant enters into the realm of mature servanthood and spiritual enjoyment.

The exegete Bursawi interprets this Quranic verse in the following: "This verse indicates that a servant is expected to cleanse his soul from all kinds of things declared by Islam as unlawful, to purify his heart from the love of the world, to direct his attention only to Lord as much as his capacities allow and to even withhold his mind from remembering anything other than the Almighty." Underlining the same quality are the words Abu Bakr Kattani uttered in his deathbed: "I would never talk about my deeds out of the fear of allowing the intrusion of hypocrisy; but since my death is just around the corner, I feel I should say a few things for your sake. I have been a watchful doorkeeper at the gate of my heart and have done my best to keep it closed to anything other than the Lord…and in the end my heart acquired such a quality that I became a stranger to everything but the Lord."

According to Ibn Abbas' interpretation, the word *tazakka* (as-Shams, 14-15) means "a person's declaration of the statement there is no god but Allah (la ilaha illa Allah)." (Qurtubi, *Jami*, XX, 22) The logic behind this interpretation lays the fact that cleansing the heart from unbelief and polytheism marks the first step of the process of purification. The first part of the declaration of the Almighty's oneness (*kalimatu't-tawhid*) begins with a negation (*la*); namely 'there is no god' (*la ilaha*). This indicates that a believer is expected to empty his heart and whole existence of all kinds of negative moral characteristics, which resemble minor deities. Then comes the confirmation 'but Allah' (*illa Allah*), which is when the heart becomes ready to receive and to be filled with the Divine light of *tawhid*. An anonymous poet voices this quite beautifully when he says:

Empty your heart of everything other than the Lord
For He does not visit a place with no proper host

Regarding this act of purification, Ibrahim Dasuqi -may Allah sanctify his secret-remarks, "Son…Do not ever fall prey to conceit, even if you

Sufism: A Path Towards the Internalization of Faith (Ihsân)

be spending your days fasting and nights praying; and even if you have a clean spirit that enjoys a close relationship to the Lord. Do not ever be defeated by pride and let your ego get the better of you; for many a dervish who has, has ended up in destruction."

Another saint Hatam Asamm -may Allah sanctify his secret- says, *"Do not ever be deceived by luxurious palaces, fruitful gardens and green pastures; for there is no garden more beautiful than Paradise. Still, remember what happened to Adam –upon him peace- right in the middle of Paradise? With a desire to stay there forever more, he stretched his hand out to the 'the forbidden fruit', only to be punished and expelled to the world by the Divine Will. Do not ever be deceived by the abundance of your deeds of worship and personal qualities. For despite his unique many personal qualities, Balaam the son of Boer ended up in destruction, even though one time the Almighty had taught him His Greatest Name. (ismu'l-azam).[21] There is an enormous lesson to be taken in that incident alone.*

Come to your senses and do not ever be deceived by the abundance of your knowledge and deeds. Have you not heard of what happened to Satan, who had erstwhile been endowed with a great amount of knowledge and had performed many acts of worship to go with it? Therefore, beware of the tricks of Satan and the ego, against which Our Compassionate Lord warns us: '[Satan] said, "Now, for Your perverting me, I shall surely sit in ambush for them on Your straight path."' *(al-Araf: 16)* And again, '[Satan] said, "My Lord, for Your perverting me I shall deck all fair to them in the earth, and I shall pervert them all together."' *(al-Hijr, 39)*

Do not fool yourself by feeling secure on the basis of sitting in the company of worshippers and ascetics; for a merely outward accompaniment is useless. Have you not heard of the story of Thaalaba,[22] who used to attend the gatherings of the Prophet Muhammad -upon him blessings and peace-?

---

21 See, al-Araf, 175-176.

22 At the beginning, Thaalaba used to spend his whole time in the Prophet's -upon him blessings and peace- mosque and listen to his teachings. But in time he started accumulating some wealth and became possessed by the love of the world. Gradually, he started missing daily prayers in the mosque and finally left the Muslim community altogether. He went so far that he even rejected to pay his required alms-giving to the community. But at the end he faced a terrible destruction. Tabari, *Tafsir*, XIV, 370-372; Ibn Kathir, *Tafsir*, II, 388.

But he would sit just there emotionlessly, for which he met a terrible destruction.

Even though he was the son of a prophet, Nuh's -upon him blessings and peace- son arrogantly played deaf to his father's message and thought he was self-sufficient. And when destruction came his way, his mere blood relation to his father did not save him.

And Lut's –upon him blessings and peace- wife…She was on friendly terms with unbelievers and sinners, though she had not the least understanding of what was going on in her own house. Blinded in the darkness of unbelief, she could not see the light of guidance.

So rely only on the Almighty and no-one else; since apart from Him, no knowledge, deed, wealth, offspring or friend can guarantee your eternal happiness."

The Quranic verses aforementioned (al-Ala, 14-15) state that only those who have purified themselves and overcome the negative desires of their lower selves will be the ones to prosper. This means that those who have not completed their act of purification will not be able to reach real happiness and salvation. Further testifying to this fact are other Quranic verses, one of which declares,

اِنَّمَا تُنْذِرُ الَّذِينَ يَخْشَوْنَ رَبَّهُمْ بِالْغَيْبِ وَ اَقَامُوا الصَّلٰوةَ وَ مَنْ تَزَكّٰى فَاِنَّمَا يَتَزَكّٰى لِنَفْسِهِ وَ اِلَى اللهِ الْمَصِيرُ

"You can only warn those who fear their Lord in the Unseen and perform the prayer; and whosoever purifies himself, purifies himself only for his own soul's good. To The Almighty is the homecoming." (al-Fatir, 18) From this, we can draw the conclusion that prophetic instructions and warnings help only those whose hearts are filled with sincerity for and fear of the Almighty; and who offer their daily prayers, as well as other deeds of worship, in this mindset.

Sinners will pay the price of their own wrong-doings and face punishment. Nobody shall be able to offer any help in having their punishments reduced. Likewise good deeds will be of benefit only to those who have offered them. Thus, those who purify their nafs are effectively doing it for their own good.

Quite meaningful in this regard is the following verse of the Quran: "Only those of His servants who have knowledge fear the Almighty." (al-Fatir, 28) The verse indicates that the more knowledgeable a servant becomes, the more he becomes conscious of the Lord in the depths of his heart. The hearts of those ingrained with heedlessness towards their Lord are, in effect, dead. Warning or counseling them is seldom of any use. The Quran (Yasin, 70) underlines this and states that the Blessed Prophet -upon him blessings and peace- and the message of the Quran are of help only to those who are alive. To become spiritually alive, a person must nurture an inward fear of Allah, glory unto Him, and complement this outwardly by offering his daily ritual prayers diligently.

The reward of becoming purified of sins are the highest ranks of Paradise, as testified by the Quran refers in the following verse: "And whoever comes unto Him a believer having done deeds of righteousness, those, for them await the most sublime degrees; Gardens of Eden, underneath which rivers flow, therein dwelling forever." (Taha, 75-76)

When a servant sets his heart only upon the Almighty, his reward becomes even greater; he becomes eligible, in the Hereafter, to witness the manifestations of Divine beauty and perfection (*jamalullah*), which are beyond the limits of linguistic description in this world. Whoever willingly directs his attention to the Lord alone and takes his Lord to be his sole concern, becomes freed of all kinds of petty, temporal concerns. As for acquiring the knowledge of the Divine (*marifatullah*), it begins with purifying the self, which then leads to a real understanding of its nature. The well-known Sufi phrase, "Whoever knows his nafs, knows his Lord" refers to this delicate relationship between the human nafs and the knowledge of the Divine.

In this day and age where human beings live under the yokes of materialism and self-centeredness that darken their soul, there are innumerable obstacles that hinder one from the all-important task of directing his focus on the reality of the human soul and other spiritual matters. There is therefore a greater need today for spiritual masters to correct our misplaced direction.

The Training of Sufism (Sayr Suluk)

Muslim history is replete with exemplary personalities to take lessons from. One such figure is the Ottoman Sultan Selim I. On his returning from the campaign of Egypt, he heard that the people of Istanbul had flocked to the streets for a huge ceremony to welcome the victorious Sultan. But feeling uncomfortable with the idea, Selim instead delayed his entrance to Istanbul, over the concern that his ego would actually enjoy the pompous reception awaiting him. Summoning his confidante Hasan Can, he told him that they shall enter the city "only after sunset when everybody has returned home to avoid their cheerful applauses and greetings, lest they flatter our egos let it have the upper hand over us." In line with the edict, the Muslim army entered Istanbul quietly after sunset without the least sign of ostentation. Selim was mindful of the dangerous aspects of the human ego and acted with due discretion. Thus, in effect, he was a 'sultan' in this regard as well.

A believer is expected to call his self to account and interrogate it on a frequent basis. He must always keep a watchful eye on his spiritual condition and progress. In Sufi terminology, this conduct is referred to as an 'inward investigation' (*at-tafahhusu'l-batini*). This cross-examination of the self, where all actions are reevaluated, should take place at least once a day. When one becomes accustomed to it, he becomes less insistent on his habitual wrongdoings. We shall now turn our attention to what Ghazzali says in this context:

"With the dawning of each day, a believer should sit together with his "self" right after his dawn prayer and reach certain agreements on the basis of certain conditions. This act is similar to a merchant's agreement with his partner regarding their share-holdings, right before him submitting his capital to the partner. Meantime, the merchant does not neglect to give certain warnings to the partner. Likewise, a person should give the following warnings and instructions to his self. 'My whole capital is my lifetime. When I lose my life, my capital also comes to an end, and profit and loss do not mean anything to me anymore. But now a new day begins. The Almighty has given me this day as a great opportunity. If he had made me dead, I would give anything just to return to this life again, even for a single day, to perform only good deeds.' Now imagine that you were dead and you were revived to come back to this life again. This is that day; do not sully it with sins and disobedience. Do not waste any second of it, because every single breath is an invaluable gift from the Almighty.

Be mindful of the fact that a day is twenty-four hours. On the Day of Judgment, twenty-four closed boxes will be brought in front of man, for each day. When he opens a box and sees the rewards of good deeds performed within that hour, he shall realize that the box is filled with light, whereupon he will feel an inexpressible joy. Then thinking of the other rewards he might receive, he becomes absorbed by an inexpressible joy; so great that if the dwellers of Hell were to partake in a single share of this joy, they would have no longer feel any pain. When he opens the second box, he smells the terrible odor of the hour he had spent in disobedience. He is the overcome by regret so deep, that if the people of Paradise were to be given a share of his regret, they would completely forget the pleasures of Paradise. When he opens the third box, he sees that it is empty; the hour he spent sleeping or doing licit activities. Still, he feels a great regret over not putting that hour to good use, which would have helped him out on this day. His regret is comparable to that of a merchant when he fails to capitalize on a huge investment. Therefore, fill your box before it is too late; do not leave it empty. Being lazy will only compound the enormity of your loss.

Bodily organs function in support of the soul. We should keep a watchful eye on them and instruct our egos on the right way of using bodily organs. We must protect our eyes from looking at unlawful and useless things so that they do not keep our hearts busy in vain. We should protect our tongues from gossip, backbiting, slander, lie, self-promotion, criticizing others and fawning; instead, we must keep them busy with the remembrance of the Lord and make sure that they utter only good things. We should protect our stomachs from unlawful and doubtful food, and even decrease the consumption of the lawful. The Blessed Prophet -upon him blessings and peace- instructs us in this regard, saying, "Refraining from useless things is the sign of a good Muslim." (*Tirmidhi*, Zuhd, 11; *Ibn Majah*, Fitan, 12) This means that a believer's speech and silence should be of Divine remembrance and contemplation.

A believer must also be careful to fasten his acts of worship upon their proper destination. When he calls his self to account, he needs to make it sure that all of his deeds are performed uniquely for the sake of the Almighty, not for the sake of any other authority including his own self.

As a result of the purification of the nafs, the heart acquires the quality of 'soundness' (*salim*). A believer with a sound heart embodies three characteristics:

1. He does not hurt anybody. This comes from a fear of the Almighty. The heart is protected from the evils of the ego, which brings exemplary character traits to the surface.

2. He is never hurt of offended by anybody. This comes from a profound feeling of love. He never pays attention to the praises or censures of ordinary people. A poet summarizes these two characteristics and versifies, "The purpose of man and jinn on the garden of Earth…is to not hurt, devotee, and not be hurt".

3. He always prioritizes the pleasure of the Lord at all costs. On being compelled to make a choice between the worldly and the Hereafter, they never hesitate in choosing the latter.

In short, the Almighty has made this life a platform of trials and has assigned man to the task of returning to Him by overcoming the obstacle that is the soul; to transform its evil to good, the reward of which is incomparable to anything in this world.

May our Lord allow us all to overcome their lower selves!

Amin!

A person with a purified soul represents a masterpiece of the Supreme Artist –the Almighty– as he has become a platform of the manifestations of Divine disclosures.

3. THE STATES OF THE SELF

According to a classification well-known to Sufi circles, in the process of spiritual training and perfection, the human nafs may assume seven types of states and stations. Now let us go into a more detailed examination of these states.

a. The Evil-Commanding Self (*an-nafsu'l-ammara*)

This is the lowest and most disobedient state of the human self. It removes a servant from his Lord and incites him to engage in evil activities. The word "*ammara*" means overly commanding. A nafs stuck in this state insatiably follows carnal and sensual desires. This is a self under the yoke of lust and a friend of Satan; it has a strong penchant for following its selfish desires and committing sin.

The mark of a person in the state of the evil-commanding self is that he inconsiderately follows the selfish and carnal desires of his ego, without showing the least resistance. Similarly, he unconditionally follows the devilish whisperings that come from within. The evil-commanding self might even be more dangerous for a person than Satan. Pointing to this reality, Ibn Ataullah al-Iskandari says, "The most you should beware of is your ego. Not only does it work against you, it also remains with you until death. Satan at least leaves man during Ramadan, the month in which all the devils are handcuffed. But by the fact that we see murder and theft even during the month of Ramadan, we understand that it is not Satan who leads man to commit these crimes, but the evil-commanding self instead."

In the Quran, the Almighty declares,

$$ اِنَّ النَّفْسَ لَأَمَّارَةٌ بِالسُّوءِ $$

"Surely the nafs of man is a persistent enjoiner of evil." (Yusuf, 53) This is the self in its evil-commanding state.

In Sufi terminology, the evil-commanding self is symbolized by the image of a poisonous serpent. Through this symbolization, Sufi calls careful attention to the venom of this self. Poet Nevizade Atai uses this image in his poetry when he says, "Each immoral character trait resembles a serpent; and the serpent king is the evil-commanding self." For this reason, every believer of right mind must be engaged in a continuous combat against the evil-commanding self. Human reason and personal will are the two essential weapons to help the believer in this combat. Many a person, who had once attained to spiritual blessings of enormous caliber, has ended up in dismay by becoming ensnared by ignorance for a mere split-second.

In this respect, the Quranic narrative of the encounter between Zulaykha, the wife of the Potiphar, and Yusuf -upon him blessings and peace- abounds in vital clues in understanding the nature of the evil-commanding self. Yusuf -upon him blessings and peace- grows up to become an exceptionally handsome man; and Zulaykha becomes passionately attracted to him, as the Quran reads, "…She, in whose house he was, sought to seduce him from his self: she closed the doors and said, 'Come, take me!' He said, 'The Almighty be my refuge. Surely my lord has given me a goodly lodging. Surely the evildoers do not prosper. For she desired him; and he would have taken her, but that he saw the proof of his Lord. So was it, that We might turn away from him evil and abomination; he was one of Our devoted servants." (Yusuf, 22-24)

Thanks to the help of Allah, glory unto Him, however, Yusuf was saved from falling weak to the seductions of Zulaykha, who represents none other than the evil-commanding nafs. Being the weaker servants of the Almighty we are, we need to turn our faces towards Him in supplication and fear, and ask for His help for immunity against the evil seductions of our own egos.

Here, the Almighty offers us words of wisdom. He commands us not to even approach misdeeds, lest their destructive natures hold sway over us. In this sense, it is forbidden for a male to stare at a female who jurisprudentially is a stranger to him, as a seemingly innocent look might actually open the door to adultery. Indeed the story between Zulaykha and Yusuf –upon him peace- comprises a multilayer of meanings, for us to reflect on the various aspects of worldly trials.

Yusuf –upon him peace- was an angel-like young man, with a majestic beauty never before seen. On seeing him for the first time, the local women cut their fingers and were too captivated to feel either the pain or the blood trickling down their palms. Had Yusuf -upon him blessings and peace- been elderly man devoid of any desire for the opposite gender, the test he was made to undergo would not have been all that difficult.

Zulaykha was had three things the ego is infatuated with the most: fortune, fame and lust. She was young and beautiful, flaunting a charm that could lure many to fall at her feet. To heighten the matter, Zulaykha had the door firmly locked, before she made her move. Amid such an enticing moment of concealed privacy that eases the path of committing the sin, Zulaykha called out to Yusuf –upon him peace-, to 'Come and take me.' Facing a sight that could melt the resistance of the strongest of wills, the Almighty tells of the difficulty of the situation even for a man like Yusuf –upon him peace-: "Had he not seen Our evidence, he too would have inclined to her…"

There and then, Yusuf –upon him peace- pleaded, 'Let the Lord be my refuge', and by so doing, he showed that the only and surest way to get out of that extremely difficult position would the haven provided by the Almighty. This equally underlines the fact that a solid practice of the Divine fear is necessary to attract Divine help. In other words, it is only through strengthening the feelings of Divine fear that a person could resist the strong temptations of the evil-commanding self. In fact, rejecting the seductions of a young, beautiful and wealthy woman, in private, is one of the most difficult things to do for a healthy young man.

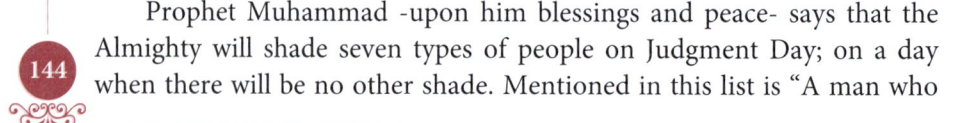

Prophet Muhammad -upon him blessings and peace- says that the Almighty will shade seven types of people on Judgment Day; on a day when there will be no other shade. Mentioned in this list is "A man who refuses the invitation of a charming, noble woman for illicit intercourse and says, 'I fear the Almighty'." (*Bukhari*, Adhan, 36)

The soft belly of human psychology is usually exposed when one receives kind compliments, upon which he loses his self-control. But this did not happen to Yusuf -upon him blessings and peace-, as Divine protection sheltered him from falling into this trap; after all, he was a God-fearing servant, with a perfected nafs (*an-nafsu'l-kamila*). Divine protection strengthened Yusuf against the deceptions that otherwise may have come from the way of the evil-commanding self.

There is a further lesson to be taken from the encounter. Zulaykha threatens Yusuf –upon him peace- with throwing him into prison, should he desist from complying with her sexual desires. With a purified self that constantly inspired in him the fear of the Divine, however, Yusuf –upon him peace- responded to her call by stating "My Lord, prison is dearer to me than that they call me to." (Yusuf, 33) Yusuf further sought refuge in the Almighty against her feminine tricks and pleaded, "Yet, if You do not turn me from their guile, then I might yearn towards them, and so become one of the ignorant." (Yusuf, 33) His preference of prison over complying with her desires gives an idea of the intensity of Yusuf's –upon him peace- fear of the Almighty.

From this Quranic story, we may conclude that the only medium of inner resistance man has against all kinds of temporal temptations is the heart. It is only the heart that can decisively reject the deceptive charms of the world and seek refuge in the Almighty.

The Holy Quran states that the strongest weapon to protect a believer against the disaster wrought by the evil-commanding self is the embodiment of Divine fear. In this respect, another Quranic instance that sheds light on the reality of the nafs is to be found in the story of Musa -upon him blessings and peace-.

Musa -upon him blessings and peace- received the mission of prophethood on the mount of Sinai, where he was told to, "'Cast down your staff'. And when he saw it quivering like a serpent, he turned about retreating, and turned not back. [The Almighty said], 'Musa, come forward, and fear not; for surely you are in security." (al-Qasas, 31) The Almighty showed a glimpse of his infinite power to Musa -upon him blessings and peace-through the staff. In turn, Musa -upon him peace- became acquainted with the power of the Almighty through what he had seen in the staff.

The Almighty appointed Musa -upon him blessings and peace- as a prophet and made him draw nearer, where He spoke to him. The Almighty entrusted Musa -upon him blessings and peace- with certain responsibilities and said to him, "And what is that in your right hand, Musa?" (Taha, 17) Musa -upon him peace- replied, "It is my staff; I lean upon it, and with it I beat down leaves to feed my sheep; other uses also I find in it." (Taha, 18) Then the Almighty said to him, "Cast it down, Musa!" (Taha, 19) Musa –upon him peace- complied with the Divine order and "So he cast it down, and behold it was a serpent sliding." (Taha, 20) When he saw this miraculous event, the frightened Musa -upon him peace- started running away, but the Almighty said to him, "Take it, and fear not; We will restore it to its first state." (Taha, 21)

Some exegetes of the Quran present allegorical and spiritual interpretations of this encounter, drawing attention to the inner meanings implied by the event. Accordingly, when Musa -upon him blessings and peace- cited some functions of the staff and mentioned that he leaned on it, the Almighty ordered him to throw it away, because in reality the only authority to lean on is the Almighty.

The ego and things related to it transpired before the eyes of Musa –upon him peace- in the form of a terrifying serpent. There, Musa -upon him peace- saw the real nature of the nafs, from which he fled in fear. In an allegoric language, Musa -upon him peace- then received the following assurance: "This serpent, Musa, stands for the attachment to temporal things; though the Almighty is the real source of attachment. Once the attachment to the world becomes materialized and the person sees it for what it is, he flees with fright. Now that you have been given the quality of *tawhid*, of the oneness of your Lord, how could it be that you depend on the staff to lean on and to see to your other needs? This is befitting of a true grasp of *tawhid*. The first step of *tawhid* is to leave all other means aside and embrace an unconditional trust in the Almighty. It is to Him you must submit yourself. Better you leave all other desires and devote yourself completely to the Almighty."

The Training of Sufism (Sayr Suluk)

The Sufis also say, "Those who have heard the Almighty's call and have seen the light of His beauty, abandon dependence on all avenues of support other than Him. On the grace of the Almighty do they lean on, whereby they salvage themselves the deceptive desires of the self."

It is the evil-commanding self that makes man feel indifferent towards real happiness and everlasting joy, by placing artificial and fleeting pleasures before his eyes. The evil-commanding self causes man to undervalue his original merit, making him plummet down from the highest degrees of Paradise to the lowest ditches of Hell.

A person dominated by the evil-commanding self is stubborn and conceited, even when meeting the means that might take him to his own eternal happiness and salvation. In a way, he finds pleasure in looking down upon people around him, lying, backbiting, and keeping himself busy with cheap and useless things. He cannot safeguard himself from impurity. The number of people dominated by this malicious nafs is quite large. They act heedlessly and ignorantly, preferring the fleeting tastes of the world to the everlasting joys of Paradise and to the indescribable delight of witnessing the Lord's Beauty in the world to come.

When dominated by the evil-commanding self, the rational soul becomes enslaved to the animal soul; and humanly qualities disappear from the scene to leave the stage to animal characteristics. Regarding this, the Holy Quran says, "We have created for Hell many jinn and men; they have hearts, but understand not with them; they have eyes, but perceive not with them; they have ears, but they hear not with them. They are like cattle; nay, rather they are further astray. Those – they are the heedless!" (al-Araf, 179)

People under the grip of the evil-commanding self also delude themselves concerning the Almighty. They continue committing all sorts of sins, but still naively hope that the Lord will show mercy and forgive them regardless. In a way, they see themselves safe from the Almighty's wrath when they say, with much sarcasm, "We will not end up with unbelief, unless we regard an unlawful thing as lawful. So there is no need for us to rush to repent; we will do that one day, anyway." Addressing this deluded feeling of safety, the Quran declares, "O men, fear your Lord, and dread a day when no father shall give satisfaction for his child, and no child shall give satisfaction for his father whatever. Surely the Almighty's promise is true; so let not the present life delude you, and let not the Deluder delude you concerning The Almighty." (Luqman, 33)

These kinds of misleading thoughts come from the insidious whisperings of the lower self and Satan, so that man may easily commit sins and use this line of logic to standardize his immoralities. Furthermore, those who are drawn within the darkness of the evil-commanding self do not feel any energy to perform charitable acts, even though they might benefit from these acts immeasurably in the world to come. And when it comes to keeping themselves away from harmful deeds, they take no action at all. If they perform a tiny piece of good deed, they regard this as a huge accomplishment, as something to be proud of. Even though they might occasionally feel repentant over their wrongdoings, the strength of their repentance is too weak to decisively change their general condition.

A believer with an evil-commanding self is similar to a sick person who needs treatment. The most basic spiritual measure he is expected to take is to call his self to account continually, so that he might promote his position from the evil-commanding self towards the self-blaming nafs (*an-nafsu'-lawwama*). The believer should be mindful of the fact that his All-Powerful Lord knows everything and think of the interrogation he will go through in the grave and on Judgment Day, and of the suffering and agony in Hell. He should accordingly repent and take resolute action. But this repentance must be serious and sincere. His whole existence, his tongue and heart, ought to participate in this action. Otherwise, repenting merely with the tongue will never provide the desired objective; it is a hypocrites' repentance, which itself is need of further repentance. The remorse of a person, who outwardly repents while continuing to commit sins, is dubious. This is disrespect to the Ultimate Authority to Whom all acts of repentance are directed. Real repentance is to feel a deep remorse about wrongdoings and to earnestly ask the Almighty's forgiveness.

On the other hand, in order for a servant to save himself from the control of the evil-commanding self, he needs to observe the rules of the Shariah and understand the real nature of the declaration of the oneness of the Almighty's (*kalimatu'tl-tawhid* i.e. *la ilaha illa Allah*). When uttering "*la ilaha*", the servant is expected to erase everything other than the

Almighty from his heart. Carnal passions, especially, are to be removed from the heart, since they distance the servant from his Lord. Once these things are eliminated from the heart, the servant is ready to establish the reality of "*illa Allah*" therein. This way, the servant realizes his innate incapability and nothingness, and thus makes a sincere effort to improve his religious degree from blind imitation to genuine comprehension. His faith thereby grows deeper and stronger in the heart and leads him servant to further good deeds and higher spiritual ranks.

b. The Self-Blaming Nafs (*an-nafsu'l-lawwama*)

Those who reproachfully call their evil-commanding self to account and strive to save themselves from its negative and evil characteristics, spiritually proceed forward to the self-blaming nafs. Such people do not deceive themselves with an unfounded reliance on the Almighty's unlimited mercy, which is what the evil-commanding self whispers to keep them away from a real commitment to make solid changes in their conditions. These people blame their self regarding their wrongdoings and asking the Almighty's forgiveness, they repent. We might mention the following two types of people who fall under this category. The first type is the knowledgeable people who do not act in full accordance with their knowledge and fail to put their theoretical knowledge to proper practice. But they are nonetheless aware of their shortcomings and feel sincere remorse. The second type are those who shed tears and ask the Almighty's forgiveness in religious gatherings; but when they leave these meetings, they go back to committing the same sins as before.

The Arabic word "*lawm*" means "to blame" or "to reproach". Accordingly the expression *an-nafsu'l-lawwama* refers to the nafs which blames and reproaches itself over its wrongdoings and shortcomings. This type of self is aware of the fact that it does not diligently follow Divine instructions, for which he blames himself remorsefully. A person with the self-blaming nafs has effectively repented and protected himself from some of the negativities peculiar to the evil-commanding self. This means that his heedlessness and desire for committing sins are less in comparison with the evil-commanding self. But still, since his level of spiritual maturity is not yet perfected, he remains vulnerable to the lure of sins.

Sufism: A Path Towards the Internalization of Faith (Ihsân)

In the state of the self-blaming nafs, the rational soul is not enslaved unconditionally to the animal soul. Each time he commits a sin, he is overcome by remorse. Laying the blame on himself, he asks the Almighty's forgiveness. But he cannot keep a secure and stable position in his repentance, as he has not yet overcome his lower self. Even though his conscience disapproves of misdeeds, he cannot completely protect himself from committing them and as is open to the negative external influences like peer pressure.

Generally stated, a person who possesses a self-blaming nafs is happy with his good deeds and sad with his bad deeds. He strives to protect himself from sensual desires and puts up a resistance. He is more strongly inclined to repentance. His heart has been enlightened by a little ray of spiritual light and his mind has been awakened, to a certain degree, against heedlessness. He has a more increased sense of observing Divine commands and offering righteous deeds, which are mostly for the sake of the Almighty. But since he is yet to receive the peace and tranquility supplied through Divine inspirations, he also carries a desire to make his deeds visible to others. This means that the evil-commanding self is somewhat still in action; though the servant does eventually blame himself over this weakness, too.

The Holy Quran cites this level of the human soul by vowing in its name:

وَ لَا اُقْسِمُ بِالنَّفْسِ اللَّوَّامَةِ

"I swear by the self-blaming nafs." (al-Qiyamah, 2) A delicate point needs emphasis, here. Self-blaming is not simply idle speech or lip service; for then, the desired result does not come true. There is a fine line between the "evil-commanding" and "self-blaming" nafs. If one feels proud of himself on the basis of the fact that he has practiced a little of self-blaming, this means that he is still under the control of the evil-commanding self. The Holy Quran refers to this occurrence in the following verse:

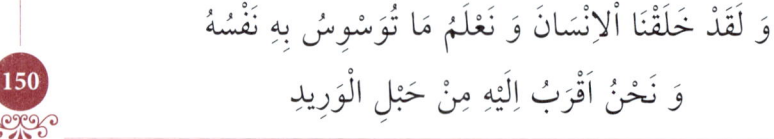

وَ لَقَدْ خَلَقْنَا الْاِنْسَانَ وَ نَعْلَمُ مَا تُوَسْوِسُ بِهِ نَفْسُهُ
وَ نَحْنُ اَقْرَبُ اِلَيْهِ مِنْ حَبْلِ الْوَرِيدِ

The Training of Sufism (Sayr Suluk)

"We indeed created man; and We know what his nafs whispers within him, and We are nearer to him than his jugular vein." (Kaf, 16) The servant should therefore be alert against the secret whisperings and deceptions that come from the evil-commanding self, and take protective measures against the destructive feeling of security.

Here, another subtlety with regard to self-blaming needs to be underlined. Some lay the blame on themselves only with the intention to attract the attention of others, who may then praise him for his humbleness. Doubtless, this is typical hypocrisy. It is only through spiritual training that a servant can stand firm on repentance and keep himself away from wrongdoings. A person whose nafs is of a self-blaming nature may protect himself from misconducts, only under a spiritual guidance and environment. Although under normal conditions he would not go back to making his previous mistakes, some immoralities like hatred, jealousy and self-conceit still lie dormant in the heart; and this keeps the risk ever alive.

Under this spiritual guidance, a servant proceeds forth from the self-blaming nafs to the inspired self (*an-nafsu'l-mulhama*), through *rabitah*, an important method in spiritual training. Here, one always remembers his promise to his master to stay away from unlawful things and to observe religious commands. This promise enables him to imagine the spiritual presence of his master at all times, which acts as a medium for him to keep his act together. Constantly calling his self to account, he must remain fixed on his resolution to leave his immoral characteristics and act in repentance. He should then strive to replace these negative character traits with positive ones; for instance, he should replace self-conceit and jealousy with humbleness and non-envious friendship. He must not seek to single out the mistakes he sees in his friends and instead keep himself occupied with his own faults. He should remember that a believer is a mirror to his fellow-believer; thus should he look at him through an evil eye, he will of course see nothing but evil. But looking at him with a good eye, he will see only good qualities.

Persistence in remembering the Lord and keeping away from sins are also essential in this station, in order to enlighten the heart with the light of Divine love.

c. The Inspired Self (*an-nafsu'l-mulhama*)

By advancing through the evil-commanding self and the self-blaming nafs one reaches the inspired self, primarily through repentance, asking the Almighty's forgiveness, staying away from sins and implementing the practices necessitated by spiritual guidance. At the level of the inspired self, the servant acquires the capacity of making correct distinctions between good and evil, which, of course, transpires thanks to the grace of the Lord. The servant also acquires a stronger resistance against the sensual desires of his self. He shuns everything that removes his heart from the Almighty. He cares little about how he is seen in the eyes of people; his sole concern is how he fares in the presence of the Almighty. The realities of faith are immovably reinforced in his heart. This particular state of the nafs derives its very name from the Quran: "By the nafs and He Who shaped it and inspired it to wickedness and righteousness!" (as-Shams, 7-8)

An inspired self is receptive to Divine inspirations. One who is graced with this spiritual station begins to experience and share the inklings of the Divine grace and insights shone upon his heart. This is made possible by none other than a sincere and consistent observation of the Divine commands. An inspired self turns his attention to love and the spiritual world, which imparts unto him the quality required to receive Divine inspirations. Still, he needs to make sure that these inspirations are coming from the Lord and not from the devil. And to make this distinction, he needs the confirmation of a spiritual guide because even though the ego is all but left powerless in this state, it still retains a small yet dangerous power to overthrow the inspired self with its tricks and insinuations. For this reason, the inspired self is not the ultimate spiritual station and the inner qualities attained to thus far are still to be perfected.

In the state of the inspired self, even though they almost never transpire, immoral character traits still lie in ambush. An inspired self is still unable to enter the realm of realities insofar as he has not yet unchained his mind from the outward and habitual cause-effect relations of the sensory world. For this reason, he is not entirely free of doubts, melancholies, inner contractions, illusions and ambitions. The peace and joy of submitting oneself to the Lord has not yet come to be for him. His heart remains distressed by concerns of livelihood and is plagued by ambitions. Though he has today's bread at hand, he is still worried about what he will eat tomorrow. His outward appreciation of the Divine attribute of "Provider" (*Razzaq*) is in conflict with his inner concerns. Such conflicts indicate that the quality and maturity of his contentment with the Almighty's dispensations, his submission to and trust in Divine regulations have not reached perfection. He is therefore in further need of inner adjustments to spiritually rectify his conflicts.

An inspired self is obtained by through a certain level of success in training the nafs, mainly through abandoning things the nafs finds attractive and performing things it finds unappealing. However defeated the animal soul may be in this station, the rational soul has not yet completely actualized its moral characteristics. This actualization does not come merely by way of leaving things that are desirable to the self and performing things that are unattractive to it. In other words this actualization is not dependent only upon abstinence and austerity. In addition to all these, it requires the practice of Divine remembrance (*dhikrullah*). But here, there is another subtlety to be discerned. So long as the heart is preoccupied with worldly concerns and ambitions, it cannot reach the real delight of Divine remembrance and enjoy the ultimate spiritual tranquility. Hence, to rid the heart of these residues and realize Divine remembrance therein in the most proper sense of the term, one needs the spiritual guidance of a qualified master.

When a servant begins to experience a profound, ecstatic pleasure during his remembrance of the Almighty, he is truly on the path of reaching its real delight. Divine inspirations then find a way into his heart, making one acquainted with the secrets of all beings, leaving him in a state of inexpressible amazement and satisfaction. This is when he starts comprehending the real meaning of the Quranic verse,

$$\text{اُدْعُ اِلٰى سَبِيلِ رَبِّكَ بِالْحِكْمَةِ وَ الْمَوْعِظَةِ الْحَسَنَةِ}$$

"Call to the way of your Lord with wisdom and good admonition." (an-Nahl, 125) By duly taking lessons from this Quranic verse, every word he utters assumes a character of wisdom; for now he has become a distinguished servant receptive to Divine inspirations. In this spiritual state, the animal soul starts yielding itself to the rational soul, whereby the person is saved from being corrupted by lowly and sensual inclinations. The praiseworthy human characteristics of tolerance, patience and endurance become more dominant; and modesty, contentment and generosity start prevailing over the overall personality.

Be that as it may, the inspired self nonetheless carries something potentially dangerous. Falsely assuming to have reached perfection and to have completed the process of spiritual purification, the servant in this state can thus regress to heedlessness and self-conceit. For this reason, the servant should continue to be mindful of the fact that he is always under Divine surveillance and regulate his mindset accordingly. He should at the same time meditate on death, a common practice in Sufism aimed toward imparting a true understanding of the temporal nature of everything in this world. The Blessed Prophet -upon him blessings and peace- says, "Frequently remind yourselves of death; for keeping death in mind purifies man of sins and makes him feel indifferent towards the world. If you remember death while you are wealthy, it will remove the disastrous aspects of your wealth. If you remember death while you are poor, it will make you feel happy with your current condition." (Suyuti, *Jamiu's-Saghir*, I, 47)

Omar –Allah be well-pleased with him- offers a similar advice when he says, "Call yourselves to account before you are called to account. Weigh your deeds before they are weighed on the Divine scale. Prepare yourselves for the Day of Judgment before you are brought to the presence of the Almighty, from Whom none of your deeds will be hidden." (Ibn Kathir, *Tafsir*, I, 27)

d. The Tranquil Self (*an-nafsu'l-mutmainna*)

The tranquil self is the type of nafs that has been saved from inner afflictions. This spiritual safety is brought about by an assiduous observing of Divine commands and prohibitions. This self has thereby reached a real and steadfast faith, which results in a genuine happiness, peace and tranquility. Through a persistent remembrance of the Lord, the heart has been purified from doubts and uncertainties; it is at ease in a sincere feeling of gratitude for and praise of the Lord.

The Training of Sufism (Sayr Suluk)

A servant with a tranquil self has effectively replaced his immoralities with positive moral characteristics, having willfully followed Prophet Muhammad's -upon him blessings and peace- exemplary character traits. His heart is now filled with patience, contentment and trust in the Almighty. The tranquil self belongs to people of piety, who have acquired certain knowledge of the Almighty. Their hearts continually busy with Divine remembrance. They have furthermore gained a profound comprehension of the inner meanings of religious instructions.

In explaining the tranquil self, Sheikh Ahmad Sirhindi (d. 1624) states, "Up until the station of the tranquil self, acts of worship are performed by way of imitation (*taqlid*). But hereon, imitation is transformed to verification (*tahqiq*)."

Before reaching this level of certitude, a servant must embody 'the state of *haqiqah*', or 'reality'. The tranquil self is a highly advanced level of spiritual maturity; a precious gift but an enormous responsibility at the same time. To draw a comparison, those whose rational faculty have not come of age cannot be held responsible for fulfilling religious duties, insofar as responsibility is dependent upon possessing the faculty of reason. In a similar fashion, a wayfarer newly initiated into a Sufi order is regarded as an innocent child with respect to the greater responsibilities of Sufism. Until he covers a certain distance in his spiritual training, his faults are treated with toleration; since in Sufism, spiritual maturity only comes with progress. But after having received a certain level of training, he is considered responsible for things that are not duties ordinary believers need to fulfill, as is the case of *Shariah* with respect to a child. Until he steps inside the door of the tranquil self, the wayfarer is not responsible for things that are regarded as shortcomings from the perspective of *haqiqah*. This responsibility begins only after the point when the wayfarer assumes the tranquil self, since it is here that he attains the maturity of *haqiqah*.

Following the same thread, there are things which are regarded permissible by *Shariah*, yet looked upon as small mistakes by *tariqah*. Furthermore, there are things regarded as small mistakes by *tariqah*, yet considered serious faults by *haqiqah* and *marifah*. For instance, according to *Shariah*, it is considered a waste to continue eating after reaching satiety. But according to *tariqah*, even eating to the level of satiety is considered waste. For *haqiqah*, on the other hand, it is a waste even if one eats just enough to survive while being unmindful of the Almighty's presence. And finally, according to *marifah*, any piece food consumed without witnessing Divine disclosures therein is a waste, insofar as the Almighty presents a sign of His existence in every single thing.

By the grace of The Almighty, the tranquil self has reached reality (*haqiqah*), peacefulness (*sakinah*), and certainty (*yaqin*)[23]. It has become protected from worldly grieves and concerns, and in addition, it has received certain spiritual unveilings and inspirations.

In the state of the tranquil self, the veils of heedlessness and ignorance over the heart are lifted. At the level of *ayn al-yaqin*, the heart beholds realities beyond appearances. Furthermore, the heart has been made secure from doubts and uncertainties. It has attained a tranquility and peacefulness through a complete submission to the Almighty. A servant in this state wholeheartedly welcomes both exoteric and esoteric religious duties and fulfills their requirements appropriately. His reception and belief in these duties are so strong that even if entire humankind were to attempt to disprove his convictions, they would fail to raise any doubt in his heart; for the servant has already eye-witnessed the underlying mysteries through the window of reality.

With such unshakable faith, believers of this ilk have no fear. They confront all kinds of afflictions and difficulties. A typical example of this is to be found in Musa's –upon him peace- encounter with the sorcerers. When the sorcerers realized the extraordinary nature of Musa's –upon him peace- feats, they acknowledged them as miracles given by the Almighty. Thereupon, they arrived at an unshakable belief in the Lord and stood steadfast thereon, regardless of its lethal consequences with which the Pharaoh threatened them. He tried to intimidate them by threatening

---

23 *Yaqīn* is an Arabic word meaning certain and evident knowledge. There is no place for doubt in *yaqīn*. In *yaqīn*, the heart has reached a satisfaction regarding the reality of the thing in question. *Yaqīn* also refers to getting beyond the apparent cause-effect relationships and seeing the reality of things clearly by means of faith. Qushayrī asserts that *yaqīn* is of three kinds:
Ilm al-yaqīn: Certainty based on report or narration.
Ayn al-yaqīn: Certainty based on eye-witnessing.
Haqq al-yaqīn: Certainty based on personal spiritual experience.

to have their hands and feet diagonally cut off and then crucifying them, unless they openly turned their backs on Musa's –upon him peace- message. The sorcerers' response to the Pharaoh was simply the following, "Surely, to our Lord we are returning. And you take vengeance upon us only because we have believed in the signs of our Lord when they came to us. Our Lord, pour out upon us patience and let us die as Muslims [in submission to You]." (al-Araf, 125-126)

The sorcerers were more than willing and ready to sacrifice their lives for the sake of their faith; for the veils in front of the appearances of all things worldly had now been lifted and they were seeing things for what they really were through the spiritual light given to them. Their souls were of the type the Almighty refers to as:

$$\text{يَا أَيَّتُهَا النَّفْسُ الْمُطْمَئِنَّةُ}$$

"O soul at tranquility." (al-Fajr, 27)

On the basis of the above verse of the Quran, we can see that the states of the nafs prior to that of the tranquil self do not receive a Divine addressing. Only the tranquil self and the states beyond are privileged with this merit. In order for a servant to be worthy of this receipt, he needs to genuinely struggle to rein in his ego. The distinguished servants who enjoy the state of the tranquil self then gradually begin to move forward towards the three higher spiritual states in line; namely, the satisfied self (*an-nafsu'r-radiya*), the satisfying self (*an-nafsu'l-mardiyya*) and the perfect self (*an-nafsu'l-kamila*), respectively. The more successful a servant is in this progress, the closer he gets to his Lord.

e. The Satisfied Self (*an-nafsu'r-radiya*)

This is the nafs that has persistently kept its focus on the Almighty; and by continually considering itself to be in Divine presence of The Almighty, it has embodied a highly advanced level of piety. The satisfied self is now content and satisfied with his Lord. Not only has it left his personal will aside, it has further annihilated it within Divine will. In the words of the Quran it has returned to its Lord

Sufism: A Path Towards the Internalization of Faith (Ihsân)

$$ارْجِعِى اِلٰى رَبِّكِ رَاضِيَةً مَرْضِيَّةً$$

"…satisfied, satisfying". (al-Fajr, 28)

The spiritual state of 'satisfaction' refers to how the servant meets all kinds of afflictions, which come from the Almighty, with patience and hospitality. After all, this is what the Almighty expects him to do; to rest satisfied with whatever Divine Will metes out: "Surely We will test you with something of fear and hunger, and diminution of goods and lives and fruits; yet give good tidings unto the patient." (al-Baqarah, 155)

Patience, in the truest sense, is to welcome everything that comes from the Lord with contentment, whether it be good or evil. Indeed, everything comes from Him alone; they comprise innumerable manifestations of His disclosures. Only those who have the ability to peer into the real nature of both blessings and tribulations merit the title "patient" mentioned in the verse. They are always satisfied with Divine fate and never show the least sign of disobedience or complaint. For them, everything, good or evil though they may seem, is predestined. This is the spiritual caliber those who possess a satisfied self.

The tests and afflictions a satisfied self undergoes are much more difficult to endure than those of the previous spiritual states; for the higher the self ascends, the thornier the path becomes. The Blessed Prophet -upon him blessings and peace- explains this delicate balance when he says, "Among mankind, it is the prophets who are subjected to the most challenging tribulations…and then come those who are closest to them. People face tribulations in proportion with their levels of piety." (*Tirmidhi, Zuhd, 57*)

Only after having overcome the obstacle of the lower self can man can reach a level of spiritual maturity that enables him to meet tribulations with endurance and rest content with Him, Who sends all these troubles. As great a reward this spiritual maturity is, it only comes at the end of an enormous show of patience and endurance. In the eyes of a believer with a satisfied self, everything in the world deserves the same treatment, regardless of whether it causes joy or grief. Since his heart is detached from the world, worldly pleasure temporal and pain are on level par to him. With a full-fledged insight into the fact that everything really comes from the Almighty, he is content with everything, both good and evil. As the poem reads:

Whatever comes from You is fine,
Whether a rosebud or a spine!
A robe of honor or a shroud,
Your grace is fine, so is your wrath!

We should keep in mind, however, that the actual practice of what has been mentioned in the poem above regarding the characteristics of the satisfied self is extremely difficult. It is only in the state of the satisfied self that a servant is allowed to speak such assertive utterances. At all times else, he should keep his lips sealed so that it may not say untimely and inappropriate things along the spiritual journey. Otherwise, such premature statements would be tantamount to nothing but unjustifiable claims; and if the Almighty were to test the truthfulness of such words, one would end up in utter failure.

In the spiritual state of the satisfied self, the servant begins to have an insight into Divine Secrets. He comprehends the meaning of Divine Oneness and spiritual realities become unfolded in front of his eyes. He is given the honor of receiving the special disclosures of Divine Names and Attributes. His character becomes an overflowing spring of goodness, beauty, and truth. He is a welcoming observant of Divine commands and prohibitions. He performs all deeds of worship purely for the sake of the Almighty and hence does not feel the least exhaustion in their practice. Outwardly speaking, acts of worship can be tiring. Yet inwardly speaking they are filled with spiritual objectives that annul their otherwise tiresome appearance; objectives that take the servant through the spiritual stations and grant him the blessing of spiritual unveilings. But even these are not really the main objectives. The ultimate objective is the Almighty alone. Should the servant forget this truth and prioritize the receiving of spiritual unveilings, for instance, it would mean that he will be thwarting nothing but his own progress. This is a loss of orientation that equally ends up exhausting the servant. Thus, from the beginning of the spiritual journey to the end, the servant should not have any kind of purpose and intention in his mind other than the Almighty.

The Almighty is nearer to us than our jugular veins. The most important thing for us is to become aware this nearness and prepare ourselves for its realization. The Almighty is satisfied with His servants, as long as they do their very best to remain steadfast on His straight path and rest satisfied with His providence.

f. The Satisfying Self (*an-nafsu'l-mardiyya*)

The satisfied self is in need of a further spiritual perfection. To receive and fully benefit from all the Divine disclosures shone upon its heart, the satisfied self must at the same time seek to become 'satisfying' for the Almighty as well. In other words, being satisfied with the Lord does not suffice; also expected, in return, is the Lord's satisfaction. The satisfaction must not be one sided and should come from both directions, as it were. Even though the attribute of "satisfying" refers to the Almighty, it is the servant who is in fact expected to make the effort to actualize this satisfaction. This nuance makes this quality attributable to the servant himself, and thus to his nafs. It could therefore be said that while the satisfied self refers to the spiritual state of those who are content with the Almighty, the satisfying self refers to the Almighty Who, in turn, is content with them.

In the state of the satisfied self, immoral characteristics have by now disappeared, replaced instead by positive qualities. Those who have reached this spiritual state see all creation through the vantages of affection, mercy, love, generosity and forgiveness. Since all creation is the artwork of the Almighty, wherever they look, they only see goodness. A servant in the state of the satisfying self calls himself to account in the most riveting correct manner and meditates on it. At every breath, he is mindful of the underlying reality of creation and the nature of his own self, with an unyielding awareness of its devilish whispers.

Also in this spiritual state, the servant also completely submits himself to his Lord under all circumstances. Whatever it be that comes from the Almighty, he welcomes it; knowing it is nothing but a Divine manifestation. And at the end of his temporal life, he is inducted among those whom are given the glad tidings of Paradise by the Almighty right before they are invited to enter it: "Return to your Lord, satisfied, satisfying!" (al-Fajr, 28) Indeed,

The Training of Sufism (Sayr Suluk)

$$رَضِيَ اللّٰهُ عَنْهُمْ وَ رَضُوا عَنْهُ$$

"...the Almighty is well-pleased with them, and they are will-pleased with Him." (al-Bayyinah, 8)

A servant who has attained such spiritual perfections sees everything from the vantage point of *haqq al-yaqin*; of an assured knowledge based on personal spiritual experience. By the will of the Almighty, he may even become acquainted with certain secrets of the unseen world. Because of his spiritual exertion, the Almighty brings him closer to Him, to the point where He virtually becomes his eyes that see, ears that hear, tongue that speaks. The words and behavior of such a person then begin to exercise a deep influence on persons around him.

The spiritual manifestations he had previously witnessed as a 'satisfied self' are now digested and internalized, becoming an integral part of his mindset. A relentless patience and trust in the Almighty have now become the dominant traits of his character.

By resorting to the exemplary moral conduct of prophets, we might to offer some examples of this spiritual state. For instance, Yaqub -upon him peace-, after having been afflicted with all kinds of sufferings, confided in his Lord, though by merely saying, "So patience is most fitting" (Yusuf, 18). Likewise was the case of Ayyub -upon him blessings and peace-, who suffered from heavy bouts of illnesses and afflictions. Even though people around him persistently encouraged him to pray to his Lord to stop his sufferings, Ayyub -upon him peace- did not follow their advice and replied, "The Lord gave me eighty years of a healthy life. The only way I would feel comfortable to ask him for a cure would be after I suffered at least eighty years of illness." Ibrahim -upon him peace- presents another splendid example. When about to be thrown into the raging fire, the angles came to offer him help, only to have Ibrahim -upon him peace- decline their offer. "The One Who has ignited this fire", he said, "knows my situation...so I do not want anything from you."

According to the conventional Sufi classification, the levels of the human nafs throughout the spiritual path of purification are divided into these six categories. But some Sufi masters talk about an additional stage called the perfect self (*an-nafsu'l-kamila*) or the pure nafs (*an-nafsu's-safiya*).

g. The Perfect Self (*an-nafsu'l-kamila*) / The Pure Nafs (*an-nafsu's-safiya*)

The perfect self is a type of soul that has become thoroughly purified by way of the spiritual process. It is a pure, mature and sublime nafs. In this spiritual state, the nafs receives all kinds of heavenly secrets. This state is only a gift from the Almighty. Personal efforts cannot guarantee the attainment of the perfect self; it is a God-given spiritual quality, a mystery of Divine predestination.

The station of the perfect self is also called "the station of guidance", insofar as the Lord entrusts those, who have attained to this state, with the responsibility of guiding other people. Their words and actions are rendered influential, to facilitate the correction of the wrongdoings and faults of others. When a person with a perfect self meets a sinner, he instantly understands his condition; and through an exemplary conduct, informs him of the remedies he needs to save him from his inner and spiritual illnesses. Feeling remorseful over his ways, the sinner then comes around to himself, and leaves acting heedlessly, so long as his heart is not sealed or locked to spiritual realities.

The heart is the battlefield of good and evil, piety and impiety, the angelic and the devilish. Hearts twist and bend for either angelic or devilish inclinations, endlessly quivering amid their manifestations.

B. THE HEART AND ITS PURIFICATION

1. THE NATURE OF THE HEART

The aim of Islam is to raise human beings of elegance and maturity, conscious of being the servants of Allah, glory unto Him. Realizing this aim entirely depends on becoming conscious of what it is to be a servant of the Almighty, in the truest sense of the word. Reaching the heights of spirituality through maturation is possible only to the degree of sublime excitement, divine fear and stirrings felt deep in the heart.

The heart is our physical and spiritual hub. It plays a vital role in sustaining our physical existence. Over four seconds of delay in pumping the required amount of fresh blood to a cell spells an end to its life; and the same goes for the billions of other cells that abide in our bodies.

Playing so important a role in our physical existence, the hearts is also a spiritual gem, the focal point of the power and ability for spiritual sensing. In this sense, the heart is virtually the king of the realm that is the body, both physically and spiritually, such that even the brain, a center of thought, produces ideas only in the shade of the emotions that emanate from the heart. This means that through the ability for spiritual sensing it possesses, the heart dominates the entire organs, including the mind. Upon a rush of panic attack, the hands begin to shake and heartbeats increase. Just how externally motivated feelings of compassion, anger or love singlehandedly influence the willpower, thoughts and consequently behavior, is vividly observable in every mode of human behavior.

Sufism: A Path Towards the Internalization of Faith (Ihsân)

In terms of its spiritual dimension, the heart is like a compass for the real and the truth. This is a function it has been given by the Almighty. Yet, once detached from this dispositional function and steered towards a direction contrary to its reason of existence, it cannot avoid being dragged to the negative. Then, instead of saving the person in both Here and the Hereafter, it works towards his destruction. Subjecting the heart to influences that will guide it to its reason for existence, nurturing and developing the inherent capabilities it has for attaining Divine pleasure, therefore forms a vital side of human education.

In the Quran, Allah, glory unto Him, sends out a warning to us, His servants, not to allow the heart to deprive us of eternal happiness by being duped by the passing pleasures of the world: "O mankind! Surely the promise of Allah is true, therefore let not the life of the world deceive you, and let not the arch-deceiver deceive you respecting Allah." (Fatir, 5)

Mawlana Rumi -may Allah sanctify his secret- expresses the need for man to tighten the reins on his egoistic desires, not to stray from his essential purpose:

"Do not look to overfeed your body and ripen it, for in the end it is but a sacrifice for earth. Look to feed your heart! That is the one to fly to soaring heights and receive honor.

Feed your body only little of greasy and sugary stuff. As those who feed the body in excess, fall in the pit of their desires and perish in disgrace.

Feed your spirit with foods spiritual. Serve it mature thought, a refined understanding and provisions of the spirit so that it can go to where it is bound to go, full of health and vigor."

Luqman (a.s) similarly advises his son against heedlessness: "The world, my dear, is a bottomless sea that has drowned many an unwise scholar, and other alike, in its torrent. Let the frame of your ship be a contented faith in Allah, glory unto Him. Let your equipment be piety and worship. Let the sails of your ship, which will allow you to ride its waves, be trust in the Divine. Only by this means, I hope, you may attain salvation." (Bayhaki, Kitab'uz-Zuhd, p. 73)

Being the center of the body as well as the center of spirituality, the heart holds an equal importance for both. Yet, since it is not so much the external appearance as it is the spirit that makes human beings who they are, the spiritual role exercised by the heart is greater than its physical role, in all its aspects. Owing to this spiritual characteristic, not to mention the subtle secrets and wisdoms it contains, the heart is the exclusive cause that enables the human being to attain to the meaning and virtue of 'humanness'. This is the underlying wisdom behind the fact that faith (*iman*) is established through the affirmation of the heart, well before the confirmation of the tongue. Noteworthy is that, here, an affirmation of the heart is considered sufficient, rather than an acceptance by thought.

Just as man, considered as the essence of the universe, carries the joint tendencies and abilities towards good and evil, the sublime and the lowly owing to his natural disposition, the heart, which is the essence of man, endures these opposite tendencies and abilities. As open as he is to angelic influences, man is also at the disposal devilish interventions. It could be said that the heart is the battlefield of good and evil, piety and impiety, forces both angelic and devilish. Hearts tremble to the sound of angelic and devilish influences until man breathes his last.

As for the heart being at the disposal of angelic and devilish influences: Angelic influences impart onto the heart spiritual impressions like faith, pleasant traits, righteous deeds, compassion and a quality of worship. As for devilish influences, they inject into it bad conditions like blasphemy (*kufr*), doubt, immorality, lust and desire. Only through worshipping and the remembrance of the Divine (*dhikrullah*) may *Shaytan* be expelled from the heart. Through the remembrance of the Almighty, hearts find their peaceful ground; and having found that peace through *dhikr*, faith becomes deeply entrenched in it, elevating the heart to the most sublime level of contentedness. And there comes a moment when the heart opens up from within, just like a drape, and the mysteries of the realms of the conceivable (*nasut*) and the inconceivable (*lahut*) lay bare and exposed. The universe, with all its mysteries, turn into a book waiting to be read.

Being the battlefield of angelic and devilish tendencies, the heart has an active and impulsive structure, ever-ready to join the ranks of the victor and embody its characteristics. The heart is different from the other organs in terms of submitting and surrendering to the will. Its natural predisposition towards both good and evil is activated not so much by internal influences as by external influences. In other words, emotions come to life not through ideas that spontaneously appear in the heart (which are called *sunuhat*) but through external factors. In this sense, the heart is like water that assumes the shape and color of its container. People of spirit, however, opt for the positive tendencies within the heart, whereby they are delivered to the land of peace.

It is stated in the Quran:

"O you who believe! Fear Allah and be with those who are true (in word and deed)." (at-Tawba, 119)

"And when thou seest those who meddle with Our revelations, withdraw from them until they meddle with another topic. And if the devil cause thee to forget, sit not, after the remembrance, with the congregation of wrong-doers" (al-Anam, 68)

"And indeed He has revealed to you in the Book that when you hear Allah's communications disbelieved in and mocked at do not sit with them until they enter into some other discourse; surely then you would be like them; surely Allah will gather together the hypocrites and the unbelievers all in hell." (an-Nisa, 140)

The will comes into play right at the beginning, to determine and choose between positive and negative influences that will have a bearing on the heart. Shaped according to the influences it is exposed to, the heart in this sense is like a weather vane placed on rooftops. Literally, *qalb* does mean to turn something into its opposite and to change in shape and color, which only reinforces this said characteristic of the heart, man's most central organ. So reveals a *hadith*: "The heart is like a feather on an empty plane, swung about hither and thither by the blowing winds." (Ibn Majah, Muqaddimah, 10; Ahmed ibn Hanbal, Musnad, IV, 408)

The below incident clearly points to the "changing" nature of the heart:

Abu Bakr -Allah be well-pleased with him- one day came across Hanzala -Allah be well-pleased with him- and asked him how he was. Hanzala replied, in a fretful tone, "Hanzala has become a hypocrite!"

"Subhanallah", replied Abu Bakr --Allah be well-pleased with him--. "What is that supposed to mean?"

The Training of Sufism (Sayr Suluk)

"When we are in the company of the Messenger of Allah -upon him blessings and peace-", explained Hanzala -Allah be well-pleased with him-, *"he reminds us of Heaven and Hell and we become so deeply affected that we virtually see Heaven and Hell before our very own eyes. But once we return to our families and become carried away in earning our living, we neglect most of what we hear."*

"Truly, I sometimes feel the same", confessed Abu Bakr -Allah be well-pleased with him-. They thereupon went to the Blessed Prophet -upon him blessings and peace- and informed him of their anxiety. The Messenger of Allah -upon him blessings and peace- said:

"By Allah, in whose Hand of Might my life lies, if you were able to maintain the state of mind you have whilst in my company and be in a constant state of dhikr, angels would have held you by the hands, while asleep and when walking about." He then added, three times:

"Sometimes it is like this, Hanzala, and sometimes like that!" (Muslim, Tawbah, 12)

The continuation of life demands that servanthood, filled with and motivated by the truths and mysteries of the Hereafter, and the pursuits of life, go hand in hand.

Such is how the Blessed Prophet -upon him blessings and peace- sheds light on the heart's *talwin*, its quality of fluctuating from one state to another. One of the main objectives of *tasawwuf* is to transform this *talwin* to *tamkin*, or stability, as much as possible through the refreshment provided by *sohbah (Islamic conversation)* and *dhikr*; to turn the heart towards the Divine direction and stabilize it thereon. Among the Companions, Abu Bakr -Allah be well-pleased with him- provides the best example of this state of mind. His unshakable conviction of heart in affirming the Blessed Prophet -upon him blessings and peace- with regard to the *Miraj*, without the least hesitation, can only be explained with the stability his heart had acquired by then.

The idolaters had erupted in a storm of denial concerning the *Miraj*. They wanted to sow the seeds of doubt in Muslim hearts and thereby turn them away from their faith. So, just as they went to numerous Companions to tell them what they thought of the *Miraj*, they also went to Abu Bakr

-Allah be well-pleased with him-: "Have you heard the latest? Your friend says he rose to the skies", they said mockingly. "What do say about that?"

A man with an ecstatic level of *iman*, Abu Bakr -Allah be well-pleased with him- then uttered the magnificent words of loyalty; words the idolaters could never imagine hearing. They only added misery to their hopeless condition: "Whatever he says is true for he never speaks a lie. Whatever it is that he says I believe him instantly!" (Ibn Hisham, as-Sirah, II, 31)

Angels are only disposed towards the good; that is how they were created. Devils work only for evil, towards deviating. Human beings are positioned right between these two beings. Safeguarding their hearts from immoderation, human beings must avoid lowering themselves into a devilish state. This does not mean they should try to overdo themselves beyond human capability in hope of attaining an angelic status. Moderation is what natural predisposition demands.

The inevitable death and the eternal beyond should be humankind's greatest concern and the objects of their greatest endeavors. Only by knowing the reality of the heart, protecting it from evil and subjecting it to spiritual influences is this possible. Balance and peace on Earth and happiness and salvation in the Hereafter depends on having a refined heart (*al-qalbu's-salim*), a heart that is on the purifying path of Islam, having retained its pure traits that come from natural disposition (*fitrah*). As indicated by the words of the Beloved Prophet -upon him blessings and peace-: "Every child is born upon the *fitrah* (of Islam). His parents then turn the child into a Christian, a Jew or a Magean…" (Muslim, Qadar, 22), the dispositional and natural structure of the heart is upon Islam right from the beginning. It is when the heart is exposed to negative influences that destroy its natural structure that the possibility of its deviation arises.

In contrast, hearts filled with spiritual manifestations through the waft of the inspiring air of spirituality develop good morals, righteous deeds and spiritual states. Only in this way does one gain insight into the mystery of '*ahsan-i taqwim*'[24] inherent in his disposition, which is when his perception of beings and surrounding events gains depth and prudence. And this means that the curtains are lifted from his 'heart's eye', alluded to by the

---

24   *Ahsan-i Taqwim*: Having been created in the best possible measure; the Quran's reference to the creation of man.

Quran[25], allowing it to gaze beyond. Undoubtedly, this vision pertains to realities beyond the field of physical vision.

Those whose heart's eyes have a potential of becoming opened, eagerly desire spiritual training and enlightening and exert a serious effort to advance in the way of the Real. But those who have no genuine desire, those oblivious from the desire to attain to spiritual certainty, turn a blind eye on the advices of prophets and saints. With a stubborn arrogance, they become more wicked, as they sink more and more in their dark swamps of ignorance. They pity the blind who cannot find their own way except through the help of another, yet they have absolutely no idea of their own spiritual blindness.

With a tendency towards both the positive and the negative, man is endowed with a will and power to choose in this world of trial in which he is subject to Divine commands and prohibitions. It is the lines of direction (*istiqamah*), be it positive or negative, embedded in the heart, that determine how the will and power to choose is to become manifest. On the other hand, the incontestable fact stands that the heart, weighed down by many external influences and egoistic tendencies, does distance itself, time and again, from its reason of existence, jeopardizing one's eternal future.

Hearts dominated by their accompanying egos are filled with unbelief, immorality, lustful desires and provoking whispers (*waswasah*). Such hearts have turned against their reason of existence. Blinded towards the sublime, they have an insatiable appetite towards the lowly. More bewildered than beasts[26] in the words of the Quran, they squander their lives in their illusions of ignorance. Hearts of this kind are diseased, in desperate need of treatment.

---

25   See, al-Hajj, 46.
26   See, al-Furqan, 44.

Our behavior reflects the mood of our hearts. We behave according to its ebbs and flows.

2. THE TYPES OF HEARTS

In the most general sense, hearts can be classified under three types:

a- Hearts that maintain their purpose and dignity of creation.

b- Sealed and dead hearts

c- Diseased and unmindful hearts.

a- Hearts that Maintain Their Purpose and Dignity of Creation

These are hearts that have awoken from ignorance through *dhikr*. Here, the spirit reigns supreme over the ego and the heart is inundated with the light of faith. Persons blessed with hearts of the kind have been effective in fulfilling what they have been called upon in the below *ayah*:

"O ye who believe! Remember Allah with much remembrance." (al-Ahzab, 41)

"And remember the name of your Lord and devote yourself to Him with (exclusive) devotion." (al-Muzzammil, 8)

"Men whom neither merchandise nor selling diverts from the remembrance of Allah and the keeping up of prayer and the giving of poor-rate; they fear a day in which the hearts and eyes shall turn about;" (an-Nur, 37)

In hearts that have acquired such a blend, the manifestation of the Divine names of beauty (*jamal*) overpowers those of wrath (*jalal*). People with hearts of this kind attain maturity through embodying the morals of Allah, glory unto Him, the Prophet -upon him blessings and peace- and the Holy Quran. These are hearts that have shed their egoistic tendencies through the grace of the love felt for Allah and His Messenger, hearts for

The Training of Sufism (Sayr Suluk)

which nothing else matters. Such hearts are referred to in the Quran as a flawless heart (*qalb salim*), a penitent heart (*qalb munib*) and a contended heart (*qalb mutmain*). Accepted in the sight of the Divine, these hearts may be explained as follows:

A flawless heart (*qalb salim*) is a heart protected or purged from the assaults of the ego. It is the heart given to man, by the Lord, accompanied by a clean predisposition, on the condition that both are protected. The heart may reach this state of refinement only through the Sufi methods known as the purification of the soul and the purification of the heart. The servant is thereby freed from the crass and heavy domination of sins and is ushered to the lightness of spirituality. Just as a myriad of beams that shine onto a lens condense themselves in a single spot to start a fire on the other side, a condensed spirituality in a heart immersed in Divine lights, burns all sins and desires of the ego to ashes. This is a sign of the attainment of a flawless heart, the very heart that will be accepted in the presence of the Real. About this the Quran states: "The day on which property will not avail, nor son. Except him who comes to Allah with a heart free (from evil)." (as-Shuara, 88-89)

Poet Ruhi of Baghdad echoes this in the below couplet:

Think not, merchant, you will be asked for gold or silver for bail,
Only a flawless heart, on a Day when nothing else shall avail...

A penitent heart (*qalb munib*) is a heart that is constantly turned to the Lord. Liberated from the captivity of mortal interests, it luxuriates in the zests of the eternal land, lovingly and enthusiastically. This heart shivers in the excitement of experiencing the Divine flows of power. The *ayah* declares: "This is what you were promised, (it is) for everyone who turns frequently (to Allah), keeps (His limits); who fears the Beneficent Allah in secret and comes with a penitent heart" (Qaf, 32-33)

A contented heart (*qalb-i mutmain*) is a heart that has covered distance towards the perfecting of good morals, under the peaceful shade of *iman*. Deeds of worship are no longer imitative (*taqlidi*); they have become comprehended at their core (*tahqiqi*) and executed in like manner. The heart is illumined through *dhikr* and the ego has laid down its guns to spirituality. The gem of *iman* is irremovably entrenched in the heart, the center of spiritual sensing. With a comprehended faith (*iman-i tahqiqi*) and contentedness, the heart has found peace and stability. The state referred to in the Quran:

$$\text{اَلَا بِذِكْرِ اللهِ تَطْمَئِنُّ الْقُلُوبُ}$$

"…Now surely by Allah's remembrance are the hearts set at rest." (ar-Rad, 28) is now fully realized. The implicit meaning of this *ayah* is that hearts distant from the remembrance of Allah, glory unto Him, will forever suffer the pain of their discontent and remain distant from attaining the true peace of mind.

The marks of those who carry one of the three types of hearts mentioned are that they are delicate, compassionate towards creation, content with the given circumstances and provide service in the way of the Truth and the good. Filled with the zest of Divine Love, they flee evil and run to the guidance of others, to the point of shedding tears on their behalf.

The asset needed to ensure that the heart attains to this blend, is genuine prayer and repentance and care to consume only the *halal*, the permissible. Protecting this asset, on the other hand, is possible only with righteous deeds. Being the human beings we are, it is impossible to steer entirely clear from sins. Yet, since sins reduce the sensitivity of the heart, rendering it spiritually blind and deaf towards the Truth, it is necessary to hold fast to sincere prayer and repentance for the heart to become the focal point of positive manifestations. Not for no reason do lessons of *tasawwuf* begin with repentance. As stated in the famous *Majalla* principle: "Repelling mischief is preferable to acquiring benefit." That is to say, repelling evil has greater priority over obtaining the good.

As regards eating only the *halal*, Sufis have said: "Allah enlightens the heart of him, who eats only what is *halal*, and flows the springs of wisdom onto his heart." Righteous deeds, on the other hand, ensure that the heart keeps possession of the level acquired. The special compliments that come from the Lord are relevant only for those in possession of hearts of this kind, and above these are the lively hearts, endowed with the light of the Lord, which belong to prophets and great saints. As their hearts are revived by Divine Love, they do not look at either this world or the

Hereafter, desirously, not even with the corner of their eyes. Allah, glory unto Him, has made prophets and their heirs, scholars and saints, inviters of humankind to *darussalam*[27] through reviving and helping them lift the veils covering their hearts, encouraging them with moral conduct and sincere deeds of worship and guiding them, thereby, to unite with their Lord (*wasl ila-Allah*).

The level desired from the *salik*, the aspirer, at the end this training of the heart, is for his heart to attain to *ihsan*, which is the consciousness of being with the Lord at all times, and in so doing, earn for himself an 'alive heart.'

b- Sealed and Dead Hearts

These are the total opposite of hearts revived through the remembrance of the Lord. The gates of faith are slammed shut for these hearts; they are sealed and dead. They are no different than some graves described as pits from Hellfire. Such hearts are the stark contrast of the hearts of prophets, saints and the righteous. Owners of these hearts, desiring nothing other than pleasures egoistic, see no other purpose in life than to eat, drink and waste their years chasing short-lived ambitions. In terms of their purpose, they are no better off than animals; some are even worse. Allah, glory unto Him, declares:

"Surely Allah will make those who believe and do good enter gardens beneath which rivers flow; and those who disbelieve enjoy themselves and eat as the beasts eat, and the fire is their abode." (Muhammad, 12)

And in another *ayah*:

"Or do you think that most of them do hear or understand? They are nothing but as cattle; nay, they are straying farther off from the path." (al-Furqan, 44)

Reserved only for egoistic ambitions and desires, the lives of such people pass amid an eternal torment. Awaiting them in the Hereafter, on the other hand, is an inexpressible disaster, set to continue until eternity. Such people are oblivious to the mysteries of life, man, and the meaningful pat-

---

27 *Darussalam*: Paradise.

Sufism: A Path Towards the Internalization of Faith (Ihsân)

terns embroidered in the universe. Not only are they deviated themselves, they also deviate others over whom they exert influence. Despite living on the property of the Almighty and amid His blessings, they revel in the ungratefulness of denying His existence and violate His commands and prohibitions. Regarding people of the kind, Allah, glory unto Him, states:

"Does not man see that We have created him from the small seed? Then lo! he is an open disputant." (Yasin, 77)

"Deaf, dumb (and) blind, so they will not turn back." (al-Baqara, 18)

"Surely you do not make the dead to hear, and you do not make the deaf to hear the call when they go back retreating. Nor can you be a guide to the blind out of their error; you cannot make to bear (any one) except those who believe in Our communications, so they submit." (an-Naml, 80-81)

That the hearts of such persons are sealed and locked is a fact established by the Quran:

$$\text{خَتَمَ اللهُ عَلٰى قُلُوبِهِمْ وَ عَلٰى سَمْعِهِمْ وَ عَلٰى اَبْصَارِهِمْ غِشَاوَةٌ وَ لَهُمْ عَذَابٌ عَظِيمٌ}$$

"Allah has set a seal upon their hearts and upon their hearing and there is a covering over their eyes, and there is a great punishment for them." (al-Baqara, 7)

This is a Divine mystery and wisdom profound enough to leave entire humankind in tremor. As the human being has a share of the Divine names *Hadi*, the Guider, and *Mudill*, the Disgracer, it is unthinkable for someone's heart to be sealed by Divine Will in the absolute sense and have the gates of guidance shut on him while still alive. For these gates were not shut even on Omar -Allah be well-pleased with him-, who had set out with the callous intent of murdering the Prophet -upon him blessings and peace- or Wahshi, the murderer of Hamza -Allah be well-pleased with him- or even Hind who viciously mutilated his corpse and sunk her teeth into his liver.

Although the Quran makes mention of people whose hearts have been sealed, it is impossible to identify them, one-by-one, in everyday life, as the

The Training of Sufism (Sayr Suluk)

condition in which people will die remains a mystery. Like the Pharaoh's magicians, there are some who lead a deviated life only to find guidance in their final years, just as there are some who lead a guided life yet end up among the deviated, as were the cases of Qarun and Balaam ibn Baura.

The point that requires attention here is that the persons mentioned by the Quran as having sealed hearts are mostly among those who engage in sins like oppression (*zulm*), disbelief (*kufr*) and perversity (*fisq*). The Quran states on twenty-six occasions that "Allah will never lead to guidance", those who possess these characteristics. Twelve of these are in reference to oppressors, eight to disbelievers, and six to the perverse. The door of guidance, however, is still open to those who abandon these sins and turn to the Lord with a genuine heart.

As for those who adamantly continue their wicked ways; they are the most miserable of all, sentenced to the greatest punishment on Earth by having their hearts sealed while still alive and breathing. Although the fact that the Quran mentions these three sins in tandem with being deprived from guidance does provide us with a clue as to the secret behind the sealing of hearts, it is best to leave the truth of it to the Almighty. However, we can infer from here the need to show greater care in avoiding these three sins. We avoid plunging deeper into the issue here, as the mystery of fate, owing to many underlying wisdoms, has been kept secret and probing it has therefore not been recommended.

Whatever the underlying wisdom of it may be, an incontestable truth still stands: hearts that have been sealed and locked are closed to the Truth and the good, and belong to those who have severed all ties with humaneness and spirituality. The only Power that could lift the seal and break the lock of their hearts is the Lord, whom they have long forgotten. Warning us, His servants, against falling into such irreparable neglect, Allah, glory unto Him, reminds: "And be ye not like those who forgot Allah; and He made them forget their own souls! Such are the rebellious transgressors!" (al-Hashr, 19) Underlined here is the fact that those who have forgotten the Lord lack the force to be conscious of even their own selves.

Because of their bestial and egoistic desires, hearts which are blinded to the truth either reject offhand the recipes of salvation and flames of guidance extended to them by prophets and saints or turn a cold shoulder to them. They deceptively console themselves by visualizing a make-believe world where there is no death and the Hereafter and try to find comfort therein. Just as bats naturally enjoy the dark, these kinds of people take misery for happiness, dominated by the negativities inherent in their characters. Their bodies are a burden on them, reminiscent of a couplet of poet Mehmed Akif:

Faith is that gem…and Lord, what great weight it is,
A rusted heart devoid of faith, a burden on the chest it is

Those who are bogged in the swamp of the ego will surely be awaken to the realm of reality with the tremendous quakes of the final moment of life and the fiery blows of the angel of death. Yet, it will serve them no benefit, as the period given the son of Adam to awake ceases the moment he sees the angel of death right before him. With that moment, the opportunity is forever lost. Remorse at that moment is too little too late, just like the belated acceptance of the Pharaoh and his subsequent prostration whilst in the throes of death. The doom awaiting such people thereafter is the lap of the raging flames of Hellfire, whose appetite for destruction only increases the more it is fed.

c. Diseased and Unmindful Hearts

They stand at the middle point between hearts that are alive and hearts that are dead. Their conditions resemble the painful lives of those suffering from illness. Neither do they have harmony in life nor inner peace. Their inner instability reflects negatively onto their outer existence and the disharmony of their outer existence takes its toll on their inner stability. The disorder in their minds reflects onto their behavior and actions. Such diseased hearts, which stagger amid the whirlpools of doubt, indecision and inconsistency, are always under the threat of falling into immorality, owing to their ignorance, lust and nagging desires. About them, the Almighty states: "In their hearts is a disease; and Allah has increased their disease: And grievous is the penalty they incur, because they are false to themselves." (al-Baqara, 10)

Stemming from an inability to land on the branch of truth, **doubt** is the disease that deprives one from a spiritual life and smites the heart with pangs of death. Again, lack of a consistency of faith that would bring the heart satisfaction afflicts them with the constant illness of unrest.

Ignorance is an utter blindness and a painful, dark road that does not allow one even to realize the pain of being deprived from the Truth. This disease spreads to their entire existence, steering them to walk a path that ends in absolute defeat and disaster.

Lust and desire is the disease of insatiability that seizes total control of the heart, as a result of it losing its refined nature and becoming unresponsive. It is a delirious obsession that will come to rest only under the dark soil of the grave, beneath the dense cypress shade.

Immorality is the spiritual cancer of the heart. If treated in time, Allah willing, it can be cured.

Hardness is another terrifying disease of the heart: the indifference to humane emotions and the delicate touches of spiritual reflections. These hearts know nothing of obeying; they play deaf to the sounds of guidance and have no notion of mercy and compassion. Even stones are softer, warmer and lovelier than these hearts, as stated by the Almighty in the Quran: "Then your hearts hardened after that, so that they were like rocks, rather worse in hardness; and surely there are some rocks from which streams burst forth, and surely there are some of them which split asunder so water issues out of them, and surely there are some of them which fall down for fear of Allah, and Allah is not at all heedless of what you do." (al-Baqara, 74)

As can be gathered from the ayah, hardheartedness is a natural outcome of forgetting the Lord and falling distant, for too long, from Divine truths. The Almighty says, in another ayah: "What! Is he whose heart Allah has opened for Islam so that he is in a light from his Lord (like the hardhearted)? Nay, woe to those whose hearts are hard against the remembrance of Allah; those are in clear error." (az-Zumar, 22)

Deeds offered with diseased and unmindful hearts lose their value in the sight of the Lord. Without the light of the Truth, hearts become blind, unresponsive. They can no longer recognize the innumerable patterns and signs of the universe that reveal Divine mysteries. Allah, glory unto Him, declares: "Have they not travelled in the land so that they should have hearts with which to understand, or ears with which to hear? For surely it is not the eyes that are blind, but blind are the hearts which are in the breasts." (al-Hajj, 46) An insightful gaze thus stimulates the heart. The window of the eye is of no benefit unless it looks with the light of the heart, as it is impossible to behold a clear vision behind a foggy window.

Even the small diseases of the heart, often overlooked, can cause the heart irreparable damage and even its death. Therefore, it is necessary to safeguard hearts with a diligent faith and submit it to the Will of the Lord. No-one other than the Lord will guide and steer a person who has fully submitted to the Creator. The below *hadith* beautifully expresses the necessity of protecting the heart:

أَلاَ وَإِنَّ فِى الْجَسَدِ مُضْغَةً إِذَا صَلَحَتْ صَلَحَ الْجَسَدُ كُلُّهُ
وَإِذَا فَسَدَتْ فَسَدَ الْجَسَدُ كُلُّهُ أَلاَ وَهِىَ الْقَلْبُ

"Be aware that there is a piece of flesh inside the body; if good so is the entire body and if corrupted, so is the entire body. And that is the heart!" (Bukhari, Iman, 39)

The world is the Lord's valley of trial and error. There blow on it various winds of trial, dragging the heart from one place to another.

Protecting the heart is necessary to prevent the heart from being swept away, like a dry leaf, before the assorted winds of events, which naturally blow as a result of the world being a land of trial. What is required is to submit the heart to the sweet zephyrs that breeze from the way of the Lord's Divine aid and support; and this is possible only by seeking refuge in Him, obeying and submitting to His commands and prohibitions.

The heart is like lucid water. But once muddied with evil deeds and sins it becomes murky. It then becomes necessary to distill it, for it to show the pearls of spirituality and the lights of truth in its bedrock.

3. THE PURIFICATION OF THE HEART

The main conditions of maintaining the characteristics of a flawless, penitent and contented heart, curing diseased hearts and avoiding the doom of sealed hearts, are:

a. *Halal* food.

b. Repentance and prayer.

c. Reading the Quran and obeying its commands.

d. Worshipping with utmost concentration (*khushuu*).

e. Reviving the nights through worship.

f. An unrelenting love of the Noble Prophet -upon him blessings and peace- and expressing that love constantly through *salawat*.

h. Contemplating death.

i. Being in the company of the pious and the righteous.

j. Embodying good morals.

k. Gazing at the Universe through a Purified Heart

To begin with, it is vital to come to a correct understanding of the nature and importance of these conditions, whose genuine and eager practice is essential.

a. *Halal* Food

> *"Brothers...Don't you be thinking you will obtain a speck of wisdom so long as you eat what is haram."*
> Ibrahim Dasuki -may Allah sanctify his secret-

As much as they depend on spiritual foods that nourish the spirit, deeds of worship also depend on the strength and vivacity obtained from physical foods. While *halal* foods inject the body with spirituality and inspiration, *haram* and doubtful foods, their direct opposites, reflect onto it gloom, density and neglect. There is a strong connection between *halal* foods and righteous deeds. The consumption of *halal* foods play a great role in the acceptance of prayers, as is expressed by the Blessed Prophet -upon him blessings and peace-: "People...Allah the Almighty is undoubtedly Pure and Clean. He therefore accepts nothing but what is pure and clean. He has enjoined the believers what He has enjoined the prophets:

"O messengers! Eat of the good things and do good; surely I know what you do" (al-Muminun, 51)

"O you who believe! Eat of the good things that We have provided you with, and give thanks to Allah if Him it is that you serve." (al-Baqara, 172)

After quoting these *ayat*, the Blessed Prophet -upon him blessings and peace- spoke about a man with unkempt hair and dusted all over from the strain of a long journey, who lifts his hands aloft and prays, 'My Lord... My Lord', and added: "How will his prayers be responded to, when what he eats, drinks and clothes himself with is *haram*?" (Muslim, Zakat, 65)

For the spiritual progress of their hearts, Sufis are extremely careful with regard to two things, as is conveyed in the saying: "Beware of what goes inside your mouth when you eat and what comes out of it when you speak!"

The below hadith succinctly yet beautifully reminds us of the level of precaution we need to take in regard to the *halal* and the *haram*.

"Doubtless, the halal has been made clear and so has the haram. But between the two, there are certain doubtful things, unknown to most.

The Training of Sufism (Sayr Suluk)

Whosoever avoids the doubtful will have protected his religion and integrity. And whosoever does not refrain from the doubtful will in time fall into haram. Just like a shepherd grazing his herd around somebody else's grove…there is always the danger that the herd will trespass. Beware that every king has a grove whose entrance is forbidden. The forbidden grove of Allah is what is haram." (Bukhari, Iman, 39)

Hearts that willingly submit to and obey the Lord's command become riverbeds of wisdom and spiritual enlightenment. In contrast, hearts unprotected from the *haram* and the doubtful turn into shelters of evil and immorality, through and through. The following examples provide enormous lessons on the importance of sensitive conduct concerning this issue:

Abu Bakr -Allah be well-pleased with him- had a slave. The slave would hand Abu Bakr -Allah be well-pleased with him- a certain amount of what he would earn for him to put to personal use. One day the slave, again, brought some food to Abu Bakr -Allah be well-pleased with him-, who began to eat them. That was when the slave abruptly asked, "Do you know what it is that you are eating?"

"No, I don't. Why don't you tell me?" responded he.

"Though I know nothing of soothsaying", the slave began to explain, "I had once soothsaid and conned this man during my Jahiliya days. I bumped into him today and he just happened to pay me with what you are eating right now!"

Immediately upon hearing this, Abu Bakr -Allah be well-pleased with him- poked his throat with his finger, and despite all the discomfort, vomited what he had eaten. (Bukhari, Manaqibu'l-Ansar, 26)

According to another report, the slave thereupon remarked, "Was this worth the trouble over just one single morsel?" Abu Bakr -Allah be well-pleased with him- replied, "Even if I had known I would die in the process, I still would have taken that morsel out." (Ahmad ibn Abdullah at-Tabari, ar-Riyadu'n-Nadra, II, 140-141)

Also meaningful is the conversation that took place between Khidr (a.s) and Abdulkhaliq Gujdawani -may Allah sanctify his secret-, during the former's visit to the latter. Khidr (a.s) does not touch the foods served to him by Abdulkhaliq Gujdawani (k.s) and draws back from the table.

"These are halal. Why are you not eating?" the astonished Gujdawani (k.s) asks him.

"True, they are halal", replies Khidr (a.s). *"But whoever prepared them has done so with anger and ignorance."*

Judging from these examples, over and above the question of whether what is eaten is *halal* or *haram*, the state-of-mind in which the food is prepared also has a bearing on a person's psyche, behavior and the quality of his deeds of worship. This only serves to further underline the importance of the delicate approach that needs to be taken towards food.

Their sensitivity towards food led the righteous to cover the edibles they bought from the market or elsewhere, while carrying them home. This is to prevent hankering eyes 'from hanging upon the food' and the yearnings of the poor and the craving stares of the underprivileged from having a negative impact on the energy and strength hoped to be acquired from the food.

As well as staying away from the *haram* and the doubtful, a believer must also maintain the balance and avoid waste whilst consuming the *halal*. The *ayah* commands: "And give to the near of kin his due and (to) the needy and the wayfarer, and do not squander wastefully. Surely the squanderers are the fellows of the Shaitans and the Shaitan is ever ungrateful to his Lord." (al-Isra, 26-27)

Using his metaphorical tone, Mawlana Rumi -may Allah sanctify his secret-, in his *Mathnawi*, gives voice to the effects of *halal* food on the spirit and the body:

"Our spiritual enlightenment came in a different form last night, as a few morsels of doubtful food that found their way in the stomach, blocked the way of spiritual enlightenment.

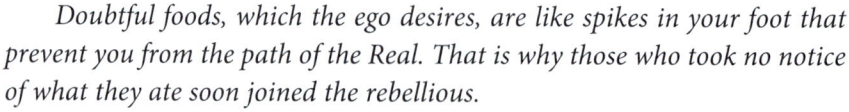

Doubtful foods, which the ego desires, are like spikes in your foot that prevent you from the path of the Real. That is why those who took no notice of what they ate soon joined the rebellious.

O body! You have such a beautiful rose in you that if you protect it, countless rose gardens of wisdom and marifa will form around, just from the fragrances it emits."

Below are similar words from Abdulqadir Jilani -may Allah sanctify his secret-, in emphasis of the importance of *halal* food in purifying the heart:

"Listen, my child! Haram food kills the heart. There are morsels that light up your heart and there are morsels that suffocate it in darkness. Again, there morsels that will keep you occupied with the world and there are others that will keep you occupied with the Hereafter. There are morsels that will turn you into a devotee of both worlds; there are morsels that will direct you to the Creator of both worlds. Eating what is haram will keep you busy with the world and make yours sins appear acceptable to you. Eating what is mubah (licit) will keep you busy with the Hereafter and endear worshipping to you. Eating halal on the other hand will draw you closer to the Lord. Only with marifatullah (knowledge of Allah) may one know the nature and influence of foods. And marifatullah is written only in the heart, not in the pages of books. Marifatullah is injected into the heart by the Creator, not the created. And this happens only after affirming the Unity of Allah and putting to practice the Divine commands."

Ibrahim Dasuki -may Allah sanctify his secret- speaks in a similar tone: *"Brothers…Don't you be thinking you will obtain a speck of wisdom, so long as you eat what is haram."*

Also noteworthy is the below words Sayyid Qasim Tabrizi -may Allah sanctify his secret- on eating what is *halal*, recounted by Ubaydullah Ahrar -may Allah sanctify his secret-:

"Sayyid Qasim one day said to me, 'Do you know why wisdom and truth displays itself only rarely these days? It is because there are just a handful of people who have purified their inner worlds. Perfection lies in the purification of the inner. And that is possible only by eating halal. Halal food is very scarce these days and there is almost nobody who has achieved inner purification. What else! How do you expect Divine mysteries to transpire in them?'"

Sufism: A Path Towards the Internalization of Faith (Ihsân)

b. Repentance and Prayer

> *"Say: My Lord would not care for you were it not for your prayer…"* (al-Furqan, 77)

The entirety of saints, the pious and the righteous, and above all prophets, have always sought refuge in Allah, glory onto Him, and prayed to Him, in good times and bad. Since even prophets have minor slipups (*dhalla*)[28], it is unthinkable for anyone to remain in no need of repentance and prayer. As repentance and prayer mean a remorse and supplication of the profoundest kind, it is the most influential means of drawing closer to the Lord. Indeed, one of the underlying wisdoms of the fact that the five daily prayers are referred to with the term *salat*, meaning 'prayer' in Arabic, is due to it being the most comprehensive form of prayer and supplication.

Prayer is preceded by repentance; seeking forgiveness from the Lord. If, of the required nature, that is, if the repentance over the sin committed comes with a sincere remorse and a stern resolution of never again recommitting it, it does away with the dirt and rust that blinds the heart and turns it into a crystal clear mirror reflecting the truth. Only in this manner does the heart become receptive to spiritual enlightenment.

An expression of how the heart, darkened from sins, is lit up through repentance is the meaningful *hadith* of the Blessed Prophet -upon him blessings and peace- below: "When a servant commits a sin, a black dot is struck onto his heart. If he abandons that sin and turns to repentance, his heart is polished. But if he does not do so and returns to committing the sin, the black dots grow and eventually cover the entire heart. This is exactly what Allah the Almighty refers to when He says:

$$\text{كَلاَّ بَلْ رَانَ عَلَى قُلُوبِهِمْ مَا كَانُوا يَكْسِبُونَ}$$

'Nay! Rather, what they used to do has become like rust upon their hearts.' (al-Mutaffifin, 14) (Tirmidhi, Tafsir, 83)

---

28 A *dhalla* is an involuntary error.

The Training of Sufism (Sayr Suluk)

On observing the world with the eye of the heart, we find that all creatures are in a state of admitting to their helplessness, before giving thanks to what the Lord provides them in their own peculiar ways. For the son of Adam, who cannot exercise his willpower without somehow falling into error, repentance is the first step of *taqarrub*, drawing closer to the Lord.

With a nature to attract Divine Mercy, prayer is enormously influential in protecting a person from likely tribulations. As aforementioned, it is for that reason that, in all Sufi orders, the spiritual lesson begins with repentance. On the importance of prayer, the Quran states:

$$\text{قُلْ مَا يَعْبَؤُا بِكُمْ رَبِّى لَوْلاَ دُعَاؤُكُمْ}$$

"Say: My Lord would not care for you were it not for your prayer…" (al-Furqan, 77)

"And when My servants ask you concerning Me, then surely I am very near; I answer the prayer of the suppliant when he calls on Me, so they should answer My call and believe in Me that they may walk in the right way." (al-Baqara, 186)

"Call on your Lord humbly and secretly; surely He does not love those who exceed the limits." (al-Araf, 55)

The Beloved Prophet -upon him blessings and peace- says in the following *ahadith*: "There can be nothing more valuable in the sight of Allah than praying to him. Prayer is the essence of servanthood." (Tirmidhi, Daawat, 1)

"Whosoever wants his prayers accepted during times of trouble should make lots of prayers during times of ease and comfort." (Tirmidhi, Daawat, 9)

"Pray to Allah with the belief in its acceptance. Know that Allah the Almighty does not accept a prayer made with an unmindful heart." (Tirmidhi, Daawat, 65)

Thus, supposing the acceptance of prayers made with an unmindful heart and in a sloppy manner is nothing but a deception of Shaytan. Imam Rabbani -may Allah sanctify his secret- says: "A war is won with the joint forces of two armies. One is the army of soldiers the other is the army of prayers." Confirming this is how the Companions would ask for the prayers of the Students of the *Suffa* to complement their own, right before setting out for battle. The Blessed Prophet -upon him blessings and peace- has stated: "There is no prayer more quickly accepted than the prayer a Muslim makes for another Muslim in his absence." (Tirmidhi, Birr, 50)

People seek the prayers of those whom they believe will have their prayers accepted. Yet, the main factor in ensuring the acceptance of a prayer is not so much the standing of the person in Divine sight than it is the sincerity of the prayer itself. This means that a genuine prayer made by someone sinful on behalf of another Muslim is better than the reluctant prayer made by another, even if he be of a way higher standing in Divine Sight. Just because a man is sinful does not mean that the Lord has abandoned him; and God forbid us ever thinking that. Had that been the case, speaking about the sins of a sinful person would not have been considered backbiting (*ghiybah*), one of the great sins. Here, the value lies in winning the heart of a person, whoever he may be, and receiving his genuine, heartfelt prayers.

"What is the most accepted prayer?" the Companions once asked the Blessed Prophet -upon him blessings and peace-. "The prayer made during the final hours of night and after each obligatory (*fard*) *salat*", he replied. (Tirmidhi, Daawat, 78)

For the prayer to be accepted, it is not enough to simply pronounce it through words. The heart must shiver through thinking of the meanings ascribed to the word chose for the prayer; and if the prayer seeks forgiveness for a sin, it should be accompanied by a stern resolution not to make the same mistake again. In addition, uprightness (*istiqamah*) and righteous deeds are crucial for the prayers to find their way to Divine presence. Hence, the *ayah*: "Whoever desires honor, then to Allah belongs the honor wholly. To Him do ascend the good words; and the good deeds, lift them up, and (as for) those who plan evil deeds, they shall have a severe chastisement; and (as for) their plan, it shall perish." (Fatir, 10)

It is necessary to, at least, try to pray in a state that is between fear (*khawf*) and hope (*rajaa*). Prayer and repentance delivers both individuals and society and prevents future disasters. For the prayer to be accepted and the heart to be cured from its diseases in the process, Mawlana Rumi

The Training of Sufism (Sayr Suluk)

-may Allah sanctify his secret- recommends the following: "Pray and repent with a heart burning in the flame of remorse and with moist eyes; for flowers bloom in places sunny and moist!"

Repentance first began with the first prophet Adam (a.s), who prayed:

$$رَبَّنَا ظَلَمْنَا اَنْفُسَنَا وَ اِنْ لَمْ تَغْفِرْ لَنَا وَ تَرْحَمْنَا لَنَكُونَنَّ مِنَ الْخَاسِرِينَ$$

"Our Lord! We have been unjust to ourselves, and if Thou forgive us not, and have (not) mercy on us, we shall certainly be of the losers." (al-Araf, 23) This prayer has set an example of repentance for his offspring to come until the Final Hour.

To awaken sleeping hearts and to provide them with a cure for their spiritual diseases, Allah, glory unto Him, invites His servants to repent, proclaiming: "O you who believe! turn to Allah a sincere turning; maybe your Lord will remove from you your evil and cause you to enter gardens beneath which rivers flow..." (at-Tahrim, 8)

Prayer and repentance are vital catalysts in making one turn to the Lord and elevating his heart to a grand level. Since the heart is vulnerable and exposed to numerous influences which may cause a 'change of heart', man has no other option than to hold fast to prayer, to ensure his heart remains firm on the path of guidance. Allah, glory unto Him, thus teaches us to repeat the below prayer:

$$رَبَّنَا لَا تُزِغْ قُلُوبَنَا بَعْدَ اِذْ هَدَيْتَنَا وَ هَبْ لَنَا مِنْ لَدُنْكَ رَحْمَةً اِنَّكَ اَنْتَ الْوَهَّابُ$$

"Our Lord! Make not our hearts to deviate after You have guided us aright, and grant us from Your mercy; surely You are the most liberal Giver..." (Al-i Imran, 8)

Repeating the gist of this Divine instruction throughout his life, the Blessed Prophet -upon him blessings and peace- would frequently pray:

Sufism: A Path Towards the Internalization of Faith (Ihsân)

يَا مُقَلِّبَ الْقُلُوبِ ثَبِّتْ قَلْبِى عَلٰى دِينِكَ

"O He who transforms hearts! Stabilize my heart upon Your religion." (Tirmidhi, Qadar, 7)

Prayer is one of the most important means of purifying the heart of its spiritual dirt. The below *ayah* reveals this beautifully: "And those who come after them say: Our Lord! forgive us and those of our brethren who had precedence of us in faith, and do not allow any spite to remain in our hearts towards those who believe, our Lord! Surely You are Kind, Merciful." (al-Hashr, 10)

It is thus necessary first to clean the heart from all that is negative, which act as obstacles on its path of reaching the ultimate aim, and make the heart's surface suitable for the ultimate goal to which it aspires. The following prayers of the Noble Prophet -upon him blessings and peace- are splendid examples for the need to cleanse the heart of indifference and negative emotions:

"My Allah! I seek refuge in You from the knowledge that does not benefit, the heart that does not shiver, the soul never satisfied and the prayer never accepted!" (Muslim, Dhikr, 73)

"My Allah! Just as you cleanse white clothes from dirt, cleanse my heart from sins and make it pure!" (Bukhari, Daawat, 39)

Obtaining a flawless heart is possible only with the blessing of the Lord. In fact, Ibrahim (a.s), who was able to present to his Lord a flawless heart, had made the following prayer, in order not to be embarrassed on the Day of Resurrection: "And disgrace me not on the day when they are raised. The day on which property will not avail, nor sons…" (as-Shuara, 87-89)

In the footsteps of his great grandfather, the Blessed Prophet -upon him blessings and peace-, too, made a similar prayer: "My Allah! I ask from you a tongue that speaks the truth and a flawless heart!" (Tirmidhi, Daawat, 23)

Equally important in prayer is repetition and persistence. It has become a method to repeat the prayer at least three times to show persistence. If sincere, the prayer is never refused. Yet, some pleas, although sincere, are at times incompatible with the Divine Will over proceedings. Still, one ought to persist with the prayer free of weariness (*futur*), as the prayers unaccepted on Earth are sure to be compensated in the Hereafter.

c- Reading the Quran and Obeying Its Commands

Filling the heart with the Quran inspired wisdom depends on the spiritual level of our heart whilst reciting it.

Subjecting him to the Quran is undoubtedly one of the greatest blessings the Lord has bestowed upon man. The perfect measures for the true peace and stability of both the spirit and the body is found in the inspiring content of the Quran. Man's happiness and salvation is possible to the extent of the share he embodies of these perfect measures. A person, who loses his inner balance by turning his back on the spirituality of the Quran instead of seeking refuge in it, has effectively laid waste on his human integrity. Responding to the greatest of all blessings with ungratefulness, he has brought about his own self-destruction in the maze of his desires and ambitions.

The Quran is a font of Divine wisdom that hands out cures and comfort to bleeding hearts and tired spirits. It is a generous Divine gift, holding the keys to welcoming the dreadful yet inevitable moment of death as a pathway, a wedding night (*shab-i arus*), for a believer to reach his Lord. The Glorious Lord presents His Divine Word to entire humankind in the following:

يَٓا اَيُّهَا النَّاسُ قَدْ جَٓاءَتْكُمْ مَوْعِظَةٌ مِنْ رَبِّكُمْ

وَ شِفَٓاءٌ لِمَا فِى الصُّدُورِ وَ هُدًى وَ رَحْمَةٌ لِلْمُؤْمِنٖينَ

"O men! There has come to you indeed an admonition from your Lord and a healing for what is in the breasts and a guidance and a mercy for the believers." (Yunus, 57)

The Blessed Prophet -upon him blessings and peace- says, in a *hadith*:

Sufism: A Path Towards the Internalization of Faith (Ihsân)

"Each feast holder desires people to attend his feast and is delighted by it. The Quran is the feast of Allah. Do not remain distant from it." (Darimi, Fadailu'l-Quran, 1)

"Read the Quran…for Allah will not punish a heart which has the Quran in it." (Darimi, Fadailu'l-Quran, 1)

"The true people of the Quran are the people of Allah…and they are His true servants." (Hakim, Mustadrak, I, 743)[29]

Hearts distant from the remembrance of the Lord and from reading the Quran become hardened and depressed, as we can gather from the words of Abu Musa al-Ashari -Allah be well-pleased with him- to those who had come to visit him: "Continue reading the Quran! Do not, ever, leave it unread for a long period of time…otherwise your hearts will become hardened like those before you!" (Muslim, Zakat, 119)

The following incident goes to show how the Quran has an effect even on animals and angels:

"I was reading Surah Baqara one night. My horse was next to me, tied. But at one stage the horse began to rear up. I stopped reading and the horse calmed down. Then, I resumed reading but again the horse began to rear up once again as I read. Fearing he might be trampled under the horse's hooves, I was forced to bring my little son Yahya closer to me. But then I looked up to the sky and saw spots that looked like lamps, which after a while, rose further up into the sky and disappeared from sight. In the morning, I told the Messenger of Allah -upon him blessings and peace- of my experience.

'Read Usayd, read,' he said to me before asking, 'do you know, Usayd, what those things were that you saw?'

'No', I replied.

---

[29] The 'people of Allah', who have not only memorized the Quran but have also obeyed its commands and embodied its morals, are provided with numerous blessings by Allah, glory unto Him. It has even been reported that the corpses of some *huffaz* remain in tact, without the least sign of decay, after their death. The beloved Mahmud Sami Ramazanoğlu -may Allah sanctify his secret- personally testified to seeing the corpse of a *hafiz* in Adana, unearthed thirty years after his death due to necessary circumstances. Not only had his corpse remained in tact, even his shroud had remained undamaged.

The Training of Sufism (Sayr Suluk)

'They were angels who had come to listen to your recital of the Quran. Had you continued reading, they would have listened to you until daybreak. They would not have remained secret to other people either, they would have seen them clearly like you did.'" (Bukhari, Fadail'ul-Quran, 15)

The Quran was revealed to man; for to a man of heart it is a deep treasure of contemplation. Aloofness to the spirituality of the Quran means a sheer and absolute destruction. To those oblivious to the ocean of wisdom and mysteries that is the Quran, the Almighty states:

$$\text{اَفَلاَ يَتَدَبَّرُونَ الْقُرْاٰنَ اَمْ عَلٰى قُلُوبٍ اَقْفَالُهَا}$$

"Will they then not meditate on the Qur'an, or are there locks on the hearts?" (Muhammad, 24)

The Quran is the manifestation of the names of Allah, glory unto Him, reflected onto our understanding in the form of speech. The Almighty expresses the Quran's infinite majesty of meaning in the following *ayah*: "And were every tree that is in the earth (made into) pens and the sea (to supply it with ink), with seven more seas to increase it, the words of Allah would not come to an end; surely Allah is Mighty, Wise." (Luqman, 27)

Filling our hearts with the Quran inspired wisdom depends on the spiritual level of the heart whilst reciting it. To attain to the truth of the Quran, it is therefore vital to raise the heart to the desired level, as the Quran has a nature that can both guide or divert a person, depending on the intention and spiritual level of the reader. Nonetheless, if recited in the appropriate manner, the *ayat* of the Quran produce a gush of spiritual excitement in believers' hearts. So states the Almighty:

"Allah has revealed the best announcement, a book conformable in its various parts, repeating, whereat do shudder the skins of those who fear their Lord, then their skins and their hearts become pliant to the remembrance of Allah; this is Allah's guidance, He guides with it whom He pleases; and (as for) him whom Allah makes err, there is no guide for him." (az-Zumar, 23)

Sufism: A Path Towards the Internalization of Faith (Ihsân)

"Those only are believers whose hearts become full of fear when Allah is mentioned, and when His communications are recited to them they increase them in faith, and in their Lord do they trust." (al-Anfal, 2)

The first condition of properly benefiting from the Quran is to approach it with respect; a kind of respect that shows the importance attached to the Word of Allah, glory unto Him. Comprising the entirety of truths and insights into all mysteries to serve the needs of humankind until the Final Hour, the Quran is undoubtedly a magnificent guide. This characteristic of the Quran is highlighted by the Almighty Himself: "Surely this Quran guides to that which is most upright and gives good news to the believers who do good that they shall have a great reward." (al-Isra, 9)

As the Quran is a Divine Book whose role as a guide is set to continue until the Final Hour, all Muslims under its guiding light are obliged to lead a Quranic way of life until death comes knocking to lead them to the life of eternity. Attaining spiritual happiness and salvation here and the pleasure of the Lord and His blessings in the Hereafter, is possible only in this manner.

Properly benefiting from the Quran is possible only to the extent that it is read with the heart. This is wonderfully expressed in the following reply of the Blessed Prophet -upon him blessings and peace-, upon being asked about the preferred voice and manner of reciting the Quran to look out for when listening to it: "The recitation of the who, when reads, evokes in you the feeling that he fears Allah." (Darimi, Fadailu'l-Quran, 34) Indeed, it was the wonderful recitation of the Quran at the home of his sister Fatima -Allah be well-pleased with him-a that stirred up feelings of awe in Omar -Allah be well-pleased with him- and guided him to the Truth.

The below *ayat* shed light on the proper manner of reading the Quran:

"A Book We have revealed to you abounding in good that they may ponder over its verses, and that those endowed with understanding may be mindful." (Sad, 29)

"…and recite the Qur'an in slow, measured rhythmic tones." (al-Muzzammil, 4)

The Training of Sufism (Sayr Suluk)

Reportedly, Omar -Allah be well-pleased with him- completed reading *surah* Baqara in exactly twelve years and sacrificed a camel in thanksgiving after he did. (Qurtubi, al-Jami, I, 40) It similarly took Abdullah ibn Omar -Allah be well-pleased with him- eight years to complete reading the same *surah*. (Muwattaa, Quran, 11)

Upon learning ten *ayat* from the Blessed Prophet -upon him blessings and peace-, the Companions would never proceed onto the next ten before thoroughly understanding and putting to practice the wisdoms and commands contained therein. In doing so, they embodied the knowledge of the Quran and gradually perfected themselves with its wisdom. (Ahmed, V, 410)

What these examples make clear is that whilst reading the Quran, one must not just pronounce the words but rather seek to acquire a share of its inner wisdoms, which allows one to devotedly obey its commands and embody its morals.

It should be borne in mind that the Ottomans, who, after the Age of Bliss, typify the most outstanding level of Islam, owe this honor to the blessings of an exceptional conduct of respect towards the Quran. It is common knowledge in history that Osman Ghazi, the founder of the State, spent a night at the house of Sheikh Edebali sleepless, supposing it would have been disrespectful to lie down in a room with a Quran hanging on the wall. In addition, the ban of touching the Quran without ablution alludes to the necessity and importance of respectful conduct towards it. Also known is the significance in Islamic etiquette (*adab*) of not holding the Quran below the waist. Conversely, let alone reading the Quran, even simply gazing at its letters is encouraged and considered reward reaping, as it engenders affinity with the Quran. One must therefore avoid disrespect towards the Quran and make a habit of reading it, even if it be a little amount each time. It must also be kept close in mind that the very first command of the Quran is to 'Read!' ('اقْرَأْ' al-Alaq, 1). The import of the command to read is also underlined by the fact that reading at least a portion of the Quran is an integral part of a proper *salat*.

The first public speech given by Sulayman ibn Abdulmalik, after being assigned as the new Caliph of the Umayyad State was: "Servants of Allah… Take the Book of Allah as guide. Accept its rulings and practice it, for

Sufism: A Path Towards the Internalization of Faith (Ihsân)

without a doubt, the Quran scatters the traps and plots of Shaytan as the morning light scatters the dark of night!" (Bayhaki, Kitabu'z-Zuhd, p. 61)

All things considered, it becomes clear that establishing a tight bond with the Quran is an essential aspect of life. We therefore must ask our Lord to flood our hearts with the sublime joy of the Divine Word. To be sure, one of the prayers of the Blessed Prophet -upon him blessings and peace- was:

"My Lord…For the sake of each of Your Beautiful Names, which You may have taught one of Your servants, revealed in Your Book or kept hidden with You, I beg You to make the Quran the spring of my heart, the light of my chest and the cure for my sorrow and anguish!" (Ahmed ibn Hanbal, Musnad, I, 391)

d- Worshipping with Utmost Concentration (*khushuu*)

"Worship Allah as if you see Him. As even though you may not see Him, He surely sees you!" (Bukhari, Iman, 37)

Deeds of worship are the testimony of loyalty to the primordial pact made by the servant with his Lord. Worshipping marks the times in which the servant is the closest with his Lord, as much as is allowed by the bounds of servanthood. It is a special realm. Clearing his mind of all problems worldly, the servant relaxes and strengthens his spirit in the peaceful thought of knowing that this is one thing he is doing for his Maker. The *takbir* made at the very beginning of salat represents just that: by lifting his hands, the servant puts everything behind him and turns to Allah, glory unto Him, only.

Worshipping provides the most effective cure and comfort for the distressing fear of death and beyond. It is a spiritual garden, through which runs the only pathway to eternal happiness; an inspiring spring that sprouts forth spiritual peace and harmony whose appreciation must never be neglected.

Offering deeds of worship with *khushuu*, or utmost concentration, is a prerequisite of obtaining the desired results. *Khushuu* is to be able to stand

The Training of Sufism (Sayr Suluk)

in Divine presence with a peaceful and serene heart, overcome with feelings of love and fear. In awe of the Almighty in whose presence one stands, it is to be able to cut all ties with everything else and be with Him alone, with the consciousness that only to worship Him was he created.

The most magnificent and comprehensive deed of worship is *salat (prayer)*. *Salat* is one of the greatest gifts of the Almighty to humankind. The *hadith* states: "Paradise is written (*wajib*) for a believer who takes a thorough ablution and offers two *rakat* of *salat* with his entire heart and soul, in complete peace and concentration." (Muslim, Taharah, 17) *Salat* is second to none in terms of the spiritual qualities it imparts to a human being. A salat of this nature would require the thought of every single entity, even one's own self, apart from the Real, to lose its value in sight and be swept aside from the heart.

Sulayman Darani -may Allah sanctify his secret- says: "If I were left to choose between two *rakat* of *salat* and the Paradise of *Firdaws*, I would choose the former. Entering Paradise would be something my ego would surely love. Yet if I offer *salat*, I will be in the company of my Lord."

Once the *salat* is underway, one cannot be occupied with anything else. *Salat* will keep all other thoughts at bay. During a *salat* offered in the truest sense, the hearts is stripped off of its veils, allowing the lights of truth to shine through. It is an inexplicable moment of intimacy with the Lord. This luxury belongs to *salat* only and is never replicated in any other deed of worship. A person fasting, for instance, can at the same time buy or sell at the market and see to his daily chores. The same goes for a pilgrim. But a person offering *salat* can neither buy nor sell. All he does is offer *salat*. He must be in Divine presence, both in matter and form.

A proper *salat* inspires and spiritualizes a believer, saving him from falling into the pits of desires egoistic, injecting in him the consciousness that the Almighty is watching him at every given moment. Highlighting this are the subsequent words of the Blessed Prophet:

"Worship Allah as if you see Him; as even though you may not see Him He surely sees you!" (Bukhari, Iman, 37)

"Remember death during your *salat*, for if a person offers *salat* with death on his mind, his *salat* will be of beauty and perfection. Offer your *salat* like the person who thinks it will be his last. Avoid everything that will later cause you regret." (Darimi, Musnad, I, 431)

A proper *salat* is described by the Quran below: "Recite that which has been revealed to you of the Book and keep up prayer; surely prayer keeps (one) away from indecency and evil, and certainly the remembrance of Allah is the greatest, and Allah knows what you do." (al-Ankabut, 45)

Salat provides protection from evil only if the peace and concentration acquired during *salat* is maintained after the *salat* as well. One who does not maintain this state of mind is not offering true *salat*. The Divine warning leveled at persons of the kind is severe: "So woe to the praying ones, who are unmindful of their prayers, who do (good) to be seen. And withhold the necessaries of life." (al-Maun, 4-7) Therefore, one who offers *salat* without doing justice to its each motion (*tadilu'l-arkan*), who is oblivious to the fact of being in Divine presence and whose mind is busy with his own petty affairs, should not expect his *salat* to produce the inspiration expected of it. A *salat* of the kind is just like paying off a debt, under duress, just because one has to. The following is how the Almighty defines a true and ideal *salat*: "Successful indeed are the believers, who are humble in their prayers…" (al-Muminun, 1-2)

Companion Abdullah ibn Shihhir -Allah be well-pleased with him- recounts the state of the Blessed Prophet -upon him blessings and peace- whilst offering *salat*: "I saw the Messenger of Allah -upon him blessings and peace- in *salat*. A sound, much like that of a boiling pot, was coming from his chest from crying." (Abu Dawud, Salat, 156-157; Ahmed ibn Hanbal, Musnad, IV, 25) When offering *salat*, Ali -Allah be well-pleased with him- would grow pale and cast aside everything, even his own flesh. For an arrow to be removed from his foot during one battle, he began to offer *salat*, knowing that only in this manner would he not feel the agonizing pain of its removal. Yet, how many have the ability to offer a *salat* that is so utterly detached from the world?

With that said those who cannot offer their *salat* with such perfection should not despair and abandon it altogether. Every person who persists in offering even a formal *salat*, with which he will have at least redeemed an obligatory debt, will more or less attain a kind of perfection.

The Training of Sufism (Sayr Suluk)

The five daily *salat*s, offered at specific times of the day, subjects one's daily schedule to a program, by which it grants one disciplined way of life with a feeling of responsibility. There can be no talk of inner balance, peace and stability for a person whose life lacks harmony and consistency. In addition, *salat* provides strong protection for faith, gives depth to contemplation, comfort in times of fear and zest in times of joy. It is an inspiring and fruitful form of worship that reinforces the spirit, gives the heart joy and lightness and increases intimacy with the Divine.

Another form of worship that perfects moral conduct by reinforcing patience, willpower and resistance to the desires of the ego, characteristics that are imperative in the course of life, is fasting (*sawm*).

In terms of its essential purpose, to fast is to combat the obstacle that is the ego with the awareness of being in a state of worship and to bridle it, reducing its influence to a bare minimum. By imparting moral virtues like patience, endurance, contentedness with the circumstances and endurance against hardships, fasting, at the same time, through deprivation and hunger, reminds one of the seldom remembered value of the Divine blessing that is food. Giving a taste of hunger to both the rich and the poor, it puts them all on level par. It helps develop feelings of compassion in the rich, by reminding them of the plight of the poor and underprivileged. It reinforces feelings of mutual gratitude.

Fasting revives feelings of piety (*taqwa*), increasing the purity of the heart. The *ayah* declares: "O you who believe! Fasting is prescribed for you, as it was prescribed for those before you, so that you may guard against evil." (al-Baqara, 183)

In training the will, there is no method more effective than fasting. The will is one of the primary means, in man, of warding off the extremities and transgressions that come from the nature of his ego. With regard to eating little to attain to the eternal treats of the eternal life, Mawlana Rumi -may Allah sanctify his secret- says: "Man's real food is love and wisdom. That is why it is not proper to feed his flesh with more food than required."

Man is in distress because he is forgotten his spiritual food and worries over food for his flesh. He is insatiable. He has grown pale from greed, his feet shake and his hearts beats with anxiety. Yet what is the food of earth compared to the food of eternity? About martyrs, Allah has said, 'They are being fed next to their Lord'.[30] Neither is there a mouth for that spiritual food, nor a body."

To attain to the truth of fasting and fully benefit from it spiritually, it is necessary that one desists from neglectful behavior detrimental to it. It is stated in the *hadith*: "Fasting is not just about abandoning eating or drinking. A perfect and rewarding fast is only through abandoning vain talk and action, and foul words. Should someone swear at or act crudely towards you, then say to him, 'I am fasting.'" (Hakim, Mustadrak, I, 595)

Also declared obligatory in addition to fasting, which trains the willpower by curbing the desires of the ego, is almsgiving (*zakat*). The underlying purpose of almsgiving is to stem likely transgressions that come with the obsession of hoarding wealth, to purge feelings of envy and jealousy the poor may nurture towards the rich and thereby sustain social life through bonding its members with love. In the Islamic social order, almsgiving and charity (*infaq*) are therefore crucial means of engendering love between the rich and the poor and eliminating malicious feelings between the two. The rich will be summoned by the Almighty, interrogated as to through which means they made their money and to where they spent it and whether or not they provided its alms and charity. Responsible with sparing a certain amount of their wealth for the poor, the rich therefore stand under a grueling financial test. Yet, passing this test, along with fulfilling the other responsibilities of servanthood yields the blessings of the Lord and entrance into Paradise.

The importance of almsgiving, mentioned numerous times throughout the Quran, is underlined by the fact that on 27 occasions it is mentioned alongside *salat*, the pillar of religion. Alms is the debt owed by the rich to the underprivileged. The Quran states: "And in their wealth and possessions (was remembered) the right of the (needy,) him who asked, and him who (for some reason) was prevented (from asking)." (ad-Dhariyat, 19) Thus almsgiving is the practice of setting aside a certain portion of wealth that passes the minimum threshold (*nisab*), as Divine tax, rendering the remainder of the wealth *halal*. The portion that is set aside is thereby transferred to the underprivileged members of society. In this way,

---

30   Al-i Imran, 169.

not only is the wealth of the rich cleansed from impurity, a social balance, justice and harmony are also established. Glancing at the following *ayah* suffices to come to terms with this matter of fact: "He indeed shall be successful who purifies (*tazakkaa*) himself…" (al-Ala, 14) Literally, *zakat* does after all mean *tazkiya*, in other words, to purify.

Almsgiving is a minimum debt the Almighty has obliged on the wealthy. In contrast, there is not a limit imposed on charity, and like fasting, the rewards awaiting those who provide voluntary charity has been kept hidden to encourage the wealthy in this regard. Different to previous nations, the Lord awards the *ummah* of Muhammad -upon him blessings and peace- one penalty for each sin committed, while ten rewards in return for each righteous deed. Additionally, there are deeds rewarded seven hundred times, even more. But the rewards of fasting and charity are concealed. About this, Allah, glory unto Him, states: "Take alms out of their property, you would cleanse them and purify them thereby, and pray for them; surely your prayer is a relief to them; and Allah is Hearing, Knowing," (at-Tawbah, 103)

It is clear from the *ayah* that almsgiving and charity purify both the wealth and the heart. The Almighty also levels a warning at those who abstain from charitable deeds, despite having the means to do so:

"O you who believe! Surely, many of the rabbis and monks devour the wealth of mankind wantonly and debar men from the way of Allah. They who hoard up gold and silver and spend it not in the way of Allah, unto them give tidings of a painful doom. On the day when it will (all) be heated in the fire of hell, and their foreheads and their flanks and their backs will be branded therewith (and it will be said unto them): Here is that which ye hoarded for yourselves. Now taste of what ye used to hoard." (at-Tawba, 34-35)

With the love of wealth setting foot deep in the heart, the wealth is held back from charity and in so doing the rights of the poor are usurped. And this incurs a pitiful end as made definite by the above *ayah*.

Only two kinds of blessings, children and wealth, have been labeled as *fitnah*, or means of tribulation. Their excessive love may permeate the heart and dominate it, a danger reminded by the Almighty as: "Your possessions and your children are only a trial, and Allah it is with Whom is a great reward." (at-Taghabun, 15)

By stopping the growth of their excessive love and keeping them outside the heart may one prevent the love of children and wealth from becoming *fitnah*. Fulfilling the Divine requirements of almsgiving and charity can only take place by depriving the love of wealth of the opportunity of setting foot inside the heart, with the awareness that wealth is simply something entrusted until a predestined time. One must therefore thoroughly reflect on the Divine warnings partly given above and seek to offer supplementary charity that will allow him to pass beyond the minimum threshold of alms. Allah, glory unto Him, declares:

وَ يَسْئَلُونَكَ مَاذَا يُنْفِقُونَ قُلِ الْعَفْوَ

"And they ask you as to what they should spend. Say: What you can spare…" (al-Baqara, 219)

The rich who are generous and thanksgiving, and the poor who are patient and dignified, partake in both human honor and Divine pleasure. In contrast, the rich who are conceited and parsimonious and the poor who are impatient and consequently always rebelling have been reproved.

Almsgiving is an expression of gratitude by those in possession of wealth. And it is a Divine promise that gratitude only increases blessings. So states the Almighty:

لَئِنْ شَكَرْتُمْ لَاَزِيدَنَّكُمْ

"If you are grateful, I would certainly give to you more…" (Ibrahim, 7)

Giving charity was in fact something dearly loved and strongly encouraged by the Blessed Prophet -upon him blessings and peace-. He says: "Son of man…Give charity so that you are treated charitably…" (Bukhari, Nafaqat, 1)

The Beloved Prophet -upon him blessings and peace- desired for generosity to become part of the essential nature of a Muslim. "Only two persons are to be envied", he says. "One is he who has been given wealth by Allah and the power over it to spend it in His way; and the other is he who has been given knowledge that he practices and teaches it to others (he who provides charity from his knowledge)." (Bukhari, Ilm, 15)

The Training of Sufism (Sayr Suluk)

In short, man is naturally disposed towards the world. The ego finds the wealth of the world dazzling. Those deceived by it can never get enough of it. The more wealth there is the greater the ambition and greed becomes. Compassion and mercy vanish when mesmerized by a hunger for wealth. Giving charity then becomes the most painstaking of tasks. Such a person is constantly vulnerable to the deceiving whispers of his ego, urging him to "make more money, become richer. You will give charity in the future!" However much he may be enjoying the comfort of the flesh, a person of the kind is spiritually ill. "Those who adjourn have perished", the Blessed Prophet -upon him blessings and peace- has said. *Zakat* is thus a definite cure for greed for the world, a malicious disease of the heart.

It is described in the Quran that at the moment of death, a person will come to his senses, as if awoken from a dream, and plead, with an eternal remorse:

رَبِّ لَوْلاَ اَخَّرْتَنِى اِلٰى اَجَلٍ قَرِيبٍ فَاَصَّدَّقَ وَ اَكُنْ مِنَ الصَّالِحِينَ

"My Lord! Why did You not respite me to a near term, so that I should have given alms and been of the doers of good deeds?" (al-Munafiqun, 10)

Furthermore, etiquette (*adab*) is central when giving alms or charity. The provider, especially, must be overcome with feelings of gratitude towards the receiver, for giving him the opportunity to reimburse a compulsory debt. At the same time, a charity given is protection for the provider against illnesses and misfortunes. In emphasis of providing for the poor with a sensitive heart, the *ayat* state:

"Do they not know that Allah accepts repentance from His servants and takes the alms, and that Allah is the Oft-returning (to mercy), the Merciful?" (at-Tawba, 104)

"O you who believe! Do not make your charity worthless by reproach and injury, like him who spends his property to be seen by men and does not believe in Allah and the last day. So his parable is as the parable of a smooth rock with earth upon it, then a heavy rain falls upon it, so it leaves it bare; they shall not be able to gain anything of what they have earned. And Allah does not guide the unbelieving people." (al-Baqara, 264)

All beings live and are survived on the dominion of the Almighty. Through a continuous transformation (*istihalah*) of the comparably meager amount of soil on Earth, the Almighty turns it into a storehouse feeding a countless amount of creatures. Do not human beings, unique among entire creation in being endowed with reason and judgment, ever see and acknowledge the fact that the Almighty feeds all beings indiscriminately, regardless of whether they are believers or nonbelievers, strong or weak, and think just whose property they are depriving others of?

Allah, glory unto Him, has created the entire universe out of love, a love for the sake of which He has bestowed countless blessings of grace. Sacrifice is a natural outcome of love. A lover perceives his sacrifice for the beloved as a pleasant duty, willingly giving up even his own life if he must. In doing so, not even for a split second does he look upon it as a great feat of sacrifice. It could be said that for the Almighty, charitableness towards His creation is the most beautiful manifestation of what the Lover does for the beloved.

Together with these financial deeds of worship, there is also pilgrimage (*hajj*), a deed that is both physical and financial. It is a sublime act which, through reviving the poignant memories from the first prophet Adam (a.s) to the Prophet of the Final Hour -upon him blessings and peace-, not only ushers hearts to perfection, but by virtue of enacting the scene of the ultimate Resurrection, hands devotees the keys to the mystery that is: "Die before you die!"

Hajj is underlain with numerous wisdoms, pertaining both to Here and the Hereafter. A true pilgrimage is a magnificent act of worship, where Muslims, forgiven through the manifestation of the eternal mercy of the Lord, come together with an ecstatic enthusiasm of a profound faith and love. *Hajj* is to shed the clothes of existence and seek a way out from the thunderstorms of the ego, by delving into the depths of spirit. *Hajj* is a deed of worship that abounds in spiritual manifestations, where man retrieves the harmony and color of his spirit, his true habitat, and where he recovers his essential identity and looks on, as his heart is cleansed with the downpour of spiritual enlightenment.

The *Kaaba*, which is the *qibla*, that is the direction of worship for believers, is the focal point of *salat*, whose offering has been commanded by the Almighty as: "Prostrate and draw near!" (al-Alaq, 19) It is the very

The Training of Sufism (Sayr Suluk)

direction to which entire Muslims turn, where the heart of the Muslim world beats. In human beings, it is the heart where the Divine Sight manifests itself, while in the universe it is the *Kaaba*. Thus in a sense, the *Kaaba* is for the universe what the heart is for man. Pilgrimage is therefore a deed of worship that calls for a sensitive heart and precision, with an appreciation of the *Kaaba*'s splendor whilst performing it. Permeated with manifestations of love and compassion, the entire schedule of *hajj* directs the heart to sensitivity, which is exemplified by keeping away from hurting the creation of Allah, glory unto Him.

Clothed in a milky white *ihram, hajj* is the attempt to acquire a share of the finesse of angels, as if to emulate them. While in *ihram*, one must not hunt or pull out shrubs and weed, or even intentionally remove a strand of hair. No *rafath* there, no *fisq*, no *jidal*…[31] Only compassion towards creation, mercy and courtesy, for the sake of the Creator.

It must not be forgotten that death is the inevitable end for all beings. Its time has been predetermined, up to the exact amount minutes to pass and breaths to be taken until its arrival. Incontestable is the fact that postponing death or bringing it forward is impossible; neither has there been news of certain man able to make a successful getaway from the hands of death. So those with the means to perform pilgrimage must thoroughly think this fact over and strictly refrain from a careless and sloppy attitude in regard. Otherwise, they would directly come under the stern warning of the Blessed Prophet -upon him blessings and peace- below:

"There is nothing preventing a person who recoils from *hajj* despite having the finances to cover the cost of food and travel, from dying as a Jew or a Christian." (Tirmidhi, Hajj, 3)

This Prophetic caution stresses that those who neglect offering pilgrimage, not because a lack of financial means but from sheer carelessness, are in a grave loss and are destined for Divine punishment, unless they mend their ways. It is indeed negligence beyond description that Muslims should remain oblivious to *hajj*, an unrivaled opportunity to purify their hearts and erase their sins.

---

31 See, al-Baqara, 197. *Rafath*: To have intercourse, to speak about intercourse or any kind of foul words. *Fisq*: All kinds of sinful conduct. *Jidal*: To engage in vain arguments.

Sufism: A Path Towards the Internalization of Faith (Ihsân)

The Blessed Prophet -upon him blessings and peace- says: "Whosoever visits the Great Kaaba with the intention of *hajj* and completes it without engaging in *fisq* or *rafath*, will return home pure as the day he was born." (Muslim, Hajj, 438)

e- Reviving the Nights

Top it up with that wine, refill it; pour it out once more,
Let the night stop, stop it my friend, for this I implore!
Enchain my sleep, shackle it; let not the moments pass
Sleepers never appreciate the night, the night they never grasp.

Introspection and shrugging off the spiritual and physical weight of the day is possible by enshrouding oneself in the peaceful silence of the night. Days are unable to give the spiritual and physical rest which nights provide so generously. Those who do not appreciate the night can never know the value of day. Entering the Divine and spiritual scenery of night calls for its purposeful revival.

For the wise people of heart, there is never a time more inspiring than the serenity of night. Spending a certain portion of the night awake is hence essential, to make the most of its abundant inspiration. The *ayah* in regard says:

$$\text{تَتَجَافَىٰ جُنُوبُهُمْ عَنِ الْمَضَاجِعِ يَدْعُونَ رَبَّهُمْ خَوْفًا وَ طَمَعًا وَ مِمَّا رَزَقْنَاهُمْ يُنْفِقُونَ}$$

"They forsake their beds, they call upon their Lord in fear and in hope, and they spend (benevolently) out of what We have given them…" (as-Sajda, 16)

"And glorify the name of your Lord morning and evening. And during part of the night worship Him, and give glory to Him a long part of the night." (al-Insan, 25-26)

The Training of Sufism (Sayr Suluk)

Immeasurable is the value the Almighty has ascribed to the time of night and countless are the mysteries He has implanted therein. The mysteries that lie behind His avowal on night, like "And the night and that which it drives on…" (al-Inshiqaq, 17), "And the night when it covers with darkness…" (ad-Duha, 2) and "And the night when it departs, and the morning when it brightens…" (at-Takwir, 17-18) are like Divine windows opened to our hearts and understanding, for us to appreciate many a reality.

Mature believers look upon the time of night as an exceptional treasure, owing to the serenity and spiritual enlightenment concealed in its chest. Those who can properly appreciate the value of this treasure find, especially after midnight, the most inspiring ground for turning to the Lord with heartfelt prayers and sincere deeds of worship, at a time when most have resigned to rest.

In his *Divan-i Kabir*, Mawlana Rumi -may Allah sanctify his secret- poeticizes the love and ecstasy he experiences at night:

Fill the goblet, cupbearer, with the love Divine
Mention nothing of bread to the reveler of the wine
Offer the kawthar and let all thirsty hearts quench
In what else but water would a fish want to be drenched?
Top it up with that wine, refill it; pour it out once more,
Let the night stop, stop it my friend, for this I implore!
Enchain my sleep, shackle it; let not the moments pass
Sleepers never appreciate the night, the night they never grasp…[32]

Regarding His fortunate servants who are bound to be treated with Divine blessings in the Hereafter for having feared Him by remaining awake at night and daybreak, the Almighty reveals:

كَانُوا قَلِيلاً مِنَ اللَّيْلِ مَا يَهْجَعُونَ وَ بِالْاَسْحَارِ هُمْ يَسْتَغْفِرُونَ

"They used to sleep but little in the night. And in the morning they asked forgiveness." (ad-Dhariyat, 17-18)

---

[32] Rendered from the Turkish translation of Divan-i Kabir by Assoc. Prof. Emin Işık, Marmara University, Faculty of Divinity.

"And they who pass the night prostrating themselves before their Lord and standing" (al-Furqan, 64)

And in another *ayah*, the Almighty informs:

"…Who sees you when you stand up and your turning over and over among those who prostrate themselves before Allah." (as-Shuara, 218-219)

Qadi Baydawi offers the following with regard to the above *ayah*: "Once the five daily salats became obligatory and the night salat voluntary (*sunnah*), the Noble Prophet -upon him blessings and peace- set out from his chamber at night to inspect the Companions. He found out that their houses were humming like beehives with the sounds of the Quran, *dhikr* and *tasbih*." (Anwaru't-Tanzil, IV, 111)

Compared to other times, Allah, glory unto Him, attaches greater value to the *dhikr* offered at dawn, as it is more difficult to occupy oneself in *dhikr* and worship at dawn compared to all times else. It is for that reason that reviving the time of dawn is a mark of one's sincere love and reverence of the Almighty. The stronger the Divine love is in the heart, the greater the desire will be in waking up for *salat* and *tasbih* at night. Therefore, awaking for *salat* and *tasbih* at night is virtually like meeting up with the beloved. To be awake when everyone else is in deep sleep, is to be among the privileged servants of Allah, glory unto Him, admitted into the courtroom of His mercy, love and knowledge.

For a believer, using the night purposefully and properly deriving the spiritual benefit of the *dhikr* of dawn means that his nights will be spiritually more light and valuable than his days. But a night spent without purpose, imprisoned to sleep alone, is a loss almost irrecoverable, like raindrops that fall on rocks, the sea and the desert and perish at the instant. If we allow the spirituality of *tawhid* that begins at dawn to encompass our hours and our hearts, the moment where we bid farewell to every single thing on Earth and breathe for one last time, will -insha-Allah- become a *shab-i arus*[33].

Abdullah ibn Amr ibn As -Allah be well-pleased with him- recalls how the Blessed Prophet -upon him blessings and peace- cautioned him:

---

33   *Shab-i arus*: Literally the wedding night but implies, here, a Divine reunion.

The Training of Sufism (Sayr Suluk)

"Do not become like so and so, Abdullah, who used to wake up for worship at night but no longer does." (Bukhari, Tahajjud, 19; Muslim, Siyam, 185)

The Beloved Prophet -upon him blessings and peace- is also reported to have said to his Companions: "Be attentive to worshipping at night, for it is the custom of the righteous before you. Waking up to worship at night is no doubt a means to get closer to Allah. It protects one from sins, atones for mistakes and rids the body of distress." (Tirmidhi, Daawat, 101) Also, the health benefits of not sleeping all the night through but rather waking up from time to time, is something medically proven. After a long, uninterrupted night's sleep one usually wakes up with a headache. This is caused by the fact that the brain is not nourished with enough oxygen during sleep, as a result of slower breathing. Dividing sleep therefore helps return the breathing speed to normal; and those who do so, wake up livelier in the morning, despite having actually slept less.

It is also to be noted that death usually comes during the very early hours of morning. This is especially the case with the elderly. Some doctors have therefore labeled dawn 'the hour of death' because that is when the sleep is at its deepest, and the heartbeat at its lowest. Awaking at that hour, coupled with a cold ablution, returns all the bodily functions to normal.

Although the commands of Islam are first and foremost underlain by the purpose of realizing servanthood to Allah, glory unto Him, each of them do come with physical benefits. The same applies for *salat*, fasting and the other deeds of worship, all imbued with countless wisdoms and benefits. But naturally, these benefits are not the reason for the existence of these deeds, but rather their byproducts.

f- *Dhikrullah* and *Muraqaba*

'...Now surely by Allah's remembrance are the hearts set at rest.' (ar-Rad, 28)

It is said that *insan*, the Arabic word for 'man', has as its origin the word *nisyan*, forgetfulness. *Nisyan* is the stark opposite of *dhikr*, or remembrance; and signifies one of the greatest weaknesses of man. This has colloquially been expressed with the expression "Man's memory is afflicted with forgetfulness" (*Hâfıza-yı beşer nisyân ile mâlüldür*). The most effectual way of reducing forgetfulness to a minimum is to 'remember' through *dhikr*.

To live in line with its reason of creation, the spirit must remain loyal to the promise made to the Lord at the *Bazm-i Alast*[34], and never leave the thought of its Creator out of its heart and mind. Consequently, making amends for the damages wrought by forgetfulness, a defect naturally present in human disposition, calls for a *dhikr* that keeps the awareness of 'Allah' and 'servanthood' ever alive; for each act of remembering only strengthens the thought and consciousness of that which is remembered. Certainly, it is not one's appearance that Allah, glory onto Him, looks at, as it is one's heart. A believer must therefore consider it a duty to protect his heart, the focal point of the Divine Gaze, from negligence and keep it occupied with Divine remembrance.

Owing to its particular importance within the duties of servanthood, the word *dhikr* is cited in over 250 places in the Quran. Proper servanthood to the Almighty and reaching, thereby, *marifatullah*, depends on the place of *dhikr* in the heart and the depth with which it is felt. It is for that reason that *marifatullah* that is, gaining acquaintance with the reality of the Lord through the heart, has been considered the noblest of all types of knowledge. After all, it is 'that' knowledge that human beings essentially need. To deter His servants from a failing to benefit from the spirituality of *dhikr*, in some of the *ayah* quoted below, the Almighty states:

$$\text{اَلَمْ يَأْنِ لِلَّذِينَ اٰمَنُوا اَنْ تَخْشَعَ قُلُوبُهُمْ لِذِكْرِ اللهِ}$$
$$\text{وَ مَا نَزَلَ مِنَ الْحَقِّ}$$

"Has not the time yet come for those who believe that their hearts should be humble for the remembrance of Allah and what has come down of the truth?" (al-Hadid, 16)

---

34   *Bazm-i Alast*, or the meeting of spirits in a time immemorial, is when the entirety of spirits affirmed the Lordship of the Almighty, by answering the Almighty's question, "Am I not your Lord?" with "Certainly. You are our Lord!" See, al-Araf, 172.

"…and certainly the remembrance of Allah is the greatest." (al-Ankabut, 45)

"Therefore remember Me, I will remember you, and be thankful to Me, and do not be ungrateful to Me." (al-Baqara, 152)

Even upon sending Musa (a.s) and Harun (a.s) to communicate the truth to the Pharaoh, the Almighty urged them not to neglect His remembrance: "Go you and your brother with My communications and be not remiss in remembering Me" (Taha, 42)

Remembering and mentioning Allah, glory unto Him, is not simply to repeat His name verbally. Much rather, it is for Divine remembrance to become embedded in the heart, the hub of spiritual sensing. The Blessed Prophet -upon him blessings and peace- says:

"The difference between one who remembers Allah and another who does not is like the difference between the living and the dead." (Bukhari, Daawat, 66)

"The mark of loving Allah is the love of *dhikr*." (Suyuti, al-Jamiu's-Saghir, II, 52)

Those detached from Divine remembrance are subjected to the threat of the Almighty, since by doing so they are equally detached from the love of the Lord. The Quran declares: "Woe to those whose hearts are hard against the remembrance of Allah!" (az-Zumar, 22)

The necessity of being in a continuous state of Divine remembrance, which provides safety from the outcome of this threat, is revealed below: "And remember your Lord within yourself humbly and fearing and in a voice not loud in the morning and the evening and be not of the heedless ones." (al-Araf, 205)

Allah, glory unto Him, again warns against the dangers of becoming detached from *dhikr*:

"And whoever turns himself away from the remembrance of the Beneficent Allah, We appoint for him a Shaytan, so he becomes his associate. And most surely they turn them away from the path, and they think that they are guided aright. Until when he comes to Us, he says: O would that between me and you there were the distance of the East and the West; so evil is the associate!" (az-Zukhruf, 36-38)

Sufism: A Path Towards the Internalization of Faith (Ihsân)

"And whoever turns away from My reminder, his shall be a straitened life, and We will raise him on the day of resurrection, blind. He shall say: My Lord! Why have You raised me blind and I was a seeing one indeed? He will say: Even so, Our communications came to you but you neglected them; even thus shall you be forsaken this day." (Taha, 124-126)

Good morals and fine characteristics are exclusive only to those who fear the Lord, who dearly love and remember Him. The Almighty proclaims: "The seven heavens declare His glory and the earth (too), and those who are in them; and there is not a single thing but glorifies Him with His praise, but you do not understand their glorification; surely He is Forbearing, Forgiving." (al-Isra, 44)

In a *hadith al-qudsi* on the value of gathering for *dhikr*, the Noble Messenger -upon him blessings and peace- says:

"Allah the Almighty states: I treat My servant according to what he thinks of Me. When he remembers me, I am with him. If he remembers me in silence I, too, remember him. If he mentions me in public I, too, mention him among a group better than his." (Bukhari, Tawhid, 15)

One day, as he was addressing his Companions, the Messenger of Allah -upon him blessings and peace- asked: "Shall I inform you of the cleanest of your deeds next to Allah, the highest of your ranks, something better than charity given from gold and silver, superior to clashing with the enemy and slaying them or them slaying you?" "Please do, Messenger of Allah", they replied, whereupon the Messenger of Allah -upon him blessings and peace- said:

"It is the remembrance of Allah". (Tirmidhi, Daawat, 6)

Dhikrullah, or the remembrance of Allah, glory unto Him, can be done individually, as well as in a group.

Muawiya -Allah be well-pleased with him- then began to explain. "There is not a single person like me who was so close to the Messenger of Allah -upon him blessings and peace- yet narrated so little from him. But once, the Messenger of Allah -upon him blessings and peace- approached a group of his Companions sitting in a circle and asked:

'Why are you sitting here?'

'We are sitting to thank and praise Allah for having blessed us with the great blessing that is Islam', they replied.

'For the name of Allah, speak the truth. Have you really sat here solely for the purpose of remembering Allah?' the Messenger of Allah -upon him blessings and peace- then asked.

'Yes. By Allah, that is the only reason', they replied, on which the Messenger of Allah -upon him blessings and peace- said:

'It was not because I mistrusted you that I repeated my question. But Jibril came to me and informed me that Allah boasts of you next to His angels. That is why I spoke that way.'" (Muslim, Dhikr, 40)

The Blessed Prophet -upon him blessings and peace- used to instruct his Companions with different forms of *dhikr* depending on their capabilities. A wonderful example of this is his advice to his cousin Umm Hani -Allah be well-pleased with him-a, the daughter of Abu Talib.

"I have become old and weak, Messenger of Allah", she said. "Can you recommend me a deed of worship I can do as I sit?" The Messenger of Allah -upon him blessings and peace- then said:

"Say Subhanallah a hundred times, Alhamdulillah a hundred times and La ilaha ill-Allah a hundred times." (Ibn Maja, Adab, 56; Ahmed ibn Hanbal, Musnad, VI, 344)

Among all kinds of *dhikr*, saying *La ilaha ill-Allah* (*kalima-i tawhid*) in an assembly holds a distinctive place, as indicated by the below *hadith* narrated by Shaddad ibn Aws -Allah be well-pleased with him-:

"Once, whilst with the Messenger of Allah -upon him blessings and peace-, he asked us, 'Is there a foreigner amongst us?' By foreigner, he meant a person of the Book (a Christian or a Jew).

'No, there isn't, Messenger of Allah', we responded.

He then commanded all doors be closed. Afterward, he told us to, 'Raise your hands and say La ilaha ill-Allah'.

We raised our hands aloft and for a while, repeated La ilaha ill-Allah. The Messenger of Allah -upon him blessings and peace- subsequently dropped his hands and prayed:

'My Allah…Thanks be to You! You have sent me with this 'sentence' and commanded me with it (to say it and comply with it). And in return, You have promised me Paradise…and You never fall back from Your promise!'

After that, he turned to us and said, 'Glad tidings to you all! Allah has surely forgiven you!'" (Ahmed ibn Hanbal, Musnad, IV, 124)

The Blessed Prophet states in another *hadith*: "*La ilaha ill-Allah* is a word whose place and value next to Allah is enormous. Whosoever says it with full sincerity and loyalty, Allah shall place him in Paradise. And whosoever says it only with his tongue without believing it, he will have only protected his life and possessions. But tomorrow, when meets Allah, he shall be dealt with." (Haythami, Majmau'z-Zawaid, I, 26)

No less significant is the following *hadith*, emphasizing the need to be engrossed in a constant awareness of *dhikr* and *muraqaba*: "Do not forget Allah and get carried away in vain conversation. For many a conversation had whilst forgetting Allah hardens the heart. And the person most distant from Allah is the hardhearted." (Tirmidhi, Zuhd, 62)

As is evident, the Blessed Prophet -upon him blessings and peace- personally taught and encouraged the practice of *dhikrullah* on more than one occasion. As enormous a loss it is to be distant from the inspiring potential of a deed so fervently encouraged, it is also a tragic deprivation, considering the awaiting rewards in the Hereafter, in return, if carried out in perfection. The more often and the deeper we remember Allah, glory unto Him, here in this world; the closer will be our reunion with Him in the Hereafter.

A lover feels the need to remember, reminisce whom he loves, proportionate to intensity of the love he feels. In tandem, each moment of remembering only serves to intensify the love felt. Those who have had a little taste of the sweetness of *iman* grow in enthusiasm for the Lord and increase their remembrances, the more distance they cover on the spiritual path. In terms of their power to satisfy, there is a difference between the desires of the ego and the desires of the spirit. While the appetite of the ego is appeased after eating, drinking and so forth, and desires them no more, the desires of the spirit only increase the more they are given. It is like drinking saltwater to quench the thirst. Each sip only aggravates the desire for more water. Persons of such ilk are in a continual state of *dhikr*, reflecting on the subtle wisdoms inherent in the creation of earth and the skies, remarking and praying:

"Our Lord! You have not created this in vain! Glory be to You; save us then from the chastisement of the fire." (Al-i Imran, 191)

The road to a life of faith and satisfaction, of reaching the joys of the Divine and ultimately meeting the Almighty with a perfected faith, runs through a continual state of *dhikr*. In whichever condition a person dies, that is how he will be resurrected, as made known by the following *ahadith*:

"Human beings are to be resurrected in the Hereafter upon the state in which they died." (Muslim, Jannah, 83)

"A person dies the way he lived and is resurrected the way he died." (Munawi, Fayzu'l-Qadir, V, 663)

In satisfying man's instinctive eagerness towards spiritual contemplation and sensing, nothing can ever come close to an appreciative understanding of the existence of the *Wajibu'l-Wujud*, the *Hakim*, the Most Wise, and *Nazim*, the Orderer, of the Universe, and love for Him. So reveals the *ayah*:

$$\text{اَلاَ بِذِكْرِ اللهِ تَطْمَئِنُّ الْقُلُوبُ}$$

"Now surely by Allah's remembrance are the hearts set at rest." (ar-Rad, 28)

g- **Love of the Blessed Noble Prophet -upon him blessings and peace- and *Salawat-u Sharifa*.**

"Allah and His angels send blessings on the Prophet: O Believers! Send your blessings on him and salute him with all respect!" (al-Ahzab, 56)

It is impossible for us to fully comprehend the Blessed Prophet -upon him blessings and peace-, a masterpiece of creation, within our capacities and power as human beings. The impressions we receive from the world would prove deficient in both understanding and explaining him. Just as it is impossible to pour the entire ocean inside a cup, it is impossible to properly understand the Muhammedan Light. Accentuating this is the following *ayah*:

$$\text{اِنَّ اللّٰهَ وَ مَلٰئِكَتَهُ يُصَلُّونَ عَلَى النَّبِيِّ}$$
$$\text{يَآ اَيُّهَا الَّذِينَ اٰمَنُوا صَلُّوا عَلَيْهِ وَ سَلِّمُوا تَسْلِيمًا}$$

"Allah and His angels send blessings on the Prophet: O Believers! Send your blessings on him and salute him with all respect!" (al-Ahzab, 56)

Compliant with the Divine edict commanded through the above *ayah*, we are required to utter *salawat-u sharifa*, with sending our blessings to and saluting *that* Prophet -upon him blessings and peace-, with whom the universe boasts. This is part of the conduct the Almighty commands the entire *ummah* to uphold and practice with respect to the Blessed Prophet -upon him blessings and peace-. It is a necessity of *iman* to draw closer to the grace and perfection of that great Prophet -upon him blessings and peace-, saluted and blessed by Allah, glory unto Him and His countless angels. For the Almighty states:

"Say (O Messenger): If you love Allah, then follow me, Allah will love you and forgive you your faults, and Allah is Forgiving, Merciful…" (Al-i Imran, 31)

The moment a believer begins to tremble before the spiritual presence of the Blessed Prophet -upon him blessings and peace- sense inexpressibly beautiful feelings budding in his heart and empties his spirit of all the appearances and shadows of the ego, he is surely on the way of acquiring a share of his love and exemplary character. To this day, the heroes of the heart from among the *ummah*, who have been able to acquire a share of his sacred character to the point of becoming one with it, have beautifully shown their love for the Blessed Prophet -upon him blessings and peace-.

Muslims continue to cherish those who reach the source of love, the Lord and His Messenger, until the Final Hour, lovingly remembering them with warm prayers even after they pass away. Of countless such devotees of

The Training of Sufism (Sayr Suluk)

the Prophet -upon him blessings and peace- privileged with this rank, the experiences of two such figures are ever etched in memory.

During his time, the Noble Prophet -upon him blessings and peace- used to send teachers to neighboring tribes, to communicate and teach the religion of truth. Some of these teachers, however, had fallen victim to sinister plots, one of which took place in the tragedy known as Raji.

The tribes of Adal and Qari had asked for teachers from the Blessed Prophet -upon him blessings and peace- to educate them in Islam. In response, the Noble Messenger -upon him blessings and peace- sent an envoy of ten Companions. But when the envoy arrived near Raji, they were ambushed. Eight were martyred, while the remaining two were surrendered to the idolaters of Mecca.

The two Companions who had fallen captive were Zayd and Hubayb -Allah be well-pleased with them-. The bloodthirsty idolaters eventually martyred both. Moments before his execution, Zayd -Allah be well-pleased with him- was asked by Abu Sufyan:

"Would you have wished for your Prophet to be in your place right now if you knew you would be spared?"

Zayd -Allah be well-pleased with him- looked at Abu Sufyan with pity and replied "Never…! I could not even bare the thought of him being spiked by a thorn in his foot in Medina, let alone hoping him to be in my place right now!"

Stunned by the response, Abu Sufyan could not help but confess, "I swear, I have never seen anyone loved more by his friends than Muhammad!"

Afterward, they went next to Hubayb -Allah be well-pleased with him-, assuring him that he would be released provided he renounced his faith.

"Not even if you were to give me the world entire", he responded. The idolaters then repeated to him the question they had moments before asked Zayd -Allah be well-pleased with him-. They received a similar response.

Hubayb -Allah be well-pleased with him- only had one last wish before he was martyred: to send a loving greeting to the Messenger of Allah -upon him blessings and peace-!

Yet, with whom could he send his message? There was not a single Muslim near him. Almost despondent, he turned his gaze towards the skies and pleaded:

"My Lord! There is nobody around to deliver my greetings to the Messenger of Allah. You deliver my greetings of peace to Him!"

*Sitting with his Companions in Medina at the time, the Blessed Prophet -upon him blessings and peace-, out of nowhere said, in an audible tone, '*وَعَلَيْهِ السَّلَامُ*', 'Peace be upon him, too!'*

"Whose greetings did you just respond to, Messenger of Allah?" the Companions wondered.

"That of your brother Hubayb", said the Blessed Prophet -upon him blessings and peace-.

Eventually, the idolaters viciously tortured both Companions to martyrdom. The final words of Hubayb -Allah be well-pleased with him- are momentous:

"Dying in this way or that is of no concern, if death comes while a Muslim!"[35]

There…the love and courage of the Companions! They felt little fear at the face of a terrifying scene enough to leave anyone in dread. Their entire concern was to capture the attention of the Blessed Prophet -upon him blessings and peace-. And in the end, their sincere and heartfelt greetings were delivered to their destination, escorted by the Lord Himself. Below is another wonderful example exposing the love and yearning of the Companions for the Noble Messenger -upon him blessings and peace-.

Abdullah ibn Zayd al-Ansari once came next to the Blessed Prophet -upon him blessings and peace- and bemoaned:

"You to me, Messenger of Allah, are dearer than everything I own, my children, my family and even myself. Had there not been the fortune of being able to see you, I would have wished to have been dead!" *He was then reduced to tears.*

---

35 See, Bukhari, Maghazi, 10; Waqidi, Maghazi, p. 280-281.

The Training of Sufism (Sayr Suluk)

"Why are you crying?" asked the Blessed Prophet -upon him blessings and peace-.

"I am crying" replied Zayd -Allah be well-pleased with him- "thinking that you, too, will one day pass away and join the high rank with all the other prophets, while I, even if I were to enter Paradise, will be somewhere lower and hence not be able to see you anymore!"

The Blessed Prophet -upon him blessings and peace-, that ocean of compassion, chose to remain silent awhile. There arrived, in the meantime, the following revelation:

"And whoever obeys Allah and the Messenger, these are with those upon whom Allah has bestowed favors from among the prophets and the truthful and the martyrs and the good, and goodly company are they!" (an-Nisa, 69)

Years later, as Abdullah ibn Zayd al-Ansari -Allah be well-pleased with him- was working away in his garden one day, his son came running and gasping for breath, informed him of the passing away of the Grand Prophet -upon him blessings and peace-, mournfully. Traumatized, Zayd -Allah be well-pleased with him- made the following wish:

"My Allah…Take my sight away, here and now, so that from here on, I do not see anyone else other than my one and only beloved, the Messenger of Allah -upon him blessings and peace-"

His prayer was immediately accepted. He lost his sight there and then.[36]

Love and affection is a like line of electricity that runs between two hearts. Lovers never leave the thought of their beloved out of their hearts and their reminiscence distant from their tongues. Up until the moment of death, they live their lives with a peace of mind brought by the level of sacrifice they have shown, with the calming satisfaction of knowing they have disposed of their wealth and entire existence in the way of the beloved. The *ayah* declares: "And keep up salat, pay the alms and obey the Messenger, so that mercy may be shown to you." (an-Nur, 56)

It is imperative to adhere to the Beloved Prophet -upon him blessings and peace-, the quintessential example, through and through; in line with

---

36 See, Qurtubi, al-Jami li-Ahkami'l-Quran, V, 271.

the principle "A lover is infatuated with everything that the beloved is fond of". Loving and adhering to him is the backbone of Divine Love.

Directly following لاَ إِلَهَ إِلاَّ الله (There is no God but Allah) in the Word of *Tawhid*, in the profession of faith, are the words مُحَمَّدٌ رَسُولُ الله, (Muhammad is His Messenger). Each Word of *tawhid*, every *salawat* is an investment towards acquiring the love of and nearness to the Real. It is this investment that yields the greatest joy both Here and in the Hereafter, that opens the door to all spiritual conquests. The universe is a manifestation of Divine Love. The core essence of this manifestation is the Light of Muhammad, the love of whom is the only road to the Essence of the Divine.

The spirituality of worship, the elegance that pervades behavior, the courtesy that governs morals, the delicacy of the heart, the beauty shone upon appearance, the exquisite charm of languages, the grace that permeates feelings, the profundity of gazes, and in short, all beauties are but sparkles of the love of that Light of Being -upon him blessings and peace- mirrored unto hearts.

Mawlana Rumi beautifully echoes this: "Come, o heart, to the real festival that is union with Muhammad…for the light you see in the universe is but a glow from the face of that Sacred Being."

Repeating *salawat-u sharifa*, at all times and places but in particular at dawn, is of immense importance in allowing the grace of Divine inspiration to leave its impression on the heart, to reinforce the bond with the Blessed Prophet -upon him blessings and peace- and allow one to imitate him spiritually.

The righteous, revived by the reality of the Prophet -upon him blessings and peace-, have enumerated the benefits of saluting the Noble Messenger -upon him blessings and peace- and thereby gaining closeness to Allah, glory unto Him, as follows:

1. A person will have complied with the Divine Command and at the same time complemented the *salawat* of the angels. The *ayah* declares: "Allah and His angels send blessings on the Prophet: O Believers! Send your blessings on him and salute him with all respect!" (al-Ahzab, 56)

It goes without saying that there is a difference of meaning between the Almighty's salutation of the Blessed Prophet -upon him blessings and peace- and the angels' salutation of him, as well as ours. The *salawat* of the Almighty is for Him to show mercy to His Messenger and elevate him. The *salawat* of the angels is for them to pray for his forgiveness. Our *salawat*, the *salawat* of his *ummah*, in contrast, is to pray for the Blessed Prophet -upon him blessings and peace-.

2. It is a means of being forgiven for sins.

The Blessed Prophet -upon him blessings and peace- avows: "Whosoever salutes me once, Allah salutes him ten times, erases ten of his sins and elevates him ten degrees." (Nasai, Sahw, 55)

3. It is a means for drawing closer to the Noble Messenger -upon him blessings and peace- on the Day of Judgment.

"The closest to me on the Day of Judgment", says the Blessed Prophet -upon him blessings and peace-, "are those bless and salute me the most." (Tirmidhi, Witr, 21)

4. The Blessed Prophet -upon him blessings and peace- personally responds to a person who sends him *salawat*. He has said:

"Allah restores me with my spirit to allow me to reply to the *salawat* one sends to me." (Abu Dawud, Manasiq, 96)

5. The name of each person who sends a *salawat* is presented to the Blessed Prophet -upon him blessings and peace-.

"Allah has angels, who journey Earth. They deliver to me the greetings from my *ummah* at the instant." (Nasai, Sahw, 55)

6. Since a person who sends *salawat* has effectively preferred the love of the Prophet -upon him blessings and peace- over any love else, he takes a great step towards embodying his conduct and eventually attains to virtue by shedding his bad habits.

7. Not only does the Prophet's -upon him blessings and peace- love for such a person increase, his love for the Blessed Prophet -upon him blessings and peace- is also preserved and continues to grow.

8. In spite of the incalculable blessings Allah, glory unto Him, has bestowed upon us through the Blessed Prophet -upon him blessings and peace- and the impossibility for us of ever repaying that, through *salawat-u*

sharifa, we will have at least showed our appreciation and taken a humble step towards giving thanks.

9. It is a means for the arrival, upon us, of the mercy of Allah, glory unto Him. The Beloved Prophet -upon him blessings and peace- states:

"Whosoever salutes me once, Allah will show mercy on him ten times the amount." (Muslim, Salat, 70)

10. It is a cause to recollect what is forgotten.

11. It is a means for the acceptance of prayers.

The Blessed Prophet -upon him blessings and peace- once saw a man who, after offering *salat*, began praying without thanking Allah, glory unto Him, and saluting His Messenger.

"The man was too hasty", he remarked, before calling the man next to him and saying, "Should one of you intend on making a prayer, let him begin with thanking and glorifying Allah and then proceed by blessing and saluting me. He can then pray in whichever manner he pleases.' (Tirmidhi, Daawat, 64)

And in another *hadith*: "A prayer does not reach its destination until the person making the prayer sends a *salawat* to the Prophet." (Munziri, at-Targhib wa't-Tarhib, III, 165)

12. It protects one from Divine reproach.

"Let the nose of he, who does not send me a *salawat* despite my name being mentioned next to him, be smothered in dirt." (Tirmidhi, Daawat, 100)

13. The Almighty will suffice for a person who has made a habit of saluting and sending blessings to the Beloved Prophet -upon him blessings and peace- in all his affairs, and will disperse his sorrow both Here and in the Hereafter.

Ubay ibn Qab -Allah be well-pleased with him- recounts:

'I send you lots of salawat'u-sharifah, Messenger of Allah. How often should I do it?' I one day asked.

'As much as you wish' he replied.

'Would it be right if I spared a quarter of my prayer for it?' I again inquired.

'Spare as much from it as you wish', he advised. 'But it will be better for you if you spared more.'

'Then I will spare half', I proposed.

'As you wish…But better if you spared more', said he.

'How about I spared two-thirds then?'

'As you wish… But better if you spared more'.

'How would it be then if I send salawat'us-sharifah in the entire time I spare for prayer?' I then asked.

'If you do', the Messenger of Allah -upon him blessings and peace- replied, 'then Allah will rid you of all your troubles and forgive your sins.'"
(Tirmidhi, Qiyamat, 23/2457)

Salawat-u sharifa enables contact with the spirituality of the Blessed Prophet -upon him blessings and peace- and an opportunity to become illumined with his light. The reward of each *salawat*, on the other hand, is proportionate with one's sincerity and love for the Blessed Prophet -upon him blessings and peace-.

O Prophet, O Messenger…An eternity of *salawat* and *salam* to You!

Dahilak ya Rasulallah…![37]

h. Contemplating Death

Neither is there a space and time, on Earth, to seek refuge from death, nor an opportunity to return from the grave, nor a safe haven from the tremor of the Day of Judgment…

In life, man finds himself constantly trembling between two stark opposites, the joy of life and the dread of death. Without comprehending the true meaning of the ever-flowing life and death, it is not possible to grasp

---

37 "I am in need for your intercession and mercy, Messenger of Allah!"

the mystery and wisdom of creation and the true nature of man. Death, the inevitable that will seize each wayfarer on Earth, is an inescapable riddle all beings with the power of understanding are called upon to solve.

It is declared in the second *ayah* of al-Mulk:

$$\text{اَلَّذِى خَلَقَ الْمَوْتَ وَ الْحَيوةَ لِيَبْلُوَكُمْ اَيُّكُمْ اَحْسَنُ عَمَلاً}$$

"He Who created death and life that He may try which of you is best in deeds…"

Similarly, in the thirty-fifth *ayah* of al-Anbiya, Allah declares: "Every soul must taste of death and We try you by evil and good by way of probation; and to Us you shall be brought back."

If Earth is a Divine school for testing *iman*, death is a necessary law of transition. For this reason Mawlana Rumi -may Allah sanctify his secret- says: "Die for revive!"

The revival of the heart is possible only through abandoning the egoistic. The Blessed Prophet -upon him blessings and peace- urges: "Frequently remember death, which destroys all pleasures from their root." (Tirmidhi, Qiyamah, 26) Contemplating death is to reflect on death before it arrives and thereby consciously prepare to meet the Lord by abandoning all that is egoistic. This is a contemplation and consciousness anchored in *iman*. Man's insatiable, never-ending worldly ambitions, passing hopes and comforts are like autumn leaves that drop on the grave by the second.

Graveyards are home to parents who have exhausted their time on Earth, to children, friends and relatives and loved ones. The grave is the final stop of all the meandering roads of life, whether it is spent on a haystack or in a palace. There is neither a dimension of time to escape it nor space. The Quran accentuates this: "Say: (As for) the death from which you flee, that will surely overtake you, then you shall be sent back to the Knower of the unseen and the seen, and He will inform you of that which you did." (al-Juma, 8)

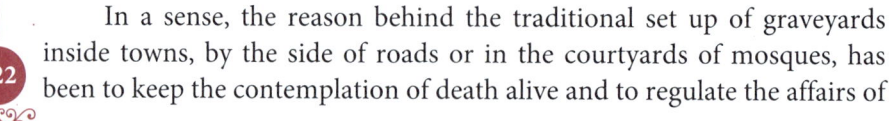

In a sense, the reason behind the traditional set up of graveyards inside towns, by the side of roads or in the courtyards of mosques, has been to keep the contemplation of death alive and to regulate the affairs of the world accordingly. Solemnly enshrouded in the silence of death, each gravestone is a fiery preacher through its presence alone. The weight of death is too intense for the weak shoulders of words to bear, a terrifying event before which all powers and sovereignties melt away.

The world is a deceitful reverie, the Hereafter a reality without death. More often than most, man is a slave to the lies that reflect from the mirror of life in its thousands of alluring images. What then is life, which continues spinning its web of lies and disloyalty, but a place of deceit?

Does not man take a lesson from the fact that the mill of time relentlessly grinds the youth and vivacity of all beings mortal? How great a deception it is to lead a life that is oblivious to the reality of the Hereafter, allured by ego provoking glitters of the world, carried away childishly playing with toys without reality! Playing during childhood, lust during youth, carelessness during maturity and hankering, with a deep set remorse, after things gone by at old age, is all to which a neglectful life amounts.

Death is one's personal Day of Judgment. We must wake up before our Day of Judgment lest we become one of those who are filled with remorse. That each mortal being will encounter the Angel of Death, at place and time unknown, is inevitable. There is no place to flee from death. Without wasting the least amount of time, man must therefore "Run to Allah..." (ad-Dhariyat, 50) and acknowledge that the one and only refuge is the mercy of the Lord.

The clearest motive for the contemplation of death is enclosed within that permanent silence, between sealed and purple lips of the dead. The only response the world can offer to the eloquent warning of death, are tears and dry sobs.

How strange it is that man is so prone to fooling himself on Earth, on which he remains only for a handful of days, as a guest. In spite of witnessing funerals almost every day, he thinks he is a far remove from death. He lulls himself in supposing to be the owner of what he possesses, things he could easily lose at any second. But man is destined for death as early as the moment his spirit is clad in flesh and ushered through a door to enter life on Earth. Although the door leads to a training road for the ultimate path, more often than not, he remains ignorant of it. Then a day comes when his spirit is stripped of the flesh and he is given a farewell to the grave, the door of the Hereafter, the journey with no return.

Each moment that ticks by takes us closer to the dawn of truth, as eloquently expressed in the *ayah*: "He whom we bring unto old age, We reverse him in creation (making him go back to weakness after strength). Have ye then no sense?" (Yasin, 68)

The *ayah* advises man in the most beautiful manner imaginable. The most discernible feature of the world is that it is disloyal. It hastily takes back what it reluctantly gives. It raises a person one day, only to throw him in a pit the next. It is like a shade that flees each time one tries to catch it. Yet, the more one runs away from it, the more it pursues him. Carried away in thinking that it is only a matter of time before one grabs hold of what he had been pursuing all along, he is suddenly interrupted by the irreversible call of death. Fall in love with the world it becomes a shrewd hag, capriciously slapping one across the face at will, whose nagging and complaining is almost ceaseless. It quickly sells out those who are attached to it.

It ought to be borne in mind that there is neither a space nor time on Earth to seek refuge from death, nor an opportunity to return from the grave, nor a safe haven from the tremor of the Day of Judgment. "Who is the most intelligent Muslim?" a Companion once asked the Blessed Prophet -upon him blessings and peace-. "It is he who frequently remembers death and prepares in the best way for the Hereafter. Those are the truly intelligent", replied he. (Ibn Majah, Zuhd, 31)

The Beloved Messenger -upon him blessings and peace- has again said, "Remember death and how flesh and bones decay after death. Whosoever desires the Hereafter should abandon the dazzle of the life on Earth." (Tirmidhi, Qiyamah, 24) "Death suffices as advice", says Fudayl ibn Iyad.

A Companion had passed away. Others spoke of him with praise, fondly reminiscing the great amount of deeds he used to offer when alive. The Blessed Prophet -upon him blessings and peace- was meanwhile listening to them, in silence. Once they finished talking, he asked them:

"Did the person, of whom you speak, frequently remember death?"

"No", they replied.

The Training of Sufism (Sayr Suluk)

"In that case, was he mostly able to abandon the unnecessary and excessive desires of his ego?"

Once again, the Companions responded in the negative. The Blessed Prophet -upon him blessings and peace- thereupon said:

"Then it seems your friend was not what you think him to be." (Haythami, Majmau'z-Zawaid, X, 308-9)

Abdullah ibn Omar -Allah be well-pleased with him- recounts how the Noble Messenger -upon him blessings and peace- held him by the arm one day and advised: "Behave like a stranger, a wayfarer even, on Earth! Count yourself among the dead, the dwellers of the grave."

Mujahid ibn Jabr r.alayh, a prominent scholar of the *Tabiun* generation, says, "Once Ibn Omar -Allah be well-pleased with him- completed narrating this *hadith*, he advised me with the following:

'Do not think of night, Mujahid, once you reach morning! And do not think of morning once you reach night! Make the most of your health before illness and life before death! For you, servant of Allah, do not know which condition (dead or alive) you will be the next day!'" (Tirmidhi, Zuhd, 25)

Anas ibn Malik -Allah be well-pleased with him- explains: "The earth exclaims ten advises to man, each day:

Son of Adam!

1. You walk on me, yet your return is to me.

2. You commit all kinds of sins on me, yet you will be punished in me.

3. You laugh and have fun on me, yet you will cry in me.

4. You take pleasure on me, yet you will grieve in me.

5. You hoard wealth on me yet will remorse in me.

6. You feed on *haram* on me, yet maggots will feed on you in me.

7. You act arrogantly on me, yet will be lowered and despised in me.

8. You joyously walk on me, yet you will be immersed in sorrow in me.

9. You walk under daylight on me yet will be left in the dark in me.

Sufism: A Path Towards the Internalization of Faith (Ihsân)

10. You walk among crowds on me, yet will enter me all alone." (Ibn Hajar al-Asqalani, Munabbihat, 37)

Speaking of Quss ibn Saida, a man of wisdom and eloquence, the Blessed Prophet -upon him blessings and peace- one day said: "One time at the Uqaz Fair, I heard Quss ibn Saida addressing people on camelback, where he said:

'People! Come, listen, learn and take a lesson! Whoever lives dies, whoever dies perishes and whatever is bound to happen happens. Rain falls, grass grows and children are born to take over the place of their parents. Then they all depart. Occurrences are ceaseless; they all follow up on one another. The skies are filled with news, the ground with lessons to be taken. The earth is a mattress stretched out and the skies a lofty ceiling. The stars will expire and the seas will come to a rest. Whoever comes does not stay and whoever leaves does not return. Who knows? Is it that they are so comfortable where they are that they remain there or are they withheld and put to sleep?

People of Iyad! Where are your fathers and forefathers? Where are the people of Ad and Thamud who built exquisite mansions and abodes of stone? Where are the Nimrod and the Pharaoh, who beside himself in worldly riches said to his people 'Am I not your greatest lord?

The Earth ended up grinding them all in its mill. Even their bones have now rotten away, scattered. Their abodes stand deserted, now inhabited by dogs. Do not ever become heedless like them! Do not tread their path! Everything is mortal, only the Almighty is not.

There is many a passage to enter the river of death, but alas, no way out!'"[38]

Death, the final curtain of the play of life, is like a mirror that shall reveal each person's own destiny. For a person who lives under the domination of his ego, with the world his only purpose, the grave appears as a dark labyrinth. Even the remembrance of death afflicts him with a pain incomparable to anything else. However, if man is able surmount the obstacle that is the ego and through the contemplation of death, covers the distance towards attaining an angelic nature, a capability hidden in his spirit, death then becomes a necessary stage of reaching Allah, glory unto

---

[38] See, Bayhaqi, Kitabu'z-Zuhd, II, 264; Ibn Kathir, al-Bidaya, II, 234-241; Haythami, Majmau'z-Zawaid, IX, 418.

Him, the Almighty and the Unimaginable. And death, which often sends cold shivers down the spines of ordinary human beings, thereby instantly turns to an excitement of reuniting with the beloved. In the words of the Sufi great Mawlana Rumi -may Allah sanctify his secret-; a death of the kind is a *shab-i arus*, a groom's night. This is a path that beautifies even the most dreadful thing man can experience, death. To beautify death, it is necessary to attain to a spiritual perfection through repentance, piety, and trust in the Lord, contentedness, Divine remembrance and patience.

In terms of the influence it wields in purifying the heart, the contemplation of death is second to none. Rabi ibn Husayn says, in this regard: "I fear my heart would become corrupted should it abandon the remembrance of death. I would have sat in the graveyard until my very last breath, had I been certain that I would not have defied the practices of my predecessors by doing so." (Bayhaki, Kitabu'z-Zuhd, p. 212)

The heart quivers amid the convulsions of the spirit and the ego until death. Death is a necessary prelude to the journey of the afterlife. Before setting out on this journey, preparing the heart for death through *marifatullah*, imparting unto it a spiritual health and serenity that would secure it from the anxiety and fear of death, are tasks one cannot afford to neglect. If successful, the underlying mystery to 'die before death' becomes unraveled, whereby man replaces the forlorn dominance of his ego with the love of and abidance by Allah, glory unto Him, in the most perfect sense of the term.

i. Being in the Company of the Pious and the Righteous

> *"O you who believe! Be careful of your duty to Allah and be with the righteous." (at-Tawba, 119)*

Guarding the heart from *masiwa* or anything other than the Lord, and rendering it receivable only to the good, requires one to accompany the pious and the righteous, from who one can receive spiritual benefit. Unlike the other parts of the body which come under the direct command of willpower, the heart recognizes no such authority and has an undying tendency to be swayed by surrounding influences.

The heart assumes the shape, color and rhythm of the environment it is in. But this is only the beginning of certain influences taking root and settling inside the heart. The influences that arise thereafter to take the heart in their command may turn out to be either positive or negative, depending on their resemblance to the tendencies that have already taken root inside the heart. So the heart is exposed to a grave danger, unless it is subjected to influences of a good nature and given thereby a certain blend. Being exposed to external influences, the heart is either swayed by them to the degree of its love for them or repels them to the degree of its hatred against them. The correct use of love and hate is therefore vital in spiritually raising or lowering a human being. Meting out love and hate to their right places does indeed play an important hand in reviving one spiritually. In contrast, showing love to those who are not worthy of it or hating those who do not deserve it in the least, renders one miserable, in proportion with the intensity of love or hate felt.

By keeping these considerations in mind, the need to, and the importance of, accompanying the righteous servants of Allah, glory unto Him, and entering their circle of influence, as demanded by spiritual perfection, becomes all the more glaring. But here, too, the benefit to be received is only proportionate to the love felt for the righteous. A dull and uninspired accompaniment barren of spiritual depth does not bring about the required end, bar some minimal benefits. Illustrative of this is the below account featuring Bayazid Bistami -may Allah sanctify his secret-:

One of his disciples one day asked Bayazid, "Would you be so kind as to give me a piece of your fur coat so I could carry it with me for spiritual benefit (tabarruk)?

"Son", replied Bayazid, "not even skinning Bayazid and entering inside him will be of any benefit if you are not upright, let alone possessing a piece of his coat!"

The entire universe displays a tendency towards unification. This stems from the fact that the essence of being is one and the same. This tendency towards unification, of becoming one with another and seeking identity thereof, is valid in both physicality and spirituality. For example, if a bottle filled with a liquid of a sharp odor is spilled in one corner of a room, the emanating smell passes through from one particle of air that has fully absorbed it to another, until it becomes equal in all parts of the air inside the room. This is a law of physics, equally valid for all opposite qualities, like hot and cold, or what have you. But for this law of identity to manifest itself in human life, a medium to enable this unification is needed. And that is love. Colloquially, this has been made famous by the saying, "There runs a path from one heart to another".

Forceful and energetic characters have generally been sources of inspiration for the weaker. The urge to imitate is in fact a tendency inherent in human disposition. A child regulates his entire actions and behavior with imitation. This tendency continues to exist in varying degrees even after childhood. Thus, the degree of concentration the pious and the righteous execute in their deeds of worship, their supreme levels of moral conduct, their spiritual eloquence and depth, rouses feelings of imitation and abidance in those around. It was through none other than this urge to imitate the Blessed Prophet -upon him blessings and peace-, the quintessential exemplar that enabled the Companions, nearly all of whom had notorious pasts, to become peaks of virtue.

We are aware from experience that by endearing himself to students, a teacher makes the subject taught both easy and enjoyable for the student. Love plays somewhat a magical role in converting difficulties to ease. If there is love, any given task is fulfilled with ease, however burdensome it may be. On the other hand, the burden of a task that is loathed feels much heavier than what it really is. Love makes a twenty *rakah salat* of *tarawih* feel like a breeze, while lack of love turns the four *rakah salat* of *fajr* into a burden. Sloppiness and laziness, here, is just an outcome of a lack of love. When all these are considered, allowing oneself to be charged with love by virtue of accompanying the pious and righteous, is sure to serve like a magic wand that turns many an imposing slope on the spiritual path into a flat, submissive plane.

On another note, to maintain the heart's peace, one must stay away from becoming intimate with the ignorant and the perverse (*fasiq*). After all, a wind that blows through carrion or a cesspool absorbs its filthy odor and spreads it around, stifling breaths and disturbing spirits.

Sheikh Ubaydullah Ahrar -may Allah sanctify his secret- gave this advice to his friends: "Being in the company of the heedless and the unmindful weakens the heart, leaves the spirit disorganized and the heart in a state of disarray."

Bayazid Bistami -may Allah sanctify his secret- once did feel such disarray and restlessness come over him. No matter what he did, he could not overcome it. Turning to those around him, he finally asked, "Check around to see if there is a stranger among us." Though they looked around, they did not come across a stranger. But Bayazid was adamant. "Look properly…especially where the staffs are", he insisted. So they did. And resting against the other staffs, they found a staff belonging to an unmindful man, which they quickly took outside. Only then could Bayazid recover his peace of mind.

Likewise, Ubaydullah Ahrar -may Allah sanctify his secret- once said to a friend who at the time was paying him a visit, "You smell of a stranger", adding, after a brief pause, "It could be that you have worn the clothes of a strange person." "That is quite true", the man replied, astonished, as he quickly went out and returned after changing his clothes.

The ability of the transmission that is characteristic of negative qualities is valid also for positive qualities. The best example of this is the case of Yaqub (a.s) and Yusuf (a.s). Seeing his own image and characteristics in Yusuf (a.s), Yaqub (a.s) grew fonder of him compared to his other children. His identification with Yusuf (a.s) was to such an immense degree that later, as Yusuf's (a.s) shirt was being delivered to him from Egypt, he was able to smell it despite being a great distance away in Canaan. No other person, even Judah, the deliverer of the shirt, could sense the mystery of that fragrance. Only when the shirt was rubbed on Yaqub's (a.s) eyes was he able to regain his sight. And this is a manifestation of the spiritual bond that has infiltrated even the seemingly lifeless matter. A simple reflection on how spirituality infuses even matter bears out the need to diligently protect the heart, doubtless more sensitive than matter.

Sufi greats say:

"Even lifeless objects receive a reflection of people's deeds and morals. There is therefore a great difference of value between a deed of worship offered in a place where sins of all kind run rife and a place that has become home to deeds of righteousness. It for this reason that a *salat* offered in the vicinity of the *Kaaba* is far more superior to that offered elsewhere."

The Training of Sufism (Sayr Suluk)

In sharp contrast to places of such inspiring spirituality, there are others that only give off heaviness and gloom. On the return from the troublesome Campaign of Tabuk, the Companions reached the Valley of Hijr, where they entered the rock-cut former dwellings of the Thamud Tribe. The Blessed Prophet (s.a) thereupon warned them:

"This is the location where Allah the Almighty destroyed Thamud", he said. *"So do not take any water from here lest you receive a share of wrath."*

"We have filled our water bottles, Messenger of Allah. And what's more, we have even prepared some dough using this water", said the Companions.

"Empty out the water and feed the dough to the camels", commanded he. (Bukhari, Anbiya, 17)

Such *ahadith* are living examples of how the spiritual state of a given location spreads and reflects even onto lifeless beings.

To develop and flourish the spiritual characteristics of the heart, one must strive to receive spiritual enlightenment and energy from the conduct of the pious and the righteous. The occasion most favorable to receiving this spiritual reflection is a *sohbah*, a spiritual talk or speech. This is verified by Luqman's (a.s) advice to his son:

"Remain by the side of the knowledgeable and try not to detach yourself from *sohbah*; for Allah revives the heart with the light of wisdom, just like He revives the parched earth with rain." (Ahmed ibn Hanbal, Kitabu'z-Zuhd, no: 551)

The following *hadith* superbly expresses the importance of *sohbah* and its awaiting benefits for a believer: "Should a group of people gather in a house among the houses of Allah to read the Book of Allah and discuss it amongst themselves, *sakina* (spiritual serenity) will surely come over them; they will be encompassed by Divine mercy and surrounded by angels. And Allah will mention them in His own presence." (Abu Dawud, Witr, 14; Ibn Maja, Muqaddima, 17)

Abu Idris al-Hawlani recounts:

Sufism: A Path Towards the Internalization of Faith (Ihsân)

"I had entered the Umayyad Mosque in Damascus. Inside was an amiable young man, with pearly teeth. Men had gathered around him, speaking to each other about certain things. Whenever they would fall into dispute, they would ask the young man and accept his adjudication. I soon found out that the young man was none other than Muadh ibn Jabal -Allah be well-pleased with him-.

In the early hours of the next day, I again went to the mosque. He was already there before me, offering salat when I happened to step inside. I waited for him to finish. Then I went next to him and after giving him my greetings, said:

'I assure you that I love you for the sake of Allah!'

'Is it really for the sake of Allah?' asked Muadh -Allah be well-pleased with him-. 'Yes', I replied. He repeated the question three times and each time I replied with the same word.

Then grabbing hold of my shirt, he pulled me closer and said, 'Glad tidings to you, then…for I heard the Messenger of Allah -upon him blessings and peace- narrate these words from his Lord:

'My love is obliged to those who love each other, remain together and visit each other for the sake of I and who have devoted themselves to My pleasure.'" (Imam Malik, Muwattaa, Shaar, 5)

The Almighty states:

$$\text{يَآ اَيُّهَا الَّذِينَ اٰمَنُوا اتَّقُوا اللّٰهَ وَ كُونُوا مَعَ الصَّادِقِينَ}$$

"O you who believe! Be careful of your duty to Allah and be with the righteous." (at-Tawba, 119)

As aforementioned, a spiritual mindset (*hal*) is transmitted in proportion with existing feelings of love and affinity. In order to perfect *iman*, it is essential to establish affinity with the pious and the righteous, to love them and be close to them as possible and allow this tendency to grow stronger to ultimately obtain the desired result.

The Blessed Prophet -upon him blessings and peace- wonderfully articulates the importance of accompanying the righteous in the following words: "The likeness of a good friend and a bad friend is like a musk-carrier and a blacksmith. The musk-carrier either offers you some of his fragrance or you buy some from him. As for the blacksmith, he either burns your clothes or spreads to you the smell of soot." (Bukhari, Buyuu, 38)

Besides the importance of being with the righteous in life, the Noble Messenger -upon him blessings and peace- also underlines the importance of neighboring them in the grave: "Bury your dead next to the righteous." (Darimi, Musnad, I, 102)

Even obtaining one's needs through the righteous has been made mention. Ibnu'l-Firasi narrates that his father had once asked the Blessed Prophet -upon him blessings and peace- whether he should ask others for what his needs.

"No, do not!" replied he, adding, "But should you fall in a situation where you must, at least ask the righteous." (Abu Dawud, Zakat, 28; Nasai, Zakat, 84)

The Beloved Prophet -upon him blessings and peace- has likewise stated: "There are men who are the keys to *dhikrullah*. Seeing them, people instantly remember Allah." (Haythami, X, 78)

Qadi Shurayh had written a letter to Omar -Allah be well-pleased with him-, asking how he, as judge, should adjudicate between people. Omar -Allah be well-pleased with him- replied in the following:

"Adjudicate between them with what is revealed in the Book of Allah. If you cannot derive a ruling from there then resort to the *Sunnah* of the Messenger of Allah -upon him blessings and peace-. If you cannot derive a ruling in either, then make use of the judgments of the righteous. Given you cannot find a ruling there either, then it is up to you whether you go ahead and adjudicate or step back. I am of the opinion that stepping back will be better for you." (Nasai, Qudat, 11/3)

A dervish once appealed to Bayazid Bistami -may Allah sanctify his secret- to recommend to him a deed that would bring him closer to Allah, glory unto Him.

"Love the righteous servants of Allah! Love them so that they return your love. Try and find a way inside their heart, for Allah, gazes at the heart of the wise three-hundred-and-sixty times a day. Let Him locate you there during those gazes!"

It is for no other reason that Sufi training demands a continuous practice of *rabitah*[39], to ensure that the *murid*, or the disciple, keeps his love for the righteous, with whom he is affined, ever alive.

It should be remembered that one, gripped by sin and wickedness, could prevent incurring many more spiritual losses to come, simply by virtue of this spiritual connection. And furthermore, through this spiritual connection, he could even obtain for himself many more spiritual benefits to come.

Proportionate with the intensity of love, *rabitah* establishes a spiritual power line, highly charged with spiritual sensing and feeling. A spiritual transaction thereupon begins between the two persons on the opposite ends of this line, conducive to unification. While the person who is the recipient in this transaction proceeds spiritually, the righteous or the pious, who is the transmitter, may suffer to a certain degree. This process is where the righteous, the source of spiritual inspiration, cleanses those who come to him, tainted with scores of spiritual dirt, a procedure comparable to washing dirty overalls. Such righteous people, who are licensed to guide (*irshad*), purify and get rid of the dirt and rust of those they are obliged to train, in the vast ocean that is their inner, spiritual world. People of this ilk play the role of purifiers in society, like plants that transform certain elements, rotten and decomposed, to colorful flowers and delicious fruits.

With that said, in the life of every righteous and pious person with the license to guide, there is a phase of seclusion, be it short or long. Not only is this from the desire to get closer to the Lord, it is also from the need to distance oneself from the ugly aspects of life, for a certain amount of time.

A love reinforced with intimacy ultimately allows the lover to become annihilated in the existence of the beloved. Only at the end of love does this come about, as elegantly expressed by Mawlana Rumi -may Allah sanctify his secret-:"A river that reaches the sea is a river no more; it becomes a part of the sea it enters. A morsel of bread we eat dissolves in our body and

---

39   For more information, see pages **249-257**.

becomes a part of us. Just the same the existence of the lover dissolves in that of the beloved, depending on the intensity of his love.'

Mawlana Rumi -may Allah sanctify his secret- continues to elaborate the condition of the spirit undergoing the experience of unification and annihilation: "Love came and like blood, filled my veins and skin. It took me away from me, filling my existence with the Beloved. The Beloved has covered the entire particles of my body. What is left to me is just a name. The rest is all Him…"

These are exactly what are referred to in *tasawwuf* as *fanafillah* and *bakabillah*[40]. But to proceed on this path that leads to the love of the Lord, it is vital for the heart to acquire a character that is both worthy of and adequate to this task. And this is acquired through exercises of humanly love.

Since it serves as a means to prepare the heart for true love, provided of course it does not transgress the legitimate bounds, love between human beings is tolerated and referred to as metaphorical love (*ashk-i majazi*); just like the love one feels for the members of his family. Yet in defining love and determining its level, one must stay true to a certain guideline, for which again the words of Mawlana Rumi -may Allah sanctify his secret- provide a superb blueprint:

"Have mercy…love is a good thing. What damages it are only your evil habits. You call lust by the name of love. Alas…if only you knew how great the distance is that separates love from lust!

Divine love and ecstasy keeps a believer awake. Worldly and licentious lusts turn man into a fool and leave him stupefied. Love is the burning and the fluttering of man who is created of water and earth. The flow of blood through the veins is unimportant…the burning of the lungs with love is."

At the peak of mortal love, the lover becomes one with the beloved, to the extent of the love felt. In *tasawwuf*, the furthermost point the disciple

---

[40] Sufi sources offer various definitions for these concepts. Just to quote one such definition: *Fanafillah* is to become annihilated in Allah; that is to shed from the heart all interests that pertain to the world and to become purified from the attributes of the ego. *Bakabillah* is for the servant, who has purged his spirit of all attributes of the ego, to embody the morals of the Lord, which is realized only by enshrouding oneself in the morals and spirituality of the Blessed Prophet -upon him blessings and peace- and the Holy Quran.

reaches in his love for his master and -virtually- becomes annihilated in the master's existence is called *fana fi's-sheikh*.

Abu Bakr -Allah be well-pleased with him- would undergo distinct feelings of ecstasy and rapture each time he met and conversed with the Blessed Prophet -upon him blessings and peace-. Even being in the Prophet's -upon him blessings and peace- presence would, far from appeasing them, only aggravate his love and yearning for him.

One time, the Noble Messenger -upon him blessings and peace- remarked, "I have never benefited from anyone's wealth as much as I have benefited from Abu Bakr's". Upon hearing these compliments, Abu Bakr -Allah be well-pleased with him- could not help but feel he was being considered as someone 'other'. Since it was he who was the person addressed and insofar as 'being addressed' implied an otherness, he felt left out of the Prophet's -upon him blessings and peace- intimacy. He erupted with a scorching feeling of agony deep inside, an agony of separation. Fretful that he might be considered as someone 'other', he exclaimed: "Are not my wealth and I for you alone, Messenger of Allah?" (Ibn Majah, Muqaddima, 11)

To depict this profound state of mind in the wonderful words of Mawlana Rumi -may Allah sanctify his secret-:

"What is love, what is one's own life…what are pearls and corals so long as they are not spent, sacrificed for the beloved?"

Similarly, at another time, Abu Bakr -Allah be well-pleased with him- had become bedridden from grief simply upon hearing that the Blessed Prophet -upon him blessings and peace- had fallen ill. It was owing to this identification that spawned the following words of the Blessed Prophet -upon him blessings and peace-, which illustrates the union of spirit and the flow that occurs between one heart and the other:

"Abu Bakr is of me, I am of him. He is my brother here and in the Hereafter." (Daylami, Musnad, I, 437)

Illustrating no less the flow from one heart to another are the words the Blessed Prophet -upon him blessings and peace- uttered while on his deathbed:

"Close all the doors apart from Abu Bakr's." (Bukhari, Ashabu'n-Nabi, 3)

The Training of Sufism (Sayr Suluk)

Sheikh Sadi Shirazi explains the transmission of *hal*, the spiritual mindset, in the following: "It was because it remained steadfast by the side of the righteous that the dog of the Sleepers of the Cave earned a lofty honor by being mentioned in the Quran. Lut's (a.s) wife, on the other hand, brought shame upon herself by remaining by the side of the perverse."

The Blessed Prophet -upon him blessings and peace- warns against the damages incurred on the heart through befriending the ignorant: "There will come a time when a certain faction from among my *ummah*, claiming to be knowledgeable in religion, will read the Quran and say, 'We will go to the governors, benefit from their worldly possessions and keep their noses out of religion'. But this will not be the case. Just like one may only collect prickles from a thorn, they will only collect what is harmful from them.' (Ibn Majah, Muqaddima, 23)

In his *Gulistan*, Sheikh Sadi uses a parable to explain the transmission of the spiritual mindset that takes place through befriending the pious and the righteous and the consequent 'identification':

"A man goes to the baths. There, one of his friends hands him a beautifully scented earthen to clean himself with. The earthen gives off an exquisite scent that enchants his soul. The man asks the earthen:

'You delightful thing…I am enchanted by your wonderful scent. So tell me, are you of musk or amber?'

'I am of neither musk nor amber', replies the earthen. 'I am simply of ordinary soil, as you know it. Yet, I was standing under the sapling of a rose, moistened every day from the dews that would drop onto me from the rosebud. The scent you smell belongs to no other than that rose.'"

As hinted at by the inner meaning of the parable, those who open their hearts to the righteous with sincerity, submission and humbleness, gradually begin to reflect the beauty they are striving to attain. Just like the side of the moon that reflects the rays of light that radiate from the sun, thereby becoming a part of the sun itself despite having no light of its own, people of such caliber virtually act like candles, lighting up the pitch dark nights of humankind, blackened from the dust of oppression.

Sufism: A Path Towards the Internalization of Faith (Ihsân)

j. Embodying Good Morals

> "*There will be nothing weighing heavier on the scales of a Muslim in the Hereafter than good morals. Allah the Almighty hates those who act and speak ill.*" (Tirmidhi, Birr, 62)

Allah, glory unto Him, has endowed human beings with an aptitude for elegance, grace and spiritual depth. The value of a human being is only to the extent he allows these attributes to flourish on the soil of his heart. Becoming a human being, not only physically but also and more importantly spiritually, makes it necessary to embody good morals and render bad habits ineffective.

Hearts replete with spirituality act as agents manifesting good morals, righteous conduct and a spiritual state of mind. It is in this manner that a servant may live up to the fact of being created in the best fashion.

In contrast, in hearts that have been vanquished by the ego, *kufr*, *shirk*, wicked habits, lustfulness and delusive whispers (*waswasah*) run rife. And eventually, the heart forgets its Lord and becomes blinded, going in the complete opposite direction of its reason of existence. Worse still, it can even become baser than witless creatures.

The Creator of the Universe addresses man with a stern warning, calling him to come to his senses and not debase himself:

يَآ اَيُّهَا الْاِنْسَانُ مَا غَرَّكَ بِرَبِّكَ الْكَرِيمِ الَّذِى خَلَقَكَ فَسَوّٰيكَ فَعَدَلَكَ فِى اَيِّ صُورَةٍ مَا شَآءَ رَكَّبَكَ

"O man! What has made you careless concerning your Lord, the Bountiful, Who created you, then fashioned, then proportioned you? Into whatsoever form He will, He casted you." (al-Infitar, 6-8)

The Almighty also declares, in the Quran:

وَ اللّٰهُ يَدْعُوٓا اِلٰى دَارِ السَّلَامِ

The Training of Sufism (Sayr Suluk)

"Allah invites to the *Daru's-Salam*." (Yunus, 25)

Yet, every invitation comes with its conditions. Not everyone is ever invited to a certain place. There are always conditions of acceptability. Only with a *qalbu's-salim*, a refined or peaceful heart, may one attend the Divine invitation to the *Daru's-Salam*, The Abode of Peace.

The sole condition for living morally, in a manner befitting of human existence, is to get hold of the sublime objectives laid down by religion. The perfection of human existence and the peak of good morals, likewise, is the Blessed Prophet -upon him blessings and peace-. Both confirming and affirming this, are the words of the Almighty:

"And you stand on an exalted standard of character." (al-Qalam, 4)

The Beloved Prophet -upon him blessings and peace- states in a number of *ahadith*:

"My Lord has trained me and how beautifully has he trained me." (Suyuti, al-Jamiu's-Saghir, I, 12)

"There will be nothing weighing heavier on the scales of a Muslim in the Hereafter than good morals. Allah the Almighty hates those who act and speak ill." (Tirmidhi, Birr, 62)

"I have been sent to perfect good morals.' (Imam Malik, Muwattaa, Husnu'l-Khulq, 8)

Prophet Muhammad Mustafa -upon him blessings and peace- is not just the only prophet, but also the only person in history to have every single, intricate detail of his life documented. His every word, action and expressed feeling was recorded and bequeathed to entire human kind as an emblem of honor. His *uswatu'l-hasanah*; that is his quintessential example; has provided a blueprint for entire humanity, declared by the Almighty in the Quran as: "Certainly you have in the Messenger of Allah an excellent exemplar for him who hopes in Allah and the latter day and remembers Allah much." (al-Ahzab, 21)

While it is imperative to seek a share of the Blessed Prophet's -upon him blessings and peace- heart-world and his impeccable morals, this may take place only to the degree of love felt for him and the extent in which one enshrouds himself in his spirituality. Through the reflection of and spiritual coloring (*insibagh*) received therefrom, a Muslim acquires a zest for character traits like compassion, mercy, benevolence, forgiveness and sharing what he has with his brothers and sisters of religion. Of this, the Companions, saints, the righteous and the pious provide consummate examples.

By drawing nearer to the reality of the Blessed Prophet -upon him blessings and peace- and virtually becoming moths around the flame of his spirituality, these believers of elegance have always considered annihilation in the Prophet's -upon him blessings and peace- spirituality as the greatest blessing one may receive in the entire world. Muslims, throughout history, who have been able to acquire a share of the quintessential example of the Prophet -upon him blessings and peace-, have thereby allowed the growth of their *iman* to its furthermost extent and by maturing the joy for the Divine embedded in their natural disposition, have acted as a torch for humankind. In loving *him* lies the most effective cure for ill and unmindful hearts.

Below are just some examples typical of his towering moral character and conduct:

The Blessed Prophet's -upon him blessings and peace- countenance was the most sparkling and attractive of all countenances. Immediately after the Hijra, Abdullah ibn Salam, then a Jewish scholar, had inquisitively asked around to catch a glimpse of him and remarked, upon finally seeing him:

"Such a face can never lie". These were his final words as a Jew, as he embraced Islam at the instant. (Tirmidhi, Qiyama, 42/2485; Ahmed ibn Hanbal, Musnad, V, 451)

Endowed with an immense degree of beauty, awe inspiring majesty and a dazzling elegance, he really needed neither an extra proof, nor a miracle to prove the fact that he was the Messenger of the Lord. Whenever the Blessed Prophet -upon him blessings and peace- would become pleased or displeased, one could immediately see it in his expression. His pure body had embodied an intense vigor, a strong sense of *haya* and a rigorous determination. He was more decent than a maiden enshrouded in her covering. As for the depth of the sensitivity of his heart, it is impossible to articulate.

Never uttering a word in vain, his every word conveyed wisdom and advice. There was not the least place for backbiting and futile talk in his

The Training of Sufism (Sayr Suluk)

vocabulary. He would talk to people according to their capacities. He was kind and modest. Though he would never express his joy through excessive laughter, his face always put a warm smile on view. Suddenly seeing him would overwhelm one in awe; though a brief conversation was enough to implant feelings of deep love and affection towards him.

He would treat the righteous with respect, according to their ranks of piety. His relatives were treated by him with honor and respect. It was habitual for him to extend the tenderness he nurtured for his family and friends to the rest of society, saying: "You will not have become a matured Muslim until you wish for your brothers what you wish upon yourselves." (Bukhari, Iman, 7; Muslim, Iman, 71-72) He would treat his servants inexpressibly well, clothing and feeding them with whatever he clothed and fed himself. Generous and compassionate, the Prophet -upon him blessings and peace- had struck a perfect balance between courage and kindness, compliant with the given circumstance.

The Messenger of Allah -upon him blessings and peace- was a man of his word, always true to his promise. Superior to all in terms of virtue, intelligence and acuteness of mind, his physical and spiritual uniqueness could not possibly be overstressed.

He had a constant look of sorrow about him. Withdrawn into an uninterrupted state of contemplation, he only spoke when necessary. His spell of silence was lengthy. With that said, he would complete every sentence he begun, collecting layers of meaning in just a few words. He would utter his words piece by piece. With a gentle predisposition, his stature was nevertheless majestically imposing.

He would never get up from his seat when angry. And never would he become angry, unless there was an infringement of right. Given there was an infringement of right gone unnoticed, his anger would never subside until the right was restored. And afterward, he would once again resign to his usual composure. Getting angry on his own behalf was not his nature; he would never develop a vendetta and become quarrelsome in a personal matter.

He would never enter the household of anyone without permission. Once he returned home, he would divide the time he would spend there into three parts: the first for Allah, glory unto Him, the second for his family and the third for himself, though only by name, as in effect he would spare that time for all kinds of people, common and elite, depriving not a single person of his precious time, leaving not a single heart unconquered.

The Blessed Prophet's -upon him blessings and peace- each state and behavior was an expression of *dhikrullah*.

At mosques, he would assume different places for seating, to prevent others from making a habit of sitting in a particular place, wary of the consecration of certain places and cites. He disliked the adoption of conceited behavior in public. Upon entering an assembly, he would take whatever seat available, insisting others do the same.

Whenever a person wanted something from him in sorting out a particular problem, irrespective of the importance of the favor, the Blessed Prophet -upon him blessings and peace- would never feel at ease until that need was aptly taken care of. Given the impossibility of sorting the problem out, then the Prophet -upon him blessings and peace- would at least comfort the person with some soothing and heartening words. He was a confidant for all. No matter what their social classes were, whether rich or poor, wise or ignorant, people would receive even treatment next to him, solely from the vantage of being a human being. All his gatherings were environments teeming with kindness, wisdom, manners, patience and trust, first and foremost in Allah, glory unto Him, then in each other.

Never would he publicly condemn a person for his shortcomings. When the need would appear to warn a particular person, the Noble Messenger -upon him blessings and peace- would do as little to subtly yet elegantly hint at it, without breaking the person's heart. He would say: "Do not rejoice over a disaster that befalls your brother…for Allah may relieve him through His mercy and test you with the same disaster." (Tirmidhi, Qiyamah, 54)

Not only was he never preoccupied with prying the concealed flaws of others, he was stern in prohibiting others from getting busy with such ignobility. Prying and suspicion of others was, after all, banned by the Almighty.

The Light of Being -upon him blessings and peace- would not speak, unless with an aim for Divine pleasure. His conversations would emit spiritual ecstasy. So attentively would the Companions listen to him as he spoke and so captivated they would be that in the words of Omar -Allah be well-pleased with him-, if a bird were to come and perch on their heads, it could have been able to remain there undisturbed for hours on end. (Abu Dawud, Sunnah, 23-24/4753) The manners and *haya* that had reflected onto his Companions were of such intensity that, more often than not, even asking him questions was deemed as impudent. They would hence wait for a Bedouin to perhaps arrive from the desert and inadvertently drop in to ask the Prophet -upon him blessings and peace- questions and spark a conversation, from whose spirituality they hoped to benefit. (See, Ibn Saad, I, 422-425; Haythami, IX, 13)

Abu Hurayra -Allah be well-pleased with him- describes the depth of his compassion:

"During the heated moment of a battle, we insisted the Messenger of Allah -upon him blessings and peace- to curse the idolaters to perish. But he said, 'I have not been sent to curse but as mercy.'" (Muslim, Birr, 87)

About the Blessed Prophet -upon him blessings and peace-, Allah, glory unto Him, states in the Quran:

$$\text{وَ مَا اَرْسَلْنَاكَ اِلَّا رَحْمَةً لِلْعَالَمِينَ}$$

"And We have not sent you but as a mercy for the worlds." (al-Anbiya, 107)

Ahmed ar-Rifai -may Allah sanctify his secret-, the great man of spirit, offers the below advice to his spiritual children:

"Expend, seeker of wisdom, all your existence in the way of the Real. Abide by the *Sunnah* of the Messenger of Allah -upon him blessings and peace-. Spend your day and night within the ambiance of worship and rightful conduct. Only in this way may you attain *marifah*. There is otherwise no share of it for you. Unable to become one with his *hal*, you will end up a defective servant."

The utterly magnificent character of the Blessed Prophet -upon him blessings and peace- which we have here attempted to summarize so far within the limited opportunity provided by words, are like mere drops trickling onto our understanding from that Great Ocean. The secret behind *wasl ila'Allah*, or reaching Allah, glory unto Him, lies in becoming intimate with the Book of Allah and the *Sunnah* of His Prophet, with a genuine heart, and in loving those whom Allah and His Messenger loves and detesting whom they detest.

For the wise, the universe is a magnificent parade of Divine manifestation and art offered up to human gaze, while for the fool, it is simply a podium of consumption and lust.

4. GAZING AT THE UNIVERSE WITH A PURIFIED HEART

By becoming increasingly purified and with the grace of Allah, glory unto Him, supplementary to the spiritual exercises of *tasawwuf*, the heart acquires such a nature at the end of the road that its possessor becomes angelic in spirit, despite continuing his physical existence. Some, who are of this acquired nature, are anonymous both to themselves and to others, much like a star among millions of others that are hidden to human gaze despite occupying space. Such persons are unidentifiable.

With that said, owing to the social responsibilities they have been entrusted with to carry out, certain other persons of the same kind are, to a certain degree, known. They thereby act as guiding lights not only during their lifetimes but also afterwards, even once they cease to exist physically, privileged with a share of the secret of eternity. They comprehend the final cause that is the will of the Lord, concealed beneath the causal chain of natural events. They thus life within the peaceful presence and serenity of having tapped into wisdom and are protected from defects like haste and anxiety, that plague human beings.

For them, nothing is absurd. Proceeding on the path of spiritual progress from the principle to 'tolerate the created for the sake of the Creator', they begin to gaze at the entire universe with a sagacious eye, to take a lesson, with love and awe.

They look upon the rising sun and the colorful portrait drawn by the rays of light at sunset with an awe-inspired gaze. They even look upon a snake with this perception; thus the fear experienced by ordinary human beings at the sudden sight of a slithering snake is replaced with an infatuation with the wonderful moirés on its skin and enchantment with its speed and agility of movement despite having no feet.

Since they gaze at creation with wisdom and love, these saintly figures are safe even from the attacks of feral animals; for love indeed acts like a radiating force in making the other succumb.

They have nothing of the general tendency of other human beings to view the wonders of the universe as ordinary. An ordinary man, who looks on impressed at manmade paintings, which after all are merely based on an imitation of nature, cannot feel the same way when gazing at the universe in connection with its Creator. Things that should evoke awe are, for him, just ordinary happenings.

The pious whose hearts are purified, on the other hand, have no business in acclaiming paintings made by artists with an interest of acquiring fame, and instead, they turn their interest and acclaim to the Real Artist and His masterpiece. They enjoy the zest of beholding the Divine art embedded in the innumerable wonders of nature. They gaze at the multicolored flowers and leaves of plants, the inexhaustible difference of color, smell and shape each tree has, the unique taste of each fruit, even though they all spring from the very same soil, and look on admiringly at the wonderful patterns on the wings of a butterfly and appreciate the incredibility of human creation. They lend an ear to the mysterious words expressed through the silent language (*lisan'ul-hal*) of countless Divine wonders like eyesight and understanding, seen by many as simply ordinary happenings.

For such people, the entire universe is like a book waiting to be read. Having surpassed knowledge of the written, they eye the knowledge of the heart; just like Mawlana Rumi -may Allah sanctify his secret- who, as a scholar buried in his books and minding his own business in the Saljuk Madrasa, was suddenly ignited by the enlightening call of an enamored, mystic dervish named Shams, and soon found himself ablaze in the fire of love. Reborn in the atmosphere of love, it was the same Mawlana in whose sight the value of written books dropped to where they truly belong, as he began reading the mysterious patterns of the universe with his very own eye of the heart. It was only after this stage that the masterpiece that is the *Mathnawi*, a cry exposing the mysteries of the Quran, universe and man, came to be.

Internalizing this state of mind is possible only if a believer discovers the potential power and love embedded in his heart.

Becoming focal points to the Divine Gaze, hearts of the kind reach their zenith. Perhaps because there is an element of human will involved in its coming to be that Mawlana Rumi -may Allah sanctify his secret- pays tribute to the value of this purified heart:

By Khalil Ibrahim, the son of Azer, was Kaaba raised
But the heart is the focal point of the Almighty's Gaze...

Frequent is the likening of the heart to *Kaaba* in Sufi hagiographic (*manaqib*) works. This stems from their conspicuous resemblance: the heart occupies a similar place in man, the essence of the universe (*zubda-i kainat*), to that of *Kaaba* with respect to the universe. Both occupy a central place in being focal points of the Divine Gaze. They are where the Gaze becomes centralized. The style of these hagiographic accounts, which tend to give the heart preeminence over the *Kaaba*, is partly from an amorous manner of expression. But more importantly, it is with the aim to encourage people by virtue of articulating the importance of uplifting the heart to this desired level, where it becomes a focal point just like the *Kaaba*.

On the subject of the heart becoming a focal point of the Divine Gaze, the words Ibn Omar -Allah be well-pleased with him- pronounced while looking at the *Kaaba* are significant to say the least:

"How great you are, *Kaaba*! How mighty is your name! But the honor a true believer has in the Sight of Allah is even greater!" (Tirmidhi, Birr, 85)

The heart is the precinct of *iman*. That the heart of a mature believer is superior even to the *Kaaba* are made clear by the words of Ibn Omar -Allah be well-pleased with him-. In virtual confirmation of this fact, Mawlana Rumi -may Allah sanctify his secret- says:

"If you have a glimmer of prudence, circumambulate the Kaaba that is the heart! It is the heart that holds the true meaning of the Kaaba which you think is just made of earth.

The Lord has obliged you to circumambulate the Kaaba, just so you acquire a heart cleansed of masiwa, a purified Kaaba of the heart.

The Training of Sufism (Sayr Suluk)

Know very well that if you break a heart, the focal point of the Divine Gaze, even the rewards of walking to Kaaba on foot will not compensate for the sin you will have reaped."

The condition of obtaining a heart of such caliber is abbreviated by Abdulqadir Jilani -may Allah sanctify his secret-:"Only the heart of he who seeks *marifatullah*, a heart that is cleansed of *masiwa*, becomes a *Kaaba*."

Ismail Hakkı Bursawi offers similar words: "He who finds a way inside a heart is superior to he who finds a way inside *Kaaba*. It is for that reason that it is common to ask the righteous and the pious to 'keep us in your heart' and plea for spiritual enlightenment (*istimdad-i fayz*) and attention (*talab-i himma*)."[41]

Imam Rabbani -may Allah sanctify his secret- expresses the fact that man is a minor universe in the following manner: "Man is a condensed summary of the universe. Whatever there is found in the universe, he thus carries a small specimen."

As has been mentioned on numerous occasions thus far, this equally underlines the bipolarity of man, of the fact of his exposure to both good and evil. The underlying purpose of religious commands and the supplementary exercises advised by *tasawwuf*, is to render good triumphant by dispossessing the tendency for evil as much as possible. In accomplishing this feat, it is vital for every organ of the human body to tow the line of Divine commands. With that said, the commands and exercises that pertain to the heart are of much greater importance, as being the hub of feelings, the heart gives direction to contemplation, which in turn regulates willpower. What this effectively means is that the primary cause of all willful conduct is the heart. Feelings indwell and take root inside the heart, allowing the heart to stand as an independent power against the will. Not only is it therefore more important to position the heart within the framework of Divine commands, it is also more difficult. Sufficient proof of this is what we have already mentioned above in relation to the difficulties that come with curing diseased hearts. Yet, since the value of each result is proportionate with the hardships endured on the way of acquiring it, disciplining the heart carries a massive value in Divine Sight.

---

41 *Istimdad-i fayz* is to aspire for spiritual enlightenment. *Talab-i himma* is to seek the attention of the Sufi master.

Sufism: A Path Towards the Internalization of Faith (Ihsân)

And in this sheer difficulty lies the reason as to why the Lord blesses those who are triumphant in this painstaking task, with angelic attributes and sometimes even more.

It is because of the crucial role it plays in ensuring man's happiness and salvation that all Sufis have regarded breaking the heart as a grave sin. This is echoed by the caution Mawlana Rumi -may Allah sanctify his secret- levels at heartbreakers:

"A broken heart which you value no more than a piece of straw is superior to the Throne… The Tablet and the Pen, just the same! Do not despise a heart, even it if be despicable! Even with its despicableness, it is supreme to all else. A broken heart is a being at which the Lord gazes. How sacred is he who mends it! Mending a heart shattered into two-hundred pieces is preferable in Divine Sight to many deeds of goodness! Be quiet! Even if each strand of your hair was to have two-hundred tongues, the heart would still remain indescribable!"

The heart has been designated as the subject of Divine manifestations and the precinct of their reflection, owing to its royal place within the human body. Indeed, as we have mentioned elsewhere, the profession of faith requires the 'affirmation of the heart'. As the subject of Divine revelation, the Quran refers not to reason, a center of contemplation, but to the heart, the hub of spiritual sensing:

نَزَلَ بِهِ الرُّوحُ ٱلْأَمِينُ عَلَىٰ قَلْبِكَ لِتَكُونَ مِنَ الْمُنْذِرِينَ

بِلِسَانٍ عَرَبِيٍّ مُبِينٍ

"The Faithful Spirit has descended with it. Upon your heart that you may be of the warners. In plain Arabic language." (as-Shuara, 193-195)

As is the case with all other activities, advancing in spiritual training is possible only through Allah, glory unto Him, complementing human endeavor with His aid, grace and benevolence. Although all human efforts and righteous deeds provide a spiritual base from which to embark, they are but means to attaining Divine grace and aid. Therefore, one who has entered this path must essentially rely on the benevolence and grace of Allah, glory unto Him. Since that 'aid' is bound to deliver the person somewhere better than where he presently is, at any rate, an improvement is certain. One must, however, strive to exert an effort that the Lord expects of him in return for the grace he anticipates.

There is an old saying: 'One must not entirely forsake that which he cannot acquire completely' (مَا لاَ يُدْرَكُ كُلُّهُ لاَ يُتْرَكُ كُلُّهُ). This is also the recommended approach to take on board in spiritual training; one ought not to neglect acquiring at least that which is in his power.

There is also a widely known parable in *tasawwuf*. A young man, aspiring to be a disciple, asks a sheikh, '*Himma* father' and the sheikh replies, '*Ghayra* (show effort) son!' A person anticipating the spiritual attention of his master must be ready to exert some effort. What the Lord expects from a servant in spiritual training is for him to realize his helplessness and nothingness before Divine splendor and make some genuine effort towards tapping into the secret expressed in the principle 'he who knows his self knows his Lord'. On the road towards vanquishing the ego, effort comes from the servant, while success from the Lord. And undoubtedly, the Almighty will hold a servant responsible only in proportion with the Divine blessings he had been granted in life. The important thing is for a person to align himself to the Truth, to the degree the blessings he has been endowed with allows him.

Lord…Light up the sparkles of Truth in the mirror that is our hearts to allow us to behold the keys to the mysteries and wisdoms of both worlds; and no less our hearts and eyes so that we are honored with Your *Jamal* in the Hereafter!

Amin…

Spiritual maturity is possible only by shedding unrefined traits and attaining a perfected character through abiding by the sensitivities and measure of the heart.

C. THE BASIC PRINCIPLES OF SUFI TRAINING

In *tasawwuf*, there are certain principles outlined by the Sufi great Abdulkhaliq Gujdawani -may Allah sanctify his secret-. Abidance by these principles followed particularly by the Naqshbandi way and which are motivated with the aim of liberating one from unrefined traits and rendering him a mature human being, is especially important. They may be enumerated as follows:

1. *Hush dar Dam*: To be spiritually awake in every breath taken.

2. *Nazar bar Qadam*: To watch one's step.

3. *Safar dar Watan*: To approach closer to the Real with every step.

4. *Halwat dar Anjuman*: To be with the Real even when in public.

5. *Yad-Kard*: For the heart be in constant *dhikr* of the Lord.

6. *Baz-Gasht*: For the pleasure of the Lord alone to become the sole purpose and desire.

7. *Nigah-Dasht*: To be protected from devilish and egoistic imaginings.

8. *Yad-Dasht*: To always consider oneself in Divine Presence.

9. *Wuquf-i Zamani*: To mind oneself and make the most of the present time.

10. *Wuquf-i Adadi*: To mind the amount of *dhikr*.

11. *Wuquf-i Qalbi*: For the heart to be relentlessly occupied with *dhikr* and to turn to the heart whilst in *dhikr*.

There is benefit in briefly explaining what these principles amount to:

1. *Hush dar Dam*: This underlines the state of being spiritually awake in each breath taken. This measure is defined by Mawlana Sadaddin Kashgari -may Allah sanctify his secret- as, "Not to fall into heedlessness even between two breaths and to consider oneself in the presence of the Lord at all times."

Being awake in every breath is for the *dhakir*, the person offering *dhikr*, to be consciously aware of Allah, glory unto Him, both during actual *dhikr* and all times else. Protecting the breath from heedlessness confers peace unto the heart. Having the Lord present in the mind in each inhalation and exhalation depends on reviving the breath through the grace obtained from obeying the Lord. As a result of the heart reaching the consciousness and peace of being with Allah, glory unto Him, all other connected conduct and behavior begins to gradually improve.

2. *Nazar bar Qadam*: This means to walk with eyes fixed on the tip of the toes. The aspirant must adopt this manner of walking, in order for his eyes and consequently his heart not to lark about in the surroundings and thus lose sight of their true aim. Unnecessary interest with the *masiwa* does away with the inner peace of the heart and brings down a curtain between the aspirant and the Real.

This manner is in fact nothing but an imitation of the way the Blessed Prophet -upon him blessings and peace- walked. When walking, the Blessed Prophet -upon him blessings and peace- never used to look around unless he had to. With his eyes firmly fixed on the tip of his toes, he would walk quickly in a dignified manner, as if pacing down a slope. Thus this principle is directly constituted by a particular aspect of the conduct of the Blessed Prophet -upon him blessings and peace-.

Wherever the gaze is directed at, that is where the heart flows; and that is a fact. The movies recorded by the eyes like a video camera, more often than not, keep the heart unnecessarily occupied. They take up unwanted space in the archives of the heart. Therefore, safeguarding the heart from disarray and confusion depends, in a sense, on the quality of the pictures reflected onto it.

Delusive whispers begin to gust through the mind, once the heart of an aspirant becomes stuck on the *masiwa (worldly things)*. If he mingles with the ignorant, the density of their hearts, their bad habits and corrupt ideas begin to reflect onto his heart, putting him in a compromising and extremely dangerous situation.

Adopting a style and manners befitting a modest human being, the aspirant must therefore not only fix his eyes on the tip of his toes when walking, he must also beware of the objects he stares at other times, too. Keeping the eyes fixed on the toes when walking is but a manifestation of modesty, knowing one's place, protecting the eyes from *haram* and most importantly, loyalty to the *Sunnah* of the Beloved Prophet -upon him blessings and peace-.

3. *Safar dar Watan*: Besides the journey embarked upon with the intention of finding a *murshid-i kamil (mature master)*, this also implies the journey undertaken by the aspirant towards casting off bad morals and the stifling density of sins and embodying good morals and sublime feelings, a journey towards his true identity, his homeland. The aspirant must never perceive the spiritual state he reaches as ultimate and must always seek improvement. Simpler put, he must always be on the move, on a journey, from one spiritual state to another higher.

Abu Othman al-Maghribi -may Allah sanctify his secret- has said:

"The aspirant must abandon his ambitions and desires and turn to obeying and worshipping the Lord. Meant by the expression *safar dar watan* is not so much a journey from one town to another as an inner journey towards reunion with Allah, glory unto Him. The moment an aspirant finds a *murshid-i kamil*, he abandons the outward journey and begins one that is inward."

During the *sayr-u suluk (spiritual training)*, the aspirant thus becomes pervaded by the consciousness of approaching closer to his Lord with every step, akin to Ibrahim (a.s), who said "I will go to my Lord." (as-Saffat, 99)

1. *Halwat dar Anjuman*: To maintain the consciousness of being with the Creator, even when among the created and leading a public existence. The aspirant must acquire an inward sense of being with Allah, glory unto Him, even whilst accompanied by other people or laboring away in his

daily work. This will enable him to continue his intimacy with the Lord without making it obvious to anybody else and at once, allow him to see to the needs necessitated by the demands of human life. Concisely yet wonderfully depicting this state of mind is the proverb, "The hands are toiling for income but the heart is with the beloved".

In the Quran, the Almighty acclaims those who are able to maintain this delicate inner sense:

رِجَالٌ لاَ تُلْهِيهِمْ تِجَارَةٌ وَ لاَ بَيْعٌ عَنْ ذِكْرِ اللهِ وَ اِقَامِ الصَّلٰوةِ
وَ اِيتَاءِ الزَّكٰوةِ يَخَافُونَ يَوْمًا تَتَقَلَّبُ فِيهِ الْقُلُوبُ وَالْأَبْصَارُ

"Men whom neither merchandise nor selling diverts from the remembrance of Allah and the keeping up of prayer and the giving of poor-rate; they fear a day in which the hearts and eyes shall turn about." (an-Nur, 37)

Sohbah (spiritual lesson) and socialization are essential in the Naqshbandi path. Therefore, maintaining the heart's intimacy and seclusion with the Lord even whilst amid public has been given preference over solitary, private seclusion.

5. *Yad-Kard*: This is for the heart to acquire a nature of *dhikr*, to become enmeshed with it; that is for it to reach a level where it is in continuous remembrance of the Lord. By virtue of the method of *nafy-u isbat* (by negating and affirming through repeating the *dhikr* of *La ilaha ill-Allah*), all the grimy residues of *masiwa (worldly things)* that act as virtual idols in the heart are cleansed, subsequent to which the idea that Allah, glory unto Him, is alone to be desired, becomes fixed in the heart.

Once the subtle heat of *dhikr* emanating from the heart takes hold of the entire body, the sublime feelings hidden in man's subconscious come alive and transform into an active conscience that reflects onto behavior. It is indeed inconceivable that a person, whose entire thought is of the Lord, to be outright deprived of divine morals like mercy, patience, generosity and forgiveness. All these are imperative conditions for becoming a matured human being. Reviving the heart through *dhikr* is therefore one of the most important principles of *tasawwuf*.

6. *Baz-Gasht*: This is for the pleasure of Allah, glory unto Him, to become the exclusive object of desire and purpose.

At the end of the *dhikr* of *nafy-u isbat*, the aspirant pronounces « اِلٰهِى اَنْتَ مَقْصُودِى وَرِضَاكَ مَطْلُوبِى » (Lord…You alone are my purpose and Your pleasure alone is my desire) and seeks to gain depth in the contemplation of the *dhikr*. This carries the aim of having the aspirant affirm the inner meaning of the *dhikr* of *nafy-u isbat* and thereby endure the mystery of *tawhid (oneness of Allah)* set a firm foot inside the heart.

By negating all other desires and ambitions that act as curtains separating one from the Lord, the satisfaction of the heart is thereby ensured. Similarly, misgivings that may arise, now and then, to delude the heart by falsely representing the purpose of the spiritual exercise of *dhikr* as receiving *karamah (miracles)* or progressing through spiritual ranks are completely set aside and the true purpose, which is to obtain the pleasure of the Lord, is indelibly embroidered once again onto the heart.

Once the inner meaning of this *dhikr* becomes embedded in conscience and manifests itself in behavior, passing obsessions instantly lose their former value, as the eyes begin to behold Divine manifestations in everything they see.

7. *Nigah-Dasht*: This is to protect the mind from devilish and egoistic imaginings, to protect the sight from staring at improper things, to prevent the imagination from visualizing things that are immoral and to keep constant surveillance over the heart, the manifestation of the Real, defending it against the invasion of the *masiwa*.

One of the purposes of *tasawwuf* is to safeguard the heart from negative thoughts and wicked imaginings. Keeping these away from the heart is very difficult undertaking, to say the least. But one who is triumphant in doing so will have reaped the true benefits of *tasawwuf*.

8. *Yad-Dasht*: This is for one to gain an awareness of being in the constant presence of the Almighty and act with this consciousness. This is also called *muraqabah*.

Allah, glory unto Him, declares in the *ayah*: "And certainly We created man, and We know what his mind suggests to him, and We are nearer to him than his life-vein." (Qaf, 16)

It is therefore vital never to lose the feeling of *ihsan*, the internalization of *iman* and the consciousness of the fact that the Lord sees one each moment and knows his each state of mind. This feeling acts like an invincible shield against sins; for how can a person sin, while his heart is constantly with the Lord, knowing he is irremovably in Divine presence?

9. *Wuquf-i Zamani*: This is to examine each bygone moment and see whether it was spent in spiritual presence (*hudur*) or heedlessness (*ghaflah*), and to put time to good use. The aspirant must be aware of the precious value of the moment he is in and reserve it for the most valuable deed of all by renouncing vain activities. On a frequent basis, he must interrogate himself to see whether he has made the most of his time.

In another sense of the meaning, *wuquf-i zamani* is for the aspirant to have a constant awareness of the state of mind that comes over him at each moment and see whether it is a state of thankfulness or a state that calls for repentance. In effect, the aspirant must every day and night reflect on his actions, one by one, and thank the Lord for allowing him to perform righteous deeds, striving at the same time to go a step further, and repent for his shortcomings, seeking remorseful refuge in the Lord. He must look upon each priceless moment of life, and especially those moments ordained by Allah, glory unto Him, as unique, as an in-compensable opportunity. And in spiritual wakefulness, he must channel his entire energy towards satisfying the demands of the given moment and bringing it to life.

In short, he must call each bygone moment to account, thanking the Almighty for each spent in spiritual presence and repenting for each wasted in heedlessness. To say the same thing differently, one must hold fast to repentance whilst undergoing spiritual constriction (*qabd*) and persist in showing thanks upon receiving spiritual revitalization (*bast*). One who refrains from heedlessness in all circumstances thus finds himself unshackled from the fetters that are the troubles of the past and anxieties of the future, and occupied with trying to revive the given moment, which the attitude expressed in the Sufi maxim, "A Sufi is the child of the present time."

10. *Wuquf-i Adadi*: This is to be conscious of the precise amount of *dhikr*. A *murshid* gives a disciple a certain amount of *dhikr*, depending on his spiritual condition.[42] To make sure it yields the desired result, each *dhikr* comes with a specific amount, a dosage if one may call it. In order for the disciple not to lose concentration during *dhikr* and to keep clear of giving in to delusive whispers, he must observe the specific measure and amount recommended by the *murshid*. Most certainly, the quality of a *dhikr* is of greater importance. Still, unless the *dhikr* comes with a specific measure and quantity, there always looms the danger of being overcome with mental and spiritual unrest. As is the case with every other activity, this state of unrest is caused by errors attributable to excess and immoderation. A *dhikr* must therefore be implemented in the best possible manner, by observing both its quality and quantity. With that said, observing a specific amount of *dhikr* is not an abstract activity of counting numbers. Much rather, it is to deepen the *dhikr* of the heart within the numerical framework. Hence, it is clear that observing a specific amount of *dhikr* not only does not stand in the way of achieving a quality *dhikr*, it moreover acts as necessary support in accomplishing it.

Interestingly enough, when the mind is engaged in various thoughts and the heart is perplexed by a variety of concerns, observing an exact amount of *dhikr* is well nigh impossible. Protecting the mind from disarray, focusing on the meaning of the *dhikr* and, at the same time, observing its specific quantity are therefore really expressions of earnestness.

11. *Wuquf-i Qalbi*: This is for the heart to be continually occupied with Divine remembrance. This marks the true internalization of *ihsan*, its becoming a constant consciousness. A disciple must inspect his heart at every given opportunity and check on its condition, as the true objective of *dhikr* is for the heart to be aware of what is uttered by the tongue. Essential during *dhikr* is therefore a constant state of *muraqabah*, an unreserved focus on the words being uttered. Sufi greats refer to *wuquf-i qalbi*, to focus all attention of the heart, as a necessary prerequisite of *dhikr*. To arrive at a taste of the true content or the zest of *dhikr*, it is a must to direct every inch of one's existence and no less his heart to Allah, glory unto Him.

---

42 On the Blessed Prophet -upon him blessings and peace- recommending different amounts of *dhikr* to people, in line with their particular conditions and circumstances see p. 196-197.

The Training of Sufism (Sayr Suluk)

The Almighty pronounces:

$$\text{وَ اذْكُرِ اسْمَ رَبِّكَ وَ تَبَتَّلْ اِلَيْهِ تَبْتِيلاً}$$

"And remember the name of your Lord and devote yourself to Him with (exclusive) devotion." (al-Muzzammil, 8)

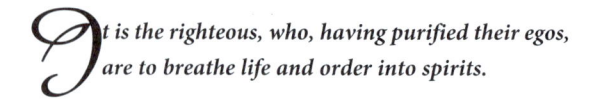

It is the righteous, who, having purified their egos, are to breathe life and order into spirits.

D. *MURSHID-I KAMIL* AND METHODS OF SPIRITUAL ENLIGHTENING

1. *MURSHID-I KAMIL*

Progressing on the spiritual path, a believer encounters diverse manifestations. The heart is like an ocean. Sometimes its waters are calm and serene; yet there are other times when its waters surge to terrifying heights amid a sudden breakout of a violent storm. Equal to the need for a reliable ship to cross this turbulent ocean is the need for an able captain. Should the captain lose control of the ship whilst trying to sail through the rising waves, it will come to know the hard way just how uncompromising the ocean is; it will bury the ship in its depths. Such manifestations are usually unbeknown to those who are new to this journey. But as one continues to sail into the open ocean, certain spiritual signs begin to show their faces, spiritual twists differing in nature from one person to another, conditions like *inqibad* and *inbisat*,[43] manifestations whose sources, whether Divine (*Rahmani*) or devilish, are unknown. Diagnosing them and taking the required precautions thus requires the guidance of a *murshid-i kamil*, a spiritually matured master.

To acquire this direction, each Muslim must come under self-discipline. The heart-world of the Blessed Prophet -upon him blessings and peace-, the exemplar beyond compare for the *ummah*, must be emulated to the extent one's capabilities and powers allow. His trust and reliance in the

---

43 *Inqibad* and *inbisat* are two opposite states that take a disciple in their grip. *Inqibad* is a spiritual constriction brought upon by fear or like anxieties, while *inbisat* is a spiritual relief through hope.

The Training of Sufism (Sayr Suluk)

Lord, patience at the face of troubles and predicaments, his distance to the treasures of the world when they flowed freely in front of him and his exceptional modesty, must be put to practice as intensely as possible. To assail the barriers that stand on the path of spiritual development, one must therefore humbly and courteously request the assistance of the wise *murshid-i kamil*s, the inheritors of the Blessed Prophet -upon him blessings and peace- and make a sincere effort to carry out their recommendations. Just as in receiving its light from the sun, the moon testifies to the existence of the sun even when it is hidden from the naked eye, saints enlightened by the Light of Muhammad -upon him blessings and peace- are witnesses and inheritors of the Blessed Prophet -upon him blessings and peace-.

The purpose of *tasawwuf* is to develop the spiritual potential, embedded in varying degrees in the natural predisposition of man. Each heart is like land concealing petrol underneath. The petrol never finds its way above the ground unless through being drilled out. The petrol that rests in the lower substratum of the ground is like the spiritual aptitude divinely given to each human being. As is the case with the intellect, it is found in varying degrees among human beings.

A *murshid-i kamil* is the one to spiritually drill this aptitude out and bring this treasure out into daylight. But for the petrol to make its way above, the drill must reach all the way to the layer where the petrol dwells. The drill must equally be strong and resilient, lest it hit upon a rock and shatter to pieces. This means that it is just as important that the *murshid*, to whose spiritual guidance one submits, be competent for the task. And this carries its certain conditions, on which we should briefly touch upon in passing:

A true *murshid-i kamil* is recognizable by three main traits:

The First Trait:

A true *murshid-i kamil* exerts a full-fledged loyalty to the Quran and Sunnah. His life and deeds consists of nothing other than bringing the morals of the Quran and Sunnah to life. Compared to other believers, the loyalty of a *murshid-i kamil* to the Quran and Sunnah is of greater intensity. His abidance by the two pillars is comparable to a man, who meticulously follows the footsteps of the guide in front of him on a snowy field, paying particular attention to step on the very ground the guide has treaded, lest he be bogged down in snow. A *murshid-i kamil* is thus rightly referred to as a *warathatu'l-anbiya*, an inheritor of prophets. It goes without saying that a loyalty of such intensity carries no room for a life that revolves around the ego.

The Second Trait:

A true *murshid-i kamil* reminds one of Allah, glory unto Him, both in his words and deeds. Because these saintly figures are recipients of the manifestation of Divine names and that they have been able to transform the Divine names of Beauty (*jamali*) names into moral behavior, they invariably remind others of the Lord. Indeed, when the Companions inquired the Blessed Prophet -upon him blessings and peace- as to who the *wali* or saintly servants of Allah, glory unto Him, are, the reply they received was:

اَلَّذِينَ إِذَا رُئُوا ذُكِرَ اللهُ عَزَّ وَجَلَّ

"They are those whose sight reminds one of Allah the Almighty".
(Haythami, Majmau'z-Zawaid, X, 78; Ibn Majah, Zuhd, 4)

The sight of a *murshid-i kamil* must therefore evoke in one the thought of Allah, glory unto Him and the Hereafter, impart peacefulness onto the heart and carry him away to a spiritual realm. This is for no other reason than that they have embodied the morals of the Lord and the Prophet -upon him blessings and peace-.

The most renowned names of the Allah, glory unto Him, are *Rahman* (the Merciful) and *Rahim* (the Compassionate). The saintly servants of the Lord, too, exert utmost compassion. The Almighty is *Sattaru'l-uyub*; He conceals sins. A *murshid*, too, does not investigate the faults of others and conceals them once made aware. The Lord is *Karim*, the Generous. A saint is likewise generous; he takes satisfaction from providing for others. Allah, glory unto Him, is *Ghafur*; the Forgiver. A *murshid*, too, forgives others' faults. The Lord is *Halim*, the Forbearing; so are saints.

Being the companions (*wali*) of the Lord, such figures are hence different to other people in more respects than one. Their hearts are closer to Allah, glory unto Him. Their deeds of worship are solemn, focused. They pay painstaking attention to their behavior. As they trek the footsteps of the Noble Prophet -upon him blessings and peace-, their prayers are more acceptable than the prayers of others. Since their bodies are engaged in a continuous state of *dhikr*, affording vigor to their whole existence, they exude a refreshing effect on the places which they enter.

A genuine believer finds himself distressed by the overwhelming spiritual weight burdened through mixing with someone of a perverse nature. Inversely, accompanying a righteous human being brings him peace. Greater still, for a genuine believer, being in the company of the Blessed Prophet -upon him blessings and peace- is bliss beyond the wildest imagination. The spiritual pleasure of being present in an atmosphere graced by the spiritual majesty of the Light of Being -upon him blessings and peace- is simply inexpressible. Still, because a *murshid-i kamil* scrupulously follows the trail of the Blessed Prophet -upon him blessings and peace-, abides consummately by his Sunnah and thereby comes the closest to the Prophetic morals, he carries a spiritual majesty and source of inspiration that comes from the Prophet -upon him blessings and peace-. Just as it is common to for a man, who makes contact with an electrical current, to shake, a true murshid must first shake the very pillars of one's spirit, then reinvigorate him and take him away on a journey across spiritual horizons.

The Third Trait:

The final mark of a *murshid-i kamil* is spiritual designation. It is not enough for an assembly to convene and chose a *murshid*. Much rather, he must be designated by an authorized *murshid-i kamil*, who himself belongs to an authentic spiritual chain that reaches all the way to the Blessed Prophet -upon him blessings and peace-. Should this kind of designation be lacking, the chain then comes to a halt at that given point. When unable to find a successor of enough competence, many a *murshid-i kamil* therefore abstains from entrusting anyone with the duty of continuing their path. At times they leave one successor, at other times many, as was the case with Khalid Baghdadi -may Allah sanctify his secret-. The wisdom underlying this is known to Allah, glory unto Him, alone.

So in brief, maturing the heart so as to render it recipient to spiritual truths is possible through certain spiritual exercises. This requires acquaintance with and the practice of the paths of spiritual maturation.

Sufism: A Path Towards the Internalization of Faith (Ihsân)

Overcoming the obstacles scattered along this path, on the other hand, requires the guidance of the righteous and pious servants of Allah, glory unto Him. Each potential disciple must search for a *murshid* to see his spiritual development through but at the same, be pay great attention to whether the suspected *murshid*, to whose he training he considers to submit himself, carries certain traits.

A Few Important Words of Note:

Since a *murshid-i kamil*, whose traits have been depicted thus far, is a distinguished servant of Allah, glory unto Him, and an exceptional man of integrity, he most certainly merits enormous respect and is required to be benefited from spiritually. But in showing this due respect and seeking to benefit spiritually from a *murshid*, one must take care not to be drowned in the torrent of excess. It must be borne in mind that even prophets, let alone the righteous and the pious, are above all servants of the Lord. They only possess whatever amount of the oceans of knowledge and wisdom Allah, glory unto Him, has privileged them with. A time comes when their eyes and hearts are exposed to the underlying wisdoms of both worlds; yet likewise, there are times when they may not be able to see what is in front of them.

In his *Gulistan*, Sheikh Sadi narrates:

"A man once asked Yaqub (a.s), 'You, who are a wise prophet with an enlightened heart! How was it that you were able get a whiff of the scent of Yusuf's (a.s) shirt as it was being brought from as far as Egypt, yet were unable to see it as he was thrown into a well just nearby?'

'The Divine share of knowledge given us in this regard', replied Yaqub (a.s) 'are like lightning strikes. Hence, truths appear crystal clear at times, yet they remain concealed at others.'"

Once, in reply to a person asking him answers to some questions unbeknown to him at the time, certain that an enlightening Revelation would soon arrive, the Blessed Prophet -upon him blessings and peace- said:

"See me tomorrow when I shall give you the answer". He did not complement his sentence with *insha-Allah*, or Allah willing.

But the expected Revelation did not arrive the day after; in actual fact, exactly fifteen days passed before it finally did arrive. Even the Light of Being -upon him blessings and peace-, for the sake of whom the entire universe had been created, was left helpless. When it did at long last arrive, it was with the following caution:

"And say not of anything: Surely, I shall do that tomorrow. Except adding if Allah wills. And remember your Lord when you forget, and say: It may be that my Lord guides me unto a nearer way of truth than this."
(al-Kahf, 23-24) (See, Ibn Kathir, III, 83; Alusi, XV, 247)

Considering that this is some measure even the Blessed Prophet -upon him blessings and peace- was commanded to follow, one must duly understand the degree of its applicability to human beings entire. Thus, it cannot be said that once a beloved servant of Allah, glory unto Him, says a prayer in general or for the recuperation of an ill person, the acceptance of that prayer is guaranteed. In order for the prayer to culminate in to what has been desired, not only must there be sincerity in both camps, the person offering the prayer and the person for whom the prayer is made, the prayer must also fall in line with Divine will. As is valid for prayers of all kinds, one must also remember that the acceptance of the prayer may in fact be adjourned to the Hereafter, instead of becoming manifest this life and that their acceptance or denial are completely dependent upon the Will of the Almighty.

Another important detail to take note of is that both prophets and saints possess distinct temperaments and dispositions and that one characteristic that comes to the fore in one prophet may not be found on the same level in another prophet. It would therefore be a mistake to expect from each and everyone them to be the same temperament and disposition.

As is mentioned in the Holy Quran, Musa (a.s) was given a kind of knowledge which Khidr (a.s) lacked; and inversely, Khidr (a.s) was privileged with a form of knowledge which was lacking in Musa (a.s). Comparably, one cannot expect a Jilani -may Allah sanctify his secret- to be a Rumi -may Allah sanctify his secret-. What has been given to both and what has been expected from both are distinct. Most certainly, however, the true purpose that underlies them all is servanthood and *marifa*. And the roads that lead to the Lord are indeed as numerous as the amount of breaths that belong to creation.

Also of great importance is the fact that no servant, bar prophets, is under Divine guarantee. Even if one was to reach the apogee of ideal servanthood, he still remains exposed to the constant threat of slipping by the wayside. One case in point is Balam ibn Baura. Formerly a righteous man, he wound up falling captive to his ego, inflicting upon himself an eternal dismay. The Quran refers to him as follows:

"And recite to them the narrative of him to whom We give Our communications, but he withdraws himself from them, so the Shaitan overtakes him, so he is of those who go astray. And if We had pleased, We would certainly have exalted him thereby. But he clung to the earth and followed his low desire, so his parable is as the parable of the dog; if you attack him he lolls out his tongue; and if you leave him alone he lolls out his tongue; this is the parable of the people who reject Our communications; therefore relate the narrative that they may reflect." (al-Araf, 175-176)

Similar is the case of Qarun, or Croesus, whose account is made mention in *surah* al-Qasas. An exceptionally upright man at one-time, he laid waste on his eternal happiness by turning into a despicable man of rebellion. Together with the lavish wealth he so depended on and boasted over, the Almighty mortified him deep into the ground. Thus whatever the spiritual rank or superiority one may be privileged with at the time, the ego, which lies in wait inside man, may rise to strike at any unexpected moment and topple one from his throne. Not for no reason did the Blessed Prophet -upon him blessings and peace- seek refuge in the Lord, by praying:

"My Allah…I am hopeful of Your mercy! Do not leave me alone with the desires of my ego even if it be for a split second! Rehabilitate my each condition! Doubtless, there is no god but You…" (Abu Dawud, Adab, 100-101)

The righteous servants of the Lord always take careful note of the meaning of the above *hadith* and never deceive themselves with the thought of 'having made it'. Those who have given in to this delusion have always found themselves left high and dry, even if they had managed to complete their *sayr-u suluk*. In contrast, those who believed they were still 'far from making it', who constantly reminded themselves of their shortcomings and weaknesses, have been able to progress relentlessly on the spiritual path. Just to think that in spite of the brilliant manifestation of the perfected nature of his humanness, even Prophet Muhammad

The Training of Sufism (Sayr Suluk)

Mustafa -upon him blessings and peace-, the pinnacle of prophets, never stopped offering *salat* to the point of having swollen feet, responding to the astounded Aisha -Allah be well-pleased with him-a, inquiring as to why he felt the need, by saying:

"Should I not be a thankful servant, Aisha?" (Muslim, Munafiqun, 79)

Again, according to report of his honorable wives, following the Revelation: "Then celebrate the praise of your Lord, and ask His forgiveness; surely He is oft-returning (to mercy)" (an-Nasr, 3) the Blessed Prophet -upon him blessings and peace- began to occupy himself with thanking and praising the Lord more with each gone second.

Therefore, regardless of the rank one attains to towards the path of the Real, he is never alleviated from the responsibilities of servanthood and may not, in any sense of the term, reduce his deeds or fabricate a self-acclaimed exemption from the duties that come with being a servant. All Divine principles and responsibilities are entrusted with human beings in all walks of life and will not be revoked up until to the moment they breathe their final breath on earth. A true *murshid-i kamil* thus strives to live his entire life abiding under the shade of the guiding command:

"Therefore celebrate the praise of your Lord, and be of those who prostrate. And serve your Lord until there comes to you that which is certain." (al-Hijr, 98-99)

Spiritual guides of such caliber do not ask for even a tiny price in return for their services. They do not even expect a return for their servanthood to Allah, glory unto Him; for those who do, depreciate the value of their deeds and spiritual ranks. Despite fasting on three days in succession, Ali and Fatima -Allah be well-pleased with him-um handed their meal away to a poor man who had come knocking on their door from hunger on the first night, to an orphan on the second night and to a prisoner on the third, making do with just water on each of those nights, as they humbly responded to the thanks of their recipients by saying:

"We did not give our food expecting thanks from you. Our sole motivation is the pleasure of our Lord..."[44]

44　See, al-Insan, 8-11; Wahidi, p. 470. Zamakhshari, VI, 191-192.

In short, true *murshid-i kamil*s are the high points of spiritual life, who continue prophets' duties of training and teaching, by virtue of putting an exemplary character on display. Acquainted with the Lord and His Sublime Attributes, these righteous servants of Allah, glory unto Him, have, at the same time, reached a level of *ihsan*. They are thus given such blessings like the knowledge of the *ladunn*, wisdom and *marifa*. Yet none of them are on level par with a Companion. Neither is a Companion on level par with a Prophet, nor are prophets on level par with the Blessed Prophet -upon him blessings and peace-. And as for the Blessed Prophet -upon him blessings and peace-, he is first and foremost a servant of the Lord and then His Messenger.

One must therefore resist the urge to ascribe greater value to human beings than they merit and treat them in accordance with their give conditions. Uways al-Qarani or even Abu Hanifa, the compiler of Islamic jurisprudence, cannot be on level par with a Companion. As for the exaggerated respect and reverence, 'supposedly' a mark of devotion, shown time and again by the ignorant towards figures they are attached to, is beyond a simple error; it is downright deviation. This deviation is something of a strange case of behavioral excess that not only runs counter to the Will of the Lord, it also distances one further away from the truth. It is owing to a concern that people may fall into an error of this kind that the Beloved Prophet -upon him blessings and peace- forbade people from singing ignorant praises of others. And should the person being praised be wary that the praises will inflate his ego, the Prophet -upon him blessings and peace- advised him to:

"Hurl dust on his (the praiser's) face!" (Ahmed ibn Hanbal, Musnad, VI, 5)

Praises that provoke the ego are but signatures of destruction placed on the heart.

The realm of existence is upheld by love and rabitah; for rabitah is none other than the manifestation of love that constitutes the core of existence. It is the perpetuation of the vivacity and sparkle of love.

2. METHODS OF SPIRITUAL GUIDANCE

a. *Muhabbah* (Love) and *Rabitah*

A look into the gist and purpose of *tasawwuf* reveals the fact that the prime catalyst in *sayr-u suluk* is love, while its ultimate objective is spiritual manners (*adab*). Love, here, is a means, while spiritual manners a result. One cannot possibly overemphasize the importance of these two concepts. When the love felt for someone intensifies, a certain degree of this love becomes projected to things around, seen as carrying a resemblance or a proximity (*nisbah*) of some sort to the person loved.

A disciple, for instance, who nurtures an extreme love for his *murshid*, cannot help but feel a similar love towards anyone who adopts a similar behavior to him, albeit in a more inadequate form. When he comes across an acquaintance of his *murshid*, he treats him like someone would treat a relative just returning from pilgrimage. Owning any single object, which his *murshid* had erstwhile used, uplifts his spirit. This is comparable to the joy felt by Uways al-Qarani upon receiving the mantle personally sent by the Blessed Prophet -upon him blessings and peace-.

Parallel with the intensification of love, the proximity (*nisbah*) that gradually increases towards the beloved becomes, at the same time, comprehensive, so as to begin from the beloved, the strongest proximity, at its core, and expand in a way that encompasses the weakest. In *tasawwuf*, the eternally expanding the perimeter of this circle of love that has the beloved as its center, in a way that encompasses all proximities near and far, is called absolute love (*ashk-i mutlaq*).⁴⁵ To recall the words of Yunus Emre,

Appreciate the created,
For the sake of the Creator

This is the state of lovingly and compassionately embracing all creation, no matter what their characteristics, natures and deeds may be, simply for the sake of the Creator. This is the final stage a lover can reach. Virtually, each station of love on the way thereto is metaphorical love (*ashk-i majazi*).

Metaphorical love begins the moment the disciple pledges loving affinity to his *murshid*. This love, too, is metaphorical. Since in its nature the heart is reserved to Allah, glory unto Him, alone, it cannot have any other beloved than the Lord. Things, other than Him, to which one becomes attached, are like steps on this ladder, exercises acclimatizing the heart to Divine Love. Overall, this is the attempt to reach the *Mawla*, or the Lord, through *Layla*, if one may use the expression. The most inspirational stage in this attempt is to encounter a true *murshid-i kamil* and to experience the spiritual excitement of love and affinity with him. And the most propitious manifestation of this is *rabitah*. *Rabitah* is the very intensification of love, where it can no longer be compared to ordinary, trivial attachments.

Literally, *rabitah* denotes ties and interest. In this respect, there is not a single being in the universe detached from *rabitah*. Everything is interconnected. On another level, *rabitah* is the manifestation of love that forms the core of existence. It is the perpetuation of the vivacity and sparkle of love.

There are three kinds of *rabitah*.

1. Natural *Rabitah*

This is the natural love felt by a person towards whom he considers close. It is an outcome of man's natural predisposition, like the love a mother feels for her child, and so forth.

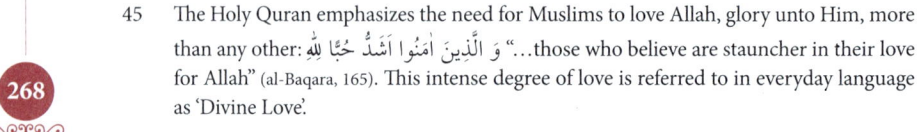

---

45   The Holy Quran emphasizes the need for Muslims to love Allah, glory unto Him, more than any other: "وَالَّذِينَ اٰمَنُوا اَشَدُّ حُبًّا لِلّٰهِ...those who believe are stauncher in their love for Allah" (al-Baqara, 165). This intense degree of love is referred to in everyday language as 'Divine Love'.

2. Base *Rabitah*

This is to become attached to forbidden, devilish tendencies; like the gambler whose heart is ever hungry with the desire to gamble to the point where he even forgets about the livelihood of his own family.

3. Sublime *Rabitah*

Motivated by the loftiest of feelings, this is the *rabitah* that steers one towards means that will eventually deliver him to the Lord. It is to accompany, either physically or spiritually, those whose hearts have been garnished (*tajliyah*) and who have thus attained to the rank of *mushahadah*, in order to benefit from them spiritually.

Here, we shall expand on this, the third type of *rabitah*. This signifies the way in which the disciple, towards acquiring a certain aptitude, keeps the love of his *murshid* ever alive in his heart, with the aim of fully benefiting from him spiritually.

A method of Sufi training, *rabitah* comes in various names and ways of practice in each *tariqah*. Generally, however, it is for the disciple to call his *murshid* to mind, right in front of his eyes, and amid sublime emotions, to try to become one with him, by recalling his spiritual state of mind and behavior. Keeping the love and respect for the *murshid* ever alive in this manner, gives the disciple a spiritual vivacity.

Man lies exposed to influences. As is the case with many diseases, inner conditions or states of mind are also contagious. The transaction that takes place between spirits is an incontestable fact of life. Especially the strong spiritual characteristics shown by active and influential figures transmit to others around, in varying degrees. This transmission does not depend on whether the 'transmitter' exudes a positive or negative character. It takes place regardless, so long as there exists a mutual bond of love and affinity between the two.

The mindsets of utterly compassionate and selfless people, for instance, wield an influence on the people by whom they are surrounded. *Rabitah*, a manifestation of love, seeks to increase and accelerate these spiritual transactions of a positive, moral nature and transform them into concrete moral behavior in the recipient. Each Muslim with a right mind must therefore nurture love towards the pious and establish affinity with them and thereby maximize the reflection of their beautiful mindsets onto their own characters.

How strange it is that a batch of mud that splashes onto a pair of clean clothes causes a person greater discomfort than bad habits invading a heart remote from the guiding light of *wahy* and thus darkened beyond recognition from sin. Since he is numbed by the delusive whispers both egoistic and devilish, he does not even become aware of his spiritual plight. At the face of what can rightly be called the 'transmission of character', it is true that man has been left free to choose from among either positive or negative examples. Regardless, the Almighty has informed of the right choice in the Quran as follows:

"O you who believe! Be careful of your duty to Allah and be with the righteous." (at-Tawba, 119)

One thing that deserves attention in the above *ayah* is that the Lord does not command His servants to 'be righteous' but to 'be with the righteous', in order for them to safeguard their piety. The first step on the way of becoming righteous is indeed to accompany the righteous, to enter a loving affinity with them. Righteousness is the natural outcome of this connection. After all, one naturally takes after the other.

In reigning in the ego, accompanying the pious and the righteous acts like radiation, impossible to witness yet unquestionably effective. Being near the righteous, witnessing moment by moment their conduct and behavior and even just looking at their lit faces, are all included in this regard. It is for that reason having the opportunity to be in the presence of spiritual elders is considered a great blessing. Mindsets transmit. The smell of roses is bound to permeate the clothes of a person who hangs around a rose garden. An assembly of the righteous, similarly, is like a bazaar of spiritual transaction.

Ubaydullah Ahrar -may Allah sanctify his secret- says:

"The expression 'be with' in the command of the Quran 'to fear Allah and be with the righteous', means a perpetual accompaniment. As it has been given mention in an absolute sense, 'being with' has two aspects, one practical and the other legal. Practical or physical accompaniment is to be physically present in the assembly of the righteous, while legal accompaniment is to evoke their mindsets in their absence."

The Training of Sufism (Sayr Suluk)

Hence, as necessary as it is to maintain sublime feelings whilst physically in the presence of the righteous, one must also continue this accompaniment in his heart, in their absence. For physically accompanying the righteous may not always be possible. To continue accompanying them in the heart, one then stands in need of *rabitah*.

But as has been previously mentioned, the training of *tasawwuf* does not approve of a physical accompaniment that is ineffectual and vain. There is many a person who is within a whisker, so to speak, of a *murshid*, yet unable to reap his due spiritual share owing to his ignorance. In contrast, there is many a disciple in a land faraway that becomes blessed with exceptional spiritual gifts, inspirations and emotions, thanks to the deep respect, longing, love and attachment he feels towards his *murshid*. The saying, as expressed by spiritual elders, that 'the one in Yemen is nearby, while the one nearby is in Yemen' articulates just that. The important thing, therefore, is not to lose the feeling of the heart, wherever one may be at the time.

On the other hand, although spiritually competent people exercise a maximum power in correcting the mindsets of those around them, this on its own is not enough. The transmission of the mindset, in *tasawwuf*, is a spiritual flow of such a nature that deriving the maximum benefit of its flow depends as much on the spiritual aptitude of the disciple and his intensity of love as it does on the competence of the *murshid*. Thus not every disciple can attain to the same level, simply because he is a disciple. Much rather the difference of spiritual level between one disciple and another, stems from the level of aptitude and intensity of love in each. To illustrate this through an example, there is essentially no difference whether a person, intent on filling his bucket with water, dips it into a lake or a boundless ocean; in both cases, he will only obtain as much water as his bucket allows. The disciple must therefore be apt and more importantly be eager to realize the full potential of his aptitude.

Yunus Emre expresses this beautifully:

Should you place your cup,
By the tap to fill,
Even if left for a thousand years
Not by itself it will

Another method utilized in both *rabitah* and *muraqabah* is reading the *silsila-i sharifah*[46]. This is carried out with a desire of receiving a share of the mercy that is hoped to descend onto the heart by mentioning the names of the righteous who make up this chain and a reflection of their beautiful mindsets. The great scholar Sufyan ibn Uyaynah has in fact said: "Mercy descends on an assembly in which the righteous are mentioned." (Ajluni, *Kashfu'l-Khafa*, II, 70)

The compiling of various books that comprise certain hagiographical accounts of the righteous, in fact has no other motivation than to inspire others, in the said manner, who approach the righteous with love. Thus the aim of *rabitah* is to spiritually inspire and enlighten hearts by having them evoke the celebrated chain of the righteous that reaches to the Blessed Prophet -upon him blessings and peace- himself. Upon getting hold of a chain of conjoint men, already quivering from a livewire in the hand of the first person in that chain, it is natural for a person to begin to shake uncontrollably from the voltage of electricity that falls to his share. Intensifying *rabitah* to the degree where it enables the disciple to embody the moral conduct of the *murshid*, by virtue of continuing the love and respect, shown to the *murshid* in his presence, even in his absence has been referred to as *fana fi's-sheikh*, annihilation in the sheikh.

Beyond the station of *fana fi's-sheikh* is the station of *fana fi'r-rasul*, annihilation in the Prophet -upon him blessings and peace-. Before becoming honored with Islam, many of the celebrated Companions, the stars of the Islamic sky, were leading lives contrary to natural disposition. But after receiving the light of guidance and having the spiritual emotions of the Blessed Prophet -upon him blessings and peace- reflect onto their own characters, they became the most virtuous persons among entire humankind. The spiritual enlightenment that has trickled from the Blessed Prophet -upon him blessings and peace- himself to the *murshid* through a successive chain is likewise transferred to the heart of the disciple, through *rabitah* and *sohbah*. This way, the exemplary character of the Noble Messenger -upon him blessings and peace- becomes reflected onto the disciple's character, as much as his aptitude can bear.

---

46 *Silsila-i Sharifah* is the term given to the chain of *murshids* that reach all the way to the Blessed Prophet -upon him blessings and peace-.

The Training of Sufism (Sayr Suluk)

On this level, one conducts himself, at each and every moment, as if in the presence of the Blessed Prophet -upon him blessings and peace- and seeks to unite with his quintessential morals. To strengthen the *rabitah* or the spiritual bond with the Prophet -upon him blessings and peace-, it is necessary to reinforce it with *salat-u salam* and a passionate devotion to the *Sunnah* and thereby establish a line of love and affinity in the heart.

It goes without saying that in Abu Bakr -Allah be well-pleased with him- one can find the most exquisite realization of *fana fi'r-rasul*. In appreciation of his spiritual mindset, the Blessed Prophet -upon him blessings and peace- has even said:

"Abu Bakr is of me, I am of Abu Bakr. Abu Bakr is my brother both Here and in the Hereafter." (Daylami, Musnad, I, 437)

Expressed beautifully by the *hadith* is the intimacy of the heart. Yet, a station even beyond this intimacy of the heart is the station of *fana fillah*, annihilation in Allah, glory unto Him. Tapping into the mysteries of the *ayat*:

وَهُوَ مَعَكُمْ اَيْنَ مَا كُنْتُمْ

"And He is with you wherever you may be." (al-Hadid, 4)

"…and We are nearer to him than his life-vein." (Qaf, 16) are possible only through attaining the station of *fana fillah*.

The heart of a *murshid* that has become annihilated in the Lord is spiritually enlightened by the manifestation of Divine names. Thus, the heart of a *murshid* is like virtually a lens that has gathered beams of light onto a single spot. The blessings of these manifestations burn all negativity to ash. Through *rabitah*, the disciple seeks to benefit from these blessings. Egoistic and selfish feelings thereby disappear from the heart and are replaced by the spiritual mindset of that model character. All things that until then had invaded the heart are banished and incarcerated where they truly belong.

This transmission of the spiritual mindset, from the *murshid* to the *murid*, signifies a progress towards spiritual unification. "One is with whom he loves", states the *hadith*.

Sufism: A Path Towards the Internalization of Faith (Ihsân)

On this subject, the Sleepers of the Cave, whose experience receives some mention in the Holy Quran[47], is noteworthy indeed. The quality of loyalty reflected onto *Qitmir*, the Sleepers' dog, because it kept watch over a group of pious and righteous men. And in return, it, too, will enter Paradise with the pious and the righteous.[48] Considering that even a dog can attain to such a level by keeping company with the pious and the righteous, the spiritual progress that beckons for a true believer through accompanying the pious and righteous servants of the Lord, is glaringly obvious.

We would like to touch upon another aspect of *rabitah*, a practice of enormous significance in *tasawwuf*.

Rabitah-i Mawt (The Contemplation of Death)

In *tasawwuf*, establishing a bond or a *rabitah* with the thought of death is referred to as the contemplation of death (*tafakkur-i mawt*). Thinking of death wields an enormous influence on one's mindset and behavior. The Blessed Prophet -upon him blessings and peace- says:

$$\text{اَكْثِرُوا ذِكْرَ هَاذِمِ اللَّذَّاتِ يَعْنِى الْمَوْتَ}$$

"Frequently remember that which uproots all pleasures; that is death." (Tirmidhi, Zuhd, 4)

Reflecting on death undoubtedly reduces the desires of the ego and the love of the world that leave a person in discomfort. Excess love of the passing possessions of the world, ambition for prestige and pursuit of things the ego finds desirable, is the beginning of spiritual disease. Towards protecting the heart from becoming infected with this disease, recalling the grave and the tribulations of the grave to which we are to be exposed in the near future will direct us to a genuine repentance and enable us to exert our deeds of worship with earnestness, guarding us at the same time from worldly ambitions and vain desires. The *dhikr* and *rabitah* we continue to practice will become the means of our eternal salvation and happiness in the Hereafter.

---

47   See al-Kahf, *ayat* 9 to 26.
48   For relevant information, refer to Ismail Hakkı Bursawi, *Ruhu'l-Bayan*, V, 226.

The Training of Sufism (Sayr Suluk)

It is reported that Ali -Allah be well-pleased with him- left the following words of advice to his son Hasan -Allah be well-pleased with him-:

"Son! Earnestly remind yourself of death and train your heart in its remembrance. Do not forget that whatever there is will eventually be reduced to nothing and remain in that nothingness! Remind your heart of the potential dangers of the world!"

Indeed, since time does not continue to flow undisturbed, like a straight line, one ought to be aware that times of trouble may quite well come to pass, just like times of joy.

Imam Ghazzali affords similar words of advice:

"Son...Live as long as you may, in any case, you shall one day die! Love who you wish, in any case, you shall one day be separated! Do anything you wish, in any case, you shall one day be called into account!

Son...Your sole purpose should be to mature your spirit, restrain your ego and prepare your body for death; for it is the grave that shall be your final station. The grave-dwellers are waiting in anticipation for the day when you will join them. Do not ever think of going there without having packed your food for the journey!"

Some of the advices Omar ibn Abdulaziz gave to Muslims in his final sermon are as follows

"People!

The Hereafter, which breathes fire, is terrible. Even prophets and angels with insight into the Jalali (Divine Wrath) mystery tremble before the tremor of that day of punishment. And who can ever keep his nerve, hold his strength together before the Wrath of the Almighty?

Still, do not despair the Mercy of the Lord, immeasurably boundless.

But know very well that deliverance in on the plain of Resurrection tomorrow is for he who fears the Allah, glory unto Him, refrains from rebellion and prefers the eternal to the passing, today. He who acts otherwise has fooled himself and has squandered the asset of life on unworthy investments, left empty-handed in the end.

Sufism: A Path Towards the Internalization of Faith (Ihsân)

Today, you have come to replace the people of the past. There will certainly come others to replace you!

As you can see, those who come depart and those who depart never return. This involuntary departure, this relentless flow in existence, is to Allah the Almighty alone.

Almost every day, you bid farewell to those who depart from amongst you to the Hereafter, carrying their corpses on your very shoulders…Do not you still take a lesson? You leave them in the bosom of earth, on their own without beds and pillows. How great a lesson there is in the mortals who have tasted the pain of death! They are gone to a realm they have no acquaintance with, separated from their loved ones, awoken from the dream of this passing life… They now see the Truth but all too little too late…The bird has flown from the cage and with it, all means of making amends…Nothing but righteous deeds remain in their otherwise empty hands. On that day of return, their sins grow in their eyes as they grievingly wait for their verdicts. Distraught, they tremor with the terror of that destined day of resurrection."

Death is passage through which one awakes in another realm and comes to terms with the truth in its nakedness. Yet, being awoken then is of no benefit on its own, unless one awakens himself before death by tearing apart the veils of ignorance.

The contemplation of death acts as a shield that protects the *murid* from ambitions, from pinning his faith on the world and all other kinds of egoistic tendencies. Since the main objective of *tasawwuf* is to vanquish the ego, the contemplation of death is a method espoused exclusively by all Sufi orders.

b. Spiritual Gathering (*Sohbah*)

Assemblies of sohbah and dhikr are gardens of Paradise on Earth, soaked by the downpour of Divine mercy and serenity.

Among the most important means utilized by many a *murshid-i kamil* in order to positively influence the heart and spirit of the *murid* is spiritual gathering and speech or *sohbah*. The words of a person who has purified his ego and heart are overloaded with the emotions of his experienced mindset. Words uttered sincerely amid these emotions find a way to the heart of the listener, influencing him beneficially.

Ikhlas, or sincerity, is the most basic factor that renders a conversation influential. The speech of a *murshid-i kamil*, most sincerely striving to transfer certain spiritual feelings onto his subject, consists of a devotion to the *Sunnah* of the Blessed Prophet -upon him blessings and peace-. The quality of *ikhlas* that wields this influence is brought about by putting what one knows to practice and to desire sincerely, from the bottom of the heart, that the listener adopts the advices given and implements them in his own life.

Another factor that makes speech influential is conciseness (*wajiz*). Achieving conciseness in speech, on the other hand, depends on mastery of the given language and a choosing the best possible words. The apogee of this power of conciseness is the Holy Quran.

In the Meccan era of Prophethood, the daughter of Imru'l-Qays, a celebrated Arab poet, was still alive. They read to her *surah* al-Zilzal. A woman very much conversant with eloquence, articulateness and concision, she became virtually petrified from wonder.

"Such words", she then said, "cannot be the words of a mortal. No mortal has to power to express words on such a high level. It is not right for my father's poems to still remain hanging on the walls of Kaaba when there are words like this on Earth. Please…go and bring those poems down!"

So states the *hadith*:

$$ \text{اِنَّ مِنَ الْبَيَانِ سِحْرًا} $$

"There is surely magic in some speech." (Bukhari, Nikah, 47) That is speech exercises a magic-like effect on the heart.

Offering spiritual guidance through speech, therefore, holds great importance. To properly come to terms with the extent of blessings of the Prophet's -upon him blessings and peace- brought about through speech, it is enough to ponder why that particular age, in which those speeches took place, and not any other in the history of humankind entire, is called the *Asr-u Saadah*, the Age of Bliss. A *muakkad sunnah* of the Blessed Prophet -upon him blessings and peace-, that is a practice that the Prophet -upon him blessings and peace- repeated consistently, *sohbah* holds a central place in all Sufi orders, especially in the Naqshbandi, as a means of transferring spiritual enlightenment from one heart to another.

Speaking of conciseness, one recalls the poetic words of Yunus Emre, which express the power of speech, both positive and negative:

With a word a war is ended,
With a word another beheaded,
A poisonous dish is turned,
To honey and butter with a word

The heart-worlds of the Companions, previously resembling an arid land, became inundated with blissful downpours of mercy through the speech of the Blessed Prophet -upon him blessings and peace-. Thanks to this, their unique seeds of virtue and spirit that until then had remained concealed beneath the soil were able to flourish. The spiritual transaction of love reflecting from one soul to another enabled the emergence of star characters. The man of ignorance, hardhearted to the point of burying his own daughter alive, who recognized no rights whatsoever, melted away and disappeared. In the same silhouette there instead appeared a teary-eyed, selfless and sensitive man.

It is significant that *sahabah*, the Arabic term for companion, and *sohbah* are derivatives of the same word. Overflowing emotions of love and respect for the Blessed Prophet -upon him blessings and peace- allowed the Companions to become the most consummate examples of the ideal benefit spiritual speech and training is hoped to yield. Yet, the state of spiritual peace and manners that would overcome them when in the presence of the Blessed Prophet -upon him blessings and peace- was of such an enormous degree, that in describing it, they would say:

"It was as if there was a bird perched on our heads and we were afraid to scare it to take flight should we make the slightest move."[49]

---

49 See, Abu Dawud, Sunnah, 23-24.

The Training of Sufism (Sayr Suluk)

They thus carried the towering character and morals of the Noble Messenger -upon him blessings and peace- everywhere they went. They displayed numerous and exceptional feats of virtue whose memories will live until the Final Hour. Regarding them, Allah, glory unto Him, declares:

"And (as for) the foremost, the first of the Muhajirs and the Ansars, and those who followed them in goodness, Allah is well pleased with them and they are well pleased with Him, and He has prepared for them gardens beneath which rivers flow, to abide in them for ever; that is the mighty achievement." (at-Tawbah, 100)

Every sohbah conducted in the feeling of worship is a reflection of many a *sohbah* of the Blessed Prophet -upon him blessings and peace-; for he is the center of all spiritual benefit obtained. Each sohbah immersed in spiritual excitement is a glimmer that successively shines forth from that center. Therefore, even if one attains a share of the light of the Prophet -upon him blessings and peace- through the medium of a righteous servant of the Lord, because the source of this light is one and the same, it is just as if he has attained that light directly from its source; just like burning other candles with the light of another. The flame that sets all candles alight is one and the same. Even the final candle to be lit reflects that very first flame, the source of the burning flame itself.

Assemblies of *sohbah* and *dhikr* are gardens of Paradise on Earth, soaked by the downpour of Divine mercy and serenity. The *hadith* states:

"If a group of people come together to remember Allah, the mercy of Allah will encompass them, serenity will descend onto them and Allah will mention them next to those in His presence." (Muslim, Dhikr, 38)

The folk of the heart, the wise and the righteous carry their love and ecstasy to their *sohbah*. They reflect the light of the mysteries in their heart to those present. And as a result of spiritual reflection (*inikas*) and coloring (*insibagh*) hearts then become filled with the light of the inspiration of truth, in varying degrees according to their aptitudes. This just like the morning zephyr that, breezing through a garden adorned with roses, cloves and all other kinds of exquisite flowers, delivers the fresh scent of spring to wherever it goes.

Sufism: A Path Towards the Internalization of Faith (Ihsân)

The Almighty says:

$$\text{وَ ذَكِّرْ فَاِنَّ الذِّكْرٰى تَنْفَعُ الْمُؤْمِن۪ينَ}$$

"And continue to remind, for surely the reminder profits the believers." (ad-Dhariyat, 55)

Having personified the above *ayah* in the most perfect manner, the Messenger of Allah -upon him blessings and peace- has said: "Religion consists of *nasihah*." (Bukhari, Iman, 42) *Nasihah* has two meanings. The first is to invite to what is good, the second sincerity.

On seeing another Companion, Abdullah ibn Rawahah -Allah be well-pleased with him- used to say to him, "Come, brother. Let's sit awhile for the sake of Allah and replenish our faith to Him."

One Companion, who could not figure out what he meant, informed the Blessed Prophet -upon him blessings and peace- of Ibn Rawaha's -Allah be well-pleased with him- words.

"May Allah have mercy on Abdullah", he commented. *"He just loves the assemblies of dhikr which the angels praise."*[50]

Also noteworthy in underlining the importance of *sohbah* is the following *hadith*:

A woman came to the Messenger of Allah -upon him blessings and peace- and bemoaned, "It is always men who reap the benefits of your speech. Could not you perhaps spare a day for us so we can gather to learn from you what you have been taught by Allah?"

"Then gather at so-and-so place on so-and-so day", said the Messenger of Allah -upon him blessings and peace-. Then the female Companions came together at that certain place, on a certain time, where the Messenger of Allah -upon him blessings and peace- taught them. (Bukhari, Ilm, 36)

Female Companions, who with the blessings of the speeches became exemplary mothers for the entire *ummah*, would reproach their children given they neglected seeing the Prophet -upon him blessings and peace-

---

50   See, Ahmed ibn Hanbal, Musnad, III, 265.

for a long time. One of them was Hudayfah -Allah be well-pleased with him-, told off by his mother, for failing to visit the Blessed Prophet -upon him blessings and peace- for a number of days. He recounts the incident as follows:

"My mother once asked me how long it had been since I had seen the Messenger of Allah -upon him blessings and peace-. 'It has been a few days now', I said. Irritated, she reproached me heavily. 'Alright, don't get angry. I will now go and visit him and offer *maghrib salat* with him and kindly request him to pray for the forgiveness of both you and I', I told her." (Tirmidhi, Manaqib, 30; Ahmed ibn Hanbal, Musnad, V, 391-2)

Muhammad Ziyauddin -may Allah sanctify his secret-, a Sufi great, would at times gather children around him and give them *sohbah*. It was at the end of one such *sohbah* that his wife commented, 'What could they understand of *sohbah*? They are still very young."

"More or less they will benefit", said he. "But my real purpose is not for them to understand. Assemblies of *sohbah* attract Divine mercy. I am only pursuing that mercy; the children are but means…"

The great Shah Naqshbandi -may Allah sanctify his secret- says: "Our path of spiritual training is paved upon *sohbah*. Goodness lies in accompanying the righteous for the sake of Allah. By continuing to be in the presence of their speech, one will attain to true faith."

Scholar Jafar ibn Sulayman r.alayh tells of the benefits he was able to secure from accompanying the righteous: "Whenever I felt hardness in my heart, I would go next to Muhammad ibn Wasi, attend his company and simply stare at his face. My heart would then soften and my laziness would be replaced by a zest for worship. That zest would last me for a week."

The words of Omar ibn Abdulaziz r.alayh are of a similar tone: "Being in the company of scholar Ubaydullah ibn Abdullah from Medina is to me better than the entire world and what is within. Being around people like him enlightens the mind, brings peace to the heart and helps one acquire manners."

A student of the great saint Abu'l-Hasan Shazali -may Allah sanctify his secret- had abandoned his company. Some time later, he saw the former student and asked as to why he had left his *sohbah*.

"What I have reaped and learnt from you until now is enough", he replied. "I no longer need you." Upset, Shazali -may Allah sanctify his secret- said:

"Listen, my dear; had it been right for a person to rest contented with the spiritual enlightenment he received from another, Abu Bakr -Allah be well-pleased with him- would have surely been content with what he had received from the Prophet -upon him blessings and peace-. Yet he remained by his side until his final breath…"

Of course, it was not just Abu Bakr -Allah be well-pleased with him- who rushed to the *sohbah* of the Blessed Prophet -upon him blessings and peace- for spiritual enlightenment, but also the Companions entire. Anyhow, the Blessed Prophet -upon him blessings and peace- would encourage them to do so at every given opportunity; for *sohbah* provided one of his primary methods of training.

Equal to the importance of showing eagerness to acquire the beauties that beckon in a *sohbah* is to look out for the right place and time. On this subject, Abdullah ibn Masud has said: "To give us advice, the Messenger of Allah -upon him blessings and peace- would look out for the most appropriate time, so as to not make us weary."

Abu Waqid al-Laysi, another Companion, recounts:

"One day, we were in the presence of the Messenger of Allah -upon him blessings and peace- inside the Masjid when there appeared three people by the door. One turned back without entering. The other two entered and drew nearer to the Messenger of Allah -upon him blessings and peace-. One of them sat on an empty spot somewhere in the circle. As there were no remaining spots left, afraid he would cause discomfort, the other assumed a seat right behind the circle.

A short while later, the Messenger of Allah -upon him blessings and peace- said, "Should I inform you of the conditions of three men? The first, who sat within the circle, sought refuge in Allah the Almighty; and Allah took him in His refuge. As for the second, he felt embarrassed before Allah the Almighty and embraced haya (spiritual manners). And Allah the Almighty became embarrassed before His servant and secured him from His punishment. And as for the other who did not enter, he turned away from the assembly and Allah, too, turned away from him." (Bukhari, Ilm, 8)

Muslim greats, aware of the wisdom underlying the above *hadith*, have allowed for the *sohbah* assemblies of the righteous to mold their hearts, never distancing themselves from such environments. Indeed, Imam Ahmed ibn Hanbal (r.a), the eminent Muslim jurist, would frequently visit the great saint Bishr ibn Khafi -may Allah sanctify his secret- and converse with him. He was attached to him, in the truest sense.

Once, his students asked, "Is it proper for you to keep on visiting an ordinary man like him when you are a *mujtahid* of the sciences of the Quran and Sunnah?"

"True. I am more knowledgeable than him in what you have just mentioned", replied the great scholar. "But he knows the Lord better than I.'

c. Service

> *To lend an ideal service is to seek the pleasure of the Lord by approaching creation with a sincere, compassionate and selfless heart.*
>
> *People of service must be courteous in all their conducts, as delicate as one tiptoeing around a minefield; for their objects are hearts, the focal point of the Divine Gaze.*

Khidmah, or service, is of enormous importance in Sufi training. The most effective way of implanting feelings of modesty, selflessness (*mahwiyah*) and mercy for the created in hearts runs through service. All *murshid*s have therefore considered it a vital means in training the disciple.

If we were to search for the pillar of Islamic morals, we would no doubt find it in turning to the Lord with love and sincerity, whose defining hallmark, in turn, is service. True to the principle 'serve to receive grace (*himmah*)', serving is an exceptional step on the ladder that delivers hearts to sublime peaks.

Such a step it is that the entirety of prophets and saints, blessed with Divine reunion and an eternity of rewards, have used for elevation. For a lifetime, they personified the Prophet's -upon him blessings and peace- words: "The notable of a tribe is he who serves it" (Daylami, Musnad, II, 324)

Sufism: A Path Towards the Internalization of Faith (Ihsân)

Thus the road to the peak and the acquiring of eternity lies in services lent with a genuine heart. There are times when a tiny service offered for the sake of the Divine can be superior to many supererogatory deeds of worship. To call to mind one such instance:

During a campaign under sweltering heat, the Blessed Prophet -upon him blessings and peace- had the Companions camp at a suitable location. Some were fasting, others were not. Tired, those who were fasting quickly fell asleep. Others, who were not, carried water for those who were and set up tents to shade them. When the time came to breakfast, the Blessed Prophet -upon him blessings and peace- said: "Those who did not fast today have received rewards greater than those who did." (Muslim, Siyam, 100-101)

The Blessed Prophet -upon him blessings and peace-, who has presented countless spurs for his *ummah* to embrace service, carried stones on his back during the construction of the mosques of Quba and Medina, despite his Companions insisting him otherwise. The exceptional modesty and spirit to serve embodied by the Light of Being -upon him blessings and peace- lays out a unique example for all Muslims. Indeed, his entire life was a sheer case of serving the Real, humankind and entire creation.

Naturally, service becomes a defining feature of the wise who take that 'sacred being' as example. Each person in love with the Real and captivated by the Prophet -upon him blessings and peace- is a person of service. People of service are like the sun and the moon, which only grow in brightness the more they light up their surroundings. The pallor of neither autumn nor winter can diminish their brightness in the least. They are like a river that traverses a great distance, serving animals, trees, the rose, the clove and the nightingale in its lengthy flow, whose delta can only be the Beloved's ocean of eternity and reunion.

Those acquainted with this truth look upon themselves as servants, even if made a ruler over the public. On being referred to as 'The Sovereign of the Two Holy Lands' (*Hakimu'l-Haramayn'is-Sharifayn*), in the first sermon after having assumed custodianship over Mecca and Medina, Sultan Selim objected, behind eyes moistened with tears, declaring, "No; rather The Servant of the Two Holy Lands'. This can only be a manifestation of a sublime perception of service and a realization of the true purpose of servanthood to the Lord.

The Training of Sufism (Sayr Suluk)

Ubaydullah Ahrar -may Allah sanctify his secret- in fact ascribes his spiritual level to the blessings of his service when he says, "We have not covered distance on this path solely from reading books of tasawwuf but from putting into practice what we read to the best of our capabilities and serving the public. Each is taken delivered from a certain path. We were delivered through the path of service."

And this shows that knowing alone is not enough without putting what is known to practice through serving. Yet Divine acceptance of the service given depends on it carrying certain qualities. An accepted or ideal service, in this sense, is to seek the pleasure of the Lord by approaching creation with a sincere, compassionate and selfless heart. In other words, serving must not be marred with self-interest and must instead be offered genuinely, eyeing exclusively the rewards of the Hereafter. If carried out with this intent, then even 'half a date' is a potential means for eternal salvation, as is mentioned in the *hadith*.

Ubaydullah Ahrar -may Allah sanctify his secret- recounts:

"I was at the bazaar one day when a man approached me and said, 'I am hungry. Could you feed me for the sake of Allah?'

I had no means at the time, except for an old, worn out imamah. So I went to a cook shop and asked him if he could feed the hungry man in return for it. 'It is worn out but clean', I said to him. 'You might use it to dry your dishes'.

Not only did the cook feed the man, he also wanted me to keep the imamah. Despite his persistent efforts, I did not take it back. I waited until the man ate to his heart's content, even though I was no better than him in needing a meal."

With the blessing of Allah, glory unto Him, Ubaydullah Ahrar -may Allah sanctify his secret- ended up with great wealth; so great that there were thousands of workers laboring away in his fields. Still, he did not step a foot away from service. He again recounts his mindset as a rich man:

"I had taken upon myself the duty of caring for four ill persons in the Qutbuddin Madrasa in Samarkand. As their illnesses had become advanced, they had begun dirtying their beds. I used to wash and clothe them with my hands. Because I served without break, I soon became bedridden myself. But even then I continued carrying water with earthenware, cleaning the ill and washing their clothes."

The lives of such great figures provide splendid examples, for us, of the virtue of spending and serving in the way of the Real. However rich a Muslim may be, he can offer what is due of his wealth only by increasing his spiritual strength and raising the level of his heart-world. Observing the standards of piety and abstinence (*zuhd*) the more one progresses spiritually and maintaining a perfect modesty despite of wealth may, then, carry a Muslim to the ideal point illustrated in the life of Ubaydullah Ahrar -may Allah sanctify his secret-.

Another level of service that is difficult to reach is highlighted in the below account of the righteous Maruf Karhi -may Allah sanctify his secret-.

An ill man, old and frail, had come to visit Maruf Karhi -may Allah sanctify his secret-. The poor old man was as pale as death; it was as if he was putting a spike through his fragile body with every breath. Maruf Karhi -may Allah sanctify his secret- laid a bed on the floor for him to get some rest.

Wailing and moaning, the old man was not able to get a blink of sleep until morning; neither could anyone else from his moans. To make things worse, he had gotten restless by each passing moment, taking his frustration out on those around. Able to put up with him only for so long, others in the house soon began heading out, in ones and twos. Maruf Karhi -may Allah sanctify his secret- and his wife were left alone with the old man.

To see to the old man's needs and serve him proper, Maruf Karhi was spending the nights without any sleep. But one night, when his lack of sleep caught up with him, he involuntarily dosed off for a while. Seeing him asleep, instead of being of thankful to a man so graceful and compassionate to see to his needs, the inconsiderate old man began grumbling to himself:

"What sort of a dervish is this? People like him only have reputations. In truth, they are showoffs. Desire is the end their deeds serve. They are clean on the outside, yet dirty on the inside. They advise others with piety, yet neglect it themselves. That is why that man over there sleeps so comfortably without thinking of my condition. How can one who sleeps contented on a full stomach understand the troubles of a bedridden man who does not blink an eye from pain?"

The Training of Sufism (Sayr Suluk)

Maruf Karhi had heard every single word. Yet, patient and magnanimous, he pretended to have heard nothing. But his wife could not put up with it any longer, as she whispered to her husband, "You have heard what the grumpy old man just said. We cannot have him at our house any longer. I cannot allow him to be a burden on you and cause you more discomfort than he already has. Tell him to fend for himself. Kind treatment is merited by those who appreciate it. It is bad to treat an ungrateful man kindly. It drives them even wilder. You do not just pamper and place a pillow under their heads. Severing them would serve them just right."

Patiently listening to his wife's outburst, Maruf Karhi smiled and replied:

"Why do the words he says hurt you, dear? If he has screamed, so be it. If he has acted rudely, it was against me. His mean words are pleasant to my ears. You can see that he is in continuous pain. Can't you see that the poor old man cannot even blink an eye? Know that true finesse, true mercy and compassion, lies in putting up with the treatment of people like him."

Sheikh Sadi, who narrates this incident, adds the below advice:

"Virtue in service is to bear the burden of the weak when strongest and healthiest, as a show of appreciation. A heart filled with compassion is forgiving. If you rest content with your dull image, with your body your name will die, too. But if you become a man of generosity, devoted to service, your life will continue even after death, in hearts where your generosity survives. Can you not see that there are many tombs in Karh, none more visited and renowned than that of Maruf Karhi?"

The righteous have already said it wonderfully: "*Tasawwuf* is to become adored, without being a burden".

The gates of mercy are opened by compassionate and benevolent service. The value of a given service depends on the greatness of the sacrifice involved and it being carried out like it is a deed of worship. Again, an ideal service is that which is lent solely for the pleasure of the Lord, with a sensitive conduct that utterly avoids disparaging the person served. As said by Abdullah ibn Munazil -may Allah sanctify his secret-: "Manners in service are more important than the service itself."

Mawlana Rumi -may Allah sanctify his secret- speaks in a similar tone: "Work for the love of Allah. Serve for the love of Allah. What is it to you if the public appreciates it or not? Does not Allah suffice as an auspicious customer in the bazaar that is the world? What can people possibly give you in comparison with what Allah shall give? So turn your gaze not to the thanks that come from the way of the people, but to the acceptance that comes from the way of Allah!"

This is exactly the beauty and greatness *tasawwuf* wishes to impart onto hearts. The words of advice given by Amir Kulal -may Allah sanctify his secret- to his student Bahaaddin Naqshbandi -may Allah sanctify his secret- for him to rid his heart of deep set egoistic tendencies are emblematic:

"Seek to win hearts; serve the vulnerable! Protect the weak and the brokenhearted! They are such that they receive no income from the public. Nevertheless, they remain in their frames of complete peace of heart, modesty and dejection. Search and find these people and serve them!"

During the first seven years of his initiation into the Sufi path, Shah Naqshbandi -may Allah sanctify his secret- in fact lead a life defined by *khidmah*, where he served the ill and weak, as well as injured animals, even sparing time to clean streets which people used, simply to reach the state of 'nothingness', the complete opposite of pride and conceit.

He recounts these years himself: "For a long time, I worked on the road as my master had commanded, fulfilling all services required of me. There came a point where, on seeing any creation of the Lord whatsoever, I would stand still where I was and wait for it to walk past. This lasted seven years all together. In return, I was engulfed by such a spiritual mindset that I could feel their inner moans of anguish, pleading the Lord."

This is a concrete manifestation of serving creation for the sake of the Creator and looking upon them through eyes of Divine love.

About righteous Muslims, the Almighty states:

"They compete with each other in what is good" (Al-i Imran, 114). The most exceptional fruits this competition has yielded are *waqf*s or charity trusts.

Most certainly, service comes in various forms. All efforts made for the pleasure of Allah, glory unto Him, are included in service. The important thing is for hearts to lend a service, be it spiritual or financial,

The Training of Sufism (Sayr Suluk)

as much as is allowed by their aptitudes, powers and suitability. The Lord has entrusted each person with a distinct kind of service to lend and has made each person suitable for the task. And no less, He has endowed each person with the required means, spiritual and physical.

There were approximately 120,000 Companions present in the Farewell Pilgrimage. Over a 100,000 of them ended up going to various lands on Earth, near and far, offering their lives as trusts in the way of the Lord, passing away in those lands. Just to cite one example among many, the tombs of the sons of Othman and Abbas -Allah be well-pleased with him- are in fact in Samarkand. Istanbul itself is home to the graves of many Companions. An overwhelming majority of those who remained in Mecca and Medina, in turn, served to protect the hubs of Islam, continuing their services there.

One of the most illustrious feats of leaving no stone unturned in calling people to guidance and striving genuinely for their happiness in Here and in the Hereafter is vivid in the life of Khalid ibn Zayd Abu Ayyub al-Ansari -Allah be well-pleased with him-, who twice arrived at the fortified walls of Istanbul, despite his old age. The love of serving and the battle to salvage their eternity steered them to four corners of the world.

Another colossal personification of the spirit of service is Wahb ibn Kabshah -Allah be well-pleased with him-. The tomb of this celebrated Companion is in China.[51] The Blessed Prophet -upon him blessings and peace- had entrusted him with the duty of carrying the light of guidance to China. Considering the circumstances of then, China was at a year's distance away from Arabia. After spending many years there, the Companion set out to Medina, in hope of appeasing the longing for the Prophet -upon him blessings and peace- burning within his heart. He made it to Medina after a grueling one year journey, only to find that the Blessed Prophet -upon him blessings and peace- had passed away. He was thus unable to see him. But fully conscious of the sacredness of the mission given him by

---

[51] There is also a post (*maqam*) attributed to Saad ibn Abi Waqqas -Allah be well-pleased with him- in Guangzhou, China. Historically renowned is the fact that the graves of Companions and the righteous, more often than not, play a vital role in keeping the religious feelings of locals animate. There are many such extant examples of this in the Central Asian towns like Samarkand, Bukhara and Tashkent.

Sufism: A Path Towards the Internalization of Faith (Ihsân)

the Prophet -upon him blessings and peace-, he returned once again to China and served until he ultimately passed away in that land.

These are magnificent portraits of *khidmah* only an ecstatic faith can explain. Their love for and spirit of service are like stars that light up our skies of eternal salvation.

There is no doubt that the Companions were able to attain to this level by minutely abiding to the nine principles of service below, in the light of the exceptional training of the Blessed Prophet -upon him blessings and peace-:

1. Serving Allah, glory unto Him and wholeheartedly abiding by His commands and prohibitions.

2. Serving the Blessed Prophet -upon him blessings and peace-; loving him from the bottom of the heart and leading a life according to his Sunnah.

3. Serving the spiritual elders of Islam, loyally and lovingly.

4. Serving parents; striving to gain their blessings without retorting even an 'ah'.

5. Serving the children by ensuring they are raised as righteous Muslims.

6. Serving relatives; visiting them and seeing to their needs.

7. Serving Muslims, sharing their joy and pain.

8. Serving entire humankind, striving to be beneficial in both speech and action.

9. Serving entire creation; taking all beings under their wings of compassion.

There is great lesson in the following words of Ali Ramitani -may Allah sanctify his secret- concerning the performance of all the above mentioned services: "There are many who mix their services with insult. But there are only a few who appreciate how great a blessing it is to serve. If you treat the opportunity to serve as a blessing and be thankful towards whom you serve, everyone will become satisfied with you and there will only be a few who complain."

The Training of Sufism (Sayr Suluk)

Whether we are aware of it or not, we are all searching for spiritual peace and serenity. And that is a profound treasure that may only be attained through services offered with the passion one has whilst offering a deed of worship. A believer who has a penchant and spirit to serve therefore always knows how to find the opportunity and means to do so. The keenness he shows in his sacrifices in the way of Allah, glory unto Him, is more intense than the ambitions of those who pursue worldly interests.

Once the desire to serve, which is nourished by the climate of love, becomes fixed in the heart, it renders one a wayfarer of eternity. The heart sheds its hardness of Hajjaj and enshrouds itself in the gentle cloak of Yunus. Knowledge, art and morals obtained in this state of mind, achieve an enrapturing life of eternity. A genuine and true service is thus a masterpiece of a mature heart. And it is such hearts that are the focus of the Divine Gaze.

How massive a loss it is then to lay waste to a life, away from the qualities of the heart! And how great a joy it is for those truly able to fill their hearts with the love to serve!

d. Favorable Inclination (*Tawajjuh*)

Tawajjuh is for the *murshid* to direct all his spiritual powers onto the *murid* and thereby pass his spiritual mindset onto him; it is the act of devoting spiritual attention. To say the same thing in another way, it is for the *murshid-i kamil* to transfer his beautiful states, in their entirety, onto the *murid* and hence exercise a positive effect on his heart and spirit. *Tawajjuh* has various means, both primary and secondary. Among these, we will talk about two in particular: the eye (*nazar*) and the essence.

The Eye

The eye is a means of seeing. The effect that comes about through seeing is conventionally referred to as 'the eye', meant by which is what the eye actually does, that is the act of 'looking'. In everyday language, 'the look' (*nazar*) is used more to refer to the negative effect brought about by looking, that is 'the evil eye'. The term 'evil eye' (*nazar* or *isabatu'l-ayn*) is commonly used to express the physical and spiritual damage incurred from the look or the eye of another. This kind of 'looking' has been made mention in some *ahadith*:

"The evil eye (*nazar*) is real." (Bukhari, Tibb, 36)

"The evil eye sends man to the grave and a camel into a pot (kills it)." (Suyuti, al-Jamiu's-Saghir, II, 60)

Knowledge based on experience on the effects of the eye is a fact accepted by all. Yet the effects of the eye are not just negative as commonly accepted; they may also be of a positive nature. The reason that brings about this effect is that the eye emits a ray onto whosoever it looks, whose nature is not quite known. And the effect is shaped according to the positive or negative nature of the ray. Facts presented by contemporary physics on rays are developed to such an extent that they leave no choice than to accept them.

The laser beam, discovered only in this century, is also a type of ray. It is now common knowledge that laser beams are used in diverse tasks of a difficult nature, from cutting thick steel to performing medical operations. Known from even way before was the diverse reactions shown by various objects, especially their colors, on exposure to rays of light.[52]

The effects caused by the rays emitted from the eye on physical objects are not always on the same level of intensity for the looker and the recipient. Just as some eyes emit rays, both positive and negative, that are of a more intense nature than others, some recipients are prone to being affected more. Some possess a greater inclination for being affected, while others do not. The public usually refers to persons identified as emitting strong yet negative rays in their looks as 'evil-lookers' and does their best to avoid their looks.

---

52 In some libraries, they lay green covers on reading desks, to prevent the eyes from getting weary. Looking at the sea or the horizon has a soothing affect on the eye; much the same is the case with looking at something green. The reason as to why people usually wear white in summer is due to the capability of the color to reflect back what the sunrays it receives. Black reacts in the complete opposite. Far from reflecting the sunrays back to whence they came, darker colors absorb them and hence keep the body warm. While wearing white, the symbol of purity, inside the hospital, surgeons are seen wearing cyan green inside the surgery. This is due to the exact same reason: green exercises a soothing effect on eyesight. Dark tones of yellow and blue, on the other hand, again have an innate tendency to absorb the rays they receive. This must be the reason as to why children are made to wear blue amulets or gold coins to repel the negative influence of sinister looks.

The Training of Sufism (Sayr Suluk)

Nazar is valid even in animals. The look of an adder, for instance, is so affective that it can result in miscarriage and even in the death of some living organisms.[53]

'The look', with which the public is intuitively or traditionally –albeit not scientifically- acquainted, plays a vital role in the training of the disciple in *tasawwuf*. As a legacy of the Blessed Prophet -upon him blessings and peace- whose inheritor he is, a *murshid-i kamil* is a person whose power of vision has reached its furthermost extent of influence, as a result of his spiritual training and inner purification.

Coming right behind the chain of Prophets in the spiritual rankings of humankind are the Companions. The term *sahabah*, the Arabic equivalent of 'Companion' which shares the same etymological root with *sohbah*, is used in reference to those who were honored to be in the inspirational presence of the Blessed Prophet -upon him blessings and peace-, in a state of having believed in what he brought. Yet, even though they owe their respect and honor, by and large, to having been in the presence of the Prophet -upon him blessings and peace-, the main cause is essentially the privilege of having been subject to his 'look'. Notwithstanding the various criteria put forth in determining the eligibility of being considered a 'Companion', the most widely accepted among them is for a person to be subjected to the look of the Blessed Prophet -upon him blessings and peace-, to have looked at him and to have been looked back on.

Even a top of the tier saint cannot, in any way, be compared to a Companion, even if he be a Companion of the lowest degree. This is because each Companion carries a distinct quality that comes with being subjected to the look of the Prophet -upon him blessings and peace-, a quality incomparable to any other, which has no other substitute. Because Muslims subsequent the generation of Companions were not privileged with this look, they were not able to attain to the privileged status of 'companionship'. Still, those fortunate to see those who had seen the Blessed Prophet -upon him blessings and peace- are referred to as *Tabiun* and their successor, *Taba-i Tabiin*.

---

53   See, Bukhari, Badu'l-Khalq, 14.

Sufism: A Path Towards the Internalization of Faith (Ihsân)

With that said, being the spiritual inheritors of the Blessed Prophet -upon him blessings and peace-, saints possess an authority and power incomparable to any of their contemporaries. To fully benefit from a *murshid-i kamil*, it is therefore not enough to simply be a number among those who feel affection for him. One must furthermore seek to attain the inspirational honor of becoming subjected to his enlightening gaze.

The Blessed Prophet -upon him blessings and peace- says: "Beware of a believer's perception; for he looks with the light of Allah." (Tirmidhi, Tafsir, 15) The perceptive power of each Muslim corresponds to his depth of *iman*. Having a maturity of faith, the perceptive powers of saints therefore exceed that of other Muslims.

The word 'beware' mentioned in the *hadith* is meant as a caution against entering the presence of mature Muslims with hidden agendas and a confused mind, as with the help of an exceptional power of perception, they will sense that which one tries to keep hidden. As external veils are parted for those whose perceptive powers have reached such a level, they instantly acknowledge things for what they are. Religious manners thus demand one to keep hold of his tongue in the presence of a scholar, and of his heart in the presence of the wise.

Since 'the eye' is one of the most important means a *murshid* utilizes to train a *murid*, being fortunate enough to be on the receiving end of that look has been considered an enormous privilege.

A Personal Memory

It was during the years I was a student at the Imam-Hatip Lyceum when I met Ahmed Can, a man of a beautiful heart. He was a Pakistani who had a deep affection for the honorable Mahmud Sami Effendi -may Allah sanctify his secret-. He was no less devoted to my father Musa Effendi -may Allah sanctify his secret-, never wanting to leave his side. He would thus frequently come to Turkey to visit Mahmud Sami Effendi -may Allah sanctify his secret- and stay in the guesthouse in our garden.

He was animated by such a profound love that even on the days where there was no *sohbah*, he would still burn with an undying desire to see Mahmud Sami Effendi -may Allah sanctify his secret-, walking around his house in hope of catching a glimpse. One night he recounted how this love came to be:

"It was a season of *hajj*. I was sitting inside the *Masjid* of Medina, in an area referred to as *Ashab-i Suffah* within the *Rawdah*. At one stage, I noticed an elegant man with a clean face, whose appearance reminded one of Allah, glory unto Him, walk towards where I was sitting, with a group of amicable people behind him. Just as he was walking past me, he threw me a look.

That look, angelic and radiating, instantly carried me away to another climate, a world of another kind. Everything had suddenly changed. The spiritual pleasure I received from that look had me on the verge of losing consciousness. Moments later, when I regained my senses, I got up, intent on finding that man. But the renowned crowdedness of the *Rawdah* made that impossible.

Yet, hoping he would come back around to that same spot, I began waiting near where I had originally been seated. And thankfully, my hope was realized. I began following him, joyously. Those around him must have thought I was a beggar, as a few of them approached me, wanting to give me charity. True, I was not a rich man; yet the blessings of that man's look made everything lose value in my sight. I felt like I had begun swimming in an ocean of contentedness. They eventually reached a house and began stepping inside. When I followed them in their wake, they, quite naturally, wanted to prevent me, as they did not know who I was. But Mahmud Sami Effendi -may Allah sanctify his secret-, that great man of wisdom, turned around and invited me inside. That day, I was exposed to many a spiritual manifestation of that man, many a look and attention (*tawajjuh*).

Alhamdulillah, my life has since changed for the better and I have become a totally different man, striving only for the life of eternity. To save up money each year to come here, in hope of benefiting from his look and attention, has now become my heart's exclusive reason for joy."

Essence

The use of 'essence' is the most shortcut and effective means utilized by a *murshid* to manage the *murid*'s heart and spirit. This is effectuated by virtue of the *murshid*, referred to as *quddisah sirruh* (may Allah sanctify his mystery), implementing his *sirr*, or mystery. The nature of this means is known only by him who uses it. As such, it belongs not to spoken *tasawwuf* (*qal*) but to its spiritual mindset (*hal*). Hence, detail of it cannot be found in books.

e. Prayer (Dua)

Prayer is another means put to use by the *murshid-i kamil* in directing the disciple to the better. This, too, has its roots in the Sunnah of the Blessed Prophet -upon him blessings and peace-.

It is well known that right before becoming Muslim, Omar -Allah be well-pleased with him- was bent on committing the most evil crime thinkable, murdering the Noble Messenger -upon him blessings and peace-. But the blessings of a prayer the Blessed Prophet -upon him blessings and peace- had previously made on his behalf, turned him away from carrying the deed out, becoming honored with the guidance of Islam instead. There are many similar examples in the life of the Prophet -upon him blessings and peace-.

Also renowned is the time when the Blessed Prophet -upon him blessings and peace- was asked during the siege of Taif to curse the Thaqif Tribe, who had exacted so much harm on Muslims. The Prophet of Mercy -upon him blessings and peace- instead prayed for their guidance, a compassionate plea whose blessings soon enabled the entire tribe to arrive at the Blessed Prophet's -upon him blessings and peace- presence to announce their wish to enter Islam.[54]

Shaybah -Allah be well-pleased with him- recounts the following:

"I was present by the side of the Messenger of Allah -upon him blessings and peace- in the Battle of Hunayn, not because I had become Muslim or accepted the Prophet but because I just could not stomach the fact that the Hawazin Tribe had mobilized an army against Quraysh. During a heated moment of the battle, to the Messenger of Allah -upon him blessings and peace- who was right beside me, I said:

'I see black and white horses!'

---

54 See, Ibn Hisham, as-Sirah, IV, 103.

The Training of Sufism (Sayr Suluk)

'Shaybah', said the Messenger of Allah -upon him blessings and peace-, 'only nonbelievers are able to see those horses that have come to the aid of Muslims.' He then patted me on the back and added, 'Lord…Give Shaybah guidance!' He did this three times. On the third, as he lifted his hand from my back, there was suddenly nobody on entire Earth, dearer to me than him." (Ibn Kathir, al-Bidayah, IV, 333)

In spite of having rejected numerous offers of guidance made by her son, the mother of Abu Hurayrah -Allah be well-pleased with him-, the eminent *hadith* narrator, ended up becoming Muslim thanks to the Blessed Prophet's prayer.[55] A prayer made by a spiritual inheritor of the Prophet -upon him blessings and peace- also exercises a maximum affect; and this acts an abundant means of spiritual rehabilitation.

Under all circumstances, a prayer reaps a result. Should a prayer be contrary to 'absolute providence' and therefore be left hanging, its compensation will be given in the Hereafter, as testified by numerous *ahadith*.[56]

On the other hand, it is not necessary that the prayer be made by a righteous man of spiritual standing for it to reap a blessing, so long as it is made sincerely, coupled with a serious desire. Hence, even a prayer made by a sinful Muslim on behalf of his brother is of enormous value. For no matter a how sinful His servant might be, Allah, glory unto Him, never forsakes him. If that were the case, backbiting (*ghiybah*) that is speaking of a misdemeanor of another behind his back, would not have been declared a great sin.

For that reason, it is not right for a person, who for one reason or another cannot manage to stay away from sin, to remain behind from praying for the *ummah* and their loved ones, falsely thinking that their prayers are of no worth because of their sinful conditions. They prayer of even the most sinful person for another may be accepted, given it is made with a sincere heart, as if wanting the thing for himself. The Lord accepts the prayers of who He wills.

On this note, there lies further benefit in talking about other characteristics of prayer.

---

55   See, Muslim, Fadailu's-Sahabah, 158.
56   See, Ahmed ibn Hanbal, Musnad, III, 18.

Sufism: A Path Towards the Internalization of Faith (Ihsân)

The Blessed Prophet -upon him blessings and peace- encouraged Muslims at every opportunity to pray for one another, both in each others presence and absence. To Omar -Allah be well-pleased with him-, who came to ask permission to perform *umrah*, the Noble Messenger -upon him blessings and peace- had even said:

"Do not forget us in your prayer, brother!" (Tirmidhi, Daawat, 109; Abu Dawud, Witr, 23)

"I became so happy to hear that", Omar -Allah be well-pleased with him- later said, "it was as if I was given the universe."

The Blessed Prophet -upon him blessings and peace- is doubtless the most honorable being in the sight of the Almighty. In spite of this, he still asked his Companions to pray for him. This is an indication that people of maturity may benefit even from the prayers of those who are of a lower spiritual rank.

The Blessed Prophet -upon him blessings and peace- again said the following to Omar -Allah be well-pleased with him-: "The best of the *Tabiun* is a man by the name of Uways. If he were to make an oath on the name of Allah, Allah would surely render his oath valid. Should any one of you come across him, ask him to pray for your forgiveness."[57] Omar -Allah be well-pleased with him- did meet Uways al-Qarani some time later and asked him to pray on his behalf.

It is thus clear that asking the righteous and pious for a prayer to repel troubles and distress and attract what is good, is something the Blessed Prophet -upon him blessings and peace- actually advised the *ummah* with.

---

57   See, Muslim, Fadailu's-Sahabah, 223-225.

Take to forgiveness and enjoin good and turn aside from the ignorant. (al-Araf, 199)

E. THE SUFI MANNERISM

1. THE MANNER OF GUIDANCE AND MERCY

*Murshid*s, well aware that the style of guiding is just as important as its content, have followed a prophetic path in this respect, too, mediating the guidance of many. By approaching, as a code, disciples with compassion and mercy to help them in their spiritual progress, they have acquired beneficial results. The lives of the righteous abound in many such examples. The below experience of the Sufi great Ibrahim Hakkı Erzurumi is noteworthy:

Ibrahim Hakkı had been invited to a nearby village in Erzurum to give sermons during the month of Ramadan. The villagers sent a young man, a non-Muslim, with a horse, to pick Ibrahim Hakkı up from his hometown and bring him to their village. As there was only one mount, Ibrahim Hakkı -may Allah sanctify his secret- took turns with the young man to ride the horse, as Omar -Allah be well-pleased with him- had once done with his slave on the way to Jerusalem, despite the continuous protests of the young man.

"If the villagers hear about this", he kept on saying, "not only will they scold me, they will also withhold my pay!"

"None of us know, son, the condition we are to be in during our last breath. You are afraid of the villagers' reaction; yet I am afraid of the account I am to give in the presence of Allah!" replied Ibrahim Hakkı. So they continued taking turns nonetheless.

As wisdom would have it and as had been the case in the journey of Omar -Allah be well-pleased with him- and his slave, it was the young man's turn to ride the mount, just as they were entering the village. Afraid of the villagers, the young man began pleading Ibrahim Hakkı, telling him that he had forfeited his turn.

"It's your turn", replied Ibrahim Hakkı, as they entered the village, with the young man on horseback and Ibrahim Hakkı walking in front of him.

Upon seeing the situation, the villagers abruptly encircled the young servant and scolded him.

"You rude, inconsiderate wretch!" they shouted. "You are just too comfortable riding the horse to give your spot up to this great man of respect, aren't you? Is this how you do your job? Was this what we paid you to do?"

But Ibrahim Hakkı -may Allah sanctify his secret- calmed them down by explaining the situation. Thereupon, a villager called out to the young man, saying:

"Seeing this sort of virtue, the least you could do is become Muslim!"

After brief silence, the young man said:

"If you are calling me to your religion, never…But if you are calling me to the religion of this great man, I have already embraced that religion on the way here!"

The above approach of Ibrahim Hakkı -may Allah sanctify his secret- sets a standard for the desired style of guidance through compassion. It is to treat another for the sake of his essence, in a sense, to look upon creation with the gaze of the Creator. Pious hearts are therefore conscious of being entrusted on Earth as the caliphs of Allah, glory unto Him, and having been, in the words of the *ayah*, "breathed with the Spirit of Allah".[58] So no matter how polluted by sin a person may be, seeing the inner perfection of his essence, they are never ones to turn a cold shoulder on him. Rarely do they lose hope in a person; they moreover help him hold onto hope until the very end. Hope, for them, is an indisputable incentive, both intellectual and emotional. We find, even in the Quran, the Almighty teaches us *ar-Rahman* and *ar-Rahim* more emphatically than all His other Names, to the point of even revealing a *surah* by the name of *ar-Rahman* that begins with the very same name, meaning 'He whose mercy encompasses entire creation.'

---

58   See, al-Hijr, 29.

The Training of Sufism (Sayr Suluk)

Being over and above a style most harmonious with Divine Pleasure, looking upon human beings from the window of the heart and offering guidance through compassion also helps revive beauties concealed within the heart of the other, providing the most blissful results. This style imparts onto both the applier and the recipient that is to both sides of the scale, an exceptional elegance, maturity, love and hunger for the Real. It is the very elixir that has transformed many a Yunus and Rumi, a potion of life for many a heart in the throes of death.

Both the content of *tasawwuf* and the use of the Sufi style in calling to Islam have thus always proved to be of great significance. It is a historical fact that emerging at a time when the social order of Anatolia came under the disrupting grip of Mongolian hordes, great Sufis like Mawlana Rumi and Yunus Emre provided virtual springs of peace and tranquility for the disturbed masses, handing out comfort and cure bleeding wounds and weary hearts. Treating many an ignorant as a patient waiting for a cure, they lead lives utterly remote from malice and hatred. Yunus says it beautifully:

I did come to lay claim,[59]
Love is all that I aim,
Hearts are where the Friend dwells,
To mend hearts is why I came

Because they strived to mend hearts, these great figures have always gazed at others from the window of the heart and emitting love and compassion all around, they were able to lead to the guidance of many. Were they to act in opposition to this wonderful and prudent conduct, they would have completely severed what was left of the already thinned ties with the public, throwing out all their chances of guidance in the process. And this would have been in defiance of Divine Will, which desires for people to be saved from the swamps they have tripped into. The Almighty has sent tens of thousands of prophets throughout history, commanding them to purify hearts in the best possible style. The righteous (*ahlullah*), entrusted with maintaining the same duty, have continued to uphold this prophetic style in spiritual training.

---

59 *Davi* in the original Turkish.

Allah, glory unto Him, the sole source of mercy and compassion, reveals the most affective style for his servants to adopt in calling to the truth:

"Call to the way of your Lord with wisdom and goodly exhortation, and have disputations with them in the best manner…" (an-Nahl, 125)

"And who speaks better than he who calls to Allah while he himself does good, and says: I am surely of those who submit? And not alike are the good and the evil. Repel (evil) with what is best, when lo! he between whom and you was enmity would be as if he were a warm friend." (Fussilat, 33-34)

The application of this style has turned many a thorny soul into a rose, many a pitch dark dungeon like heart into a sunlit garden.

Embarking from this principle, Mawlana Rumi -may Allah sanctify his secret- underlines the importance of setting sinful human beings right on the path of truth and no less the style of conduct in doing so:

"Even if he be like iron, black and rusted, his rust will be cleansed once rubbed and polished. Polish a mirror and it will begin to shine beautifully, even if it be of iron; reflecting wonderful shapes and patterns.

Do not muddy the waters of the lake of the heart, if you wish to see the moon and the stars float above it! Humans are like a river; once the water is muddied, you will not be able to see any reflection!"

As Mawlana Rumi -may Allah sanctify his secret- says, human spirit is like clear water; if muddied by sin, it becomes murky, reflecting nothing of goodness. It then becomes necessary to refine the water to expose the spiritual gems and the light of truth in its waterbed. The aim of *tasawwuf* is therefore to rein in egotistic and selfish feelings and deliver the individual and in due course entire society to peace and harmony. The Lord has indeed adorned man with elegance and a sublime depth. Man's true worth is to the degree he flourishes these traits implanted in his heart-world. Hearts pervaded by spirituality are gifted with good morals, righteous deeds and spiritual manifestations. Only in this way can man meet the terms of having been created in *ahsan-i taqwim*, in the best fashion thinkable.

The Training of Sufism (Sayr Suluk)

Hence, no matter how far a person may have gone in disbelief and sin, he may not be deprived of his right of invitation to the truth. One of many such examples in the life of the Blessed Prophet -upon him blessings and peace- is recounted in the following:

The Noble Messenger -upon him blessings and peace- had sent a Companion to call Wahshi to Islam; the same man who had sent the Prophet -upon him blessings and peace- into enormous grief by martyring his beloved uncle Hamza -Allah be well-pleased with him-. Somewhat astounded, Wahshi responded:

"How can you call someone like me to Islam when Allah says, 'And they who do not call upon another god with Allah and do not slay the soul, which Allah has forbidden except in the requirements of justice, and (who) do not commit fornication and he who does this shall find a requital of sin. The punishment shall be doubled to him on the day of resurrection, and he shall abide therein in abasement' (al-Furqan, 68-69). I am a man who has committed all these ugly deeds. How can there be a way out for me?'

Revealed thereupon was the following ayah:

قُلْ يَا عِبَادِيَ الَّذِينَ اَسْرَفُوا عَلَى اَنْفُسِهِمْ لاَ تَقْنَطُوا مِنْ رَحْمَةِ اللهِ اِنَّ اللهَ يَغْفِرُ الذُّنُوبَ جَمِيعًا اِنَّهُ هُوَ الْغَفُورُ الرَّحِيمُ

"Say: O my servants who have acted extravagantly against their own souls...! Do not despair of the mercy of Allah; surely Allah forgives the faults altogether; surely He is the Forgiving the Merciful." (az-Zumar, 53)

Relieved by the message of the ayah, Wahshi emotionally exclaimed:

"How great is your mercy, o Lord!" After a sincere repentance, he then embraced Islam with his friends.

Wahshi, who had martyred Hamza -Allah be well-pleased with him- at Uhud, had now become a Companion. Engrossed in the spiritual pleasure of receiving guidance and with the hope of making amends for his martyring of Hamza -Allah be well-pleased with him-, Wahshi -Allah be well-pleased with him- risked all dangers and killed Musaylamatu'l-Kadhdhab, the false prophet, and ended a tumultuous unrest.

"Is this compassionate pardon valid only for Wahshi, Messenger of Allah?" inquired the Companions.

"It is for all Muslims", he answered.[60]

As seen in the above narration, hearts that turned to a sincere repentance at the time heard the most affective testimonies of true compassion and love from the lips of the Blessed Prophet -upon him blessings and peace- himself. From those lips have entire humankind likewise heard refreshing words of cure and consolation. It is again from the grace of the Light of Being -upon him blessings and peace- that mankind is able to see the infinite ocean of mercy and generosity and the shore of hope. That they are addressed in the most compassionate manner by the Almighty –'O My servants!'- is again only for the sake of that Noble Being -upon him blessings and peace-.

So in this day and age, giving priority to the mercy and compassion of the Lord and spreading hope is of crucial importance in dispersing the widespread spiritual crisis brought about by the materialistic influences of the West. It is much more realistic to win people over emotionally than to steer them into rational debates. Today, many are rationally conditioned for the worse, which makes it almost impossible to persuade them through argumentation. When a person is rationally conditioned to respond to something in a pre-established way, it prevents him from accepting rational proofs. In warming hearts to the truth, it would therefore be more affective to first approach people leniently and then help them flourish their inner spiritual tendencies.

One must give priority to winning the heart of a person swamped in error, rebellion and sin before criticizing, censuring or even asking him to fulfill religious commands. For this, one must try to establish a bond of love with the person, the ground of personal closeness. Once the person's heart begins to acquire a certain blend, one may then begin to gradually correct his mistakes. One must not underestimate the spiritual blessings compliments and treats, both spiritual and physical, bring. In this regard,

---

60 See, Haythami, Majmau'z-Zawaid, X, 214-215.

one must grasp the subtlety of the following words of the Blessed Prophet -upon him blessings and peace-, a virtual window of hope opened to hearts stifled under the smoke of sin, offering them a fresh breath of life:

"My intercession is especially for those among my *ummah* who have committed great sins." (Abu Dawud, Sunnah, 20)

Mawlana Rumi -may Allah sanctify his secret- wonderfully elaborates the Prophet's -upon him blessings and peace- merciful attitude towards sinners: "Medicine looks for the ill and wounded, to heal them. To sickness is where the cure goes. To a ditch is where the water flows. If it is the water of mercy and compassion you need, then be like that, too!"

But for the medicine to be effective, the wound must first be cleaned from all bacteria. Cleaning ill hearts from the bacteria of sin is for them to be washed with the water of repentance. The medicine, that is the Prophet's -upon him blessings and peace- intercession, takes place only afterwards.

In another *hadith*, it is said: "A repenter from sin is like he never sinned." (Ibn Majah, Zuhd, 30) This is an expression that brings glad tidings on the one hand, while indicating the depth of Divine compassion on the other.

The delicate measure of guiding through compassion implemented by all prophets has also been diligently followed by the righteous. Accordingly, the first fruit of faith has come to be considered as compassion and servanthood has concisely been defined within the two standards below:

Ta'zim li-amrillah; or to observe the commands of Allah, glory unto Him, delicately and full of respect.

Shafqat li-khalqillah; or to show mercy and compassion to the created for the sake of the Creator.

Fudayl ibn Iyad -may Allah sanctify his secret- offers a splendid example of a Muslim who leads a life within this measure:

Seeing him crying one day, they asked him the reason.

"I am crying because I am upset on behalf of another Muslim who has done me wrong", he replied. "I fear he will suffer in the Hereafter."

Shedding light onto what it exactly is that sends mature Muslims of such ilk to feel such mercy and compassion, Mawlana Rumi -may Allah sanctify his secret- says: "Once the seas of mercy surge, even stones drink the water of life. Corpses dead for a hundred years rise from their graves and faces, dark and devilish, assume an angelic beauty envied by even the houris of Paradise."

It is reported that Ibrahim Adham -may Allah sanctify his secret- once washed the grimy mouth of a drunken man, responding to those who could not understand why he did so, by saying:

"It would be disrespectful for me to leave a mouth and tongue, created to mention the name of Allah, grimy!"

When the man regained consciousness, they told him that "Ibrahim Adham of Khorasan just washed your mouth!"

Feeling embarrassed, the man was suddenly awoken spiritually, as he murmured, "In that case, I hereby repent for good!"

Ibrahim Adham -may Allah sanctify his secret-, who mediated the guidance of the man, that night heard a voice in his dream:

"You washed his mouth for us; so We washed his heart for you!"

In the Quran, Allah, glory unto Him, advises the Blessed Prophet -upon him blessings and peace- and in his person the entire Muslims with the following: "Take to forgiveness and enjoin good and turn aside from the ignorant." (al-Araf, 199)

In putting this command to practice, the most perfect example is without a doubt provided by the Blessed Prophet -upon him blessings and peace-. The morals, compassion and forgiveness he displayed were of a kind that would make even angels envious, so to speak. Here is just one among many:

On the day of the liberation of Mecca, the Noble Prophet -upon him blessings and peace- had declared a general amnesty. Mecca, having witnessed nothing but oppression, mockery and enmity for years on end, was now making the most of the sweet breeze of compassion and mercy, ensured by the great forgiveness gusting throughout. But a Meccan by the name of

The Training of Sufism (Sayr Suluk)

Fadala, with the intention of casting a grim shadow over this pleasant day, approached the Blessed Prophet -upon him blessings and peace- with the intention of killing him. Yet, possessing insight to his malicious intention all along, without showing any sign of panic or anger, the Blessed Prophet -upon him blessings and peace- spread his wings of mercy for Fadala and, placing his graceful hands on Fadala's chest, said:

"Repent, Fadala, from the plot you have contrived in your mind!" The malicious intention disappeared from Fadala's mind there and then. His heart melted and was thereby filled with the light of iman. In his sight, the Messenger of Allah -upon him blessings and peace- suddenly became the most beloved of all beings.[61]

This is, without a doubt, exceptional maturity of conduct that puts into action the principle 'Let he who has come to kill you, be revived through you'; and the history of Islam abounds in such examples. Many, including Omar -Allah be well-pleased with him-, are fruitful results of this wonderful style of approach. Mawlana Rumi -may Allah sanctify his secret- says:

"From the perfection of the mercy of Allah and the billowing waves of the ocean of benevolence, each arid land receives rain and each arid soil is united with water."

"You who calls to guidance…! Know that the medicine for an evil eye is a good eye! A good eye and a beautiful gaze stomp on the evil eye and destroy it. A good eye and a clean gaze owe their being to the fact that the mercy of Allah is superior to His wrath. It is from mercy. An evil eye is from wrath, curse. As a beautiful gaze is from Divine mercy, it reigns supreme over the evil eye. This is but a manifestation of what is expressed in the hadith al-qudsi as 'My mercy has overtaken My wrath' *(Bukhari, Tawhid, 55)*. Know that under all circumstances, the mercy of Allah is superior to His wrath. It is because of this that every prophet has reigned supreme over his enemies.

So ridding troubles is not through complaining or oppressing. Its cure is to show benevolence and forgive. Let the warning of the Prophet -upon him

---

61   Ibn Hisham, IV, 37; Ibn Kathir, as-Sirah, III, 583

blessings and peace- 'Charities rid one of troubles'[62] wake you up. Realize the way to treat illnesses and troubles!

But do not forget that forgiving the oppressor is to oppress the exploited! To feel sorry for the thief and the wretch is to beat the weak and deprive them of mercy!"

One must therefore establish a delicate balance. True, the Almighty is *Ghafuru'r-Rahim*, the Forgiver and the Merciful; yet He is also *Azizun Dhu'ntiqam*, The Dignified Avenger of the rights of the exploited from the oppressors.

The Blessed Prophet -upon him blessings and peace- has hence said:

"On seeing two of your brothers fighting, run to the aid of both the oppressor and the oppressed."

"We see how we are meant to aid the oppressed, Messenger of Allah; yet how can we help the oppressor?" asked the Companions, on which the Prophet -upon him blessings and peace- said:

"By preventing him from oppressing…" (Bukhari, Ikrah, 7; Muslim, Birr, 62)

What we wish to say, in short, is that both faith wise and islamically, humanity today, including Muslims, is like a wounded bird. It is therefore necessary to approach them with care and sensitivity and dress their wounds. And this can only be done observing the content and style we have tried to convey above.

---

62 See, Tirmidhi, Zakat, 28; Suyuti, al-Jamiu's-Saghir, I, 108.

Tolerance for the sinner should not be carried over to the sin; and hostility to the sin should not be reflected onto the sinner. A Muslim of this mind should direct criticism to himself and tolerance to another, as an adopted manner of calling to the truth.

2. THE MANNER OF GENTLENESS AND AFFECTION

Looking at human beings with the Sufi eye, calls for showing attention to their essence, not their sinful existence. This is one of the deep underlying wisdoms as to how the style of *tasawwuf* compassionately embraces the sinner, though not the sin. A true Sufi perceives a sinner like a bird with a broken wing, in desperate need of compassionate care. He feels deep inside the concern to give the sinner back his health, attend to his troublesome spirit and let him fly once again. Leniency and compassion for the created for the sake of the Creator is, after all, the most influential means for a Muslim to attain to virtue and maturity.

It is reported that during his time as judge in Damascus, Abu'd-Darda -Allah be well-pleased with him- heard a group publically condemning another man, supposedly a sinner.

"If you were to see a man fallen in a pit", he asked them, "what would you do?"

"We would hang down a rope and try to drag him out", they replied.

"In that case, do not speak ill of him. Instead, thank Allah for your well-being and try to save your brother who has fallen into the pit of sin."

"Wouldn't you be hostile towards this sinner?" they asked, astounded.

A Companion reared by the unique training of the Blessed Prophet -upon him blessings and peace-, Abu'd-Darda -Allah be well-pleased with him- gave them the magnificent response below:

*"I am an enemy of his sin, not his person. He is again my brother of religion, the moment he abandons his sin."*⁶³

These are profound qualities Abu'd-Darda -Allah be well-pleased with him- wishes to convey. Such qualities are glimmers from the Prophet's -upon him blessings and peace- exceptional moral conduct, in harmony with the command and pleasure of the Lord. Falling on the fertile soil of righteousness, these qualities have been perceived throughout the history of Islam as measures of spiritual maturity and means for providing the light and joy of guidance.

This style is an attempt to purify the sinner in the waters of tolerance, forgiveness, compassion and love, without drowning him in his sin. The Blessed Prophet -upon him blessings and peace- approached even the most ingrained idolaters like Abu Jahl with this sensitivity, never meddling with their debauchery or dragging their sins into light, only inviting them to swim to utter purification in the cleansing waters of *iman*, the sea of salvation and happiness. Awaiting us is indeed great lesson in the fact that Allah, glory unto Him, completely erases the past sins of those who sincerely repent, as if they were never committed in the first place, even turning past misdeeds into rewards, depending on the level of sincerity shown by the repenter. The *ayah* states:

"Except him who repents and believes and does a good deed; so these are they of whom Allah changes the evil deeds to good ones; and Allah is Forgiving, Merciful" (al-Furqan, 70)

Those who do not have an inkling of this grand compassion are enemies to both themselves and humankind. Ruthless persons of the kind, without the least mercy and compassion, are to be pitied for blocking the avenue for their eternal happiness with their very own hands. In contrast, people like Yunus and Mawlana, triumphant in tapping to the source of mercy, are like the sweet roses of Paradise, adored not only by human beings, but also by animals, from the savage wolf to the gentle wren. Even with their thorns, they emit beauty to their surroundings, treating wounded souls. Embodying the nature of a rose, that is the key. Not to be a thorn from top to bottom due a feeling of dejection from seeing to many

---

63   See, Abdurrazzaq, Musannaf, XI, 180; Abu Nuaym, Hilyah, 1/225.

The Training of Sufism (Sayr Suluk)

thorns in the garden that is the world, but to embrace them all and bud as a rose, even in spite of the freezing winter that disrupts the coming of spring. Mawlana Rumi -may Allah sanctify his secret- says it wonderfully:

"It was because it did not fear the night and flee the dark that moon became lit and began to spread light. And the rose acquired that wonderful scent for getting on well with the thorns.

Listen to this truth from the rose; look, it says, 'Why should I feel down and lose myself in grief for being with the thorn? I acquired this smile for nothing other than putting with the thorn's company. It is through him that I am able to give out beautiful scents to the world…'"

Eşrefoğlu Rumi -may Allah sanctify his secret- gives poetic voice to the approach needed to acquire this mindset:

For that Friend, one ought
To swallow poison like sweet

Fed up from punishing a man, time and again, for drinking, a Companion had cursed him. On hearing this, the Blessed Prophet -upon him blessings and peace- said: "Do not curse him. I promise in the name of Allah that if there is one thing I know about him, it is that he loves Allah and His Messenger." (Bukhari, Hudud, 5)

A student of the late Mahmud Sami Ramazanoğlu -may Allah sanctify his secret-, suffering from depression, had a lapse in judgment and arrived at the door of his master, drunk. The person who happened to open the door reproached him.

"Look at you!" he said. "Do you know to whose door you have just come?"

"Yes, I do" the helpless and forlorn student then replied. "But is there any other door that can give a warm hug?"

Sami Effendi -may Allah sanctify his secret-, hearing the entire conversation, quickly came to the door and took his emotionally hurt student inside, ushering him to the palace of his heart. He revived his desolate heart with love, mercy and compassion. Privileged to receive such sensitive treatment, the student, in no time, abandoned his bad ways and joined the ranks of the righteous.

The gist of 'looking at the created through the sight of the Creator', an exceptional approach exemplified in the lives of the righteous, is beautifully expressed in the following *hadith*:

"By Allah in whose Hand of Might my life resides, you cannot enter Paradise unless you are compassionate towards one another."

"We are all compassionate, Messenger of Allah" said the Companions.

"What I mean by compassion", explained the Blessed Prophet -upon him blessings and peace- *"is not just compassion towards one another in the sense you understand. Much rather, it is a compassion that encompasses entire creation...a compassion that encompasses entire creation."* (Hakim, Mustadrak, IV, 185)

No matter how remote a human being may be from his essential purpose, he is still honorable, since he is a 'human being'. That he is bogged down in the swamp of sin, unaware of the highness embedded in his essence, is perhaps comparable to the Black Stone, hanging on the wall of Kaaba, falling down and becoming dirty. Should such a thing occur, it would be inconceivable for any Muslim conscience to remain indifferent and carry on as if nothing has happened. Even when in dirt, Muslims still would not remain back from treating the Stone with respect. They would pick it up from the ground along with its dirt, clean it up with tears in their eyes and vie with each other to replace it to the high spot where it belongs. Remembering that it originated from Paradise, they would overlook its outward dirt and regard its essential worth. Yet, just like the Black Stone, a human being, too, is from Paradise. Regardless of how fallen he becomes through sin, his essential worth remains intact.

No competent doctor would become angry with a patient for having caught an illness. Even if the illness may have been caused by the patient's recklessness, he would ascribe the cause to the patient's vulnerability, be it physical or mental. So instead of becoming angry with a patient for any role he may have played in becoming infected, the doctor sympathizes with his pain and gets his treatment under way, kindly and compassionately, without wasting any time. He feels responsible for the patient's

The Training of Sufism (Sayr Suluk)

recovery. A Sufi, too, lives in society in the mindset of a doctor walking inside a hospital ward, a mindset that acts like a lifejacket for those strayed offshore.

Extending a lifejacket of the kind and pulling one out of the billowing waves of sin, provides an enormous means of eternal happiness. The advice the Blessed Prophet -upon him blessings and peace- gave Ali -Allah be well-pleased with him- on the battlefield of Khaybar is of immense importance: "Ali…For a person to be guided through you is better than you owning a valley of red camels." (Bukhari, Jihad, 143)

This truth is further reverberated in an *ayah*:

وَ مَنْ اَحْيَاهَا فَكَاَنَّمَا اَحْيَا النَّاسَ جَمِيعًا

"…and whoso saves the life of one, it shall be as if he had saved the life of all mankind." (al-Maidah, 32)

This is an issue of faith. Disbelief is doubtless the heaviest crime thought and emotions can commit. Since a kinder, more lenient approach offers a greater chance of rescue from disbelief, when the Almighty sent Musa (a.s) to the Pharaoh to advise him with belief, He commanded the Prophet speak with a lenient tone (*qawl-i layyin*). The Almighty was certainly not unaware of the intensity of the Pharaoh's unbelief. So even if the person be as stubborn and ingrained as the Pharaoh, we must not let our emotions get the better of us and use a threatening, intimidating tone. Instead, we must let ourselves be guided by the Divine teaching that strongly encourages us to adopt a soft tone of speech. Mawlana Rumi -may Allah sanctify his secret- underlines this beautifully:

"Fully comprehend the Lord's words to Musa, 'speak softly with the Pharaoh, show him leniency'.

By pouring water onto boiling oil, you will wreck both the stove and the pot."

The following *ayah* where the Almighty addresses His Messenger -upon him blessings and peace- and the entire *ummah* in his person, gives voice to this very fact:

Sufism: A Path Towards the Internalization of Faith (Ihsân)

$$\text{فَبِمَا رَحْمَةٍ مِنَ اللهِ لِنْتَ لَهُمْ وَلَوْ كُنْتَ فَظًّا غَلِيظَ الْقَلْبِ}$$
$$\text{لَانْفَضُّوا مِنْ حَوْلِكَ فَاعْفُ عَنْهُمْ وَاسْتَغْفِرْ لَهُمْ}$$

"It was by the mercy of Allah that you were lenient with them (O Muhammad), for if you had been stern and fierce of heart, they would have dispersed from round about you. So pardon them and ask forgiveness for them..." (Al-Imran, 159)

Adopting this approach is necessary not only towards nonbelievers and sinners, but also towards Muslims carrying certain weaknesses and faults of human nature, who otherwise lead exemplary Islamic lives. An approach that puts down a person and hurts him emotionally, when it was supposed to simply correct him in the first place, may even have the opposite effect and contrary to the original intention, push the person further down the path of sin. Persons, who are told off in this manner, can become restless even towards their own parents; and it is indeed more difficult from them to put up with this approach when it comes from the way of another. Even truths said in a stern manner act like knives shredding through the skin, losing all their benefit and appeal. Mawlana Rumi -may Allah sanctify his secret- says:

"Even your father appears like a monster, savage and ruthless, when he cautions you over a fault. This is the effect of the grief emitted by his harsh reprimand. Even though a father's reprimand is for your benefit, the harshness of his reprimand makes the compassion and pity in his heart, appear to you like a monster."

This psychological nature of man must always be borne in mind and no matter how deeply bogged in sin a person may be, his essential worth must never be forgotten. It is for this reason that the Blessed Prophet -upon him blessings and peace- says:

"Belittling a Muslim brother suffices for one as sin." (Muslim, Birr, 32)

Inspired by the above *hadith*, Bezmialem Valide Sultan founded a trust in Damascus, to compensate for the things her servants may break, lest they felt humiliated over they accidentally caused. And this is an exemplary mindset that speaks for itself.

The Training of Sufism (Sayr Suluk)

A Muslim of such consciousness ought to direct criticism to himself and tolerance to another; for the Almighty declares: "And spy not, neither backbite one another. Would one of you love to eat the flesh of his dead brother? You abhor that (so abhor the other)!" (al-Hujurat, 12)

Ideal human beings, who have been able to conduct themselves within these Divine guidelines, have been able to become heroes of virtue and morality, never detaching a consideration of the world from the Hereafter. One such example is Sheikh Edebali, a sultan of spirituality and the spiritual guide of Osman Gazi, one of the most prominent commanders to have given shape to history. The Sheikh's profoundly meaningful advices to Osman Gazi are of immense value to all administrators, from the highest to the lowest rank, and above all, to family members in their conduct towards one another:

"Son…You are a chieftain! From now on, anger is onto us, meekness onto you. Resentment is onto us, restoring relations onto you. Accusing is onto us, forbearance onto you. Helplessness and error are onto us, tolerance onto you. Discord, clashing and disagreement are onto us, justice onto you. Malicious looks and words and unjust remarks are onto us, forgiveness onto you.

From here on, son, dividing is onto us, uniting onto you. Laziness is onto us, cautioning, encouraging and shaping onto you…"

These unique advices are nothing but an exceptional manifestation of a richness of heart and the highness of virtue that can easily forgive personal mistreatment for the sake of Allah, glory unto Him, and regardless of the given circumstances, perceive the servants of the Lord compassionately, with love and affection.

Even when there was a case where it was obvious a certain person was guilty of a misdeed, in order not to humiliate him, the Blessed Prophet -upon him blessings and peace- never used to point the finger at him publicly, instead making him virtually anonymous by cautioning the entire group over the fault. At times, to suggest he was far from impressed over a given misdeed, he would even go as far as ascribing to himself an error vision, and say:

"What is it with me that I see you like this?" (Bukhari, Manaqib, 25; Muslim, Salat, 119)

This is the delicate manner of protecting the guilty person from embarrassment and humiliation, a common quality of all who understand and live a Sufi life in the truest sense. The road to the Lord runs not through wrecking hearts but mending them, as elaborately said by Yunus Emre:

The heart is God's throne,
On the heart God shone,
In both words will bemoan,
He who wrecks a heart…

To be sure, many an outcast, condemned and alienated over his faults, has been won back over to the land of mercy, solely through the blessings of this delicate method.

It is reported that once a student of Junayd Baghdadi -may Allah sanctify his secret- had been caught red handed in a compromising situation. Embarrassed, the student then left the lodge, never to return. Some time later, while passing through the local bazaar with his other disciples Junayd Baghdadi -may Allah sanctify his secret- caught sight of the dejected student. On becoming aware of his master's presence in the bazaar, the student quickly walked away, too embarrassed to face up to him. This did not escape Junayd's -may Allah sanctify his secret- notice, as he turned to his disciples and said:

'You go; a bird has fled from the cage of my heart!' He then began pursuing the student. Looking behind his back after a while, the student realized he was being pursued by his master. He got all the more anxious and picked up his pace. Too anxious to take notice of where he was headed, he ended up in a deadened road and bumped his head on the wall, at the end of the road, falling to the ground. When he looked up, he saw his master standing. Feeling humiliated, he lowered his gaze.

"Where are you headed, my dear…who are you running from?" asked Junayd -may Allah sanctify his secret- with the softest of tones. "It is times of trouble this that a teacher proves his worth in lending a helping hand to his student." Compassionately, Junayd -may Allah sanctify his secret- then

The Training of Sufism (Sayr Suluk)

helped his student get back up on his feet and took him back to the lodge. The remorseful student then repented and assumed his righteous ways of old.

This is an indication of the fruitful results that come with the maturity of approaching another, regardless of the gravity of his sins, as a father would approach his son.

A step even beyond forgiving others' faults is to respond to evil with good, even praying for the spiritual rehabilitation of whom he has been afflicted with harm; and this should be a defining characteristic of a mature Muslim. Sufficient as example for this is the manner in which the Blessed Prophet -upon him blessings and peace- prayed for the guidance of the very people he was stoned by at Taif. Again, his request for the people of Mecca to be spared from perishing by Divine wrath and be given, instead, guidance through Islam, was the sole cause behind the salvation of many a transgressor.

A *hadith* states: "It is no virtue for you to respond to good with good, to evil with evil. Virtue is to respond to evil, not with evil, but with good." (Tirmidhi, Birr, 63)

Should the person responded to with goodness be a foe, he will become a friend. Be he in the middle, he will draw ever closer; and be he already close, he will grow deeper in love. This is the main reason as to why people today, who are caught in the uncompromising grip of materialism, seek to calm their spirits by appealing to the mystical way of viewing the world. There thus beckons great benefit in using the style of tasawwuf in introducing and conveying Islam. The majority of people in the West who have entered the fold of Islam resort to the works of great Sufis like Ibn Arabi and Mawlana Rumi to fill the emptiness in their spirits. Heading the list of books on Islam that are currently in demand in the Western hemisphere are books on *tasawwuf*. Our times therefore stand in desperate need to a depth of heart that, in the words of Mawlana Rumi -may Allah sanctify his secret- below, can embrace humankind entire:

Come! Come! And still come, whatever you may be...
A fire worshipper, an idolater or if it is nothing you believe,
Our lodge is not that of despair, so come, even if
You repented a hundred times only to renege...

Sufism: A Path Towards the Internalization of Faith (Ihsân)

Rumi's -may Allah sanctify his secret- kind invitation above is inspired with the aim of introducing man to his essential substance and, on the inspirational ground of affection and tolerance, saving him from his errors and ushering him through to embracing the honor that is Islam. Otherwise, it is not a purposeless declaration of accepting anyone on the condition they remain in their flawed ways of old. The purpose is to rehabilitate their inner worlds. After all, only if a device has broken down does one take it to a repairer. The heart-worlds of figures like Mawlana Rumi -may Allah sanctify his secret- are like repair shops. Since, the work there is aimed at repairing what has broken down; it is only natural that the invitation above be extended to people spiritually flawed.

At a time when religious life has become skin and bones and when people carry numerous flaws when judged at the backdrop of religious criteria, it becomes essential to approach another with a Sufi-styled selflessness, compassion and leniency. Such an approach is the most fruitful means in increasing the potential of rehabilitation of those engulfed in sin and rebellion.

But it must be expressed that tolerating the sinner should strictly be on personal terms. Otherwise, condoning sinners and sins that involve violating the rights of others and wreak havoc on society and social harmony is unthinkable. Moreover, it is undoubtedly not wrong for a person who leads a life within the apparent bounds of Islam, to look upon the sinner with feelings of 'anger'. This is in fact necessary for him to stay away from the sinner lest his heart be exposed to the dangers that come with befriending him. For people, who lead lives in a manner unaware, sins are as enchanting as a sweet tune and many a person in this state readily commits a sin without feeling its crumbling weight in the least. Tolerating the sin of a sinner is therefore dangerous for most, as it might lead to them taking Divine measures lightly and even to their hearts leaning towards the sin. So tolerance for the sinner should not be carried over to the sin; and hostility to the sin should not be reflected onto the sinner.

Our final words on this subject will be to quote the *hadith*:

"Make ease, do not make difficult. Relieve do not cause disgust." (Bukhari. Ilm, 11)

This is, of course, on the condition of not harming the core of Islam and diverting from the path of truth…

O Lord! Render us among the true people of love whose hearts are filled with wisdom and make us acquainted with the mysteries of both worlds! Make our hearts sources of compassion, mercy and charity towards the created for the sake of the Creator!

O Lord! Compliant with the mystery 'My Mercy has surpassed My Wrath', direct us onto the path of forgiveness and include us among the flanks of the righteous, the guides of truth!

Amin…

CHAPTER THREE

Marifatullah and Divine Awards

A- ***MARIFATULLAH* OR KNOWLEDGE OF THE DIVINE**
  1- Divine Essence
  2- Divine Attributes and Their Manifestations
  3- Knowledge of the Divine and Its Manifestation in the Wise

B- **DIVINE AWARDS**
  1- Knowledge of the *Ladunn*
  2- *Firasah* or Spiritual Foresight
  3- Spiritual Disposal and *Karamah*
  4- Truthful Dreams

من عرف نفسه فقد عرف ربه

"he who knows his self knows his Lord."

Marifatullah and Divine Awards

So manifest is the Lord that He is hidden virtually due to the intensity of His manifestation.

A. *MARIFATULLAH* OR KNOWLEDGE OF THE DIVINE

1. DIVINE ESSENCE

The impossibility of grasping the essential nature of Allah, glory unto Him, is made evident by the following words of the Blessed Prophet -upon him blessings and peace-: "Contemplate on the creation of Allah. Do not reflect on His Essence, for you will never be able to grasp its value as befits Him." (Daylami, Musnad, II, 56; Haythami, Majmau'z-Zawaid, I, 81)

After all, knowledge of Allah, glory unto Him, that will deliver understanding to the land of faith and wisdom and allow it to unite with the light of guidance, pertains not to His Essence but to His Attributes. This is due to the fact that the Lord infinitely transcends space and time. Human understanding, on the other hand, functions only through the impressions it receives from the world of sense perception. Accordingly, in order for the understanding to grasp a given thing, the thing needs to resemble another thing in the sensory world and that needs to engender an impression on the mind. Allah, glory unto Him, in contrast, has the attribute of not resembling any created being (*mukhalafatun li'l-hawadith*). This means that the Lord does not bear any resemblance whatsoever to a subsequently created being and is infinitely and absolutely distinct, superior and perfect in comparison. An appreciation of the perfection of the order that reigns supreme throughout the universe is sufficient to render this a logical fact of the matter. It would be utterly absurd to compare the Almighty Creator, the First Cause possessing a power to create such an orderly universe, with something He created. His perfection, glory and power stand above all things created, an imperative fact necessitated by both reason and logic. It is therefore neither possible nor right for the human mind to opinionate with regard to the essential nature of the Almighty, simply because He is unlike any other.

What we are obliged with regard to the Lord, however, is to grasp and accept, through His Attributes, the existence of His Essence. The analogies and explanations the Almighty provides us in the Quran about Himself, conduce to this purpose. The *ayah* reveals:

"Allah is the light of the heavens and the earth; a likeness of His light is as a niche in which is a lamp, the lamp is in a glass, and the glass is as it were a brightly shining star, lit from a blessed olive-tree, neither eastern nor western, the oil whereof almost gives light though fire touch it not… light upon light! Allah guides to His light whom He pleases, and Allah sets forth parables for men, and Allah is Cognizant of all things." (an-Nur, 35)

It should be observed that the analogy provided by the Quran first familiarizes the human understanding with impressions it can relate to; and then by abstracting the understanding from those impressions, it proceeds to uplift it to a reality beyond imagination and comprehension, which it refers to as 'light upon light'. Contrary to how one might be tempted to understand the expression, His Light is not exhausted by a specific kind or multiple kinds of light; neither by all the species of light for that matter. Being infinitely above all types of light; the Lord's Light is rather an indefinable light that eludes all efforts of describing it. Since, however, perceiving any observable thing requires as much vision as it needs light, not everyone can see the proof of the Real, discern His signs and succumb to His Will. After all, the blind are held back from seeing the things light readily presents to vision, to the sight of anyone and everyone privileged with the ability to see. A seeing eye, then, is as great a requirement for observation as the light that presents to its vision the existence of reality. Only a spirit privileged with a seeing eye can therefore perceive and appreciate.

On the other hand, that the Almighty refers to Himself in the verse as 'Light' and declares Himself as 'the Light of the heavens and earth', denotes the fact that it is only Him who created entire existence, presented the vast universe to observation, revealed innumerable realities both hidden and open and brought joy to hearts in their revelation. If it were not for the Great Light of the Lord, nothing would have been known or even found; and joy would never have found its way inside the heart.

All species of light that act as visible causes in making entire existence appear for observation are therefore nothing but manifestations from that Great Light. Comparable to the ranking that exists between different lights in the heavens, which is based on a difference of intensity, there also exists a similar scale between the lights visible on earth. For instance, if the rays of the sun were to shine upon the moon, then reflect from there onto a mirror inside a house on earth, then ricochet from the mirror to another mirror straight across the room, then further onto a bowl full of water lying on the ground and then finally back onto the ceiling, the first rank in terms of possessing the most intense shining power would belong to the sun and then to the moon and so on. With each one of these entities, that which is closer to the source of power is stronger than the one following it. The way in which the lights of the heavens are ranked follows a similar pattern; that is the light benefited from is stronger than the light that draws its radiance from it. And, vertically exceeding in intensity, all these lights find their ultimate perfection in the infinite and greatest light, the light of Allah, glory unto Him.

So the appearance of all things and their knowledge comes about only by virtue of the Lord, the enlightener of the heavens and earth, making them appear and known. Without His Light, the manifestation of existence and knowledge thereof is impossible. Still, while gazing say at a forest in broad daylight during spring, a person can only remark, despite seeing multifarious shades of colors: "I did not see anything but greenery!" He is too caught up in the luscious greenery of spring to take note of the light that makes that greenery appear; when it is only thanks to that light that he is able to perceive all the colors before his eyes. In this situation, the light remains hidden only because of the intensity of its appearance.

Embarking from this fact, Sufis say:

"Allah, glory unto Him, is not really hidden. Yet, in terms of our capacity to comprehend, He is hidden because of the intensity of His appearing."

Aziz Mahmud Hudayi -may Allah sanctify his secret- says:

His Manifestation veils the manifest,
For proof of light, would one with sight, request?

Simpler put, one would not be able to see any objects inside a room lit with a bulb of five-thousand volts. The Almighty, infinitely superior in radiance even to a light of millions of volts, therefore unquestionably remains unseen to human comprehension. The Quran underlines this fact when it refers to believers as:

"Those who believe in the unseen…" (al-Baqara, 3)

Yet for the prudent, this invisibility is of a kind that is more visible than even the most apparent beings. Such that: We live with air but we are unable to see it in spite of the fact that it really encompasses us. We can only feel it while breathing in and out. Yet, going further than not rejecting the existence of air because of an inability to see it, we even exclaim with a do-or-die desperation: "We cannot live without air!"

Maritime creatures are similar to us. They perhaps do not take much notice of the sea, despite living inside of it. But what else are they encompassed by other than the sea?

This means that wherever a given being may be located, to our right or left, in front of or behind us, we may perceive it. But when it comprehensively encompasses us, it sheds all limitations of direction and the manifestation of its existence transcends our perception and withdraws, in a sense, to invisibility. Had it been otherwise or to give an example, had air not been hidden from our vision, life would have become unbearable; it would have been like an intense fog that concealed the sight of every object in its mist. Simpler put, the appearance of a being by which we are comprehensively encompassed would bring upon invisibility to other beings. It is for that reason that the Lord has remained invisible, hidden to human eyesight on earth. Had He been apparent, owing to the splendor of His Beauty (*jamal*) by which they will have been comprehensively encompassed, human beings would not have been able to see anything but Him. And there would have been no such thing as the life of the world, whose purpose is to put human beings on trial.

Thus, the Almighty, who is transcendent in the sense of being beyond imagination and understanding, is both hidden and apparent. Or rather, He is hidden in Essence but apparent in His manifestation.

He is apparent; for all beings come to be through the light of His Essence.

He is hidden; for eyes do not have the power to look at Him.

He is apparent. Whatever there is other than Him becomes manifest only through His attributes.

He is hidden, for there is nothing like Him. Human reason is conditioned to perceive objects through their opposites. Thus it is only natural for the Lord, the Unchangeable for whom there is no opposite, to remain hidden.

Most certainly, no conscious being in entire creation has enough aptitude to comprehend a Being of such nature. It is owing to this reason that faith consists in accepting the existence of His Essence and not a comprehension of its reality; for to exist or not to exist is one thing, while to pass judgment on its nature is another thing.

The Lord has thus endowed human beings with the power of reason, to discern and acknowledge His Divinity. Moreover, He has made the world of sense abound in the manifestations of His attributes, making it possible to for reason to proceed from these effects to the Cause. Illustrating this is the case below:

The great Sufi Junayd Baghdadi -May Allah sanctify his secret- one day saw a large number of people anxiously and excitedly rushing somewhere.

"Where are you going?" he asked them.

"A scholar has arrived from a so-and-so place. The word is that he explains the existence of Allah using many proofs. We are going to make the most of his proofs and explanations. Join us, if you want!" they replied.

Junayd -May Allah sanctify his secret- thereupon looked at them and said, with a dry smile:

"There are countless proofs in the universe chanting the Divine for eyes that can see, ears that can hear and hearts that can feel. Better still, there are even many testimonies given by the Almighty about Himself. So folks... He who is still riddled with doubts can go! As for us, there is not a speck of doubt in our hearts!"

In a word, the Lord has made manifest a myriad of His attributes in man the essence of the universe, in the universe a silent Quran, and in the Quran a vocal universe. To make matters even easier, He has sent numerous prophets to guide and help man locate the manifestations of His attributes and draw benefit from them. And through prophets, the Almighty has disclosed the realities of worlds seen and unseen to human understanding in the most appropriate manner, in the form of 'speech', as is exemplified by the Holy Quran.

So concerning the essence of Allah, glory unto Him, we may merely stay put with the following, as much as is allowed by the limited scope of speech:

The Absolute Being cannot be restricted by any limitation; He cannot be attributed with anything apart from what He attributes Himself. Since it is conditioned by our limited faculty of understanding, even calling Him 'Absolute' is to, in fact, restrict Him; yet for the sake of explanation, we have no other choice. But in truth, Allah, glory unto Him, is different from anything and everything that may come to mind, any word that can be articulated.

It is due to His Essence that this Absolute Being, infinitely glorified, manifests His attributes; just as a glimmering candle shines forth its light. All beings are concisely determined in the knowledge of the Absolute Being, of which the universe is a manifestation. Beings in this realm, which we refer to as the world of observation (*shahadah*), exist only relatively; none of them can exist through their own existences alone. They are considered to exist only as recipients of the attributes, works, decrees, power and creativity of the Absolute Being. Although the Essence of the Divine manifests His power, wisdom, providence and disposal in every single being, the realm of existence is never the manifestation as such of that Essence. In other words, the realm of existence is the manifestation of the attributes of the Divine and not His Essence.

The Essence thus has a glory above anything else. Were it not for the sun, its rays would never have been. Yet, although the rays do not exist independently from the sun, they are not quite the sun. It should be noted, however, that to recognize everything as Him would be tantamount to accepting the universe and the realm of existence entire as god, which leads to a materialism that reduces 'One' to 'all'. The belief ascribed to Plato and referred to as pantheism stems from his grave misunderstanding. Although some have tried to drag *Wahdat-i Wujud* into the pantheistic system and recognize it therein, true Sufis have always been stern to reject what could at best be called a deviation. For although everything has come to be through His existence, glorifying and negating the Essence from everything else is from which the true *Wahdat-i Wujud*[64] doctrine consists. Simpler said, though it is true that the universe is a recipient of the attributes of the Real, the Essence of the Real is not the universe itself; for the Creator may never become manifest in the form of a created. And since Allah, glory unto Him, is *mukhalafatun lil'hawadith*, that is, He does not resemble the created in any shape or form, accepting a notion that is the complete opposite of the above is blatant disbelief (*kufr*). The Lord thus has a glory that cannot be sullied by any kinds of anthropomorphic attributes with which He may wrongly be ascribed. It is well known that thrusting this truth aside has led both Jews and Christians to go as far as formulating a 'son of God' –Allah forbid-, by which they refer to Uzayr (Ezra) –upon him peace- and Isa (Jesus) –upon him peace-, respectively. As a Divine response to these similar deviations which the human mind tends to conjure in his private world of imagination, Allah, glory unto Him, declares:

"And they have not honored Allah with the honor that is due to Him; and the whole earth shall be in His grip on the day of resurrection and the heavens rolled up in His right hand; glory be to Him, and may He be exalted above what they associate (with Him)." (az-Zumar, 67)

---

64   *Wahdat-i Wujud* is a Sufi conception systematized by Muhyiddin ibn Arabi -may Allah sanctify his secret-. There is yet another conception called *Wahdat-i Shuhud*, belonging to Imam Rabbani -may Allah sanctify his secret-, who is celebrated as the *Mujaddid Alf-i Thani*, the Restorer of the Second Millennium. Both conceptions are, in fact, explanations of the very same thing from two different windows; both seek to grasp and elucidate the difference between the Divine attribute of Being with the being/existence perceivable in the world of sense. With that said, there is one important difference between the two. Whereas *Wahdat-i Wujud* is to feel Divine Oneness (*tawhid*), *Wahdat-i Shuhud* is to observe the manifestations of Oneness. Since both conceptions essentially pertain to *hal* or the spiritual mindset, they must not be confused with philosophical reasoning or be tainted by it.

For that reason, the Word of *Tawhid*, which constitutes the foundation of the Islamic creed, serves, first, to eradicate from the heart all kinds of deviant beliefs in false deities with the words 'there is no god…' (*la ilaha*) and, second, to implant a true belief in a transcendent God, as accepted by Allah, glory unto Him, with the words 'but Allah' (*il-Allah*). The Quran is unquestionably clear:

"Allah is He besides Whom there is no god, the Ever-living, the Self-subsisting by Whom all subsist; slumber does not overtake Him nor sleep; whatever is in the heavens and whatever is in the earth is His…" (al-Baqara, 255)

"…there is nothing whatever like unto Him, and He is the One that hears and sees (all things)." (as-Shura, 11)

"Say: He, Allah, is One. Allah is He on Whom all depend. He begets not, nor is He begotten. And none is like Him." (al-Ikhlas, 1-4)

In short, what we are obliged with concerning the Essence of the Lord is simply to acknowledge and submit to Him, within the framework of the impressions and wisdoms we derive from our own world. However great one's intellectual capabilities may be in this temporal world, he is forever helpless in comprehending the Essence…simply helpless.

As is referred to in the Quran, speaking with Allah, glory unto Him, on Mount Sina, gave Musa –upon him peace- an enormous spiritual delight. Amid the Divine manifestation he was privileged with, he lost control over his senses. Forgetting whether he was still on earth or had in fact gone beyond, he virtually overstepped the bounds of space and time. Suddenly yearning and scorching with an avid desire in his heart to see the Essence of the Lord, he pleaded the Almighty to be given that opportunity. But Allah, glory unto Him, replied:

"You shall never see me! (*lan taraanii*)" and commanded Musa –upon him peace- to throw a glimpse at the mountain. If the mountain could withstand this manifestation, said the Almighty, he, too, would be able to gaze at Him. Behind countless veils according to reports, a ray from the Lord then reflected onto the mountain. The mountain erupted at the instant and Musa –upon him peace- fainted from tremor. On regaining consciousness, he glorified the Lord repented to Him for having overstepped the bounds.[65]

This Quranic reality attests to the helplessness to which man is forever doomed in comprehending the Divine Essence.

With that said, there are numerous saying of the Blessed Prophet –upon him blessings and peace- which reveal that in Paradise, believers will get to gaze at the Essence of the Divine, as clearly as they would see the full moon on a clear night. There is no contradiction between this and what was said above, as the conditions of the world are not the same as the conditions of the Hereafter. Muslims are thus to be given a distinct aptitude and faculty to allow them to observe the Essence of the Divine. That the Blessed Prophet –upon him blessings and peace- was not left upon a worldly state and was made to undergo a spiritual operation by having his chest cleft by Jibril –upon him peace- was, in a sense, to impart onto him a structure and aptitude that would enable him to undertake the great task of prophethood to come. Otherwise, his powers of a natural human being would not have been sufficient either for that enormous task or for a massive manifestation of the caliber of the *Miraj* (Ascension).

Thus, those who are able to proceed from *iman* to *ihsan*, from faith to its internalization, are those to attain to the truth and wisdom under the light of these Divine mysteries. Such servants become essences and darlings of the universe. These are the truly perfected human beings (*insan-i kamil*). They constantly search and long for the eternal realm, for reunion with the Absolute Being. To have fallen into this world of limitations, into the relative world of existence, is like exile for them. In this world, they have nonetheless been triumphant in shedding their temporary existences, in acknowledging that only with the Existence of the Real do they exist and have hence submitted their will to the Will of the Real.

May the Lord grant all of us a faith of certainty, in the truest sense! May He adorn our gardens of faith with the buds of righteous deeds in line with His pleasure! May He make us neighbors to His Beloved Messenger in the Hereafter and honor us with the privilege of gazing at the Beauty of His Essence!

Amin...

---

65   See, al-Araf. 143

One who looks with the light of the Real beholds eternity in a speck, the entire ocean in a drop. (Mawlana Rumi)

2. DIVINE ATTRIBUTES AND THEIR MANIFESTATIONS

The Essence of the Lord is one, while His attributes are inexhaustible. His attributes are not reserved to a certain number; they are infinite. Their entirety is known to Him alone. Some of these have been revealed exclusively to prophets. Others, like the Ninety Nine Names, have been revealed to mankind entire. Scholars, on the other hand, are acquainted with many Divine attributes that are not included in the 'ninety nine'.

All Divine attributes, both known and unknown, have the primary aim of communicating the fact that the one and only Creator of the universe is unsullied by deficient attributes and is of a transcendence, an unimaginable excellence, endowed only with attributes that are perfect. It is hence impossible for any attribute of Allah, glory unto Him, classified under the headings Essential (*Dhati*) and Positive (*Thubuti*) to be deficient or to be supplemented by another attribute improper.

Such that:

The perfection of His existence is through Him being alive; an aliveness that is perennial and absolute. The Lord's attribute of Life (*al-Hayah*) is not a kind that has death as its opposite; it is rather a life exclusive to Him alone. The Quran describes this as:

"And put your trust in Him Who lives and dies not; and celebrate his praise; and enough is He to be acquainted with the faults of His servants." (al-Furqan, 58)

His Knowledge (*al-Ilm*) is indisputably not a product of thought or ideation. Standing as the most unswerving proof to the infinite knowledge of the Almighty is the delicate harmony and order profuse throughout the universe, impenetrable to any other power of will or reason. Even the tiniest discovery on Earth by man, requires the toil of numerous minds and the successive passage of a number of centuries, with the aid of the gradual development of various scientific principles. Only after the passage of epochs following the creation of man and the piling up of countless efforts on top of one another, for instance, has it become possible to communicate via mobile phones, an activity so widespread today. Such is scientific progress in general. Scientific discoveries, inventions up till now and the countless mysteries yet to be exposed, are nothing but the unveiling of qualities the Almighty, through his Knowledge, has embedded in the order of the universe, just in the blink of an eye.

The infinite difference between the Knowledge of the Almighty and the knowledge of creation is beautifully elaborated below:

During the incredible and mysterious journey of Khidr and Musa –upon them peace- an episode, of which the underlying wisdom is concealed, a sparrow came and landed on the edge of the ship's deck. Shortly afterward, it beaked out a few drops of water from the sea. Khidr –upon him peace- thereupon turned to Musa –upon him peace- and commented: "Compared to the knowledge of Allah, the knowledge of you, I and entire creation is only as much as the water beaked out from the sea by that bird." (Bukhari, Tafsir, 18/4)

Mawlana Rumi –may Allah sanctify his secret- articulates the wisdom as to why humankind was taught the attributes Knowledge, Hearing and Sight;

"In order for you not to give in to fear and engage in mischief, the Lord has informed you that He is the Knower; that He knows everything through and through.

In order for you to seal your lips against ugly and vile speech, He has informed you that He is the Hearer; that He hears everything perfectly.

In order for you not to get caught up in wickedness, both hidden and open, He has informed you that He is the Seer; that He sees everything vividly."

All existent speech is nothing but a manifestation of the Divine attribute of Speech (*kalam*). Allah, glory unto Him, thereby not only makes manifest the infinite power of His Speech; He also makes His Sublime

Sufism: A Path Towards the Internalization of Faith (Ihsân)

Name reverberate in countless languages. From His Speech, the Almighty has endowed each being a language peculiar to it, including those thought of as being lifeless. The Quran declares:

"The seven heavens declare His glory and the earth (too), and those who are in them; and there is not a single thing but glorifies Him with His praise, but you do not understand their glorification; surely He is Forbearing, Forgiving." (al-Isra, 44)

Since all modes of *tasbih*, the verbal glorification of the Lord, are performed through the articulation of names, the only possible way open for man to get to know the Lord is the manifestation, in our realm of comprehension, of the Divine Attributes. Insofar as their meanings are concerned, these attributes are 'adjectives'; yet in terms of their reference to the Essence, they are 'nouns'. In other words, the Lord is attributed with them to such an extent that they are, for Him, names. It may be compared to how certain people, in time, become synonymous with their well-known attributes or titles, which are used to refer to them directly: *as-Siddiq* for Abu Bakr –may Allah be well-pleased with him-, *Imam-i Azam* for Abu Hanifa, *Meyyitzade* etc.

Thus, manifestations of Divine Attributes are also called the manifestation of Divine Names. In this regard, the Almighty Himself has referred to His Attributes as Names, in the medium of which He presents Himself to the comprehension of His servants:

وَلِلّٰهِ الْأَسْمَاءُ الْحُسْنٰى

"And Allah's are the best names…" (al-Araf, 180)

To be sure, it is through the name that the servant establishes connection with the Divine. This goes to show that the Lord's Name is an indispensable element in negating deficient qualities from Him. Good or bad actions the servant performs are therefore directed not to the Reality of the Divine but to His Name. The Lord's Reality thus always remains free of smear.

If it were not for the proper Name of the Almighty, man would sure find it difficult to regulate his conduct for Him. Man, after all, is accustomed to discern a being in a name and express that same being through that name. For man, a name is the registration of that being. It is for no other reason than this; that upon creating Adam –upon him peace-, the Lord taught him all the names, knowledge of which thereby gave the prophet superiority over angels, as alluded to by the Almighty. In an important sense, to know the name of a being is, after all, to acknowledge its essential being. Indeed, were it not for knowing the Lord through His Glorious Names, what could have we known about Him?

Man is, hence, forever in need of names that express the characteristics of his Lord. In whatever situation one may find himself in, he seeks to call upon the Lord with a name fitting with the situation. Were it not for these names, one's connection with the Lord would have only been weak, if not entirely missing. It could even be said that these Names, to a certain degree, do away with the muteness of man at the face of the Essence and the Divine and provide keys that open the deadlock of human comprehension. Without a doubt, even mentioning or repeating the names of Allah, glory unto Him, effectively nourishes one's faith and brings a divine serenity into the heart, increase the love for and focus towards the Lord and desire for the blessings next to Him and turns one to the eternal at the expense of the world and its passing pleasures, igniting one with the desire for the reunion with the Real. These benefits are proved by the fact that the prayers and rememberings (*dhikr*) recommended by the Blessed Prophet –upon him blessings and peace- abound in the names of Allah, glory unto Him.

On finding himself in the grip of a dire situation, a believer, who is in desperate need of Divine compassion, looks for an expression that would best sum up his circumstance and clutches on to, say, the Divine Names Merciful (*ar-Rahman*) and Compassionate (*ar-Rahim*). On feeling of being on the verge of losing all spiritual ties under the crushing weight of sins, he rummages for a means to get closer to the Real and grips the Names the Forgiver (*al-Ghaffar*) the Concealer of sin (*as-Sattar*). When beholding the Divine manifestations in both the universe and in his spirit, he looks for an expression, unfound in books, to give voice to his emotions and roars '*Allah-u Akbar*' to appease his billowing spirit. Shortly said, in all kinds of emotional states, a servant unlocks the locked doors of his spirit through the means of the various names of Allah, glory unto Him, and treats the spiritual convulsions he may feel time and again.

It is for this reason that the Almighty has presented Himself compliant with the truth of the matter yet in a way human beings can understand. In the fact that He presents Himself as the Knower, the Wise, the Powerful, the Forgiver and etcetera and that human beings know Him as such, there lies a reason humane; as human beings can personally identify with many of these names, although to a very limited degree. And this can only be a Divine gift presented to comprehension of humankind for its guidance and salvation.

In a way, the manifestation of the Almighty's attributes and actions is nothing but a 'Divine condescending for human understanding'. The manifestation explains that which is manifested. But this manifestation does not take place as it does in His Essence; it rather is a condescending for our understanding to accommodate. Under the shade of this truth fall the below words of Mawlana Rumi -May Allah sanctify his secret-:

"One who looks with the light of the Real beholds eternity in a speck, the sun as an eternity, and the entire ocean in a drop."

Aware of this subtle truth, Ibrahim Gülşeni –May Allah sanctify his secret- chants the couplet below:

How is it that you are an ocean within these drops?
Or a radiant sun within these tiny dots?

The answer to this question lies hidden in the below words of Mawlana Rumi -May Allah sanctify his secret-:

"Just how can anyone understand the works of the Real when His wisdom is unquestionable? Who can ever penetrate the core of the matter? Even these words I utter are words spoken necessarily for the sake of explaining.

To engage in the affairs of religion is essentially to be left in admiration and awe. But this admiration is not to turn a cold shoulder on the qiblah of truth simply because reason cannot cope with it. On the contrary, it is to fall in to the depths of awe as an enchanted and ecstatic admirer of Him.

When we sleep, it is because of His love that we lose our consciousness, as souls enchanted by Him. Should we be awake, we live through countless mysteries in the epic written by Him.

When we weep, we are clouds loaded by His nourishments and blessings. Smile and we are His brilliant lightning.

Should we become angry and make war, it is the manifestation of His wrath. When we make peace and ask to be pardoned, it is but the revelation, the appearance of His love.

Who are we in this baffling universe? We are each shadow beings, mere nothings, like the letter alif that does not connect with any other letter or take any dots. Every action and state that emanate from us are the manifestations of His Divine Names and Attributes."

What commits Mawlana Rumi -May Allah sanctify his secret- to plunge into the deep end of admiration and awe, are the magnificent and infinite manifestations of the names and attributes of the Divine, both in the universe and his own soul, which are of a nature mind blowing. The abundance of Divine names makes it easier to understand the abundance of His actions; they express the boundlessness inherent in the content of Divineness. They distance the Almighty from constricting, narrow perceptions. Attributes opposite to created beings, especially, act as an effective bulwark against perceptions with a tendency to impose limits on the Divine. Some only wish to see Him as Outward. Outward He is indeed; but Allah, glory unto Him, is at the same time Inward.

The Almighty is the *Jamiu'l-Azdad*, the Combiner of Opposites; He has brought all opposite attributes together in His Being. It is owing to such Glory that all created beings are different to one another. Accordingly, anything that permits comprehension by the human mind can be done so only through its opposite. The sharper the opposition is, the better the comprehension.

On another note, the opposites that we know in our world of understanding are devoid of the ability of harmonious coexistence and are charged with tendency to vanquish one another and seek unity. Valid for realities in realms both physical and metaphysical, this inherent tendency stems from the fact that the origin of being is one. Simply put, it is the outcome of the *adatullah*, the laws of Allah, glory unto Him, operating throughout the universe. Just as night seeks to subjugate the day and heat looks to overcome the cold to find unity therewith, the spiritual transactions that take place through contemplation and sensing, in the spiritual meaning of the term, are all occasioned by this Divine law. Yet, the opposites in the Essence of the Divine are not charged with a tendency to destroy one another. Rather, they have the nature of and power for coexistence. Thus considered from that angle, the Almighty has no attributes that pose any contradiction in themselves. To give an example, He is Alive. Yet, His Life is free of having death as opposition. A life-death opposition is applicable only for beings created and mortal. He Exists though His Existence is not sullied by nothingness. He Knows but this is not a knowledge burdened by an opposite in ignorance. He sees to all needs but never stands in need of anything. The same goes for each of His attributes.

When all is said and done, since we do not have the power to access the absolute content of the Essential attributes of the Almighty and are able to think only through the impressions we receive for the world of sense, analyzing and comprehending their nature is forever beyond our mortal grasp.

We might illustrate this with the following example: From a single cable of electricity, it is possible to obtain two opposite results: we may plug one end of the cable into, say, a freezer and obtain cold and the other end into a heater and obtain heat. Presuming we were to carry this out inside the same room, the battle that would emerge between the heat and the cold where each proceeds to vanquish the other, would not affect the cable of electricity, their mutual source of power, which would remain indifferent. Similarly, as the Almighty has endowed all beings with a distinct aptitude and power to generate a certain effect, each created being receives the manifestations of His Names within the framework of its aptitude. And this, in turn, results in the perpetual battle of opposites, where the one with greater intensity subdues its lesser.

This means that the battle of opposites prevalent in our universe is not so much a battle where one seeks to reduce the other to nothingness, as it is a battle to defeat the other. Since each opposite quality is founded upon one or more Divine Names and since these Names are eternal, this opposition can never be abolished.

A natural outcome of this line of consideration is that while it is the Divine Name Guider (*al-Hadi*) that prevails over believers, it is the Name Deviator (*al-Mudill*) that reins dominant in nonbelievers. The opposition between faith and disbelief, then, is set to continue until the Day of Judgment. It is impossible for the defining quality of this battle to go beyond 'seeking triumph' and become a war of attrition, of total annihilation, as the manifestation of each Divine Name is ceaseless and eternal.

Another outcome of this is that no matter how much strength nonbelievers may possess, they may never vanquish faith. The same goes for Muslims, too. What we have touched upon here regarding the human tussle between faith and disbelief is a fact equally valid for all oppositions throughout the universe.

On another note, in receiving the manifestation of Divine Names, the universe, which exists through their composition, is not alone. Both the Quran and man are recipients of equal measure.

Whereas the universe constitutes a concrete cosmos through this manifestation, the Quran is a prose of truths that expresses all the realities embedded in the universe in the form of 'speech'. As for man, he is not only like the universe in terms of being a recipient of the manifestation of the Divine Names he is furthermore the kernel to the shell that is the universe, its core and essence. It is due to this reason that man is called the minor universe (*alam-i saghir*).

It is essential for the opposition in Divine Names to exist in man, their perfect precinct of manifesting. Accordingly, a believer in whom the Divine Name Guider (*al-Hadi*) reins dominant, at the same time imperatively carries a portion of the Name Deviator (*al-Mudill*). The faith a person of the kind has is nothing but the result of that specific Name, the underlying cause of his faith, gaining supremacy in that person. In a nonbeliever, this situation is totally the opposite.

A natural consequence of this is that every believer has, more or less, an aptitude for disbelief and every disbeliever for belief. It is therefore vital for a believer to adopt a mindset that is halfway between fear and hope and live compliantly. A believer must therefore never put out of his mind the likelihood that he might lapse into deviation at any second. Together with that, he must never rule out the possibility that there might come a day when the Divine Name *al-Hadi* will claim its ascendancy in the soul of even the most stubborn disbeliever. He must therefore treat every non-believer under the light of this glimmer of hope.

Emphasized by the Blessed Prophet –upon him blessings and peace- is exactly that:

"A person, for a long time, offers the deeds of Paradise but ends his life with the deeds of Hellfire. A person, for a long time, offers the deeds of Hellfire but ends his life with the deeds of Paradise." (Muslim, Qadar, 11)

That is why it is crucial for each believer to position his heart somewhere between fear and hope and adopt the below command of the Almighty as a motto:

"And serve thy Lord until there come unto thee the Hour that is Certain!" (al-Hijr, 99)

Because of the unknown nature of fate in terms of whether one ends up a believer or not, feeling absolute security from Divine punishment or counting oneself absolutely bound for it are both tantamount to *kufr*. No-one is secure apart from prophets and those, like the *ashara-i mubassharah*, who were given by prophets the glad tidings of Paradise whilst still alive.

As we have already mentioned above, while opposite attributes coexist harmoniously and tranquilly in the Essence of the Divine, these attributes have manifested on Earth, the temporary land of trial, with a tendency to seek victory over one another. Such is the case with the victory, now and again, of those guided through the manifestation of the name *al-Hadi* or of those obstinate in their disbelief through the manifestation of *al-Mudill*. Even despite the superhuman efforts of prophets, societies have always had their fair share of nonbelievers; and in contrast, believers have always been able to sustain their existence, even during periods when nonbelievers and oppressors reigned sovereign.

The Quran solemnly testifies to many who struggled in the cause of *iman* even in their last breaths without buckling; to the People of Ukhdud when being thrown into pits of fire, to the first followers of Isa (Jesus) –upon him peace- whilst being gnawed to death between the teeth of lions, to the *Habib'un-Najjar* as he was stoned by his own townsmen and to the magicians of the Pharaoh, hung upon date trunks simply for heeding to the call of Musa –upon him peace-, whose final words before reuniting with their Lord as martyrs were:

$$رَبَّنَا أَفْرِغْ عَلَيْنَا صَبْرًا وَتَوَفَّنَا مُسْلِمِينَ$$

"Our Lord: Pour out upon us patience and cause us to die as Muslims!" (al-Araf, 126)

From all this, we can gather an important lesson of creed and conduct. No matter how intense a person may be in his denial, nobody has the right to deprive him of the call to Islam; for a moment may come when the Divine attribute the Guider may emerge from beneath his subconscious and lead to a momentous change in his character. In other words, even the most chronic disbeliever has the possibility of being guided. This fact of the matter is expressed by the Almighty in the below Quranic verse, in His advice to Musa and Harun –upon them peace- just before sending them to talk some sense into the Pharaoh:

$$فَقُولَا لَهُ قَوْلًا لَيِّنًا لَعَلَّهُ يَتَذَكَّرُ أَوْ يَخْشَىٰ$$

"Then speak to him a gentle word haply he may mind or fear." (Taha, 44)

Undoubtedly, the Quranic verse above at the same time presents us with a perfect method in communicating Islam, a method which has two principles:

1. The person, who is the subject of the call to the truth, must be spoken to with a soft, delicate and non-provocative tone.

Indeed, in spite of leaning towards embracing the call of Musa –upon him peace- on numerous occasions after witnessing his miracles, the Pharaoh was prevented by his vizier Haman and other notables. Yielding to his conceit and vanity, he never ended up believing. But as he was being swallowed by the waters of the Red Sea caving in on him, in a state of utter hopelessness, he tried to catch hold of the Divine Name the Guider, and said:

"…I believe that there is no god except Him Whom the Children of Israel believe in: I am of those who submit." (Yunus, 90)

But a lifetime seeking the manifestation of the Divine Name Deviator meant that the Pharaoh's faith, confessed amid the throes of death, was never to be accepted. And the notorious oppressor migrated to the Hereafter as a nonbeliever.

The Quran reinforces this method in another verse:

"Call to the way of your Lord with wisdom and goodly exhortation, and have disputations with them in the best manner; surely your Lord best knows those who go astray from His path, and He knows best those who follow the right way." (an-Nahl, 125)

2. Irrespective of their circumstances, the call to Islam must be generalized so as to encompass humankind entire.

As wretched as he was in declining the call to believe, the Pharaoh was also a ruthless murderer, having slain thousands of newborns just to kill Musa –upon him peace-. Still, this did not mean he be denied of the call to the truth. The prophets entrusted with the duty of delivering to him the call were even told to:

"Then speak to him a gentle word haply he may mind or fear." (Taha, 44)

In the same way, the Blessed Prophet –upon him blessings and peace- personally communicated the call to Abu Jahl on numerous occasions. Despite accepting deep down the truth of the Prophet's call, Abu Jahl could not defeat his ego and pride to admit to it. Yet, this exceptional manner of conduct of the Blessed Prophet –upon him blessings and peace- lead to the guidance of many former ingrained disbelievers, like Omar ibn Khattab, Abu Sufyan, Hind and Wahshi.

Marifatullah and Divine Awards

In both serving the Islamic cause and in all social relations in general, this manner of conduct thus opens possibility of implementing a style of beauty and elegance and moreover takes into consideration the specific circumstances involved. And this is an influential, and no less inspirational, outlook integral to the behavior of Sufis observed to this day.

As a natural and compulsory consequence of believing in Him through an affirmation of the heart and a verbal confirmation of the tongue, the Almighty has desired that He be glorified through worship, a duty for whose fulfillment, He has endowed, among entire creation, only man and *jinn* with enough competence. He has bestowed upon them intelligence and comprehension, proportionate to which He has held them responsible.

Despite the fact that jinn significantly outnumber human beings and are invariably mentioned before their human counterparts wherever they are cited together in the Quran, priority of honor nonetheless belongs to human beings. With that said, jinn are responsible, like man, to carry out their duties of servanthood and worship, the common reason of existence for both.

The Almighty reveals this in the Quran as:

$$\text{وَمَا خَلَقْتُ الْجِنَّ وَالْإِنْسَ إِلاَّ لِيَعْبُدُون}$$

"I created the jinn and humankind only that they might worship Me." (ad-Dhariyat, 56)

What is more, Allah, glory unto Him, whose infinite Mercy has surpassed His Wrath, has not just left man and *jinn* alone, only with the power of reason and comprehension and a sense of discerning right from wrong, He has also reinforced them with further Divine aids. As if the universe alone was not splendid enough a display proving of the existence of the Allah, glory unto Him, in all its aspects, the Almighty has sent a convoy of prophets and saints, to alleviate the difficulties man and *jinn* may encounter in connecting these proofs to Him. And indeed, so that no person is excluded from this supplementary aid, the Almighty inaugurated it with the first man, crowning Adam –upon him peace- the ancestor of mankind, with the laurels of prophethood. Because of the superiority of man over jinn, all prophets have hailed from the species of man, some of whom have been responsible also with the guidance of *jinn*.

Although the messages of each prophet is the same in terms of the abstract truth they communicate, their social rulings have followed a parallel course with the progress of human life, finding their consummate perfection in the Prophet of the Final Hour –upon him blessings and peace- and the Holy Quran revealed to him. Thus, the Holy Quran will remain until the end of time a miracle of expression never to be annulled. Likewise, as the Blessed Prophet –upon him blessings and peace- presides over both man and jinn as prophet, he has also been referred to as *Rasulu'th-Thaqalayn*. The term *thaqalayn* signifies the species of both man and *jinn*.

The universe, the embodiment of a composition of Divine Names, is at once a dazzling exposition of Divine Power. As sciences progress, the magnificent manifestations of Divine art are grasped more extensively and in greater depth, allowing one to infer a stronger conviction of the power of the Almighty. Confirming this are scientific activities of all kinds, from contemporary research of outer space to the progress of genetic sciences and the wonder of computers. It is for such reason that Allah, glory unto Him, declares:

"…among His servants only who are possessed of knowledge fear Allah; surely Allah is Mighty, Forgiving." (Fatir, 28)

With each step taken on the path of progress, sciences present more evidences of Divine power and glory to human comprehension. Endowed with such a character, the universe is like an infinite source of realities at the service of the human mind; an epic work of elaborate poetry that has not been committed to words. Those who achieve depth in knowledge by adhering to Divine commands transcend the realities that have been to put to words and, with a spiritual authority, begin to read the wisdoms and mysteries written in the book of the universe.

Natural sciences aim at decoding the Divine Order that regulates the universe under 'laws of nature'. By grasping these realities known as 'laws of nature' from a more universal standpoint, those with depth of knowledge, however, attain to the Divine Purpose which governs the universe.

Man, a minor universe, is also an infinite prose of realities presented to human comprehension, akin to the other realms. This is the reason as to why he is called *zubda-i kainat*, a condensed universe, its essence and seed. Just as a seed contains all the characteristics of what it will engender, man is implanted with all the mysteries and realities that exist in both the universe and the Quran, in the form of a nucleus.

The Almighty, whose existence does not resemble the existence of what He has created, whose Essence is impenetrable to the mind and who has left open only the door of appreciating Him through His works and art, has created man as *khalifah* or vicegerent on Earth. Making him the most honorable of all creation, the Lord has created man as the kernel of the universe. In terms of the realities embedded in him, man is a minor universe. Science must therefore make man acquainted above all with his own self and informing him of the reason of existence, push open the door to *marifatullah* or Divine knowledge.

The essential purpose science should strive to attain is elaborated by Yunus Emre as:

To know is to learn knowledge,
To learn is to know oneself,
If you do not know yourself,
What sort of a read is that?

'I read and I know', say not
Or that 'I worshipped in lots'
If you do not know the Real
All that is, is vain talk

This particular value and rank the Lord has graced man with has found its voice, more generally, in works produced in Sufi milieus, works that echo their depth of heart. Perhaps the first to come to mind among all works that duly describe man with his inherent worth is the famous poem of Sheikh Ghalib, the renowned Sufi poet of the 18th century. In this poem, the Sheikh addresses 'man' in the following:

In you lies the cellar of the mysteries of love,
The glimmer and bounty of creation, its well

And many more states lay hidden in you, all secret,
Knowledge, skill and reality…in you they indwell

Just look and you'll see that in you lies the earth and skies
The throne and angels…and certainly, heaven and hell

Look after your essence, then, for you're the universe's core,
The apple of the eye of being, the kernel of its shell

So in short, man is a succinct summary of the Lord's glorious realities that are manifest in this temporary world. Endowed with this quality, man is a universe of a distinct kind, with an exclusive potential to become the Quran come to life.

Yet, scientific research has not been able to implement the relative success it has enjoyed in bringing the unseen facts of the universe out into the open, in the realm of the 'human being'. This is due to the fact that man is a compound of body and spirit and that the Lord has revealed man only little information concerning the enigma that is spirit. Therefore, in terms of his inner world, man poses a greater mystery than the universe itself. The rapid increase in knowledge of the human body over the course of the past two millennia has not followed a similar course regarding knowledge of the spirit. This is nothing but a confirmation of the Quran's declaration:

"And they ask you about the spirit. Say: The spirit is one of the commands of my Lord, and you are not given aught of knowledge but a little." (al-Isra, 85)

As for the universe, it is systematically interwoven by a set of intricate and perfect principles, which we refer to as *adatullah* or *sunnatullah*, the Laws of Allah, glory unto Him. These are, at the same time, laws of wisdom pertaining to both the physical and metaphysical realms, referring the mind to the infinite knowledge and power of the Lord. Their common unchangeable denominator is that they are proofs attesting to the fact that they have been set down by One Being, from whose power the entire artwork of the universe has come to be. Since the Almighty presents Himself to us, His servants, through the wisdoms and mysteries of what He has

Marifatullah and Divine Awards

created, Islam naturally invites man to discern these manifestations in the universe, as if he is reading the lines of the Quran. The Quran professes:

"Do they not see the earth, how many of every noble kind We have caused to grow in it?" (as-Shuara, 7)

"Look then at the signs of Allah's mercy, how He gives life to the earth after its death, most surely He will raise the dead to life; and He has power over all things." (ar-Rum, 50)

"Who created the seven heavens one above another; you see no incongruity in the creation of the Beneficent Allah; then look again, can you see any disorder? Then turn back the eye again and again; your look shall come back to you confused while it is fatigued." (al-Mulk, 3-4)

"Will they not then consider the camels, how they are created? And the heaven, how it is reared aloft? And the mountains, how they are firmly fixed? And the earth, how it is made a vast expanse?" (al-Ghashiyah, 17-20)

"Do they not look at the sky above them? How We have made it and adorned it, and there are no flaws in it?" (Qaf, 6)

That there prevails in this boundless universe a harmonious order that shrinks minds in stature and leaves them in awe is indisputable. This harmonious order has been in tact since the time the universe was created, in the eternal balance of a delicate and meticulous calculation. Had the Earth not been on 23.5 degree tilt, for instance, there would have been no such thing as seasons; an endless summer or winter would have been all there was. Again, had the distance separating the Earth from the Sun been only a little more, every single spot on Earth would have come under the freezing grip of a glacial climate. Less and everywhere would have scorched to crisp. These and many more characteristics unmentioned here suffice to verify the fact that all bodies in space have been programmed in a way to facilitate human life.

Eyes that can see thoroughly acknowledge that in the face of Divine sovereignty and order, the Earth is just one of billions of dust floating in space. Mountains, planes, oceans and even human beings are just tiny specks in amid this floating pool of dust. Afflicted with such vulnerability, man is thus nothing apart from the privilege of being a servant of the Lord.

Sufism: A Path Towards the Internalization of Faith (Ihsân)

Programmed according to a calculated mechanism of many interwoven layers, thus created in a perfection that befits the glory of the Almighty, human beings will better appreciate the Glory that reigns supreme in the skies and on Earth with the progress of science. The Quran declares:

"We will soon show them Our signs in the Universe and in their own souls, until it will become quite clear to them that it is the truth. Is it not sufficient as regards your Lord that He is a witness over all things?" (al-Fussilat, 53)

And without a doubt, the advance of space research is truly bringing with it a more comprehensive understanding of the subtleties pointed out to by the Quran. Not only does every new scientific discovery confirm the Quran, they, at times, also throw light on many unclear verses.

Many a right minded scientist in the fields of embryology, anatomy and biology has indeed felt compelled to give credit where it is due, dazzled before the verses of the Quran that provide methodical detail on each stage of embryonic development in the mother's womb:

"And certainly We created man of an extract of clay, Then We made him a small seed in a firm resting-place, Then We made the seed a clot, then We made the clot a lump of flesh, then We made (in) the lump of flesh bones, then We clothed the bones with flesh, then We caused it to grow into another creation, so blessed be Allah, the best of the creators." (al-Muminun, 12-14)[66]

---

[66] Prof. Marshall Johnson, renowned for his research in the field of anatomy, was one to feel astounded upon reading the particular Quranic verses which describe the embryonic development of humans. Especially striking his attention were the details given on the characteristics of *mudhgah* (foetus, literally 'chewed flesh'):

A single chew of meat (*mudghah*)… precisely shaped according to the alignment of teeth; as if they are teeth marks on chewed meat. Its entire length is a centimeter, virtually the size of a single chew.

Found in a *mudghah* are the entire characteristics of a human being. Some are actual while others are potential, not yet activated. The science of medicine cannot find words to explain this phenomenon. Should it go ahead and say that the organs of the *mudghah* are active, it would not be true to the point as there are some that lay dormant; and vice versa. In contrast, however, the Quran elaborates it as a "…a lump of flesh, complete in make and incomplete" (al-Hajj, 5), an expression that comprises all relevant information on the *mudghah*; an expression revealed many centuries ago.

Impulsively rejecting the Quran to begin with, Prof. Marshall then felt obliged to accept it in its entirety as he could not help but confess:

Marifatullah and Divine Awards

Since the Quran is not a book reserved to sciences like astronomy, botanic, biology, geology and so forth, and since it's characteristic feature is to be *jawamiul'-kalim*,[67] it is exempt from the duty of affording specific details on science and technology. Yet each scientific and technological discovery and development effectively corroborates the truths and wisdoms the Quran has pointed out to in concise –not in detail-, serving to throw greater light on Divine realities with every passing day. The realm in which exhibits these realities in their most explicit and detailed fashion is the universe itself. The reason for this despite the comparatively clearer manner in which the Quran lays open the realities essentially embedded in the core of the human being, many of its truths have nonetheless been left somewhat concealed.

The concise nature of the Quran is due to the fact that it comprises infinite realities. Had the realities that are gradually exposed through scientific toil, been laid out in the open by the Quran, a couple of problems would have emerged as a result:

a. Considering the level of knowledge of their times, people would have found it difficult to accept them and consequently would have perhaps chosen the option of impulsively refuting them. Divine Mercy and Compassion has therefore disguised these truths in a way to allow for them to be exposed gradually, through the passage of time.

b. Had the Quran provided meticulous details on all realities, its content would have become enlarged to a point where it would have been almost impossible to read it from start to end, let alone commit it to memory. By declaring:

"…and We have sent down to thee the Book explaining all things, a Guide, a Mercy, and Glad Tidings to Muslims." (an-Nahl, 89)

"…and there falls not a leaf but He knows it, nor a grain in the darkness of the earth, nor anything green nor dry but (it is all) in a clear book."

"Yes; this Quran, which throws light on the pursuit of scholars, has definitely been revealed by God. When their times come, each of its realities will reveal themselves, one by one, and come out into the open. That which God declares in the Quran as "For every prophecy is a term, and you will come to know (it)." (al-Anam, 67) will then become manifest. (See, Abdulmajid Zindani, Kur'ân'da İlmi Mûcizeler, p. 31-36).

67 *Jawamiul'-kalim* denotes the ability to express great meaning in just a few words.

Sufism: A Path Towards the Internalization of Faith (Ihsân)

(al-Anam, 59) the Almighty conveys that the Quran points out to all realities throughout the universe in concise; and by stating:

"Do they not then meditate on the Quran? And if it were from any other than Allah, they would have found in it many a discrepancy." (an-Nisa, 82), He invites all His servants to breathe the true air of contemplation the Quran emits.

To use its own expression, the Quran is the *Furqan*; that is, it is *the* Book that draws the definitive line between guidance and depravity, good and evil, the light and the dark and brings their differences to the fore. It yields results according to the shares, intentions and aptitudes of those who approach it. Approached with an uncorrupted heart, it is then sure offer added proofs to increase and strengthen the *iman*; and to this the Quran itself attests:

"Those only are believers whose hearts become full of fear when Allah is mentioned, and when His communications are recited to them they increase them in faith, and in their Lord do they trust." (al-Anfal, 2)

In contrast, those who approach the Quran conditioned by a negative prejudice will only add further fuel to their deviation. Looking upon anything with the eye of love serves to bring its beauty to the forefront. An opposite look of hatred, on the other hand, obscures its otherwise unmistakable beauty; similar to Abu Jahl's perception of Islam. The more such people read the Quran the more ossified their feelings of disbelief and deviation become, as they quiver in the helplessness of not being able to attain to the heights of the Quranic beauty. They are comparable to those who are defeated in a game by a sworn archrival; they grow in fury and the fires of their inexpressible anger rages even higher. And consequently, they become all the more deserving of punishment. As regards, the Quran declares:

"And We reveal of the Quran that which is a healing and a mercy to the believers and it adds only to the perdition of the unjust." (al-Isra, 82)

"Say: "It is a Guide and a Healing to those who believe; and for those who believe not, there is a deafness in their ears, and it is blindness in their (eyes): They are (as it were) being called from a place far distant!"" (Fussilat, 44)

Thus, as much as the Quran is an unmistakable light of guidance for the pious, it only serves to increase the corruption of those whom stubbornly close their eyes to its light.

Marifatullah and Divine Awards

Concerning such people is again the below Quranic verse:

"Have they not travelled in the land so that they should have hearts with which to understand, or ears with which to hear? For surely it is not the eyes that are blind, but blind are the hearts which are in the breasts." (al-Hajj, 46)

As mentioned above, the universe is a system of creation that has come to existence as the compound of the manifestation of Divine Names, while the Quran is the reflection of the realities, both hidden an open, of this system onto speech. As for man, he is the core, essence and seed, as it were, of both and as such, he carries a share of its opposite manifestations, in varying degrees.

❦

Having created the universe through the compound of the manifestations of His Names, the Almighty has endowed only human beings with the perfected manifestations of these names. This is the reason as to why man is the *ashraf-i makhluqat*, the most honorable of creation. Depending on his aptitude, man, in turn, is endowed with opposite attributes, being a *jamiu'l-azdad*. He laughs and cries, loves and hates, and so forth. In other words, man's existence, in the broadest sense, is permeated by attributes both of mercy and of wrath. Hence, he may give expression to a richness of heart and generosity and at the same time, incinerate in the flames of anger and malice. He is ever exposed to the ebb and flow of calm and fury.

Man has received his fair share of many a Divine attribute. But their degree of manifesting poses an infinite difference in one human being to another. From the lowest end of the scale to the highest, the amount of share received of this manifesting makes up the social classification.

To give an example, each human being undoubtedly holds a manifestation of the Divine Names Merciful (*ar-Rahman*) and Compassionate (*ar-Rahim*). But their level of intensity varies from one person to another, posing contrasting ratios. Some are 'merciful' and 'compassionate' only towards themselves or at most, to their family members of close circle of friends, while there are others whose 'mercy' and 'compassion' are vast enough to embrace humankind entire, even the animal kingdom. On the manifestation of the attribute 'Merciful', we may cite the accounts below:

Once traveling to certain destination, Bayazid Bistami -May Allah sanctify his secret- decides to take a break under a tree to eat. After finishing his food, he gets up and carries on his journey. But a while later and after having covered a great distance, he notices an ant crawling on his bag, upon which he remarks with angst:

"I have exiled this creature of the Lord from its homeland"; as he returns all the way to that same tree to drop the ant off where it belongs.

Here is another immeasurable display of mercy:

One day, as Sari-i Saqati -may Allah sanctify his secret- was explaining to his students the Prophetic saying, "He who does not trouble himself with the troubles of believers is not one of them" (Hakim, Mustadrak, IV, 352; Haythami, Majmau'z-Zawaid, I, 87), *another student of his fretfully rushed inside and said:*

"Sir…Your entire neighborhood has burnt down. Only your house has survived the fire!"

"Alhamdulillah (Thank God)", sighed Sari-i Saqati, blissfully.

Thirty years down the track, he would be seen confessing to a close friend:

"By saying alhamdulillah in that time of anguish, I had thought of merely my own wellbeing and remained aloof from identifying with the troubles of others who were struck by that disaster. And my last thirty years, my friend, has been nothing but a repentance for that mistake!"

Therefore, regardless of where and when the mercy and love one feels may have sprung from and who its focal point may have originally been, if they are allowed to flourish and expand as to embrace entire creation, they will undeniably turn one into a 'true Muslim' or in other words, a true person of love. Even if it may have blossomed from a specific passion or attraction, like a sapling sprouting from a slapdash sprinkle of water, love will be set on the path of becoming 'real love', if it is extended to entire creation for the sake of the Creator.

Unless the limits of that unfathomable connection of mercy and affection that is 'Divine Love' are expanded to an infinite horizon, any mercy and affection felt will not become love in the truest sense. At best, it will remain at the phase called metaphorical love, an elementary form of real love.

Marifatullah and Divine Awards

The compound of the manifestation of Divine Names has resulted in the surfacing of different temperaments, as many as the number of human beings. Just as mixing different paints with one another brings out the tone of the dominant color, similarly, the coalescence of these Divine Names surface, in a human being, according to the dominant manifestation that prevails over him. Quite naturally, therefore, Sufi paths are branched out; each branch or order (*tariqah*) attends to a given temperament, easing the path of the spiritual progress of an aspirant by attracting him to an order that complements his disposition. This also underlines the necessity of espousing a different method of training each *murid*, compliant with his temperament.

In a similar manner to which organisms are classified under human beings, animals or plants, or living and non-living organisms at the very top, temperaments may also be subjected to a classification in terms of their fundamentally defining characteristics. But it should be borne in mind that the difference between the minimum and the maximum ratios of any given qualities possessed by any two organisms belonging to the same category may be radically greater than the difference between two categories themselves. For instance, the difference of ranking between the lowest human being and the highest is more striking than the difference between the human being and animal as such. Behind this significant difference lies a tremendous disparity of manifestations that surface in each. This holds equally for all attributes both positive and negative. Truly dizzying is the difference between a person in the deep end of oppression or disbelief and his counterpart, who is on the highest end of the scale.

A nonbeliever, in whom the Name Deviator (*al-Mudill*) prevails, for example, lives a life debauched within the narrow confines of his existence. He could not care less about the believers' faith. But as was the case with Abu Lahab and those alike, once his disbelief escalates in intensity, that carelessness turns to resentment and incites him to battle with righteous believers and even taking up arms against Prophets if he must, simply to appease that resentment. The same is the case with oppression. A hunter who hunts not out of need but out of pleasure will soon become hard-hearted and even sadistic. The callous emperors of Rome, who would look on in bloodthirsty pleasure as the first believers of Jesus –upon him peace- were being devoured by ravaging lions, provides a case in point for the diagnosis of the Quran:

« بَلْ هُمْ اَضَلُّ »

"They are even more bewildered than animals."

The infinite diversification between the manifestations that surface in all organisms, living and non-living, including human beings, exposes 'difference' as an integral law of the universe. Equating any two beings with one another, let alone the entire realm of existence, is thus nothing but a futile undertaking, given that the infinite manifestation Divine Names means that there are no 'twins' in the universe; twins in the sense of complete and utter sameness. In terms of matter and spirit, no two human beings are one and the same. Much is the same case with two trees of the same species, always differing in the amount of branches, leaves and fruits they bear.

Coming to an understanding of the Almighty, man and the universe from this fundamental perspective, enables one to endure his opposites and even refines him to a maturity of treating them with compassion and leniency. *Tasawwuf* is just that: the maturity of being able to look lovingly and compassionately upon things that leave others in anger; others who have not set out on this path of love. This is a virtue acquired from having probed the underlying wisdom of external appearances.

This virtue and maturity, in turn, impresses us with many qualities. First and foremost, it makes us commiserate with the sinner instead of feeling personal anger towards him. It renders us gentle towards the nonbeliever, making us consider his deprivation; from guidance it gives us hope at the same time. It instills us with power and courage to call to the way of truth. It makes us look upon anyone needing to hear the call, like the blind who are in need of others to help them walk and guide their way. It allows us to comprehend the absurdity of not carrying the natural pity felt upon seeing a bird with a broken wing, to a person of whose spirit has been broken under the gnashing weight of sin. It turns our emotions of love and compassion to a grand waterfall, founded high above all interests of kinship, falling generously on humankind entire. In a society made up of human beings of such magnitude, murder and conflict make way to benevolent solidarity. And in tandem there will come a rise of the number of righteous souls most of whom now belong to the yesteryears. The praiseworthy moral conduct, which they embody by emulating the Blessed Prophet –upon him blessings and peace- will be spread to the rest of society. Behavior towards people of with faults will gain the maturity exemplified in the case below:

Khatam-i Asamm -May Allah sanctify his secret-, a scholar from Balkh, is an illustrious figure of Sufi history for having refined himself through the spiritual legacy of the Blessed Prophet –upon him blessings and peace- and elevating his moral conduct to an exceptional level. That he was famous with the nickname Asamm, or deaf, despite being a man of sound hearing, is based on an outstanding experience:

One day, he was visited by a distressed woman, who had come with a request. Just when she had begun to explain to him her troubles, she involuntarily broke wind. The embarrassment she felt was beyond words; she virtually melted like a candle. But in order to prevent the woman suffering an even greater embarrassment, Khatam -May Allah sanctify his secret- acted as if he heard nothing. And taking his hand to his ear, he said:

"I have bad hearing, sister. Raise your voice a little…I cannot hear!"

Thinking that her moment of embarrassment had gone unheard, the woman then heaved a huge sigh of relief. Raising her voice, she resumed explaining her trouble.

It is reported that Khatam acted deaf for an entire fifteen years following the incident, when the woman eventually passed away, Khatam -May Allah sanctify his secret- acted as if he was deaf to prevent her from finding out and feeling humiliated. Hence, he came to be known as Khatam-i Asamm or Khatam the Deaf.

It is of course improbable that the profound level of moral conduct and sensitivity displayed by Khatam -may Allah sanctify his secret- was a result of him bringing what he had read in books to life. Khatam's behavior may only be explained by his success in transforming the share Khatam had received from the Divine Attribute the Concealer of Sins (*Sattaru'l-Uyub*) into moral conduct. Such conduct has been labeled, especially in *tasawwuf*, as 'embodying the morals of Allah.'

True saints, therefore, surrender their will to the Will of the Lord, absorbed in the manifestations of His magnificent attributes. Knowing that whatever the Lord wills is proper, they instill this knowledge to those around and set them right on this knowledge. On this subject, the following account is replete with wisdom:

"Suppose that the Lord made you preside over the universe...what would you do?" Sunbul Sinan -may Allah sanctify his secret- one day asked his disciples.

Each came up with an answer.

"I would destroy all nonbelievers" retorted one.

"I would smite all drinkers" said another.

"I would not leave one person who smoked", exclaimed another. Muslihiddin Effendi, a scholar and a disciple of Sheikh Sinan, was meanwhile keeping silent. His silence was broken by the Sheikh, who turned to him and asked:

"And you...what would you do?"

With his usual propriety, Muslihiddin Effendi replied:

"Master...Is there a deficiency in the Lord's will and governance that I should think of placing another measure? I can only reply that I would keep everything as they are!"

Delighted with his answer, Sunbul Sinan -may Allah sanctify his secret- said:

"Only now has the issue found its core (merkez)! (i.e. only now has the question been settled)"

Muslihiddin Effendi came to be known as Merkez Effendi after that day. And after the passing away of Sunbul Sinan -may Allah sanctify his secret-, he became his successor, assuming his spiritual duties.

In a virtual summary of this mindset, Ibrahim Hakki Erzurumi -May Allah sanctify his secret- articulates his submission to the Real in the following:

All His works supreme
With one another fitting
Whatever He does, convenes
Wait, what the Lord does, and see
What He does, He does splendidly

Hence, attaining to this beauty of character is possible only through embodying the manifestations of the attributes of Allah, glory unto Him, in the heart. Otherwise, we would be no different to a piece of paper oblivious to what is being written and drawn upon it. Mawlana Rumi -may Allah sanctify his secret- says it beautifully:

"If you were to draw the picture of an unhappy man on a piece of paper, both the picture and the paper would remain ignorant of the sorrow or happiness of what is drawn.

On the surface, the picture is of sorrow; yet neither the picture nor the paper has any clue. The picture of a smiling man has no idea of his smile."

So regardless of how deeply we may be inundated with the manifestations of Divine attributes, which we owe to the honor of being human, we will be no different to a paper and a lifeless picture thereon, unless we are aware of it. We must therefore melt all the mortal and relative attributes we have been given as part of a trial, in the pot that is the manifestation of the glorious attributes of the Lord. We must be fully aware that the contents of each attribute belonging to the Essence of the Lord are of an indefinably infinite extent. They are all without beginning (*azali*) and end (*abadi*). They are all absolute in Him, attributed with infinite qualities. Simpler said, no Divine attribute recognizes any limit. Therefore, His Knowledge, Speech, Power, Creativity and all attributes alike a free from all comparisons and efforts of explanation. Our world and its features, on the other hand, are both limited and mortal; a fleeting shadow is all they are. Still without success in perfectly understanding the nature of himself, it is certainly unthinkable for man to be able to comprehend the attributes of the Lord that are exclusive to Himself, in their proper nature. Just as we cannot comprehend the reality and nature of the Essence of Allah, glory unto Him, we are equally inept in comprehending the reality and nature of each of His attributes.

Those triumphant in coming to terms with this truth and in realizing that their sight, hearing, understanding, speech and all other abilities are but crumb-like manifestations of the attributes of the Lord, live amid the climes of nothingness, inhaling the inspiring winds of wisdom breezing there about. Annihilating their existence in the deep satisfaction of *iman*, they say:

لَا مَوْجُودَ إِلاَّ هُوَ

"There is no other being than Allah."

Molding their minds and spirits is the wisdom of acknowledging:

"Lord…You are the way You are, whatever that may be!"

Consequently, free from all apprehensions and delusions, they return to their Lord with a purified heart, recorded in the books of the righteous.

"Which are the greatest names of Allah?" a dervish once asked Bayazid-i Bistami -may Allah sanctify his secret-.

"Which of His names are small? Do not be a fool. All of Allah's names are great. If you want your wishes accepted by Him, seek to clean your heart of anything other than Him. His Names do not manifest in hearts that are oblivious. But at hearts which have been revived by His Light, Allah gazes at each moment with many of His names."

In fact, the name of Allah is ascribed with greatness in many a Quranic verse:

"Therefore glorify the name of your Lord, the Great." (al-Waqia, 96)

The Blessed Prophet –upon him blessings and peace- complied with this command by saying, while bowing down in ritual prayer, *Subhana Rabbiya'l-Azim* (I glorify my Majestic Lord from all deficient attributes) and while prostrating, *Subhana Rabbiya'l-A'la* (I glorify My Sublime Lord from all deficient attributes).

O Allah! Grant us a share of the secret of Divine knowledge and love for the sake of Your beautiful names and in particular, for the sake of Your genuine name!

Amin…

Since a mature person who has attained to marifatullah now stands beneath the manifestation of the love of the Real, he incinerates all egoistic tendencies in his spirit, just like a paper ablaze under a lens reflecting the rays of the sun.

3. KNOWLEDGE OF THE DIVINE AND ITS MANIFESTATIONS IN THE WISE

Marifatullah, or knowledge of the Divine, is a boundless and infinite knowledge from the Divine that comprises all the mysteries and wisdoms prevalent in the universe entire. Any effort to perfectly define it would be a task beyond human capability. Yet each person enjoys a share of this knowledge to the extent allowed by his power, aptitude and effort. Hence, the Blessed Prophet –upon him blessings and peace- has prayed:

لاَ أُحْصِى ثَنَاءً عَلَيْكَ أَنْتَ كَمَا أَثْنَيْتَ عَلَى نَفْسِكَ

"(My Lord) I am powerless to glorify and praise as befits You! In whichever manner You have glorified and praised Yourself, that is how you are!" (Muslim, Salat, 222)

Indicating the importance of *marifatullah* are also the following words narrated as a *hadith al-qudsi*: "I was a secret treasure. I loved to be known and thus created creation for them to know Me."[68]

After the words of the Holy Quran and the sayings and behavior of the Blessed Prophet –upon him blessings and peace-, there are no better words and behavior than the genuine servants of the Lord who have attained to *marifah*, that knowledge spoken of. That is because their unique words and behavior are profound and of a *ladunni* nature; they are not acquired. They are thus called the 'inheritors of prophets' (*warathatu'l-anbiya*). The

---

68   See, Ajluni, Kashfu'l-Khafa, II, 132.

Sufism: A Path Towards the Internalization of Faith (Ihsân)

hearts of those who witness the behavior of these genuine persons, who hear their words, become inundated with spiritual inspiration. With an increased eagerness, they gradually ridding themselves of devilish whispers and worldly ambitions, whereby the secrets slowly become unraveled.

Some of these righteous souls Adam's –upon him peace- temperament, others are of Ibrahim's -upon him peace-. There are some who characteristically take after Musa –upon him peace-, while there are others who resemble Jesus –upon him peace-. And there are some who are of the temperament of Muhammad –upon him blessings and peace-.

The distinctive attribute of those who are of a Muhammadan temperament is that they are persons of knowledge, love and unity (*tawhid*). Among them are such persons who virtually elude all efforts of describing them through a single attribute, simply because they have embodied all the defining attributes in their existence. Any further explanation would be redundant.

The Lord has endowed these beloved servants of His with different manifestations depending on their particular spiritual states. He has turned some into a Shah Naqshiband, boundless and unique oceans of inspiration in knowledge of the Divine, and others into a Majnun wandering in the deserts of love. There are some made by the Lord to stroll across the valleys of awe and others muted before the presence of His Majesty. Some have been rendered a Yunus Emre, a nightingale chirping the tunes of love, while others a Mawlana Rumi, whose tongues bursts with wisdom, scattering rare pearls of spirituality all around. Equipping all of his saints with the knowledge of *marifah* and privileging each with a distinct manifestation, the Lord has blessed them to entire humankind as outstanding lights of guidance.

Since a mature person who has attained to *marifatullah* now stands beneath the manifestation of the love of the Real, he incinerates all egoistic tendencies in his spirit, just like a paper ablaze under a lens. As he thereby becomes an illuminating center of attraction, others naturally grow fond of and respect him. But because he has disengaged himself from the grip of passing compliments and interests, he does not fall into the destructive whirlpool of pride, conceit and self-importance. Though in public, he is with the Real. He lives amid feelings of *ta'zim li amrillah*, respectfully

Marifatullah and Divine Awards

abiding by the commands of Allah, glory unto Him, and *shafqah li khalqillah*, nurturing compassion and mercy to the Almighty's creation. But as is demanded by his love of the Lord, never does she show any love and affection to the oppressor and the ingrate, his counter opposite in perfection. Yet, as is demanded by his compassion, he feels sorry for them and prays for their guidance.

He only needs the wealth and possessions the world has to offer to spend as charity in the way of the Divine. A mature person of perfection devotes himself only to the knowledge of the Divine and reuniting with the Real. From now on, he is a genuine servant who takes pays no attention to the pains and agonies of the world.

Mawlana Rumi -May Allah sanctify his secret- beautifully uses the below parable to emphasize how spiritual aptitudes always differ from one person to another, how each person behold the patterns embroidered by the Lord throughout the universe from different perspectives as reflected by their own mirrors of the heart and how some manage to continue being with the Lord despite seemingly being among crowds:

"A Sufi went to an adorned garden, to raise his spirits and to thereby throw himself deep in contemplation. He became infatuated with the vibrant colors of the garden. Closing his eyes, he began his muraqabah and contemplation. An ignorant man passing by thought the Sufi was asleep. Astonished and upset, he scolded the Sufi:

'Why are you sleeping?' he asked. 'Open your eyes and stare at the vines, the booming trees and the greening grass! Gaze at the works of Allah's mercy!'

The Sufi replied: 'Know one thing very well, you ignorant man, that the heart is greatest work of Allah's mercy. The rest are like its shadow. A stream flows amid the trees. From its crystal water, you can see the reflection of trees on both sides. What is reflected on the stream is a dream garden. The real garden is in the heart, for the heart is the focus of Divine gaze. Its elegant and slender reflections are to be found in this worldly life, made of water and mud. Had the things in this world not been the reflection of the cypresses of the heart's joy, the Almighty would not have called this dream world the place of deception. It is said in the Quran:

'Every soul shall taste of death, and you shall only be paid fully your reward on the resurrection day; then whoever is removed far away from the fire and is made to enter the garden he indeed has attained the object; and the life of this world is nothing but a provision of vanities.' (Ali Imran, 185)

The ignorant who presume the world to be Paradise and exclaim 'here is Paradise!' are those fooled by the sparkle of the stream. Those who are left distant from the true gardens, who are the righteous servants of Allah, incline to that reverie and are deceived. A day will come when this slumber of ignorance will come to an end. The eyes will open, the truth shall be seen. But what is the worth of seeing that sight during the final breath? A great joy to he who has died before death and whose spirit has had a scent of the truth of this garden…"

And without a doubt, should a person take no heed of the pleasures of the world that appeal to the ego and turn away from them, Allah, glory unto Him, will purify his spirit and enlighten his heart.

When the Blessed Prophet –upon him blessings and peace- said, "The heart that is visited upon by light will open up and expand", the Companions asked, "What is its sign, Messenger of Allah?" The reply was:

"Distancing oneself from the passing world, becoming devoted to the eternal life of the Hereafter and preparing oneself for death before it comes to pass." (Tabari, Tafsir, VIII, 37)

The hearts of these loyal journeymen of this honorable road of *marifah* are like nacres that produce pearls larger than drops of April rain. They do not shrink back from turning many a raw heart, which nurtures fondness towards them, into a sizeable piece of pearl; as long as these aspiring hearts can understand the drop of rain that deserves to be kept in that nacre!

In the commentary of the *Mathnawi*, it is said:

"Allah, the possessor of Speech, whispered a secret into the cloud's ear and tears began pouring out of its eyes like an emptied water skin. He whispered a secret into the rose's ear and adorned it with the beauty of color and scent. He whispered a secret to the stone and turned it into an agate among all minerals. That is to say, the Lord manifested with His attribute al-Latif (the Subtle, the Graceful) and made the cloud downpour with water, the rose beautiful and the stone precious.

The Lord also whispered a secret into the human body and elevated to infinity the folk of marifah who protect that secret. Inspired by the Divine realm and salvaged from the physical, these saints of the Lord have tapped into the secret of closeness to the Real."

Undoubtedly, these secrets are the secret of love, which, through numerous manifestations, conduce to the attaining of *marifah*. In its inspirational climes, the secret of love keeps hidden the perfection and beauty of everything.

Top-level saints experience, more intensely, the manifestations of essential love. Essential love, in the ordinary sense, is when a person inadvertently falls in love with another and establishes an affectionate connection. But in the real sense, essential love is an attraction towards the Lord in a like a manner and to become annihilated in Him.

The righteous, the privileged recipients of these manifestations of essential love, are not the types who love only when things are sailing smoothly and grow weaker in love when things begin to get tough. The allegory below offers a wonderful example of true, essential love:

Mawlana Jami -may Allah sanctify his secret- recounts:

"There was a young man who used to frequent the circle of our master Sadaddin Kashgari. He excelled in self-discipline, contemplation and love. But there came a day when he, like me, fell in love with a beautiful woman; and in a single moment, he transferred to her all the treasures he had amassed in his heart up until then.

So he one day bought a present of gold and diamonds and left it on the street she habitually walked past, hiding it, at the same time, to ensure nobody else saw it and picked it up instead of her. His beloved, he thought, would then collect it as she strolled past, without knowing who it was from and why it had been left there. Once I heard about this, I said to him:

'What a strange thing is you are doing! You are leaving on her path that which took you so much effort to amass, just like that! Even if she saw and collected it, she is still not going to know who it is from and why it had been left there. At least leave a sign so she knows it is from you!'

Shaken, the young man responded in tears: 'What are you talking about? Do you suppose that I do not know just how strange what I am doing is? I do not expect anything in return, for I do not want to discomfort her by making her to feel obliged towards me because of those gifts!'

I quivered. If the love felt for a mortal, I thought, could exude such depth, elegance and beautiful behavior, there is no guessing how magnificent a manifestation one may see from those who are enraptured in 'essential love'".

In explaining the spiritual levels of the heart by recollecting on his own experiences and the spiritual stages he outgrew, Mawlana Rumi -may Allah sanctify his secret- has used the term *raw* for the time he excelled as a *dersiam* (professor) in the Seljuk Madrasa mastering books of exoteric content, *cooked* to label the phase when he received the manifestations of Divine Knowledge whereby the mysteries of the universe became exposed, and *burnt* for the state in which he was virtually burnt to ashes in the flame of essential love.

Attaining to *marifatullah* is possible only through a contented belief in the Essence of the Divine and an understanding of Divine manifestations, to the degree allowed by human capacity.

O Allah! Allow us to sufficiently live up to the trusts You have entrusted us with! Hand us possession to enough righteous deeds that would usher us through to receive a maximum of Your Mercy in the Hereafter! Turn our hearts into stages exhibiting the magnificent manifestations of Your Love! Make us tap into the mystery of being created in the 'best of mold' so as to forever revive our hearts with the dews of Your Compassion!

Amin…

Attaining Divine awards depends on the blend of the heart.

B. DIVINE AWARDS

All beings other than Allah, glory unto Him, have been created through the manifestation of His attribute *al-Latif* (the Graceful); in other words, through His grace. No being among entire creation has come into existence through merit, by paying its due price. The mortal and relative existence of beings, as well as their entire characteristics and prospects spawned by the underlying wisdom of their creation, are to be defined entirely as Divine awards.[69] This means that existence of all that which exists, is merely the grace, generosity and favor of the Almighty.

Although the existence of entire creation and the qualities they possess is, in effect, a 'Divine award', we will use this term here to refer to the grants received by those progressively travel on the Sufi road, corresponding to the distance they cover. Persons with aptitude begin to receive unique favors and characteristics the more they progress on this path, even before they pass away to 'the other world'. However much one may think that receiving these Divine awards is a matter of merit –since a person uses his particular willpower to enter the path to begin with-, in the final reckoning, grace overpowers merit, which is the reason why it has become custom to conceive them purely as Divinely given and confine the term 'award' to refer to them. The enormous difference between being awarded with something and meriting something has led to suppose merit nonexistent. This approach is not really off the mark, considering that the opportunity a person is given, which makes meriting possible, is essentially also a 'Divine award'.

---

69   Divine Awards (*mawhibatu'l-ilahiyyah*): Divine favors and grace.

Some inherently able persons, who acquire a spiritual level through the training of *tasawwuf*, attain to many a rank of perfection during this spiritual journey. Such that the wisdoms of many mysteries are bared open for many a saint and many knots are untied. What was previously unknown is discovered anew, enigmas are conquered. Enlightening inspirations that glimmer onto a purified heart steers its possessor to the core of the Real and reality. Truthful dreams, which are generated through the Protected Tablet (*Lawh-i Mahfuz*) reflecting many of its future insights onto the heart, begin to be seen. Its possessor acquires a profound contemplation and a vision that feels the Divine purpose in everything of which it catches sight.

These states, obtained through Divine Grace complementing genuine effort, come in many more forms of manifestation. Expressed in the form of knowledge, they have been referred to as *ladunni*. Although they are of a content that transcends human comprehension and grasp, those, who through the grace and benevolence of the Lord have been privileged with a share of *ladunni* knowledge, at the same time attain to a comprehensive comprehension and understanding, parallel with the distance they have progressed. We will now try to expand on the nature of this *ladunni* knowledge, as much as is allowed by human capability and permitted by religion.

Once I love My servant, I (virtually) become his tongue that speaks, heart that comprehends, ears that hear, eyes that see, hands that hold and feet that walk. I give him whatever He wants from Me. If he seeks refuge in Me, I protect him. (Hadith al-Qudsi, Bukhari, Riqaq, 38)

1. *LADUNNI* KNOWLEDGE

This special kind of knowledge is purely God-given, a divine endowment, an award. In reference, the Quran uses the expression "knowledge from Our presence".[70] The term *ladunni*, meaning "from Us, form Our presence", comes from that.

The truths revealed by the Lord to the Blessed Prophet –upon him blessings and peace- are chiefly comprised of three categories. The first category marks the truths that can only be comprehended with the light of prophethood; they have thus remained a mystery known only to Allah, glory unto Him, and His Messenger. The Prophet –upon him blessings and peace-did not disclose these truths to any one of his Companions.

The existence of these truths, whose disclosure is both impermissible and impossible – even if they were disclosed, it would be impossible to comprehend them- may be gathered from a number of sayings of the Blessed Prophet –upon him blessings and peace-.

"If you knew what I knew, you would laugh only little and cry in lots", the Noble Messenger –upon him blessings and peace- told his Companions. (Bukhari, Kusuf, 2; Muslim, Salat, 112)

And in another hadith, he says, "I have such moments with my Lord that neither a close (muqarrab) angel nor a prophet could ever comprehend." (Munawi, Fayzu'l-Qadir, IV, 8)

---

70   See, al-Kahf, 65.

Sufism: A Path Towards the Internalization of Faith (Ihsân)

There is a further second set of truths that the Almighty revealed to His Prophet, which may only be truly comprehended by a selected and capable few who have acquired a spiritual and intellectual ability and depth, whom are referred to as *khawas* and *khawasu'l-khawas*.[71] The truths of this category is the knowledge the Blessed Prophet –upon him blessings and peace- is known to have conveyed to a few great Companions of the likes of Abu Bakr and Ali –may Allah be well-pleased with them-. Their passage from one heart to another is a tradition. If written books were to be their mode of passage, it would have been accessible to those incapable, as yet, of understanding it, causing a misunderstanding that would steer them to error as a consequence. Be that as it may, each and every person is responsible with learning it as much as is allowed by his spiritual aptitude and power, which he must develop for the sake of his wellbeing.

The third set of truth the Blessed Prophet –upon him blessings and peace- was revealed with are the truths of religion or the law (*sharia*). With respect to this category, entire humankind is obliged to affirm faith in it and put it to practice. Since it comprehensively binds entire humankind, the Almighty has taken into consideration the weakest, rendering the observing of these truths physically possible. And as they are needed by everybody, they have been announced to the entire world, to determine the obligations of all.

Time and again, the Blessed Prophet –upon him blessings and peace- would inform his Companions of the events set to take place until the Day of Judgment, yet many of them would not be able to properly understand. There were others who would simply forget.[72]

In contrast, it is a known fact that the Blessed Prophet –upon him blessings peace- disclosed many a truth difficult in nature to the certain Companions of aptitude, many of which they have conveyed from their hearts to the hearts of others who were of similar caliber. These truths are not needed by the general public, added by the fact that they are of a nature that exceeds the comprehension of most. Their transfer among the spiritually apt is not by a public address but rather through one heart to another;

---

71 *Khawas*: The selected, righteous servants. *Khawasu'l-Khawas*: The selected among the selected; figuratively, the cream of the crop.
72 See, Bukhari, Qadar, 4.

Marifatullah and Divine Awards

that is from one able person to another person with spiritual ability. And historically, this is how this tradition has survived.

In addition to Abu Bakr and Ali, Ibn Masud, Abu Hurayrah, Muadh ibn Jabal and Harith ibn Malik –may Allah be well-pleased with them- are other Companions who received certain secrets of this unique knowledge.

To the hearts of His servants who properly obey Him and successfully fasten their natural desires and wants to Divine Will, the Lord offers many treats, never before seen and inconceivable in nature. The Almighty indeed reveals in the Quran that he grants a special knowledge and wisdom to such of His righteous servants:

يَآ اَيُّهَا الَّذِينَ اٰمَنُوا اِنْ تَتَّقُوا اللّٰهَ يَجْعَلْ لَكُمْ فُرْقَانًا وَ يُكَفِّرْ عَنْكُمْ سَيِّاٰتِكُمْ وَ يَغْفِرْ لَكُمْ وَ اللّٰهُ ذُو الْفَضْلِ الْعَظِيمِ

"O you who believe! If you fear Allah, He will grant you a distinction and do away with your evils and forgive you; and Allah is the Lord of mighty grace." (al-Anfal, 29)

"O you who believe! Fear Allah and believe in His Messenger: He will give you two portions of His mercy, and make for you a light with which you will walk" (al-Hadid, 28)

The *hadith* says:

"He who puts to practice what he knows will be taught by Allah what he does not know." (Abu Nuaym, Hilyatu'l-Awliya, X, 15)

And a related *hadith al-qudsi* states:

"Whosoever nurtures enmity towards one of My righteous servants, I will declare war on him. My servant may not get closer to me, in any way lovelier, than the obligatory deeds I have commanded him with. And through supererogatory deeds, My servant continues to get closer, until I love him. And when I do love him, I become (virtually) his eyes that see, his ears that hear, his hands that hold and his feet that walk. I then give him *whatever he wants from Me. Should he seek refuge in me, I shall protect him."* (Bukhari, Riqaq, 38)

As is obvious, offering supererogatory deeds with love and passion, after of course earnestly offering those that are compulsory deeds in their proper manner, provides a means to receiving such magnificent blessings and awards of the Lord. For this, it is necessary to repel the lowly desires of the ego and abstain from the impermissible and doubtful and, at the same time, embrace the Sunnah as a way of life. Pleasures of the flesh must likewise be confined to where they belong, diverting attention instead to developing the inner, spiritual world. After all, what is at stake is so enormous a blessing that once obtained, it lifts the curtains of human shortcomings that veil the understanding to reveal a window that opens to the truth, the real and wisdom. It grants a precision of judgment and foresight. Outward causes and excuses, and external appearance in general, can no longer deceive a person who has melted in the Will of the Divine. Henceforth, he begins to discover the underlying reasons of all happenings, endowed with exceptional forethought.

Along with the ability to pass precise judgment and offer foresight through the inspirations that arise in the heart, there are also pleasantly subtle ideas that emerge in the mind, delicate messages pertaining to the heart-world, which are conveyed not so much through words as through signs. These are called *latifah* or *lataif* in its plural. These are guiding signs with which the Lord gifts his servants who strive on the path of spirituality.

The Almighty may also help His righteous servants in desperate situations by warning them with externally inaudible sounds. These have been called *khatif*, meaning a secret sound that comes from who knows where, whose speaker is unseen.[73] They are sounds that emerge in the heart of an aspirer on the Sufi path, which invite him to the Real.

The below incident attests to the truth of hidden sounds:

Wanting to give the corpse of the Blessed Prophet –upon him blessings and peace- an ablution, following his bereavement, the Companions were unsure whether to remove his shirt, as had been the case with other corpses, or to leave it on and perform the ablution like that. A voice was then heard

---

73   It is for this reason that the telephone, in modern Arabic, is called *khatif*.

Marifatullah and Divine Awards

from the unseen telling them not to remove his shirt, clearing the minds of the Companions.[74]

Through His messengers, Allah, glory unto Him, has taught human beings the 'Book' and 'Wisdom'. This teaching has, at times, been open and at others as *ladunni*, in the form of inspirations that shine upon the heart. But as aforementioned, insofar these states generally transpire in a way difficult for human understanding to bear, they have remained a secret to most. Yet, both the Quran and Sunnah testify to the truth and reality of *ladunni* knowledge. In fact, the below encounter between Musa and Khidr –upon them peace-, recounted both in the Quran[75] and in some sayings of the Prophet –upon him blessings and peace-, offers some magnificent glimmers of the nature of *ladunni* knowledge:

The Pharaoh and his army, in pursuit of Musa –upon him peace- and the believers, had drowned in the billowing waves of the Red Sea, right before the eyes of the Israelites. Following this Divine blessing, Musa –upon him peace- gathered his people, giving them an eloquent and fiery sermon, melting the hearts of the listeners, drawing tears from their eyes. It left them in awe of their prophet's depth of knowledge and wisdom. Under the inspiring effect of the talk, one of them asked:

"Messenger of Allah…Is there anyone more knowledgeable than you on the face of Earth?"

Taken in by the question, instead of replying "Allah knows", Musa –upon him peace- instead remarked, "No…I do not know anyone who is". He thereby committed a slipup.[76] *The Almighty did not approve of his response and, at that instant, revealed to his messenger of His "…servant, at where the two seas meet, who is more knowledgeable than you. I have given him knowledge from my presence (ladunni)."*

With an avid desire to learn this knowledge, Musa –upon him peace- said, "I will not give up until I reach the junction of the two rivers or I will go on for years." (al-Kahf, 60)

---

74 See, Abu Dawud, Janaiz, 27-28; Ahmed ibn Hanbal, VI, 267; Ibn Majah, Janaiz, 10.
75 See, al-Kahf, 60-82.
76 A slipup or a *dhallah* as it is called signifies unintentional words and behavior seldom expressed by prophets which do not accord with Divine Pleasure.

Accompanied by his nephew Yusha ibn Nun, he then set out. After undergoing many experiences during their journey, they finally found the man they were looking for. The Quran depicts that moment of union as:

"Then they found one from among Our servants whom We had granted mercy from Us and whom We had taught knowledge from Ourselves." (al-Kahf, 65)

The man, of whom Musa –upon him peace- had been made aware through revelation, was sitting on a rock, shrouded in a green mantle. Musa –upon him peace- approached him. Greeting him, he then said, "I am Musa".

"So you are Musa, the Prophet of the Children of Israel", replied Khidr –upon him peace-.[77]

"Are you the man my Lord has referred to as the most knowledgeable among all men?" asked Musa –upon him peace-.

"Allah has given you a knowledge I do not have", replied he, "and I have been given a knowledge you do not have, Musa."

"Shall I follow you on condition that you should teach me right knowledge of what you have been taught?" (al-Kahf, 66) *then insisted Musa –upon him peace-.*

That was how Musa –upon him peace- expressed his desire to be trained by Khidr –upon him peace-. As can be seen in the Quranic verse, the foremost condition of acquiring this knowledge is to be willing to follow; for this knowledge is transferrable only from one heart to another, which demands an accompaniment, both physical and spiritual. So it continues:

Musa –upon him peace- wanted to acquire the ability to discern the inner wisdoms of seemingly bizarre events impossible to make sense of

---

77 *Khidr*, in Arabic, means green or something that has to do with the color green. The Blessed Prophet –upon him blessings and peace- has said, "The reason as to why he was called Khidr was that whenever he would sit on yellow grass, it would turn to green." (Bukhari, Anbiya, 27; Tirmidhi, Tafsir, 18; Daylami, Musnad, I, 345) Mujahid, a prominent Tabiun scholar, has narrated, "Whenever he stood to offer ritual prayer, his surroundings used to turn green." It is thus understood that the name Khidr was not his real name but rather a nickname given to him later on.

externally. So Khidr –upon him peace- said to him, "Surely you cannot have patience with me… and how can you have patience in that of which you have not got a comprehensive knowledge?" *(al-Kahf, 67-68)*

Through these words, Khidr –upon him peace- had effectively made the first discovery concerning Musa's –upon him peace- psychological condition; he was really explaining to him what he was, words that were to be proven right in the end. After all, this knowledge demanded patience and Musa –upon him peace- was coming from a tumultuous life. The lesson Musa –upon him peace- was to learn was his own helplessness at the face of the science of Divine reality.

Meanwhile, Musa –upon him peace- was adamant to join. "Allah willing, you will find me patient and I shall not disobey you in any matter." *(al-Kahf, 69)* he pleaded.

"If you would follow me, then do not question me about anything until I myself speak to you about it." *(al-Kahf, 70)* advised Khidr –upon him peace-.

So they walked awhile on the shore, boarding a ship owned by two brothers before too long. The two men were allowed to travel free of charge. In return, Khidr –upon him peace- began puncturing the lower deck of the ship.

"Do you want to drown all these people aboard?" Musa –upon him peace- protested anxiously. "Why did you just do that? The ship's owners are two poor men and this ship is their only means for a living. You have really done something strange!"

Khidr –upon him peace- said nothing except to remind Musa of his previous warning.

"Did I not tell you that you would not be able to remain patient with me?"

"Do not interrogate me for something which has slipped my mind" said Musa –upon him peace- apologetically. "Do not be hard on me over this!"

It was right at that moment that a sparrow came and perched on the side of the ship and began dipping its beak into the sea, hoisting a few drops of water. Bringing the sparrow to Musa's –upon him peace- attention, Khidr –upon him peace- then said, "Next to the knowledge of Allah, the knowledge of you and I and entire creation is merely as much as the water that bird has just beaked out from the sea."

After some time, they got off from the ship and began walking. They soon encountered a male child. Khidr –upon him peace- killed him at the instant.

"What?" exclaimed Musa –upon him peace-. "Do you now take an innocent child's life, when he has not killed anyone? You have done something horrible!"

"Did I not tell you that you would not be able to bear patient with me?" responded Khidr –upon him peace-. Embarrassed for failing to keep his word, Musa –upon him peace- said:

"If I ask you for an explanation once more, banish me from your company. I have truly reached the end of excuses with you!"

So they resumed walking until arriving at a village. Hungry by now, they asked the villagers for something to eat. Not only did the villagers refuse to host them, they also treated them unkindly. Just as they were about to leave the village, Khidr –upon him peace- noticed a wall, made of mudbrick, on the verge of collapsing. So he took to the task of rebuilding the wall from scratch. Musa –upon him peace- could not contain himself.

"You are serving people who disdained hosting us and would not give us so much as a few loaves of bread to stem our hunger…You could have at least asked for a wage for your labor!"

"Time has come for us to part ways", responded Khidr –upon him peace-. "I will now tell you the inside story about the things that made you impatient:

The ship which I put a hole through belonged to the poor men of the sea. I wanted to make it look defective…for they were being pursued by a king who was taking all the fine ships on the sea by force.

As for the child…he was set to become a rebel. His parents, on the other hand, were righteous folks. We feared that their child might lead them to transgression and ingratitude, and cause them distress. So we wished that their Lord give them a purer and more compassionate child in return for him.

And the wall I set right…It belonged to two local orphans. Underneath was a hidden treasure belonging to them. Their father was a good man. So your Lord willed for the orphans to expose their treasure once they come of age. I did nothing of my own doing. There…the insight into the events with which you could not remain patient."[78]

Many explanations have given and commentaries written concerning the subtle and mysterious wisdoms contained in the above encounter. We may expand upon some of them below:

Ladunni knowledge is to view phenomena and external conditions beyond human criteria, according to the measure of an order unknown to most. When, for instance, asking questions is considered the key to learning in almost all sciences, this knowledge does not tolerate questioning and debate. It instead promotes silence, patience and submission. It looks at the end result of all affairs. Ibrahim Hakki Erzurumi depicts this wonderfully:

The Real renders good all vice
Think not He does otherwise
To look on, is for the wise
Wait, what the Lord does, and see
What He does, He does splendidly

Ask not 'why is this so unseemly?'
Only proper that it should be
Just wait till the end and see
Wait, what the Lord does, and see
What He does, He does splendidly

The righteous brothers of the sea had allowed Musa and Khidr –upon them peace- to travel on their ship for free. By doing two honorable men a small favor, they in the end received the far greater blessing of the protection of their ship, at the expense of a minor, compensable damage. In other words, the *halal* asset, which was put to a lofty service, did not go to waste.

In the *ishari* sense, or in its spiritual interpretation, that the ship was inflicted with a minor damage and consequently protected from being forcefully seized by the king, alludes to the fact that perceiving the ego, the ship that sails on the sea of life, as flawless, will drag it to spiritual ruin

---

78 For the *ahadith* which dwell on this encounter, see Bukhari, Tafsir, 18/4; Muslim, Fadail, 170.

amid the whirlpool of conceit and arrogance; and that one must therefore continually confess to his shortcomings and flaws to protect himself from spiritual destruction.

There are likewise numerous wisdoms underlying the killing of the innocent child by Khidr –upon him peace-.

Man must make sure that his natural yet innocent love for his spouse, children, friends and relatives is kept where it belongs and is not allowed to rise above his love of the Lord. They will otherwise hold him back and even stray him from his true purpose.

One of the great names of Allah, glory unto Him, is *ar-Raqib*, which refers to His discontent at seeing even a shadow of the love of others clouding the love for Him, in the hearts of those whom He loves. Divine Love, in other words, allows of no partners.

There was a time when Yaqub –upon him peace- nurtured an intense love for his son Yusuf –upon him peace-, especially after catching sight of the light of prophethood on his forehead. But his excessive love for his son was defiant of Divine Will. The Lord hence willed that Yaqub –upon him peace- go through an ordeal. The consequence is well-known: long years of separation from his beloved son. An excess love brought a painful separation.[79]

Through social inheritance, some great truths become universal realities common to all and consequently find expression in the cultural artifacts of a society. One such case is the proverb 'excess love brings swift separation', which hints at the imminent damages wrought by loving someone immoderately, to the point of idolization.

It is noteworthy that the parents of the child killed at the hands of Khidr –upon him piece- would presumably have been reduced to enormous grief to hear of their son's death; just as they were once so elated to hear his birth. Yet, had the child lived, he was going to end up ruining their lives both in this world and in the Hereafter. Had the decision been left up to the parents, they surely would have not wanted their son's death. But as the Compassionate Allah loves His righteous servants infinitely more than

---

[79] See, *Ruhu'l-Bayan*, v. IV, p. 218.

Marifatullah and Divine Awards

any parent could love their own children, by ruling the death of that child only to compensate with another more righteous, the Lord had really done them an enormous favor. Since the deceased child departed the world innocently, unsullied by sin, the Lord compensated his very short life by securing, in return, his eternal happiness in the Hereafter, along with his parents. A blessing in the guise of a wrath meant that a minor damage was preferred over a greater damage.

It turns that, most of the time, humans err when assessing external events, as they have no access to Divine Wisdom. In the Quran it is declared:

وَعَسٰى اَنْ تَكْرَهُوا شَيْئاً وَهُوَ خَيْرٌ لَكُمْ وَعَسٰى اَنْ تُحِبُّوا شَيْئاً وَهُوَ شَرٌّ لَكُمْ وَاللّٰهُ يَعْلَمُ وَ اَنْتُمْ لاَ تَعْلَمُونَ

"…and it may be that you dislike a thing while it is good for you, and it may be that you love a thing while it is evil for you, and Allah knows, while you do not know." (al-Baqara, 216)

Murdering an innocent person is certainly a great crime, for which Islamic Law requires retribution. So implementing the example of this Quranic narration solely on the back of esoteric knowledge, an act which the exoteric, the legal side of Islam could in no way tolerate, is impossible for Muslims who are responsible only with acting in line with the external. Hence, even great figures who possess the knowledge of the heart, do not act unless the external causes are fulfilled; in other words, they never digress from the world of causality. The limits set by Islamic jurisprudence are undeniable measures for all.

Musa –upon him peace- was a prophet revealed with a law, which he was ordered to implement. Khidr –upon him peace-, on the other hand, was acting in line with a knowledge divinely taught; that is, he was not acting out of his own desire, but rather according to the desire of the Almighty. Musa's –upon him peace- objection against him was motivated by his reflexes to observe the limits set by the Lord. It is again the Lord who has revealed, to humankind, the encounter of the two in the Quran. This means that the events recounted in the encounter are different manifestations of the same reality, however they may appear as defying the legal facts of religion. Indeed, the moment Musa –upon him peace- found out the inner secrets of these bizarre manifestations, he abandoned all protest, realizing that *shariah* was the body to *haqiqah*, its spirit. As the law extends to everyone and most people cannot penetrate the gist of esoteric realities, their obliged with only so much as the law.

In spite of the malicious treatment of the villagers, that Khidr –upon him peace- proceeded, just the same, to repair an almost derelict wall in the village without expecting any financial return, highlights how important a duty and lofty a virtue it is to protect orphans. It equally voices the fact that a *halal* earning may never go astray. The earnings the righteous earn through legitimate means are, indeed, always under Divine protection.

Othman –may Allah be well-pleased with him- narrates the following with regard to the treasure that was buried in the wall: "The treasure was a tablet made from gold, written on which were the following seven lines:

1. Amazing is he who is still able to laugh despite being aware of death.

2. Amazing is he who pursues the world despite knowing it is mortal.

3. Amazing is he who grieves, knowing that everything is predestined.

4. Amazing is he who hoards wealth, knowing he is to be called into account.

5. Amazing is he who sins, knowing of Hellfire.

6. Amazing is he who talks about another, despite being certain about Allah.

7. Amazing is who expects a rest on Earth, despite being certain about Paradise; and so is he who obeys the Devil, despite knowing he is the enemy." (Ibn Hajar Asqalani, *Munabbihat*, p. 29)

Again in the light of the *ishari* meaning of the encounter, 'the point where two seas meet', the meeting spot of the two, alludes to Musa –upon him peace-, a profound sea of exoteric knowledge, and Khidr –upon him peace-, a profound sea of the esoteric.

The fact that Musa –upon him peace- abided by Khidr –upon him peace- for the purpose of *ladunni* knowledge is noteworthy in its

Marifatullah and Divine Awards

resemblance to the *murshid-murid* or master-disciple relationship, in Sufism. It may therefore be concluded that even if a person may possess a depth of knowledge like Musa –upon him peace-, he should still be willing to humbly and respectfully kneel down before a saint and seek his enlightening.

"What shall we do", the Companions once asked the Blessed Prophet –upon him blessings and peace- *"if we are faced with a problem for which we cannot find a solution either in the Quran or Sunnah?"*

"Consult jurists and the righteous and seek their judgment", he replied. *"Do not refer the matter to your personal views."* (Haythami, Majmau'z-Zawaid, I, 178)

Imam Shafii, the great scholar of Islamic jurisprudence, used to frequently visit Shayban-i Rai -May Allah sanctify his secret-, a man of profound spiritual depth, and kneel before him, like a loyal student, to discuss specific matters, in hope of benefitting spiritually. At times, his students would object, saying:

"Look at you Imam and look at Shayban…Why do you show him so much respect?"

"For he knows things we do not", the Imam would say.

In like manner, Ahmed ibn Hanbal and Yahya ibn Main would consult Maruf Karhi on many issues.

Spiritual masters are sought, not for studying exoteric sciences, but the sciences of the heart, as they are guides that shed light on the paths leading to the Lord. Many a celebrated exegete, a scholar of hadith and jurisprudence, like Ibn Abidin and Alusi among numerous others, in fact entered the Sufi path, accepting the guidance of saints to lead them out of intricate matters they could not resolve on their own.

Imam Abu Hanifah, one of the greatest jurists the world has ever seen, similarly sought inspiration in the company of Jafar Sadiq -may Allah sanctify his secret-. The following illustrates the enormous respect the Imam had for the men of spirituality:

It is reported that Ibrahim Adham -May Allah sanctify his secret- one day chanced upon Imam Abu Hanifah. The Imam's students began staring at Ibrahim Adham -may Allah sanctify his secret-, somewhat disdainfully.

Sensing this, the Imam called out to Ibrahim Adham, invitingly: "Please master...come closer. You have honored our lesson!"

Ibrahim Adham -may Allah sanctify his secret- timidly greeted him and walked off. Once he disappeared out of sight, his students asked the Imam, "To what does that man of such praises? How can someone like you call him master?"

"For he is constantly occupied with Allah", humbly replied the Imam. "And we are occupied with Him simply on the level of words."

As is valid for all other branches of knowledge, it is necessary to comply with the divinely determined manners whilst receiving training in *ladunni* knowledge. Comprising the most important aspect of these manners is to embody a humbleness that allows one to be constantly aware of his vulnerability and nothingness.

How striking it is that a prophet of the caliber of Musa –upon him peace-, honored as the *Kalimullah* (the one directly spoken to by the Almighty), never thought to himself, "I need to remain and tackle the problems of my people for which the Torah is sufficient. Besides, I am a recipient of Divine revelation and if I wished, I could just ask the Lord to teach me directly". Instead, displaying an utmost humbleness, he willingly obeyed the Divine Will, setting a splendid standard for people to come after him. A clear testimony to this state of mind is his resolution to '… walk for years on end if that is what it takes to find him (Khidr)'. Musa's –upon him peace- humility sets an excellent example for all seekers of knowledge.

Had Allah, glory unto Him, wished, He could have made Musa –upon him peace- find Khidr –upon him peace- instantly, without toil. The Almighty instead willed for His prophet a tiring journey, which means that this path demands a tenacious love and determination and, of course, Divine Grace.

The experience of the two also indicates the need to seek esoteric training from a master, compliant with the etiquette and the causal nature of the knowledge involved. More often than not, it is impossible to disregard this nature and obtain this knowledge without a *murshid*, a guide. Only those of the disposition of Uways al-Qarani are excluded. Triumph on this path requires an immense help as much as it does a strong determination.

On the other hand, that Musa asks Khidr –upon them peace- for training may tempt one to ask how a great prophet could seek the knowledge of a saint, however great the standing of the latter may be. But it must be noted that the desire of Musa –upon him peace- to learn from Khidr –upon him peace- certainly does not mean that he possesses no knowledge and wisdom whatsoever and that he has not been granted any share of spiritual insight (*kashf*) and inspiration. This is similar to a case where one seeks training from another person, who has greater expertise in the knowledge sought. To give an example, Sinan's prowess and depth in architecture is undoubtedly greater than all the artists and laborers who took part in the construction of the Suleymaniye Mosque. Nonetheless, Sinan would not know the art of marble engraving as much as an expert-in-the-trade who worked in construction. But this does not imply a deficiency on Sinan's part, as all the artists and laborers stand under his command.

So, just because Khidr –upon him peace- temporarily became a master to Musa –upon him peace- does not mean he was superior to him. In essence, there cannot even be a comparison of superiority-inferiority here, as Musa and Khidr –upon them peace- are wayfarers of two different realms, incomparable and irreducible to one another. The essential wisdom to be taken note of here is that all created beings, including prophets, stand helpless before Divine Knowledge; and it is this that shines through the recounting of their experience.

Together with being human, prophets are selected persons, the privileged recipients of Divine revelation. These unique servants of the Lord do not commit sin. But because they are also human, helpless before the Lord, they do rarely commit blunders or slipups referred to as *dhalla*. Through these slipups, which serve to throw light on the nature of a given situation and thus sets an example for humankind, the Almighty gives them a taste of their humanness and thereby trains them, in a nature unknown to us. Here, Musa –upon him peace- is to understand, in due course, the meagerness of human knowledge compared to the Lord's and realize the existence of many levels of knowledge unrevealed to him. This realization of his is to provide an ideal blueprint for humankind until the Final Hour.

Indeed, in spite of possessing so great a power and authority like prophethood, prophets were only aware of as much knowledge as they were given and were provided insight into the unseen (*ghayb*) only as much as the Almighty allowed them. Since *ladunni* knowledge is after all awarded, they may only know that which has been revealed to them and remain unaware of what is kept secret. It is mentioned in the *Gulistan* of Sheikh Sadi that a person once asked Yaqub –upon him peace-:

"You, the wise prophet with an enlightened heart…How was it that you were able get a whiff of the scent of Yusuf's –upon him peace- shirt as it was being brought from as far as Egypt, yet were unable to see him being thrown into a well just nearby?'

"The Divine share of knowledge given us in this regard", replied Yaqub –upon him peace- *"are like lightning strikes. Truths appear crystal clear at times, yet they remain concealed at others."*

The expression Musa –upon him peace- used when seeking knowledge from Khidr –upon him peace- was in fact 'the knowledge that *you have been given*'. This means that knowledge must be ascribed to the Almighty, not to mortals. Allah, glory unto Him, is the absolute source of all knowledge. He grants a share to whom He wills, as much as He wills. For some of this knowledge, He renders external causes as means, while for some, He directly inspires to the heart of His servant.

On another note, if a person who is fasting consumes something through forgetfulness, his fast remains intact. Similarly, Musa's –upon him peace- objections to Khidr –upon him peace- did not bring an end to their accompaniment. But it was Musa –upon him peace- who thwarted the probable share he may have reaped from this knowledge by urging, from a mixture of embarrassment and excitement, despite not being compelled to:

"If I ask you about anything after this, keep me not in your company…" (al-Kahf, 76) He laid down a condition and therefore had to make do with only that much a share of knowledge.

The Blessed Prophet –upon him blessings and peace- has said, "May Allah have mercy on Musa. Had he been able to keep patient, through them, Allah will have informed us about many more (mysterious and

Marifatullah and Divine Awards

bizarre) incidents." (Muslim, Fadail, 170; Bukhari, Tafsir, 18/2) Patience and poise on this path is therefore a must.

Another explanation provided by Sufis on the encounter is such: It is reported that the young man who accompanied Musa –upon him peace- in his search for Khidr –upon him peace- was Yusha ibn Nun, his nephew and a prominent figure among his companions. He ended up succeeding Musa –upon him peace- after his passing away. Similarly, the Noble Messenger –upon him blessings and peace- had chosen Abu Bakr –may Allah be well-pleased with him- to accompany him during the Hegira; the most virtuous of his Companions and referred to as "the second of the two whose third was Allah". (Bukhari, Ashabu'n-Nabi, 2) These examples draw attention to the importance of establishing true friendships, only for the sake of Allah, on the spiritual path.

Just this experience of Musa –upon him peace- alone gives us a fair idea of the profound nature of *ladunni* knowledge.

The Blessed Prophet –upon him blessings and peace- has said:

"I undoubtedly see things you do not see and hear things you do not hear. The sky has squeaked and so it should…for there is not a spot as small as four inches in the skies that an angel has not placed its forehead upon to fall prostrate to Allah. I promise by Allah that had you known the truths I knew, you would have laughed only little and cried in lots…You would have left your homes and dashed towards plains to plead to Allah at the top of tour voices."

On hearing this, its narrator Abu Dharr al-Ghifari –may Allah be well-pleased with him- commented, "How I truly wished I was a tree being cut!" (Ibn Majah, Zuhd, 19)

Other Companions put their feelings of awe and utter helplessness before the *ladunni* realities into the following words:

"If only I was a piece of date birds beaked away at", said Abu Bakr –Allah be well-pleased with him-. The distraught Omar - Allah be well-pleased with him- wished to be a "piece of grass…or better still, nothing!" Aisha -Allah be well-pleased with her- hankered to be simply "a leaf on any old tree."

What made them buckle and bend before the Power and Majesty of the Almighty is the spiritual station of helplessness and fear.

Another Companion enchanted by the spirituality of the company of the Blessed Prophet –upon him blessings and peace- was Harithah ibn Malik al-Ansari -Allah be well-pleased with him-. One morning, the Prophet –upon him blessings and peace- asked him:

"In what condition did you wake, Harithah?"

"As a true believer" answered he.

"Every truth, Harithah, comes with a proof. What is the proof of your faith?" the Prophet –upon him blessings and peace- then asked.

"After I gave the world up", he answered, *"my days became parched and my nights sleepless. It was as if I could clearly see the Throne of my Lord. It is as if I can see the dwellers of Paradise visiting one another and the folk of Hell cursing at each other."*

The Blessed Prophet –upon him blessings and peace- thereupon said, "Very well then, Harithah. Maintain your condition…You are person whose heart Allah has illumined." (Haythami, Majmau'z-Zawaid, I, 57)

Again, in reference to Harithah, the Prophet –upon him blessings and peace- said, "Whosoever wishes to see a person whose heart Allah has illumined, let him look at Harithah." (Ibn Hajar, al-Isabah, I, 289)

This incident is depicted by Mawlana Rumi -may Allah sanctify his secret- in the language of love:

"Harithah asks the Messenger –upon him blessings and peace- for permission to '…describe what he saw' and begins:

'Messenger of Allah…Let me begin to depict, right now, the day of resurrection people believe will take place tomorrow. Let me expose the secrets of resurrection. Command me and I will rip open the veils of these secrets… so that the gem of Divine wisdoms inside me may sparkle like the sun in the skies…

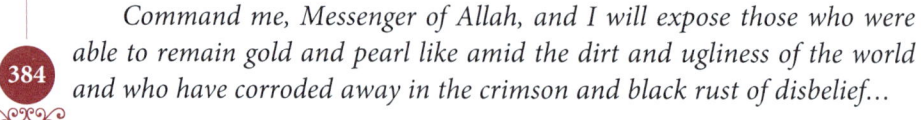

Command me, Messenger of Allah, and I will expose those who were able to remain gold and pearl like amid the dirt and ugliness of the world and who have corroded away in the crimson and black rust of disbelief…

Allow me to make known the seven abysses of hypocrisy in the inextinguishable light of prophethood...

Let me show everyone the clothes the rebellious will wear in the Hereafter. Let me make them hear the sounds of the drum and the kettledrum that will roll for prophets...

Allow me to show them the ebullient and overflowing Pool of Kawthar so that a splash of it may lick at their faces and its sounds echo in their ears.

Please, let me show them the thirsty souls running to and fro around the Pool...Their shoulders are brushing up against mine. Their screams are filling my ears...

The elated dwellers of Paradise are hugging each other and shaking hands right in front of my eyes.

The moaning screams of the dwellers of Hell, their cries of agony, are about to deafen me!

These are signs I express from deep within me. I would say more, if only I was not afraid that the Messenger of Allah –upon him blessings and peace- might reprimand me.'

He was saying these as he was engrossed in spiritual intoxication. He had lost himself in incredible ecstasy; he had little control over his consciousness. He was ready to expose all secrets.

To awaken him for this state, the Messenger –upon him blessings and peace- said, 'Get a grip on yourself and be quiet'. Pulling Harithah by the collar, he then added:

'Come to your senses! Hold the bridles of your tongue for you are at the verge of saying things you should not. The mirror of your spirit has burst outside of the casing of your skin. But never forget that exposing the secrets you are given is because of your inability to digest them. One of Allah's names is Sattar, the Concealer. Be aware of this and do not sacrifice the joy of living up to this name to a dry indigestion.'"

Just as each particle in the universe exhibits a Divine balance, in the face of the manifestations of the spiritual realm, one is obliged to maintain a balance and moderation. The quintessential example for his *ummah* under all circumstances conceivable, the Blessed Prophet –upon him blessings and peace- never wandered out of the confines of a moderate standard, the upright path, even when at the peak of spirituality.

The Prophet –upon him blessings and peace- would be overcome with so enormous a spiritual inspiration that it would be impossible for him to endure it for too long. In particular, he would suffer great pains during the arrival of Divine revelation, breaking pearl-like drops of sweat. At times, when inspiration and rapture would reach its peak, he would say:

"Spirituality has inundated me, Aisha. Come and talk to me awhile"[80] and return to the human climes.

In contrast, upon feeling overcome with too much worldliness he would say, "Call us to prayer, Bilal, so we may freshen up!" (Abu Dawud, Adab, 78) He would thereby establish a balance between the human and spiritual dimensions.

As well observing a perfect measure in his inner world, the Noble Prophet –upon him blessings and peace- was also moderate towards those around. He took care not to reveal the sublime truths the Almighty granted him, which transcend reason, to anyone apart from those who could grasp it. Owing to the importance of this aspect, Ali –Allah be well-pleased with him- has said: "Speak to people in a way they can understand" (Bukhari, Ilm, 49); that is not according to your level of comprehension but theirs.

In relation to these mysterious truths, Abu Hurayrah –Allah be well-pleased with him- states how he held back from narrating a number of the Prophet's –upon him blessings and peace- words over a concern that people might not understand:

"I learnt two urns full of knowledge from the Messenger of Allah. The first I spread among public. As for the second, if I were to spread it, my throat would have been cut." (Bukhari, Ilm, 42)

The Blessed Prophet –upon him blessings and peace- has stated: "Passing wisdom onto those whom it is not due is tyranny." (Darimi, Muqad-

---

80   See, Munawi, *Fayzu'l-Qadir*, V, 228.

Marifatullah and Divine Awards

dimah, 34) It may also be gathered that withholding wisdom from the proficient is equally tyranny. The Quran declares:

"He grants wisdom to whom He pleases, and whoever is granted wisdom, he indeed is given a great good and none but men of understanding mind." (al-Baqara, 269)

Sufi greats of poise have not offered to share this knowledge they received to those of shallow understanding. These intimate secrets, which wit fails to grasp, after all, have to be concealed from the inept. In fact, Hallaj Mansur, who was entrusted with these secrets the Lord privileges some of His servants with, paid the price of revealing just a ray of them with his life. He was executed.

Having plunged into the ocean of Divine Oneness, Hallaj was overcome with an intense state of ecstasy and spiritual intoxication and the tumultuous manifestations taking place in his spirit when he exclaimed *'Ana'l-Haqq'*, 'I am the Real'. The verbal exposure of an intimate secret, led people to judge his words according to the standard of reason which, by its nature, could not duly weigh their delicate nature.

Many saints have also undergone the spiritual state in which Hallaj had found himself engrossed. But this state is neither fixed (*tathbit*) nor an utter identification (*tashkhis*). It is a passing phase that transpires in saints who, during the station of *fana'fillah*, or annihilation in Allah, fail to retain their poise and lose control over their reason. A person is not liable under the law of religion during this phase when the power of reason runs out, when it departs the world of external standards and analogies, as the first requirement for being obliged by the law of religion is to be 'rational'. Reason, on the other hand, plays no part in uttering such words. These spiritual states are utterly incomprehensible through reason.

Since these states are a result of coming under an intense Divine charm (*jazbah*), a person under the effect of such a state is referred to in Sufism as a *majzub*.[81] Although this spiritual state, which surpasses any

---

81 A *majzub* is a person who, allured by the Divine charm, has lost control of his reason, but whose heart nonetheless remains firmly attached to Allah, glory unto Him. Even though a *majzub* may have been dragged into a state that could be considered strange when measured against the standard of human life, he has surpassed many an ordinary man in his depth of comprehension. It is like his will, comprehension and

external standard, may be condoned by those with insight, the public dislike it causes is nonetheless justified. Not for no reason has it been said regarding the execution of Hallaj that 'Hallaj was in the right but so were his executioners'. Poise has therefore been overly advised in Sufism, which regards the state of being a charmer (*jazib*) superior to that of being charmed (*majzub*).

It is reported that Abu'l-Harith, the hangman, approached Hallaj from the front to execute him and fiercely struck him across the face, leaving his face and nose bloodied and broken. Right at that moment, Sheikh Shibli, who was standing by, let out a scream and fainted, for some reason unknown.

The manifestation witnessed in Hallaj is a state-of-mind (*hal*). Once this state passes, the Real is the Real and matter is matter. Sheikh Shibli says:

"Hallaj and I went through the same stages. They called me insane and left me on my own. As for Hallaj, they ascribed him with sanity and hanged him." He further explains:

"After Hallaj was executed, I went to his grave at night and offered ritual prayer until daybreak. Come dawn, I prayed, 'My Lord…Hallaj was faithful and wise servant of Yours who believed in your Oneness. Why is it that You inflicted him with such misery?'

Right then, I became drowsy and fell asleep. I saw a dream where the Day of Judgment had broken, where I heard the Real declare:

'We put him through that tribulation for spreading Our secret among the inept!'"

It is understood, then, that what is undesirable is not attaining to the mysteries of the truth by becoming annihilated in the Real but rather their dissemination among the public, caused by the spiritual intoxication these acquired mysteries may cause. It is therefore extremely wrong to generalize a few exceptional cases of overexcitement, caused by a failure to

---

discernment have come under the force of an intense voltage otherwise unbearable. Persons of the kind are walking examples of human helplessness at the face of Essential Manifestations.

observe this standard, and speak ill of saints and the devotees of the Sufi path. Speaking ill of the beloved servants of Allah, glory unto Him and failing to appreciate their value stems from ignorance and shortsightedness. It is unthinkable for a believer to disclaim them.

Thus the fundamental principle on the spiritual path is a strict abidance by the sacred standards without, however, rejecting the truth of the eternal secret. It is also necessary not to let words in on the intimate secrets between the Lord and His servant. All these are experiences undergone amid a spiritual ecstasy, beyond the access of reason. Once they subside and the sense of mind returns, this spiritual frenzy makes way for calm.

Under the influence of exceptional manifestations that have called on their spirits, some saints were steered to display certain unusual behavior. But once awoken from that realm, in which reason and will are momentarily relinquished, they continued on their essential direction.

Junayd -may Allah sanctify his secret- was once asked, "Some saints enter a state of spiritual ecstasy and display unusual behavior. What do you have to say about that?"

"Let them be", answered Junayd -may Allah sanctify his secret- "so that they find their peace with Allah. Except over things the law of religion explicitly prohibits, do not condemn them. Bear in mind that this path has burnt their lungs, their efforts have left them exhausted and parched, and they have endured many tribulations. They behave like that for no other reason than to overcome the spiritual state overwhelming them. And there is no harm in that."

The prayer Hallaj reportedly made moments before he was executed gives us an idea of his sincerity and soaring spiritual level:

"My Allah...Your servants have gathered to kill me for no other reason than their devotion to You and Your religion. Forgive them...for had You let them in on the secrets You blessed me with, they would not have thought ill of me. And had You withheld from me the secrets You withhold from them, I would not have exposed them. Forgive them, o Lord... for they are only allowing me to reunite with You!"

It is narrated from those who observed Hallaj's state from the vantage of the spiritual realm that the moment Hallaj was hung upon the gallows, Iblis came to him and said:

"You said Ana[82] and I said Ana. How is it that you receive mercy for pronouncing the same word while I am pelted with curse?"

"By saying Ana, you saw yourself superior to Adam and in so doing, spilled your conceit", replied Hallaj. *"But I, on the other hand, said Ana'l-Haqq, and in so doing, annihilated myself in the Real. Conceit, which is nothing but a claim to selfhood, is the sign of Hell. But getting rid of it and becoming annihilated in the Real is the expression of 'nothingness'. That is why my share is mercy, while yours is a debasing curse."*

Ibrahim ibn Fatiq recounts how Hallaj advised him with the following when at the verge of being executed:

"'Some people have declared me to be an infidel, son, while others are convinced of my sainthood. But those who accuse me of disbelief are dearer to both Allah and me than those who call me a saint.'

'Why do you say that?' I asked him.

'Those who look upon me as a saint only do so because of their benefit of the doubt (husn-u zan). But the others are calling me an infidel purely from their loyalty to the religion. A person who is loyal to the religion is dearer to Allah than he who only gives a benefit of the doubt."

Mawlana Rumi -may Allah sanctify his secret-, who went further beyond the manifestations experienced by Hallaj, has said, "Had Hallaj knew about the manifestations between my Lord and I, he himself would have turned around and stoned me."

These and spiritual states alike are simply expressions annihilation in the Real or *fana fillah* spilled out to words. *Fana fillah* is depicted by Mawlana Rumi as:

"Upon seeing the infinite river of life, empty out the water inside your cup of life into it. Can water ever flee the river?

---

82 *Ana*, in Arabic, is the subjective pronoun I.

Marifatullah and Divine Awards

Once the water in your cup mixes into the river, it is saved from its existence and becomes the water of the river. The water in the cup, then, loses its quality and attributes and is left only with its essence. Henceforth, it shall neither decrease, nor become dirty nor stink."

Since all their emotions and ideas are directed to Divine Wisdom, for Mawlana Rumi -may Allah sanctify his secret- and alike persons who have kneaded into their hearts the ideal spiritual blend, the Lord virtually becomes the eyes that see and hands that hold.

A Rumi enthusiast thinker elaborates how his profound state of mind eludes the understanding of most:

"We have listened to the screams of Mawlana Jalaladdin's ecstasy. But we have no way of seeing the depths of the ocean of peace into which he had dove. We only see what has been washed upon the shore from the deepest end of that ocean. We have acquired not the love of Mawlana but the screams voiced from his love. What we try to convey with our lisped tongues is merely that. It was only he who delved into the ocean of peace. We are left only with the sounds released by the storm of his ecstasy…and alas, we identify that with Mawlana."[83]

The state of spiritual love, rapture and ecstasy is such a mysterious ocean that what lies below the surface is known only to those who have dived into it.

Similarly, Muhyiddin ibn Arabi who put into words a mere portion of this mysterious science, albeit in the form of signs, has been cherished by saints and wayfarers of the Sufi path, looking on at the realities underlying in the bosom of his timeless expressions, reminiscing him as the *Shaikhu'l-Akbar*, the Greatest Master. Those aloof from the esoteric world, on the other hand, have imputed him infidelity, as they have been unable to untie the knot of his mysteries.

Given there is no confidant around to confide in, who can endure the secrets, it is better to keep silent. It is necessary to speak to each according to their intellectual capacities. Otherwise, to speak about wisdom

---

83 Nurettin Topçu, *Mevlana ve Tasavvuf*, p. 139.

and *marifah* to someone who can never appreciate the spiritual mindset involved, is to do injustice to the truth.

Muhyiddin ibn Arabi has thus said, "Those unacquainted with our mindset should not read our books."

Similar are the words of Mawlana Rumi -May Allah sanctify his secret-. "I have voiced this mystery", he says, "in a manner obscure and succinct…for he who tries to elaborate will end up with a burnt tongue and its listener with a burnt comprehension."

To prevent readers of shallow understanding from being steered into false paths, in his *Mathnawi*, a book offered to the understanding of people possessing varying degrees of intellectual aptitude, Mawlana Rumi -may Allah sanctify his secret- has either used simple and concrete parables to express the otherwise complex and abstract Divine mysteries and truths, or has concealed them under the rubric of signs accessible only to their spiritual experts. He has thereby covered the subtle meanings of the *Mathnawi* from those lacking a depth of heart. He states:

"My rhymes are not rhymes; they are an ocean of meaning. Neither is my satire mere satire; it is educational. My parables are not simple, run of the mill words; they are instructive. They are there to explain the mysteries and allow for their comprehension."

Omar –Allah be well-pleased with him- recounts an incident he witnessed:

"I one day entered the presence of the Messenger of Allah –upon him blessings and peace- and found him conversing with Abu Bakr –Allah be well-pleased with him- on the Oneness of the Divine. I sat with them. But I felt like a man who knew no Arabic; I could barely understand what they were talking about.

'What was that all about?' I later asked Abu Bakr. 'Do you always converse with the Messenger of Allah in that manner?'

'Yes, sometimes' he replied. 'When we are alone…'"[84]

---

[84] For information, refer to Ahmed ibn Abdullah at-Tabari, *ar-Riyadu'n-Nadrah*, II, 52.

Marifatullah and Divine Awards

If a person of the ilk of Omar –Allah be well-pleased with him-, whose genius is incontestable, can barely understand a conversation taking place in his native tongue, one may have a proper idea the difficulty hearing something of the kind would pose an ordinary human being.

Putting onto paper the realities spoken of during such spiritual conversations and their public dissemination in that manner has therefore been regarded undesirable; seen as something adverse. Only in that manner has it been possible to enable the passage of these truths to proper persons, ensuring it was kept secret from the general public. Therefore, a mention of the name of a person thought of as having attained spiritual perfection is always coupled with the expression *qaddas'Allahu sirrah*, that is 'May Allah sanctify his secret, or inner world, from all kinds of spiritual dirt.'

Occupied with heart-world of people in terms of its purpose, *tasawwuf* is thus naturally obliged to use love, the reason of the universe's existence. It has therefore also been dubbed the path of love and affection. But since love is an exuberant emotion, it may reduce power over the will and bring about an ecstatic and unrestrained excitement.

One such example from the deep love between the Blessed Prophet –upon him blessings and peace- and Jafar Tayyar –Allah be well-pleased with him- is as follows:

Jafar Tayyar –Allah be well-pleased with him- had returned from Abyssinia to Medina, accompanied by a group of Companions On finding out that the Blessed Prophet –upon him blessings and peace- was actually at Khaybar, he proceeded there, without taking any timeout to rest. His arrival at Khaybar gave the Blessed Prophet –upon him blessings and peace- enormous joy, as he said:

"Should I feel happy over the fall of Khaybar or the arrival of Jafar?" (Ibn Hisham, as-Sirah, IV, 3)

On his return from the *umratu'l-qada*,[85] the Blessed Prophet –upon him blessings and peace- discussed, with his relatives, who would be the

---

85 The *umratu'l-qada*, or the compensatory *umrah* is the supererogatory pilgrimage the Blessed Prophet –upon him blessings and peace- had originally intended for in the year of the Peace of Hudaybiyah but which he could only perform in the year after.

most suitable person to take care of Fatimah, the orphan of Hamza –Allah be well-pleased with him-. He ultimately decided on Jafar; and kissing him on the forehead, he complimented:

"You are so much like me both in appearance and disposition!" (Bukhari, Maghazi, 43)

So elated was Jafar –Allah be well-pleased with him- to hear this compliment that he virtually lost consciousness. He began hopping like an innocent child, spinning around himself like a moth around a flame. (Ahmed ibn Hanbal, Musnad, I, 108; Ibn Saad, IV, 35; Waqidi, II, 739)

Hence, just as one may very well become ecstatic at hearing such an enormous compliment and become beside himself, he may also shed the external world and become immersed in rapture upon receiving the graceful blessings of divinely manifestations. This is only natural. The important thing is to maintain the balance and to keep sight of the main direction and not spill over outside the standards being a human being demands, even amid that torrential flood of excitement.

Maintaining this balance necessitates guidance by those who, on the Sufi path, have combined exoteric sciences with the spiritual life.

Unless persons entrusted with the duty of enlightening attain to a required level and prowess in exoteric sciences, the danger on the path of spiritual love and affection remains ever alive. To avoid this danger, in some orders like the Naqshibandiyya, it has been custom for masters to be designated among those with equal depth in exoteric sciences, so that they may protect themselves and others from the ominous dangers spoken of.

The methods of spiritual training espoused by saints are various. Naqshibandiyya, one of the most prominent of the all the orders of the Sufi path, trains the disciple without ever letting him fall into spiritual enchantment (*jazbah*). This is alluded to by the words of Abdulkhaliq Gujdawani -may Allah sanctify his secret-:

"Had Hallaj lived in our times and come under our training, Allah willing, we would have protected him from spiritual intoxication (*sakr*)."

Insofar as the law of religion is concerned, emotions of overexcitement time and again observed in some Sufi orders, which are nothing but the spilling over of an intensity of spiritual enchantment, are merely slips of the tongue. What they essentially indicate is that although favorable and even recommended in their moderate dosage, excessive spiritual excitement and exuberance may come with some consequences.

Besides the attributes common to all prophets, it is evident that each prophet possesses a quality exclusive to himself. The same goes for saints, in comparison to each other. For instance, a saint may be of *jalali* or *jamali* temperament. But in their hearts, they nonetheless all know the Almighty in a way different to the comprehension and grasp of an ordinary person and strive to gain closer to Him, by abandoning all things mortal. They are constantly aware of their helplessness upon the boundless plane of Divine Knowledge. Be that as it may, not only are all saints not on the same spiritual level, they are also not obliged with carrying out the same duties. Some return to the public once they reach the final destination of their *sayr-u suluk*, their spiritual journey. They are obliged with enlightening the public. As has been mentioned before, similar to a teacher who teaches a child in a gradual manner, in their social interactions, they act as if they are unaware of most of the truths they in fact know. Feigning ignorance in this manner is referred to as a *tajahul-i arifana*; literally 'a wisely feigned ignorance'.

Since they are not obliged with enlightening the public, other saints remain on the station of awe (*khayrah*) and remain in continual silence. It is like they are mute before the flows of Divine Power impressed throughout the universe. There are yet other saints, entrusted with the duty of guiding the public, who are like waterfalls in their speech. Divine secrets and wisdoms begin to overflow ceaselessly from the tips of their tongues.

In some, on the other hand, these states are variable. Their lives exhibit various stages. One such example, as it manifested itself in the life of Muhammad Parisa -may Allah sanctify his secret-, is below:

After the ritual prayer of *isha*, Muhammad Parisa -May Allah sanctify his secret- would stand at the courtyard of the mosque for a while and return home after a short conversation. Yet sometimes such a mood would come over him that he would come to a standstill, virtually frozen, in the courtyard until the *adhan* of *fajr*, immersed in a profound state of awe. On hearing the *adhan*, he would enter the mosque once again.

Similar to the difference visible in their lives and emotions, each saint has also adopted a different stance towards death. While Mawlana Rumi -may Allah sanctify his secret- looked upon death as a reunion and a wedding night due to his burning with the love of the Divine, Hasan Basri -may Allah sanctify his secret- carried the persistent anxiety of not knowing what was to become of him during his final breath, beset by the manifestation of Divine fear.

All we may know of *ladunni* knowledge are mere crumb-like reflections onto words, as much as words themselves allow, from its manifestations observed first and foremost in the lives of prophets and their sprinkling in the lives of saints. Since the absolute truth of this knowledge lies with the Almighty, grasping it in its real meaning transcends the bounds of our comprehension.

Spiritual foresight is the ability to observe what lies behind the veils, the secrets of beyond. Only those who are able to look inside the nacre may become aware of the pearl.

---

2. SPIRITUAL FORESIGHT (*FIRASAH*)

Firasah is a light with which the Lord awards the hearts of His beloved servants. In other words, it is the transpiring of an incisive intelligence, genius, sensitivity, a depth of knowledge and understanding in the heart, in the form of spiritual comprehension. Through the genuine feelings and inspirations that emerge in the heart, it is the ability to discern the hidden truth of things that take place and accurately foresee and determines the thoughts passing through hearts and minds.

The Blessed Prophet –upon him blessings and peace- has stated:

اِتَّقُوا فِرَاسَةَ الْمُؤْمِنِ فَإِنَّهُ يَنْظُرُ بِنُورِ اللهِ

"Beware of the foresight of a believer…for he gazes with the light of Allah" (Tirmidhi, Tafsir, 15). Undoubtedly, attaining this prudential foresight, which enables one to look with the penetrating light of the Lord, is reserved only for those who are triumphant in shedding the conceit of their egos. The history of Islam presents many such cases in regard:

On the report of Anas –Allah be well-pleased with him-, while going to visit Othman –Allah be well-pleased with him- one day, he happened to notice a woman on the street. He was taken in by her beauty. With that thought in his mind, he entered Othman's presence, who, the moment he saw Anas, said:

"You are coming here, Anas, with traces of fornication on your eyes." The astounded Anas –Allah be well-pleased with him- exclaimed:

"Is Divine revelation still continuing to arrive after the Messenger of Allah?" To that Othman –Allah be well-pleased with him- replied:

"No…this is simply prudence and an accurate foresight."[86]

It is also renowned that the foresight of Omar –Allah be well-pleased with him- on many issues fell in harmony with Divine commandments revealed afterwards. The Noble Messenger –upon him blessings and peace- indeed attests to this when he says:

"Among the people who lived before you, there were those who received inspiration. If there is any such figure person among my nation, it is surely Omar." (Bukhari, Ashabu'n-Nabi, 6)

Abu Abbas ibn Mahdi explains:

"As I was journeying through the desert once, I came within an arm's length of another man ahead of me, barefoot and bareheaded, who was not carrying a water-bottle. 'How is he supposed to offer ritual prayer without any water?' I thought to myself; he must have no notion of ablution or prayer, I supposed. Then the man suddenly turned around and recited the Quranic verse, '…know that Allah knows what is in your hearts' (al-Baqara, 235). *I simply lost consciousness and fell to the ground. When I regained my senses, I sought repentance from Allah and continued on my way. Not long after, I caught up with the same man once more. Seeing him, this time, impressed me with an enormous feeling of awe. I came to a standstill. He turned around, as he had done before and recited, 'And it is He Who accepts repentance from His servants and pardons the evil deeds and He knows what you do'* (as-Shura, 25) *after which he disappeared from sight. I never saw him again."*

Dhunnun-i Misri -may Allah sanctify his secret- recounts a similar experience:

"At one time, I saw a young man in worn out clothes with patches all over it. Though my ego wanted to despise him, it was as if my heart was testifying to his sainthood. Caught between my ego and my heart, I had begun thinking, when the young man became aware of my secret. Giving me a look, he said:

---

86 Qushayri, *ar-Risala*, p. 238.

Marifatullah and Divine Awards

'Do not throw your gaze at me, Dhunnun, to catch sight of how worn out my clothes are. The pearl always lies hidden in the nacre!' He then slipped away out of sight."

A young man who had come to the *sohbah* of saint Abdulkhaliq Gujdawani for the first time and who was concealing his Christian faith, had asked him of the inner meaning of the Prophet's words, "Beware of the foresight of a believer…for he gazes with the light of Allah." The reply was: "Remove the zone around your waist and become a Muslim!"

Stunned by his crystal clear foresight, the young man uttered the Word of *Tawhid* in the presence of the great sheikh and became Muslim on the spot.

It has been similarly reported that Junayd Baghdadi -may Allah sanctify his secret- foresaw, at first sight, that a young man, disguised as a Muslim, was in fact a Jew and that he would end up a Muslim in a very short time.

Foresight is hence a Divine award that may increase or decrease depending on the intensity of faith and piety in the heart.

Uprightness and toil is superior to countless feats of spiritual insight and karamah. It should also be known that a spiritual insight and karamah that does not bring about a greater loyalty to the commands of religion is nothing but a disaster and tribulation. (Mawlana Khalid Baghdadi)

3. SPIRITUAL DISPOSAL (*TASARRUF*) AND *KARAMAH*

Being Omnipotent, when the Lord wills for something to be, He simply says 'Be' (*Kun*) and it becomes. Together with this, in accordance with His Divine Will, the Almighty has at the same time entrusted some of His servants with disposal over certain events. Essentially, however, these disposals can never take place without the intervention of the Lord as the 'Creator'. So with regard to these disposals, these certain human beings act only as means, as is the case with the four archangels.

Among these archangels, for instance, Jibril –upon him peace- is entrusted with the duty of conveying revelation to prophets, Mikail –upon him peace- with directing and managing natural phenomena, Azrail –upon him peace- with taking the lives of the living and Israfil –upon him peace- with blowing the horn to signal the beginning of the Hereafter.

The Almighty could most certainly have executed all of these directly without there being a need for angels. Still, through His Divine Will, the Almighty has invested them with such duties and authority. The power of angels stems essentially from the power of the Lord. It is He who gives them the power they have. The same goes for entire creation.

Allah, glory unto Him, has similarly handed His prophets with distinct authorities of disposal. Famous among all these, is Sulayman's –upon him peace- knowledge of the language of animals and his command over the winds and *jinn*.

Marifatullah and Divine Awards

The Noble Messenger –upon him blessings and peace-, the imam of all prophets, was also endowed with many unique powers, from which the elite among his *ummah* have also reaped a share, as much as was allowed by the Almighty. The disposals of some prominent saints like Abdulqadir Jilani and Ahmed ar-Rufai, both in their lifetimes and after their death, has frequently been reported.

A spiritual disposal is not brought about by the control and willpower of any given person. Much rather, it occurs through the Almighty manifesting His attribute 'Creator' in that disposal and intervening in the action. A disposal is thus no different than any other happening. The only difference lies in its unusual nature, in that not everyone is privileged with it.

Karamah, a type of spiritual disposal, is a supernatural occurrence unexplainable through the laws of nature, awarded by the Almighty to saints as a result of the perfected quality of their faith, piety and spiritual knowledge. This constitutes the formal aspect of *karamah*. As for the real *karamah* as acknowledged by saints, it is to live unswervingly upon uprightness (*istiqamah*). In terms of the spiritual disposal they have attained to, the righteous saints are different to other human beings in perceiving, thinking and even conduct.

As can be understood from the above definition, *karamah* as it transpires in saints are of two kinds:

1. **Spiritual *Karamah***: This is to cover distance on the way of acquiring of knowledge, both exoteric and spiritual, moral behavior and a quality of worshipping, so as to attain to a spiritual level that ensures a share is received of the inner sense of the verse, "Continue then in the right way as you are commanded." (Hud, 112) Simpler put, it is *istiqamah*; to stand firm on the upright path. The words of enlightening wisdom that spill from the mouth of a saint, for instance, are uttered in a style that does not hurt the feelings of anyone, even when they are voiced to caution the listener.

It is impossible to obtain this state through reason and rational contemplation. Allah, glory unto Him, graces this only to who He selects.

2. **Existential (*Kawni*) and Formal *Karamah***: These signify the extraordinary occurrences that takes place in the physical world, like relo-

cating from one place to another (*tayy-i makan*), having wild animals see to personal duties and so forth.

The true experts of Sufism do not pay much attention to this type of *karamah*. Besides, displaying a *karamah* of the kind is not a prerequisite of sainthood. The Lord, again, bestows this type of *karamah* to servants whom He chooses. In any case, displaying a formal *karamah* has not been looked kindly upon by Sufis, unless it be necessary; and exhibiting a *karamah* of the sort is the last thing a saint wishes to do, as it comes with public admiration and applause. Ignorant people then begin to expect everything from the saint.

However much the public may esteem the *karamah* of the second kind, it is the first that is more desirable. It is consensus among Sufis that 'The greatest *karamah* is uprightness.' The toil of an aspirant, who is not upright, is only in vain.

Mawlana Khalid-i Baghdadi -may Allah sanctify his secret- states:

"Uprightness and toil is superior to countless feats of spiritual insight and *karamah*. It should also be known that a spiritual insight and *karamah* that does not bring about a greater loyalty to the commands of religion is nothing but a disaster and tribulation."

Karamah have a sublime purpose; to 'shock' the onlookers, so to speak, and steer them to uprightness. But Islam consists of a Divine Offer, to persuade human beings to come under obligations. This will continue to be its prevailing quality until the Final Hour. Extraordinary feats, on the other hand, which are somewhat compelling, are detrimental to this aspect. It is owing to this reason that neither prophets have ever resorted to miracles nor saints to *karamah* unless it was deemed necessary.

A true *karamah* generally brings about the following effects:

1) It trains the ego.

2) It rids the heart of ugly habits and inclinations, adorning it with divinely inspiration.

3) It lets the heart in on secrets and wisdoms.

Alternately, one of the most important means in manifesting a *karamah* is the *Ism-i Azam*, the greatest name of Allah, glory unto Him, which He reveals to His servants as secret. We would like to briefly touch upon the theme of *Ism-i Azam*, to the degree it holds a significant place in the discussion of Divine awards.

Ism-i azam is one of the names of the Lord that renders a prayer, made by mentioning it, accepted. Yet, it remains a secret as to which name of the Lord it specifically is and many narrations have come in regard. The strongest of these reports is the one that suggests that the *Ism-i Azam* is 'Allah', the Name of the Almighty's Essence, which unites all His other names in its scope.

One relevant conception in Sufism is as follows:

Having given human beings a share of His Power by breathing into them His Spirit, the Almighty has made 'man' the most comprehensive manifestation of His Divine Names. The perfected human being is thus he who is able actualize the potential of these Divine Names embedded in his natural disposition and thereby attain to the honor of embodying the morals of the Lord Himself. It has therefore been suggested that whichever Divine Name reigns supreme in a person that is his *ism-i azam*. A person, for instance, in whom feelings of mercy and compassion are full-fledged, is dominated by the manifestations of the Divine Names *Rahman* (the Merciful) and *Rahim* (the Compassionate). For such persons, those names are the *ism-i azam*. But true merit lies in embodying what is demanded by the beautiful names of the Lord and turning them into a lively moral existence. Otherwise, many can straightforwardly read the *Ism-i Azam* from books or from memory and carry on like normal. Hence, if the heart has absolutely no share of mercy and compassion while the tongue is busy uttering them, it is futile to expect the realization of the prayer made.

On this subject, an incident that took place between Ali –Allah be well-pleased with him- and a bedouin is momentous:

A poor bedouin one day asked for some charity from Ali –Allah be well-pleased with him-. Without the means to provide him anything else at the time, Ali –Allah be well-pleased with him- picked up a handful of sand from the ground and reading a certain prayer and breathing into the sand, poured it out to the open hands of the bedouin as gold. The bedouin was stunned. He began begging Ali –Allah be well-pleased with him- to let him in on how he was able to do what he did and what the prayer was he read into the sand. Full of composure, Ali –Allah be well-pleased with him- told him it was al-Fatiha. The bedouin, brimming over with joy, then picked up a handful of sand from the ground, read al-Fatiha and breathed into it. But to his dismay, the sand remained sand. So, he once again asked for the underlying wisdom behind all this, in response to which –Allah be well-pleased with him- said:

"This is a difference of heart."

Mawlana Rumi -may Allah sanctify his secret- recounts a similar incident:

"A man once accompanied Jesus –upon him peace- on a journey. On the way, he noticed a pile of bones heaped on the side of the road and begged the Prophet to teach him "…the Ism-i Azam you know so that I may bring the bones to life!"

"You are out of your depth", replied Jesus –upon him peace-. "To pronounce the Ism-i Azam and bring the dead back to life, you need a breath purer than rain and a servant-hood more sensitive than that of angels. The Ism-i Azam demands a clean tongue and a pure heart…a person with a soul untainted by the haram and free of rebellion and sin, just like the angels. Only if a person has a pure soul may his prayer be accepted. The Lord makes him an overseer of His treasures. You may very well hold Musa's staff in your hands. But do you possess the power he has that you may turn it into a dragon and have the force to control it? Even Musa had felt a fear upon seeing his staff turn into a dragon and had the Lord reassure him 'Do not fear, Musa' (an-Naml, 10) So no benefit lies in you learning the Ism-i Azam Jesus knows, without having the breath he has!"

But the ignorant man remained adamant. "Since, I am without the power as you say, can't you at least read it onto the bones lying over there and bring them to life?"

Amazed to hear the ignorant man still insisting, Jesus –upon him peace- said, "What is the wisdom underlying this insistence, my Lord? Why is this fool so inclined to debate? He wants to revive bones, when he really should try to revive his heart which is lying dead, skin-and-bones. Instead *of praying for his own revival, he wants to bring bones back to life. What ignorance!"*

Thus, the true righteous servants of the Lord are those who have attained to this maturity. Whenever a *karamah* transpires through a saint, his feelings of gratitude for the blessings of the Lord, therefore, increase all the more. It provides for them a source of inspiration in the struggle they have undertaken. True saints are never led by their *karamah* to suppose that their eternal lives are secured. On the contrary, they become filled with feelings of helplessness and humility before the Lord, despising their egos even more than before. Because they can never be sure of the danger of falling into conceit and tribulation, they carry a relentless fear.

The tragic fate of Balam ibn Baura, to whom the Almighty had revealed the *Ism-i Azam*, in fact presents many lessons. This man was acknowledged among the Israelites as a scholar and saint. But in time, he fell into conceit and became deceived by the dazzle of the world, as a result of which he lost his respected status; he even died a nonbeliever. His circumstances are depicted by the Quran as:

"And recite to them the narrative of him to whom We give Our communications, but he withdraws himself from them, so the Shaitan overtakes him, so he is of those who go astray. And if We had pleased, We would certainly have exalted him thereby; but he clung to the earth and followed his low desire, so his parable is as the parable of the dog; if you attack him he lolls out his tongue; and if you leave him alone he lolls out his tongue; this is the parable of the people who reject Our communications; therefore relate the narrative that they may reflect." (al-Araf, 175-176)

Excess admiration for a saint, who has command over *karamah*, has therefore been considered extremely dangerous. It is mostly this danger that underlies the saints' dislike for exposing *karamah*. In any case, *karamah* is not the ultimate spiritual level and does not, by any means, demonstrate the spiritual depth of a saint. Those righteous souls know very well that nobody, except for prophets, have their eternal happiness guaranteed. Many a person enters Paradise when having come within an inch of Hell; and many another is toppled down to the pits of Hell after having come within a step of entering of Paradise. As a way of life, a believer must therefore firmly adopt the standard:

Sufism: A Path Towards the Internalization of Faith (Ihsân)

"And serve your Lord till the Inevitable (death) comes to you." (al-Hijr, 99)

As is the case with every other issue, our sole measure with regard to these Divine blessings which manifest in the form of *karamah* is the Quran and Sunnah. The truth of *karamah* stands, nonetheless, as an incontestable, authentic fact.

A few proofs from the Quran attesting to the factuality of *karamah* are below:

Asaf, the vizier of Sulayman –upon him peace- had assured him that he would be able to bring the throne of Bilqis "in the blink of an eye" (an-Naml, 40) and was true to his word.

Zakariyya –upon him peace- had been entrusted to take care of Maryam –upon her peace-, who had devoted herself to the Temple to worship. Each time he would enter the Temple, however, he would find various food items by her side. On asking her where they were coming from, he received the answer:

"From Allah…" (Al-i Imran, 37) Again, the 24th and 25th verses of Al-i Imran, which reveal how Maryam –upon her peace- was nourished directly by Allah, glory unto Him, testify further to *karamah*.

Evidences presented by the Sunnah are even more: "Three people have spoken whilst still in the cradle", says the Blessed Prophet –upon him blessings and peace-. "Jesus son of Maryam, the baby ascribed to Jurayj and another baby." He then goes onto give further detail.[87]

Explained in another authentic *hadith* is the ordeal of three journeymen, trapped in a cave into which they had retreated at night; a massive rock had rolled down, blocking the entrance. As a means for their way out, each journeyman prayed with a mention of a past deed they had offered exclusively for the sake of the Lord, and as a result, the rock gradually made way to the point of fully opening the passage.[88]

Anas –Allah be well-pleased with him- explains:

---

[87] See, Muslim, Birr, 8.
[88] See, Bukhari, Adab, 5; Anbiya, 53; Dhikr, 100.

"Usayd ibn Khudayr and Abbad ibn Bishr were by the side of the Prophet –upon him blessings and peace- during a dark night. When they left his presence, they saw two sets of light in front of them, lighting their way. And when they parted ways with each other, one set of light followed one, and the other followed the other." (Bukhari, Salat, 79; Masajid, 78, Manaqib, 28, Manaqibu'l-Ansar, 13)

Another incident confirming a *karamah* of a Companion is the fact that while detained as a captive by the Meccan idolaters and during a season when no fresh fruits were available, Hubayb –Allah be well-pleased him- was seen helping himself to a bunch of fresh grapes. (Bukhari, Jihad, 170; Maghazi, 10, 28)

It has again been reported that while addressing the public on the *minbar*, Omar –Allah be well-pleased with him- out of nowhere called out, "To the mountain, Sariya, to the mountain!" As he was saying these words, which had nothing to do with what he had been saying until that point, Sariya was in the heat of battle, commanding an army of Muslims at a month's distance away from Medina. But Allah, glory unto Him, made these words audible to him. (Ibn Hajar, al-Isabah, II, 3)

The Companions' lives abound in such examples.

As the stark opposite of *karamah*, there may transpire from the hands of certain persons, who are either nonbelievers, perverse or carry a pretention for sainthood, certain extraordinary feats similar in appearance to authentic *karamah*. These feats of extraordinary nature, which transpire in line with their pretensions, are referred to as *istidraj*.

These are brought about through certain spiritual exercises. In other words, it is possible to actualize the potential for certain capabilities inherent in the spirit through certain nonreligious influences. Hindu fakirs, for example, are known to acquire a spiritual force mostly through abstinence. At times, this is made possible through magic or mobilizing a *khuddam*[89] from among the jinn. Distinguishing feats of this kind from real *karamah*

---

89   Through certain recitations, it is possible to subject a *jinn* to personal command and use him like a servant. A jinn of the kind is called a *khuddam*, a servant. A *khuddam* executes the command of the person, by whom he has become bounded, as much as his powers allow.

is a matter of knowledge. But this much can be said that the lives persons who exhibit istidraj never measure up to the standard of *taqwa* or piety. They lack in abiding by the Sunnah of the Prophet –upon him blessings and peace-. This is the first dividing line to watch out for. Junayd Baghdadi -May Allah sanctify his secret- has fittingly said:

"If you see a person flying in the air and know that his condition does not measure up to the Quran and Sunnah, do not be fooled for it is *istidraj*."

Besides, a person privileged by the Divine with command over *karamah* would never flaunt it with an air of showing off. Since true saints are unblemished by the defective urge to show off, they never exhibit a *karamah* unless it is necessary. They instead persistently conduct themselves with a perfection of moral behavior, which other people can emulate. This is comparable to the fact that Blessed Prophet –upon whom blessings and peace- acted within human conditions in order to set a quintessential example for his *ummah* and only rarely displayed miracles –with the permission of Allah, glory unto Him- when the need for it arose. The righteous servants of the Lord do not stray a whisker's length from the path of the Prophet –upon him blessings and peace-. Paying attention only to this much is more than sufficient in order to distinguish *karamah* from *istidraj*.

The Pharaoh was one who had command over *istidraj*. Throughout his four-hundred year life (according to some accountings), he did not suffer even from a headache. His teeth were all intact at the time of his sudden death. It is even said that when striding downhill on horseback, the front legs of his horse would grow lengthier.

An *istidraj* only aggravates the conceit and self-importance of a non-believer and a perverse, worsening his inevitable end. Seeing Musa –upon him peace- strike his staff across the Red Sea and open, with the permission of the Lord, a dry path through it, the Pharaoh turned to his soldiers and yelled:

"Look! The sea has parted before my majesty!" Little was he aware that once he would charge his horse onto that path, the Red Sea would swallow both him and his men in its depths.

The Blessed Prophet –upon him blessings and peace- has also informed that Dajjal will also put many an *istidraj* on show, in an attempt to deceive people.

There are further circumstances where the outcome of an attempted *istidraj* turns out to be the total opposite of what the person had intended. These are called *ikhanah*, a humiliating betrayal. Musaylamah the Liar, who had falsely staked a claim to prophethood, for instance, had once spat in a well with the intention of increasing its water. But to his dismay, the well dried up altogether.

Just as it was possible for *karamah* and *istidraj* to transpire during the time of the Noble Messenger –upon him blessings and peace- and the Companions their manifestation during later periods remains equally possible. The spiritual disposals and *karamah* which some saints manifest with the purpose of guiding the willpowers of those who witness it take place only through the blessings of the prophet they follow; thus, in a sense, they are at the same time a continuation of his miracles.

It is an incontestable historical fact that spiritual disposals and *karamah*, manifested both during the time of the Companions and later periods, have led to the guidance of many. Many an onlooker has even felt compelled to confess, 'If this religion boasts saints like this, there is no guessing how great its prophet must be', by which they, at once, confirm the true center of each *karamah*: the Prophet –upon him blessings and peace-.

Some Specific Cases of Disposal and *Karamah*

To worship Him alone and to work on Earth, Allah, glory unto Him, the Creator and the Ruler of the Universe, designated human beings as His vicegerent (*khalifah*). This fact is recounted by the Quran as:

$$وَ اِذْ قَالَ رَبُّكَ لِلْمَلٰٓئِكَةِ اِنّى جَاعِلٌ فِى الْاَرْضِ خَلٖيفَةً$$

"And when your Lord said unto the angels: I am about to place a vicegerent on Earth" (al-Baqara, 30)

The 'vicegerency' of man carries the following meanings:

Sufism: A Path Towards the Internalization of Faith (Ihsân)

'I shall give Him some authority from My Power and Attributes; and he, as My representative, will possess a command of disposal over My creation, implementing My law on My behalf. But he shall not be the main actor; he will not implement the law on his own behalf and for his own sake. He shall be only My agent and regent. Through his will, he shall be responsible with implementing My Will, My command and My law. And those who come after him will be obliged to continue the same duty as their successors, which will expose the secret of, 'It is He Who has placed you as vicegerents on Earth...' (al-Anam, 165)" (Elmalılı, *Hak Dini*, I, 299-300)

Both the miracles that transpire in prophets and the disposals and *karamah* observed in saints, offer insights into the mystery of man being the vicegerent of the Lord. Among a countless cases of their manifestation, some are given below:

Mansur ibn Abdullah recalls the following about Abu Abdullah ibn Jalla: "Ibn Jalla had once recounted to me an experience of his:

'I had come to Medina, destitute and penniless. I went to the sacred grave of the Prophet –upon him blessings and peace-. After saluting him, I said, 'I am in poverty, Messenger of Allah, and I have come as your guest.'

Moments later, I became drowsy and fell asleep. In my dream, the Messenger of Allah –upon him blessings and peace- offered me a muffin. I ate half of it. And when I woke up, I found the other half by my side.'"[90]

Another noteworthy incident to take place after the passing away of the Blessed Prophet –upon him blessings and peace- is retold by al-Utbi:

"I was sitting by the Prophet's –upon him blessings and peace- sacred grave, when a bedouin arrived and said, in a tone I could hear:

'Peace and blessings to you, Messenger of Allah! I heard Allah the Almighty say, '...and had they, when they were unjust to themselves, come to you and asked forgiveness of Allah and the Messenger had also asked forgiveness for them, they would have found Allah Oft-returning, Merciful.' (an-Nisa 64). So I have repented for my sins and asked forgiveness and have come to ask you to intercede on my behalf to my Lord.'

---

[90] See, Kalabazi, *Taarruf*, translated by S. Uludağ, p. 214

Marifatullah and Divine Awards

He then recited a moving poem and left. Soon after, I was overcome with sleep. In my dream, I saw the Messenger of Allah –upon him blessings and peace- who told me to, 'Catch hold of the bedouin and give him the good news that Allah has forgiven him.'" (Ibn Kathir, Tafsir, I, 532)

❦

As the war raged high during the Battle of Gallipoli, army major Lutfi Bey shouted, "Come o Muhammad! Your Book is all but lost!"[91], desperately seeking the aid of the Blessed Prophet –upon him blessings and peace-. Just how that genuine plea for help was to materialize is made evident in the below incident:

The year is 1928…Exactly thirteen years had passed since the victory at Gallipoli.

Cemal Öğüt Effendi of Alasonya, an erudite man of wisdom, was at hajj, in Medina, where he had the good fortune to meet many important people. Among those was the caretaker of the Blessed Prophet's –upon him blessings and peace- sacred gravesite. The man was at the same time a loyal admirer of the Ottomans, an admiration he would express at every given opportunity. After some conversation, Cemal Öğüt Effendi could not help but ask the reason for his love for the Ottomans.

The elderly caretaker, behind a radiant face, said to him the following, without a moment's hesitation:

"Only one memory of mine, of which I will tell you know, is enough incentive for me to love the Ottomans for the sake of Islam. It would have been the year 1915 when a scholar from India arrived for hajj. The richness of the man's inner world needed no further evidence; he was a saint in all likelihood. It was by the grave of the Grand Prophet –upon him blessings and peace- that I first saw him; he had arrived here after completing his pilgrimage. He looked very sad. The tears rolling freely from his eyes would never stop, I thought. I had to ask him what the reason of his grief was. So I did. He began crying even more and said:

---

91   See, Mehmed Niyazi, *Çanakkale Mahşeri*, p. 352-355.

Sufism: A Path Towards the Internalization of Faith (Ihsân)

'Only after so many years have I found the opportunity to visit the Noblest Man of all worlds. But my insight tells me that he is not in his usual position. Is it that the eye of my heart has gone blind? Why can I not feel the presence of the Prophet –upon him blessings and peace-? I have been devastated by these thoughts since the day I stepped foot inside Medina!'

The same night I had the greatest fortune of seeing the Messenger of Allah –upon him blessings and peace- in my dream. I remembered the words of the Indian scholar. The Prophet –upon him blessings and peace- did not leave me much in suspense. 'What he feels is right', he said. 'Right now, I am not in Medina. My heart could not bear the thought of leaving my children, in a desperate situation, alone on the battlefield. I am currently aiding them.'"[92]

The confession British General Ian Hamilton after the defeat at Gallipoli stands as a virtual testimony to the above account: "We were not defeated by the physical strength of the Turks; it was their spiritual strength that defeated us. They did not even have any ammunition left to fire at us. But we indeed saw without very own eyes, the forces that arrived from the skies."

These types of occurrences are disposals the Almighty gives His prophets after their passing away from Earth. Prophets continue to live, in their graves, in a nature we cannot comprehend through the spectacles of our sensory impressions. The below *hadith* in fact bears this out in no uncertain manner:

The Blessed Prophet –upon him blessings and peace- has said, on the report of Aws ibn Aws –Allah be well-pleased with him-:

"The most virtuous of days is Friday. Therefore, make sure to send me lots of salutations on that day, as your salutations are brought directly to me." On hearing this, the Companions asked:

"How will our salutations be brought to you after you have passed away and nothing physical shall remain of you?"

"Allah the Almighty" he replied "has made the bodies of prophets invulnerable to decay below earth." *(Abu Dawud, Salat, 201; See, Nasai, Juma, 5)*

---

92 From the Zaman newspaper of 18 March 2001.

Marifatullah and Divine Awards

This state of aliveness is valid equally for martyrs, as is stated in the Quran:

"And reckon not those who are killed in Allah's way as dead; nay, they are alive (and) are provided sustenance from their Lord." (Al-i Imran, 169)

With that said, the prophets' state of aliveness is far more intense to that of martyrs.

The manifesting of disposal and *karamah* by saints, the inheritors of prophets, has continued to this day. Just some of the countless cases in point are as follows:

Ubaydullah Ahrar -may Allah sanctify his secret- relocated from Central Asia (*tayy-i makan*) to take active part in the conquest of Istanbul. This is recounted by his grandson Khawaja Muhammad Qasim:

"It was on a Thursday afternoon, when out of the blue Ubaydullah Ahrar ordered for his horse to be prepared. Mounting his horse, he then galloped out of Samarkand. Mawlana Sheikh, a renowned student of his, pursued him awhile. It was not long before he returned, telling the others that Ubaydullah Ahrar's horse steered left and then right and disappeared from sight. Some time later, he returned to Samarkand, greeted by his students who were anxious to know the reason behind his sudden journey.

'Mehmed Khan, the Sultan of the Turks, asked for my help' he explained. 'So I went to help him. And with the permission of Allah the Almighty, victory was granted.'"

Khawaja Abdulhadi, Ubaydullah Ahrar's grandson, who years later came to Istanbul from Samarkand, recounts the following:

"When I went to Istanbul, I visited Sultan Bayezid II, who after describing to me my grandfather's physical appearance, explained:

'This, my father told me once: Amid the most violent phase of the Siege of Istanbul, I prayed to the Lord to send me the qutb of the time for help. He soon appeared in such and such stature on a white horse and assured me that I need not fear for the victory would be ours.

'They have lots of soldiers repelling us', I said to him. He then opened his caftan and told me to look inside. Inside the sleeves of his caftan, I saw a massive army, streaming like a great flood.

'This army has come to aid you', he said, after which he added, 'Now go to the top of that hill, strike the kettle three times with the drumstick and command your army to attack'.

I did exactly as he told me. And he, too, took part in the offensive along with his army. The fath of Istanbul was soon realized…"[93]

It is thus a historical matter of fact that Sultan Mehmed received the spiritual aid of saints in their entirety. Especially renowned is the vital physical and spiritual assistance provided by Akşemseddin -may Allah sanctify his secret-.

One specific incident indicating the spiritual disposal of Aziz Mahmud Hudayi -May Allah sanctify his secret- is retold below:[94]

It is the year 1975. The time for zuhr prayer was near, when a stout and swarthy young man with an amicable appearance arrived at the tomb of the Great Saint. By accident, he came across Muharrem Effendi, the imam of the Aziz Mahmud Hudayi Mosque, in whom he confided his request.

"Excuse me sir", he said. "I have come to see Aziz Mahmud Hudayi. Is it possible for me to see him now? Is he here at the moment?"

Astounded to be posed with a question of the kind, Muharrem Effendi simply paused and said, "Yes, son. Aziz Mahmud Hudayi is here."

The young man, noticeably delighted to hear these words, begged the imam to "Allow me to see him…please!"

Still unable to make sense of the situation, the imam repeated his previous words, hoping that the young man would realize that they were standing right beside the tomb of the man he wanted to see.

---

[93] See, Mawlana Sheikh, Manaqib Khawaja Ubaydullah-i Ahrar, 4b-5a; Majdi Mehmed, Khadaiqu's-Shaqaiq, p. 272-273; Molla Jami, Nafakhatu'l-Uns, p. 764-765.

[94] I heard this incident personally from Muharrem Kır Effendi, my former classmate at the Imam Hatip Lise (High School).

"Aziz Mahmud Hudayi is indeed here", he said. But the young man simply repeated his request.

"In that case, let me see him. I want to see him".

Hoping to get to the bottom of the matter, the confused Muharrem Effendi then asked, "Do you actually know, son, who Aziz Mahmud Hudayi is?"

Annoyed by these seemingly meaningless questions and the imam's inexplicable stubbornness to prevent him from seeing the Sheikh, the young man, whose purity of heart matched the genuineness of his appearance, exclaimed:

"I know Aziz Mahmud Hudayi in person. He personally invited me here. I had promised him I would come and he knows about this all too well."

At last, Muharrem Effendi realized that the matter had a delicate and mysterious twist.

"How did you promise him that you would come?" he asked curiously, upon which the young man began to explain:

"I was among the team of commandos who were airdropped into battle during the Cyprus Peace Operation of 1974. Amid the frenzied warfare between our troops harbored at the sea and the Cypriot Greeks trying to repel us from their bases in the Beşparmak Mountains, we jumped off with parachutes. But the strong wind meant that each of us was dragged here and there, far from where we had intended to land. I landed right in the heart of the enemy line. I was caught in the middle of a hellish crossfire from both sides. As I stood petrified not knowing what to do, there appeared a tall, imposing man with a comforting expression. He looked at me with a delightful smile and said:

'What on earth are you doing here, son? This is the enemy line. Why did you come here all by yourself?'

'Baba', I said, 'it was not me who landed here…I was dropped here by the wind.'

Shaking his head a little, the bright-faced old man said, 'I have come to fight, too. I was sent here long before you. I know this area like the back *of my hand. Which platoon are you from? Come…Let me take you to your platoon!'*

So I followed him into a trail, with balls of fire flying over our heads. But that great man was strolling along, as if walking on a quiet road. I was taken aback by his overall attitude. He asked me a great number of questions on the way; my name, where I was from, and so forth. I answered them all. Afterwards, I asked him a question myself.

'And who might you be, Baba?'

'They call me Aziz Mahmud Hudayi', he replied.

'Baba', I added, 'you have done me an enormous favor. Should I end up returning home safe and sound, I would love to visit you as a show of appreciation. Can I have your address?'

'Come to Uskudar and ask for me', he said. 'Anyone will tell you where I am!' That was all the address he gave me.

Meanwhile, we had made it to our platoon. I kissed the great man's hands with love and respect. We bade farewell to each other, after which I checked in with my commander.

Suddenly seeing me in front of him unharmed and supposing it would have been impossible for anyone to make it alive from that scorching line of fire, my commander exclaimed,:

'How were you able to come here?'

'An old, beautiful Baba brought me here', I responded.

After ceasefire, I returned home. But I could not help thinking about the enormous favor of Aziz Mahmud Hudayi; so I came to Uskudar to visit him in appreciation. The people who I asked directed me here, telling me he is a holy man'".

The young man paused awhile. Taking a deep breath, he then repeated his previous request:

"That was how we met each other, sir. Now, please…Allow me to see him!"

Deeply moved by now, Muharrem Effendi could not say anything to the young man staring at him behind pleading eyes. Then doing the best to regain his composure, he could only give him a short explanation and that by stuttering:

"Son…Aziz Mahmud Hudayi is not someone who is physically alive. He is a great saint who lived between 1543 and 1628. He must have called you here so you could recite Fatiha. His grave is over there…"

Hearing this reply, the loyal and faithful young man became extremely saddened by the news he had found about only then. There was only the tomb of the great man, whom he had longingly come to visit and to whom he owed his life. It was only then that he came to terms with the incredible spiritual disposal he had experienced in the raging heat of battle. He began to sob. Covering his face with his hands, he cried for many minutes.

He was not alone in his tears. The imam was also crying…

A memory of the great saint Mahmud Sami Ramazanoğlu, which we had the fortune to hear personally during one of his *sohbah*s, runs as follows:

Mahmud Sami's -May Allah sanctify his secret- sister, two years his junior, was crippled in both feet. Close to where they were was the tomb of a famous saint known as Kaplanci Baba, frequently visited by the public. Accompanied by his mother and younger sister, he too one day went to visit the tomb, spending the night there. As they were fast asleep at night, they woke up to the scream of her crippled sister. His mother rushed to ask her what was wrong. The young girl explained, excitedly, that an old man had risen from the tomb and pressed and applied pressure on both her feet. Sami Effendi, recounting this memory, said that from that day onwards until her death, her sister was able to walk without ever feeling the least ache in her feet.

The incidents explained thus far and those alike are the Divine blessings of the authority of spiritual disposal the Almighty has graced some of His servants with. Yet it must not be forgotten that the absolute doer is invariably the Almighty Himself. The aid He has given His servants, both through the medium of angels and saints, have continued to this very day.

The truthful dream seen by a believer is one-forty-sixth of prophethood.
(Bukhari, Tabir, 26; Muslim, Ruya, 6)

4. TRUTHFUL DREAMS

Among the Divine awards are truthful dreams, considered as a way of comprehending the realities of the unseen. During sleep, connection with the material world is reduced to a bare minimum and spiritual emotions, trapped inside the body, are strengthened. The clouds of the ego, which veil the panorama of the sublime, disperse and allow for clearer vision. Gazing at the realm of the unseen in this manner is made possible for certain righteous persons. Verification of what the insights seen during these dreams comes later on, after awaking.

The Blessed Prophet –upon him blessings and peace- has said:

"Only glad tidings (*mubashshirat*) are left behind from prophethood", on which the Companions present asked what exactly was meant by these glad tidings.

"A truthful dream", responded the Prophet –upon him blessings and peace-. (Bukhari, Tabir, 5; Muslim, Salat, 207-208)

Mubashshirat are seen when the hearts of genuine believers become receptive to Divine inspirations and glad tidings during the dream.

In clarifying the meaning of the expression 'glad tidings in the life of the world' as it comes to pass in the verse "For them are glad tidings, in the life of the world and in the Hereafter…" (Yunus, 64), the Blessed Prophet –upon him blessings and peace- has said:

"They are the truthful dreams a Muslim sees or is made to see." (Tirmidhi, Ruya, 3)

Dreams are of three types:

Marifatullah and Divine Awards

1. Devilish Dreams: These are dreams inspired by the devil with the purpose of casting fear, distress and sorrow; like a dream where one falls of a cliff or sees scenes of disaster and chaos that sends him into despair. These dreams are baseless. Should one see a hazy, complicated dream the details of which he can barely remember, he should not tell anyone about it and seek refuge in the Almighty from the lure of the *Shaytan*.

On the report of Abu Said al-Khudri –Allah be well-pleased with him- the Noble Messenger –upon him blessings and peace- has stated: "If anyone of you sees a dream he enjoys, let him know that it is from Allah the Almighty. Therefore, he should thank Allah and recount this dream."

According to another narration:

"He should tell this dream only to who he loves. If he sees a dream he dislikes, that is from *Shaytan*. He should therefore seek refuge in Allah from his evil and not tell the dream to anyone. That way, the dream shall not harm him." (Bukhari, Tabir, 3, 46; Muslim, Ruya, 3)

It is further said in yet another *hadith*:

"Should anyone of you see a dream he dislikes, let him spit three times to his left, seek refuge in Allah from the evil of the devil three times and change his position from one side to the other." (Muslim, Ruya, 5)

2. Dreams Caused by an External Influence: These are scenes reflected onto a dream from one's imaginings or daily circumstances; like drinking lots of water in a dream after having eaten a salty dish before falling asleep or the reflection onto a dream of a problem that has kept the mind busy during the day. These have no interpretation. They are baseless.

3. Truthful Dreams: These dreams are remembered clearly. Inspired by the Lord, their nature is either that of glad tidings or warning. Certain designated angels receive these images from the Protected Tablet (*lawh-i mahfuz*) and instill them in the spirit of the sleeper with the command and permission of the Lord.

Truthful dreams are glimmers from the Protected Tablet that throw light on the future. The first stages of the prophethood of the Noble Messenger –upon him blessings and peace- consisted of truthful dreams, lasting for about six months.

The Prophet –upon him blessings and peace- says:

"As the Time[95] draws near, the dreams of a believer are almost never belied (they occur as they are seen). The truthful dream seen by a believer is one-forty-sixth of prophethood…and that which is from prophethood can never be a lie."[96]

"Dreams are of three kinds: The first are the truthful dreams, glad tidings from Allah. The second are the fear and sorrow whispered by the devil. And the third are things a person communicates to himself. Whosoever sees something in a dream he dislikes, should not tell his dream to others…he should immediately get up an offer ritual prayer." (Bukhari, Tabir, 26; Muslim, Ruya, 6)

"The truest dreams are seen by those who speak the truth most." (Muslim, Ruya, 6)

"The most truthful dream is seen during the approaching dawn." (Tirmidhi, Ruya, 3/2274)

Truthful dreams need to be interpreted by their experts; their signs need to be deciphered. Interpreting dreams is likewise a God-given expertise. There were times after ritual prayer when the Blessed Prophet –upon him blessings and peace- would listen to and interpret the dreams of some of his Companions and provide insight into the forthcoming events signaled by their dreams.

Interpreting dreams is without a doubt a special science founded upon certain principles. Those with insight into this science are known as a *muabbir*; that is, an interpreter. Many books have been written on interpreting dreams for the benefit of the general public. The most famous of these are the works of Ibn Sirin and Muhyiddin Arabi -may Allah sanctify his secret-, often quoted by many other books of dream interpretation compiled up to this day. Be that as it may, interpreting dreams by simply

---

[95] According to scholars of *hadith*, the expression 'as the time draws near' may refer to the equinox or the closing in of time either with the approaching Day of Judgment or at dawn towards sunrise.

[96] Regarding the fact that truthful dreams are one-forty-sixth of prophethood, it has been said that the Blessed Prophet –upon him blessings and peace- saw truthful dreams during the first six months of his twenty-three years of prophethood; and a period of six months is equal to one-forty-sixth of twenty three years.

drawing from the information provided in such works is not entirely a correct line of approach; as the gist of interpreting dreams is spiritual insight (*kashf*). The interpreter must therefore possess a spiritual command. One would otherwise face the dangers of a wrong interpretation, as pronounced by the Blessed Prophet –upon him blessings and peace-:

"A dream comes true as said by its first interpreter." (Ibn Majah, Tabir, 7) Dreams must therefore not be told to those who lack expertise. And the experts of this science have stated that 'the first interpretation is valid and it cancels out the rest'.

According to what is explained in the epistle *Mizanu'n-Nufus*,[97] the science of dream interpretation is comprised of two parts: subjective (*anfusi*) and objective (*afaqi*). Anyone, elite or not, may acquire knowledge of objective interpretation; that is, it is possible to be trained in it by virtue of collecting interpretations made previously by spiritual experts from books or word of mouth. This way, many similar dreams may be decoded in light of previous interpretations.

Each entity seen in a dream is like a word in a language. In other words, each is virtually a language of its own. The meaning ascribed, by the dream language, to an entity seen during a dream is based on a distant relation. That is to say, this relation is not without a ground, a foundation. A snake, for instance, is taken to signify an enemy; and this meaning has its source in the narrative of Adam –upon him peace-. Each mode of behavior and movement the snake exhibits is thereby taken as signifying a specific attitude of the enemy. If the snake appears dead straight or motionless, for instance, it is then interpreted as a road.

On the other hand, many factors play a vital role in interpreting dreams; like the specific day, night or the season of the year in which the dream is seen. For example, whereas the realization in life of a dream seen during winter is delayed, a dream seen towards daybreak is generally quick to come true. Yet, more often than not, such interpretations are deficient as they do not take into regard the different temperaments of the dream seer.

---

[97] Written by Hafiz Hulusi Effendi, the chief *mudarris* of Bayezid Mosque, the epistle was printed in 1305 (AH) in Istanbul.

The science of objective dream interpretation is, in contrast, exclusive to the elite (*khawass*) and always needs the assistance of spiritual insight (*kashf*), as distinguishing a divinely (*rahmani*) dream from a devilish (*shaytani*) requires Divine inspiration. Moreover, since human beings drastically differ from one another in temperament, even the same dream seen by two different people may carry different meanings. Appreciating this subtlety demands a spiritual command.

This calls to mind how two people had once come to Ibn Sirin, telling him that they had both dreamt that they were offering a sermon on the pulpit. Ibn Sirin told one of them that he would be undertaking pilgrimage and the other that he would be hanged. Both interpretations were soon realized.

Aisha –Allah be well-pleased with her- explains:

"I had once dreamt of three moons falling into my room. I recounted it to my father Abu Bakr –Allah be well-pleased with him-. He kept silent and did not give me an answer. Only when the Messenger of Allah –upon him blessings and peace- passed away and was buried in my room, did he say, 'There…the first and the best of the three moons you had dreamt about!'" (Muwatta, Janaiz, 30)

When the *Muhajirun* arrived in Medina, lots were drawn to nominate their brothers from among the *Ansar*. Othman ibn Mazun –Allah be well-pleased with him- fell to the family of Ummu'l-Ala al-Ansariyya –Allah be well-pleased with her-. They immediately took him and lodged him at their home. A short time later, however, he was struck down by an illness. The family saw to his treatment but to no avail, as he passed away not long after. Ummu'l-Ala then saw Othman –Allah be well-pleased with him- in her dream where he had a flowing tap. She immediately explained her dream to the Blessed Prophet –upon him blessings and peace-, who said:

"That is his deeds, flowing for him." (Bukhari, Tabir, 13, Janaiz, 3, Shahadat, 30, Manaqibu'l-Ansar, 46)

Another woman had come to the Prophet –upon him blessings and peace- for him to interpret her dream in which the central pillar of her home broke and fell in front of her. The Blessed Prophet –upon him blessings and peace- asked the lady whether or not she was married, and if she was mar-

ried, where her husband was. The lady told him that her husband had gone out on a journey but still had not returned. The Prophet –upon him blessings and peace- thereupon informed her that her husband would soon return safe and sound and they would rejoice over it. The dream was realized exactly as it was interpreted.

The woman saw the same dream again, while her husband happened to be on journey, during the caliphate of Abu Bakr –Allah be well-pleased with him-. This time, she went to the Caliph to have her dream interpreted. Like the Blessed Prophet –upon him blessings and peace- before him, the Siddiq –Allah be well-pleased with him- inquired the lady for some information about her husband. He afterwards told her that her husband had died on the road.

Confused and in panic, the woman said, "The Messenger of Allah –upon him blessings and peace- had interpreted the same dream as referring to my husband's safe return!"

"True", replied he. "That was the insight he was given and this is what I am inspired with." It was not long before the news of her husband's death reached Medina.

Correctly interpreting dreams is an extremely difficult and even impossible undertaking without a spiritual command, in that the dream-world presents things and states of extraordinary nature, illusory, obscure and almost illegible.

The Almighty declares in the Quran how He had endowed Yusuf –upon him peace- with expertise in this science.[98] While in prison, Yusuf –upon him peace- had listened to a baker and a former cupbearer of the palace tell him their dreams. The baker explained to him how he had dreamt of carrying a tray full of bread on his head when a flock of flying birds closed in and ate all the bread. Yusuf –upon him peace- informed the baker that he would end up being hanged and that a flock birds would pick away at his head. The cupbearer, on the other hand, told Yusuf –upon him peace- that in his dream he was serving the king as cupbearer, like before, which the Prophet interpreted as signaling his "return to the palace as cupbearer." These insights were soon realized in the exact manner foretold.

---

98 See al-Yusuf, 6-111.

As has been mentioned above, the science of dream interpretation is based chiefly on spiritual insight (*kashf*). For this reason, the interpreter must possess a spiritual ranking. It was said that the late Celaleddin Ökten, who I had the good fortune to study under during my years at Istanbul Imam Hatip Lise (High School), used to exert great expertise in interpreting dreams. He would mention that dreams could only be interpreted with a lucid and spiritual heart and that the accuracy of an interpretation always depended upon the piety of the interpreter.

During his youth, Celaleddin Ökten –may Allah have mercy on him- used to teach courses on religion at high schools; leading a pious life with a spirited heart. It was during those years he became famous with his accurate dream interpreting. After giving some examples of his experiences in interpreting dreams, he would go on to lament:

"Then came a time when the curtains came down…as courses on religion were abolished by the state and I was appointed a teacher of philosophy. And once I began swimming in the murky sea of reason-engendered philosophical theories, the springs of my heart all dried up."

Another renowned case of a truthful dream is as follows:

Imam Busiri, the poet behind the famous Qasidah-i Burda, one day came across a spiritually enlightened old man while on his way home.

"Busiri!" the old man called out to him. "Did you see the Messenger of Allah –upon him blessings and peace- in your dream last night?"

"No, I did not", replied Busiri. The old man parted ways without saying another word. But his question had ignited the fiery love and affection the Imam had in his heart for the Blessed Prophet –upon him blessings and peace-.

That night, however, the Imam did see the Blessed Prophet –upon him blessings and peace- in his dream. When he woke up, he felt an inexpressible joy and peace take over his heart. Thereafter, he began writing many poems paying homage to the Blessed Prophet –upon him blessings and peace-, a read of which would throw many devotees of the Prophet into the ocean of his love.

But a short time later, he became hemiplegic; he lost sensation in one half of his body. No longer able to walk, he could not even move a finger without a struggle. It was then that he wrote the celebrated Qasidah-i Burda,

Marifatullah and Divine Awards

through which he sought a healing from the Lord. The night he completed the qasidah, he saw a dream, where he read to the Blessed Prophet -upon him blessings and peace- what he had written; and happy to hear the poem, the Blessed Prophet -upon him blessings and peace- stroked the part of his body that was paralyzed. It must have been some love, as upon waking up, Imam Busiri saw that he was fully cured, on which he offered his deep thanks to Allah, glory unto Him.

While walking to the mosque for the fajr prayer that morning, elated to be cured, he came across Sheikh Abu'r-Raja -may Allah sanctify his secret- who asked to him to recite the qasidah in which he praises the Best of Creation -upon him blessings and peace- .

"I have many poems like that. Which one are you asking for?" inquired Imam Busiri.

"The one you read to in the presence of the Messenger of Allah", said Sheikh Abu'r-Raja. "I noticed he was greatly delighted to hear it."

Knowing very well that nobody had yet heard the qasidah, Imam Busiri was stunned.[99]

There are many cases in the Islamic world where many secrets pertaining to the realm of the unseen (*ghayb*) are exposed to the righteous, be it through spiritual insight, foresight, inspiration or truthful dreams. But then again, there stands the immutable Divine declaration that:

"Say: No one in the heavens and the earth knows the unseen but Allah" (an-Naml, 65). This, then, calls for a few explanatory words.

In actual fact, the core of this explanation is comprised in the *hadith al-qudsi*, "…and when I love him, I (virtually) become his tongue that speaks, heart that comprehends, ears that hear, eyes that see, hands that hold and feet that walk…" (Bukhari, Riqaq, 38) The center of spiritual insight and inspiration is the spirit the Lord has breathed into man. The eyes placed on the head may seem to be the medium only of external vision; but facing the 'divine light' placed in those eyes, the curtains of the unseen may become dysfunctional, to the degree the Almighty allows. In such a case, it is again the Almighty who is exposing the unseen; man has otherwise no

---

[99] See, Ilhan Armutçuoğlu, Kaside- Bürde Manzum Tercümesi, p. 7-10.

power to see, hear or know what remains behind the curtain. Only through the grace of Allah, glory unto Him, and His informing does man know end up knowing what was previously hidden.

The Almighty indeed reveals in the Quran that He does reveal certain information concerning the unseen: "This is of the declaration relating to the unseen which We reveal to you…" (Al-i Imran, 44)

With that said, the unseen is of two kinds: the absolutely unseen and the relatively unseen.

The unseen, which can be known to no other than the Lord, is referred to as the absolutely unseen. Knowing something of it has nothing to do with one's personal aptitude. What can ever be known of it may only be through the informing of the Lord. So an insight into the absolutely unseen is only as much as the Lord allows.

The relatively unseen, on the other hand, are things known by some and unknown by others. For example, only a person himself, and nobody else, may know how much money he has in his pocket. Certain facts which may be unseen and therefore unknown to some may be simple knowledge for others.

The unseen spoken of here in relation to the saintly servants of the Lord is the unseen in the absolute sense. And anything known thereof is known only to the degree the Almighty allows.

No matter how accurately they may foresee and pass judgment on certain events before they happen, true saints never make a public claim to possessing a command of spiritual insight and foresight. There are such men, staring at whose faces remind one instantly of the Lord. Pearls of wisdom spill forth from their tongues. They do not speak, as it were, but are rather made to speak. Still, they are humble in the face of the blessings of the Lord, certain that man is a weak and may easily give in to conceit and transgress his limits. The feeling of self-importance is, without a doubt, the greatest danger. When this danger becomes a lively threat, the Almighty may give one the taste of helplessness in order to warn him.

Spiritual foresight, insight and truthful dreams are really nothing but Lord gracing His righteous servants by virtue of inspiring them with unseen realities.

CHAPTER FOUR

Some Questions Concerning Sufism

A- MEDIATION (*TAWASSUL*)
B- SEEKING SPIRITUAL BLESSINGS (*TABARRUK*)
C- VISITING GRAVES

الا بذكر الله تطمئن القلوب

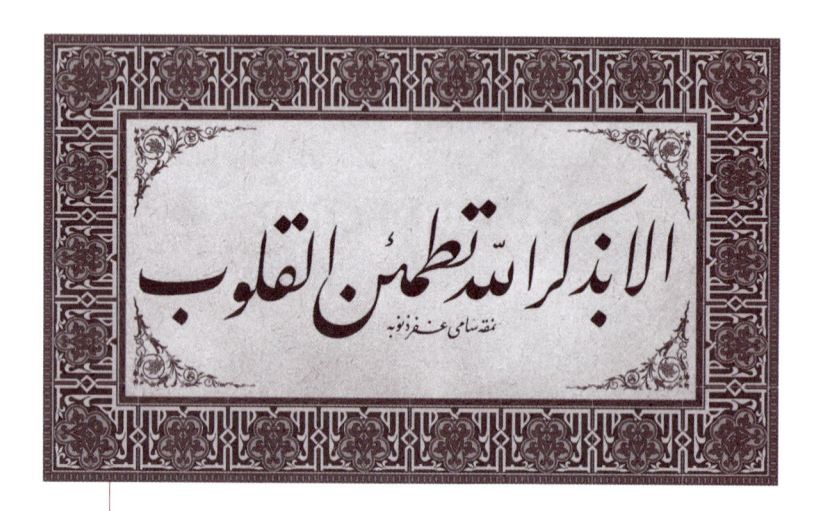

"…Now surely by Allah's remembrance are the hearts set at rest." (ar-Rad, 28)

Some Questions Concerning Sufism

O you who believe! Be careful of your duty to Allah and seek means of nearness to Him!
(al-Maidah, 35)

A. MEDIATION (*TAWASSUL*)

Every path and vehicle that delivers the servant to the essential purpose of his existence is considered a means (*wasilah*). To mediate, or to seek *tawassul*, is the act of seizing these means to gain closeness to the Almighty. More specifically, it is to ask something from the Lord through the mediation of His Beautiful Names, the Quran, righteous deeds, prophets and saints, with the hope of increasing the likelihood of the acceptance of what is asked, to seek His refuge and aid in acquiring something desired or repelling something unwanted.

The 35th verse of al-Maidah states:

يَآ اَيُّهَا الَّذِينَ اٰمَنُوا اتَّقُوا اللّٰهَ وَ ابْتَغُوا اِلَيْهِ الْوَسِيلَةَ

"O you who believe! Be careful of your duty to Allah and seek means of nearness to Him!"

The term *wasilah* is mentioned in the absolute sense; that is to say, without any limitations. Thus, the means one is required to search for in gaining closeness to the Lord are righteous deeds like ritual prayer, fasting and striving in His path (*jihad*). Some exegetes have also added that coming under the training of a *murshid* with the aim of embodying the moral conduct of the Blessed Prophet –upon him blessings and peace- is likewise a means.

The manner in which saints and scholars direct one to the path of the Lord is not priestly. It serves only to enlighten and to warn. They are like guides directing travelers on a beaten track. Catholicism, in contrast, has priesthood, according to which the priest serves as a necessary means between man and God. Islam rejects this; that is to say, between the Lord and man, a third person is unthinkable. One may personally and immediately turn to the Lord at any given moment and worship Him.

Be that as it may, some objections have been voiced concerning the role of the *murshid*, supposing that he, like a priest, comes in between the Lord and the disciple progressing on the spiritual path. But it must be remembered in the clergy, one is unable to do one's duties of servanthood to the Lord without the intervention of a priest. This is a misconception wrought by the corruption of Christianity. The role carried out by scholars and saints therefore can never be compared to that of the clergy.

Related criticisms are therefore improper and irrelevant, and are caused by bringing to the fore the literal meaning of the term *tawassul*. This overlooks the true nature of mediation. In any case, such criticisms are generally raised by those outside the Sufi milieu, unable to understand the mindsets of the true *murshid-i kamil*. This prejudice is sometimes caused by the improper behavior of certain members of Sufi sects with a failure to properly internalize the methods of Sufism. Still, this cannot serve as an excuse. Just as it is unthinkable to criticize an entire movement based on the shortcomings and, at times, malicious intentions of a few of its members, it is equally wrong to ascribe personal faults to the movement itself. It is moreover illogical to attribute the personal mistakes of a few to the sublime values they claim to represent. No person of sound mind, for instance, could hold Islam responsible for the mistakes of Muslims.

As indicated above, true *murshid*s offer guidance on the paths of spirituality, similar to that carried out by scholars in exoteric sciences. This is not to come in between the Lord and His servant. It simply consists of the *murshid* using his experience and expertise to warn the aspirant on the way to the Lord and throw light on the path, ensuring he passes the obstacles safe and sound, free of danger. Just as the vehicle we chose to take on a journey is not an end but only a means, a spiritual guide is a teacher who trains the heart of a disciple and adorns it with the morals of

Some Questions Concerning Sufism

Allah, glory unto Him, and His Messenger. If able, many a disciple makes swift progress on the spiritual path to the point of even leaving behind his master, who had opened up new horizons for him in the beginning; as is the case with Shams Tabrizi and Mawlana Rumi -may Allah sanctify his secret-, when compared externally.[100]

So regardless of his importance and value, a *murshid* is never an end, but only a means.

In a sense, seeking means is to adopt a *murshid-i kamil*, which means none other than a mature and experienced believer, as a guide, to seek his support in passing unscathed the fine roads on which one may otherwise easily lose his footing and to make the most of the inspiring supervision he provides. In yet another sense, to seek means is for one to disclose his desire to the Lord and ask for its acceptance for the sake of those whom the Lord loves; it is thus an effort to ensure the prayer is thereby accepted. Otherwise, it is not to ascribe sacredness to the righteous servants of Allah, glory unto Him.

"Adopt the Messenger of Allah –upon him blessings and peace- in your prayers", says Imam Malik –may Allah have mercy on him-.

Similar are the words of Imam Jazari -May Allah sanctify his secret-: "Adopt prophets and the righteous as means to have your prayers granted."

In his *Shifau's-Saqam*, Imam Subki writes:

"Mediating through the Noble Prophet –upon him blessings and peace- is permissible under all circumstances. Adopting the Prophet as means was possible before he was even created and afterwards during his life, just the same. The same goes right now following his passage from Earth while he is in *Barzakh*, as it will be when he is resurrected on the Plain of Judgment and in Paradise."

Ibn Abbas –Allah be well-pleased with him- recounts:

---

[100] Shams Tabrizi, who discovered the spiritual ocean hidden in Rumi's spirit, was virtually like a flame, long awaited, to set alight a sea of petrol. That was what his duty and authority consisted of. Once he did set that sea alight, he met such a raging spiritual explosion that even he became trapped amid its roaring flames.

Sufism: A Path Towards the Internalization of Faith (Ihsân)

"There was an ongoing war between the Jews of Khaybar and the tribe of Ghatafan, where the Jews were always routed. In the end they prayed, 'Lord…we ask for victory in the name of the Unlettered Prophet whom You have promised will appear near the Final Hour'. After this, they decisively defeated Ghatafan. Yet, once Allah, glory unto Him, did make appear the Messenger of Allah –upon him blessings and peace- who they had used as means in their prayer, the Jews rejected his prophethood and the book revealed to him. Thereupon Allah the Almighty proclaimed:

$$\text{وَكَانُوا مِنْ قَبْلُ يَسْتَفْتِحُونَ عَلَى الَّذِينَ كَفَرُوا}$$

$$\text{فَلَمَّا جَاءَهُمْ مَا عَرَفُوا كَفَرُوا بِهِ فَلَعْنَةُ اللهِ عَلَى الْكَافِرِينَ}$$

'And when there came to them a Book from Allah verifying that which they have, and aforetime they used to pray for victory against those who disbelieve, but when there came to them (Prophet) that which they did not recognize, they disbelieved in him; so Allah's curse is on the unbelievers.'"
(al-Baqara, 89) (Qurtubi, II, 27; Wahidi, *Asbabu'n-Nuzul*, p. 31)

Medina was struck by a severe famine following the passing away of the Blessed Prophet –upon him blessings and peace-. The locals sought the opinion of Aisha –Allah be well-pleased with her-, who advised them that they should "…open up a hole in the ceiling above the grave of the Messenger of Allah –upon him blessings and peace- so that nothing stands between him and the skies."

They did just that. They were soon inundated with heavy rain. Medina was covered in green and camels became fleshier than ever. The year came to be known as *Amu'l-Fatk*, the Year of Abundance. (Darimi, Muqaddimah, 15)

There was a man who would frequently go to Othman ibn Affan –Allah be well-pleased with him- to ask him to take care of what needs he would have; only to have Othman –Allah be well-pleased with him- all but ignore him. The man later came across Ibn Hunayf –Allah be well-pleased with him- and complained over the situation, but he was told to:

"Take ablution and offer two rakat of salat at the mosque and then say the following in your prayer:

'O Allah…I am asking from You and turning to You in the name of our Messenger Muhammad –upon him blessings and peace-, the Prophet of Mercy. O Muhammad! I am turning to Your Lord with you…Take care of my need!' And then mention what it is that you want."

The man did exactly as he was told and appeared before the door of Othman ibn Affan –Allah be well-pleased with him- once again. The doorkeeper took him by the hand to Othman, who had him seated on the cushion next to him.

"What do you need?" he then asked the man. The man told him what he needed. His wish was granted immediately. As he was leaving, Othman –Allah be well-pleased with him- said:

"Why did you not tell us all this time that you were in need? Come to us, should you need anything else in the future!"

The man decided to go to Ibn Hunayf to thank him. On seeing him, he appreciatively said, "May Allah reward you with the best! He took little notice of me before I spoke to you!"

"I assure you by Allah", said Ibn Hunayf, "that what I advised you with was not my personal opinion. It is based on what I had witnessed once. A blind man once arrived next to the Messenger of Allah -upon him blessings and peace- and pleaded, 'Pray to Allah to take this blindness away from my eyes. Life is difficult for a blind man!'

'Keep patient, if you wish…that will be better for you', counseled the Beloved Messenger –upon him blessings and peace-.

'I have nobody to hold me by the hand, Messenger of Allah, and take me where I want to go', he replied. 'And this puts me under great duress. Please…Pray that I am cured!' The Messenger of Allah –upon him blessings and peace- then told him to:

'Go, take ablution and offer two rakat of ritual prayer. Then pray: O Allah! I am asking from You and turning to You in the name of Muhammad, Your Messenger, the Prophet of Mercy. O Muhammad! I am turning to Your Lord with you…My Allah! Allow him to intercede for me!'" (Tirmidhi, Daawat, 118; Ahmed ibn Hanbal, Musnad, IV, 138).

According to the narration of Hakim, by the time he completed his prayer, he was no longer blind. (Hakim, Mustadrak, I, 707-708)

Utbah ibn Ghazwan –Allah be well-pleased with him- reports the following words from the Blessed Prophet –upon him blessings and peace-:

"Should any one of you lose something in a place where there is nobody around or is left with no other option than to ask for help, call out' Servants of Allah…help me ;'!for Allah has servants you cannot see". (Haythami, Majmau'z-Zawaid, X, 132; Imam Nawawi, al-Adhkar, 201)

Imam Nawawi, who narrates the above, adds his own personal experience:

"The man from who I took this *hadith* told me that he had undergone a similar encounter and testified that acting in line with the Prophet's –upon him blessings and peace- advice was sure to acquire the desired result. I was somewhat astounded. Some time after, a camel belonging to this man next to me had fled. Though it was within reach, it would gallop every time someone drew near. I thereupon recounted this *hadith* to him. And then, for no observable reason, the camel came to a complete standstill, allowing its owner to freely grab its bridles."

On the report of Ibn Abbas –Allah be well-pleased with him-, the Noble Messenger –upon him blessings and peace- has said:

"Apart from the guardian (*hafazah*) angels, Allah the Almighty has certain angels on Earth who record everything, to each falling leaf. Should anyone of you face a difficult situation in the desert or somewhere else, call out « عِينُونِى عِبَادَ اللّٰهِ Servants of Allah…help me '"!(Haythami, Majmau'z-Zawaid, X, 132)

It has also been reported that during his own prayers, the Blessed Prophet –upon him blessings and peace- would often say: "For the sake of Your Prophet and the prophets before me…" (Haythami, Majmau'z-Zawaid, X, 132)

In another *hadith*, the Blessed Prophet –upon him blessings and peace- explains:

Some Questions Concerning Sufism

'"Lord...I ask Your forgiveness for the sake of Muhammad!' pleaded Adam –upon him peace- after realizing his error for committing the blunder that led to his expulsion from Paradise.

Then Allah, glory unto Him, asked:

'How do you know Muhammad when I have not yet created him?'[101]

'When You created me,' said Adam –upon him peace- 'and breathed into me from Your Spirit, I looked up and saw the words La ilaha ill'Allah Muhammadun Rasulullah inscribed above the pillars of the Throne. I knew there and then that You would only mention the most beloved of all creation next to Your Name.' Thereupon Allah, glory unto Him, declared:

'You have spoken the truth, Adam! Surely, he is the most beloved for Me of all creation! So implore me for his sake; and since you have, I hereby forgive you. Had Muhammad not been, you would not have been created!'
(Hakim, Mustadrak, II, 672)

On another note, according to the manners of prayer advised by Islam, all prayers begin and end with thanking Allah, glory unto Him, and saluting the Blessed Prophet –upon him blessings and peace-. A salutation (*salawat*) of the Prophet –upon him blessings and peace- is a prayer made to the Lord on his behalf. There is an established conviction that Allah, glory unto Him, never turns down a *salawat'us-sharifah*, which, in essence, is a prayer and plea to the Almighty; the precise reason as to why prayers are adorned with it, both in the start and in the end. That is to say, squeezing in personal prayers amid two, whose acceptances are highly expected, is to ensure their acceptance as well.

---

101 Existing alone in pre-eternity, the Almighty created the *masiwa*; that is everything other than Him, as He wished to be known by man and *jinn* to the degree of their capacities. The first to be created was the Muhammedan Light. It is for this reason that the Blessed Prophet –upon him blessings and peace- says. "I was a prophet when Adem was still between spirit and body." (Tirmidhi, Manaqib, 1). In contrast to the fact that the Muhammedan Light, meaning the essence of the Blessed Prophet –upon him blessings peace-, was the first to be created, his appearance on Earth in the shroud of a body, marks the final link in the prophetic chain. The 'not yet created Muhammad' referred to above, therefore implies the physical 'self' of the Prophet and not his essence, the Muhammedan Light.

Indeed, the Noble Prophet –upon him blessings and peace- one day happened to see a man who, after ritual prayer, was praying without expressing thanks to Allah, glory unto Him, and sending blessings to His Messenger.

"The man rushed it", the Prophet –upon him blessings and peace- then said, before calling him over to give advice:

"Upon wishing to make a prayer, one should first thank and praise Allah and send blessings to His Prophet…and then afterward continue in whichever manner desired." (Tirmidhi, Da'awat, 64/3477)

Asking for the acceptance of a prayer for the sake of the honor of prophets, saints and the righteous servants of the Lord have in Divine Sight, to emotionally turn to and plead the Lord by resorting to them as means, is one of the most effective ways in attracting Divine Mercy and ensuring that the prayer is accepted. But a prayer is made to Allah, glory unto Him, alone. In seeking the mediation of the beloved servants of the Lord, one must therefore be careful not to refer their needs personally to them, but to the Almighty alone. Mentioning the beloved servants of the Lord in a prayer is only a method utilized to have a prayer, made exclusively to the Lord, accepted.

Mediating through persons of virtue, in actual fact, is nothing but seeking their righteous deeds and praiseworthy traits as means. After all, it is these deeds and traits that have rendered them precious in the sight of the Lord to begin with.

Thus, even the Blessed Prophet –upon him blessings and peace- himself use to mediate through the poor persons among the *Muhajirun* when praying for aid or victory,[102] and would say: "Bring to me your weak; for it is only for the sake of your weak that you are nourished and aided." (Abu Dawud, Jihad, 70; Ahmed ibn Hanbal, Musnad, V, 198)

It is certain that seeking, as means, these brokenhearted but righteous people, who rest content with the riches of their hearts despite not having a presence or a financial power that would yield them a social standing, would render a prayer worthier of acceptance.

---

102 See, Bukhari, Jihad, 76; Tabarani, Mujamu'l-Kabir, I, 292.

Some Questions Concerning Sufism

With regard to seeking the dejected and brokenhearted as means in attaining to the pleasure of the Lord, the following parable of Malik ibn Dinar is deeply meaningful:

"*Whilst praying to the Almighty, Musa –upon him peace- asked, 'Where should I search for You, o Lord?'*

'*Search for Me next to the brokenhearted*' answered He. (Abu Nuaym, Hilyah, II, 364)

Anas –Allah be well-pleased with him- reports that during the severe drought that struck during his caliphate, Omar –Allah be well-pleased with him- took the Prophet's uncle Abbas –Allah be well-pleased with him- by his side and sought him as means while praying the Lord for a downpour of rain, pleading:

"My Lord…We use to seek our Prophet as means and You used to give us rain! Now, we are seeking the uncle of our Prophet as means. Give us rain!" The downpour soon came and the locals found their much needed water. (Bukhari, Istisqa, 3)

Another report depicts Omar –Allah be well-pleased with him- as shedding tears whilst humbly and emotionally pleading:

"My Allah…Both the cloud and the water is by Your side. Send the cloud and shower us in rain!" Shortly after the prayer, clouds of mercy began to cluster from all sides and hover above, releasing a massive rain. In response to this Divine blessing, Omar –Allah be well-pleased with him- addressed the crowd with the following:

"People! The Messenger of Allah –upon him blessings and peace- used to love and respect his uncle Abbas like a father and would consider an oath made by his uncle as if it was an oath made by himself. So people! Uphold the respect the Messenger of Allah –upon him blessings and peace- had for his uncle…Adopt him as means in praying to Allah to repel what troubles you may encounter!" (Hakim, Mustadrak, III, 377)

There is a further narration reported by Ibn Abdilbarr, which throws further light on the issue:

"Omar went outside with Abbas –Allah be well-pleased with them- by his side and prayed, 'O Allah…We are seeking Your closeness (taqarrub) *through the uncle of our Prophet and we wish for him to intercede (istishfa). Watch over him for the sake of Your Messenger, just as you watched over the two orphans for the sake of their parents' virtue and goodness.[103] We have come to You having repented and seeking intercession!' Turning towards the people who were present, he then recited the following from the Quran:*

'Then I said, Ask forgiveness of your Lord, surely He is the most Forgiving. He will send down upon you the cloud, pouring down abundance of rain. And help you with wealth and sons, and make for you gardens, and make for you rivers.' (Nuh, 10-12)

Abbas –Allah be well-pleased with him- then also stood up and prayed. Tears were flowing freely from both his eyes, like a gushing spring. Once the long-awaited rain did fall, the public began patting him, remarking, 'Congratulations to the cupbearer (saqi) of the Sacred House!' (Ibn Abdilbarr, Istiab, II, 814-815)

The above incident serves as a clear evidence of a Companion seeking means through another Companion. But this has led some to argue that mediating through a righteous person is possible only as long as the person is alive and that seeking means through him after his death is impermissible. But restricting mediation through the Blessed Prophet –upon him blessings and peace- only to his life on Earth alone is merely a subjective opinion that does not reflect the truth of the matter. The words of Omar –Allah be well-pleased with him- where he suggests, in his prayer, how they used to seek mediation through the Prophet –upon him blessings and peace-, incorporates the periods both before his passing away and after. In any case, the sole reason as to why they nominated Abbas –Allah be well-pleased with him- as means was nothing other than that he was the uncle of the Blessed Prophet –upon him blessings and peace-. Simpler put, because it is this kindred with the Prophet that underlies their motiva-

---

103 Omar –Allah be well-pleased with him- is referring to the Quranic verse where Khidr explains to Musa –upon them peace- the reason as to why he repaired an almost derelict wall: "And as for the wall, it belonged to two orphan boys in the city, and there was beneath it a treasure belonging to them, and their father was a righteous man; so your Lord desired that they should attain their maturity and take out their treasure, a mercy from your Lord, and I did not do it of my own accord. This is the significance of that with which you could not have patience. " (al-Kahf, 82)

tion for choosing Abbas, the means sought is actually that of the Blessed Prophet –upon him blessings and peace- himself. The same applies for some great saints; adopting them as means even after their death is possible and at times demanded.[104]

One of the most glaring examples of this is as follows:

It was common for scholars and people to visit the grave of the great Imam Abu Hanifah, seek him as means, a practice they found to be of benefit. One of them was Imam Shafii, who later said:

"On feeling in need for something, I would offer two *rakat* of ritual prayer. Then I would pay the grave of Abu Hanifah a visit, where I would pray to Allah the Almighty. And through his abundance, my need would be taken care of."[105]

Also serving as means for salvation, on the other hand, are righteous deeds. In a *hadith*, the Blessed Prophet –upon him blessings and peace- recounts past the ordeal of three journeymen:

"Three friends, who were caught in the rain during their journey, entered a cave in order to spend the night. But then a large rock toppled down the mountain and blocked the entrance. One of them suggested, 'We have no other choice than to pray to Allah through our righteous deeds; none other than Allah can rescue us from here.'

The first used his caring service to his parents as means. The rock moved slightly, yet not enough to provide a passage out. The second offered his fear of Allah, purity and virtue as means. The rock shifted a little more though the gap was still not wide enough. Then the third prayed to Allah using his observance of the rights of others as means. The rock thereupon moved completely out of the way and they were able to make their way out."[106]

Another influential factor in having a prayer acknowledged and accepted are the beautiful names of Allah, glory unto Him. It is therefore common to pray to the Lord, by the means of repetitiously mentioning the Divine Names.

---

104   For more detail on the subject, see, Zekeriya Güler, "*Vesile ve Tevessül Hadislerinin Kaynak Değeri*", ILAM Academic Journal, v. II, n. 1, p. 83-132.
105   al-Haytami, al-Khayratu'l-Hisan, p. 94.
106   See, Bukhari, Adab 5, Anbiya 53, Dhikr, 100.

The Quran declares:

"And Allah's are the best names, therefore call on Him thereby…" (al-Araf, 180)

In relation, Aisha –Allah be well-pleased with her- narrates that the Blessed Prophet –upon him blessings and peace- used to pray with the following words: "My Allah…I implore You for the sake of Your Name that is pure, pleasant, sacred and most adorable to You! It is that Name to which You respond when a prayer is made with it, give when something is wanted, provide Your mercy when needed and offer a way out, a breadth, when help is sought through that Name."

In what follows, the Prophet –upon him blessings and peace- asked Aisha –Allah be well-pleased with her-:

"Did you know, Aisha, that Allah had taught me the name of His which is always responded to when a prayer is made with it?"

"May my parents be ransomed for you, Messenger of Allah! Please, teach me that name", she insisted, on which the Blessed Prophet –upon him blessings and peace- said:

"You ought not to be taught that name!" Aisha –Allah be well-pleased with her- then moved away and sat by herself for a while. She returned a few moments later; and kissing the Blessed Prophet –upon him blessings and peace- on the forehead, repeated:

"Please, Messenger of Allah…Teach me that name!"

"I should not be teaching you that name, Aisha, for it would be inappropriate for you to pray for something worldly through it!" Aisha –Allah be well-pleased with her- explains what unfolded afterwards:

"I then got up and taking ablution, I offered two rakat of prayer. Afterwards, I prayed to Allah the Almighty as follows: 'My Lord…I refer and pray to you as Allah…as the Merciful (ar-Rahman), the Compassionate (ar-Rahim), the Good (al-Barr). I hereby call onto You with all the names I know and I do not know. I pray to You to forgive me and show mercy!' When I completed my prayer, the Messenger of Allah –upon him blessings and peace- smiled and said:

'You most definitely mentioned that name in your prayer!'" *(Ibn Majah, Dua, 9)*

Anas ibn Malik –Allah be well-pleased with him- recounts the following:

"The Messenger of Allah –upon him blessings and peace- once heard a man pray, 'My Allah…Praise is to You alone! There is no god but You! You are One, without any partners! You are the Benefactor (al-Mannan). You are the Creator of the heavens and earth (al-Badi'). You have Glory and Honor…' The man then followed up by stating what he wanted in his prayer. The Messenger of Allah –upon him blessings and peace- thereupon said:

'By Allah, the man asked with the Greatest Name of the Lord. Such is that Name that Allah gives whatever is wanted through it and responds to a prayer made with it." *(Ibn Majah, Dua, 9; Nasai, Sahw, 58)*

It is therefore clear that seeking means through the beautiful names of the Divine is part of the *Sunnah* of the Prophet –upon him blessings and peace-.

Some scholars have states that there is essentially no difference in meaning between the Sufi terms *tawassul, istianah, istighathah, istishfa, tashaffu, tawajjuh* and *tabarruk*, which, in terms of content, denote seeking aid.[107] They express the desire for spiritual help (*himmah*) from saints, who possess a spiritual command, both in their presence and in absentia. Asking for *himmah* from a righteous servant of the Lord believed to be in possession of spiritual command, is to ask him to act as means (*wasilah*) on the path towards attaining to the ultimate purpose. And this attainment is brought about through his prayers and spiritual attention.

The word *himmah*, denoting spiritual aid, is generally used in reference to the help provided by the saintly servants of Allah, glory unto Him. Used to express the aid of the Lord, in contrast, are the terms *nusrah* and *tawfiq*, which mean Divine help and assistance.

---

107 See, Subki, *Shifau's-Saqam fi Ziyarati Khayri'l-Anam*, p. 133-134.

Sufism: A Path Towards the Internalization of Faith (Ihsân)

Essentially, it is only Allah, glory unto Him, who can help. It would therefore be unbecoming to consider seeking means in prayers as asking the aid of someone else. It is only the Real who is called for help throughout.

The Quran is clear-cut on the matter:

$$وَمَا النَّصْرُ اِلاَّ مِنْ عِنْدِ اللّٰهِ$$

"…and there is no help except from Allah" (al-Anfal, 10)

"If Allah assists you, then there is none that can overcome you, and if He forsakes you, who is there then that can assist you after Him? And on Allah should the believers rely." (Al-i Imran, 160)

Abdullah ibn Abbas –Allah be well-pleased with him- remembers the following advice given him by the Blessed Prophet –upon him blessings and peace- one day as he was riding behind him on his saddle:

"Let me teach you a few words, my dear. Observe Allah (His commands and prohibitions) so that He observes and protects you. Make the pleasure of Allah a priority in all your affairs so that You find Him in front of you. If you are to ask for something, ask it from Allah. If you are to seek aid, seek the aid of Him. And know that even if entire humankind was to gather to obtain something of benefit to you, they can only obtain that which is predestined for you by Allah. Again, if entire humankind was to convene to harm you, they may only inflict as much harm as predestined for you by Allah." (Tirmidhi, Qiyamah, 59)

Since all Muslims embrace this reality as it is, they continually repeat it in the al-Fatiha which they recite in every *rakah* of their ritual prayers:

$$اِيَّاكَ نَعْبُدُ وَاِيَّاكَ نَسْتَعِينُ$$

"You alone we worship and You alone we ask for help."

Indeed, concerning the Divine aid the Blessed Prophet –upon him blessings and peace- was given during the Battle of Badr, the Almighty revealed, "…and you threw not when you threw but Allah threw" (al-Anfal, 17); that is, the real and the absolute doer and provider of all spiritual aid and grace is the Lord alone.

Some Questions Concerning Sufism

The sincere prayers made by some Muslims, motivated with the desire to gain closeness to the Lord without any intention of *shirk* of *kufr* whatsoever, which involves the anticipation of the spiritual aid of the righteous, is underlain by nothing but a hope of receiving Divine mercy, which mentioning the righteous is hoped to bring. In a sense, this is to bring about a spiritual atmosphere that would yield an abundance and inspiration spiritual. Everything occurs with the permission of the Lord; and the Lord alone. The person, through whom a spiritual aid is sought, is not an absolute doer and it is the Almighty alone who essentially provides the aid sought.

Asking directly from the righteous in absentia or during a visit of their graves and calling unto them by saying, "So-and-so! Cure me! Take care of this need of mine", which some people tend to do, is extremely wrong and can open the door to *shirk*. Although some interpretations can no doubt be given to mitigate these statements, one must nonetheless categorically refrain from uttering them, in order not to harm the utterly delicate core of the belief in the Oneness of Allah, glory unto Him. Expressions alike which leave an impression that beings other than the Almighty, may possess absolute disposal in clearing troubles and governing the universe.[108]

---

[108] Those who have stated that such expressions can be used, have suggested that each of these expressions is to be regarded as rational simile (*majaz-i aqli*), a type of speech in the science of rhetorics. A rational simile is when an action is referred not to the real doer and agent of the action in question but to its visible cause as perceived in space and time. A striking example of the use of a rational simile in the Quran figures in the verse, "And when the earth throws up her burdens" (az-Zilzal, 2), where the act of 'throwing out her burdens' is ascribed to the space, or the Earth, in which this action is to take place, and to the Almighty, the real agent, in spite of Him being the One throwing the burdens out of Earth. Still, the reference is really to the Almighty, albeit in an indirect manner.

Sufis, therefore, affirm and believe that the person through whom they are seeking means is not the real doer, who, in reality, can only be the Lord; and it is only the Lord whose aid they seek. They agree that any opinion contrary to this would be tantamount to brazen *shirk*.

In relation, Muhammad Abu Zahra says:

"The words of ordinary and naïve Muslims must be interpreted according to the nearest meanings they signify. Instead of downright prohibiting them from visiting the grave of the Prophet –upon him blessings and peace-, it would be better to instruct them. Explaining and informing them is preferable to indicting them with *shirk*. There is not a shadow of doubt that Allah the Almighty will preserve *tawhid* until the

Respect shown to the loving memory of the Blessed Prophet –upon him blessings and peace- comes from the strength of the bond of love and affection felt for him.

B. SEEKING SPIRITUAL BLESSINGS (*TABARRUK*)

Tabarruk is to ask from one's abundance for blessings. It is the attainment of spiritual benefit and inspiration through the means of something else.

Seeking Spiritual Blessings from Leftover Food

Consuming the leftover foods of saints has been a means utilized to lay oneself open to spiritual disposal. Contrary to what some think, this is not an unauthentic (*bidah*) practice. Literature on *hadith* and Muslim history attest to many cases of this practice during the life of the Blessed Prophet –upon him blessings and peace-.

In various times and places and, in particular, during the Hudaybiyah Campaign, the Companions sought spiritual benefit from the hallowed leftovers of the Prophet –upon him blessings and peace-.

Jabir -Allah be well-pleased with him- recounts:

Final Hour. In his final days, the Prophet –upon him blessings and peace- gave believers the glad tidings that the Devil has forever lost hope of being worshipped, once again, in these lands. Ibn Taymiyya may therefore rest at ease regarding the well-being of *tawhid*." (Abu Zahra, *Ibnu Taymiyya*, p. 326).

'*Meded ya Rasulallah*' (help, o Prophet), a phrase often repeated in Islamic literature, is a request made to the Blessed Prophet –upon him blessings and peace- in hope of receiving his intercession in the Hereafter. Considering this as *shirk*, as some do, is unwarranted, as each believer readily believes that even the intercession of the Prophet –upon him blessings and peace- may take place only with the permission of Allah, glory unto Him.

"*People were worn out by thirst on the Day of Hudaybiyah, so they came to the Messenger of Allah, who, at the time, had a water container made of leather in front of him. He had just taken ablution when people moved closer toward him.*

'What is bothering you?' asked the Messenger of Allah.

'We have no water left to drink and to take ablution except the little amount in front of us', they explained.

The Prophet of Allah placed his hands inside the container. At the instant, water then began to spring forth from between his fingers; it was exactly like a jetting spring. We all drank and took ablution from it."

"*How many were there of you that day?*" *Jabir -Allah be well-pleased with him- was asked.*

"*Had we been a hundred-thousand, the water would still have been enough; but at the time, we were one-thousand-five-hundred all together.*"
(Bukhari, Manaqib, 25)

Without a doubt, the water that flowed from the fingers of the Noble Messenger –upon him blessings and peace- is better and more curative than the *zamzam*, since it flowed directly from the sacred hands of the Prophet –upon him blessings and peace-.

According to many a *hadith*, upon drinking from a container full of milk, the Blesssed Prophet –upon him blessings and peace- would offer the remaining milk to the Companions nearby, initiating a transfer of spiritual inspiration, a benefit that would reflect equally onto the milk, which would not decrease even a bit.

Sahl ibn Sad –Allah be well-pleased with him- testifies:

"*The Messenger of Allah –upon him blessings and peace- was once offered a cup of beverage. He drank some of it. To his right, there was a child while to his left were some elderly Companions. Elegant and courteous as ever, he turned to the child and asked:*

'*Would you allow me to offer this drink to your elders first?*'

But the intelligent child gave an astounding response. 'Messenger of Allah', he said, 'I can never think of passing the share you have given me to anyone else!'

The Messenger of Allah –upon him blessings and peace- thereupon handed the cup to the child." (Bukhari, Ashribah, 19)

Asma bint Abu Bakr –Allah be well-pleased with her- explains:

"While pregnant with Abdullah ibn Zubayr, I had set out to migrate next to the Messenger of Allah –upon him blessings and peace-. On reaching Medina, I stopped over near Quba, where I gave birth. I eventually arrived next to the Messenger –upon him blessings and peace-, with my baby. He took the baby in his arms and asked for a piece of date. After slightly chewing the date, he placed it in Abdullah's mouth. This was the first morsel Abdullah ever consumed. The Prophet –upon him blessings and peace- then prayed for abundance (barakah) on the baby's behalf."[109]

Whilst they had the Noble Messenger -upon him blessings and peace- as guest, Abu Ayyub al-Ansari and his family would offer him from the meals they prepared. When the leftover food was returned, Abu Ayyub would search for the parts of the food which the Messenger of Allah -upon him blessings and peace- had touched, specifically eating from those parts for *tabarruk*. (Muslim, Ashribah, 170-171)

Jabir –Allah be well-pleased with him- recounts a memory of the difficult times prior to the Battle of Handak while they were digging trenches:

"While digging trenches in the days preceding the Battle of Handak, we were thwarted by a rather hard rock. A few Companions went to the Messenger of Allah and told him they had come upon a hard rock they were unable to break.

'I will go down in to the trenches myself' the Messenger of Allah told them. He then got up. He had a stone tied to his belly from hunger. It had been three days since we had eaten anything. The Messenger of Allah -upon him blessings and peace- grabbed hold of the pickaxe and struck a blow at the rock, which then shattered, turning into something like a sand dune.

---

109 See, Bukhari, Aqiqah, 1.

'Allow me to go home, Messenger of Allah', I asked afterwards. Given permission, I went home and told my wife of seeing '...the Messenger of Allah in an exhausted condition. Do we have something to eat?'

'Some barley and a kid', she said.

So I slaughtered the kid and served the barley. We placed the meat in a pot. Just as the bread was nearly baked and the pot was beginning to boil on the rocks on which it was placed, I rushed to the Messenger of Allah and said:

'I have some food, Messenger of Allah. Please, honor us with a couple of other persons...'

'How much food is there?' he asked. I told him what we had. He then said, 'Good and plenty...Tell your wife not to take the pot away from the fire and keep the bread in the furnace until I arrive!'

Then turning to his Companions he called out, raising his voice, 'People of the trenches; come...Jabir has prepared a feast for us!' Everyone present made a move.

Anxious, I ran home to my wife and said, 'Look what has happened now...The Messenger of Allah is coming with the entire Ansar, Muhajirun and others alike!'

'Did the Messenger of Allah ask how much food there was?' she asked.

'Yes' responded I.

'Then not to worry', she said calmly, 'for he knows more than you!'

They arrived a short while after. The Messenger of Allah -upon him blessings and peace- told them to enter without cramming each other. The Companions entered in tens. The Messenger of Allah -upon him blessings and peace- then began splitting a loaf of bread, putting some meat on it and giving it to each of the awaiting Companions; and each time he would close the lid of both the pot and the furnace once he was done. Until each and every Companion, around a thousand all together, ate to their hearts content, the Prophet -upon him blessings and peace- repeated the same procedure. There was even some food left over in the end. Then turning to my *wife, he said, 'Eat this and offer some to your neighbors, too; for hunger has really devastated everyone!'* (Bukhari, Maghazi, 29; Muslim, Ashribah, 141)

Below is another narration:

On the return from the Campaign of Taif, the Blessed Prophet –upon him blessings and peace- reached Jiranah, lying on the road from Mecca to Medina. There, he gave Abu Musa al-Ashari and Bilal –Allah be well-pleased with them- a container filled with water, some of which he had used, and told them to:

"Drink from this water and splatter it on your faces and chests. Glad tidings if you do". They took the water and did as they were advised. Behind a curtain, Umm Salamah –Allah be well-pleased with her-, the wife of the Prophet, then called out to them, saying:

"Offer some of that water to your mother, too". The two Companions then presented some of it to the noble Umm Salamah. (Bukhari, Maghazi, 56)

Seeking Blessings through Belongings

It is an incontestable fact that a personal item, which evokes memories a loved one, intensifies the love felt, by imparting feelings of reminiscence. This is part of human nature. Yet, it is also historically proven that over-indulging in these feelings can lead all the way to idolatry.[110] At the same time, it is a natural tendency to be fond of a personal item belonging to a loved one. However, the important thing is not to go overboard.

The most vivid example mentioned in the Quran of a spiritual impression on a personal item is Yusuf's –upon him peace- shirt. When dispatched from Egypt to be taken to Yaqub –upon him peace-, despite

---

[110] In fact, what is referred to as fetishism in the history of religions, which is the deviant practice of worshipping and ascribing a divine status to the personal items left behind by deceased heroes, is a historical depravity born from an excess of this natural tendency. Since it is diffuclt to grasp abstract realities, many have resorted to identifying the abstract Creator with tangible entities; and this has lead to the deviation that is idolatry. With that said, abstract realities do exert a spiritual manifestation on the tangible. The correct approach for those with clarity of judgment is to grasp these spiritual reflections and patterns impressed on physical entitites, in a way that leads the mind from the effect to the cause. Such is how Allah, glory unto Him, is known; and so is spirit. The same applies for all abstract truths.

being in Canaan, Yaqub –upon him peace- was able to smell its scent; and once he rubbed the shirt on to this blinded eyes, he regained his sight.[111]

This spiritual influence brought through a personal item therefore serves the *murshid* with a mean to keep the disciple firm upon an ideal spiritual blend. Internalizing these reflections only strengthens the spiritual bond. At the same time, this is an expression of Prophet's –upon him blessings and peace- encouraging of Muslims to give presents to one another.

Whilst in the Banu Saidah quarters with his Companions, the Blessed Prophet –upon him blessings and peace- asked Sahl ibn Sad –Allah be well-pleased with him- for a cup of water. Judging by the testimony below of Abu Hazim –Allah be well-pleased with him- Sahl must have held onto and cherished that cup for the rest of his life:

"Sahl took out the cup and showed it to us; and we drank water from it. Omar ibn Abdulaziz later insisted Sahl to give the cup to him as present. And he did." (Bukhari, Ashribah, 30)

Sahl ibn Sad –Allah be well-pleased with him- recounts:

"A woman once brought the Messenger of Allah –upon him blessings and peace- a mantle, telling him of her wish to give it to him as present. The Prophet –upon him blessings and peace- accepted her present and wore the mantle. But then a Companion said:

'What a beautiful mantle, Messenger of Allah. Can I have it?'

'Certainly', replied the Messenger –upon him blessings and peace-, as he presented the mantle to the Companion. After the Messenger of Allah –upon him blessings and peace- left, the other Companions scolded the man.

'That was not right what you did', they said. 'The Messenger of Allah accepted the mantle only because he was in need of one. And then you asked for it, knowing that the Messenger of Allah never withholds anything that is asked from him.'

'I only wanted to reap its spiritual blessings (tabarruk) because the Messenger of Allah –upon him blessings and peace- had worn it', explained the

---
111   See, Yusuf, 93-96.

man. 'And I am hoping that it will serve as my shroud when I die.'" *(Bukhari, Adab, 39)*

Aisha –Allah be well-pleased with her- narrates:

"There was nothing more pleasant to Quraysh than sleeping on a sarir. On arriving at Medina and temporarily settling in the house of Abu Ayyub, the Messenger of Allah –upon him blessings and peace- asked him if they had one. It turned out that he did not.

Hearing about this, Asad ibn Zurarah of the Ansar sent the Messenger of Allah –upon him blessings and peace- a straw-covered sarir made from oak and weaved with linen.

The Messenger of Allah –upon him blessings and peace- used the sarir for the duration of his stay at the house of Abu Ayyub and after he moved to his own chamber by the Masjid. After his passing away, he was washed and shrouded on this serir, on which he lay, as the Companions offered his funeral prayer.

People used to personally ask to borrow the sarir to carry their dead and thereby seek its spiritual blessings. The corpses of both Abu Bakr and Omar –Allah be well-pleased with them- were carried on the very same sarir to their graves. (Balazuri, Ansabu'l-Ashraf, I, 525)

A similar incident is as follows:

Abu Hurayrah –Allah be well-pleased with him-, the Companion to have narrated the most number of ahadith, used to remain by the side of the Blessed Prophet –upon him blessings and peace-, observing his every action and behavior. One day, he complained to the Prophet –upon him blessings and peace- of not being able to remember most of what he would utter, despite committing them to his memory upon hearing them.

"Lay down your cloak", the Blessed Prophet –upon him blessings and peace- then said to him, before praying for him and making a hand gesture as if he was collecting some things with his palms and throwing them into the laid out cloak.

"Pick up your cloak", he then said. Afterwards, Abu Hurayrah –Allah be well-pleased with him- was granted such a strength of memory that he no longer forgot what he heard. (Tirmidhi, Manaqib, 46)

Some Questions Concerning Sufism

A Companion by the name of Firas also wanted to own a personal item belonging to the Blessed Prophet –upon him blessings and peace-. On one occasion, he saw the Blessed Prophet –upon him blessings and peace- eating from a plate in front of him; so he decided to ask to have that plate as present. Never one to refuse the request of anyone, the Blessed Prophet –upon him blessings and peace- presented the plate to Firas.

Omar –Allah be well-pleased with him- would occasionally go to Firas' house and ask him to bring '…that sacred plate'. Then filling the plate once touched by the blessed hands of the Prophet –upon him blessings and peace- with zamzam, he would drink from it, splattering the remainder of the water on his face. (Ibn Hajar, al-Isabah, III, 202)

Recounting what follows in Abu Juhafah –Allah be well-pleased with him-:

In the midday heat, the Messenger of Allah –upon him blessings and peace- went out to Bathah, where he took ablution, and offered the prayers of *zuhr* and *asr* in two *rakat*. Pinned to the ground in front of him was a short spear. People all around suddenly rose to their feet and began holding the hands of the Prophet –upon him blessings and peace- and wiping their faces with them. I, too, took hold of one of his hands and placed it against my face; and lo and behold, his hand was cooler than snow and more beautifully scented than musk. (Bukhari, Manaqib, 23)

In his recounting of the Prophet's –upon him blessings and peace- Anas ibn Malik -Allah be well-pleased with him- recaps how the Companions vied with each other to get hold of the strands of his hair, in hope of attaining the spiritual blessings thereof:

"After stoning the devils, the Messenger of Allah -upon him blessings and peace- slaughtered his sacrifice and had his hair cut. The barber held his lock of hair on the right and cut it. The Messenger of Allah -upon him blessings and peace- called Abu Talha and gave him that lock. The barber then held the hair on his left side. 'Cut', the Messenger of Allah -upon him blessings and peace- told him; and he did. He also gave that to Abu Talha, telling him to 'Distribute it among people!'" (Muslim, Hajj, 323-326)

Anas –Allah be well-pleased with him- testifies to how the Companions were rushing around the Blessed Prophet –upon him blessings and peace- as he was getting a haircut, to make sure that not a single strand of hair fell to the ground without it being picked up by someone. (Muslim, Fadail, 75)

Indeed, the Companions sought spiritual blessings not only through the strands of hair belonging to the Blessed Prophet –upon him blessings and peace- but also through his personal items. They carried this excitement even during the heated moment of war. One of the most splendid examples of this mindset is provided by Khalid ibn Walid –Allah be well-pleased with him-, who kept a few strands of the Prophet's –upon him blessings and peace- in his *imamah* as spiritual memento.

It is reported that as the fringes of the Prophet's -upon him blessings and peace- hair were being cut, Khalid ibn Walid -Allah be well-pleased with him- insisted he be their recipient. "Please give those to me, Messenger of Allah", he pleaded. "Do not prefer anyone else above me in this regard... may my parents be ransomed for you!"[112]

Upon receiving the Blessed Prophet's -upon him blessings and peace- fringes he had desperately wished for, he rubbed them over his eyes and placed them in the front of his cap beneath his imamah. Thereafter, he never encountered an enemy force he did not ultimately vanquish. "Wherever I directed them towards", Khalid -Allah be well-pleased with him- later said, "that place was ultimately taken!"[113] *(Waqidi, III, 1108; Ibn Athir, Usd'ul-Ghabah, II, 111)*

---

112 In the meantime, Abu Bakr -Allah be well-pleased with him- was looking on in amazement, comparing Khalid's -Allah be well-pleased with him- misdemeanors at Uhud, Handak and Hudaybiyah to what he had become now. (Ibn Saad, II, 174)

113 Hikmet Atan testifies to a recent, similar instance of the blessings provided through the Blessed Prophet's -upon him blessings and peace- hair and beard:
"In 1983, I heard Ali Yücel Efendi explain the following incident. 'It was during my time as imam at Suluova Central Mosque, when another imam from one of the neighboring villages came to me and said, 'Something just happened of which I could make little sense', he said as he began explaining to me the following.
"Recently, some people from a village close to the village where I am imam came to me with a fair number of books. 'Our father has just passed away', they said, 'and he has left us these. But we cannot read them. You are a scholar; only you can benefit from these books around here. So we thought we would give them you as present'. So I took the books and went home. I then sat in front of the stove, which was burning at full blast, and began to examine the books. Inside them were some letters and enveloped belonging to the deceased imam. They were personal, I thought, and decided to gather them and throw them all into the stove burning ferociously in front of me.

Some Questions Concerning Sufism

At one stage during the fierce Battle of Yamamah, Khalid –Allah be well-pleased with him- lost his imamah. He then ordered his soldiers to find it. Despite searching the battlefield, they could not locate the imamah. So Khalid –Allah be well-pleased with him- reissued the order. After a grueling search, they eventually found the imamah, old and worn out, much to their surprise. They could hardly make sense of their commander's insistence on finding something seemingly worthless. Sensing their disbelief, Khalid –Allah be well-pleased with him- explained:

"The Messenger of Allah –upon him blessings and peace- had his hair cut and the Companions were scrambling for the strands. I, too, managed to get hold of a few strands, which I placed inside this imamah. This brought me such blessings that I never fought a war wearing it that I did not eventually win. The secret of my victories is nothing other than my love for the Messenger of Allah –upon him blessings and peace-." (Haythami, Majmau'z-Zawaid, IX, 349)

Such occurrences, which took place right before the Companions' very own eyes, are further proofs that matter can be spiritually and emotionally infiltrated. The key is to possess an awake heart that is able to receive the inspiration radiating forth from that spiritual reflection, on the condition, of course, that one does not resort to extremities.

The righteous predecessors –may Allah have mercy on them- continued the Companions' practice of seeking spiritual blessings. Below are just a few examples:

Ibn Sirin says:

"I once informed Ubaydah of having in my custody 'a strand of the Prophet's –upon him blessings and peace- hair, inherited to us from either

---

But as soon as I did, the stove suddenly went 'tissss' and was put out. Horrified, I ran outside. Only later did I find enough courage to enter back inside the house."

"So I told the *hodja*", continues Ali Efendi, "that there was a strand of the beard of the Blessed Prophet -upon him blessings and peace- inside one of those envelopes".

After a while, I saw the *hodja* once again, who straightaway asked me, "How did you know that there was a strand of the beard of the Blessed Prophet -upon him blessings and peace- inside one of those envelopes? The people that gave the books came again later on and said, 'We were unaware at the time but it turns out there is a strand of the beard of the Blessed Prophet -upon him blessings and peace- inside the envelopes. Could we have it back?'"

Anas' mother or family.' With great excitement, he said: 'By Allah, to have a single strand of his hair is dearer to me than the entire world and what's within.'" (Bukhari, Wudu, 33)

Abdullah, the son of Ahmed ibn Hanbal, recounts:

"My father used to take hold of a strand of the Prophet's –upon him blessings and peace- hair, place it against his lips and kiss it. And at times, he would place it above his eyelids. There were also times when he would dip the hair in a cup of water and then drink the water; and through its spiritual blessings, he would ask Allah for a cure of what illness he may have been suffering from at the time. I also remember a time when he took the cup used by the Messenger of Allah –upon him blessing and peace- and washed it in a bucket, from which he later drank. With the intention of receiving a cure, he would likewise drink *zamzam* and run the water across his hands and face." (Dhahabi, Siyari Alami'n-Nubalam Beirut, 1986-1988, XI, 212)

The same Abdullah once asked his father Ibn Hanbal whether it was permissible to touch the knob of the Prophet's –upon him blessings and peace- pulpit (as he used to rest against it whilst giving a sermon) and the Prophet's Chamber, hoping for spiritual blessings.

"I see no harm in that", was the reply. (Dhahabi, Siyar, XI, 212)

Qadi Iyad testifies that "Ibn Omar –Allah be well-pleased with him- was seen rubbing his face against the spot on the pulpit upon which the Messenger of Allah –upon him blessings and peace- used to sit."[114]

The following incident reported to have taken place between Imam Ahmed ibn Hanbal and Imam Shafii –may Allah have mercy on them- serves as another wonderful example. Recounting it is Rabi ibn Sulayman, a student of Imam Shafii.

"Imam Shafii one day handed me a letter, telling me to deliver it to Ahmed ibn Hanbal and to return with the reply. So, I took the letter and headed out to Baghdad. I met with the Imam at fajr prayer and offered the prayer behind him. Afterwards, once the Imam made his way out of the mihrab, I presented him the letter, saying:

'This is a letter sent from Egypt from your brother Imam Shafii.'

---

114 Qadi Iyad, Shifa, II, 47, 71; Ibn Taymiyyah, Majmuu'l-Fatawa, I, 230.

'Do you know what is written?' he asked.

'No', I replied. The Imam then unsealed the envelope and began reading the letter. He was suddenly overcome with tears.

'What does the letter say?' I asked curiously.

'He says that in his dream', he began explaining, 'he saw the Messenger of Allah –upon him blessings and peace- who told him to '...write a letter to Ahmed ibn Hanbal and send him my greetings; and tell him that he will be subjected to a great tribulation where he will be asked to claim that the Quran is created. Tell him not to give in to this demand, at any cost. Allah will honor his name and make it live on until the Final Hour."

'What great news that is for you', I commented. Delighted, the Imam then removed his shirt and gave it to me; and after receiving his shirt as a reply to the letter, I returned to Egypt. When I presented the shirt to Imam Shafii, he said:

'I would hardly wish to upset you by taking this shirt away from you. But perhaps you could dip the shirt into some water and give that water to me so we could share its spiritual blessings (barakah)'"[115]

The strands of the Prophet's –upon him blessings and peace- beard, reverentially kept and protected in the pulpits of various mosques around the world, act as mercy for entire Muslims, like a refreshing wind that has persistently blown from his time to ours. Respecting the loving memory of the Blessed Prophet –upon him blessings and peace-, in turn, only strengthens the bond of love and devotion for him in the heart. Many a loyal devotee of the Blessed Prophet –upon him blessings and peace- has made the most of the spiritual blessings offered by these mementos.

The splendor of the Ottomans, which lasted over six centuries and has never been matched by any Muslim state, essentially stemmed for its deep respect to matters spiritual. As the spiritual causes underlying the legendary Ottoman magnificence one can recall, among others, the famous incident where Osman Gazi kept awake all night, supposing it would be disrespectful to put his feet up in a room in which there was a copy of the Quran, and the time when Sultan Selim reverentially brought

---

[115] See, Ibnu'l-Jawzi, Manaqibu'l-Imam Ahmed ibn Hanbal, p. 609-610.

the Sacred Trusts of the Blessed Prophet –upon him blessings and peace- to Istanbul and designated forty *huffaz* to incessantly recite the Quran by their side, day and night, a practice that would continue uninterrupted until the fall of the Empire.

The fact that the Sacred Trusts, including the mantle of the Blessed Prophet –upon him blessings and peace-, are today accessible for Muslims who wish to see them, provides an added means of spiritual blessings for the entire Muslim world.

I had forbidden you from visiting graves. But now you may, for visiting graves will remind you of the Hereafter. (Tirmidhi, Janaiz, 60; Muslim, Janaiz, 106)

Graveyards are schools of wisdom and grave visiting offers the most effective training in the art of contemplating death.

C. VISITING GRAVES

In his journey through life, man quivers amid two incredibly opposing poles: the joy of living and the fear of dying. Without comprehending the true natures of the ever-flowing life and death, there can be no understanding of the true nature of man and the mysterious secret behind his creation.

Human comprehension, stuck between the twofold riddle of 'coming to the world and exiting the world', must raise itself to a proper and real judgment regarding the world and regulate all behavior accordingly. Only then will it be rescue itself from the deceitful shadows of the worldly life and embark upon a spiritual journey towards the real world.

For a believer, death is a pathway for reuniting with the Lord and a joyous, wonderful and desirable transition from one state to another. For a nonbeliever and a perverse, death is a painful and humiliating demise, a storm of punishment that blows right from the pits of Hellfire.

The most vital wisdom for man begins at the point he solves the riddle lying underneath the earth. The mysterious realm of the land of the dead does not disclose its secrets, unless man's ideas, efforts, search, depth of heart and spiritual sensing centers on the inevitable reality of death.

Undoubtedly, man has two important advisers in life. One speaks, while the other remains silent. The vocal adviser is the Quran. And that, which gives advice through its deep silence, is death. It was due to this fact that Muslims, throughout history, established graveyards in town centers, by roads and in the courtyards of mosques, to give the living enough opportunity to benefit from the silent advices of death. The preferred choice of greenery was the evergreen and durable cypress, to act as symbols of the Hereafter; symbols of a never-ending life.

Death has no known language; yet what profound meanings are buried in its perplexing silence! Graveyards are now the abodes of mothers, father, children, lovers, friends and kindred, who have taken up residence therein, after exhausting their time on Earth.

Concerning the realm of the grave, whose nature will be shaped according to out stringency in following the commands of the Lord, the Blessed Prophet –upon him blessings and peace- says:

"The grave is either a garden of Paradise or a ditch of Hellfire." (Tirmidhi, Qiyamat, 26) This indicates the tight relationship between the deeds of life and the experiences of after-death.

Whilst standing next to a grave, Othman –Allah be well-pleased with him- would cry until his tears would leave his beard soaked. Someone once said to him, "You do not cry when you remember Heaven and Hell; yet you bawl your eyes out when with a single thought of the grave!"

"That is because' he replied 'I heard the Messenger of Allah –upon him blessings and peace- say, 'The grave is the first station of the Hereafter. If one is able to pass it, the rest is easier. If not, the rest is even more difficult and intense. Nothing I witnessed was more dreadful and terrifying than the grave!'" (Tirmidhi, Zuhd, 5/2308; Ahmed, I, 63-64)

Aisha –Allah be well-pleased with her- reports that one day a Jewish woman came to her and said to her, after speaking awhile about the punishment of the grave, "May Allah protect you from its ordeal!"

Thereupon, Aisha –Allah be well-pleased with her- asked the Blessed Prophet –upon him blessings and peace- about the punishment of the grave.

"Yes", he said. "The punishment of the grave is a fact."

"After that day, I never saw the Messenger of Allah –upon him blessings and peace- offer a ritual prayer without seeking refuge from the punishment of the grave", Aisha –Allah be well-pleased with her- would later state. (Bukhari, Janaiz, 87; Muslim, Masajid, 123)

Bara –Allah be well-pleased with him- recounts:

"We were with the Messenger of Allah –upon him blessings and peace- during a funeral. Sitting by the grave, he began crying so much that it dampened the soil underneath. He then said, 'Brothers…Prepare well for what (death) will inevitably come to all of us!'" (Ibn Majah, Zuhd, 19)

To be sure, graveyards are schools of wisdom and lesson and grave visiting offers the most effective training in the contemplation of death. As an act of loyalty, the Blessed Prophet –upon him blessings and peace- would frequently visit the graves of his Companions to have passed away before him and pray for their eternal well-being.

On visiting the graves of the martyrs of Uhud, he would say, "Peace to you in return to what you have kept patient with! How beautiful, for you, is the land of the Hereafter!" (Tabari, Jamiu'l-Bayan, XIII, 186; Ibn Kathir, Tafsir, II, 529)

Likewise, he would visit the Baqi Cemetery, time and again; after greeting the deceased, he would state: "Peace to you, dwellers of the land of believers! Allah-willing, we, too, shall reunite with you. I ask Allah the Almighty for well-being and peace on behalf of you and us." (Muslim, Janaiz, 104)

In fact, while asleep in Aisha's chamber one midnight, the Blessed Prophet –upon him blessings and peace- was delivered by Jibril –upon him peace- a Divine command: the Almighty was ordering him to visit the Baqi Cemetery and pray for those buried there. So, the Prophet –upon him blessings and peace- quietly got up, making little noise in order not to awaken the sleeping Aisha –Allah be well-pleased with her-. But she had not yet fallen asleep; and curious as to where the Prophet –upon him blessings and peace- was headed at such late a time in the night, she decided to secretly follow him. Seeing the Blessed Prophet –upon him blessings and peace- enter the cemetery and shed tears for the eternal well-being of the believers buried therein, the previous suspicion of Aisha soon turned to embarrassment. She stood there for a while, watching the Blessed Prophet's –upon him blessings and peace- emotional pleading from a distance. She then ran back to her chamber and snuggled under the quilt, acting as if she had been sleeping all along. Yet hearing her gasping for breath from all that running, the Blessed Prophet –upon him blessings and peace- understood what had just happened, and lamented:

"Were you afraid that Allah and His Messenger would wrong you?" (Muslim, Janaiz, 103) In saying this, he was also indicating that his conduct was under the constant surveillance of the Almighty.

The below account is provided by Muadh ibn Jabal –Allah be well-pleased with him-:

"Sending me off to Yemen as governor, the Messenger of Allah –upon him blessings and peace- accompanied me to the outskirts of Medina to say farewell to me. I was astride my mount and he was walking by my side. After giving me some advice, he said:

'Who knows, Muadh, you might not be able to see me again after this year. But perhaps you will visit my Masjid over there and my grave…'

Hearing those words, coupled with the grief of his separation, reduced me to tears.

'Do not cry', consoled the Messenger of Allah –upon him blessings and peace-. Then turning his gaze toward Medina, he said:

'Closest to me among people are the pious who, wherever they are, uphold their piety for Allah.'" (Ahmad, V, 235; Haythami, IX, 22)

Dawud ibn Abi Salih explains:

"Marwan once saw a man who had placed his face against the gravestone of the Prophet –upon him blessings and peace-. Holding the man by the scruff of his neck, he roared, 'What do you think you are doing?'

The man looked back; and it just happened that he was none other than Abu Ayyub al-Ansari –Allah be well-pleased with him-. Staring at Marwan, the illustrious Companion said:

"I know exactly what I am doing. I have come to visit the Messenger of Allah –upon him blessings and peace-, not a stone. I once heard the Messenger of Allah –upon him blessings and peace- say, 'Do not fear over the fate of religion when the competent undertake its duties. But when the incompetent begin to see to the affairs of religion, no anxiety felt or tears shed can ever be enough!" (Ahmed ibn Hanbal, V, 422)

Above is a case of Companion brushing his face against the Blessed Prophet's –upon him blessings and peace- gravestone during his visit.

Not only did the Prophet –upon him blessings and peace- visit graves on a frequent basis, he also encouraged his Companions and entire Muslims to do the same:

"I had forbidden you from visiting graves. But now you may, for visiting graves will remind you of the Hereafter." (Tirmidhi, Janaiz, 60; Muslim, Janaiz, 106)[116]

Grave visiting provides a lesson for the visitor and a means of mercy for the deceased; for a buried corpse pleas for help, like a person who has fallen abruptly into quicksand.

Ibn Abbas –Allah be well-pleased with him- narrates:

"Passing by two graves, the Messenger of Allah –upon him blessings and peace- once said, regarding them, 'They are both being punished but not over a major sin. One is punished for sowing discord and the other for not duly protecting himself from his urine while urinating.' He subsequently asked for a green date branch. Severing it into two, he then placed them one by one on each grave, adding, 'It is hoped that their punishment will be lessened, so long as they do not dry out.' (Muslim, Taharat, 111)

Qurtubi, the exegete, interprets the above as:

"The expression 'so long as they do not dry out' alludes to the fact that the branches glorify the Lord, for the duration they remain green. Scholars have thus commented that planting trees on graves and reciting the Quran thereby, provides benefit for the deceased buried therein. If even planting a tree alleviates the punishment of the dead, who knows how much he will benefit from a recitation of the Quran? The deceased receive the rewards of whatever deed dedicated to them." (Qurtubi, Tafsir, X, 267)

---

116 During the period of Ignorance, people used to boast with their dead, supposing that they had acquired a sacred status, and would visit their graves in this mindset. In order to eradicate this superstition, the Blessed Prophet –upon him blessings and peace- had at first banned grave visiting. Yet, once the remnants of this superstition no longer existed, he lifted the ban, specifically encouraging it for the purpose of contemplating death.

Sufism: A Path Towards the Internalization of Faith (Ihsân)

Reciting, especially, chapter Yasin is a method common to and practiced by all, in allowing the deceased to benefit from the Divine mercy that is brought about by a read of the Quran. The *hadith* indeed states:

"Yasin is the heart of the Quran. If one is to read it solely for the pleasure of Allah and with a desire for the Hereafter, he will sure have his sins forgiven. Recite Yasin unto your dead." (Ahmed ibn Hanbal, Musnad, V, 26)

"Once someone from among you passes away, take him to his grave without too much delay. And once you have buried him, let one person recite al-Fatiha beside his head and last part (the final two verses) of al-Baqara beside his feet." (Tabarani, al-Mucamu'l-Kabir, XII, 340; Daylami, Musnad, I, 284; Haythami, Majmau'z-Zawaid, III, 44)

Ala ibn al-Lajlaj reports that before his father Lajlaj, a Companion, passed away, he left the following will:

"When you place me in the grave, say *Bismillah wa ala sunnati Rasulillah*[117] and shovel earth on me. Beside my head, recite the opening and final part of al-Baqara. I have personally witnessed the fondness of Abdullah ibn Omar with this practice." (Bayhaki, as-Sunanu'l-Kubra, IV, 56)

Noteworthy are the final wishes of Companion Amr ibn As –Allah be well-pleased with him-:

"Once you place me inside the grave, wait by my side for a time that takes to slaughter a camel and cut apart its meat, so that your presence heartens me to get accustomed to my new life and that I can prepare the answers I am to give to the messengers of my Lord." (Muslim, Iman, 192)

Imam Nawawi, who cites the above in his book, further narrates the following from Imam Shafii –may Allah have mercy on him-:

"Reading from the Quran by the grave side is recommended (*mustahab*). But reciting the Quran entire is better." (Nawawi, Riyadu's-Salihin, 293)

The Blessed Prophet –upon him blessings and peace- says, as reported by Ibn Abbas –Allah be well-pleased with him-:

---

[117] In the name of Allah, glory unto Him, and upon the *sunnah* of the Messenger of Allah –upon him blessings and peace-.

"The dead in the grave is like a person on the brink of being drowned at sea, terrified and gasping for help. He anticipates a prayer from his father, mother, siblings and intimate, loyal friends. An incoming prayer is dearer to him than the entire world and what is within. Allah doubtless gives mountain-like rewards to grave dwellers, through the blessings of the prayers of the living. The best present the living can ever send to the dead is to pray for their forgiveness and give charity on their behalf." (Daylami, Musnad, IV, 103/6323; Ali al-Muttaqi, XV, 694/42783; XV, 749/42971)

It is reported from Othman ibn Affan –Allah be well-pleased with him- that immediately following a burial, the Blessed Prophet –upon him blessings and peace- would wait by the side of the grave and say:

"Pray for the forgiveness of your brother and plea Allah to allow him to correctly answer the questions he is posed with in the grave…for he is being interrogated at this moment." (Abu Dawud, Janaiz, 67-69/3221)

Jabir ibn Abdullah –Allah be well-pleased with him- recounts:

"When Saad ibn Muadh –Allah be well-pleased with him passed away-, we went with the Messenger of Allah –upon him blessings and peace- to offer our final duties. After leading his funeral salat and burying Saad in his grave, the Messenger of Allah -upon him blessings and peace- continued reciting tasbihat for a while; and so did we. Then the Prophet of Allah -upon him blessings and peace- pronounced a takbir.

'Why, Messenger of Allah, did you recite some tasbih and then a takbir?' some Companions then asked.

'Until Allah gave it breadth, the grave squeezed and further squeezed this righteous servant", replied he.'" (Ahmad ibn Hanbal, III, 360)

Ibn Abbas –Allah be well-pleased with him- narrates:

"The day Saad was buried, the Messenger of Allah –upon him blessings and peace- said, whilst standing by his grave:

"Had there been a person immune to the trial of the grave", the Blessed Prophet -upon him blessings and peace- then continued, "it would surely have been Saad. But the grave squeezed even him until Allah gave it breadth." (Tabarani, Mujam'ul-Kaabir, X, 334)

As can be understood from all the above, visiting graves, praying for the forgiveness of the dead buried therein, doing charitable work in their name and reciting Quran unto them act as a means of mercy for the deceased. In the Quran, the Almighty commands us to pray, in the following, for believers who have migrated to the eternal realm before us:

"Our Lord! Forgive us and those of our brethren who had precedence of us in faith, and do not allow any spite to remain in our hearts towards those who believe! Our Lord, surely You are Kind, Merciful" (al-Hashr, 10)

But while visiting a grave, it is vital is to refrain from certain false and innovated (*bidah*) practices. Even though Muslim scholars have said and written copiously to protect Muslims from indulging in excessive and deficient behavior during grave visiting, both kinds of unwanted behavior have, unfortunately, prevailed to this day.

Refining grave visiting from excessive and deficient behavior, a matter that confuses the minds of those with a shallow knowledge of religion, is a difficult undertaking. Human incompetence of grasping abstract realities has turned the nature of grave visiting into something of a *shirk*, at least according to some; like lighting candles by and tying rags around the graves and seeking aid directly from the person lying therein. This is a manifestation of a defect, similar to how Christians ascribe divinity to Jesus –upon him peace-, simply due to their incompetence in appreciating an abstract concept of God. A stark contrast of this excessive behavior, on the other hand, has seen the emergence of a deficient approach, which takes the protestation far enough to downright equate grave visiting with *shirk*.

Reminiscent of its approach in all other issues, Islam embodies the principle of moderation with regard to grave visiting. As was mentioned above, the verbal and applied standard of grave visiting set by the Prophet –upon him blessings and peace- and followed by the Companions clearly illustrates the proper approach to be adopted in visiting graves, without falling into either excess or deficiency.

Ibn Abbas –Allah be well-pleased with him- explains:

"Saad ibn Ubadah –Allah be well-pleased with him-, whose mother had passed away only recently, came to the Messenger of Allah –upon him blessings and peace- and asked:

'My mother died, Messenger of Allah, at a time when I happened to be away. Will it benefit her if I were to give charity in her name?' And when the Messenger of Allah –upon him blessings and peace- answered 'Yes', Saad said:

'Then bear witness, Messenger of Allah, that I am offering my fruit garden as charity in the name of my mother.'" (Bukhari, Wasaya, 15)

Abdurrahman ibn Abi Amra reports that her mother had vowed to set a slave free overnight but had postponed it until morning. However, she did not make it to daybreak and passed away. So he approached Qasim ibn Muhammad and asked whether it would benefit her mother if he was to set a slave free in her name. Qasim thereupon said:

"Saad ibn Ubadah had approached the Messenger of Allah –upon him blessings and peace- and asked, 'My mother has just passed away. Would it be to her benefit if I were to set a slave free in her name?' to which the Messenger of Allah –upon him blessings and peace- replied, 'Yes'". (Muwattaa, Itq, 13)

Abdurrahman, the son of Abu Bakr –Allah be well-pleased with him-, had suddenly died in his sleep. Aisha –Allah be well-pleased with her- gave away lots of charity on her deceased brother's behalf. (Muwattaa, Itq, 13)

Ibn Abbas –Allah be well-pleased with him- explains:

"A man once came to the Messenger of Allah –upon him blessings and peace- and inquired, 'My mother has passed away, Messenger of Allah, with a month of fasting overdue. Should I fast on her behalf?'

'If your mother owed a debt', said the Messenger of Allah –upon him blessings and peace- 'would you not have covered the debt in her name?'

'I would have', replied he, whereupon the Messenger of Allah –upon him blessings and peace- said:

'Allah is more deserving to have His debt paid off'" (Muslim, Siyam, 155)

Another narration of the same event reports the Blessed Prophet –upon him blessings and peace- as asking, "Had your mother owed a debt and you had paid it off, will that have been valid?" With the man agreeing that it would have, the Blessed Prophet –upon him blessings and peace- stated, "Then fast to compensate for your mother". (Muslim, Siyam, 156)

The Noble Messenger –upon him blessings and peace-, our guiding light, has furthermore declared:

"All of man's deeds are terminated with death; except for three things: A charity from which others continue to benefit (*sadaqah-i jariyah*), a knowledge which serves and a virtuous child who sends his prayers." (Muslim, Wasiyyah, 14)

These statements of the Prophet illustrate the rewards a deceased believer reaps from charities given in life and which continue beyond his death, and moreover, that they do benefit from the prayers and charities intended for them by their living loved ones and Muslim brothers, whom are therefore encouraged to engage in charitable activities in their name.

It is indeed important to continue charitable work in the name of Muslims who have passed on to the Afterlife. Compliant with the last *hadith* aforementioned, a Muslim's book of deeds does not close, as long as his charities continue to flow in life. Giving charity in the name of a believer, who has bode farewell to the world to enter the grave all on his own, is among the most virtuous and loyal deeds his inheritors and true friends can ever offer.

Closing the outstanding debts of the deceased, in particular, is a righteous act recommended personally by the Blessed Prophet –upon him blessings and peace-. The first inquiry the Blessed Prophet –upon him blessings and peace- used to make at a funeral was whether the deceased person had an outstanding debt; and he would proceed to offer his funeral *salat* only after the debt had been closed. How delicate an instruction of mercy this serves us, in regard to restoring the unsettled duties of the deceased.

An analogy based on the ransom a Muslim is allowed to pay as compensation for the fasts he was physically prevented, both on time and at a later date, from offering, led Imam Muhammad to a jurisprudential ruling (*ijtihad*) known as *isqat-i salat*, where the inheritors of a deceased Muslim may pay ransom in compensation for the ritual prayers he failed to offer in life. Accordingly, a ransom is to be given for each unoffered ritual prayer;

either a days feed for the poor or an equivalent amount of money. This charity must furthermore be transferred to the needy without there being any decrease or altering of the required amount. There are three noticeable benefits in Imam Muhammad's ruling:

a) An encouragement to offer charity, in whose rewards the presenter of the charity partakes.

b) Its bringing joy to the needy and their ensuing prayers for the deceased.

c) An anticipation of the Lord's mercy and forgiveness.

Yet, it is unfortunate that this practice of *isqat*[118] has today become distanced from its original purpose, having been transformed to an exercise known as *dawr*[119], something that conflicts the spirit of Islam.

The practice of *dawr* has been turned into a form of trickery. This false practice depicts an unoffered deed of worship as if it is compensated by a charity that itself is not, in actual fact, given. What takes place is that a certain amount of money, intended for absolving the deceased of his debt over the ritual prayers[120] he failed to offer in his lifetime, is placed

---

118 *Isqat* is to relieve the deceased from the debts he accrued through ritual prayers, fasts, vows etc. he had failed too offer while alive, by handing the needy, in cash value, their compensation. (Hayrettin Karaman, Ebediyet Yolcusunu Uğurlarken, p. 81-85)

119 In contrast to handing the amount in cash value to the poor, *dawr* is to place a certain amount of money in a piece of cloth which is presented to the needy, only for the needy to re-present it to the benefactor; and for this circulation to continue until the specific amount of debt is closed off. This innovative practice neither existed during the time of the Prophet –upon him blessings and peace-, nor during the Companions, nor during the Tabiun generation that followed. *Isqat* was ruled permissible by the end of the second century following the Hegira, while *dawr* as late as the fifth century. Today's widespread practice of *dawr*, thought by many as stemming from the ethos of Islam, is really a harmful innovation that encourages stinginess and laziness in offering deeds. It is therefore necessary to abandon the custom of *dawr* and to instead offer direct charity in the name of the deceased and pray the Lord that he be forgiven. This way, one will have complied with the Sunnah, and at the same time ensure that the charity is delivered to its true owner, the one in need. (Hayrettin Karaman, Ebediyet Yolcusunu Uğurlarken, p. 81-85)

120 Meant by the debts of ritual prayer are the prayers that the deceased either failed to offer in life or those he did offer without observing its inner guidelines like sincerity and concentration. Otherwise, it does not, in any way, imply the ritual prayers one consciously neglected, by counting on this as means of potential compensation.

in the middle, which instead of being permanently given to the needy, is then made to circulate between the two parties: the presenter to the recipient and then back to the presenter and then, once again, to the recipient, repeatedly; and with each circulation, the amount of charity supposedly becomes inflated. Handing a small amount of money to the recipient, often many in number, only to take it back -which incidentally is the intention carried to begin with- and then to reoffer the money to the same recipient or another, only to have him hand it back once again, and presuming that by doing so the amount of this pseudo charity increases the more recipients there are, is nothing short of an ugly innovation; and the persons involved can only deceive themselves. Especially astonishing is how some wealthy people resort to this means and expect the desired result. This is nothing but a vain endeavor, which from the outside, appears as absurd and illogical as a plot to trick the Almighty.

O Lord! Reconcile our intentions with Your pleasure! Protect us from the doom of those who have dived into the world and have thus drowned themselves in a puddle! Our Lord, the Most Merciful of the Merciful! Adorn and perfect our lives and deaths with the blessings, grace, sublime beauties You have given Your righteous servants and, above all, with Your reunion!

O Lord! Allow us the privilege of beholding the universe with the gaze of Divine love, of observing it from the vantage of spiritual consciousness and feeling; with the shiver of conscience and the excitement of faith…And allow us to make it to the climes of mercy, to Your presence, through the tears of remorse that flow from our eyes, with a clean name and a peace of mind!

Amin…

CHAPTER FIVE

Advice from the Righteous

خوش کود

"Appreciate"

The cautions and advices of the righteous are reflections from the climes of the Quran and the words of the Prophet.

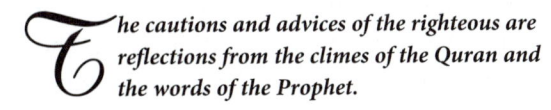

Advice from the Righteous

The righteous servants of the Lord, who have attained to an excellence of conduct by virtue of perfecting exoteric and the esoteric knowledge on the Sufi path, are those who are privileged with the good fortune of receiving the honor of being 'the inheritors of prophets'. They are embodiments of the prophetic perfection of conduct and guidance spread over the course of time. In other words, they are tangible guides for those who have not been fortunate enough to live in the times of the Blessed Prophet –upon him blessings and peace- and his Companions. The *hadith* states:

"Scholars (with inner and outer perfection) are the inheritors of prophets." (Abu Dawud, Ilm, 1)

Being the recipients of an intense manifestation of the Divine names Merciful and Compassionate, mercy and compassion become part of their original nature. Having unshackled themselves from an egoism that considers and values nobody other than the self, these matured believers attain to a lifelong selflessness, where they rather think of everyone apart from themselves. Their lives, devoted exclusively to guiding others, thus continue beyond their mortal bodies. Consequent upon their taming of their egos, they utilize their spirits as bridges that deliver not only themselves to the Lord but also the rest of the *ummah*, for whose eternal salvation they strive. They are teachers for masses awaiting rescue, heroes who carry on in their consciences the responsibility of the masses towards their Creator.

The cautions and advices of the righteous are reflections from the words of the Prophet –upon him blessings and peace-; for he is the hub of spiritual benefit. Their speeches, cautions and advices, imbued with spiritual vigor, are all glimmers reflecting from that hub. It is therefore vital to seize the assemblies of the righteous as god-sent; since they reenact for the *ummah* the twenty-three year prophethood of the Beloved Messenger –upon him blessings and peace-, in their words, actions and emotions.

A saint sheds his willpower in the love of the Lord, like a moth spinning uncontrollably around a flame, whereby the Lord, henceforth, becomes his eyes that see and ears that hear. As he stands under the manifestation of the Lord's love and affection, his egoistic tendencies burn to crisp, like a paper under a sunlit lens. Thereby, he becomes a spiritual center of attraction loved, intentionally or unintentionally, by others, whose sympathies flow towards him. His cautions and advices act as relieving cures for injured spirits.

The cautions and guiding words of advice uttered by righteous saints, who have attained to his horizon and spiritual command, are of greater value and influence in sending a wakeup call to ignorant hearts, compared to advices of those who do not practice what they preach. One must therefore cherish their enlightening advices like a lost treasure and devote himself to their enlightening words, with love and sincerity. Below are only a handful of examples from the advices of the righteous, which shed precious light on the eternal path of happiness:

Hasan Basri –May Allah sanctify his secret- (642-728)

Son of Man! A true believer wakes in the morning with fear, even if he be a man of *ihsan*. This is befitting for him, in any case. A believer makes it to the next night, again, with fear. He is always tremors amid the fear of two things:

1. Past sins: He can never be sure how the Almighty will treat him over these.

2. Future life: How is he to live and how will he end up dying? He continuously reflects over the answers to these questions he can never foretell.

Men! Realize this truth and offer righteous deeds: Allah and His Messenger see all things you do and there will come a day when you shall be returned to Allah, who knows the hidden and the open. And that day, you will be informed of all things that you had done.

Beware of your hearts. Renew them with through a constant remembrance of the Lord, for they are quick to rust. Tame your egos, as they are wild. Should you fail to curb the evil desires of your ego, it will only be a matter of time before it rolls you down a terrifying abyss.

You will not attain a perfected faith, as long as you continue to condemn others over their faults when you have your own faults waiting there unresolved. Take a look at your own faults before you ever set your eyes on the faults of others; begin by correcting them!

Men! The Quran is a cure for believers, a guide for the pious. Whoever follows it will be lead to guidance and the right path. Whoever turns away from it will end up a wretched destined for disaster.

Son of Man! Alone you shall die, alone you shall be resurrected and alone you shall be called into account!

Malik ibn Dinar –May Allah sanctify his secret- (d. 748)

No longer is there pleasure on Earth, except for two things:

1. Meeting and conversing with brethren.

2. Waking up for the prayer of *tahajjud* and being occupied with Divine remembrance and reciting the Quran at that inspirational time of night.

Jafar-i Sadiq - May Allah sanctify his secret- (699-766)

Keep a righteous deed you offer a secret and let it lose value in your sight; for if you consider it worthless, it may not lead you to conceit. And if you keep it a secret, it will make up for its shortcomings and increase its virtue. By hastening to offer a righteous deed, you will have reached it without delay. Otherwise, your ego may fall weak and make you postpone it; or worse still, abandon it.

If you hear something unpleasant about your brother, persevere to convince yourself that he might have an excuse. If you fail to find one, then assume that the excuse is of a nature you cannot understand and strive to conceal his fault!

Sufyan-i Sawri –May Allah sanctify his secret- (713-777)

Seeking knowledge should be with the purpose of attaining piety for Allah, fulfilling His commands and fearing Him. The superiority of knowledge comes from its ability to endow one with these supreme emotions. Had this been lacking, knowledge, too, would have been on level par with all things else.

Going to Khorasan to preach is better than living in the vicinity of Mecca.

The first condition of knowledge is to look for ways of attaining it. Once it is found and attained, practice comes next…and then silence and contemplation…and after that observing the universe through the gaze of wisdom.

Junayd Baghdadi –May Allah sanctify his secret- (d.909)

Sohbah with Allah, that is being with Him, comes through beautiful conduct and a continuation of a solemn and contemplative mindset.

Advice from the Righteous

Sohbah with the Messenger of Allah –upon him blessings and peace- comes through adhering to his *Sunnah*.

Sohbah with saints comes through respect and service.

Sohbah with the family comes through beautiful morals.

Sohbah with the brethren comes through a constant smile and cheering them up.

And *sohbah* with the public comes through prayer and mercy.

Imam Ghazzali –May Allah sanctify his secret- (d.1111)

Keep your heart awake upon these three deeds of worship, son; do not let your heart and mind stray elsewhere: whilst reciting the Quran, whilst remembering your Lord and whilst offering ritual prayer. When occupied with these three deeds, do not lend your heart and mind to any other, even if for a moment. Do not forget being in the presence of Allah! The value of what you do will diminish, should you let your mind wander while your face is turned towards the *qiblah*. Turn your face to the Kaaba, the first temple from which Islam was born, and fasten your heart to Allah, glory unto Him. And if you want to join the ranks of the wise, fill your silence with contemplation, reserve your gaze for taking lesson and let your wishes be to worship. These three traits are the signs of the wise.

Abstain, son, from breaching the rights of others! A penny of debt steals the rewards of many an accepted act of worship! The Prophet –upon him blessings and peace- never used to offer the funeral prayers of those who had died with unsettled debts. His purpose was to cast mercy in the hearts of the rich, so that they would withdraw their claim over the debt. But Allah most certainly helps one, who borrows a loan out of need with the intention of paying it back. Even if he ends up dying whilst striving to pay the loan back without quite making it, Allah will aid him in the Hereafter.

One must thank the Lord for tribulations; for apart from disbelief and sin, there is never a tribulation which does not come with a goodness of

Sufism: A Path Towards the Internalization of Faith (Ihsân)

which you do not know. Allah knows what is better for you, more than you can ever know for yourself! There are many things you suppose to be evil which are in fact good for you. And there are many things you deem to be good which are in fact bad for you. The safest way is to rest content with Divine destiny and to offer thanks no matter what the situation may be.

Son…If there was ever a thing you needed to be wary of, it would be to watch out for who you befriend. Know that a basketful of fresh apples cannot turn a single rotten apple into a fresh one; yet a single rotten apple can rot the rest away. Therefore, always accompany the righteous!

A good friend is like a person who sells rose oil; you will either you buy some from him or he will offers some to you, or at least, the fragrance will rub off on you so long as you remain by his side. One is with whom he loves. You shall be resurrected in the Hereafter with whoever you had loved and befriended on earth. Persist, therefore, to accompany the scholars and the righteous, who put their knowledge to practice!

Everything in life, son, is through the allocation of Allah. Allah has made some wealthy and others poor, some healthy and others disabled, some knowledgeable and others ignorant. This is the only way to maintain the order of the world. On seeing people lower than you, do not become arrogant and despise them! You could have been in their shoes and they could have been in yours. Think of this and befriend the poor! Always try to be humble towards them! Protect the dignity of being a human and a Muslim! This is the only way to happiness. If you want peace in both worlds, do not break anyone's heart! When you see someone younger, say to yourself, 'he has fewer sins than I'; and upon seeing someone older, say, 'he has more rewards than I and is more virtuous than I in ways I do not know'. Look at them with these thoughts! When you see a scholar, think to yourself that 'he has knowledge which shall save him'; and upon coming across an ignorant, think that 'he will be forgiven for he does not know'! Even when you stumble upon a nonbeliever, think that 'all his sins will be forgiven should Allah grant him guidance and that he may reach the presence of the Lord as innocent as a dove…but who knows in what condition I shall breathe my last?' And thereby reflect on your own finale! The more you know yourself and the greater you look down upon yourself, the higher your rank will be in the sight of the Lord.

See to the needs of your brethren of religion, son, to the best of your ability; for the Honorable Prophet –upon him blessings and peace- has said:

"Whosoever takes care of the need of his brother in religion, Allah will take care of a need of his." (Bukhari, Mazalim, 3)

And in another *hadith*, the Honorable Prophet –upon him blessings and peace- has stated: "Whosoever takes conceals the flaw of a Muslim, Allah will take conceal a flaw of his both Here and in the Hereafter." (Muslim, Birr, 72)

A wise man ought to say to himself: The only capital I have is my life; I have no other. This capital is so precious that each breath exhaled is gone forever, never to return. Breaths are numbered and they decrease by the moment. Capitalize, therefore, on each breath and act as if you will be dead by tomorrow. Protect your each limb from sin and clutch onto piety!

My Lord…End our lives with happiness! Make us attain to Your pleasure and Splendid Countenance (*jamal*)! Do not detach us from wellbeing, day or night! Make piety our fodder and direct our trust and hope towards You! Keep us firm on the path of truth! Only You are worthy to be worshipped! I glorify You from all deficiencies! I am among those who have wronged themselves, for being unable serve you as befits Your Majesty!

Praise be to Allah, the Lord of the worlds; and salute and peace to Muhammad Mustafa, the pride and joy of the universe!

Abdulqadir Jilani –May Allah sanctify his secret- (1077-1166)

Son! Piety is what you need. Strive to fulfill the terms of piety so that your heart is cleansed of inner conflicts and bad habits…and becomes bound for the good.

While earning the goods of the world, son, do not be like he who collects wood in the dark of night without knowing for sure what he is collecting. Be cautious as to whether it is permissible or impermissible, legitimate or illegitimate. Allow the sun of *tawhid* and piety to shine a light upon all your deeds.

Putting the Quran to practice, son, will elevate you to the status of the Quran; raise you onto its throne. Practicing the Sunnah, on the other hand, will draw you closer to the Messenger of Allah –upon him blessings and peace-, whose spiritual aid will thereby ensure that you will not be banished from heart-worlds of saints even for a moment. It is him who beautifies the hearts of saints.

Haram food kills the heart, son, while *halal* revives it. There morsels that will keep you occupied with the world and there are others that will keep you occupied with the Hereafter. Again, there are morsels that direct your interest to the Creator of both worlds.

Son…Become friends with him who helps you in the struggles against your ego! Be in his company! Do not befriend him who fans the flames of the desires of your ego! First, occupy yourself with your own ego; benefit yourself and set your ego straight…and then occupy yourself with others. Do not be like the candle which lights up its surroundings only to melt away!

O he who wishes to offer righteous deeds in the way of Allah! Be sincere! Otherwise, you will have tired yourself for nothing.

Not by words are people enlightened; but by a genuine belief and eagerness in the heart. All this is attained solely through seclusion, worship, Divine remembrance, abstinence and contemplation. They are otherwise not the consequences of certain ceremonial deeds which never go beyond an external show and infiltrate the spirit. The tongue and heart, the words and essence and the inner and the outer of a wayfarer on the path to the Lord must therefore be one and speak in one voice.

Ahmed ar-Rifai –May Allah sanctify his secret- (1118-1182)

Friends…Try and gain a closeness to the saints of the Lord; for to love a saint is to love the Lord and to be hostile to him is to be hostile to the Lord.

Continue your *dhikr* of the Lord; for *dhikr* is a magnet that pulls towards reuniting with Him, a strong rope that binds to His closeness.

Those who continue their Divine remembrance are on good terms with the Lord; and whosoever is on good terms with the Lord has effectively reunited with Him. *Dhikr* settles in the heart through the blessings of *sohbah*, as a person shares the same path as his friend and is lead to wherever that path shall take him.

Contemplation was the very first deed of the Noble Prophet –upon him blessings and peace-. Before there were ever any obligatory deeds, his worship consisted of reflecting on the creation and blessings of Allah. So hold a firm grip on contemplation and render it a means of self-improvement.

Be careful not to be like a sieve that sifts out the fine part of the flour only to be left with its dregs. Do not let your hearts be filled with deceit and malice while words of wisdom roll of your tongues, lest the *ayah* "So do you enjoin men to be good and neglect your own souls?" (al-Baqarah, 44) acts as your prosecutor.

Clean your hearts thoroughly, as a cleanliness of heart is much more important than a cleanliness of clothes. Besides, Allah gazes directly at one's heart, not at his clothes. Observe the boundaries of uprightness and do not desire anyone else than Allah.

Friends…The door opens for he who knocks on it humbly and with poise; and he is allowed inside. He who enters dejected shall be hosted with honor.

Abdulkhaliq Gujdawani –May Allah sanctify his secret- (d.1189)

Son…My will for you is that you let yourself be guided by knowledge, upright conduct and piety under all circumstances! Read the works of people bygone and pursue the path of *Ahl-i Sunnah wa'l-Jamaah*! Learn the law (*fiqh*) and *hadith* and take flight from the ignorant and crude! Make sure to offer your ritual prayers in congregation! Abstain from fame as much as your strength allows; for fame comes with catastrophe. Do not eye ranks of authority and always keep a low-key! Do not take on a duty beyond your power! Do not interfere with public affairs which do not concern you in the least! Do not associate with perverse officials! Maintain a

Sufism: A Path Towards the Internalization of Faith (Ihsân)

balance in all affairs! Do not disrupt that balance and lend unnecessary ear to beautiful voices, for they darken the spirit and give birth to hypocrisy! Still, do not reject a beautiful voice altogether, for a call to prayer and a read of the Quran made with it, revives the spirit.

Eat little, speak little and sleep little; and flee the ignorant like a gazelle flees a lion! Seek solitude in times of tribulation and keep your distance from jurists who pass legal judgments to protect only their own interests and in so doing bring about a trifling with religion, from the supercilious wealthy and from the ignorant! Eat only *halal*, abstain from things doubtful and make piety your primary criteria in marriage! Otherwise, you will become attached to the world and ruin yourself for it!

Do not laugh a lot; especially be careful not to chuckle! Laughing in lots kills the heart. But do not ever abandon a smile.

Look upon everyone with mercy; do not look down on anyone. Do not go to great lengths to prettify your outward appearance, for an outer gloss hides an inner destruction. Do not get into arguments. Do not ask anything from anyone; rest content and let contentment be your riches. Protect your dignity!

Stay loyal to those who have contributed to your development and training. Serve them with your wealth and life and share their pains! Their detractors shall never find peace! Do not lean towards the world and the ignorant who strive for it!

Your heart should always be delicate and somber, your body resilient for the duty of servanthood and your eyes tearful. May your deeds be genuine, your prayers be of seeking refuge, your clothes be of modesty, the righteous be your companions, exoteric and esoteric knowledge be your capital and your house be a mosque!

Fariduddin Attar –May Allah sanctify his secret- (1119-1220)

Accept the apologies of those who hurt you. Allah does not like one who hurts the public. Such a trait is unbefitting for a religious man.

Wounding another heart with tyranny is to wound your own heart. He who is able to see his own faults acquires a certain strength in his spirit.

The signs of foolishness are to search for others' faults without noticing one's personal faults…and to expect generosity whilst having sowed the seeds of miserliness in one's own heart.

He who does not please others through his moral conduct has no value in the sight of the Lord.

Visit the ill, for it is the way of the Prophet. If it is within your power, quench the thirsty in water. Serve the public in assemblies. Inquire the states of orphans so that Allah will grant you honor. Know that the cry of an orphan, even if it be for a split second, shakes the Throne. A tyrant who reduces an orphan to tears becomes wood for Hellfire. One who gives joy to an orphan opens the door of Heaven ajar for himself.

Whatever you give in the way of Allah is your true property. For the rest, you shall be called into account.

Muhyiddin Ibn Arabi –May Allah sanctify his secret- (1165-1240)

If you accustom your heart to the remembrance of Allah, then your heart will surely be enlightened by the light *dhikr* shall grant you. It is that light opens the eye of your heart.

Treat the servants of Allah with mercy and compassion. Scatter your mercy unto entire creation. Do not say, 'this is simply weed, lifeless and without benefit'. They truly harbor benefits you may not appreciate. Leave the created alone and have mercy for it, with the mercy of its Creator.

Do not turn anyone away empty-handed. Console them even if it be with a kind word and act pleasantly. Think that you will one day meet the Lord.

Do not allow anyone to enslave you for a piece of worldly dazzle. You are a servant only of Allah, who has accepted you as servant.

Show love to the faithful servants of Allah by feeding them and taking care of their needs. Know that, in their unity, the entire believers are like one person, one body.

Accustom yourself to congregation. Try and shed tears from a fear of Allah. Grab hold of the rope of Allah and tend towards things that please Him.

Mawlana Rumi –May Allah sanctify his secret- (1207-1273)

Allah the Almighty has sent messengers and saints to the world as mercy. For that reason, they persistently and tirelessly counsel the public. For those who block their ears to their counseling, they plea, 'Have mercy on them, o Lord, and do not shut the gate of mercy on their faces!'

Get your act together and pay attention to the advices of saints! Listen to them, so that you are saved from fear; and that you attain to spiritual peace and security!

Before letting the opportunity slip and without hesitation, seize the robes of a perfected man who has cast off the deceit of this fleeting world and has utterly surrendered himself to the Real, so that you are rescued from the tribulations of these bad times, the troubles of this final hour!

The words of saints are like a pure, crystal-clear river brimming with the font of life. While you still have the opportunity at hand, drink from it to your heart's content, so that the flowers of spirituality blossom therein.

Know that spiritual propriety is like the spirit that dwells inside the body. For saints, it is the light of the eye and the heart. If you wish to crush the head of the devil, know that this is the weapon you need.

Open your eyes and throw a gaze at the Quran, the word of Allah, from head to toe! Each of its verses teaches and trains one in spiritual propriety.

Give all you have, your body, soul and riches in return for a mended heart! Mend a heart so that it shed lights upon you in the pitch dark of the grave.

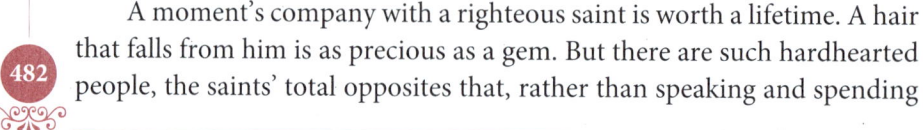

A moment's company with a righteous saint is worth a lifetime. A hair that falls from him is as precious as a gem. But there are such hardhearted people, the saints' total opposites that, rather than speaking and spending a moment with them, keeping a distance from them is more precious than the entire riches of the world.

I said to my heart, "Do not desire to be at the forefront; and instead act as a balm of generosity. Do not be the thorn that spikes. If you wish never to be inflicted with harm by anyone, then do not be a person who speaks, thinks and teaches evil. Strive for righteous deeds, no matter which mood you may come under.

Ibrahim Dasuki –May Allah sanctify his secret- (d.1277)

What you need, son, is the prayer of saints; the desire to come under their spiritual aid for the sake of your own wellbeing.

You, who has read and memorized the Quran, do not be proud that you have done so! Instead, look at yourself: Are you able to sufficiently put it to practice or not?

Son! Become a man of silence and refrain from indulging in the futile, like the arts of argumentation and glittery words! Choose sincerity and do not listen to your ego while offering righteous deeds with that purpose!

Hang around with him, who has combined the law (*shariah*) and the truth (*haqiqah*) in his essence. Never forget that it will be such persons that will offer you the greatest help on this path!

I would wish for you, son, that you practice in line with the Sunnah at all times and observe the spiritual propriety so essential in this way!

You must be brave! Do not be a coward who shirks even from his own shadow! No trouble, no matter how great, should knock you out with the first blow!

Become filled with the love of the Lord; be with him, even, in a state of ecstasy.

Should you ever search for people to backbite, let them be your parents; for they are more deserving than anyone to take away the rewards of your good deeds.

Allah the Almighty gazes at the hearts of His servants seventy-two times in a single day and night. So keep your heart clean and bright; for it is the precinct of the Divine gaze.

Do not fool yourself, brother, in thinking you have achieved something by yourself! When you fast, it is Allah who has made you fast; and when you offer prayer, it is Allah who has made you do so. So is the case with the rest of your deeds. If you have attained to the level of piety or if you have obtained anything, spiritual or material, it is only because Allah has privileged you with it.

Refrain from saying 'I', my dear, even if you have amassed deeds of goodness equivalent to that of entire men and *jinn*! For Allah consigns the self-important who stake a claim to I-ness to humiliation! It will diminish your material-spiritual rank…Always keep that in mind!

Bahaaddin Naqshiband –may Allah sanctify his secret- (1318-1389)

Our path is the path of salvation shown by Allah the Almighty; as much as it is the path of adhering to the Sunnah and following the Companions. Our path hence offers great revenue in little time.

Our path is that of *sohbah* and love, as was the path of the Companions. Goodness and blessings lie in company and company is achieved through *sohbah*. Seclusion comes with the danger of fame; and fame is catastrophe.

Those who journey on our path must take of three things:

First is propriety towards Allah the Almighty; that is he must be immersed in servanthood, inside and out. He must fulfill all the commands of Allah and keep away from what He has prohibited; and removing all else other than Allah from the heart, he must mobilize all his means in His path.

Second is propriety towards the Beloved Messenger –upon him blessings and peace-. This is none other than to follow him, lovingly, in all affairs and behavior.

Third is propriety towards the righteous man who has enlightened you.

Advice from the Righteous

Nothing good comes through food prepared or obtained ignorantly, unwillingly or with anger; for the devil and the ego have found their way inside of it. If eaten, it will surely come with consequences disruptive of spiritual inspiration and peace. Good comes from food prepared and eaten free of ignorance and with the thought of Allah. The reason as to why people cannot gather enough energy to do good and offer righteous deeds is because they are not careful enough in observing the *haram*, the doubtful and the rights of others in eating and drinking. No matter what the circumstances may be, attaining peace and concentration in ritual prayer, to offer it with pleasure and tears, depends on eating *halal*, preparing it as if preparing it in the presence of Allah and eating in a like mindset. A body nourished with the *haram* can find no pleasure in ritual prayer.

The Prophet's –upon him blessings and peace- words, "*Salat* is a believer's ascension" (Suyuti, Sharhu Ibn Majah, I, 313) alludes to the levels of proper ritual prayer. While chanting the opening *takbir* of the prayer, one must be in a state of concentration, overcome in Divine presence, by thinking of the splendor and the majesty of the Almighty. He must improve this mindset to the point of losing control (*istighraq*). The peak of it is exemplified by the Beloved Prophet –upon him blessings and peace-.

The truth of saying 'there is no god but Allah' is to not let anything other than Allah become idolized in the heart. Executing the order of Islam, that is, to fulfill its commands and refrain from its prohibitions, is to abandon the *haram*, the doubtful and even a majority of the licit; it is to keep a distance from permits (*rukhsah*) allowed under stringent circumstances and to make use of the licit only as far as they are necessary. Now, not only is that light and purity, it is also a vehicle that elevates one to the ranks of sainthood; ranks which are attained by these means. The entirety of those who fail to attain to these ranks, fail only because they fail to observe these and acquiesce in their desires that people are kept off limits to these ranks. Otherwise, inspiration from the Lord comes by the minute.

Mawlana Khalid Baghdadi –May Allah sanctify his secret- (d. 1826)

I advise you with a constant worship of Allah and piety, not to cause anyone harm wherever you may be and to be attentive especially to the Two Sacred Precincts (*Haramayn-i Sharifayn*).

Do not backbite, even if you are backbitten. Do not seize anyone's property. Take only that which the Law has decreed permissible and spend it in the way of good. Do not spend money to appease your desires, when your brethren are hungry and needy. Do not lie, ever. Do not look down upon anyone. Do not ever think yourself to be superior to others.

Exert all your power in offering deeds of worship, both physical and spiritual. But at the same time, convince your ego of never having done anything of worth; for the spirit of all deeds of worship is intention and a sound intention may only come about through sincerity. How can you not need sincerity, when those superior to you needed it? I pledge by Allah that I personally do not believe that I have offered any deed of worth, since the day I was born, that has been accepted in the sight of the Lord, so as to keep me exempt from being called to account.

If you do not see yourself bankrupt in all deeds of goodness, then know that you are in the lowest end of ignorance. But should you know that you are bankrupt, do not despair the mercy of Allah the Almighty.

Musa Effendi –May Allah sanctify his secret- (1918-1999)

The heart-world and spiritual perfection of a believer is exhibited in his behavior. Among the foremost signs of this admirable behavior are:

Being down-to-earth at all times, having an awareness of the value of each moment and breath and not letting them go to waste, loving the servants of Allah and keeping amicable relations, treating another according to his religious depth, concealing faults, being cautious of the *halal* and the *haram* and regarding as a great sin a thing considered by others as trivial; for trivializing a sin is to –Allah forbid- trivialize the Almighty.

Advice from the Righteous

Compliant with the pleasure of our Lord, let's adorn our dawns with prayer and Divine remembrance. Let's lend our services, first and foremost to our families and elders. Let's reduce the times we spend with the lovers of the world and accompany instead the righteous. Let's offer an equal share of our services to our relatives and the needy. Most importantly, let's be meticulous in observing the *halal* and the *haram*. Let's also be diligent in our social relations so that we do not slack off from our essential duty of servanthood.

Error, forgetfulness and instability come only in moments when we are absentminded from *dhikr*. Those who perpetuate the spiritual state of *dhikr* are unaffected by the grief and sorrow of the world; they do not even have more worldly joy than needed. A constant state of spiritual presence, generosity and mercy towards the created fill that gap. In other words, love; love of a continual kind. Allah the Almighty dips a servant besotted with Him in the ocean of love. After that, the person loves only those who deserve to be loved; and that, as much as the Lord allows.

One must consider it a valuable duty to properly serve the community he is a member of, for the sake of the Divine. One who works to better the social life, order and prosperity of a community, holds a precious existence in that community; and corresponding will be his rewards in the Hereafter. It is stated in the *hadith* that:

سَيِّدُ الْقَوْمِ خَادِمُهُمْ

"He who serves people is their noblest." (Daylami, Musnad, II, 324)

Many, who despite the abundant deeds of worship they offer, neglect embodying the trait '*sattaru'l-uyub*', the Divine Attribute of concealing the faults of others. And for that reason, they cannot progress spiritually as much as they would wish. Yet, forgiving and hiding others' faults is one of the most important features of good morals. Just as Allah the Almighty conceals and forgives innumerable faults committed by us His servants, we must also be forgiving. Only those touched by Divine Love may know how to forgive.

All skill lies in the ability to be with the Real, amid the turmoil of the world and daily activities; a wonderful state, which is a blessing, an award given by the Lord. If only we can properly reflect on the important duty awaiting us, we could restrain ourselves from being duped by the toys the world has to momentarily offer.

One of the greatest gifts the Lord can give his servant is to convince him of his own helplessness. Perhaps the greatest gain I ever acquired on the path of spirituality was to be able to see my own faults. I realized my bankruptcy towards my Lord, through which I no longer had the power to see and fiddle with the faults of anybody else. I can only thank Allah that I am ever so grateful for that…

O Lord! Give us a share of the fire of love burning in the hearts of Your beloved servants! Grant us the ability to give ourselves direction through the inspirational cautions and advices of the saints by whose spiritual aids we are trained!

Amin…

CHAPTER SIX

Sufi Narratives and Lessons

True Education
The Method in Spiritual Training
Ibrahim ibn Adham and the Fawn
Not to Stain the Path of the Real
Karamah
Affecting Ignorant Hearts
The Friend's Door
To Obey, To Serve, To Advise
Serving Creation
Courtesy in Saints
Will in Presence
Propriety
Propriety in Serving
Propriety…No Matter What
The Morals and Service of a Saint
Let the Immortal Know, Not Mortals!
Do Not Look Down On Anyone!
Do Not Condemn Anyone!
Cheering Up an Orphan
Friendship
The Purpose of Friendship
Full Submission
Receiving the Prayers of a Believer
A *Majzub* and the Cure of an Ailing Heart
Faces like Angels
The Condition of the Heart during Charity
The Righteous Deed that Reaches the Throne
A Constant Awareness of the Real
The *Karim* is All I Need
The Responsibility of Forerunners
Attending the Invitation of the Lord
The Importance of *Halal*
Halal Earnings

SUMMARY

"Edeb yâ hû"

Saints, who reach the core of companionship through the Lord, remain the companions of entire humankind for eternity.

Sufi Narratives and Lessons

Sufism, as has occasionally been touched upon in the preceding chapters, is a science pertaining not so much to words as to the perfection of one's inner essence and mindset; it is therefore replete with beauties and inspirations that reflect onto life from the charming heart-worlds of saints. These beauties, which since times immemorial have been conveyed under the name of 'narratives', have undertaken an active role in maturing faith in the Lord, perfecting moral conduct, galvanizing the springs of Divine love and affection in the heart and nourishing sublime emotions like compassion, mercy and selflessness. The narratives frequently recounted by the Quran in fact set Divine blueprints to steer man to spiritual maturity in his journey in life; and effectively so, since the narratives themselves are taken directly from actual life experiences.

Encouraged by this Divine method and true to our purpose to convey the truths of Sufism not merely as they exist in written words but also, and more importantly, in the manner in which they exists in heart-worlds, we have so far quoted various narratives based on actual life experiences in preceding chapters, which we wish to complement in this chapter by citing further examples of such concrete experiences. We will moreover attempt to provide succinct interpretations of the core lessons comprised by these narratives, the cautions and lessons we are called upon to take on board. Our purpose in what is to come, in short, has been to extend to the reader a few drops from the vast ocean of moral and virtue straight from the hearts of various Sufis.

True Education

The great Sami Effendi had just completed his bachelor's degree at the Faculty of Law, at the Daru'l-Funun University in Istanbul. Noticing his upright conduct and wonderful demeanor, a righteous man said to him:

"This education is fine, too, but you really should look to complete the real education, son. Let's enroll you in the school of wisdom, where you can receive training in the sciences of the heart and the secrets of the Hereafter", after which he added:

"I really do not know how they train one in that school and what they teach. But if there is one thing I know, it is that the first lesson of this education is to not hurt, and the last lesson not to be hurt."

Moral of the Story:

Not hurting is relatively easy. But not being hurt is seldom in one's control; for it is a matter of heart. Avoiding being hurt and heartbroken, therefore, is possible only by becoming immune the poisonous, heart-piercing arrows shot by mortals. The strength of this immunity depends on the level acquired in cleansing the soul and purifying the heart. On being stoned and insulted in Taif, the Blessed Prophet –upon him blessings and peace- was met with an angel, who assured him that he could, with a word, "…strike the two mountains, surrounding Taif together, and destroy the locals".

But being the mercy to the worlds he was, the Honorable Prophet –upon him blessings and peace- not only declined that offer, he moreover turned towards Taif and compassionately pleaded for the eventual guidance of her locals.[121]

Similarly, as he was being stoned to death, Hallaj, a devoted lover of the Prophet, was heard pleading, "My Lord…They know not; so forgive them even before You forgive me!"

---

121 See, Bukhari, Badu'l-Khalq, 7; Muslim, Jihad, 111.

This is a mindset acquired only through education in its truest form; a mindset belonging to a heart purified through spiritual training.

On being asked about the traits of a purified heart (*qalb-i salim*), Abu'l-Qasim al-Hakim replied:

"A purified heart has three traits: It is a heart that does not hurt, a heart that is not hurt and a heart that does goodness only for the sake of Allah without accepting anything in return. For a believer reaches the presence of his Lord with dignity (*wara*), if he has not hurt anyone; with loyalty, if he has directed his heart solely to his Lord and protected it from being hurt by anyone; and sincerity, if he has not ascribed any mortal as partner to his righteous deeds."

The poet says it beautifully:

The purpose of man and jinn on the garden of earth
Is to not hurt, devotee, and not be hurt!

The Method in Spiritual Training

Shah Naqshiband –may Allah sanctify his secret- explains the intricate details he observed whilst aiding others in purifying their hearts and cleansing their souls:

"We train a disciple in the most appropriate means necessary; that is, according the condition he is in. At times, we prefer the way of enchantment (*jazbah*), and at others, the way of a steadier path (*suluk*). We know that many a person comes to us with seeds of love in his heart, while many another carries none of these seeds whatsoever or they have been left to decay under the musty layer of the ego and its worldly desires. Our duty is hence to purge these mortal interests and to plant the seeds of love in their place; and should these seeds already be planted there, it is to ensure that they blossom to become a sapling of sincerity, watered by the rain of truth, under the rays of the sun of *marifatullah*.

As for teaching *dhikr*, it is like giving one a flint stone. Whether or not a spark of love is ignited depends thereafter on the prowess of the disciple in using it."

Moral of the Story:

The diseases of the body come in various types and with a range of treatments; so are the illnesses of the spirit and the heart. Saints with foresight and prudence, therefore, diagnose and treat the spiritual illness of a person in accordance with his specific condition. Whereas some, like Ibrahim Adham, are advised to:

"Abandon your crown and throne", in stark contrast, others like Sultan Mehmed the Conqueror, are told:

"You will incur blame on yourself, should you abandon your crown and an inept person then comes to assume it after you".

Some are trialed by water, some by fire. No matter how grueling the trial may be, curing a spiritual disease, as is the case with physical illnesses, requires a trust in the doctor and precision in using the recommended remedy; and more. Negligence in taking medication for a physical illness may only inflict harm that will, at worst, last as long as one lives on earth; yet negligence in taking the vital medication to treat an illness of the heart is tantamount to wasting a life of eternity.

Ibrahim ibn Adham and the Fawn

Ibrahim ibn Adham was previously a king in Balkh, lavishing in the luxury of the palace. The Sufis of the time used to counsel him, time and again, to save him from his destructive lifestyle and revive his eternal wellbeing. According to a famous report, while lying down on his bed on night, Ibrahim overheard some strange noises coming from the rooftop. Unable to sleep, he stuck his head out of the window and shouted:

"What on earth is going on there?" He was responded to with an odd answer.

"I am searching for my lost camel", a man said.

"What are you thinking", Ibrahim retorted, "searching for your camel on a rooftop?" This time around, the response was startling:

"You know very well, Ibrahim, that it is only foolish to search for a lost camel on a rooftop, yet you never stop to think how foolish it is to search for eternal happiness in the life of pomp and extravagance you lead!"

In comparison with the advices he had previously heard, these words left Ibrahim staggered. Nonetheless, all it took was a few days for him to forget and he carried on living his life as usual, without any noticeable change.

Many days had gone by when Ibrahim one day decided to set out from the palace, with his cohorts, to go hunting for fawns. At one stage, he rode off alone, in search for a good game. It was then he heard a whisper in his ear. 'Wake up', said the voice. He took no notice. But the voice reverberated again, and again. Suddenly, the voice became ubiquitous; it was coming from everywhere:

"Wake up before death wakes you up", they echoed.

Ibrahim ibn Adham was both stunned and scared. But then, a beautiful fawn suddenly appeared before his prying eyes, which momentarily made him forget the voices. Gathering his poise, he enthusiastically took aim at the delicate fawn with his arrow, keen on hunting it down. He was only a fingertip away from letting go of the arrow. But then the fawn, directing its poignant stare at Ibrahim, murmured:

"Did the Merciful Allah create me so you could hunt me down, Ibrahim?"

Petrified, Ibrahim began to tremble, from head to toe. With eyes welled up with tears, he came down from his horse and fell prostrate on the ground in deep remorse and prayed:

"My Lord, whose grace and benevolence is infinite! For a long time, I have wasted the breaths of my life in lavishness and pomp! Wash my heart with Your grace, o Allah, and leave nothing therein except for Your love!"

Ibrahim ibn Adham's eyes had now been awoken to an entirely different world; he found himself gazing deeply at a Divine realm. This truly beautiful sight erased from his mind all the conceptions of beauty he had previously entertained. The caftan of kingship, which he would don every morning with great care, and the pride of being the sultan of Balkh, had now suddenly lost all their glitter and significance. They suddenly appeared as awkward extras he could very well do without.

With eyes still moist from tears of repentance and a heart burning in the fire of remorse, Ibrahim ibn Adham set out towards the wilderness. He had walked a tremendous distance when he came upon a shepherd, wearing a woolen cloak as was customary. He approached the shepherd, without hesitation, and swapped his woolen cloak for his exquisite caftan. The moment Ibrahim put on the cloak, he felt an enormous relief. The shepherd, in the meantime, was astounded. "Our sultan has lost his mind", he thought to himself. Yet, far from having lost his mind, Ibrahim ibn Adham had much rather come to his senses. He had gone hunting for a fawn, only to be awoken by Allah, glory unto Him, through a fawn.

Moral of the Story:

When faced with a choice between the Here and the Hereafter, those who choose the Hereafter become sultans of eternity, awarded with infinite rewards. As for those who choose the world, even though they may appear as kings on the outside, they are in reality beggars of a life of eternity, which they shall never lay claim to, regardless of how avidly they may beg. It was this secret that Ibrahim ibn Adham came to terms with; and once he did, he made the due sacrifice required to become a sultan of eternity. As for the external warnings he was encountered by in the lead up to this decision, they were, in a sense, brought about by the gem of sincerity he had carried in his heart up to that time. More correctly, the condition of his heart served as means in enabling him to meet the causes that were to trigger him to take a step through the threshold of spiritual enlightenment and bring about the enormous blessings of the Lord, which made a sacrifice as great as giving up a throne easy for him. And the moment he did, he became graced with innumerable blessings in return.

Not to Stain the Path of the Real

The path of Sufism is a glittering road shone upon by the light of the Real, which thus accepts no stain whatsoever. Those who are able to see the essence and appreciate the spirit of this path can never find anything there that contravenes the ethos of Islam.

The spiritual circle of Shah Naqshiband –may Allah sanctify his secret- abounded with a vast number of students from all walks of life. Prominent scholars of Bukhara like Khawajah Yusuf were always eager to attend his circles. Still, the popularity of Shah Naqshiband became a matter of controversy for some scholars, who began speaking ill of him, alleging his teachings were defiant of the principles of Islam. They eventually met with Shah Naqshiband and voiced their concerns.

"Listen while we explain our path to you", Shah Naqshiband said to them. "Should you find anything contrary to the Quran and Sunnah, just name whatever it is and we shall abandon it!"

The scholars then listened to Shah Naqshiband explain to them what the great Sufi path was all about and thinking over them at length, they could not find anything to dispute.

"It seems your path is none but the upright path (*sirat-i mustaqim*). You will no longer hear any objections from us", they concluded.

Moral of the Story:

Understood from the above incident is that the true Sufi path is delicate in its adherence to the Quran and Sunnah and carries a sensitivity of heart in upholding them. Advising his disciples to conduct themselves with uncompromising loyalty to this principle, Shah Naqshiband moreover underlines how integral it is to remain loyal to the Quran and Sunnah, when, instead of disputing the skeptic scholars, he invites them to point out the aspects of the Sufi way which they think contravenes the two principles, so he could forego them. It is therefore essential for the devotees of this path to conduct themselves with the same sensitivity in order not to stain what is otherwise a pure path. It should be noted that the scholars referred to in the above encounter are righteous scholars and not the wicked scholars (*ulama bi's-suu*) who squander their knowledge, along with their hearts, in the way of evil, by acting in defiance of the commands of the Almighty, by failing to observe the measures of sincerity and piety, by rejecting the virtues of the righteous and in the words of the Quran, by selling the *ayat* of Allah, glory unto Him, in return for meager pleasures of the world.

Karamah

His disciples one day insisted Shah Naqshiband to display a *karamah*, to which the Sheikh responded by saying:

"Our *karamah* is clear. Just take a look: We are able to stand on our feet and walk on Earth despite the crumbling weight of sin we carry on our shoulders. Could there ever be a greater *karamah*?"

He then reminded his disciples that the gist of the Sufi path was not *karamah* but rather uprightness (*istiqamah*), stating:

"Even if you were to enter a garden and hear the trees proclaim, leaf by leaf, 'Welcome, saint of the Lord', you still should not take any notice, either internally or externally. You should instead intensify your perseverance in servanthood."

Some of his disciples, thereupon, commented:

"No matter how much you try to conceal it, master, you still display some *karamah*, from time to time."

"What you witness", replied that great pillar of modesty, "is nothing but the *karamah* of my disciples".

The Sheikh was so sensitive to keeping his spiritual standing a secret that he did not allow his disciple Husamaddin Khawajah Yusuf to record his words and *karamah* whilst he was alive.

Moral of the Story:

The greats of Islam were able to acquire their spiritual standing by embracing, not *karamah*, but uprightness as a standard. By showing

Sufi Narratives and Lessons

karamah, they have said, one does not necessarily acquire a value more than that of a flying bird or a swimming fish; and that true *marifah* is not to imitate what, say, a bird or a fish can do with natural ease. It is rather to lead a life of integrity and uprightness devoted to the pleasure of the Lord alone and stirred by an intense consciousness of servanthood. This was what the spiritual greats underlined at every given opportunity and exhibited in their lives.

Affecting Ignorant Hearts

On a holy day in the year 1340 AH, there was a special event including Quran and *mawlid* inside the Ayasofya Mosque in Istanbul. The mosque was packed all the way up to the tiers. Present were numerous scholars and students, as well as a group of the most selected *huffaz* (memorizers of the Quran) of the time, reciting the Quran and *mawlid* to the eager audience.

Sitting somewhere near the pulpit was one Adil Bey of Beylerbeyi, a man of spirituality with a receptive spiritual insight. A while later, Adil Bey became overwhelmed by a state of spiritual constriction; strange, since an atmosphere filled by a recitation of the Quran really should have been the last place for someone to come under such spiritual distress. Adil Bey curiously looked around. Before long, he realized that sitting opposite to him was an ignorant, hardhearted man. They were facing each other. Adil Bey recognized that it was the negativity reflecting from the man's heart that was culpable for his own constriction. He quickly changed spots. Relieved though he was, he still could not shrug off the affects for some time.[122]

Moral of the Story:

Just as the righteous exude peace and serenity, the unmindful reflect onto others instability and restlessness and a hardness of heart. Strolling

---

[122] The affects of ritual prayer is only as great as the condition of the heart. In chapter al-Maun, the Almighty declares, "So woe to the worshippers…who are unmindful of their prayers". It is therefore natural to find the unmindful, that is persons ill-of-heart, or even hypocrites, inside mosques.

inside a garden leaves one delighted with the wonderful scents of the flowers, whereas hanging around dirt smears one in stench. Concerning those whose hearts have decayed and therefore do give off anything other than bad influences, the Almighty therefore declares:

"And when you see those who enter into false discourses about Our revelations, withdraw from them until they enter into some other discourse, and if the Shaitan causes you to forget, then do not sit after recollection with the unjust people" (al-Anam, 68)

The subtlety of the Divine command above is more apparent to true servants who are governed by a sensitivity of heart. The more sensitive the heart becomes, the deeper the inner standards become; the sight begins to see the realities behind the curtain and sense truths hidden to most. A splendid example of this is provided by the experience of Seyfi Baba:

Seyfi Baba, who used to dearly love Sami Effendi –may Allah sanctify his secret-, was a man of profound spiritual insight. He left his house in the Istanbul suburb of Topkapi, one day, to pay one of his usual visits to Sami Effendi. But the moment he stepped inside the Sami Effendi's Erenköy home, he collapsed on the floor unconscious. The person, who had let Seyfi Baba inside, desperately splashed some water onto his face, enabling him to regain consciousness.

"We must call a doctor", he afterwards suggested, only to be prevented by the exhausted Seyfi Baba, who said:

"There is no need for a doctor, son, for this has nothing to do with a medical condition. The rebellious people and the density of the places of rebellion I encountered on the way took their toll on me and the moment I stepped inside this door, I was struck by the intensity of the pure spirituality here…But my heart could not take that either. With the help of the beloved Sami Effendi and the blessings of the spiritual atmosphere here, I will be better in no time."

Thus, similar to how the negativity generated by the unmindful leave a distressing and constricting effect on the heart, the positive and inspiring affects the righteous emit relieve and refresh it. Spiritually right-minded persons should therefore try and keep away from the unmindful, as much as they can, and keep with the righteous. Dawud –upon him peace- used to, time and again, pray Allah, glory unto Him, in the following:

"My Lord…Should you see me headed towards a gathering made up of unmindful people, break my feet before I ever make it there so I never end up joining them. It would truly be a great blessing for me if You do that!"

The Friend's Door

"Prepare our mounts", Abu Said Nishaburi –may Allah sanctify his secret- one day instructed his disciples. "We are heading to the town."

The preparations were made and the Sheikh, accompanied by a group of his disciples, headed out. Some time later, they arrived at a village in Nishapur.

"What is the name of this village?" asked the Sheikh.

"*Dar-i Dost*", the locals replied, which means 'the friend's door'.

The Sheikh thereupon decided to stop over. After a day, some his disciples said:

"We thought we were going to the town, master. Aren't we going to move on?"

Abu Said –may Allah sanctify his secret-, whose heart was brimming with the keys to many spiritual secrets, explained:

"It takes a long, grueling journey for the lover to reach the door of the beloved, the friend. Since we have reached the friend's door here, where else could we need to go?"

They ended up staying for forty days, experiencing many spiritual events in the process. Many villagers made the most of the Sheikh's inspiring company, repenting for their past sins and joining the group as his disciples. What the Sheikh had meant by 'the friend's door' was exactly that: to win hearts…for opening the door of the Friend's palace was possible only if one had the key: a heart that had been won over.

Sufism: A Path Towards the Internalization of Faith (Ihsân)

Moral of the Story:

Opening the door of the 'Friend' ajar by winning a heart, has always been the sole desire of righteous servants burning with the love of the Real and the crown on the jewels of righteous deeds that enable them to attain to the eternal reunion. Shah Naqshiband –may Allah sanctify his secret-, for instance, used to exert his duty of enlightening others so caringly and with such exceptional effort that he would concern himself with all his students' problems, regardless of how trivial they may have seemed. Whenever he would visit someone, the Sheikh would inquire the personal problems of whom he was visiting, then those of his family and even his mounts and chickens. He would thereby seek to win the person's heart. If there was some food being served at a gathering, the Sheikh would personally serve its preparers with his very own hands.

To Obey, To Serve, To Advise

A righteous man, who used to frequent the *sohbah* of Dawud-i Tai, once advised Maruf-i Karhi against "…abandoning deeds, for they bring one closer to the pleasure of the Lord."

"What exactly do you mean by deeds?" asked Maruf-i Karhi.

"To remain in a state of obeying the Lord under all circumstances and to serve and advise Muslims", replied the man.

Moral of the Story:

A small deed offered with an obeying and submissive mindset is more valuable in the sight of the Almighty than mountains of deeds offered without. Servanthood begins with obeying and submission. After all, was not the devil expelled from Divine presence because of a lack of obeying and submitting to the Lord and not because of a shortage of deeds?

Serving, on the other hand, is so great a virtue that all prophets and saints have clutched onto it, abandoning it neither during times of illness, nor even on their deathbeds. For the people of wisdom, this is sufficient example of the proper way in which one should continue to serve. Serving, in short, is a hallmark of compassionate and benevolent hearts.

A mature believer is a serving person, a soldier of heart who having cast off his mortal existence, considers himself in the rearmost end of the army of servers. He is by the side of the ill and the troublesome, always close to the mourners, a call away from the dejected, the brokenhearted and the outcast.

Advising, in contrast, is characteristic only to its experts; for what is preached exercises an influence only to the extent it is practiced personally. It is therefore not right for just anyone and everyone to offer advice. The competent in this regard, that is those who have enshrouded themselves in prophetic conduct and morals, exercise a command to do so. Evading this responsibility despite being privileged with the command to advise, on the other hand, incurs enormous blame and liability; for the Blessed Prophet –upon him blessings and peace- states:

"Religion is to advise (*nasihah*)". (Bukhari, Iman, 42)

Therefore, to abandon the duty of advising is tantamount to destruction, to refer to the Divine warning given in chapter al-Asr. Not listening to advice is just the same; it is a cause of destruction.

Aspirants on the way of the Real must therefore accept obeying, serving and advising as indispensable standards and seek these eternal means to acquire the pleasure of the Lord.

Serving Creation

A righteous man saw Pertevniyal Valide Sultan, the benefactor of the Aksaray Valide Mosque in Istanbul, in his dream, shortly after she had passed away, where she had attained to high ranks in the Hereafter.

"Was it because of the mosque you had built that Allah lifted you atop this rank?" he asked her.

"No", replied she.

Sufism: A Path Towards the Internalization of Faith (Ihsân)

"Then with which deed?" asked the man curiously.

"It was a rainy and muddy day", she began explaining. "We were on our way to Ayyub Sultan Mosque when I noticed a scrawny kitten, grasping for breath inside a puddle of water on the side of the pavement. I had the cart stop and told the *baji*[123] next to me to, 'Go and take the little kitten out of the water…lest the poor thing drowns.'

Disinclined to step out of the cart, she replied, 'But my lady we will have our hands and clothes dirty should we step outside in this rain!'

So, without wanting to break her heart, I stepped out of the cart myself, and plunging myself in the mud, took the kitten out of the puddle. The poor thing was quivering. Feeling sorry for it, I placed it on my lap and warmed it up, not letting it go until it came back to its senses.

It is because of that small piece of compassion I showed to the kitten that Allah the Almighty graced me with this high rank."

Moral of the Story:

The glittered path to the skies of spiritual maturity and perfection runs through the ladder of compassion and service. Each Muslim must therefore make compassion and service a part of his nature and let them be his distinctive characteristics.

Courtesy in Saints

Musa Effendi –may Allah sanctify his secret- recounts:

"It was a season of pilgrimage. With the respected Sami Effendi –may Allah sanctify his secret- we were staying at the house of Abdussattar Effendi of Turkistan, in the Mecca suburb of Jiyad, close to the Kaaba. The room Sami Effendi –may Allah sanctify his secret- was staying in

---

[123] In the Ottoman palace, Sudanese women were employed as caretakers of valide sultans, whom were referred to as a *baji*. Being known for their honesty and integrity, the Sudanese were especially chosen to serve in the Palace.

overlooked the street, while our rooms were situated on the opposite side of the house.

At midday during one of those days, Sami Effendi appeared before our door and said, "It seems there is someone outside in need of something to eat."

I quickly prepared some food and rushed outside the door. But there was nobody in sight. Thinking the person had left without waiting, I returned inside. Ten minutes, give or take, had passed when Sami Effendi once again appeared outside of our room.

"That needy person has returned and is looking inside", he said.

This time around, when I stepped outside with the food in my hand, I was finally able to see the person in need: a dog, looking tiredly through the door, panting from starvation. I instantly emptied the food out in front of it. It must have been very hungry, as it quickly ate it all up.

Moral of the Story:

Such is the courtesy and humbleness of spiritual elders. Sami Effendi –may Allah sanctify his secret- did not refer to the dog as a 'dog' but rather as a person. On most occasions, he would speak of animals not as 'creatures' but as 'the servants of Allah'.

A beauty of moral conduct towards a created being for the sake of the Creator is, in essence, presented to the Creator Himself; it is the beauty of a purified heart attached unconditionally to the Lord. Reaching a purified heart, on the other hand, is to reach the inexhaustible, the infinite source of companionship, in the truest sense. Purified hearts pulsate with Divine pleasure, for they are precincts for the manifestation of the Real, magnificent artworks of generosity and compassion.

Will in Presence

A rumor had spread that Sheikh Muhammad Nuru'l-Arabi, a 19th century Sufi, was denying the existence of a particular willpower (*irada-i*

Sufism: A Path Towards the Internalization of Faith (Ihsân)

juziyyah) in human beings. The Ottoman Sultan Abdulmecid then 'willed' for the Sheikh to present in his case at the Palace, during one of the regular lessons of *huzur*.[124•] So, the Sheikh arrived and was asked for an explanation, on which he said:

"A person most certainly exercises a particular power of will; and that is the very reason for his responsibility before the Lord…but not everyone and not all the time. I, for example, possess a particular willpower and freedom of choice but I have come only because of the Sultan's command. Even if I wanted to leave, it is out of my control. They say 'Come' and we come…they say 'leave' and off we go. So it is clear that my willpower means nothing here, concerning a certain choice of movement. Likewise, being in the presence of the Sultan, the things I can do are limited. In exact manner, there are some who continuously live in the consciousness of being in the presence of the Lord. Many a person, knowing that Allah the Almighty is omnipresent and that He watches everything, consider themselves in Divine presence only when offering ritual prayer. But there are those who have obtained a certain spiritual rank, who live with a genuine awareness of being in Divine presence at every moment. Now, it is up for you to decide whether such persons exercise a particular willpower or not!"

Much fond of his words, the Sultan saw the Sheikh off with generous gifts.

Moral of the Story:

A servant exercises a willpower given to him by Allah, glory unto Him. Even though the Will of the Almighty features in every happening, His pleasure rests only with the good. The aim of a teacher is to endow the student with knowledge that would enable him to pass the course. There is nothing a teacher can do if the student slacks off. Again, the duty of a doctor is to ensure that the patient is cured; yet, the patient has nobody else to blame other than himself should he neglect to take the required medicine. Over the negligence, the doctor may not be charged.

Submitting one's willpower, on the other hand, to the Lord in whose presence we stand, brings about a far greater revenue than what is given.

---

[124] The *huzur* lessons were scholarly meetings conducted in the presence or *huzur* of the Sultan; and hence the name.

In other words, if the servant genuinely submits his vision to the infinite gaze of the Lord, his hands to His irrepressible Hand of Might, his tongue to His infinite attribute of Speech and his hearing to the endless Hearing of the Lord, his senses and comprehension will assume an entirely different nature. Simpler put, he will never be at a loss for what he has given. In contrast, each thing presented will transform into eternal blessings right from the heart of eternity. For that reason, in reference to His righteous servants who are unremittingly conscious of being in His presence and have been able to submit their particular willpower to his Will, the Almighty has metaphorically said, in a *hadith al-qudsi*:

"I will become their eyes that see, ears that hear and hands that hold".
(Bukhari, Riqaq, 38)

Propriety

Dawud-i Tai recounts:

"I accompanied Abu Hanifah for twenty odd years. It struck my attention that during this time, I never saw him bareheaded or putting his feet up to rest, either next to others or by himself. I once asked him what wrong could there be in putting your feet up when alone.

"It is better to have propriety in the presence of the Allah the Almighty" he replied.

Moral of the Story:

When in the presence of a person of high rank, people do not act as they normally would and take great care to display behavior suitable to the environment they are in. Being in the presence of any given person, in other words, requires proper conduct. Because they live every moment in the consciousness of being in Divine presence, saints do not ever neglect proper conduct. Propriety, therefore, encompasses their entire lives, for they possess hearts of wisdom through which they see and feel, with certainty, that they are being watched by the Great Beloved at all places and times. They are accustomed to the secret:

$$وَهُوَ مَعَكُمْ اَيْنَ مَاكُنْتُمْ$$

"And He is with you wherever you may be…" (al-Hadid, 4); and they thereby live every moment in the presence of the Lord.

What we are basically trying to say is that, while there are some who feel that they are in the presence of Allah, glory unto Him, only during ritual prayer, who are guided to propriety so long as the prayer lasts depending on the depth in which they feel this presence, there are others truly righteous, whose every behavior and conduct is of propriety, as they prolong this mindset even outside ritual prayer. In honor of such people, the Quran states:

$$اَلَّذِينَ هُمْ عَلٰى صَلَاتِهِمْ دَائِمُونَ$$

"Those who are constant at their prayer" (al-Maarij, 23) Not only do they never neglect their ritual prayers, it is said they are in a constant state of prayer even when not praying. This denotes their ability to maintain the consciousness of being in Divine presence in and outside of ritual prayer.

Propriety in Serving

Abu Abdullah Rugandi says:

"Do not ever underrate any service you receive. After all, service is service; and it may just be that something which seems unimportant to you is regarded highly by the Lord for reasons you know not. It is unknown to us in which of service the pleasure of Allah is to be found. Therefore, continue to serve until you obtain your desire and your desire ought not to be anything than the pleasure of Allah. The blessings and advantages you attain to on the way should only intensify your gratitude to the Lord and your service."

Moral of the Story:

It is not so important to simply offer service as is it is to offer it with a sincere heart and in the best possible manner. People who put their hands up to serve must therefore be motivated not just with the desire to serve but to embody a behavior that would acquire for them the pleasure of the Lord. Carrying out service only with a vested interest in return for winning somebody's favor at the expense of turning a cold shoulder on all the other types of service seen as serving no personal ends, is tantamount to laying waste on eternal happiness. Although these people may end up winning the favor of certain others for whom they strive, the Mercy of the Lord is lifted from them and they consequently attract Divine Wrath. Serving must not be motivated by the desire to acquire the praises and favors of mere mortals on Earth. Much rather, it should be driven with the desire to accomplish such deeds on Earth that would grant one a kingdom of spirituality in the Hereafter.

The aspirant must therefore treat every opportunity to serve as a lost and found treasure. It is possible that a service looked down upon by everyone on Earth could be hiding rewards greater than the earth and the heavens. To test the sincerity of His servants and to see where their hearts flow, the Lord does, after all, conceal many an ocean sought after in a drop.

Propriety…No Matter What

Ibn Ata –may Allah sanctify his secret- explains:

"It was not simply because of their ritual prayers and fasts that those who have progressed on this spiritual path have been able to do so. They progressed by complementing these obligations with virtuous deeds and behavior. The Prophet –upon him blessings and peace- in fact says:

"The closest to me from among you on the Day of Judgment is he with the most beautiful traits and morals." (Tirmidhi, Birr, 71)

Sufism: A Path Towards the Internalization of Faith (Ihsân)

Moral of the Story:

The poet says it wonderfully:

Propriety…a God-given crown,
Wear it, lest in troubles you drown.

Another wise poet says:

Among the spiritually minded, I asked and sought out
All is accepted, they said, only with propriety no matter what.

True heroes of propriety and morals are prophets and saints, and also those who know how to follow in their footsteps, through which they exert a will for moral conduct. The pillar of morality is not something detached from a maturity of religiosity. Morality is to rescue one's self from animalistic traits and to be adorned with human qualities in their place. Being Muslim in the truest sense is to embody the morals of Islam, to exhibit its beauties in behavior and conduct.

When viewed from the vantage of the intellect and wisdom, it is not difficult to see that the main theme of the Quran is propriety and morals. Even its narratives recounted from the depths of history are motivated towards conveying a perfection of behavior.

Mawlana Rumi –may Allah sanctify his secret- says:

"'What is faith?' asked my heart. My intellect kneeled down and whispered to my heart's ear, 'Faith is nothing but propriety.' Improper people not only harm themselves…but through their improperness, they are perhaps setting the entire world on fire."

The Morals and Service of a Saint

Ahmed ar-Rifai –may Allah sanctify his secret- used to greet every person he came across. On hearing about someone ill in a village or a town, near or far, he would use to the first opportunity to visit them. When he came across a blind person on the street, he would hold his hand and take him to his intended destination. Should he come across an elderly person, he would help him carry his load and narrate, to those around, the following saying of the Blessed Prophet –upon him blessings and peace-:

"Whoever respects and helps an elderly person will be granted but Allah the Almighty with someone to respect and help him in his elderly years." (Tirmidhi, Birr, 75)

Upon returning from a long distance journey, he would head straight to the forest, chop some wood and carry it back to the town on his donkey. He would then personally distribute it among the widows and the poor.

He would run to the help of the mentally ill and the crippled, wash their clothes and sit with them, listening to their problems. He would then serve them food with his very own hands and ask for their prayers. He would say to his disciples:

"Visiting these vulnerable people is not just commendable (*mustahab*) it is obligatory (*wajib*)."

While playing on the street one day, a few kids had happened to walk past him. Scared of his awe-inspiring appearance, the kids ran off. But Ahmed ar-Rifai –may Allah sanctify his secret- quickly ran after them and hugging them compassionately, one by one, he even apologized, saying:

"As you can see, dear kids, I am a vulnerable soul just like you. Forgive me…I never meant to scare you!"

Moral of the Story:

The way of spiritual wisdom, proceeding on which one acquires the pleasure of the Real and the key to His reunion, is like blank sheet of white paper. The ink used for writing on this paper is also white and is read only by Allah, glory unto Him. For that reason, saints embark on a lifelong struggle not to drop a black stain on that piece of paper; so much so that they avoid harming even an ant and offer the moral conduct and service to the Lord as purely as they can, in order to attain to His pleasure. For, the Almighty declares:

إِنَّ اللهَ يُحِبُّ التَّوَّابِينَ وَيُحِبُّ الْمُتَطَهِّرِينَ

Sufism: A Path Towards the Internalization of Faith (Ihsân)

"For Allah loves those who turn to Him constantly and He loves those who keep themselves pure and clean" (al-Baqarah, 222)

Let the Immortal Know, Not Mortals!

During the first years of Islam, an unidentified person used to drop off a sack of food items in front of the homes of certain poor people. This continued uninterrupted for a long time, until one morning the poor woke up to find that nothing had been left in front of their doors. As they began thinking about the possible reason, Medina was suddenly shaken with the death of Zayn'al-Abidin –may Allah sanctify his secret-, the grandson of Ali –Allah be well-pleased with him-. The news sent everyone to grief.

They solemnly began performing the final services for this beloved grandson of the Prophet –upon him blessings and peace-. When it was time to wash his body, the person entrusted with this honorable duty was taken aback by a number of blistered scars on the back of the corpse. He could not make sense of them. He decided to ask his family members and one of them, who had insight into the matter, said:

"Every morning, Zayn'al-Abidin would prepare sacks of food-items, carry them on his back to the doors of the poor and return without anyone noticing. Not even the poor knew the identity of the person leaving sacks of food in front of their doors. The scars you saw on his back were caused by the heavy sacks of food he carried."

Moral of the Story:

Those who offer their deeds simply for the pleasure of the Lord, keep a tight lid on them, like a sworn secret, from the public. Deeds exposed to the knowledge of the public despite initially being carried out for the pleasure of the Lord, leave behind their value by the time they reach Divine presence, for they then assume an egotistic character and are exposed to the onslaught of pride and self-importance. Each righteous offered deed in the way of the Real should therefore be offered to 'let the Immortal know, not mortals'; only then will it be accepted. And neither pens nor inks would be sufficient to record the rewards of a deed offered in such a mindset.

Blissful are the true heroes who, while striving to better the conditions of people through the genuine services they offer, seek the pleasure of the Real and not their egos.

Do Not Look Down On Anyone!

It is reported that one day Jesus –upon him peace- journeyed out of town, accompanied by a man regarded as righteous and looked up to by the Israelites. Another man, a notorious sinner known for his debauchery, followed them, beset with a feeling of remorse over his ways. When they stopped over somewhere for rest, the sinner sat someplace else where, brokenhearted, he sought refuge in the mercy of the Most Merciful and repentantly prayed:

"O Lord…Forgive me for the sake of that great prophet over there!"

Once the supposedly righteous man overheard his prayer, he looked down on him in despise and made his own prayer:

"My Lord…Do not resurrect me with that man on the Day of Judgment!"

The Lord thereupon revealed the following to Jesus –upon him peace-:

"Inform my two servants that I have accepted both their prayers. I have forgiven my sinful yet remorseful servant and made him bound for Paradise. As for the other looked upon as righteous, I have banished him from Paradise for not wanting to be in the company of someone I have forgiven."

Moral of the Story:

Looking down on any servant of the Almighty apart from those who have already met Divine wrath, is a murder the heart commits. Only hearts of stone, distant from Divine Love, can commit this murder. By looking down on another, one does not bring him down; he only serves to bring himself down and signal his own self-destruction. Indeed, the Blessed Prophet –upon him blessings and peace- states:

بِحَسْبِ امْرِئٍ مِنَ الشَّرِّ أَنْ يَحْقِرَ أَخَاهُ الْمُسْلِمَ

Sufism: A Path Towards the Internalization of Faith (Ihsân)

"Looking down on and despising a Muslim brother suffices as sin." (Muslim, Birr, 32)

The poet says it eloquently:

Do not despise the men of sin
For many treasures are hidden in ruin

Do Not Condemn Anyone!

Khamdun Qassar –may Allah sanctify his secret- says:

"Should you see a drunkard staggering along, beware not to condemn him…for it is possible you might one day find yourself on the same boat!"

Moral of the Story:

The Sufi way and training is grounded in compassion and mercy; it allows for no contempt, belittling and hurting others' feelings. The Lord reveals that His servant is a mystery from His Eternal Power. It is therefore important to look upon a sinner as a jewel that has fallen in a swamp, waiting to get picked up. Contempt would only mean that the jewel is pushed further down the mud. In commanding His servants to avoid such a destructive attitude, the Almighty states:

"O you who believe! Let not (one) people laugh at (another) people perchance they may be better than they, nor let women (laugh) at (other) women, perchance they may be better than they;" (al-Hujurat, 11)

Rather than weighing the sins of others, which is thus prohibited by the Quran, one must weigh up and come to terms with his own, personal sins. Furthermore, it has been frequently observed that people who spend all their time judging others with contempt end up falling into the same position themselves. Not for no reason do they proverbially say, "Laugh at your mate, suffer the same fate."

Cheering Up an Orphan

Sari-i Saqati recounts:

"On *eid* day once, I saw Maruf-i Karhi collecting date seeds on the street. I asked him what he was going to do with the seeds, to which he replied:

'I saw a small kid crying over there. When I approached him and asked why he was crying, he told me that he was an orphan who neither had the clothes nor the toys his peers had. Before he even finished his sentence, he began crying again. His situation was heartrending. So I decided to collect the seeds which you see. I shall sell them and with the money, purchase the clothes and toys the kid wants.'

His word touched my heart, too, and I insisted the Sheikh to allow me to '…personally take care of the child.' He was kind enough to let me, on which I took the kid to the bazaar and purchased his needs."

Sari-i Saqati further adds the impact this righteous deed had on his soul:

"The blessings of my serving the orphan engulfed my heart in such a light, with which I felt spiritual zests I had never before experienced."

Moral of the Story:

Cheering up orphans and protecting them is an initiative strongly encouraged by Islam, the rewards of which are unimaginable. The following promise of the Blessed Prophet –upon him blessings and peace- for those who take up this initiative is enough to put hearts in a sweet trance:

"He who protects an orphan of his own or of another shall be side by side with me in Paradise *just like this*." As he was narrating this *hadith*, Malik ibn Anas –Allah be well-pleased with him- reenacted the hand gesture the Prophet -upon him blessings and peace- had made as he said 'just like this', by joining his index and middle fingers together. (Muslim, Zuhd, 42)

The Blessed Prophet –upon him blessings and peace- further says:

"Should a person caress the head of an orphan simply for the sake of Allah, he will receive ten rewards for each strand of hair his hands make contact with." (Ahmed ibn Hanbal, Musnad, V, 250)

'Caressing the hair of an orphan' implies taking close interest in all his needs, be they material or spiritual.

Friendship

Sahl ibn Ibrahim explains:

"We were friends with Ibrahim ibn Adham. I was once struck down by a severe illness, whereupon Ibrahim spent all he had, simply to ensure that I regained my health. In time, I slowly began to recuperate. There was one occasion when I felt like eating a few things, so I asked him if he could obtain them. Because he did not have any means at the time, it turned out that he sold his donkey in order to purchase the things I wanted. It was only later on when I got back up on my feet that I found out about this. I needed to go somewhere, for which I decided to borrow his donkey. When I asked him where the donkey was, he replied:

"We have sold it."

As I felt the burden of the journey would prove too much for my health, I asked him:

"What am I to do now?"

"No stress, brother", he said. "I will carry you on my back!" He ended up carrying me on his back across three villages.

Moral of the Story:

In good times, everyone is a friend. But true friendship shows itself only in bad times and its value is incomparable with any other. The secret of sainthood, therefore, lies in remaining the friend of Allah, glory unto Him, His Messenger and righteous persons, in the often difficult and unpleasant days of our lives.

Sacrifice and philanthropy especially towards Muslims who are in need attracts the mercy of the Lord, who is infinitely merciful and compassionate towards His servants, and who has sent His Messenger –upon him blessings and peace- for no other reason than for him to be a mercy to the worlds. The Blessed Prophet –upon him blessings and peace- says:

"Allah shows mercy to people of mercy and compassion." (Abu Dawud, Adab, 58)

The Purpose of Friendship

Abdullah ibn Mubarak –may Allah sanctify his secret- had gone on a journey with a man with certain bad habits. When their journey came to an end and both went their own ways, Abdullah ibn Mubarak began weeping. His friends affectionately asked the reason behind his tears:

"Despite such a long journey", he explained behind misty eyes, "I could not mend any of the bad habits of my friend for the road. I could not help him improve his behavior. And now, I cannot help it but think it could have been because of my own shortcomings that I was unable to be of any benefit to him…If it is because of my own error that he was unable correct himself, what is to be of me tomorrow when we are resurrected?" He then continued sobbing helplessly.

Moral of the Story:

Friendships should always be constructed upon a spiritually beneficial purpose. Accordingly, befriending and accompanying the righteous should be with the aim of benefiting from them and befriending persons of spiritual weakness and shortcomings should be with the intention of offering them spiritual help. Friendships established purely upon passing pleasures and oblivious to spiritual benefit are tantamount to laying waste to the happiness of both worlds. Even the least damage one is inflicted with through such friendships can never be taken lightly: behavior and action rubs off from one friend to the other.

Yet, should all attempts towards bettering them prove unfruitful, the method to be followed in attempting to correct persons with shortcomings is not to hurt their feelings by laying the blame on them. One should instead question himself to see whether the fault in fact lies with him. For if it is because of our own shortcomings and flaws that we have been unable to set another person right, it means that we are seriously accountable in the Hereafter. The purpose is not to act as a veil but to part all veils and point to the truth.

Full Submission

The Quran recounts how the Almighty commanded Musa –upon him peace- to:

"Go to the Pharaoh; for he has indeed transgressed…" (Taha, 24)

As Musa –upon him peace- could not think of anyone to leave his family and sheep with, he asked:

"What about my family and sheep, o Lord?"

Allah, glory unto Him, thereupon reminded His messenger of being the best of protectors, declaring:

"What else can you wish for, Musa, after you have found Me? Run to fulfill My command! Become attached to Me and show submission! If I wish, I could place a wolf to shepherd your sheep and angels to guard your family! What is it that worries you, Musa? Who saved you when your mother threw into the river? And Who reunited you with your mother afterwards? Remember the time you had killed a man by accident and the Pharaoh was after your head…Who protected you from him at that time?"

Attentively listening in the meantime, Musa –upon him peace- was answering each question by saying:

"You, You, You, my Lord!"

Moral of the Story:

Musa –upon him peace- was of course at the peak of submission, like all prophets. But since prophets act as exemplars for humankind, the Lord

Sufi Narratives and Lessons

makes transpire through them many important and enlightening standards for us to take note of and behave accordingly when faced with similar situations. The lesson expressed by the above narrative is that no personal excuse is valid at the face of the commands of Allah, the Lord of the Worlds. With Him is to be found all the blessings and protection one may ever need when striving to execute His command. If a servant genuinely struggles to fulfill a Divine command only for the pleasure of the Lord, he will see that the Lord does help him whatever the circumstances may be. The Absolute Protector in fact had Musa –upon him peace- raised in the Pharaoh's palace, immersed Ibrahim –upon him peace- in a garden of roses amid the scorching fire of Nimrod, put the righteous young men of the Cave into a slumber of over three-hundred years to protecting them from the harm of tyrants and safeguarded Muhammad Mustafa –upon him blessings and peace- from many a threat, including concealing him from the prying eyes of his enemies in the Cave of Sawr. The poet expresses this beautifully:

I expect the help of no other, let the Lord be my guard,
In Him I trust, 'for Allah is the Best Protector'[125]

Sayri

Receiving the Prayers of a Believer

It was a day when Maruf-i Karhi was fasting voluntarily. Just as he was walking past the bazaar late afternoon, he saw a water-bearer, praying:

"May Allah treat him, who drinks from this water, with His blessings and mercy!" So Maruf heeded the call; and breaking his fast, he drank from the water the man had to offer.

"Why did you break your fast?" asked those next to him.

"So I could attain to the blessings of the man's prayer", he answered.

After Maruf-i Karhi passed away, a friend of his saw him in his dream; and recalling the incident, asked him, "How did Allah treat you?"

---

125 A reference to Yusuf, 64.

"Because of the blessings of the water-bearer's prayers", he responded, "my Lord forgave me and treated me with compassion."

Moral of the Story:

There is many an outcast, whose heart is constantly with the Lord, whose prayers can at times be more precious than the rewards of voluntary deeds of worship. But it must be borne in mind that voluntary fasts broken with the hope of attaining to a greater virtue must be compensated at a later date, as completing an unfinished fast is obligatory (wajib), even if it may have been voluntary to begin with. Underlined by the above incident is to be able to choose something more important over another thing of lesser importance. For there may come a moment when seemingly small things may be loaded with enormous benefits. On the other hand, just as there may be treasures buried inside desolate buildings, there may also be persons, who although may look as if they are desolate on the outside, may in fact be precious gems on the inside. One must beware not to ignore such persons. This is splendidly voiced in the below couplet:

Consider each night a Qadr, every person a Khidr,
You are being watched, the eight Heavens awaiting

Sayri

The Blessed Prophet –upon him blessings and peace- says:

"Should I tell you of those who are Heaven bound? They are those who nobody takes seriously, as they are weak and are seen as weak; yet if they were to vow that 'such and such will happen', Allah would surely make their vows come true.

Should I tell you of those who are Hell bound? They are the hard-hearted, the rude, the miserly and the conceited, who swagger as they walk." (Bukhari, Ayman, 9; Muslim, Jannah, 47)

A *Majzub* and the Cure of an Ailing Heart

Bayazid-i Bistami –may Allah sanctify his secret- came across a doctor preparing some medicine and asked him:

"Do you have a medication, doctor, for my illness?"

"What is your illness?" counter asked the doctor.

"Sin", replied he.

Helplessly extending his arms to both sides, the doctor then said, "I do not know of a medication for the illness of sin."

Meanwhile, a young *majzub* nearby, who overheard their conversation, interrupted and said:

"I know of some medicine for your disease!"

"Tell me, young man", urged Bayazid joyously. Despite being looked upon as deranged, it was evident that the young man was in fact a man of wisdom. So he began describing the ingredients of the medicine to cure sin:

"Take ten dirhams worth of remorse roots and ten dirhams of repentance! Place them onto the tray of your heart and beat it up with the gavel of *tawhid*. Then sift it through the sieve of fairness and knead some tears into it. Afterwards, cook it in the oven of love! You will acquire a paste from which you should take five spoonfuls a day. Do as I say and soon, you will have nothing left of your disease!"

Bayazid-i Bistami heaved a deep sigh and remarked:

"Pity the fools who think you are deranged and suppose themselves to be intelligent!"

Moral of the Story:

When perception in the sight of the Lord becomes more important, for one, than public reception, the paths of maturity and wisdom become wide open. One's sight, hearing and feeling then begins to assume a profound and mysterious depth. Many a person of the kind becomes something of an Uways al-Qarani, ignored by the public and looked upon as deranged.

But in reality, it is only because he has attained to the special friendship of Allah, glory unto Him, and His Messenger that he appears that way.

The above incident further reflects the blessings of the Divine command, "Accompany the righteous!" (at-Tawbah, 119) As was seen in the young man's words of wisdom, the medicine given by the righteous provides a cure for many an ailing heart, binding it to the Real, healthier and stronger than ever. Further, the fact that Bayazid-i Bistami asks for a medicine for the heart in spite of possessing a spiritually alive and healthy heart himself, is a manifestation of his own humbleness, and no less, it is motivated with the aim of actually curing the doctor's heart.

Faces like Angels

With the late Sami Effendi and my late father Musa Effendi –may Allah sanctify their secrets-, who was accompanying him, we were returning from Bursa to Istanbul. To board the car ferry at Yalova to cross to the other side of the Marmara Sea, we were about to line up with the rest of the cars. The attendant at the dock, assigned with the task of making sure that the cars lined up in neat rows, suddenly caught sight of Sami Effendi and Musa Effendi, as he was signaling the proper position for our vehicle. Astounded, he paused. He then came closer. Taking a curious look inside the car, he heaved out a deep sigh and remarked:

"Good Lord, what a strange world! There are faces like angels…and there are faces like the Nimrod…"

Moral or the Story:

The above incident shows that the sign of being a 'friend' of Allah, glory unto Him, is for the heart and face to be enlightened by His Divine Light. In other words, saints are those who, when seen, remind one of the Lord, insofar as their path is the path of the Divine. They are upon the towering morals of Prophet Muhammad Mustafa –upon him blessings and peace-, the great guide of the entourage of truth. Indeed, simply the Prophet's –upon him blessings peace- face and expression were inviters to the Lord, without him needing to put the invitation to words. In fact, the moment he saw the Prophet –upon him blessings and peace- Abdullah ibn Salam –Allah be well-pleased with him, an erstwhile prominent scholar among the Jews confessed:

"Such a face cannot lie". This alone was enough motivation for him to embrace Islam. (Tirmidhi, Qiyamah, 42; Ahmed ibn Hanbal, Musnad, V, 451)

Everywhere he goes, each servant thus leaves an almost endless amount of impressions, be they positive or negative; his behavior and mindset speak for themselves and he comes under numerous glances, both attentive and inattentive. There is not telling how many people will take a liking for the way one conducts himself in public and take it as an example.

It must be born in mind that the universe is the source of Divine joy, whose wonderful manifestation the beautiful mystery we call man is. The righteous and the mature souls, who are comprised in the content of this Divine joy, are people who are never consigned to the rubble of history; their lives continue after their death, as a reward of having led exemplary lives for humankind.

The Condition of the Heart during Charity

Musa Effendi –may Allah sanctify his secret- recounts:

"We were on a journey with Sami Effendi –may Allah sanctify his secret-. Somewhere in the town of Ürgüp, a man stopped the car and asked for some cigarette money. In spite of the silent protests of some of the journeymen, Sami Effendi said:

'Since he is asking for it, we must give him what he wants', and ensured the man received the money. Receiving the money, the delighted man then had a sudden change of heart and remarked:

'I will now go and but bread with this money instead'. He was visibly happy as he walked into the distance."

Sufism: A Path Towards the Internalization of Faith (Ihsân)

Moral of the Story:

Actions executed simply for the pleasure of Allah, glory unto Him, find ways inside a person's heart and serve to better their morals. What is therefore important in charity is not the inner condition of the receiver but the inner condition of the benefactor. The Blessed Prophet –upon him blessings and peace- states:

"A man once promised to himself that he would give charity. At night time, he left his house with the charity in his hand and unknowingly gave it to a thief. The word on the street next day was '…how strange it is that a thief was given charity last night!'

Hearing this, the man said, 'Thank you, my Lord. Surely, I will offer another charity.'

He, again, left his house with the charity in his hand and unknowingly placed it inside the palm of a prostitute. Next day, people were chitchatting about the oddness that 'a prostitute was given charity!'

'Thank you, my Lord', responded the man, 'for handing me the opportunity to give charity even if it were to a prostitute. I will surely offer another charity.'

That night, he left his house once more with the charity in his hand and again, unknowingly, handed it to a wealthy man. 'What is going on?' grumbled the townsfolk the next day. 'This time a rich man was given charity!'

'Thank you Allah', the man said, 'for allowing me to give charity even if was to a thief, a prostitute and to an affluent!'

In return for his sincerity, it was said to the man, in his dream:

'The charity you gave to the thief may perhaps make him feel ashamed of his thieving and make him abandon it. The charity you gave to the prostitute may perhaps make her leave her ways and lead her to virtue. And the rich man may perhaps draw a lesson from your charity and dispense from his wealth to the needy!'" (Bukhari, Zakat, 14; Muslim, Zakat, 78)

Since the influence of a given charity is only as great as the benefactor's sincerity, the benefactor must therefore be in a state of gratitude towards the Lord.

The Righteous Deed that Reaches the Throne

One day a disciple of Dawud-i Tai, who was seeing to the personal chores of the Sheikh, said, "I have cooked some meat. Would you like me to bring some?"

Seeing his master remain silent, he then brought a plateful of meat and placed it in front of him. But without throwing even a little glance at the meat in front of him, Dawud-i Tai –may Allah sanctify his secret- asked:

"What about the so-and-so orphans, my dear?"

The disciple sighed and to indicate that they were without sufficient means, replied, "Their situation is the same, master."

"In that case, take this meat to them!" advised the great saint.

"But it has been a very long time since you ate meat, master", said the disciple, genuinely wanting his master to consume the food he had prepared for him. Yet adamant, Dawud-i Tai said:

"If I were to eat that meat, my dear, it will only find its way outside. But if the orphans were to eat it, it would find its way to the Throne of the Lord!"

Moral of the Story:

Just as it is impossible for the sun not to provide warmth, it is impossible for high-spirited human beings not to feel sorry for others and to remain indifferent to their pains and troubles. Compassion is a Divine treasure effervescent throughout the universe. The hearts of the righteous, for that matter, are inexhaustible chests of the treasure of compassion. In their eyes, the awaiting profit in casting aside the fleeting interests and desires that only serve to aggravate the ego and focusing on good deeds that not only nourish the spirit but also serve to eternalize the deeds is infinitely more beautiful. The greatest profit a human being can ever acquire on Earth is through righteous deeds. Other gains are merely trusts placed temporarily in the hands of man, as is testified by the below incident:

The family members of the Blessed Prophet –upon him blessings and peace- once had a sheep slaughtered. After most of its meat was handed out in charity, the Blessed Prophet –upon him blessings and peace- inquired what was left of the sheep.

"Only a single shoulder blade", informed Aisha –Allah be well-pleased with her-.

"That means", declared the Prophet –upon him blessings and peace- "all is ours except for a single shoulder blade!" (Tirmidhi, Qiyamah, 33)

A Constant Awareness of the Real

Abdulqadir Jilani –may Allah sanctify his secret- recounts a personal experience:

"A light, one day, appeared right in front of my eyes and soon covered the entire horizon. Still trying to make out what it was, I suddenly heard a voice coming from the light:

'I am your Lord, Abdulqadir', it said. 'I am so pleased by the righteous deeds you have offered until this day that, from now on, I have made all that is *haram*, *halal* for you!'

But as soon as the sentence finished, I realized that the voice belonged to the cursed devil and said:

'Go away, you wretched creature! The light you show is nothing but eternal darkness for me!'

'You have gotten away from me once again through the wisdom given to you by your Lord', he said. 'Yet, to this day, I was able to deceive hundreds of people with this trick!' The light then subsided.

Sufi Narratives and Lessons

I lifted my hands aloft and thanked my Lord, knowing that this was a blessing from Him."

Hearing him recall this incident, a man asked, "How did you know that the voice belonged to the devil?" Abdulqadir Jilani –may Allah sanctify his secret- replied:

"When he said, 'I have made all the *haram*, *halal*!'"

Moral of the Story:

In all times and places, there have always been people who have maliciously tried to obscure the religion of Allah, glory unto Him. At times when this destructive activity becomes more intense than ever, the criterion or the ability to discern right from wrong, the good from evil and the beautiful from ugly gains an added importance for a believer. Today, the above incident is reenacted in similar fashion, with supposed scholars acting with vested interest who strive to transform the *haram*s of Islam to *halal*s and vice versa, damaging the social fiber in the process. The prudent attitude and acute judgment of Abdulqadir Jilani –may Allah sanctify his secret- is therefore of special importance for all of us. In fact, his method of approach is unmistakably clear: The Almighty never privileges anyone with a right He has not privileged even the Prophet with. Could the devil and the pretentious scholars, who are virtually the human embodiments of the devil, exercise greater insight into the nature of the *halal* and the *haram*, the right and the wrong, the beautiful and the ugly than the Prophet? No way! The Almighty sends a stern warning to people who think the contrary:

Say: "What! Will you instruct Allah about your religion? But Allah knows all that is in the heavens and on earth: He has full knowledge of all things." (al-Hujurat, 16)

The *Karim* is All I Need

Bayazid-i Bistami explains:

"One day, I needed to cross to the other side of the Tigris. When I came near the shore, both sides of river joined together to ease my path across. Quickly coming to my senses, I said to myself:

"I will surely not be fooled by this; for the boatmen deliver one to the other side of the river for half a dime. But by coming together, you are asking for my thirty years of righteous deeds! Sorry to say but I cannot waste the deeds I have prepared for the day of resurrection in return for as little as half a dime! The *Karim* (the Generous) is all I need, not a *karamah*."

Moral of the Story:

Karamah, for which the ego takes a liking, poses a really sensitive problem for saints. The price to be paid by brushing aside *karamah* is either a temporary tiredness, a little cost out of one's pocket or to go unnoticed in the public eye. But the price of seizing *karamah*, on the other hand, may at times be as much as the entirety of the righteous deeds offered up until that time, a spiritual bankruptcy that leaves nothing in the hand to take to the eternal realm. Except for the *karamah* whose exhibiting was necessitated by the Will of the Lord, saints have always consciously shunned all interest in showing such feats, which are tantamount to gaining public approval and applause, focusing instead on acquiring the pleasure of the Lord, the ever *Karim*.

Meaningful are the below comments made by Sahl ibn Abdullah at-Tustari on the issue:

"Changing bad habits with good ones is the greatest of all *karamah*. Indeed, some *karamah* are like toys given to appease a crying child. Saints never desire this; only the ignorant do. They amuse themselves and often many others with it."

The most important point above all, therefore, is to:

"…stand firm on the right path as you are commanded" (Hud, 112)

The Responsibility of the Forerunners

Imam Abu Hanifah one day came across a child walking in the mud. Throwing a compassionate smile at the child, he said:

"Watch out, dear, so that you do not trip and fall!"

Sufi Narratives and Lessons

The child turned to the Imam with eyes gleaming with intelligence and gave the following unexpected reply:

"For me to fall is no big deal, Imam. But it is you who should be careful…for should you trip, those who follow you and hang on your every word will fall and helping them up would be awfully difficult!"

Captivated by the prudent words of the child, the Imam began to cry. He turned to his students and said:

"Should you receive stronger evidence on a given issue, do not follow my ruling. That is the sign of maturity in Islam…and only by this means will your love and attachment to me transpire…" (Khashiyat'u Ibn Abidin, I, 217-219, Dimashq, 2000)

Moral of the Story:

Being at the forefront on the way of truth comes with a blessing, though also with a great responsibility. Forerunners influence others through their good characteristics; yet their errors and evils may often be misconstrued as correct and good and find a breeding ground. Thus, the greats of Islam like Abu Hanifah have not only taken note of this delicate aspect whilst passing legal judgment, they have also led their lives strictly within the measure of piety. In fact, after being spotted cleaning a tiny speck of dirt from his shirt, Imam Abu Hanifah was asked:

"According to the ruling you have made on the issue, Imam, the size of the dirt on your shirt does not prevent you from offering ritual prayer. So, why do you make such a fuss?"

"That was a ruling", replied the Imam. "But this is piety!"

Such is the sole standard, sufficient to turn all the obligations to the Creator as well as the created into reasons of the joy in the eternal life of the Hereafter!

Attending the Invitation of the Lord

Hasan Basri –may Allah sanctify his secret- says:

"Sheep are more sensitive than men, for when a shepherd calls, they stop grazing and pay attention. What could be said to a man who fails to take a lesson from this and ignorantly remains deaf to the invitation of the Lord?"

Moral of the Story:

An invitation can be of many kinds. If the call is made by someone disliked, the situation would be different compared to the call of a beloved friend. Attending the call, the invitation of Allah, glory unto Him, should therefore be with an exuberant heart overflowing with the joy of submission. We must especially weigh the excitement and enthusiasm of our hearts, on the scale of Divine love and attachment, in heeding to the invitation of the *adhan* heard five times a day. Mawlana Rumi voices this beautifully:

"Get your act together! Since the Lord demands you, turn your head into feet, if that is what it will take, and run…for His invitation exalts man, gives him spiritual exuberance and eternal blessings!"

The Importance of *Halal*

A financially wealthy disciple of Abu Abbas Nihawandi –may Allah sanctify his secret- one day asked the Sheikh who should be the worthy recipient of his alms.

"To whomever your heart warms to", advised the Sheikh.

The disciple took this advice to heart and left. On the way, he came upon a blind man begging on the street. Taking a liking towards the man, the disciple took out a pouch full of gold coins from his pocket, the sum total of his alms, and gave it to him. Inspecting the pouch with his hands, the blind beggar walked away delightedly. The next day, while he was walking through the same street, the disciple happened to overhear a conversation between the same beggar from yesterday and another blind man.

"A gentleman gave me a pouch full of gold yesterday", the man was saying to his friend. "And I went to the tavern and got blind drunk…"

Annoyed and disgruntled, the disciple headed straight next to Abu Abbas –may Allah sanctify his secret-. He was just about to recount the incident to him, when the Sheikh, without giving him an opportunity to speak, handed him a dime he had received from selling his *taqiyah*, telling the disciple to:

"Give this dime to the first person you come across!"

Unable to utter even a word, the disciple left the scene to fulfill the charitable task he had been given. Compliant with the request of his Sheikh, he handed the dime to the first person he saw on the street. Yet, with a gnawing curiosity, he decided to follow the man. Eventually, the man ended up at the outskirts of the town, where he entered a derelict house. There, he took out a dead quail from his inside pocket and left it on the ground. He was just about to leave the scene when the disciple confronted him and said:

"For God's sake, tell me the truth. What is the dead quail that you just left on the ground over there, all about?"

Suddenly confronted by the disciple by whom he was given the dime, the man stuttered as he explained:

"For seven days, I was not able to find anything to feed my family. My wife and I were doing our best to keep patient but our children could not take it anymore…Still, begging people was something I could never get myself to do. While craving in agony, I found that almost decayed and rather inconsumable dead quail. Out of desperate need, I was on the verge of taking that to my children, for them to eat. But in my mind, I was pleading the Lord, beseeching him to help me…And that was when you appeared and gave me the dime. For that, I thanked the Lord and came here to drop off the dead quail. I now intend on heading to the bazaar to buy something for us to eat…"

Almost petrified, the disciple wasted no time to go to his Sheikh. Before he could even utter a word, the Sheikh said:

"Son, it seems then that you did not pay enough attention to whether your earnings were muddled by the *haram* and the doubtful. Hence, you alms were squandered for wine, even though you did take care to find the right person. The way you earn something is the way it ends up being spent. The reason as to why a single dime of mine found the hands of a righteous man in contrast to your pouch full of gold that ended up in the hands of a drunkard, is only because it was the fruit of elbow grease…in other words, it was *halal*."

Moral of the Story:

Everything gains and loses value in accordance with the positive or negative characteristics it possesses. This fact is more conspicuous with regard to the *halal* and the *haram*. There is an old proverbial saying pertaining to wealth and property that catches hold of the inner gist of fact:

"What comes from *Hayy*, goes to *Hu*." (*Haydan gelen huya gider*)

This has two meanings. Firstly, that which comes from *Hayy* (the Alive) or the Lord returns to *Hu*, literally to Him who is again, no-one other than the Lord. The second meaning is 'easy come easy go'; that is, earnings acquired on the back of impermissible or doubtful means eventually go to waste. In short, while *halal* engenders nothing but *halal*, *haram* only brings about another *haram*. Voicing this fact are the evocative words of Abu Bakr Warraq –may Allah sanctify his secret-:

"When I wake up in the morning, I observe people around and realize who is living off *halal* and who is living off *haram*".

"How so?" he was asked.

"On seeing someone", he explained, "who scuttles into vain talk, backbiting and cursing as soon as he wakes up in the morning, I just know that this state is caused by the *haram* he consumes. And whosoever wakes up in the morning and busies himself with the remembrance of the Lord and remorseful repentance, is able to do so only because of the *halal* he consumes. Both the *halal* and the *haram* transpire in people's behavior according to the specific characteristics they possess."

Halal Earnings

Imam Abu Hanifah was quite a wealthy man, who made a living as a merchant. Being a busy scholar, however, he would manage his business through his proxy and personally inspect and see whether his business transactions were undertaken according to *halal* standards. So sensitive was he to this issue that on one occasion, before sending his partner-in-trade Hafs ibn Abdurrahman to sell some fabric, he advised him to:

"Sell these at a reduced price, as the fabrics are slightly defective."

Hafs ended up selling the fabrics at the price specified by the Imam, yet forgot to inform the customer about the flaws of the goods he had purchased. On finding out, the Imam asked Hafs whether he knew the customer so they can get in touch with him. It turned out that Hafs did not know the man. So, wary that the legitimacy of his earnings might be clouded, Imam Abu Hanifah gave the entire money he had made from the transaction as charity. The Imam's level of piety accrued for him enormous blessings in all his transactions, both financial and spiritual.

Moral of the Story:

In order to find out whether someone is an upright and pious person with a clean heart, one need not look so much at the deeds of worship he offers as to the spiritual level with which he offers those deeds. More specifically, one must observe and see whether or not his behavior complies with the morals of Islam and his earnings are made in a *halal* way. Upon hearing a person speaking highly of another man, Omar –Allah be well-pleased with him- asked the person whether he had done any of the three things that would justify his praises:

"Have you neighbored him, traveled with him or traded with him?"

When the person replied in the negative for all three, Omar –Allah be well-pleased with him- went on to say:

"In that case, do not praise him, for you do not know him properly!"

Sufyan-i Sawri –may Allah sanctify his secret- has therefore said:

"The piety of a person is to the degree of the *halal*-ness of his earnings."

He was once asked to explain the virtue of offering ritual prayer, in congregation, in the first row.

"First look at where you earn your bread from, brother" he replied. "As long as your earnings are *halal*, feel free to pray in whichever row you want…no trouble."

The late Musa Effendi –may Allah sanctify his secret- would recount a personal experience of his in underlining the vitality of ensuring that earnings are made through *halal* means and are kept distant from the corrupting elements of the *haram*:

"We used to have a neighbor. Earlier a non-Muslim, he had later converted to Islam. When I one day asked the motivation behind his embracing of Islam, he explained the following:

'I became a Muslim thanks to the business ethics of my land neighbor Molla Rebi in Acıbadem. Molla Rebi was a man who made a living by selling milk. One night, he came to our house with a container full of milk and said:

'Here…this milk is yours!'

'How can that be?' I asked. 'I do not remember asking milk from you!'

That is when the graceful man began explaining:

'One of my cows sneaked into your land and grazed and it was only later that I became aware of it. For that reason, this milk belongs to you. Plus, I will continue to bring its milk to you until its digestive cycle comes to an end…in other words, until the grass and weed it consumed from your land completely exits its system.'

Sufi Narratives and Lessons

'Do not even mention it, my friend', I said. 'Grass is grass. You owe me nothing…' But Molla Rebi would not take that as an answer.

'No way', he said. 'This milk is part and parcel yours!' So he placed in my hands the container of milk and many more over the next few days, until the cow's digestive cycle came to an end.

I was exceptionally moved by his conduct. Consequently, the veils of ignorance that had clouded my sight until then made way and the sun of guidance dawned in my heart. I just thought to myself, '…a religion that imparts such grand morals must surely be the most sublime religion; and nobody can doubt the integrity of a religion that raises such elegant, sensitive, just and wholesome people.' So I pronounced the *kalima-i tawhid* and became a Muslim.'"

These lessons of wisdom make evident the sensitivity and precaution we must take on board with regard to making a *halal* living and shunning the corrupting elements of *haram*. For *halal* earnings, are among the fundamental pillars of piety. The Blessed Prophet –upon him blessings and peace- therefore states:

"An honest and reliable merchant is in the class of prophets, the righteous (*siddiq*) and martyrs." (Tirmidhi, Buyu, 4)

A merchant with a sensitive heart, who has acquired the privilege of being mentioned in the same breath as prophets, the righteous and martyrs, becomes a means of peace and blessings for those around and at once, acquires for himself the joy of both worlds, Here and the Hereafter. Yet, those who fall victim to worldly greed are doomed for poverty in the eternal life, however much they may seem to be leading a glittered life of riches in this passing life on earth.

The Blessed Prophet –upon him blessings and peace- further says:

"There will come a time when a person will not pay the slightest attention to whether his earnings are *halal* or *haram*." (Bukhari, Buyu, 7, 23)

Thus, in this day and age, where the dangers the Prophet –upon him blessings and peace- had indicated are running rife, and where they do not seem to let go of a person however great the person may strive to get away from them, abiding by the *halal* becomes the most primal issue and the greatest of all deeds of worship.

Hearts triumphant in fulfilling this deed of worship and remaining steadfast in a state of abidance and submission to the command of Allah, glory unto Him, provide sources of goodness and inspiration, much like a rose that weaves through dozens of thorns to blossom. Contrastingly, hearts immersed in the *haram* and doubtful are as such that they have settled for a place among the thorns, relinquishing their potential to blossom; and as such, they have become hotbeds of evil and immorality.

May Allah, glory unto Him, protect is all!

Amin…

Tasawwuf is a zest…only those who taste it may know.

SUMMARY

In a Word

Innumerable wisdoms underlie the below revelation of the Almighty's to the Blessed Prophet –upon him blessings and peace-:

"The Faithful Spirit has descended with it (the Quran)…upon your heart that you may admonish.[126]" (as-Shuara, 193-194)

The core of all wisdom is comprised by the fact that all knowledge, especially Divine knowledge and wisdom, may flourish only in the heart-world. In other words, knowledge exposes its inner meaning and beauty only through the medium of hearts that are overcome by love, ecstasy and inspiration. On this fact does the below, oft-quoted Sufi perspective rest:

"Knowledge is basic element but the aim of acquiring it is nothing other than righteous deeds. Most concisely, this lies in the secret of reverently abiding by the commands of the Lord (*tazim li-amrillah*) and being compassionate to all His creation (*shafqah li-khalqillah*). Otherwise, knowledge is nothing but a useless burden."

Hence, all written knowledge is in fact like a seed. If uncultivated and kept in a storehouse, a seed continues to remain only a seed, no matter how many years go past. Much is the same with written knowledge uncultivated in the heart-world and relegated instead to the lines of books lying dormant on bookshelves. In contrast, seeds planted into the ground

---

[126] Translated as 'admonish', the actual Quranic term is in *indhar*, which denotes the act of commanding and prohibiting through casting fear, by reminding of the gloomy consequences that come with abandoning them in the Hereafter.

flourish according to their inner capacities and many end up becoming colossal plane trees. Seeds of knowledge planted into the soil of the heart grow to become gardens of spirituality and only then do the true fruits of knowledge and wisdom become ready to be picked.

It is for that reason that the Holy Quran was descended onto the heart of the Blessed Prophet –upon him blessings and peace- and the Companions read the Divine warnings and commands not from the lines of books but directly from the heart-world of the Light of Being –upon him blessings and peace-. In so doing, their hearts and eyes were illumined with many a unique manifestation of the Divine word on that sacred heart-world, whereby the sublimely profound realities of Islam, its secrets and wisdoms, reflected onto their spirits in all their beauty. In a sense, the Companions affirmed belief in the Messenger of Allah –upon him blessings and peace- by virtue of becoming captivated by his quintessential character and become moths around his flame. As such, by virtue of taking a share of this reflection, the norm of the Sufi way has been to keep Islam alive in the heart-world of spirituality and inspiration and convey the enlightening glimmers of this light reflected from its source, the heart of the Blessed Prophet –upon him blessings and peace-, to the hearts of saints, to future ages and generations.

Thus, the jurisprudential aspects of Islam are the main columns of this building, its aspect of piety stand for the complementary elements built around these columns, which, at once, are its facets of beauty and elegance. By uniting these two aspects, *tasawwuf* not only articulates the essentials of good deeds and a perfection of conduct, it moreover discloses the secrets of man, life and the universe, enabling a perceptive realization of the responsibilities human beings are entrusted with to fulfill. Inherent with this quality, with regard to the questions of Divine love (*muhabbatullah*) and knowledge (*marifatullah*), the Sufi way is like a window in the heart that opens up to the heavens.

As we have already mentioned on a few occasions, *tasawwuf* consists of living Islam according to the measures of an internalized (*ihsan*) sincerity and piety, as well as contemplation, abstinence, submission and love. But the gist of this all is not so much to explain them, as it is to reflect them onto our lives to the extent allowed by our means and capabilities. It was common

Sufi Narratives and Lessons

for righteous scholars to conclude their advices wisdom aimed towards perfecting hearts through divine beauties and morals, with the words:

"It is easy to say and easy to listen…but incredibly too difficult to act accordingly!"

Viewed from this vantage, writing, too, is easy, as it is to read the written lines; though it is incredibly difficult to live accordingly and to adopt these beauties as the defining characteristics of our lives. Expressing the command 'to keep patient' is not demanding for the tongue that articulates it; nor is it burdensome for the ears that hear and eyes that read it. But when it comes to manifesting what the command signifies in hearts, already weary from being exposed to numerous troubles and excruciating distress, many are left all the more tormented and eventually choose the easier option of impatience. What matters, therefore, is not simply learning and teaching the knowledge of *tasawwuf* but to consume it as a potion that instills life into our hearts.

Inviting His servants to righteous deeds, Allah, glory unto Him, states in the Quran:

"He Who created Death and Life, that He may try which of you is best in conduct; and He is the Exalted in Might, Oft-Forgiving…" (al-Mulk, 2)

Significant is the fact that the Quranic verse does not resort to expressions like 'best in learning' or 'best in expression' or even 'best in listening', but rather says 'best in conduct', which is none other than righteous deeds.

The most basic aim of the Sufi way, therefore, is to blossom the petals of the heart through the life-potions of wisdom, piety and love, so as to ensure that man is reunited with his Lord before he becomes mired in the desert of ignorance that is the life of the world. Comprehending and putting to practice this reality is, at once, to comprehend and to live the Sufi way. As the greats of *tasawwuf* say:

"*Tasawwuf* is a zest…only those who taste it may know!"

Thus, the essence of the Sufi way which we have heretofore tried to explain consists of serving Allah, glory unto Him, in the best possible manner and making a serious preparation for the eternal life. Simpler put, *tasawwuf* is to live servanthood in the most consummate manner thinkable, for the Lord created

Sufism: A Path Towards the Internalization of Faith (Ihsân)

man for no other reason than to serve Him. Sufism is therefore nothing but removing the obstacles standing in the way between man and servanthood and acquiring the channels to provide means for becoming a servant as such. Dressing many wounds, the Sufi way renders many an arid soil a lusciously green and lavishly flowered garden, turning many a derelict heart into an exquisite palace. In short, while we journey on this land of separation to the eternal realm of reunion, *tasawwuf* is the gilded path that hands human beings the keys to becoming 'wonderful servants' (نِعْمَ الْعَبْدُ) in the sight of the Real.

The awaiting task is nothing but casting away the ego and all claims egoistic, and to lead a life of nothingness in the presence of Divine Majesty. This is a sensation that instills in one an unwavering feeling of helplessness and trust in the Lord, which proceeds to lift the heart onto the peak of spiritual perfection. Hearts which reside in the palace of nothingness may never fall off the cliff of deprivation, humiliated and ashamed; much rather, they attain to the awaiting heights of the heavens, to the degree of their humbleness and the intensity by which they suppress their egos. The poet expresses this beautifully:

By humbly falling onto earth does the seed become graced,

By the mercy of the Merciful are the humble raised

O Lord…Include us among those who You praise as 'wonderful servants'! Make our hearts, which we strive to protect from the aridness of the ego and all claims egotistical by placing them inside the habitat of nothingness, blossom through Your eternal mercy! Reconcile our words with our hearts and our hearts with our words! In our hearts, flourish the buds of Truth, which we have humbly tried to put into words here under the auspices of the eternal manifestation of Your attribute of Speech! Include all of us among your beloveds and among the righteous crew; and resurrect us by their sides! Do not let us digress from the lighted path of the Blessed Prophet –upon him blessings and peace-! Grant us the privilege of his great intercession! Give us the mindset and conduct which pleases You and do not allow us to offer any deeds other than those which please You! Reconcile all our feelings with your majestic Will! Distance us from a mindset and behavior You do not like! Allow us to lead our lives on the straightest of all paths up until we breathe our last! Let our humble, feeble work serve as a means to good, guidance, wisdom, truth and divine knowledge!

Amin…

Bibliography

Abdurrahman Güzel, Mustafa Tatçı, **Yunus Emre**, Ankara, 1991.

Abdülbaki Gölpınarlı, **Mesnevi ve Şerhi**, İstanbul, 1973-1974.

Abdulqadir Jilani, **al-Fathu'r-Rabbani**, (translated by Yaman Arikan), Istanbul, 1987.

Abdulkarim al-Jili, **İnsan-ı Kamil**, (translated by Abdülaziz Mecdi Tolun; prepared by Selçuk Eraydın, Ekrem Demirli, Abdullah Kartal) Istanbul, 1998.

Abdulmajid Zindani, **Kuran'da İlmi Mucizeler** (translated by Resul Tosun), İstanbul, 1995.

Abu Dawud, Sulayman ibn Ashas as-Sijistani, **Sunanu Abi Dawud**, I-V, Istanbul, 1992.

Abu Nasr as-Sarraj at-Tusi, **al-Luma** (translated by Hasan Kamil Yılmaz), Istanbul, 1996.

Ajluni, Ismail ibn Muhammad, **Kashfu'l-Khafa**, I-II, Beirut (undated).

Adem Ergül, **Kalbi Hayat**, Istanbul, 2000.

Ahmad ibn Hanbal, **al-Musnad**, I-IV, Istanbul, 1992; **Kitabu'z-Zuhd** (published by Muhammad Said Basyuni Zaghlul), Beirut, 1986.

Ahmed Davudoğlu, **Sahih-i Müslim Tercüme ve Şerhi**, I-XII, İstanbul, 1979.

Ahmed ar-Rifai, **Onların Alemi** (translated by Abdülkadir Akçiçek), Istanbul, 1996.

Ahmed Taşgetiren, **Altın Öğütler**, Istanbul, 1992.

Ali ibn Husayn Waiz Kashifi, **Rashahat Aynu'l-Hayat** (edited by Ali Asghar Muiniyan), I-II, Tehran, 1977.

Ali Can Tatlı, **Zühd Açısından Dünya Nimetleri**, Istanbul, 2005.

Ali Himmet Berki, **Açıklamalı Mecelle: Mecelle-i Ahkam-ı Adliye**, Istanbul, 1982.

Ali Özek, Hayrettin Karaman, Ali Turgut, Mustafa Çağrıcı, İ. Kafi Dönmez, Sadreddin Gümüş, **Kuran-ı Kerim ve Türkçe Açıklamalı Meali**, Saudi Arabia, 1992.

Asad Sahib, **Maktubat-ı Mawlana Khalid**, (translated by Dilaver Selvi, Kemal Yıldız), Istanbul, 1993.

Balazuri, **Ansabu'l-Ashraf**, Egypt, 1959.

Baydawi, Abu Said Nasruddin Abdullah ibn Omar, **Anwaru't-Tanzil wa Asraru't-Tawil**, I-IV, Beirut, (undated).

Bayhaki, Abu Bakr Ahmed ibn al-Husayn, **as-Sunanu'l-Kubra** (undated), Daru'l-Fikr; **Kitabu'z-Zuhdi'l-Kabir**, Beirut, 1996.

Bukhari, Abu Abdillah Muhammad ibn Ismail, **al-Jamiu's-Sahih**, I-VIII, Istanbul, 1992.

Darimi, Abu Muhammad Abdullah ibn Abdirrahman, **Sunanu'd-Darimi**, I-II, Istanbul, 1992.

Daylami, Abu Shujaa Shiruyah ibn Shahridar, **al-Firdaws bi-Ma'suri'l-Khitab**, Beirut, 1986.

Elmalılı Muhammed Hamdi Yazır, **Hak Dini Kuran Dili**, Istanbul, 1971.

Ethem Cebecioğlu, **Tasavvuf Terimleri ve Deyimleri Sözlüğü**, Ankara, 1997.

Fariduddin Attar, **Tadhkiratu'l-Awliya** (prepared by Süleyman Uludağ), Istanbul, 1985.

Ferit Devellioğlu, **Osmanlıca-Türkçe Ansiklopedik Lugat**, Ankara, 1997.

Ghazzali, Abu Hamid Muhammad ibn Muhammad, **Ihya-u Ulumi'd-Din**, I-VI, Beirut, 1990.

Hakim, Abu Abdillah Muhammad ibn Abdillah an-Nisaburi, **Mustadrak ala's-Sahihayn**, I-V, Beirut, 1990.

Hasan Basri Çantay, **Kuran-ı Hakim ve Meal-i Kerim**, I-III, İstanbul, 1996.

Hasan Kamil Yılmaz, Anahatlarıyla Tasavvuf ve Tarikatlar, İstanbul, 2000.

Hayat Neşriyat İlmi Araştırma Merkezi Meal Heyeti, **Kuran-ı Kerim ve Muhtasar Meali**, Istanbul, 2001.

Hayrettin Karaman, **Ebediyet Yolcusunu Uğurlarken**, Ankara, 1999.

Bibliography

al-Haythami, Hafiz Nuraddin Ali ibn Abi Bakr, **Majmau'z-Zawaid wa Manbau'l-Fawaid**, I-X, Beirut.

Ibn Ataullah Iskandari, **al-Hikamu'l-Ataiyyah** (translated by Saffet Yetkin), Ankara, 1963.

Ibn Hajar al-Asqalani, Shihabuddin Ahmed ibn Ali, **Hadyu's-Sari Muqaddimatu Fathu'l-Bari Sharhi Sahihi'l-Bukhari**, I-XXVIII, (undated); al-Isabah fi Tamyizi's-Sahabah, Egypt, 1379; Munabbihat, Istanbul, 1960.

Ibn Hibban, Abu Khatim al-Busti, **al-Ihsan bi Tartibi Sahihi Ibn-i Hibban**, I-X, Beirut, 1987.

Ibn Hisham, **as-Siratu'n-Nabawiyyah**, Beirut, 1992.

Ibn Jawzi, Abu'l-Faraj Abdurrahman ibn Ali ibn Muhammad, **Manaqibu'l-Imam Ahmed ibn Hanbal** (prepared by Abdullah ibn Abdulmuhsin at-Turki), Cairo, 1409.

Ibn Kathir, Imaduddin Abu'l-Fida, **Tafsiru Qurani'l-Azim**, I-IV, Beirut, 1988; **al-Bidayah wa'n-Nihayah**, I-XV, Cairo, 1993; **as-Siratu'n-Nabawiyyah**, I-IV, Cairo, 1964.

Ibn Majah, Abu Abdillah Muhammad ibn Yazid al-Qazwini, **Sunanu Ibn Majah**, Istanbul, 1992.

Ibnu Abdilbarr, Abu Omar Yusuf ibn Abdullah ibn Muhammad, **al-Istiab fi Marifati'l-Ashab**, I-IV, Cairo (undated).

Ibnu'l-Asir, Muhammad ibn Abdulkarim ibn abdulwahid as-Shaybani, **al-Kamil fi't-Tarih**, I-XIII, Beirut, 1965.

İbrahim Canan, **Hadis Ansiklopedisi**, I-XVIII, Istanbul, (undated).

İlhan Armutçuoğlu, **Kaside-i Bürde Manzum Tercümesi**, Konya, 1983.

Imam Malik, **Muwattaa**, I-II, Istanbul, 1992.

İsmail Fenni Ertuğrul, **Vahdet-i Vücud ve İbn-i Arabi** (prepared by Mustafa Kara), Istanbul, 1991.

İsmail Hakkı Bursevi, **Ruhu'l-Beyan**, I-IX, Istanbul; Kenz-i Mahfi, Istanbul, 1727.

Kadir Mısıroğlu, **Külliyat**, Sebil Yayınevi.

Kalabazi, Taju'l-Islam Abu Bakr Muhammad ibn Ishaq Bukhari, **at-Taarruf li Madhhabi Ahli't-Tasawwuf**, (translated by Süleyman Uludağ), Istanbul, 1992.

M. Aziz Lahbabi, **İslam Şahsiyetçiliği** (translated by İ. Hakkı Akın)ö Istanbul, 1972.

Mahir İz, **Tasavvuf**, Istanbul, 1969; **Yılların İzi**, Istanbul, 1975.

Mahmud Sami Ramazanoğlu, **Külliyat**, Erkam Yayınları.

Majmuu'l-Hadith, Damascus Maktabatu'z-Zahiriyyah Library, no: 59.

Maqdisi, Izzuddin Abdussalam, **Sırların Çözümü ve Hazinelerin Anahtarları**, (translated by Hayri Kaplan), Istanbul, 2001.

Mawlana Sheikh, **Manaqib-i Khawajah Ubaydullah-i Ahrar**, Bayazid State Library, Bayazid Section, no: 3624.

Mecdi Mehmed, **Hadaiku'ş-Şakaik**, Istanbul, 1853.

Mehmed Doğan, **Büyük Türkçe Sözlük**, Istanbul, 1994.

Mehmed Niyazi, **Çanakkale Mahşeri**, Istanbul, 1999.

Molla Jami, **Nafakhatu'l-Uns**, (simplifed by Abdülkadir Çiçek), Istanbul, 1981.

Muhammad Abid al-Jabiri, **Arap-İslam Kültürünün Akıl Yapısı**, Istanbul, 1999.

Muhammad ibn Abdullah al-Hani, **Adab**, Istanbul, 1995.

Muhammad Abu Zahra, **Ibnu Taymiyyah Hayatuhu wa Asruhu wa Fikruh**, Beirut, (undated).

Muhammad Asad, **Kuran Mesajı**, (translated by Cahid Koytak, Ahmet Ertürk), I-III, Istanbul, 1999.

Muhammad Fuad Abdulbaqi, **al-Mujamu'l-Mufahras li Alfazi'l-Qurani'l-Karim**, Cairo, 1988.

Muhammad Hamidullah, **İslam Müesseselerine Giriş**, Istanbul, 1981.

Muhammad Salih az-Zarqan, **Fakhruddin ar-Razi ve Arauhu'l-Kalamiyya wa'l-Falsafiyya**, Beirut, 1963.

Bibliography

Muhammed Esad Erbili, **Mektubat**, (simplified by H. Kamil Yılmaz, İrfan Gündüz), Istanbul, 1983; **Risale-i Esadiyye**, Dersaadet, 1924.

Munawi, Muhammad Abdurrauf, **Fayzu'l-Qadir Sharhu'l-Jamii's-Saghir**, I-IV, Beirut, 1994.

Mundhiri, **Abdulazim ibn Abdulqawi, at-Targhib wa't-Tarhib**, I-IV, Cairo, 1934.

Muslim, Abu'l-Husayn ibn Hajjaj al-Qushayri, **al-Jamiu's-Sahih**, I-III, Istanbul, 1992.

Mustafa Kara, **Metinlere Günümüz Tasavvuf Hareketleri**, Istanbul, 2002.

Nasai, Abu Abdirrahman Ahmed ibn Shuayb, **Sunanu'n-Nasai**, I-VIII, Istanbul, 1992.

Nawawi, Abu Zakariyya Yahya ibn Sharaf, **Riyadu's-Salihin**, Beirut; **Riyazü's-Salihin** (translated and annotated by Yaşar Kandemir, İsmail Lütfi Çakan, Raşit Küçük), I-VIII, Istanbul, 1997; Sharhu Sahih-i Muslim, I-XVIII, Egypt, 1981.

Necip Fazıl Kisakürek, **Veliler Ordusundan 333**, Istanbul, 1976; **Reşahat (Şeyh Safiyyüddin)**, Istanbul, 1995.

Nurettin Topçu, **Mevlana ve Tasavvuf**, Istanbul, 1998.

Osman Nuri Topbaş, **Külliyat**, Erkam Yayınları.

Ömer Rıza Doğrul, **İslamiyetin Geliştirdiği Tasavvuf**, Istanbul, 1948.

Qurtubi, Abu Abdillah Muhammad ibn Ahmed, **al-Jami li Ahkami'l-Quran**, I-XX, Beirut, 1985.

Qushayri, Abdulkarim, **ar-Risalatu'l-Qushayriyyah**, Beirut, 1990.

Razi, Fakhruddin Muhammad ibn Omar, **Mafatihu'l-Ghayb (at-Tafsiru'l-Kabir)**, I-XXXII, Beirut, 1990.

Roger Garaudy, **İslam'ın Vaad Ettikleri** (translated by Nezih Uzel), Istanbul, 1983.

Rudani, Imam Muhammad ibn Muhammad ibn Sulayman, **Jamu'l-Fawaid**, (translated by Naim Erdoğan), Istanbul, 1996.

Sadık Dânâ, **Külliyat**, Erkam Yayınları.

Sayyid Sharif Jurjani, **Kitabu't-Tarifat**, Beirut, 1990.

Selçuk Eraydın, **Tasavvuf ve Tarikatlar**, Istanbul, 1994.

Suat Yıldırım, **Kuran'da Uluhiyyet**, Istanbul, 1987.

Subqi, Taqiyyuddin Abu'l-Hasen Ali, **Shifau's-Saqam fi Ziyarati Khayri'l-Anam**, Egypt, 1318.

Suyuti, Abu'l-Fadl Jalaladdin Abdurrahman ibn Abi Bakr, **al-Jamiu's-Saghir**, Egypt, 1306; **Sharhu's-Sudur bi Sharhi Hali'l-Mawta wa'l-Qubur**, Istanbul, 1986; **Sharhu Ibn Majah**, Karachi, (undated).

Süleyman Ateş, **İslam Tasavvufu**, Ankara, 1972.

Süleyman Uludağ, **Tasavvuf Terimleri Sözlüğü**, Istanbul, 1991.

Şefik Can, **Mesnevi Tercümesi**, I-VI, Istanbul, 1997.

Sheikh Ashraf Ali Tanawi, **Hadislerle Tasavvuf** (prepared by Zaferullah Davudi, Ahmed Yıldırım), Istanbul, 1995.

Sheikh Sadi Shirazi, **Bostan**, Istanbul, 1995.

Shihabuddin Ahmed ibn Hajar al-Haytami al-Makki, **Khayratu'l-Hisan fi Manaqibi'l-Imam'l-Azam Abi Hanifati'n-Numan**, Beirut, 1983.

at-Tabarani, al-Hafiz Abu'l-Qasim Sulayman ibn Ahmed, **al-Mujamu'l-Kabir**, I-XXV, 1983.

Tabari, Abu Jafar Muhammad ibn Jarir, **Jamiu'l-Bayan an Tawili Ayi'l-Quran**, Beirut, 1995.

Tahanawi, Muhammad Ala ibn Ali, **Kashshafu Istılahati'l-Funun**, Beirut, 1861.

Tahiru'l-Mevlevi, **Şerh-i Mesnevi**, I-XIV, Istanbul, 1963-1973.

Tirmidhi, Abu Isa, Muhammad ibn Isa, **Sunanu't-Tirmidhi**, I-IV, Istanbul, 1992.

Waqidi, **Maghazi**, Egypt, 1948.

Zekeriya Güler, **"Vesile ve Tevessül Hadislerinin Kaynak Değeri"**, ILAM Academic Journal, January-June, 1997, v. 2, no. 1, p. 83-132.

Contents

PREFACE 7

CHAPTER ONE

WHAT IS SUFISM? 13
A. THE ORIGIN OF SUFISM 13
B. THE DEFINITION OF SUFISM 31
   1. The Sufi way personifies exemplary
      charactertraits (*akhlaq*) and propriety (*adab*). 32
   2. The Sufi way is about purifying
      the heart and the soul. 35
   3. The Sufi way is a ceaseless spiritual combat 38
   4. Sufism means sincerity (*ikhlas*) 39
   5. Sufism means standing upright
      on the straight path (*istiqamah*) 42
   6. The Sufi way is (*rida*) and submission (*taslimiyyah*) 45
C. THE SUBJECT MATTER OF SUFISM 50
D. THE AIM OF SUFISM 52
E. THE NECESSITY OF SUFISM 55

F. THE RELATION OF SUFISM TO
OTHER SCHOLARLY DISCIPLINES...............................73

   1. SUFISM AND OTHER ISLAMIC DISCIPLINES...............73

      a. Sufism and Theology..74

      b. Sufism and Quranic Exegesis (*Tafsir*).........................76

      c. Sufism and the Sayings and Actions of the Blessed
Prophet-upon him blessings and peace- (*Hadith-Siyar*).........79

      d. Sufism and Islamic Jurisprudence (*Fiqh*)..................81

   2. SUFISM AND NATURAL SCIENCES.................................85

   3. SUFISM AND LITERATURE...90

   4. SUFISM AND FINE ARTS..93

      a. Music..93

      b. Architecture...96

      c. Calligraphy...97

   5. SUFISM AND PHILOSOPHY...100

G. BENEFICIAL KNOWLEDGE...105

CHAPTER TWO

THE TRAINING OF SUFISM (*SAYR SULUK*)...................................117

A. THE SELF (*NAFS*) AND ITS PURIFICATION (*TAZKIYA*)......121

   1. THE REALITY OF THE NAFS..121

   2. THE PURIFICATION OF THE LOWER SELF, OR NAFS......126

      a. Purification by the Almighty......................................131

      b. Purification by the Messenger of Allah
-upon him blessings and peace-....................................132

      c. A Person's Own Purification of His Self..................134

   3. THE STATES OF THE SELF..142

Contents

    a. The Evil-Commanding Self (*an-nafsu'l-ammara*) 142

    b. The Self-Blaming Nafs (*an-nafsu'l-lawwama*) 149

    c. The Inspired Self (*an-nafsu'l-mulhama*) 152

    d. The Tranquil Self (*an-nafsu'l-mutmainna*) 154

    e. The Satisfied Self (*an-nafsu'r-radiya*) 157

    f. The Satisfying Self (*an-nafsu'l-mardiyya*) 160

    g. The Perfect Self (*an-nafsu'l-kamila*)/
       The Pure Nafs (*an-nafsu's-safiya*) 162

B. THE HEART AND ITS PURIFICATION 163

  1. THE NATURE OF THE HEART 163

  2. THE TYPES OF HEARTS 170

    a. Hearts that Maintain Their Purpose
       and Dignity of Creation 170

    b. Sealed and Dead Hearts 173

    c. Diseased and Unmindful Hearts 176

  3. THE PURIFICATION OF THE HEART 179

    a. *Halal* Food 180

    b. Repentance and Prayer 184

    c. Reading the Quran and Obeying Its Commands 189

    d. Worshipping with Utmost Concentration (*khushuu*) 194

    e. Reviving the Nights 204

    f. *Dhikrullah* and *Muraqaba* 207

    g Love of the Blessed Noble Prophet -upon him blessings and
       peace- and *Salawat-u Sharifa*. 213

    h. Contemplating Death 221

    i. Being in the Company of the Pious and the Righteous 227

    j. Embodying Good Morals 238

4. GAZING AT THE UNIVERSE WITH A PURIFIED HEART	244
C. THE BASIC PRINCIPLES OF SUFI TRAINING	250
D. *MURSHID-I KAMIL* AND METHODS OF SPIRITUAL ENLIGHTENING	258
1. *MURSHID-I KAMIL*	258
2. METHODS OF SPIRITUAL GUIDANCE	267
a. *Muhabbah* (Love) and *Rabitah*	267
b. Spiritual Gathering (*Sohbah*)	276
c. Service	283
d. Favorable Inclination (*Tawajjuh*)	291
e. Prayer (Dua)	296
E. THE SUFI MANNERISM	299
1. THE MANNER OF GUIDANCE AND MERCY	299
2. THE MANNER OF GENTLENESS AND AFFECTION	309

CHAPTER THREE

MARIFATULLAH AND DIVINE AWARDS	323
A. *MARIFATULLAH* OR KNOWLEDGE OF THE DIVINE	323
1. DIVINE ESSENCE	323
2. DIVINE ATTRIBUTES AND THEIR MANIFESTATIONS	332
3. KNOWLEDGE OF THE DIVINE AND ITS MANIFESTATIONS IN THE WISE	359
B. DIVINE AWARDS	365
1. *LADUNNI* KNOWLEDGE	367
2. SPIRITUAL FORESIGHT (*FIRASAH*)	397
3. SPIRITUAL DISPOSAL (*TASARRUF*) AND *KARAMAH*	400
4. TRUTHFUL DREAMS	418

Contents

CHAPTER FOUR

SOME QUESTIONS CONCERNING SUFISM 429
A. MEDIATION (*TAWASSUL*) 429
B. SEEKING SPIRITUAL BLESSINGS (*TABARRUK*) 444
C. VISITING GRAVES 457

CHAPTER FIVE

ADVICE FROM THE RIGHTEOUS 471

CHAPTER SIX

SUFI NARRATIVES AND LESSONS 491
True Education 492
The Method in Spiritual Training 493
Ibrahim ibn Adham and the Fawn 494
Not to Stain the Path of the Real 497
Karamah 498
Affecting Ignorant Hearts 499
The Friend's Door 501
To Obey, To Serve, To Advise 502
Serving Creation 503
Courtesy in Saints 504
Will in Presence 505
Propriety 507
Propriety in Serving 508
Propriety...No Matter What 509
The Morals and Service of a Saint 510
Let the Immortal Know, Not Mortals! 512

Do Not Look Down On Anyone! 513
Do Not Condemn Anyone! 514
Cheering Up an Orphan 515
Friendship 516
The Purpose of Friendship 517
Full Submission 518
Receiving the Prayers of a Believer 519
A *Majzub* and the Cure of an Ailing Heart 521
Faces like Angels 522
The Condition of the Heart during Charity 523
The Righteous Deed that Reaches the Throne 525
A Constant Awareness of the Real 526
The *Karim* is All I Need 527
The Responsibility of the Forerunners 528
Attending the Invitation of the Lord 530
The Importance of *Halal* 530
Halal Earnings 533

SUMMARY 537

BIBLIOGRAPHY 542